INDEPENDENT T

BRITAIN
& IRELAND

THE BUDGET TRAVEL GUIDE

INDEPENDENT TRAVELLERS

BRITAIN
& IRELAND

THE BUDGET TRAVEL GUIDE

Thomas Cook
Publishing

Published by Thomas Cook Publishing,
a division of thomascook.com Limited
PO Box 227
Unit 15/16
Coningsby Road
Peterborough PE3 8SB
United Kingdom

Telephone: 01733 416477
E-mail: books@thomascook.com

Text:
© 2003 Thomas Cook Publishing

Country, route and area maps:
© 2003 Thomas Cook Publishing
City maps: © Lovell Johns Ltd, Witney, Oxfordshire
London Underground map:
© Transport for London

ISBN 1 841573 70 1

Head of Publishing: Donald Greig
Series Editor: Edith Summerhayes
Text design: Tina West
Layout: Peter Cooling, Cooling Brown
Cover design: Liz Lyons Design, Oxford
Cover layout: Studio 183, Thorney, Peterborough
Copy editor (first edition): Jane Egginton
Proofreader: Colin Follett
Country map: Lovell Johns Ltd, Witney, Oxfordshire
Route maps: Pixel Cartography and Studio 183

Text typeset in Book Antiqua and Gill Sans
    using QuarkXPress
Picture research: Michelle Warrington
Colour repro: PDQ Digital Media Solutions, Bungay
Text revisions: Cooling Brown
Printed and bound in Italy by Legoprint S.P.A.

Mini CD design: Laburnum Technologies Pvt Ltd,
    New Delhi, India
CD manufacturing services: business interactive ltd,
    Rutland

First edition (2002) written and
researched by:
**Eric and Ruth Bailey; Katy Carter;
Alison Farthing; Kerry Fisher;
Rebecca Ford; Sarah Hay;
Nerys Lloyd-Pierce; Tim Locke;
Joani Walsh**

Updating and revisions for 2004
edition:
Tim Locke; Robin McKelvie

Mini CD written and researched by:
Tim Locke

Transport information:
Kevin Flynn,
Thomas Cook European Timetable

THE AUTHORS

Eric and Ruth Bailey are a husband-and-wife travel writing team with a score of guidebook titles to their credit. They live in North Norfolk and have visited each of Ireland's 32 counties.

Katy Carter, travel writer and editor, is now Surrey-based after living and working in Oxford, London and Cheshire. She has written and co-authored numerous travel guides to the UK.

Alison Farthing works in the tourism and leisure industry. Based in the Hope Valley in Derbyshire, she enjoys independent travel. Her favourite places are Nepal and South America.

Kerry Fisher is a freelance journalist who writes for women's magazines and travel books. She has written several guides in the Thomas Cook *Hotspots* series, is the author of *Discover Sydney* and has worked on a number of DK and AA travel guides.

Rebecca Ford is a freelance journalist and travel writer who specialises in writing about Britain and Italy. She has contributed to a large number of guidebooks and is the author of *Discover Edinburgh and Glasgow*, published by Thomas Cook Publishing for WH Smith.

Sarah Hay has written for magazines such as *Dazed & Confused* and *The Face* and has reported for worldpop.com. She lives in Manchester.

Nerys Lloyd-Pierce is an award-winning freelance journalist, based in Cardiff. She writes regularly for national newspapers, including the *Independent on Sunday* travel section.

Tim Locke has written and contributed to numerous guides on Britain. He is also the editor of Thomas Cook's *Independent Travellers Europe by Rail* and is an enthusiastic walker and cyclist. He contributed the chapters on Birmingham and Plymouth–Penzance for this guide, and compiled the CD.

Joani Walsh has been a journalist for 15 years and has worked on many of the UK's leading women's magazines as well as contributing to national newspapers. She lives in Liverpool and is currently deputy editor and travel editor of the women's monthly *Candis*.

ACKNOWLEDGEMENTS

Thomas Cook Publishing would like to thank Spectrum Colour Library for supplying the photographs used in the book (to whom the copyright belongs) and the Thomas Cook Archives for supplying the historical illustrations.

Thanks also to Helen Hipkiss of Marketing Manchester, Sara Mason-Parker and the Bristol Tourism and Conference Bureau.

COVER PHOTOGRAPH

White cliffs of Dover, Robert Harding/Digital Vision

CONTENTS

GENERAL INFORMATION

ROUTES & CITIES

Routes are shown in one direction only but can, of course, be travelled in the opposite direction. See pp. 14–15 for a diagrammatical presentation of the routes.

HELP IMPROVE THIS GUIDE

This guide is updated each year. However, the information given may change and we would welcome reports and comments from our readers. Similarly we want to make this guide as practical and useful as possible and are grateful for any comments, criticisms and suggestions for improving future editions.

A free copy of this guide will be sent to all readers whose information or ideas are incorporated in the next edition. Please send all contributions to the Editor, *Independent Travellers Britain and Ireland*, Thomas Cook Publishing, at PO Box 227, Unit 15/16, Coningsby Road, Peterborough PE3 8SB, United Kingdom, or e-mail books@thomascook.com.

INTRODUCTION – ABOUT THIS BOOK

Great Britain and Ireland surprise many visitors for their sheer variety, brought about by a combination of a complex history and an amazing diversity of landscapes. With careful selection there is enough to fill a lifetime of travelling.

ENGLAND

Almost any prolonged journey across England reveals contrasts of some kind. The most obvious changes in mood are supplied by the landscapes, which range from watery fens beneath wide skies in East Anglia, the craggy heights of the Lake District fells, the tor-punctuated moors of Dartmoor, the rugged sea cliffs of Cornwall and the manicured countryside of the Cotswolds.

Architectural styles also change perceptibly from one region to the next. The most striking are the great stately homes, along with the golden-coloured stone cottages of the Cotswolds, Devon's cob walls and thatched roofs, and the distinctive black and white half-timbering that appears towards the Welsh borders.

There are layers of history just about everywhere. When the Romans colonised the country they left a network of towns and roads, as well as Hadrian's Wall. In the wake of the last invasion of Britain in 1066 the conquering Normans erected a chain of castles, and medieval England witnessed a spate of church building.

Many monasteries were destroyed by King Henry VIII after his break with the Pope and now stand as eerily beautiful ruins, but the cathedrals and churches have survived better, displaying a range of styles from Saxon via Norman to late Gothic.

A UNITED KINGDOM?

The distinction between Great Britain and the United Kingdom (UK) confuses many visitors and even the British themselves. Technically Great Britain means England, Wales and Scotland. The UK includes Northern Ireland as well, although people from Northern Ireland can also be described as British. Since 1999 some power has been devolved to Wales, Scotland and Northern Ireland although all three countries still also send members of parliament to London's Westminster.

The industrial revolution started in Ironbridge gorge in the 18th century and changed the world. The world's first canals and railways were in England too. Today industrial heritage is an industry in itself, with scores of restored mills, heritage steam railways and similar sites to visit.

With money came pleasure: one legacy of this is the array of peculiarly English seaside resorts, with their Victorian piers and promenades. And the English still lavish time and money on their gardens, from the smallest cottage plots to the expansive country parklands of stately homes.

WALES

Green, hilly Wales changes in mood as soon as you are over the border from the fertile English plains. In medieval times the English pushed rebellious Welsh tribes back into the uplands and erected a ring of castles to keep them under control. Apart from the numerous sheep, one of the first things you will probably notice is the Welsh language which is still taught in schools. By law all signs and official documents and notices have to be in Welsh as well as English. Welsh place-names can be real tongue twisters (try Llanwrtyd – 'chlan-oor-tid' – for instance).

Wales is mainly rural. Its three national parks – Snowdonia, the Brecon Beacons and the Pembrokeshire Coast – have the best scenery. Snowdonia offers challenging walks, some astonishing medieval castles and heritage railways. The Brecon Beacons are slightly less dramatic but with some exhilarating peaks, thunderous waterfalls and green dales. For the best of the coast, head towards Pembrokeshire, with its cliffs and sandy beaches, or to the Gower peninsula west of Swansea.

Architecture is nothing like as diverse as it is in England. Most Welsh towns are a mixture of grey stone and railway-age yellow or red brick beneath roofs of dark grey Welsh slates. The centre might be punctuated by a Gothic clock tower and overlooked by a nonconformist chapel. Most people live in the southern coastal strip, especially around the capital city of Cardiff, and in the former coal-mining and steel-making towns of the Valleys, renowned for choral singing and rugby.

SCOTLAND

Scotland has had a long bloody history of warfare with the English, but only relinquished its independence in 1707. To this day Scotland remains somewhat apart from the rest of the UK, with its own laws and established church, and the nation embraced devolution more warmly than Wales in 1999.

For visitors there is the dual attraction of its two very different major cities – Edinburgh and Glasgow – and some of the most stunning mountain and coastal landscapes in Europe. Then there are the classic Scottish golf courses, malt whisky distilleries, tartan shops, weather-beaten castles and remote fishing villages. The downside is the climate. It is possible to spend a week touring around and see nothing but rain and mist, even in the height of summer. There's also the minor irritation of midges that make themselves painfully known in mountainous areas in summer.

The most famously Scottish scenery lies in the Highlands and Islands. The Highlands contain the highest and most majestic peaks in the British Isles. Oban is a convenient base for ferries out to many of the islands such as Mull, Coll and Tiree, Bara and South Uist, Colonsay, Jura and Islay. Further north there is much more, including the Orkney Isles and their superb Neolithic sites.

IRELAND

The many clichés about Ireland are mostly true. Famously green because of the almost daily falls of soft rain, it is also very friendly. Visitors do get talking to locals over a pint of Guinness and you get the feeling that everyone has plenty of time to chat. In Ireland it doesn't pay to be in too much of a hurry.

Ireland was never colonised by the Romans; it moved straight from the Iron Age to the Viking era. As a result, its Celtic roots have survived strongly. Poetry and folk music are widely celebrated and there are many early Christian sites.

The **Republic of Ireland** achieved independence from Britain in 1921 after centuries of colonisation. Here agriculture and Catholicism are still huge influences. With EU money it has boomed and many overseas firms and people have moved in over the past 20 years. The scenery is wild, unspoilt and often spectacular on the west coast, notably around Killarney. Dublin is the one big, bustling city, enormously popular for short breaks.

ISLAND NATION

Ireland is an island consisting of Northern Ireland and the Republic of Ireland. The Republic – also known as Eire, Southern Ireland or simply Ireland – is an entirely separate country to the UK. The term British Isles refers to Great Britain and Ireland, plus the Channel Islands and the Isle of Man. These latter two have a peculiar in-between status; reigned over by the British monarch but not represented in the UK parliament.

In 1921 the part of the north where Protestants were in a majority was partitioned and **Northern Ireland** remained part of the UK. Since the 1970s there has been intermittent violence between the Catholic republican and Protestant loyalist extremists, and progress towards peace has been stuttering, though signs of some sort of reconciliation have begun to emerge. The troubles are confined to small areas of Belfast, Londonderry and a few other places.

Large areas of the country are completely peaceful (and some, such as the coast around the Giant's Causeway, astonishingly beautiful), but the stories of sectarian violence deter holidaymakers. If you travel, you'll get a lot of it to yourself.

KEY TO ICONS	
RAIL	Rail stations
🚗	Car
🚌	Public transport
⛴	Ferry services
✈	Airports
i	Information
🛏	Accommodation
🍽	Food and drink

STOPS ON ROUTE

ROUTE

START/FINISH POINT

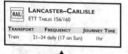

LANCASTER–CARLISLE
ETT TABLES 156/160

TRANSPORT	FREQUENCY	JOURNEY TIME
Train	21–24 daily (17 on Sun)	1 hr

PUBLIC TRANSPORT DETAILS

Mode of travel, journey time, frequency of service and *Thomas Cook European Timetable* numbers are given (see p. 39).

Independent Travellers Britain and Ireland provides you with information, advice and detailed routes to show you an interesting way to see and enjoy cities and regions independently and at your own pace. Some routes take advantage of the network of rail routes. Others use cross-country bus, local bus and even boats to show you the cream of a smaller region. Other areas are most easily explored by car. In each case, interesting stopovers, side trips and places to look for en route are described so that you get the most out of your journey.

Carefully selected highlights of each place are given, including attactions and their opening times and price range. Large cities and areas of interest, such as some national parks, have their own chapters. Most chapters are accompanied by a map, showing the route, city or area and the stops described in the text. In all cases we have given detailed information on how to get there, get around by local transport and make the most of your time there. All chapters give details of the best in characterful budget accommodation and places to eat, as well as local entertainment.

PRICES

In order to provide you with information for budgeting for your trip, price indicators (shown right) have been used throughout the book. Prices do change, so use these symbols for guidance only.

Accommodation

£/€	=	under £15/€24
££/€€	=	£15–30/€24–48
£££/€€€	=	£30–50/€48–80
££££/€€€€	=	over £50/€80

Based on price per person, with breakfast.

Food

£/€	=	under £5/€8
££/€€	=	£5–10/€8–16
£££/€€€	=	£10–15/€16–24
££££/€€€€	=	over £15/€24

Based on the cost of a mid-range main course.

Attractions

£/€	=	up to £3/€4.8
££/€€	=	up to £6/€9.6
£££/€€€	=	over £6/€9.6

Throughout the book you will see notes and tips in the margins. These suggest places to stop and worthwhile side trips. They tell you things to do for free and fill you in on interesting local facts. At the end of chapters, a 'Where Next?' section often points out other places to explore for yourself and suggests how to link up with other routes in the book.

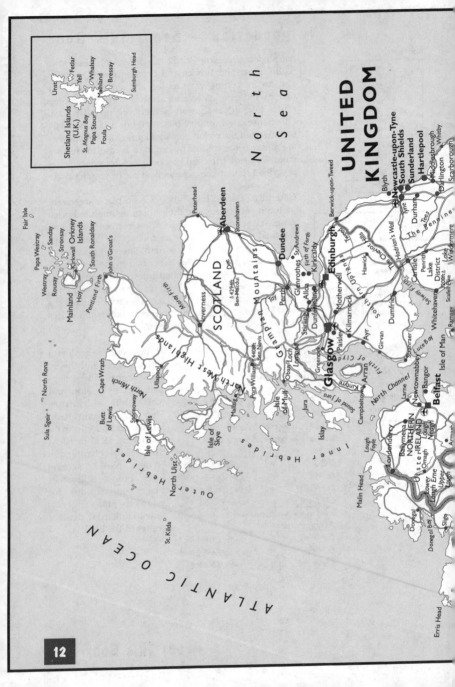

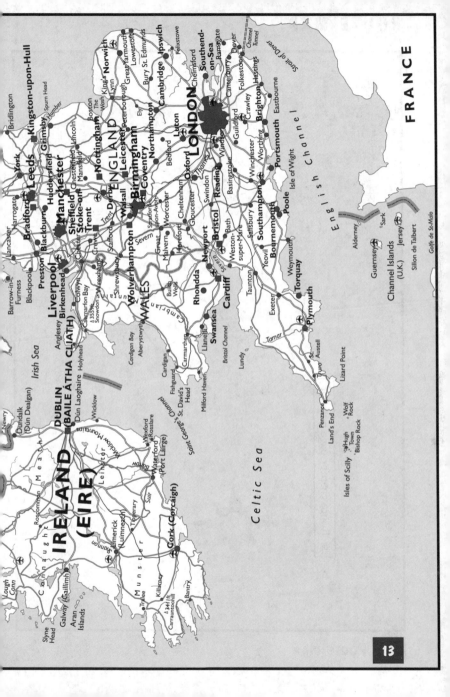

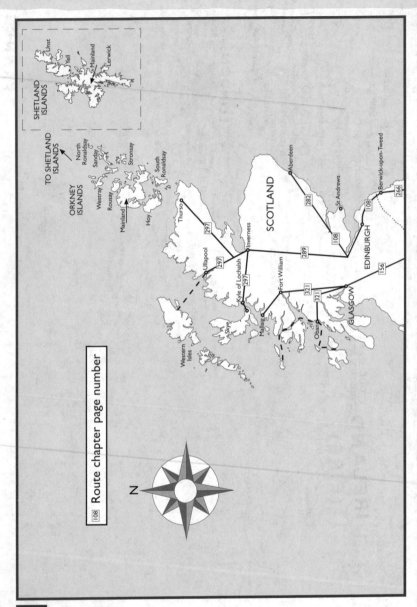

Route chapter page number

108

SHETLAND ISLANDS

Unst
Yell
Mainland
Lerwick

TO SHETLAND ISLANDS

ORKNEY ISLANDS

North Ronaldsay
Sanday
Stronsay
Westray
Rousay
Mainland
Hoy
South Ronaldsay

Thurso

297

Ullapool

297

Kyle of Lochalsh

297

Skye

Mallaig

Western Isles

Inverness

289

Fort William

321

321

Oban

Aberdeen

282

St Andrews

108

108

SCOTLAND

Berwick-upon-Tweed

266

108

EDINBURGH

156

GLASGOW

N

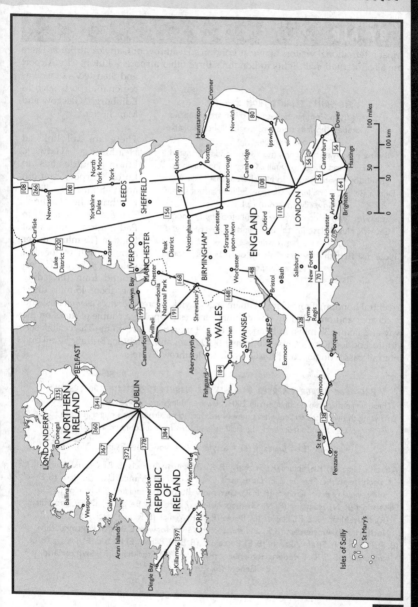

REACHING BRITAIN

BY AIR

Most international visitors arrive at London's Heathrow or Gatwick airports. There are also international flights to London's three other airports – Luton, City Airport and Stansted – as well as regional airports such as Edinburgh, Glasgow and Manchester.

There are rail links at Heathrow, Gatwick, Luton (shuttle bus to Luton Airport station) and Stansted. From Heathrow the Heathrow Express runs to Paddington in west London (15 mins), or for about a fifth of the cost you can take an Underground train (Piccadilly line, about 45 mins direct to central London). From Gatwick there are Gatwick Express services as well as slightly cheaper and only slightly slower other services (stopping a couple of times on the way and taking 35 mins) to London Victoria. Luton trains are on the Thameslink service to London King's Cross (40 mins), Blackfriars and Brighton. Britrail, Eurail and Interrail passes do not cover the Gatwick or Heathrow Express.

NO-FRILLS FLIGHTS FROM EUROPE

If coming from Continental Europe, there are cheap 'no frills' (ticketless, no free on-board meals) flights bookable online through:

Ryanair (www.ryanair.com) mostly to London Stansted; also European flights to Dublin, Glasgow and Shannon

bmibaby (bmibaby.com) to Manchester, East Midlands, Dublin, Belfast, Cork, Jersey, Glasgow, Edinburgh and Cardiff

Now (fly-now.com) to Luton

easyJet (easyjet.com) mostly from Luton and London Gatwick, plus Belfast, Bristol, East Midlands, Liverpool and Newcastle

Note that **British Airways** deals are often as cheap, sometimes cheaper.

EUROPEAN AIRPORTS SERVED BY NO-FRILLS FLIGHTS TO BRITAIN AND IRELAND

These were the main destinations in 2003; however things are always changing, so it's worth browsing the websites to see what's new. Note that some airports are not that close to the places mentioned; check the airlines' websites for transport connections.

Key: (B) = bmibaby, (E) = easyJet, (N) = Now, (R) = Ryanair

Austria: Graz (R), Klagenfurt (R), Salzburg (B, R). **Belgium**: Brussels (B, R), Ostend-Bruges (R). **Czech Republic**: Prague (B, E). **Denmark**: Copenhagen (E). **France**: Lyon (E), Paris (B, E) and several regional airports (B, E, R). **Germany**: Berlin (R), Frankfurt (R), Munich (B, E), Düsseldorf (R, N), Hamburg (R, N). **Greece**: Athens (E). **Ireland**: Belfast (E), Dublin and others (R). **Italy**: Milan (B, E, R), Naples (E), Rome (E, N, R), Venice (E, R) and several others (E, R). **Netherlands**: Amsterdam (B, E) and three others (R). **Norway**: Oslo (R). **Portugal**: Faro (B, E), Lisbon (N). **Spain**: Alicante (B, E), Barcelona (B, E, R), Bilbao (E) Madrid (E), Malaga (B, E) and others (B, E, R). **Sweden**: Gothenburg (R), Malmö (R), Stockholm (R). **Switzerland**: Geneva (E), Zurich (E).

From outside Europe flight fares vary seasonally (highest in summer and lowest in the depths of winter). From North America you would probably be looking at about $300–$600 return. There are some good deals on the Internet. Courier flights, where you take a package across with you, are rockbottom, but are often hard to find.

BY SEA

Several ports serve ferries from continental Europe, mostly from France and Belgium, plus some from the Netherlands, Norway, Sweden and Spain. The busiest, and closest to the continent, is Dover, to where there are dozens of crossings every day. **Hoverspeed** (tel: 08705 240241) catamarans whisk passengers across from Calais, France, in 55 mins. The ferry only takes about 30 mins longer and gives excellent views of the White Cliffs of Dover as you arrive. Operators are **P&O Ferries** (tel: from UK 08706 000600) (tel: from France (00 33) 802 010 020) (online booking: www.posl.com) and **SeaFrance** (tel: from UK 08705 711711) (online booking: www.seafrance.com). Booking is advisable if coming by car, but rarely necessary for foot passengers. There are price reductions for BritRail and Eurail holders.

OTHER CROSSINGS

Ostend to Dover.

Esbjerg, Hamburg and Hook of Holland to Harwich.

Rotterdam and Zeebrugge to Hull.

Amsterdam, Bergen (via Stavanger) and Gothenburg to Newcastle.

Dieppe to Newhaven.

Roscoff and Santander to Plymouth.

Cherbourg to Poole.

Bilbao, Cherbourg, Le Havre, Ouistreham and St Malo to Portsmouth.

Zeebrugge to Rosyth.

BY CHANNEL TUNNEL

The Tunnel runs from near Calais in northern France to the edge of Folkestone in Kent. **Eurostar trains** (tel: 08705 186 186; from outside UK tel: (00 44) 1233 617575; website www.eurostar.com) run from Paris and Brussels to London Waterloo via Lille Europe, Calais Fréthun and Ashford (with no other intermediate stops); holders of Eurail and Interrail and BritRail passes get a discounted fare. Journey time from Paris or Brussels to London is about 3 hrs.

Drivers can take their vehicles through the Tunnel on the **Eurotunnel shuttle** between Calais and Folkestone. There is no need to book, you can just turn up; you can also book a specific crossing in advance. Tel: (from UK) 08705 353535; tel: (from France) (00 33) 321 006 100; website: www.eurotunnel.com. There are departures every 15 mins, 24 hrs a day. At the other end you just drive off and join the motorway.

TRAVELLING AROUND BRITAIN

TRAINS

The rail network is operated by some 25 companies. However, you can buy a through ticket to and from anywhere on the network, and staff at ticket offices are obliged to inform you of the cheapest fare. All trains have standard (second) class, and many long-distance ones have first class too. Light refreshments are often available. Generally you don't need to reserve seats; however some main lines can get crowded, notably the west coast route from London Euston to Glasgow.

> For **national rail enquiries**, tel: 08457 48 49 50 (24 hrs); Textphone for the deaf or hard of hearing; tel: 0845 60 50 600 (24 hrs).

Day return fares are usually only slightly more expensive than singles. They apply to journeys begun after 0930, and you are not normally allowed to break your outward journey. **Five-day** and **saver** (one-month) **returns** are also sold. Full-price **returns** for peak period travel cost twice the price of a single.

RAIL PASSES   **BritRail Passes** are the best value if you are exploring Britain by rail, but cannot be purchased by UK residents, and are sold only outside the UK. The prices vary according to the type of pass and where you buy it; for details see the website www.britrail.com. The BritRail Classic Pass gives freedom of

---

TICKET TYPES

'Open' tickets offer the greatest flexibility but are the most expensive option

Open Single no restrictions; valid on the date shown on the ticket or on either of the following two days
Open Return no restrictions; outward validity as for Open Single; return within one month

If you are prepared to accept some time or date restrictions, a range of cheaper tickets is available, including:

Day Single and Day Return no time restrictions; valid only on the date shown on the ticket
Cheap Day Return peak-time* travel restrictions; valid only on the date shown on the ticket
Saver Return peak-time* travel restrictions; valid outwards only on the date shown on the ticket; return within one month
SuperSaver Return peak-time* and peak-day** travel restrictions; valid outwards only on the date shown on the ticket; return within one month
Network AwayBreak Return (London and South-East only) peak-time* travel restrictions; valid outwards only on the date shown on the ticket; return within five days

* peak time usually means before (around) 0930
** peak day means Fridays, summer Saturdays and peak holiday dates

If you are able to buy your ticket three or more days in advance (the longer the time, the greater the reduction) and commit yourself to travel by a particular train, 'Apex' (advance purchase) tickets offer even greater savings.

SCENIC JOURNEYS ON THE MAIN NETWORK

The *Thomas Cook Rail Map of Great Britain and Ireland* highlights the most scenic rail routes in the country. Classic trips include:

Swansea to Conwy through the heart of Mid Wales, via the spa town of Llandrindod Wells, to the sea at Aberdovey (Aberdyfi), then north past Harlech Castle; joining the private narrow-gauge Ffestiniog Railway at Minffordd, through central Snowdonia to the walled town of Conwy.

Leeds to Carlisle via Settle, traversing the Pennines, and crossing the famous Ribblehead Viaduct on the way, before the section along the Eden Valley.

Carnforth to Carlisle via Barrow-in-Furness, crossing low viaducts around the north side of Morecambe Bay, then hugging the Cumbrian coast with views into the Lake District and towards southern Scotland.

Glasgow to Mallaig (see pp. 321–326) the celebrated 264-km West Highland Railway takes in the watery wilderness of Rannoch Moor, the forests of Glen Spean, Fort William and the 21-arch Glenfinnan Viaduct before finishing along the shores of Loch Morar.

Bradford to Burnley passing the Victorian textile-making towns of Calderdale, including Halifax and Hebden Bridge: industrial heritage at its most scenic.

Inverness to Kyle of Lochalsh (see pp. 297–299) across the neck of Scotland, snaking up sizable gradients, dropping to Loch Carron and the ferry port for Skye.

travel over 4, 8, 15 or 22 consecutive days or a calendar month, while the BritRail FlexiPass entitles you to choose 4, 8 or 15 days to travel over a two-month period. There are also Party Passes (with 50% off for the third and fourth passengers), Family Passes and regional passes covering Britain and Ireland combined or south-east England. Other passes (also available to UK residents) cover Scotland, Wales and various other regions. Alternatively you can get a third off all off-peak travel by purchasing a **Young Person's Railcard** if you are aged 16–25; it costs £18 and is valid for a year (website: www.young-persons-railcard.co.uk). There are similar deals for the over-60s. All ages are entitled to buy a **Network Card**, giving a third off off-peak travel for a year in south-east England (and Dorset), price £20.

NOSTALGIA RAILWAYS In addition to the mainline companies, there are a number of privately run railways (not covered by rail passes), operated as nostalgia attractions (mostly steam-hauled). Many of these are great fun, but few actually take you anywhere useful or cover much ground. The best ones include:

The **Bluebell Railway** from Horsted Keynes (bus shuttle to East Grinstead rail station) to Sheffield Park (a fantastic National Trust garden), between London and Brighton. The track was opened in the early 1960s by enthusiasts. As Britain's first nostalgia railway it got a lot of the most characterful and oldest rolling stock and engines, and the stations are well done out in period adverts and signs.

The **North Yorkshire Moors Railway** from Pickering to Grosmont, through the North York Moors (north-east of York). This is quite a useful way of getting into the Moors if you want to explore the national park.

The **Severn Valley Railway** from Kidderminster to Bridgnorth (west of Birmingham), via the attractive town of Bewdley. Bridgnorth with its cliff-top position is well worth a visit.

The **Romney, Hythe & Dymchurch Railway** from Hythe to Dungeness, Kent (west of Dover). Not scenic, just plain odd. The line, built by two racing drivers in 1927, is said to be the world's smallest scale public railway. Tiny locos and toytown-like carriages make the 13½-mile (22-km) journey to Dungeness. This is perhaps Britain's most surreal place, a vast shingle bank dotted with old railway carriage shacks and fisherman's huts and dominated by a vast nuclear power station.

BUSES

National Express, tel: 08705 808080, 0800–2200 (or book online, website: www.gobycoach.com), operates much of the national bus network, connecting most major towns. Generally long-distance bus travel is cheaper than rail travel, though as you are travelling mostly along motorways and other major roads it's not exactly a bundle of fun, and there's always the risk of getting delayed in heavy traffic.

Local bus services are run by a bewildering number of private companies. National TravelLine (tel: 0870 608 2 608) will be able to help with local bus service enquiries or you can look on the website: www.showbus.co.uk/timetables/index.html. For many counties you can get free public transport maps from tourist information centres and bus stations, showing bus numbers and giving an indication of frequencies. The density of networks varies enormously. For example, there are excellent services on the Isle of Wight, while much of Mid Wales is a bus desert.

> ### BUS PASSES
> If you plan to do a lot of bus travel consider purchasing a **National Express card**. The **Tourist Trail Pass** gives unlimited travel throughout the country for a stated period; additionally there are cards on sale giving discount travel for young persons (aged 16–25), students, lone parents, families and over 50s.

DOMESTIC FLIGHTS

You can get up to Scotland in only 1½ hours from London by plane. There are some very good deals with budget no-frills airlines. easyJet (tel: 0870 600 0000; website: easyJet.com) run domestic flights to Aberdeen, Belfast, Bristol, Edinburgh, Glasgow,

Liverpool, Newcastle, London Luton, London Stansted and London Gatwick. Ryanair (tel: (0541) 569569; website: www.ryanair.com) fly to to Ireland (see p. 16), Blackpool, Glasgow and London Stansted; they also fly from Dublin to London Gatwick and London Luton.

CYCLING

It takes careful planning to explore Britain by bike, to dodge the busiest roads and to take in the best countryside. Britain hasn't been the most cycle-friendly place in Europe, but things are improving with the development of a 9,500-mile (15,000-km) **National Cycle Network** by the charity **Sustrans**, 35 King Street, Bristol BS1 4DZ; tel: (0117) 929 0888 (website: www.sustrans.org.uk), due for completion in 2005. Large parts of the Network are already open, taking in quiet roads and specially created cycle paths; Sustrans sell a range of excellent maps showing where these go.

Cyclists' interests are catered for by the **CTC** (Cyclists' Touring Club), 69 Meadrow, Godalming, Surrey GU7 3HS, UK; tel: (01483) 417217; website: www.ctc.org.uk. They can advise members on cycle hire, transporting bikes on planes and trains, cycle routes and cyclist-friendly accommodation.

Recommended areas for cycling are East Anglia (Suffolk and Norfolk particularly), the Cotswolds, Northumberland, the Isle of Wight and (for the fit) Mid Wales and the Welsh borders. The whole of the South Downs Way (Winchester to Eastbourne, 112 miles/180 km) is open to cyclists, providing a superb off-road experience over chalk downland.

Taking bikes on trains is mostly feasible, subject to space; many rail companies take cycles free of charge, though often not during weekday rush hours. Some companies, including First Great Western, Great North Eastern Railway and Hull Trains require reservation and a payment of £3 (sometimes reduced to £1 if you book in at least two hours in advance. Folding bikes, however, can always be carried free. You cannot take a bike on a bus used to replace a train service during weekend engineering works. For details, get a leaflet on the subject from any major station.

WALKING

Britain is one of the most walked countries in the world, and there is an admirable degree of access. There are three types of **right of way** in England and Wales, on which you have a legal right to walk: public footpaths (open to walkers only; often waymarked with yellow arrows), public bridleways (open to walkers, cyclists and horse riders; waymarked with blue arrows), and byways (open to all traffic). The routes are clearly marked on Ordnance Survey (OS) maps.

Britain also has an amazing number of **long-distance paths**. These include the famous National Trails (official long-distance paths maintained by the Countryside Agency) such as the Pennine Way and Offa's Dyke Path; others signposted by local authorities (such as the Cotswold Way), plus many others created by enthusiasts who cobbled together existing footpaths to make their own routes.

Additionally, you are also allowed to walk on some open land such as commons and moorland, along canal towpaths, and through countryside owned by the National Trust. In Scotland the rules are more nebulous: there is a tradition of access in open country, but routes are subject to closure in the deer-stalking and grouse-shooting seasons (1 July–15 Feb and 12 Aug–10 Dec). So generally you can go where you like in upland areas, but few rights of way as such exist, and not many walkers' routes are shown on OS maps.

WHERE TO WALK Britain's scenery is so varied that there's really something for all tastes. This list highlights areas accessible by rail or good bus services.

Snowdonia National Park has the highest peaks in England and Wales, with some seriously challenging walks and climbs, as well as easier ascents. Betws-y-Coed station is at the heart of it all, with good bus links to the walking area around Snowdon – the highest summit, interesting whichever way you ascend (there's even a steam train up). Another magnificent area is at Idwal Cottage Youth Hostel (A5 between Betws y Coed and Bangor; plenty of buses), where there's a nature trail around the stunning mountain lake of Llyn Idwal as well as sterner climbs to the summits of Glyder Fawr and Glyder Fach. Barmouth station is handy for the unspoilt and easily walked Mawddach Estuary. The coast is only intermittently worthwhile, but it gets exhilarating just out of Conwy, where Conwy Mountain has great views and is a straightforward stroll up. Northwards across the bay and above Llandudno, Great Ormes Head is even easier to access thanks to its chair lift and tram.

The Lake District National Park is wonderfully varied, with an incredible concentration of walks, from easy strolls along lakes and valleys to demanding hikes up rocky fells; the train network doesn't penetrate that far, but you can travel to Windermere for buses to Ambleside and Keswick to get you in the middle of things. Good walking areas accessible by bus include Grasmere, Derwentwater (ringed by a series of contrasting hills and mountains, and with a boat service linking places around the lake, including Keswick) and Langdale. You can also get the bus from Penrith to Ullswater, where you can approach the famous peak of Helvellyn from its most challenging and interesting side, as well as lovely walks on the eastern shore (you can return to base by steamer service).

RAMBLERS' ASSOCIATION

For information on all walking matters in Britain, contact the Ramblers' Association, Camelford House, 87–90 Albert Embankment, London SE1 7TW, tel: (020) 7339 8500; website: www.ramblers.org.uk.

The **Scottish Highlands and Islands** include Britain's highest mountain, Ben Nevis (4406 ft/1343 m), easily reached from Fort William, itself a useful base with buses to Glen Coe and elsewhere. The long-distance West Highland Way (from Milngavie, at the edge of Glasgow) ends here, with a finale section taking in the majestic valley of Glen Nevis. The isle of Arran is reached from Ardrossan station and has a pearl of a hike up to its highest point, Goat Fell. On the rail line from Perth to Inverness, Dunkeld and Pitlochry are popular walking centres.

The North York Moors National Park is easy terrain, with gently rolling moorland cut into by green valleys, and a coastal section of high, sandstone cliffs and delightful seaside towns and villages. The long-distance Cleveland Way from Helmsley to Filey takes in the best of it, with a coastal finale from Saltburn southwards; the route can be completed in a week by reasonably fit walkers. You can get to the coast by train to Saltburn, Whitby, Scarborough and Filey, and there are good bus services linking up these and other places. Good stretches of coast to head for include between Ravenscar and the old fishing village of Robin Hood's Bay.

The Pennines These hills run from the south end of the Peak National Park in central England, through the Yorkshire Dales National Park and Northumberland National Park. The Peak District is the best served for public transport, though being ringed by large cities it doesn't feel as remote as some of the other areas. Edale station is at the start of the long-distance Pennine Way, which takes a long, arduous course up the 'backbone of England' to the Scottish Borders; for something less daunting, walk over Mam Tor to Castleton, in the heart of the cave country. North of the Peak District the moors get steadily austere, broken by the partly wooded valley of Calderdale, where there are fascinating walks rich in industrial heritage around the former mill town of Hebden Bridge (rail connections to Bradford and Leeds). The Yorkshire Dales have limited train access, though the scenic Settle–Carlisle line passes through Horton in Ribblesdale, close to the distinctive cave-riddled mountains of Pen-y-ghent and Ingleborough. There are decent bus services getting you into Wharfedale (where Grassington is a good walking centre) and to Malham Cove for some exciting limestone scenery. Into Northumberland it gets very remote, although you can get the train to Hexham and the bus to get onto Hadrian's Wall for a walk along this extraordinary Roman relic; the best stretch is around Housesteads Fort.

Eastern England is low-lying and flat, with most of interest along the coast or beside rivers (this area features some of the great bird sites of northern Europe): head for the marshes and dunes of the North Norfolk Coast west of Sheringham station, along the waterways of the Broads National Park around Wroxham or the incredibly remote station of Berney Arms, or along the water meadows of the Stour valley near Manningtree station, at the hub of the countryside immortalised by the painter John Constable.

Around London are plenty of possibilities, with superb cliff walks accessible from

Hastings, Eastbourne and Dover, the South Downs reached from Lewes and Arundel, Knole Park near Sevenoaks, Windsor Great Park from Windsor and the Thames valley from Henley-on-Thames.

The Pembrokeshire Coast Path can be reached easily from Fishguard, Tenby and Milford Haven stations; Fishguard is closest to the most dramatic sections.

The 600-mile (970-km) **South-West Coast Path** follows the entire coast of Dorset, Devon and Cornwall and much of Somerset, with Penzance, St Ives, Falmouth and Weymouth making handy access points.

DRIVING

Driving in Britain is a real mixed bag: wonderfully unspoilt routes through the back of beyond, as well as tedious bumper-to-bumper jams along main roads carved up by endless roadworks. In many rural areas driving is the only feasible way of covering much ground, but if you are sticking to major cities you may have an easier time on public transport.

Car hire and driving licences. Car hire is widely available through the standard chains such as Avis, tel: 0870 606 0100; Budget, tel: 0800 626063; Hertz, tel: 0990 996699; and National, tel: 0990 565656. Holiday Autos, tel: 0870 400 4453 (website: www.holidayautos.com), can be good value, and easyJet run a bargain car rental agency with online bookings (website: www.easyrentacar.com) with locations at Birmingham, Glasgow, Liverpool, London (London Bridge and Chelsea) and Manchester. Or pick up a local Yellow Pages directory and shop around.

> Weekends are generally the quietest times to travel, though Sunday evenings are busy with weekend traffic returning to London and other major centres of population. Sunday mornings and lunchtime are very quiet, however.

Most foreign driving licences are acceptable. If you hold a licence written in a foreign language, it is a good idea to get an official translation from an embassy or recognised automobile association before leaving your country, or get an international driver's licence. Car hire firms require you to have held your licence for at least a year. Remember that the vast majority of rental cars are manual; if you want an automatic, you'll need to request one specifically.

Driving conditions. Those unused to driving in Britain would do well not to start in central London, as it is one gigantic maze to escape from. However, major airports such as Gatwick and Stansted are well out of the city, and even Heathrow is not too bad to drive out of, as long as you're not going straight into London itself. The general standard of signposting on roads is very good. There is a wide range of road atlases. Michelin road maps highlight scenic routes in green, which can be useful for planning a tour.

If you have never driven in Britain before, you'll find a few different things here. The obvious difference from most foreign countries is that traffic drives on the left. British roads are full of roundabouts (or rotaries): give way to any traffic already on the roundabout and go round it clockwise, indicating left before you turn off onto your exit. If your exit is the third one on a four-way roundabout, indicate right as you drive onto the roundabout, get in the right-hand lane if there are two lanes, then after the second exit move over to the left and indicate left to leave the roundabout.

At traffic lights you must always stop on red unless there is a green filter arrow indicating traffic moving in a particular direction may go. Cars are often parked down one side or both sides of a narrow street, so you'll often have to pull out onto the other side of the street. On motorways and dual carriageways, use the inside (leftmost) lane for normal driving and the outside lane(s) for overtaking. Don't sit in the middle or outside lane if there's room to move back into the inside one as this can make drivers behind impatient.

Speed limits. Britain may have gone metric, but all road signs and speed restrictions are in miles; speedometers also give speeds in miles per hour. Speed limits are 70 mph (113 km/h) on motorways and dual carriageways (divided highways), 60 mph (97 km/h) on country roads, and 30mph (48 km/h) in built-up areas (unless stipulated otherwise: sometimes it's 40 mph (64 km/h) or 50 mph (80 km/h), so look out for signs). Speed traps and speed cameras are everywhere and it is illegal to break the speed limit.

Parking. Finding an on-road space in a town or city centre can be tricky, though usually there's no shortage of paying car parks. Yellow lines along the edge of the road denote parking prohibitions (although you can stop to load/unload): double or single lines mean waiting is restricted to times specified on nearby signs; if there is no sign for a double line it means no parking at any time.

TOLLS

Motorways are all toll-free, though you have to pay tolls for some bridges and tunnels, such as the Dartford river crossing (taking M25 traffic) and the Severn bridges used by M4 and M48 traffic to cross between England and Wales. Though the tolls can seem a bit hefty, it is not worth the extra fuel and time expended making elaborate detours to avoid them.

FUEL

Most cars take lead-free petrol, although some take diesel. Fuel is more than twice as expensive as in the US. Supermarket filling stations are often the best value.

Never stop on roads with red lines along the edge, except at specified parking bays. Do not park within the zigzag lines at approaches to zebra crossings, or in designated residents' parking zones. Fixed penalty notices for parking offences are issued by traffic wardens: if you get one, pay the fine by post straight away, otherwise the fine will be increased. In London, cars are frequently clamped or towed away for breaking parking regulations, involving extortionate fines.

REACHING IRELAND

BY AIR

Flights are very busy in the morning and evening when advance booking is essential. Discounted fares are available on some off-peak flights but again it is wise to book ahead. Student/youth fares operate year round. Check with STA Travel Ltd; tel: (020) 7361 6161.

Ireland's major gateways for travellers arriving by air are Belfast, Dublin and Shannon airports. There are very frequent flights from London and other cities in the UK, as well as direct links to regional airports at Cork, Kerry, Waterford, Galway, Knock, Sligo, Londonderry and Carrickfinn. More than 25 UK airports, including London City, Gatwick, Heathrow, Luton and Stansted and places as far apart as Aberdeen and Southampton, have links with Ireland.

The main airlines operating between Britain and Ireland are Aer Lingus, British Airways, British Midland and Ryanair. Few flights last much longer than an hour. Services from the United States and Canada are operated by major airlines into Belfast, Dublin and Shannon airports, and there are direct flights to Belfast and Dublin from many European centres.

Belfast International Airport is at Aldergrove and there is a regular Airbus service into the centre 15 miles (24 km) away.

Dublin Airport is only 6 miles (10 km) from the city centre, but heavy traffic can make the journey by car or taxi frustratingly long. An Airlink bus service runs between the city centre and the airport.

Shannon Airport is 16 miles (26 km) west of Limerick. Bus Éireann runs a regular service between the airport and city.

All three airports have foreign exchange and banking services, car hire facilities and tourist information centres.

BY FERRY

Car and passenger ferry services offer an economical alternative method of reaching Ireland from Britain for families and groups of three or four. About a dozen companies operate services from ports in England, Wales and Scotland. Fast, modern vessels – including giant catamarans – are used on the crossings. All of them have drive-on/drive-off facilities, carry foot passengers and are equipped with comfortable lounges, restaurants and shops.

Sailing times vary between an hour and 4 hours and most companies offer several sailings a day. The crossing between Swansea in South Wales and Cork takes 10 hours, but is a viable alternative for those touring south-west Ireland. Travellers from mainland Europe can sail with Irish Ferries and P&O Irish Sea Ferries from Cherbourg to Rosslare. The crossing takes about 18 hours. Brittany Ferries offer a 14-hour crossing between Roscoff and Cork once a week in summer.

REACHING IRELAND

Holyhead on the island of Anglesea to Dublin and Dún Laoghaire.

Fishguard and Pembroke in Wales to Rosslare in County Wexford.

The Scottish ports of Stranraer, Cairnryan and Troon to Belfast and Larne in Northern Ireland.

Other routes operate between Liverpool and Belfast; Liverpool and Dublin; and from Campbelltown, Scotland, to Ballycastle in Northern Ireland.

Most ferry ports in Ireland are reasonably handy for the centres they serve. In Belfast vessels tie up within walking distance of the city centre. In Dublin a short taxi ride will take you to the city's heart, and from Dún Laoghaire you can take a suburban DART train or bus to central Dublin.

BY TRAIN

Fast and comfortable rail services connect all parts of Britain to ports with ferry services to Ireland, where Irish Rail services provide connections to stations throughout the island.

For information on train services to British ferry ports contact National Rail enquiries; tel: 08457 48 49 50; website: www.nationalrail.co.uk/travel (information); or 0845 722 2333; other websites: www.qjump.co.uk, www.thetrainline.com (credit card bookings). Combined rail and ferry reservations can also be made through Stenaline Rail/Ferry Reservations; tel: 0870 545 5455. Information on rail and bus connections to Irish ferry ports can be obtained from the London office of the Irish national transport authority, CIÉ; tel: (020) 8686 0994.

BY COACH

Reservations can be made in person at Eurolines, 52 Grosvenor Gardens, London SW1, or with any National Express agent. For enquiries and credit card reservations; tel: 0870 514 3219. In Ireland contact Bus Éireann, Busaras, Store Street, Dublin 1; tel: (01) 836 6111; website: www.buseireann.ie.

Coach services are available between Britain and Ireland. Daily services are operated between London and Birmingham to Dublin, Galway, Cork and more than 100 other destinations. Operated by Eurolines in conjunction with National Express and Bus Éireann, all services have modern coaches with large windows, reclining seats and on-board toilets. Smoking is not permitted.

Regional departure points in Britain include Bradford, Bristol, Chester, Leeds, Liverpool, Luton, Manchester and Reading in England, Cardiff and Newport in Wales, and Glasgow in Scotland.

TRAVELLING AROUND IRELAND

Ireland is generally well served by public transport, though rail services are sparse compared with mainland Britain.

In the Republic, bus and train services are provided by CIÉ, the national transport authority, which has responsibility for Iarnrod Éireann (Irish Rail), Bus Éireann (Irish Bus) and Bus Átha Cliath (Dublin Bus). The integrated public transport company in the north is Translink, comprising Northern Ireland Railways, Ulsterbus and Citybus (Belfast). Public transport services on both sides of the border are modern, efficient and clean.

TRAINS

There are two classes on Irish trains: standard and super standard. A supplement of €8.25 is charged for travel to all destinations for super standard class, which is the equivalent of first class. Cycles can be transported on trains at a cost of €2.50–€7.60 each way, depending upon distance. Inter-rail, Eurrail and Euro Domino passes are valid in Ireland.

Iarnród Éireann (Irish Rail) (tel: (01) 836 6222; website: www.irishrail.ie) operates services to most cities and major towns, with Dublin as the hub. Travel between centres in the west of Ireland often involves a trip east to Dublin to make a connection at Dublin. To avoid this it is advisable to use Bus Éireann as a link.

DART (Dublin Area Rapid Transit) serves 30 stations from Malahide and Howth, County Dublin, south along the coast to Greystones in County Wicklow. Trains are frequent and fast. Multiple journey tickets, including the Dublin Explorer, which allows unlimited travel on DART trains and Dublin Bus routes over a four-day period, may be bought at any DART station.

Northern Ireland Railways has four main routes from Belfast Central Station (tel: (028) 9089 9411): north to Londonderry via Ballymena and Coleraine; north-east to the ferry port of Larne; east to Bangor along the shores of Belfast Lough; and south to Dublin via Newry.

The Dublin–Belfast express does the trip in 2 hours with a standard fare of €29 one way and day return and €43 monthly return. There are eight trains a day in each direction. Busy times to avoid if possible are holiday weekends and the last trains on Fri and Sun. Seats may be reserved.

BUSES

Bus Éireann (Irish Bus) has a comprehensive network serving all cities and most towns and villages outside Dublin. It also provides services in the cities of Cork, Galway, Limerick and Waterford; tel: (01) 836 6111; website: www.buseireann.ie.

SPECIAL DEALS

A wide range of special tickets covering rail and bus travel is available in Northern Ireland and the Republic. Some deals cover travel on both sides of the border.

The **Emerald Card**, valid for bus and rail travel throughout Ireland, offers either 8-days travel out of 15 consecutive days or 15 out of 30 consecutive days.

The **Irish Rover train ticket** is valid for journeys on Irish Rail and Northern Ireland Railways and provides 5 days travel out of 15 consecutive days.

The **Irish Rover bus pass** covers travel on all Iarnród Éireann and Ulsterbus services, including cross border services and city routes in Belfast, Cork, Galway, Limerick and Waterford. There are three deals, offering either 3 days travel out of 8 consecutive days, 8 out of 15, or 15 out of 30.

In the Republic the **Irish Explorer** ticket offers 5 days rail-only travel out of 15 consecutive days or 15-days rail and bus travel out of 30 consecutive days.

The **Irish Rambler**, valid on Bus Éireann provincial routes and on Cork, Galway, Limerick and Waterford city services, offers 3 days travel out of 8 consecutive days, 8 days out of 15, or 15 out of 30.

Bus Átha Cliath (Dublin Bus) operates all public services in the greater Dublin area, which includes parts of counties Wicklow, Kildare and Meath. A wide range of discounted pre-paid tickets, valid for a day to a month, may be bought at the CIÉ information desk at Dublin Airport, the Dublin Bus head office at 59 Upper O'Connell St, Dublin 1, or at more than 200 bus ticket agencies throughout the city and suburbs.

Ulsterbus (tel: (028) 9033 3000) provides an excellent network of regular services, with good express links between those towns not served by a rail link. Cheap day returns and Freedom of Northern Ireland tickets offering unlimited bus and rail travel are available at Ulsterbus depots.

COACH TOURS A wide variety of day and half-day coach tours operates from the Europa Bus Centre in Belfast to such places of interest as the Glens of Antrim, the Giant's Causeway, Fermanagh Lakeland, the Sperrin Mountains, the Mountains of Mourne and Armagh city. Tours take place mostly in summer.

Information on open-top summer bus tours, steam train trips and tours of Belfast city is available from tourist offices.

Full day and half-day guided tours are organised from the cities and larger towns in the Republic to some of the most interesting and scenic places in Ireland. Bus Éireann operates day tours all year round from Dublin to the Boyne Valley (Newgrange) and Glendalough. Various escorted coach tours are operated by many companies.

DRIVING

In spite of high petrol prices and the comparatively high cost of car hire, motoring remains an attractive option, especially for families or small groups. Apart from the freedom from timetable tyranny and fixed itineraries, driving provides true flexibility and the opportunity to visit on a whim many of the fascinating sights and places that lie off the main routes in Ireland.

IRISH MILES

Distances on road signs in Northern Ireland are always in miles. In the Republic most of the old black and white finger posts show distances in miles, while the newer green and white signs are in kilometres.

Some very old milestones on both sides of the border are marked in Irish miles. At 2240 yards (2048 m), the Irish mile is 480 yards (439 m) longer than the standard British mile.

Signs in the Republic are bilingual, with information and place names in English and Irish.

Rules of the road – speed limits seat belt wearing, drink/drive laws, etc. – are the same in Northern Ireland and, with minor differences, the Republic as they are in mainland Britain. The basic rule, of course, is 'Drive on the left, overtake on the right'.

Speed limits are 30 mph (48 km/h) in towns, unless signs show otherwise, 60 mph (97 km/h) on single carriageways and 70 mph (113 km/h) on dual carriageways and motorways. Car drivers and passengers must wear seat belts, and motor cyclists must wear crash helmets.

Traffic volume is noticeably lower than on the mainland. Roads are generally well surfaced, though some lanes in remote areas in the Republic may be dotted with potholes.

PARKING Outside Belfast, Dublin and some of the larger towns parking is rarely a problem. You will find a free car park or unrestricted street parking in many smaller places. In Northern Ireland and the Republic car parks and lay-bys are indicated by a large white 'P' on a blue sign. Dublin, Belfast and some other centres have multi-storey and open car parks as well as parking meters, but parking tends to be expensive. Disc parking operates in some places in the Republic. Discs can be bought at petrol stations, tourist offices, newsagents and some other shops.

As in mainland Britain, on-street parking restrictions are indicated by yellow lines painted along the roadside. A single yellow line means parking is allowed for restricted periods or at certain times; a nearby sign will give details. Double yellow lines indicate that parking is strictly forbidden.

CAR HIRE International and local car hire companies operate on both sides of the border. Rental desks will be found at Belfast, Dublin and other major airports and lists of hire companies can be supplied by tourist offices.

Rates vary according to the type of vehicle and time of year. Book early if you will be travelling in Ireland during mid-July to mid-Aug. The best rates may be obtained by booking a fly-drive or rail-sail-drive package.

Make sure you know the total price of renting a car, since insurance and tax are often added to the quoted price. In addition to the third party, fire and theft insurance that comes with the basic rental deal, it is wise to take out a Collision Damage Waiver (CDW) to cover all costs in the event of an accident.

RED PLATES

In Northern Ireland you will see some cars bearing red R plates. 'R' stands for Restricted and indicates that the driver has passed his or her test within the past 12 months and must keep to low speeds. The plates also help other road users to identify inexperienced drivers and make allowances for them.

To rent a car, drivers must be at least 21 (some companies say 25) with at least a year's full licence experience. Some companies will not rent to drivers over 70 or 75. If you intend crossing the border make sure this is allowed under the terms of the rental agreement and insurance cover. And don't forget your licence!

CYCLING Ireland's peaceful countryside and quiet roads are ideal for cycle tours or even the odd day out on a bike. You can rent a bike in many places for about £12/€19 a day or £50/€79 a week. Information on cycle hire is available from the Irish Tourist Board, 150 New Bond St, London W1S 2AQ; tel: 0800 039 7000; fax: (020) 7493 9065; www.kerna.ie/wci; e-mail: wci@kerna.ie.

TRAVEL BASICS

ACCOMMODATION

Many tourist information centres provide **accommodation booking services**. Often these are free (the hotel or guesthouse owner pays the commission), although sometimes there is a small charge. These centres only deal with accommodation that has been inspected – the owner has to pay a hefty annual fee to be on their books, so many smaller establishments miss out.

In comparison to much of mainland Europe, hotel and guesthouse accommodation in Britain and Ireland is quite expensive. It can be better value if you are sharing a room, though rates tend to be per person rather than per room, and you can get reasonable deals for singles.

The tourist boards for England, Wales, Scotland, Northern Ireland and the Irish Republic grade hotels and guesthouses according to facilities. Rooms with private bathroom are becoming more the norm but are by no means universal.

Hotels tend to be particularly pricey in big cities, notably London. If you are touring around and want the occasional splurge, there are many highly characterful country house hotels scattered around rural areas such as the Lake District and Dartmoor, which can make memorable stopovers. Wolsey Lodges (9 Market Place, Hadleigh, Ipswich, Suffolk, IP7 5DL; tel: (01473) 827500; wolsey@wolseylo.demon.co.uk; www.wolsey-lodges.co.uk) is a non-profit making consortium of nearly 200 privately-owned houses offering good accommodation in an atmosphere more akin to a house-party than a hotel; locations are spread across the country. A full listing of AA (Automobile Association) inspected hotels and guesthouses in Britain and Ireland is on the AA website: www.theaa.co.uk/getaway/hotels/hotels_home.jsp. For a list of **hotel chains** see the Directory, page 405.

A distinct notch down in price (typically £15–£30 per person), and often better value than hotels, are **guesthouses** providing **bed and breakfast ('B&B')**. Sometimes for an extra charge they offer evening meal (usually served quite early, at around 7pm).

Northern Ireland has just eight hostels (website: www.hini.org.uk). In the Republic of Ireland there's a fair scattering, particularly around Dublin and along the west coast. The Irish website is: www.irelandyha.org.

These range from a couple of spare rooms in a private home or in a farm to rooms over pubs and buildings fully given over to the accommodation business. Rooms often have tea-making facilities and TV, and for breakfast you get a hefty fry-up of bacon, eggs, sausages and more. If you're travelling solo and arrive late in the day you are sometimes given a twin or double for the price of a single. Such accommodation is in plentiful supply, though in July and August it can be hard to find a bed in tourist areas like the Scottish Highlands where all the holiday traffic winds round a few roads and ends up at places like Oban and Fort William.

An extensive network of **youth hostels** spreads across Britain. The vast majority are run by the Youth Hostels Association (covering England and Wales, tel: 0870 870 8808; website: www.yha.org.uk) and Scottish Youth Hostels Association (tel: (01786) 891400; website: www.syha.org.uk). There is no upper age limit, but prices are lower for under 18s: typically £4.75–£6.90 for under 18s and £6.75–£12.50 for adults, with a £1 reduction for student cardholders. Some city locations are more expensive.

CARRY ON CAMPING

Campsites are well scattered, although there are few within larger towns and cities. Tourist information centres have lists of approved sites, which range from relatively luxurious to a flat area of grass with a cold water tap. The Camping and Caravanning Club, Greenfields House, Westwood Way, Coventry CV4 8JH; tel: (024) 7669 4995; fax: (024) 7669 4886; website: www.campingandcaravanningclub.co.uk; publishes a book of camping and caravan sites. Camping in the wild is often possible, but remember that even open land is owned by someone and you do not have a right to pitch your tent where you like: always enquire locally first if possible.

Beds are normally within dormitories, although individual rooms may be available. Some hostels have curfews and require that you carry out daily chores. You can usually choose between the hostel food (very good value, with evening meals around £5) or use the self-catering facilities. If you plan to do a lot of hostelling, it is worth taking your own sheets or sheet sleeping bag to avoid the small sheet hire fee. You can get annual membership (£12.50 adult, £6.25 under 18s) through the national offices given above, or at any hostel. Book ahead during the school holidays (especially July and Aug). You can book up to six months in advance using Hostelling International's free online service, www.hostelbooking.com.

DISABLED TRAVELLERS

The Royal Association for Disability and Rehabilitation (RADAR), 12 City Forum, 250 City Road, London EC1V 8AF (tel: (020) 7250 3222; minicom: (020) 7250 0212; website: www.radar.org.uk) is the national organisation for people with disabilities. Useful RADAR books are *Getting There* (£5 including postage) and the annual *Holidays in Britain and Ireland: A Guide for Disabled People*. Information in the USA is available from the Society for Accessible Travel and Hospitality (SATH), 347 5th Avenue, Suite 610, New York, NY 10016; tel: (212) 447 7284; www.sath.org.

FOOD AND DRINK

British and Irish cuisine has become so cosmopolitan over the last 20 years that it can be hard to find characteristically local food. There are still regional and national

Eating out regularly can be a major drain on finances, but you can save a lot by picking up picnic items at supermarkets, greengrocers and market stalls, and if you want a restaurant meal by eating a set-menu lunch rather than an evening meal.

specialities – such as fresh fish and shellfish in many seaside towns, cakes such as bara brith (a Welsh fruit loaf) and parkin (a Yorkshire gingerbread), Scottish haggis and West Country clotted cream (served with jam and scones for a not exactly healthy 'cream tea'). That great British institution, fish and chips, is still going strong. Pizza, burgers and kebabs lead the way in fast food, and Indian, Hong Kong Chinese and Italian eateries are pretty much everywhere. Vegetarian food is increasingly popular, and even in towns without specialist veggie restaurants you will find vegetarian items on the menus.

Sandwich bars are found in most towns and cities: in London they are usually the cheapest option. Note that you don't pay tax on takeaway cold food, but you do if you consume it on the premises.

Many museums and other attractions such as stately homes have inexpensive cafés, generally serving very pleasant light lunches, cakes and teas: the standards at National Trust properties are almost invariably high.

Most pubs serve food, often 1200–1400 and around 1900–2100, varying from bought-in fare to imaginative home cooking. Many pubs have two menus – basic bar food and more expensive restaurant offerings. In smaller towns there can be nowhere to eat between 1700, when cafés close, and 1900, when pubs start serving. If you're on the road, motorway service stations are convenient and well signposted, though the food is mostly forgettable and is often over-priced.

Ireland has plenty of specialities, including the nutty-textured soda bread, barm brack (a fruit loaf) and such alcoholic drinks as stout (famously Guinness) and Irish whiskey. The Irish are great meat-eaters, although fish and shellfish – particularly oysters and salmon – are widely on offer. Dublin and larger cities have plenty of vegetarian restaurants, and elsewhere there is usually something non-meaty on the menu. Eating out can be expensive, but pub food is often good value.

Food festivals, fairs and gourmet events with local contacts are listed at www.aboutfood.co.uk.

BOOZE

Alcohol is famously represented by 'real ale', a naturally conditioned draught dark beer that you can only get in pubs and is served direct from the barrel or pumped up from the cellar by tall wooden handpumps. Served cool rather than ice-cold, real ales vary greatly in character from one brewery to another and come in a range of styles. The most widely available is bitter (brown and hoppy), but there are numerous strong brews, old ales, golden-coloured summer ales, dark, sweetish mild beers and black, dry stouts. You can also sometimes find 'real' draught cider (or scrumpy) – a deceptively strong dry or sweet alcoholic drink made of apples. The fizzier bottled, canned and pasteurised draught versions are much more widely available.

HEALTH

All visitors to Britain and Northern Ireland are entitled to free emergency treatment on the National Health Service (NHS) through hospitals and surgeries. Additionally, for free advice from a qualified nurse on medical matters you can call NHS Direct; tel: 0845 4647.

Chemists such as Boots or Superdrug and larger supermarkets stock a fair range of drugs available without a doctor's prescription. Own-brand products are usually the cheapest.

HITCH-HIKING

Some rural areas have such sparse public transport networks that a passing driver may well give you a lift, but generally hitching is a risky business and is not recommended.

LANGUAGE

In parts of Wales, particularly in the north and west, you will hear Welsh spoken, and throughout Wales signs and information are given in both Welsh and English. In parts of Western Scotland and the Islands Gaelic is still spoken. However, Welsh and Gaelic speakers are all at ease with English too.

MAPS

You can pick up road atlases covering Britain and Ireland, including plans for major cities and towns, for well under £10 (the *AZ* one is among the clearest). Tourist information centres are a good source of (often free) local town maps, which sometimes include recommended town walks.

Ireland is covered by the Ordnance Survey of Ireland *Explorer* maps at 1:50,000 scale, with 71 sheets for the Republic of Ireland and 18 for Northern Ireland. The OS also publish city maps, including a street atlas of Dublin and a good road atlas of Ireland.

Ordnance Survey (OS) maps cover the country in great detail. 204 *Landranger* sheets covering Britain at 1:50,000 scale (2 cm = 1 km), or about 1¼ inches to the mile are ideal if you are touring or cycling. These sheets are contoured and show footpaths and bridleways, so you can also use them for walking. Even better for walking or exploring landscapes in detail are the 1:25,000 maps (4 cm = 1 km), or about 2½ inches to the mile; orange-covered *Explorer* maps. These show every field boundary and, outside large settlements, every building.

MONEY AND BANKS

Sterling is the general term given to the UK currency (for Britain and Northern Ireland), with 100 pence (p) to the pound (£). Scotland and Northern Ireland issue their own banknotes, which can be spent in England and Wales, although they are not often seen there. Eventually the UK may well join the European Monetary System and scrap the pound in favour of the euro.

The euro is the currency of the Irish Republic and is divided into 100 cents. The euro is also the currency of Austria, Belgium, Finland, France, Germany, Greece, Italy, Luxembourg, the Netherlands, Portugal and Spain. Euro notes and coins are legal tender in each of these countries, although the designs of the coins vary.

The main credit cards such as Visa and MasterCard, as well as some debit cards, are widely accepted and convenient means of withdrawing cash from cash dispensers. There is a flat transaction fee per exchange on top of any interest charged, so it is best not to use your card to make lots of small withdrawals.

Additionally you may like to take traveller's cheques, either in your own currency (in which case you pay a money change commission each time you cash them) or in £ sterling (where you pay all the commission when you purchase the cheques). If you lose them they will be replaced as long as you have the counterfoil, which should obviously be kept in a separate place, together with a note of which cheques you have cashed. You can change money in banks, branches of Thomas Cook and bureaux de change.

MoneyGram is a money transfer service offered by Thomas Cook, where money can be sent within 10 minutes to or from thousands of locations abroad to or from main Thomas Cook branches (or to most larger post offices). This is useful if you need more money to be sent from home. For information, tel: (01733) 294822.

SMOKING

Lighting up is becoming increasingly regarded as antisocial. You cannot smoke on trains or buses, or in most public buildings. Many restaurants have a no-smoking policy, or no-smoking areas. Smoking is more prevalent in pubs, although even some of these have no-smoking areas.

SAFETY

Violent crime is rare in Britain and Ireland, and generally fear of crime is more a problem than crime itself. At night when the pubs close the atmosphere in some city and town centres can be raucous but is seldom threatening. Petty theft is rife, however. Take care with bags and valuables in any crowded place, particularly tourist sites, airports, rail stations and London tube stations. Avoid putting handbags on the floor or around a chair back in a restaurant, and be on guard while withdrawing money at cashpoint machines.

RECOMMENDED READING

Some good reads which set the scene include:

Fiction

Brideshead Revisited, Evelyn Waugh (1945). Poignant tale of a doomed aristocratic family in one of England's stately homes.

How Green was my Valley, Richard Llewellyn (1939). Elegy for the lost world of coal-mining in a South Wales valley, based around family, chapel and pit.

Nice Work, David Lodge (1988). Industry meets academia in the industrial West Midlands in a precisely observed and humorous exploration of British cultural divides.

On the Black Hill, Bruce Chatwin (1982). The story of twin brothers growing up on a remote Welsh borders farm, and their changing relationship through the 20th century.

The French Lieutenant's Woman, John Fowles (1969). Lyme Regis, Dorset, is the setting for a saga of repressed sexuality in Victorian England.

Trainspotting, Irvine Welsh (1993). Surreal no-holds-barred evocation of junkie lifestyles on the deprived fringes of Edinburgh.

Troubles, J G Farrell (1970). The crumbling British grip on Ireland in the years after World War I, and the beginning of the Troubles.

Non-fiction

Cider with Rosie, Laurie Lee (1959). Haunting autobiography of childhood in the Cotswolds in the pre-petrol era.

McCarthy's Bar, Pete McCarthy (2000). Popular and entertaining journey of discovery around Ireland, with a few pub stops on the way.

Notes from a Small Island, Bill Bryson (1995). An American's hilarious re-encounter with Britain's inhabitants.

The English, Jeremy Paxman (1998). Incisive look into the nature of Englishness by a leading TV journalist.

The Kingdom by the Sea, Paul Theroux (1983). Quirky tour of Britain's coastline, seen through an American's eyes.

Two Degrees West, Nicholas Crane (1999). A dead-straight walk down the central meridian, giving a cross-section of contemporary England.

If you are hiking into remote rural areas, you are most unlikely to encounter any danger from wildlife. There is only one poisonous snake, the adder, and even that is rare and very shy. Mosquitoes are non-malarial and no more than annoying; the Scottish midge gives tiny, mildly irritating bites during summer (especially prevalent in watery areas). Bulls can appear daunting, but farmers are banned from

VARIABLE CLIMATE

The climate has a lot of regional variation, with more rain falling in the west than in the east, and the temperatures generally getting colder as you proceed north. The Scottish mountains and hills and mountains of northern England and north Wales often get a fair amount of snow in winter – enough for skiing to be feasible in Scotland – while it generally stays mild in winter towards the south coast. In Ireland it famously rains intermittently a lot of the time – shower, shine, shower, and so on.

putting dangerous ones on land crossed by rights of way – the non-dairy breeds (such as the docile brown Hereford) and young bulls you may encounter are nearly all harmless. It might be useful to carry a stick to wave at frisky cattle and horses.

As yet the sun is not the danger that it is in places like Australia, but it is still wise to use sun cream when venturing outdoors in summer.

WHEN TO GO

Britain's and Ireland's seasons are not that clear cut. It can be chilly or mild, wet or dry in summer or winter, and extreme temperatures are not that common. That said, the most popular time for visiting the country is May to Sept. Daily high temperatures generally peak in the low to high 20s Celsius (70s to mid-80s Fahrenheit) for some days during July and Aug and maybe June, May or Sept too). Autumn is cool (daily highs often around 10°C/50°F) and in recent years has witnessed severe storms and floods, possibly an effect of global warming. Dec to Feb is rather bleak and wintry with daily highs typically around 0–10°C/32–50°F); during Mar and April it is often a cocktail of wind, rain, milder weather and sunshine until things warm up in May.

Top tourist cities such as London, Bath, York, Oxford, Cambridge, Dublin and Canterbury can get absolutely packed in high summer, and scenic areas such as the Scottish Highlands, Yorkshire Dales, the Irish west coast and Lake District are pretty busy during this time too. You may find that out of season some places can have more atmosphere, but beware that many attractions close between Nov and Mar inclusive, including most National Trust properties.

LITERARY ISLES

Britain and Ireland constitute the most written-about part of the world. Classic writers whose works relate to specific places include:

Thomas Hardy (mostly in and around Dorset)

Jane Austen (Bath, Dorset and elsewhere)

William Wordsworth (the Lake District)

Dylan Thomas (South Wales)

James Joyce (Dublin)

Charles Dickens (London)

Emily Brontë (her only novel *Wuthering Heights* is set in the moors around Haworth, Yorkshire).

Daylight hours vary considerably. In late Dec in southern Britain it gets light some time before 0800 and is dark again by 1600, while in mid-June dawn breaks around 0400 and dusk sets in well after 2100. In the far north it is even more extreme, with very short winter days and very long daylight hours in summer.

THOMAS COOK PUBLICATIONS

The **Thomas Cook European Timetable (ETT)**, published monthly at £10.50, has up-to-date details of rail services throughout Britain and Ireland, as well as the whole of Europe. It is of great practical use both for pre-planning and for making on-the-spot decisions about independent rail travel around Britain and Ireland. A useful companion to it is the **Thomas Cook Rail Map of Great Britain and Ireland** (£7.95). These publications are available by phoning (01733) 416477 in the UK. In North America contact the **Forsyth Travel Library Inc.**, Westchester 1, 44 South Broadway, White Plains, New York 10601; tel: (0800) 367 7984; www.forsyth.com.

Europe's largest city, London has over 7 million inhabitants, and is roughly 50 miles (80 km) across. Fortunately for the visitor, however, most of the main attractions are central, and transport by bus and tube is easy to get to grips with. The river Thames, London's *raison d'être* and running through its heart, helps to make sense of the city's geography.

Whatever you like to do, London offers an enormous choice. The traditional tourist attractions – Buckingham Palace, Big Ben, St Paul's Cathedral, Westminster Abbey, the Tower of London and the British Museum – together with all the pageantry, are reason enough to come and visit. But to these can be added exciting developments which sprang into being at the dawn of the new millennium, and which have given a new buzz to the city. The London Eye, the world's largest ferris wheel, and the Tate Modern art gallery, in particular, have helped to bring the South Bank of the river to life.

You need to allow plenty of time to see London properly, as well as money – like most capitals, London has many ways of parting you from your cash. If the pace, and expense, seem to be getting too frenetic, you are never far away from one of the great parks and quiet, leafy squares that can provide havens of tranquillity in the midst of this busy city. Take time, too, to explore the back streets with their beautiful and varied architecture, and you will discover what Londoners already know, that it is these quiet parts, still almost village-like, which have the strongest charm.

GETTING THERE

London is served by five international **airports**: Heathrow, Gatwick, Stansted, Luton and London City; the first three are the most commonly used for international flights. There are frequent train services from all three into the centre of town, except during the small hours. From Heathrow there is also an Airbus service with three buses an hour to 15 destinations in central London, and there are hourly Jetlink 777 buses into Victoria Coach Station from Gatwick and Stansted. Taxis are pricey, so avoid them unless you have a lot of baggage.

London's principal railway stations (clockwise from Waterloo) and the destinations they serve are **Waterloo** – the Southwest (Southampton, Salisbury); also international trains to Brussels and Paris; **Victoria** – Gatwick Airport, the South Coast (Brighton), Kent (Canterbury, Dover); **Paddington** – Heathrow Airport, the South Midlands (Oxford, Stratford-upon-Avon), the West of England (Bristol, Devon, Cornwall), South Wales, Ireland via Fishguard; **Marylebone** – the West Midlands (Birmingham) via Banbury; **Euston** – Birmingham Airport, the West Midlands, the Northwest (Liverpool, Manchester, the Lake District), North Wales, Ireland via Holyhead, Scotland via the West Coast; **St Pancras** – Luton Airport, the East Midlands (Leicester, Nottingham, Derby); **Kings Cross** – Cambridge, Yorkshire (Leeds, York), the Northeast (Newcastle), Scotland via the East Coast; **Liverpool St** – Stansted Airport, Cambridge, East Anglia (Ipswich, Norwich); **Charing Cross** – the Southeast (Hastings, Dover); **London Bridge** – same destinations as Charing Cross, also very frequent cross-London services linking Bedford and Luton Airport north of the Thames to Gatwick Airport and Brighton in the south.

London's **Victoria Coach Station**, with services to all parts of the country, is less than half a mile (800 m) from the railway station of the same name.

GETTING AROUND

For most of your stay you will find it easiest to get around by bus and by underground railway, known as '**the tube**'. If you are doing any travelling at all buy a Travelcard, valid on buses, the tube and the Docklands Light Railway. A one-day pass, available at any tube station, can be used after 0930. Weekly and monthly Travelcards, for which you will need a Photocard (bring a spare passport photo and your ID), can be bought at underground stations and some newsagents. Fares are based on a zone system: most of the main attractions lie within central zone 1. A carnet of ten zone 1 tickets can be bought at a discount.

THE DOCKLANDS LIGHT RAILWAY (DLR)

Linked to the tube, the DLR runs from the City of London via Docklands to Greenwich. A ride on this modern driverless system (make a beeline for the front, like everyone else) is an attraction in itself, giving great views, and you can buy a Sail & Rail ticket for a round trip to Greenwich, combining riverboat and DLR.

So long as you avoid travel in the rush hours (0800–1000 and 1600–1900 weekdays), you

BUS TOURS

Several companies offer tours of London using open-top buses, giving running commentaries in various languages. These include the **Big Bus Company**, tel: (020) 7233 9533, and the **Original London Sightseeing Tour**, tel: (020) 8877 1722). You can hop on and off – tickets are valid for 24 hours. Leaflets are available from tourist information centres, and you can get on anywhere: all buses pass through Trafalgar Square and most near Victoria station.

A cheaper way of doing a bus tour, though without the commentary, is to choose one of the standard bus routes. Bus no. 11 from Chelsea to the City is a good one, passing Westminster, Trafalgar Square and St Paul's Cathedral, as is no. 25 (Victoria to St Paul's).

should find the tube easy to navigate and a fast way of getting about. Trains are frequent and run until after midnight.

Buses may take longer, but you will get to know London much faster above the ground than below it, particularly from the top of a double-decker. On some older buses, boarded from the rear, you pay a conductor; on the more modern type you pay the driver on boarding, so have some coins ready. Pick up a bus map at a tourist information centre or the London Transport information centre at Piccadilly Circus.

ON THE RIVER

Oddly for a city that owes its existence to the Thames, Londoners make little use of their river to get about. However, there are many pleasure cruisers – offering everything from a one-way journey to dinner-dances – which are an unrivalled way of seeing the city. The main piers are at Westminster Bridge (north), Embankment (north), the South Bank, the Tower and Greenwich. For cruises, unless you are booking an evening one, you can just turn up and buy a ticket at the pier.

Taxis can be useful, though expensive: fares in black cabs are based on a combination of distance and time, so they can mount up fast in traffic jams. Generally you should stick to licensed, black cabs: you can flag one down if its yellow sign is illuminated. Tipping is expected.

Finally, do some **walking** in London, and you may find that places are closer together than you might have thought from travelling underground. Take short cuts through the parks, and arm yourself

WALKING TOURS

There are several companies offering guided walks all over London and on many different themes. Listing magazines like *Time Out* have details, or ask at tourist information centres – there is no need to book, just turn up at the start point. Well-established companies include **London Walks**, tel: (020) 7624 3978, www.walks.com; **Historical Walks**, tel: (020) 8668 4019; and **Stepping Out**, tel: (020) 8881 2933.

with an *A–Z* street map or guide (from newsagents). One of the best walks in London is the exhilarating **Thames Path**, which runs along the south bank: walk the stretch from Lambeth Bridge to Tower Bridge for some of the best views in London.

INFORMATION

CITY AND TRANSPORT MAP
– inside back cover

There are **London Tourist Board** tourist information services at Victoria Station, open Mon–Sat 0800–2100 (2000 Mar–May, 1900 Oct–Feb), Sun 0800–1815; Liverpool Street tube station, open Mon–Fri 0800–1800, Sat 0800–1730, Sun 0900–1730; Waterloo International Terminal, open daily 0830–2230; and Heathrow tube station, open daily 0800–1800.

The **Britain Visitor Centre** (1 Regent St, Piccadilly Circus) offers free transport maps and information: open Mon 0930–1830, Tues–Fri 0900–1830, Sat 0900–1700 (1000–1600 Nov–May), Sun 1000–1600. The London Tourist Board's London Line, tel: 09068 663344 (60p a min), is a 24-hr recorded information service. The London Tourist Board's website is useful for just about everything (www.visitlondon.com).

Listings **magazines**, the best and most venerable of which is *Time Out*, give full information on everything from street markets to art exhibitions. *Time Out*'s website (www.timeout.com) is also comprehensive.

SAFETY Central London is generally safe, though you should always stay alert. Pickpockets operate in all the obvious places, especially busy shopping areas like Oxford Street, so try not to look too much like a tourist. Keep your belongings about you, keep bags with valuables zipped up, etc. At night, public transport is relatively safe, but steer clear of unlit streets and parks. The area around King's Cross is best avoided at night.

If you are unlucky, report all crimes to the police and get a copy of their report for your insurers.

MONEY Many hotels and most banks and bureaux de change will change travellers' cheques. Credit cards are accepted in most shops, restaurants and tourist attractions and there are ATMs everywhere. When changing money, use a bank for the best rates or a reputable bureau de change. There are 24-hour bureaux at the airports offering good rates. 'No commission' bureaux usually offer the poorest exchange rates.

POST/PHONE You will find British Telecom and Mercury boxes on streets, in stations, and in large department stores. The phone code for London is 020. *Poste restante* facilities are available at the Chief Office, King Edward Building, King Edward St, EC1 (tube: St Paul's) or at the Trafalgar Square Branch Office, 24–28 William IV St, WC2N 4DL (tube: Charing Cross).

INTERNET London has numerous Internet cafés. The easyEverything cafés are among the cheapest, although they are completely soulless. They have branches at Victoria (Wilton Rd), Trafalgar Sq. (7 Strand), 358 Oxford St, 9–16 Tottenham Court Rd and 160 Kensington High St. **Public libraries** usually have free Internet access.

ACCOMMODATION

As with most capital cities, it is more expensive to stay in London than anywhere else in the country. As a general rule, cheaper places are likely to be found around Victoria and Paddington stations, or Earl's Court; Bloomsbury, around the British Museum, also has some reasonably priced options, and is both pleasant and central. The West End (Westminster, Mayfair and Marylebone) and Kensington and Knightsbridge tend to be most expensive.

To make booking easier you could make a reservation through the London tourist information centres which offer a **room-booking service** for £5 plus a percentage of the first night's fee in advance), or through the Thomas Cook accommodation desks at Gatwick, and Charing Cross, Victoria, King's Cross, St Pancras and Paddington stations. You can also use your credit card to book in advance via the London Tourist Board booking line, tel: (020) 7604 2890, or their website, www.visitlondon.com.

BUDGET ACCOMMODATION

If your budget is tight, hostels may be the answer, especially with a family as there are usually bunk-bedded family rooms. There are several centrally placed YHA hostels with excellent facilities, including the purpose-built **St Pancras** (££, 79–81 Euston Rd, NW1; tel: 0870 7706044; e-mail: stpancras@yha.org.uk); **Holland House** (££, Holland Walk, W8; tel: 0870 7705867; e-mail: hollandhouse@yha.org.uk), in a historic mansion; and **City of London** (££, 36 Carter Lane; tel: 0870 7705764; e-mail: city@yha.org.uk), close to St Paul's Cathedral.

Other budget options include the **Museum Inn** (£, 27 Montague St, WC1; tel: (020) 7580 5360; www.hostelslondon.org), the quietest and best situated of the Astor independent hostels, for the under 30s; and **County Hall Travel Inn** (££, Belvedere Rd, SE1; tel: (020) 7902 1600; www.travelinn.co.uk), in a very convenient South Bank location.

St Christopher's Inns (tel: (020) 7407 1856; www.st-christophers.co.uk) form a small chain of private hostels, with meals, Internet access and laundry facilities. There are locations in Camden (48–50 Camden High St, NW1), Borough High St, SE1, on the South Bank near London Bridge (three hostels), plus (out of the centre) Greenwich and Shepherd's Bush.

For reasonably priced B&Bs try SWA (££), tel: (020) 7385 4904, www.thewaytostay.co.uk, or the London Bed & Breakfast Agency, tel: (020) 7586 2768, www.londonbb.com.

FOOD AND DRINK

London's fast-changing food scene is as varied and exciting as any capital city's. The most comprehensive guide to it all is the *Time Out Guide to Eating and Drinking in London*, sold in newsagents (magazine format). You will find queues almost everywhere in central London on Friday and Saturday nights, so go early, or book.

Apart from restaurants, cafés – many part of international chains – have recently sprung up everywhere: among the best are Aroma, Caffè Nero, and Pret à Manger. For lunches, some of the museums and galleries offer a very high standard of food, whether you want a coffee and croissant or a full hot meal – recommended are **Tate Britain** and the **National Gallery**. Many big department stores have excellent cafés (**John Lewis**, Oxford St, **Dickens and Jones**, Regent St, and the most famous of them all, **Harvey Nichols Fifth Floor Café**). You can buy good sandwiches and other take-away snacks from **Boots**, **Marks and Spencer** (M&S) and **British Home Stores** (BHS). The focus in the list below is largely on independent cafés and budget places to eat.

WESTMINSTER AND MAYFAIR	**Café in the Crypt** ££ St Martin-in-the-Fields, Trafalgar Sq., WC2. Good value self-service restaurant beneath the church.
	Momo £££ 25 Heddon St, W1. Trendy Moroccan restaurant; the **Mô** café/tearoom is next door.
	Wren at St James's £ 35 Jermyn St, SW1. Nice vegetarian café with outdoor seating.
KENSINGTON, KNIGHTSBRIDGE AND CHELSEA	The French quarter of South Kensington (around Bute St) is a good place to find authentic French cuisine.
	Chelsea Kitchen and **Stockpot** £ 98 and 273 King's Rd, SW3. Two branches of the same chain, selling filling food at bargain prices.
	Fifth Floor Café ££ Harvey Nichols, Knightsbridge, SW1. Good place for posing and celebrity spotting; delicious snacks.
	Pizza on the Park ££ 11 Knightsbridge, SW1. Flagship restaurant of the upmarket Pizza Express chain.
COVENT GARDEN, SOHO AND HOLBORN	Chinatown, around Gerrard St and Wardour St north of Leicester Square, is a good place to browse for Peking-style, Cantonese and *dim sum* dishes, while Old Compton St offers every type of restaurant, from the upmarket to the coffee bar. Covent Garden has many restaurants to choose from.
	Café Pelican ££ 45 St Martin's Lane, WC2. Reasonably priced brasserie, good for people watching.
	Centrale ££ 16 Moor St, W1. Good for comforting portions of pasta.
	World Food Café £ 14 Neal's Yard, WC2. Delicious vegetarian recipes from around the world.
MARYLEBONE AND BLOOMSBURY	**Drummond St** (behind Euston station) has several restaurants with an exciting range of southern Indian food (including vegetarian) at ridiculously low prices. The **Diwana Bhel-Poori House** (££) at no. 121 and **Raavi Kebab Halal** (£) at no. 125 are recommended. There are many good cafés in **Museum St**, handy for the British Museum.
	Wagamama ££ 4 Streatham St, WC1. One of several branches across London, serving Japanese noodles canteen style.

LONDON

	Pizza Express ££ 10 Dean St, WC1. Perhaps the most famous branch of the chain, renowned for its live jazz.
THE CITY	**Fatboy's Diner** £ 296 Bishopsgate, EC2. Heavenly American-style burgers.
	The Place Below ££ St Mary-le-Bow, Cheapside, EC2. Gourmet vegetarian restaurant in the crypt of a Wren church.
SOUTH BANK	**Honest Cabbage** £££ 99 Bermondsey St, SE1. Wholesome, seasonal English fare.
	Oxo Tower ££–££££ Barge House St, SE1. A mix of eateries is offered in this river-frontage landmark. There are superb views from the 8th-floor brasserie.
	fish! ££££ Cathedral St, SE1. Trendy fish restaurant on the edge of Borough Market.

HIGHLIGHTS

WESTMINSTER AND MAYFAIR Westminster, the hub of political (and tourist) London, will be for many the first port of call. If you can, go early in the morning or late afternoon to avoid the crowds. On Parliament Square, dominated by Big Ben's clock tower, are the **Houses of Parliament**, built in the 1860s in flamboyant Gothic revival style to replace the old Palace of Westminster, destroyed by fire. A recent cleaning programme has revealed Parliament's mellow, honey coloured stonework – walk across Westminster Bridge for classic views. You can watch the often unseemly spectacle of democracy in action for free from the Strangers' Gallery of the House of Commons, by joining the queue outside St Stephen's Entrance. Sittings easiest to get into are on Mon–Wed after 1800, or head for the more civilised (and sumptuous) House of Lords. There are also guided tours during the summer recess (££, early Aug to late Sept; tel: (020) 7344 9966).

Across Parliament Square lies **Westminster Abbey**, a Gothic masterpiece crammed with the monuments and tombs of the great and the good. ££, Broad Sanctuary; open Mon–Fri 0930–1645 (also 1800–1945 Wed); Sat 0930–1445; closed Sun. The restful abbey cloister includes the beautiful **Chapter House**, £, open daily 0930–1700 (Apr–Sept); 1000–1700 (Oct); 1000–1600 (Nov–Mar).

Leading off Parliament Square is **Whitehall**, where many of the government offices are found. Off to the left are the **Cabinet War Rooms**, a warren of underground rooms that served as a nerve centre of British operations during World War II. ££, Clive Steps, King Charles St; open daily 0930–1800 (Apr–Sept); 1000–1800 (Oct–Mar). The next turning on the left is **Downing Street**, home of the prime minister and protected by forbidding gates. The austere **Cenotaph** in the middle of Whitehall honours Britain's war dead. On the right is the **Banqueting House**, the only survival of the old Whitehall Palace, from which Charles I stepped out onto the scaffold for his execution (££, open Mon–Sat 1000–1700). Beyond on the left, at

TOP TEN FOR KIDS

There are plenty of places to keep children amused in London, depending on their tastes. High on the list will probably be the **Natural History Museum** (see p. 48) – head for the dinosaurs early in the day to avoid the queues – the **Science Museum** (see p. 48), **Madame Tussaud's and Planetarium** (see p. 49 – book in advance so you don't have a 2-hour wait), and **London Zoo** (see p. 49).

Very young children find **London's Transport Museum** (see p. 49) enthralling. For those old enough to climb vertical ship's ladders **HMS Belfast** (see p. 51) is a must. The nearby **Tower Bridge Experience** (see p. 51) is also fun and the **London Dungeon** a treat for the unsqueamish (see p. 51). Also south of the river are the **London Aquarium** (see p. 51), and the **Imperial War Museum**, which should capture the imagination (see p. 52). Kidsline can provide more ideas on how to entertain children (tel: (020) 7222 8070), and listings magazines detail events targeted at younger age groups.

If you want to take them shopping, **Covent Garden** with its free street entertainment should prove diverting. For mainstream shopping with older children and teenagers, take them to Oxford Circus. **Hamleys** and **Virgin**, **Top Shop**, **New Look** and **H&M** should provide shopping heaven for kids while you head off to the nearby department stores.

CHANGING THE GUARD

The popular spectacle of changing the Queen's Guard takes place at Buckingham Palace on alternate mornings at 1130 and daily Apr–July. Arrive early to get a good vantage point near the railings. For more information on the 40-minute ceremony, tel: 09068 663344.

Horse Guards, colourful mounted sentries make popular subjects for photographs.

At the far end of Whitehall lies **Trafalgar Square**, where despite attempts to disperse them by banning the sale of feed, the traditional pigeons refuse to go away. Across to the north of the square is the **National Gallery**, housing one of the most comprehensive collections of paintings in the world. It's free, so go several times rather than try to see it all at once; open daily 1000–1800 (Wed until 2100). Around the corner and also free is the **National Portrait Gallery** (St Martin's Pl.; open Mon–Wed, Sat–Sun 1000–1800, Thur–Fri 1000–2100; nice restaurant with view on top floor).

Next, head west down the Mall into lovely **St James's Park**: from the bridge across the lake there are views of the domes and turrets of Whitehall in one direction and **Buckingham Palace** in the other. The palace's State Rooms, sumptuous but soulless, are open Aug–Sept 0930–1630; £££; tel: (020) 7321 2233 to book in advance. More accessible are the **Royal Mews** (££, Buckingham Palace Rd; open Mon–Thur 1200–1600; Aug–Sept 1030–1630) where the gilded state carriages, including the Gold Carriage used at coronations, and liveried horses are kept. The **Queen's Gallery** displays masterpieces from the Royal Collection.

LONDON

It is worth taking a detour to Millbank, which runs south off Parliament Square, to take in **Tate Britain**, which houses the nation's greatest collection of British art (free; open daily 1000–1750). North of the pleasantly informal **Green Park** lie Piccadilly and Park Lane, the Mayfair domain of bespoke tailoring, gentlemen's clubs, upmarket hotels and the Royal Academy of Arts. The Academy is home to prestigious art exhibitions which are often very popular, so book in advance; tel: (020) 7300 5959. (Variable charges; Piccadilly; open Sat–Thur 1000–1800, Fri 1000–2030.)

KENSINGTON AND CHELSEA South Kensington is the home of three of London's great museums, all housed in grandiose Victorian buildings. Admission is free, except for special exhibitions. The **Natural History Museum** (Cromwell Rd; open Mon–Sat 1000–1750, Sun 1100–1750) could absorb you for hours. Don't miss the realistic animatronic dinosaurs (arrive early to avoid queues), the Creepy Crawlies gallery and the earthquake experience in the Earth Galleries. The **Science Museum** also manages to be both enormously entertaining and informative (Exhibition Rd; open daily 1000–1800). The more traditional **Victoria and Albert Museum** is an Aladdin's cave of decorative arts, from medieval stained glass to 20th-century fashion (Cromwell Rd; open daily 1000–1745, and Wed 1830–2200).

Exhibition Rd leads northward to **Hyde Park** and the contiguous **Kensington Gardens**, divided by the Serpentine Lake. This is London's largest open space, cutting a green swathe through the heart of the city. To the west, **Kensington Palace**, formerly Princess Diana's London home, houses the Royal Ceremonial Dress Collection. £££, open daily 1000–1800 (mid-Mar–mid-Oct); 1000–1700 (mid-Oct–mid-Mar). The ornate, circular **Royal Albert Hall** and the dazzling **Albert Memorial** across the road were built in memory of Queen Victoria's consort. At Hyde Park's north-east and south-east corners are London's two triumphal arches. Both **Marble Arch** and **Wellington Arch** were designed in 1825 as entrances to Buckingham Palace.

FOR FREE

All London's national museums admit visitors free, except to temporary exhibitions. These are the Natural History Museum, the Science Museum, the Victoria and Albert Museum, the Imperial War Museum, the Theatre Museum, the National Maritime Museum, the British Museum and Library, the National Gallery, National Portrait Gallery, Tate Britain and Tate Modern. Other free museums are the Wallace Collection, Kenwood House and the Sir John Soane's Museum.

Some of the other London museums which charge adults admit children free. These include the Cabinet War Rooms, HMS *Belfast* and the Museum of London.

Chelsea, to the south, is one of London's most desirable areas: the streets near the river – Cheyne Walk, Cheyne Row and Tite St – make a lovely place to wander. The slightly tacky King's Rd, Chelsea's high street, caters for the hip.

BLOOMSBURY AND MARYLEBONE Renowned for its literary and academic connections, Bloomsbury has a distinctly intellectual air. Its principal site is the treasure trove of the **British Museum**, repository of the infamously pilfered Elgin Marbles, the newly redisplayed Egyptian mummies, and the Anglo-Saxon Sutton Hoo burial hoard. The recently opened central Great Court is a triumph. Free; Gt Russell St; open Mon–Wed, Sat–Sun 1000–1730, Thur–Fri 1000–2030.

West of Tottenham Court Road, **Fitzrovia** is a characterful maze of streets. One of London's best-kept secrets, the **Wallace Collection** (Manchester Sq., free, open Mon–Sat 1000–1700, Sun 1200–1700) has an outstanding array of paintings and furniture. To the north, on Marylebone Rd, lies **Madame Tussaud's**, the world's best-known waxworks and still the best place in London to see the famous and infamous throughout history. A combined admission ticket gives access to the **Planetarium**, a spectacular virtual reality space show using the latest technology. Queuing for the two is traditional, but it's better to book a timed ticket in advance; tel: (0870) 400 3000. £££, open daily Mon–Fri 1000–1730, Sat–Sun 0930–1730 and from 0900 Jun–Aug. Planetarium open Mon–Fri 1230–1700, Sat–Sun 1030–1700.

Regent's Park to the north – one of London's finest open spaces – is surrounded by John Nash's elegant Regency terraces. Within the park lies **London Zoo**, whose popular draws include the big cats, elephants and the Penguin Pool. £££, open daily 1000–1730 (Mar–Sept); 1000–1600 (Oct–Feb). East along Euston Rd is the modern **British Library**, where some of Britain's most famous books and manuscripts, from the Lindisfarne Gospel's to Sir Paul McCartney's lyrics for *Yesterday*, are on display (free, open all year daily 0930–1730).

> **LONDON AND THE FAMOUS**
>
> Look up at the walls of the buildings you pass and you may spot one of the 400 or so **blue plaques**, which mark the houses where well-known people once lived. Among the famous commemorated in this way are Karl Marx (28 Dean St, W1), Charles Dickens (48 Doughty St, WC1) and Wolfgang Amadeus Mozart (180 Ebury St, SW1).

SOHO, COVENT GARDEN AND HOLBORN Soho, south of Oxford Street and east of Regent Street, has few formal sights, but is a great place to wander with no particular purpose, despite the clubs and porn with which it has long been associated. Historically the area has always been a home for émigrés and refugees, who have brought a taste for books (check out the many shops, new and secondhand, along **Charing Cross Rd**) and for food.

Covent Garden, with its bazaar-like atmosphere, is now mainly devoted to shopping (see p. 53). The magnificent Victorian **Royal Opera House** has recently been restored, and the Floral Hall has been transformed into a magnificent foyer, with free lunchtime concerts. **London's Transport Museum**, just south of the piazza, is just the thing for small children, with its old buses and trams to clamber on and plenty of interactive displays (££, open Sat–Thur 1000–1800, Fri 1100–1800). Round the corner and with free admission, the **Theatre Museum** (Russell Street, Tues–Sun, 1000–1800) is a fascinating look back at London's thespian history, with props and pictures and demonstrations of stage make-up and costume. South of the Strand, the classical palace of **Somerset House** now contains the Impressionist paintings of the **Courtauld Institute Galleries**, the **Hermitage Rooms** with changing displays of items from the Winter Palace in St Petersburg, and the **Gilbert Collection** of decorative silverware (joint ticket £££; Strand; open Mon–Sat 1000–1800, Sun 1200–1800, free Mon until 1400). The River Terrace, opened to the public in 2000 for the first time in 100 years, is part of a pedestrian link along the river. Tucked away to the east are the **Inns of Court**, the historic heartland of England's legal system. Although they are private institutions, you are welcome to stroll around the grounds. On Lincoln's Inn Fields, London's largest square, **Sir John Soane's Museum** is a wonderfully eccentric time warp, filled with the 18th-century architect's collection of antiquities (free, open Tues–Sat 1000–1700 and 1800–2100 first Tues of the month).

The City The City of London, known as the Square Mile and a global financial centre, is buzzing with activity Monday to Friday but hauntingly quiet and atmospheric at weekends. This was where the Romans founded the original Londinium. Located alongside a length of Roman wall, the **Museum of London** (££, 150 London Wall; open Mon–Sat 1000–1750, Sun 1200–1750; free after 1630) gives an excellent introduction to the capital – the Roman gallery is especially good. (The entrance is on a raised walkway of the Barbican complex, a relic of 1970s town planning.)

The Great Fire of London

The Great Fire in 1666 almost totally destroyed the buildings of the medieval city. In the rebuilding the medieval layout of streets and alleys was retained, along with the street names: gigantic office blocks thus stand incongruously on Milk St, Bread St and Poultry. The 311-step **Monument** (£, Monument St; open daily 1000–1740) is close to the spot on Pudding Lane where the fire started; there are great views from the top.

After the Great Fire of 1666 had almost destroyed the old city, Sir Christopher Wren was commissioned to design 51 new churches. His masterpiece, completed in 1710, was the innovative **St Paul's Cathedral**, the City's greatest monument (££, open Mon–Sat 0830–1600, galleries from 1000). Climb up to the famous dome for panoramic views, and watch what you say in the Whispering Gallery (additional charge). North, near the still-functioning Smithfield meat market, lies a gem of a church, **St Bartholomew the Great**. Dating from the 12th century, it was used for the final wedding scene in the film *Four Weddings and a Funeral*.

The City is centred around Bank underground station and the Bank of England, which has a free museum for budding capitalists (Bartholomew Lane; open Mon–Fri 1000–1700). Eastwards on the waterfront looms the **Tower of London**, the 900-year-old palace and infamous former prison, which houses the Crown Jewels. £££, Tower

Hill; open Mon–Sat 0900–1700, Sun 1000–1700 (Mar–Oct); Tues–Sat 0900–1600, Sun–Mon 1000–1600 (Nov–Feb). To avoid the often horrendous queues, you can buy your ticket for the Tower in advance from any underground station – or make sure you arrive early on the day. If time is short, don't miss the Jewel House and the White Tower, the 11th-century keep; or get your bearings by taking a free guided tour with one of the quaintly dressed Beefeaters. Spanning the Thames nearby is the splendid Victorian Tower Bridge, famous both for its profile and for its revolutionary design that allowed the bridge to be raised for tall ships to pass beneath. **The Tower Bridge Experience** explains all this with the aid of animatronic characters, and the high-level walkway gives great river views; £££, open daily 1000–1830 (Apr–Oct); 0930–1800 (Nov–Mar).

THE SOUTH BANK Ten years ago much of the South Bank of the Thames was a dreary wasteland, created by the closure of the docks in the 1960s. But an amazing burst of regeneration, partly timed to greet the year 2000, has now created the finest riverside walk in London linking a number of new and exciting attractions. East of Tower Bridge, the modish **Design Museum** (££, Butler's Wharf, off Shad Thames; open Mon–Fri 1130–1800, Sat–Sun 1030–1800) is the only museum in the world devoted to 20th-century design. Butler's Wharf, the quayside here, is full of fashionable restaurants. Between Tower and London bridges is docked **HMS Belfast**, a World War II armoured warship that can be freely explored. ££, Morgan's Lane; open daily 1000–1800 (Mar–Oct); 1000–1700 (Nov–Feb). **Southwark Cathedral** is one of London's oldest churches (£, Montague Close; open daily 0800–1800). The popular, macabre **London Dungeon**, presenting the darker side of London's history (£££, 34 Tooley St; open daily 1000–1830, mid-July–Sept 1000–2100), is not for the squeamish. Wine lovers can spend hours studying wine-making history and sampling its products at **Vinopolis** (£££, 1 Bank End; open daily 1000–1730).

Continuing westwards past a reconstruction of Sir Francis Drake's *Golden Hind*, **Shakespeare's Globe Theatre** is a faithful reconstruction of the Elizabethan theatre where the Bard's plays were first staged: as well as guided tours it boasts a superb multimedia exhibition (£££, New Globe Walk; open daily, 0900–1200 (May–Sept) 1000–1700 (Oct–Apr). For performances (May–Sept), tel: (020) 7401 9919. Opposite the sleek **Millennium Footbridge** is the triumphant **Tate Modern**, imaginatively converted from a former power station to house Britain's leading collection of contemporary art (free; open Sun–Thur 1000–1800, Fri–Sat 1000–2200).

Further west still, beyond the South Bank Centre, London's biggest arts complex, is the **British Airways London Eye**, a spectacular addition to the London skyline which offers hugely popular 30-min rides within its glass capsules: £££ (advance booking only; tel: 0870 5000 600; www.londoneye.co.uk), Jubilee Gardens; open daily late May–mid-Sept 1000–2200, rest of year 1030–2000. Close by in former County Hall, the **London Aquarium** has an impressive collection of sea creatures (£££, open daily 1000–1800). **Hungerford Bridge** provides another superb viewing platform.

LONDON

It's worth taking a 15-minute walk south of Waterloo station to the **Imperial War Museum**, a balanced account of 20th-century warfare, with poignant Blitz and Trench Experiences (Lambeth Rd; free, open daily 1000–1800).

GREENWICH AND THE DOCKS Allow a day to head out to riverside Greenwich, taking a picnic if it's fine to verdant Greenwich Park. A good way to get here is via the overhead Docklands Light Railway (see p. 41), which passes through former docklands that were spectacularly redeveloped in the 1980s as offices, symbolised by the massive tower of Canary Wharf. You could stop short of Greenwich at Island Gardens, and then walk below the Thames through the curious **Greenwich Foot Tunnel**, to emerge right beside the *Cutty Sark* tea clipper.

THE THAMES BARRIER
Hop on a cruise boat at Greenwich (by the *Cutty Sark*) for a trip to the **Thames Barrier and Visitors' Centre** at Woolwich. This remarkable piece of engineering, built in 1984, has a series of ten movable gates to prevent London from flooding. £, 1 Unity Way; open 1030–1630 (Apr–Sept); 1100–1530 (Oct–Mar).

Greenwich is a focal point for the nation's maritime heritage. Highlights include the **National Maritime Museum**, arranged by well-chosen theme and with two excellent interactive galleries (Romney Rd; free, open daily 1000–1700). On top of the hill is the fascinating **Royal Observatory**, where you can enjoy the novel pleasure of standing astride the Greenwich Meridian (Greenwich Park, open as museum, also free). Alongside the Thames lies the *Cutty Sark*, a beautifully restored relic of the great days of sail; ££, King William Walk; open daily 1000–1700.

KEW AND RICHMOND These are two riverside villages that have now been engulfed into the west London suburbs. They retain bags of charm in themselves, and both have Georgian buildings; you can walk from one to the other via the delightfully verdant Thames towpath. Kew, however, is famed primarily for **Kew Gardens** (£££, daily except 25 Dec, 1 Jan; website: www.kew.org; rail station: Kew Gardens), one of the world's foremost botanical collections, begun in 1759 and also known as the Royal Botanic Gardens. Highlights include the Pagoda, the glasshouses – especially the elegant 19th-century Palm House, the Evolution House and the modern Princess of Wales house.

Richmond is a larger place altogether, with some pleasant riverside pubs around Richmond Bridge. The best walk is to go up Richmond Hill, where blue plaques on the large houses proclaim that it has for long been home to the rich and famous, and into **Richmond Park**, a huge deer park with free access in daylight hours. It is surprisingly rural, and is still the haunt of herds of deer (who should not be approached); seek out the Isabella Plantation, where azaleas burst into bloom in early summer, and Pen Ponds. Richmond is easily reached by rail or District Line underground (Richmond station).

HAMPSTEAD   Hampstead (just north of central London) has for long been the preserve of writers, artists and intellectuals. It has some fascinating back streets for wandering. Church Row and Hampstead Grove take you up to the edge of **Hampstead Heath**, a countrified expanse of woodland and parkland, crisscrossed by a bewildering maze of paths. On the northern side is **Kenwood House** (free, daily), an 18th-century mansion with a superb art collection. A walk across the Heath can tie in with a visit to **Highgate Cemetery**, burial place of many famous people including Karl Marx; the west part of the cemetery is dramatically overgrown, with crumbling masonry peeping out from the ivy, and is open by guided tour only; tel: (020) 8340 1834. Back in Hampstead, you can also visit the former homes of psychoanalyst **Sigmund Freud** (££, 20 Maresfield Gardens, Wed–Sun afternoon), and Modernist architect **Ernö Goldfinger** at (££, 2 Willow Road, 1200–1700, Thur–Sat, Apr–Oct, plus Sat in Mar). Hampstead station is on the Northern Line, 15 mins or so from central London.

SHOPPING

Oxford Street (tube: Marble Arch/Bond St/Oxford Circus) is where all the big names have their flagship stores. Regent Street has more upmarket clothing plus **Liberty** (famous for its Liberty print fabrics) and **Hamleys** (five floors of toys). For those with serious money, or aspirational window shoppers, **New Bond Street** and **South Molton Street** house world-leading fashion designers. In Knightsbridge, **Harrods** and **Harvey Nichols** are two of the classier department stores; Harrods' Food Halls are renowned for selling just about everything, in a splendidly luxurious setting. The memorial to Dodi Al Fayed and Diana, Princess of Wales, on the lower ground floor is another point of interest in Harrods.

Covent Garden's pedestrianised piazza – a former fruit and vegetable market – has a quirky mix of shops and stalls selling clothing, crafts and bric-à-brac, with street entertainment thrown in. Covent Garden's side streets are well worth exploring for designer fashion plus **Stanford's** (12 Long Acre), probably the best map and travel guidebook shop in the world. One of the best street markets to head for is **Spitalfields** (opposite Liverpool St station), a friendly place to browse for clothes, crafts, records and organic foods, which is less commercialised and crowded than the famous **Camden Markets** (north of Camden Town tube). Farmers' markets are a fairly recent phenomenon; tel: (020) 7704 9659, www.lfm.org.uk for details of markets in London.

EVENTS AND FESTIVALS

Innumerable special exhibitions and events, from royal pageantry to the Notting Hill street Carnival in late August, take place throughout the year. These are listed in *Time Out* and other weekly listings magazines; London's daily paper, the *Evening Standard*, also has a good listings supplement every Thursday.

ENTERTAINMENT AND NIGHTLIFE

Going out after dark is half the point of being in London: few other cities have such a rich choice of entertainment, from pub theatre, drag acts and comedy clubs to world-class opera, dance and classical music.

If you have time to plan, book ahead. For those last-minute decisions, however, there are some excellent bargains to be had. Unsold tickets are often sold off cheaply within an hour or so of the start of the show. The half-price ticket booth in the clock tower on Leicester Square (open Tues–Sun 1200–1830) sells same-day theatre tickets.

BOOK AHEAD

For the most popular and prestigious events – rock concerts and sell-out musicals – you simply will not get in unless you book well in advance. This is made easier by the large ticket agencies, which (although imposing a hefty surcharge) may have tickets for events that are otherwise sold out. There are agencies all along Charing Cross Rd and Shaftesbury Ave, or contact **First Call**, tel: 0870 906 3838; www.firstcalltickets.com, or **Ticketmaster**, tel: (020) 7316 4709; www.ticketmaster.co.uk.

Major venues for concerts include the **Barbican Centre**, Silk St (tel: (020) 7638 8891; www.barbican.org.uk), the **Royal Albert Hall**, Kensington Gore (tel: (020) 7589 8212; www.royalalberthall.com), and the **Royal Festival Hall** complex on the South Bank (tel: (020) 7960 4242; www.sbc.org.uk). For theatre there's the **Royal National Theatre** (South Bank; tel: (020) 7452 3000; www.nationaltheatre.org.uk). Smaller theatres, clubs and venues all over London are the setting for a very lively alternative arts scene. Listings magazines such as *Time Out* carry exhaustive details of what's going on, week by week.

SIDE TRIPS

HAMPTON COURT Henry VIII's vast riverside palace was originally built by Cardinal Wolsey, who had to hand it over to his monarch when it turned out to be bigger than anything the king owned. Highlights of the various tour routes available are the Tudor kitchens, real tennis court and Henry VIII's State Apartments. The 60 acres (24 ha) of grounds include a famous maze and the formally patterned King William's Privy Garden. £££, open Mon 1015–1800, Tues–Sun 0930–1800; closes 1630 mid-Oct–mid-Mar. The Palace is a short walk across the Thames from Hampton Court station, some 30 mins from London Waterloo. You can also travel to Hampton Court as Henry VIII would have done – by boat. The ride from Westminster Pier to the palace is a beautiful one through the semi-rural outskirts of London. It takes about 3 hours, so make a day of it; tel: (020) 7930 2062 for times, which vary with the tides.

WINDSOR **Windsor Castle**, dominating the town's skyline, is both the largest royal residence and the oldest, inhabited for over 500 years. Although visitors may be surprised by how little is open to the public, the visit is worthwhile to see the State Apartments, meticulously restored after a serious fire in 1992; the exquisite Queen Mary's Doll House; and St George's Chapel, an outstanding example of late Gothic architecture. £££, open daily 0945–1715 (Mar–Oct); 0945–1615 (Nov–Feb); may be closed for official engagements. Windsor is easily reached by train from London Waterloo or Paddington, taking 30–50 mins.

ST ALBANS Located just north of the London suburbs and less than a 30-minute train ride from Kings Cross St Pancras rail station, St Albans is in the thick of commuter country, but has a rewarding old centre (10 mins' walk from the station; turn right along the main road from the station access road), with Georgian and timber-frame buildings, at their best along Fishpool St. Primarily though, it is of interest for its Roman remains within Verulamium Park (named after the Roman town of Verulamium, in its day one of the largest settlements in Britain), which include the only completely exposed **Roman theatre** in Britain (£, Gorhambury; open daily 1000–1700, Mar–Oct; 1000–1600, Nov–Feb), used in its time for ceremonies and theatrical entertainment. Close by are a section of town wall and the **Verulamium Museum**, which vividly evokes Roman life here, with displays of everyday artefacts.

BRICKS AND MORE BRICKS

Highly recommended for families with children aged up to 12 is **Legoland**, near Windsor, whose main attraction apart from imaginative theme park rides is Miniland, where famous world landmarks are recreated with millions of little bricks. For money-saving tickets (£££) including rail travel from Waterloo and shuttle bus to the park, tel: 0845 6000 650.

LONDON – HASTINGS

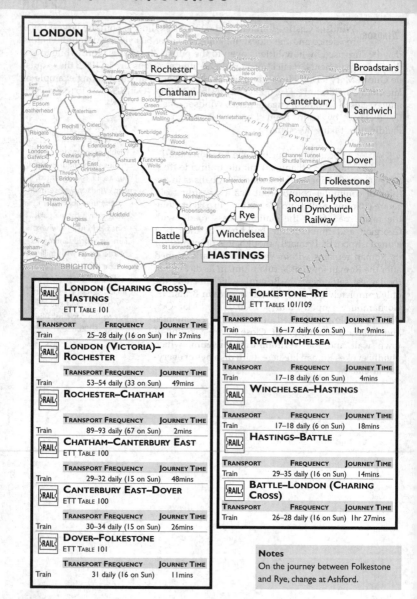

LONDON (CHARING CROSS)–HASTINGS

ETT TABLE 101

TRANSPORT	FREQUENCY	JOURNEY TIME
Train	25–28 daily (16 on Sun)	1hr 37mins

LONDON (VICTORIA)–ROCHESTER

TRANSPORT	FREQUENCY	JOURNEY TIME
Train	53–54 daily (33 on Sun)	49mins

ROCHESTER–CHATHAM

TRANSPORT	FREQUENCY	JOURNEY TIME
Train	89–93 daily (67 on Sun)	2mins

CHATHAM–CANTERBURY EAST

ETT TABLE 100

TRANSPORT	FREQUENCY	JOURNEY TIME
Train	29–32 daily (15 on Sun)	48mins

CANTERBURY EAST–DOVER

ETT TABLE 100

TRANSPORT	FREQUENCY	JOURNEY TIME
Train	30–34 daily (15 on Sun)	26mins

DOVER–FOLKESTONE

ETT TABLE 101

TRANSPORT	FREQUENCY	JOURNEY TIME
Train	31 daily (16 on Sun)	11mins

FOLKESTONE–RYE

ETT TABLES 101/109

TRANSPORT	FREQUENCY	JOURNEY TIME
Train	16–17 daily (6 on Sun)	1hr 9mins

RYE–WINCHELSEA

TRANSPORT	FREQUENCY	JOURNEY TIME
Train	17–18 daily (6 on Sun)	4mins

WINCHELSEA–HASTINGS

TRANSPORT	FREQUENCY	JOURNEY TIME
Train	17–18 daily (6 on Sun)	18mins

HASTINGS–BATTLE

TRANSPORT	FREQUENCY	JOURNEY TIME
Train	29–35 daily (16 on Sun)	14mins

BATTLE–LONDON (CHARING CROSS)

TRANSPORT	FREQUENCY	JOURNEY TIME
Train	26–28 daily (16 on Sun)	1hr 27mins

Notes

On the journey between Folkestone and Rye, change at Ashford.

This tour of the south-eastern corner of England packs in an astonishing cross-section of history, from the Romans to the Industrial Revolution. Beyond the historic naval dockyard at Chatham lies Canterbury, a great religious centre from the Middle Ages; by the coast are quieter, unspoilt towns such as Broadstairs and Sandwich. Dover is home to a Norman Castle that was an important base in World War II. Beyond the well-preserved old ports and smugglers' haunts of Rye and Winchelsea are the atmospheric, slightly decaying town of Hastings and the village of Battle, where in 1066 the most important battle ever to take place on British soil was fought.

LONDON

See p. 40.

ROCHESTER

Of the three Medway towns, Gillingham, Chatham and Rochester, the latter is the oldest and most attractive, and the main reason to visit this otherwise dreary corner of Kent. It was originally settled by the Romans, and the city walls follow the line of their original fortifications. Rochester's star attraction is its **castle**. The square, 100-ft-high (30 m) Norman keep is one of the best preserved in England, and the curtain walls also survive – one of the towers was famously undermined by King John (££, The Keep, open Apr–Sept 1000–1800, Oct–Mar 1000–1600). Running a close second is the superb **Rochester Cathedral** (The Precinct; open daily 0730–1700; donation); though much altered, many of the cathedral's Norman elements remain.

CHARLES DICKENS
Rochester features in several of the novels of Charles Dickens, who spent many years in the area. He is remembered in the excellent **Dickens Centre** (££, High St, open daily 1000–1645), where many scenes from his books are recreated. Free **guided walks** of Rochester depart from here.

i **Tourist Information Centre** 95 High St; tel: (01634) 843666, website: www.medway.gov.uk; e-mail: visitorcentre@medway.gov.uk. Open Mon–Sat 1000–1700, Sun 1030–1700.

TO There is not a lot of choice in Rochester, but good places to try on the High St are **Casa Lina** at no. 146 for Italian food and the bar **City Wall** at no. 122. In Chatham, head straight for the dockyard for refreshments.

CHATHAM Chatham, the next stop down the line and about 2 miles (3 km) east of Rochester, is well worth a stop for the vast **Historic Dockyard**. Once an important naval base, this is now a major working museum. Attractions include a World War II destroyer, a Cold War submarine, many lifeboats, a working ropery and a new museum. £££, Dock Rd, open daily

1000–1800 (Apr–Oct); Wed, Sat and Sun 1000–1600 (Feb, Mar and Nov); closed Dec–Jan. To get there, take a bus from Chatham town centre.

CANTERBURY

Three major events have shaped Canterbury's character: the arrival of St Augustine from Rome in AD 597 to begin the conversion of the English peoples, the brutal despatch of Henry II's 'turbulent priest', Thomas Becket, in 1170, and German bombing in 1942. Despite the latter, much of the medieval streetscape of this compact city survives in its narrow, crooked alleys, clustered around the impressive cathedral, which was the destination of Chaucer's pilgrims. Tourists in their millions follow in their footsteps, so try to avoid summer weekends and bank holidays. But don't miss Canterbury out because of the crowds, and allow a whole day to explore.

Head first for the **cathedral** (£, open Mon–Sat 0900–1900, 1700 in winter; Sun outside service times), entering the precinct via the ornate, heraldic **Christ Church Gate**. The cathedral at the heart of the Anglican church dates from around 1070 and has been much added to. Its chief glories are the beautiful 12th- and 13th-century stained glass; a forest of late Perpendicular pinnacles and towers, including Bell Harry, the 235-ft (71-m) central tower; and the largest Norman crypt in the country. The shrine where Becket was murdered is in the north-west transept.

Long stretches of the medieval **city wall**, built on Roman foundations, survive. Just beyond the wall lie the ruins of **St Augustine's Abbey**, where the saint himself and other early archbishops and kings of Kent were buried (£, Longport, open daily Apr–Sept 1000–1800, Oct 1000–1700, Nov–Mar 1000–1600). Some Saxon remains survive as well as a later Norman church, and there is an excellent new interpretive centre. The city's Roman history is explained in the **Roman Museum**, on the site of an excavated Roman house (£, Butchery Lane, open Mon–Sat 1000–1700 and Sun June–Oct 1330–1700).

The Canterbury Tales is a popular attraction purporting to provide a 14th-century experience in order to bring Chaucer's verses to life. ££, St Margaret's St, open daily 0900/0930–1730 (Mar–Sept), Mon–Fri and Sun 1000–1630, Sat 0930–1730 (Nov–Feb). The excellent **Canterbury Heritage Museum**, in Stour St, £, open Mon–Sat 1030–1700 all year, Sun 1330–1700 (June–Oct), housed in the lovely Poor Priests' Hospital, is one of many medieval hostels built along the river to accommodate pilgrims.

> *i* **Canterbury Visitor Information Centre** 34 St Margaret's St; tel: (01227) 766567; website: www.canterbury.co.uk; e-mail: canterburyinformation@ canterbury.gov.uk. Open Mon–Sat 0930–1700 (1730 Jul–Aug), Sun 1000–1600 (Easter–Dec). Daily guided walks.

🚆 **Canterbury East** station, for the London Victoria and Dover trains (which run about every 30 mins), is on Station Rd East, 5 mins from the city centre.

🛏 Canterbury has a good range of accommodation, with cheaper B&Bs mainly on the outskirts, though you should book ahead in July and Aug.

Magnolia House £££ 36 St Dunstan's Terrace; tel: (01227) 765121. B&B with walled garden in quiet, central side street.

Kingsbridge Villa ££ 15 Best Lane; tel: (01227) 766415. Central and comfortable.

Canterbury Youth Hostel £ 54 New Dover Rd; tel: 0870 7705744; e-mail: canterbury@yha.org.uk. Half a mile from city centre.

🍴 There is no shortage of places to eat and drink in every price range. St Peter's St is a particularly good area for restaurants.

Flap Jacques £–££ 71 Castle St. Inexpensive French bistro.

Caffè Venezia £ 60–61 Palace St. Italian café selling delicious snacks.

Café St Pierre £ 41 St Peter's St. Good French bakery with garden.

SIDE TRIPS FROM CANTERBURY
Broadstairs (12–14 trains from Canterbury West daily, journey time 28 mins) is a delightfully old-fashioned seaside resort lining a series of tiny bays, and much of it dating from the pre-railway age. Charles Dickens lived here, and his house is now Bleak House where you can see the desk where he penned *David Copperfield* (££, daily except mid-Dec–mid-Feb). From here you can walk along the coast for half an hour or so to **Ramsgate**, a dozy little Regency resort that has seen better days but has some very pretty side streets; there's a station here too.

🛏 Broadstairs Youth Hostel is at 3 Osborne Rd, tel: 0870 7705730; e-mail: broadstairs@yha.org.uk.

Sandwich (15–16 trains from Canterbury West daily, 12 on Sun (change at Ramsgate), journey time 53 mins) was once a port, but silting up has stranded it some way inland. It has survived the passage of time better than most towns in southern England, and unlike Canterbury has the air of being undiscovered by tourists. You can walk along a section of the medieval wall, and there are three ancient churches to explore, one dating from Norman times. About 1½ miles (2.4 km) outside town, the remains of **Richborough Roman Fort** (£, open daily except 25, 26 Dec and 1 Jan) date back to the invasion of Britain in AD 43; here at the very entrance to Roman Britain were a now vanished town and a huge triumphal arch.

DOVER

Millions today pass through Dover on their way to foreign parts, but for centuries its role, as guardian of the shortest sea passage to the European mainland, was to keep invaders out. Though not a particularly enticing town, Dover's historic importance has left it with several attractions that make it well worth a look. Chief among these is **Dover Castle**, one of the most impressive medieval fortresses in western Europe. You can explore everything from the Roman lighthouse and Norman keep (which houses the 'Live and Let's Spy' interactive exhibition, popular with children) to Hellfire Corner, the labyrinth of underground passages which were the HQ of secret operations during World War II, including the Dunkirk exodus. The castle is vast, so allow a good half-day and take a picnic. £££, open daily 1000–1800 (Apr–Sept), 1000–1700 (Oct), 1000–1600 (Nov–Mar).

Otherwise, Dover's surviving old buildings include the well-preserved **Roman Painted House**, a Roman guesthouse, with the oldest frescoes in Britain. £, New St, open Tues–Sun 1000–1700 (Apr–Sept) and daily 1000–1700 (July–Aug). **Dover Museum** tells the town's story and includes the Bronze Age Boat Gallery; £, Market Sq., open daily 1000–1800 (summer); 1000–1730 (winter). The **Grand Shaft** is a quite extraordinarily ingenious triple spiral staircase giving fast access (originally for the Victorian army) up and down the famous white cliffs. £, South Military Rd/Snargate St; open Tues–Sun 1400–1700 (July–Aug).

> **ℹ️ Tourist Information Centre** Townwall St; tel: (01304) 205108; website: www.whitecliffscountry.org.uk; e-mail: tic@doveruk.com. Open daily 0900–1800.

> **🚆** The station is Dover Priory, 10 mins from the town centre. Trains run here about every $\frac{1}{2}$ hour from London Victoria via Canterbury East.

> **🛏️** There are plenty of guesthouses, should you need to stay here. Two close to the castle are **Castle House** ££ 10 Castle Hill; tel: (01304) 201656; e-mail: dimechr@aol.com, and **Cleveland** ££ 2 Laureston Place; tel: (013040) 204622; e-mail: albetcleve@aol.com. There is also a busy **hostel**, 306 London Rd; tel: 0870 7705798; e-mail: dover@yha.org.uk.

FOLKESTONE

A 20-min train ride along the coast from Dover is the port of Folkestone, with frequent buses to Hythe (p. 61). Another 19th-century resort, it has vestiges of charm around the church and the old High St, and along the clifftop promenade known as **The Leas**.

i **Tourist Information Centre** Harbour St; tel: (01303)
258594; website: www.kents-garden-coast.co.uk; e-mail:
tourism@folkestone.org.uk. Open daily 0900–1730 (Sun
1000–1600 in winter).

Folkestone Central is on Cheriton Rd; for the SeaCats
use Folkestone Harbour. (The Shuttle terminal is on another
line, and outside the town.)

SIDE TRIP FROM FOLKESTONE Another good reason to stop off at Folkestone is to take
a bus to **Hythe** (from Folkestone Central), terminus of
the 14-mile (22.5-km) **Romney, Hythe & Dymchurch Railway** (RH&DR) which runs
via nine stations along the coast to Dungeness. This popular miniature railway uses
steam engines which are replicas of full-size locomotives. It is highly recommended,
both for the railway itself and because the track runs along the edge of **Romney
Marsh**, a mysterious, once malarial marshland well below sea-level, now home to
extra-large frogs not seen elsewhere in Britain.

New Romney has a museum of model railways (open as railway), while the desolate promontory of **Dungeness** is home to an isolated community of makeshift
homes, a vast nuclear power station. and huge colonies of seabirds. The RH&DR
runs daily Apr–Sept and weekends in Oct and Mar. £££ for round trip; tel: (01797)
362353 for train times.

i **Tourist Information Centre** En Route Building, Red
Lion Sq., Hythe; tel: (01303) 267799; fax (01303) 26161. Open
summer only Mon–Fri 0900–1730, Sat 0900–1700, Sun
1000–1400.

RYE

The enchanting historic town of Rye is perched above the waterline near the mouth
of the Rother. Rye was once an important Channel port, and rife with smugglers, but
silting eventually stranded the town over 2 miles (3.2 km) away from its harbour.

Today, **Mermaid St**, with its picturesque cobbles and lopsided, clay-tiled buildings,
is one of Rye's prettiest streets. Many others have Georgian houses, or medieval
relics such as the 14th-century **Land Gate** and **Ypres Tower**, a former lookout, which
now houses the **Rye Castle Museum**. £, East St, open Thur–Mon 1030–1730
(Apr–Oct), Sat and Sun 1100–1600 (Nov–Mar). **Lamb House** was the home of the
American novelist Henry James during his later life; £, West St; open Wed and Sat
1400–1800 (Apr–Oct only).

THE CINQUE PORTS

In Saxon times Edward the Confessor granted special privileges to five Channel ports – Hastings, Romney, Hythe, Sandwich and Dover. In return, their duties were to defend the Channel, and keep the royal fleet equipped with ships and men. The Cinque (pronounced 'sink') Ports still retain some ceremonial status, along with a Lord Warden. Other ports co-opted later included Deal, Walmer, Rye and Winchelsea. Only Dover is an active port today.

[i] **Tourist Information Centre** 21 Lion St; tel: (01797) 226696; website: www.rye.org.uk; e-mail: ryetic@rother.gov.uk. Open Mon–Sat 0900–1730, Sun 1000–1730 (summer); daily 1000–1600 (winter). Also houses a local museum (£) which tells the story of Rye.

[RAIL] The station is just north of the town. There are no trains direct from Folkestone and Dover (change at Ashford).

[🛏] Rye's choice of accommodation is excellent.
Jeake's House ££ Mermaid St; tel: (01797) 222828; e-mail: jeakeshouse@btinternet.com. Characterful B&B in this pretty street.
Little Orchard House ££ West St; tel: (01797) 223831. Period B&B with a lovely garden.

[🍴] Don't miss the 15th-century **Mermaid Inn** ££ Mermaid St for atmosphere. Or try the **Old Forge** ££ 24 Wish St for seafood dishes. **The Peacock** ££ Lion St has a good range of food.

WINCHELSEA

This smaller, even quieter version of Rye is a fascinatingly odd place built in the 13th century as a planned town around a regular grid plan. The Black Death and French raids pretty much killed off the town's commerce, and it was mostly rebuilt in the 17th and 18th centuries, although medieval cellars and three town gates survive. The church occupies the central square, and is itself a strange hotchpotch, partly ruined; the nearby Winchelsea Court Hall Museum (£, May–Sept, Tues–Sat, plus Bank Holidays and Sun afternoons) tells the town story.

[RAIL] Turn right out of the station, then right again; ³/₄ mile (1.2 km) walk.

HASTINGS

Although William the Conqueror landed at Pevensey, and the famous battle that changed English history took place up the road at Battle, the name of Hastings is forever associated with 1066. The town today is a mixture of rather rundown seaside resort and attractive, still functioning fishing port. A distinctive feature of **The Stade**, which runs behind the shingle beach, are the weatherboarded net shops, built to store fishing nets.

East of the pier is Hastings' best feature, the **Old Town**, which preserves some picturesque old houses and narrow, winding streets, especially **All Saints St** with its timber-framed 15th-century houses. The Old Town nestles between two hills, one of which can be climbed by Victorian funicular railway; there are great walks along the cliffs from here to Fairlight Cove. On top of West Hill is **Hastings Castle**, the site of William I's first motte-and-bailey in England. **The 1066 Story** within the castle brings to life the events of that year (£, open daily 1000/1100–1700). The warren of tunnels under the hill houses **Smugglers' Adventure**, a fascinating recreation of the town's long associations with illicit imports (St Clements Caves, West Hill; ££ or £££ joint ticket with the 1066 Story. Open daily 1000–1730 (Easter–Sept), 1100–1630 (Oct–Easter).

---

i **Tourist Information Centre** Queens Sq., Priory Meadow. Open Mon–Fri 0830–1815 (1700 Tues–Thur in winter), Sat 0900–1700, Sun 1000–1630. The Stade, Old Town, Open summer only, Mon–Fri 1000–1800, Sat 0900–1700, Sun 1000–1630. Both tel: (01424) 781111; website: www.hastings.org.uk; e-mail: hic–info@hastings.gov.uk.

🚉 The station is on Havelock Rd, 10 mins from the seafront. There are hourly trains from Rye.

🏨 Hastings has a good range of guesthouses and B&Bs, especially away from the seafront. Try **Lavender and Lace** ££ 106 All Saints St, Old Town; tel: (01424) 716290.

🍴 There are many places to choose from around the High St and George St.

WHERE NEXT?

Instead of returning to London, from Hastings you could continue west along the coast on the Hastings–Arundel route (see p. 64).

BATTLE

Battle Abbey was built by William I in atonement for the slaughter of the battle of Hastings; the high altar is said to mark the spot where Harold fell. As well as exploring the abbey remains you can take an audiotour around the battlefield itself, and try to imagine how it all happened (about one mile walk). ££, open daily 1000–1800 (Apr–Sept), 1000–1700 (Oct) and 1000–1600 (Nov–Mar). Battle is about a 10-min train journey from Hastings. The station is ¼ mile (400 m) from the abbey.

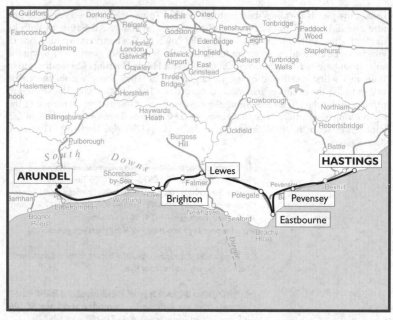

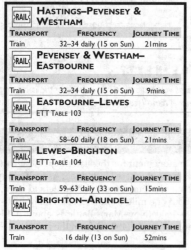

RAIL	HASTINGS–PEVENSEY & WESTHAM		
TRANSPORT	FREQUENCY		JOURNEY TIME
Train	32–34 daily (15 on Sun)		21mins

RAIL	PEVENSEY & WESTHAM– EASTBOURNE		
TRANSPORT	FREQUENCY		JOURNEY TIME
Train	32–34 daily (15 on Sun)		9mins

RAIL	EASTBOURNE–LEWES ETT TABLE 103		
TRANSPORT	FREQUENCY		JOURNEY TIME
Train	58–60 daily (18 on Sun)		21mins

RAIL	LEWES–BRIGHTON ETT TABLE 104		
TRANSPORT	FREQUENCY		JOURNEY TIME
Train	59–63 daily (33 on Sun)		15mins

RAIL	BRIGHTON–ARUNDEL		
TRANSPORT	FREQUENCY		JOURNEY TIME
Train	16 daily (13 on Sun)		52mins

Notes

On the journey from Brighton to Arundel, change at Ford.

Colour Section

(i) The Union flag, red, white and blue; the white cliffs of Dover (p. 60)

(ii) The Houses of Parliament, Westminster, from the South Bank, London; double-decker buses at Victoria Station, London (pp. 40–55)

(iii) King's College, Cambridge, seen from 'The Backs'; punting on the river Cam in Cambridge (pp. 90–94)

(iv) Clifton Suspension Bridge, Bristol (p. 124); St Michael's Mount, Cornwall (p. 146)

This journey skirts the Sussex coast and heads through the rolling green chalky landscapes of the South Downs, passing through Brighton and on to Arundel, from where you can continue to Chichester to join the route to Lyme Regis (see p. 70). There are direct trains to and from London from each of the places featured.

HASTINGS

See p. 62.

PEVENSEY

It was at Pevensey Bay that William the Conqueror is thought to have landed prior to defeating the English at Battle in 1066. The castle is a bewildering mixture of dates: the outer walls are Roman, the inner castle is of various medieval phases, and is topped by a World War II gun emplacement. The audio tour, which takes you down into the prisons, fleshes out the history. £, daily except 25, 26 Dec and 1 Jan.

> [RAIL] Pevensey Bay and Pevensey & Westham stations are each
> ¹/₂ mile (0.8 km) from the castle. Pevensey Bay is near the old
> part of the village.

EASTBOURNE

Eastbourne has taken good care of its graceful Victorian architecture and retains a fine **Pier**. Despite its reputation as a retirement town it boasts a number of lively family activities, such as the **Miniature Steam Railway Fun Park**, free, train ride £, Lottbridge Dr.; open daily 1000–1700 (Easter–Sept). Authentic street scenes containing a bewildering array of merchandise are recreated at the **How We Lived Then Museum of Shops**, £, 20 Cornfield Terrace, open daily 1000–1730. The history of life-saving vessels is displayed at the **RNLI Lifeboat Museum** on King Edward Pde; free (but donations to RNLI welcomed); open daily 1000–1600/1700.

Near Eastbourne is a spectacular stretch of coast where the South Downs hit the sea. Just a short walk west of Eastbourne or a 15-min bus ride from its pier is the sheer 575-ft (175 m) **Beachy Head**, famous as a suicide spot. Beyond are the well-known chalk cliffs known as the Seven Sisters, and the whole area offers wonderful walking. **Beachy Head Countryside Centre** is open daily 1000–1730 (Apr–Sept), daily 1000–1730 (Oct), weekends 1100–1600 (Nov–Dec), and offers guided walks.

> [i] **Tourist Information Centre** Cornfield Rd; tel: (01323)
> 411400; website: www.eastbourne.org.org/tic;

e-mail: eastbournetic@btclick.com. Open Mon–Sat 0900–1730,
Sun 1000–1300 (summer); Mon–Fri 0930–1730, Sat
0930–1600, closed Sun (winter).

[RAIL] **Eastbourne station** is on Terminus Rd, a 10-min walk
from the seafront. There are hourly trains to London, Lewes
and Hastings; more frequent trains to Brighton.

[TO] There are many restaurants around Terminus Rd. Try
Luigi's ££ 72 Seaside Rd for Italian fare or the Thai **Seeracha**
££ 94 Terminus Rd.

LEWES

Thomas Paine, author of *The Rights of Man*, promoter of American independence and
and co-author of the American Declaration of Independence, lived here during his service as an excise officer. Surprisingly untouristy, Lewes is quite unlike anywhere else
in the south-east, a town of remarkably steep alleys and narrow ancient-feeling streets,
centred on its hilltop castle. There are plenty of antique shops for browsing.

Lewes Castle has a Norman keep – climb to the top for some magnificent views of
the surrounding South Downs; ££, High St; open Mon–Sat 1000–1730, Sun
1100–1730. A combined ticket (££) also gives access to **Anne of Cleves House**,
Southover High St (open daily). The house was part of Henry VIII's divorce settlement to his fourth wife, who famously did not live up to her portrait in Henry's
eyes. It now houses a folk museum. A good place for a peaceful picnic (between castle and house) are the gardens of **Southover Grange** at the bottom of steep, cobbled
Keere St. The house was built of Caen limestone taken from Lewes Priory, which
stood nearby; it was also the boyhood home of 17th-century diarist John Evelyn.
Free; open daily until dusk.

[i] **Tourist Information Centre** 187 High St; tel: (01273)
483448; website: www.lewes.gov.uk; e-mail:
lewestic@lewes.gov.uk. Open Mon–Fri 0900–1700, Sat
1000–1700, Sun 1000–1400 (summer); Mon–Fri 0900–1700, Sat
1000–1400, closed Sun (winter).

[RAIL] **Lewes station** is south of High St, down Station St. Trains
run frequently along this line. It's just 15 mins to Lewes from
Brighton, and about 40 mins to Eastbourne.

[TO] Lewes has many pubs serving beer from the local brewery,
Harvey's; there is an excellent brewery shop in High St. Try the
funky Snowdrop, at the far end of South Street, or the friendly

SOMETHING'S BURNING

Communities all over Britain celebrate Bonfire Night on 5 November as the anniversary of the unsuccessful Gunpowder Plot of 1605 to blow up the Houses of Parliament. But in Lewes the event also commemorates the Lewes Martyrs, 17 Protestants burned at the stake in 1556, and remembered with riotous pyrotechnics. On Bonfire Night today revellers in Lewes indulge in the ceremonial burning of effigies of Guy Fawkes and the Pope. More universally reviled targets, like prominent politicians and terrorists, are sometimes also set on fire in effigy in this unique ceremony, which also includes huge costumed torchlit processions.

Lewes Arms, behind the castle. Restaurants include:
John Harvey Tavern £ 1 Bear Yard, Cliffe High St, tel: (01273) 479880. In the town centre by the river and close to Harvey's, the old-fashioned brewery that owns it. Well-kept seasonal Harvey's beers and excellent value pub food.
Pailin Thai £ 20 Station St; tel: (01273) 473906. Good value Thai food.

BRIGHTON

Vibrant Brighton has long been known as 'London by the Sea', although it only acquired city status in 2000. It began to develop after a local doctor extolled the curative powers of sea bathing, which kickstarted the trend for seaside holidays. Its fashionable status, bestowed by the Prince Regent, later George IV, never really left it, although it has always had a slightly bohemian air. The elegant Georgian and Regency terraces, which sprang up after the prince built the exotic Royal Pavilion, give Brighton its unique architectural character. This, along with its seaside attractions and buzzing nightlife, make it well worth at least a day's exploration.

There are three must-sees in Brighton: the Royal Pavilion, Brighton Pier, and the Lanes. **The Royal Pavilion**, George IV's bizarre seaside palace, is an exotic monument to Regency high living. Its mass of oriental-inspired onion domes, pagodas and minarets were contributed by the famous architect John Nash between 1815 and 1822, and the carefully restored interior, famed for its elaborate chinoiserie and rich decor, is one of the most extraordinary in Europe. ££, Old Steine, open daily 1000–1700/1800.

Between the Pavilion and the seafront are the attractive narrow streets of the original fishing village, now transformed into the pedestrianised **Lanes**, a warren of bijou shops selling antiques, gifts and designer wear. For the more eclectic shops of **North Laine**, which spreads north of North Street, head towards Kensington Gardens.

The train station, at Queens Rd, is ½ mile (0.8 km) north of the seafront, with a good bus link to the centre. Most attractions are within easy walking distance. If you are driving, it is a good idea to use one of the Park and Ride schemes, since parking can be difficult in the city centre.

Tackiness plunges to its depths at **Brighton Pier**, but for traditional arcade games and fairground rides there is nothing to beat it, and you will have a hard task dragging children away. Free, open daily, weather permitting. The earlier and architecturally superior **West Pier**, built in 1866, was seriously damaged by fire twice in the spring of 2003 but there are plans to restore it using lottery funding.

Across the road from Brighton Pier is an unusually good **Sea Life Centre** (££, 33 Marine Pde; open daily 1000–1800). From a long transparent tunnel you can watch sharks and rays lurk eerily close to your head. **Volk's Electric Railway** (£, Madeira Dr.; operates daily Apr–Sept), the first electric railway in Britain, will take you 1 mile (1.6 km) east along the seafront on its elderly rolling stock. To see typical and unspoilt Brighton Regency architecture, head east towards **Kemp Town**, where the white stuccoed terraces centred around Lewes Crescent are a good example of 19th-century speculative building.

i **Visitor Information Centre** 10 Bartholomew Sq.; tel: (01273) 292590; website: www.visitbrighton.com; e-mail: brighton-tourism@brighton-hove.gov.uk. Open Mon–Fri 0900–1730, Sat 1000–1800, Sun 1000–1700 (summer); Mon–Fri 0900–1700, Sat 1000–1700, closed Sun (winter).

Places to stay are plentiful for every budget, although it is advisable to book ahead for bank holidays and weekends.
Topps Hotel £££ Regency Sq.; tel: (01273) 729334. Comfortable Georgian townhouse near the West Pier.
Four Seasons ££ 3 Upper Rock Gardens; tel: (01273) 681496. B&B in upmarket Kemp Town area.
Brighton Backpackers £ 75 Middle St; tel: (01273) 777717. Independent, popular hostel, with a quiet annexe overlooking the seafront.
Youth Hostel £ Patcham Place, London Rd; tel: 0870 7705724, is 4 miles (6.5 km) out of town, in a grand Queen Anne mansion surrounded by parkland.

You are spoilt for choice for food in Brighton, whatever your price range or food preference. For cheap places look around North Laine. In the Lanes and out towards Hove the restaurants tend to be more upmarket and pricier.
Al Duomo ££ 7 Pavilion Buildings. Great pizzas.
Black Chapati ££ 12 Circus Parade, New England Rd; tel: (01273) 699011. Well-established restaurant serving carefully prepared oriental cooking; Japanese and Thai as well as Indian. Worth seeking out, although it's off the beaten track.
Browns £££ 3–4 Duke St; tel: (01273) 323501. Wide range of dishes and background jazz.

Mock Turtle £ 4 Pool Valley; tel: (01273) 327380. Traditional teashop with homemade cakes, which also serves light lunches.

ARUNDEL

Romantic **Arundel Castle** dominates this picturesque little town from a wooded mound overlooking the Arun valley. The seat of the dukes of Norfolk for over 700 years appears medieval; in fact most of the castle's fabric was reconstructed in the 19th century as it was ruined in the Civil War. There is plenty to see inside including paintings by Holbein, Van Dyck and Gainsborough. £££, open Sun–Fri 1200–1700 (Apr–Oct).

Arundel's other charms are its Catholic **cathedral** and its unspoilt brick, flint and timbered buildings lining hilly narrow streets, which are good for antique hunters. To the north the Arun flows through a nature reserve belonging to the **Wildfowl and Wetland Trust** (££, Mill Rd, open daily 0930–1630/1730) where there are many species of waterfowl, some tame enough to hand feed.

[i] **Tourist Information Centre** 61 High; tel: (01903) 882268; website; www.sussex-by-the-sea.co.uk; e-mail: tourism@arun.gov.uk. Open Mon–Sat 0900–1700, Sun 1000–1600 (summer); daily 1000–1500 (winter).

Boat cruises can be taken up the Arun to Amberley from the Tea Rooms by the bridge.

[RAIL] Trains run hourly from London to Arundel. The station is ½ mile (0.8 km) south of the town centre on the A27.

[🛏] **Arundel Youth Hostel**, tel: 0870 7705676 (e-mail: arundel @yha.org.uk) is out of town at Warningcamp, but a pleasant 20-min walk along the river from the town (from the station, turn right on A27, then first left).

[🍴] There are many good tearooms for snacks and high tea. The **White Hart** ££ 3 Queen St serves good food at moderate prices.

WHERE NEXT?

Continue along the Sussex coast from Arundel to Chichester (hourly trains, journey time 20 mins), to join the Chichester–Lyme Regis route (see p. 70). Arundel has hourly services to London Victoria (1hr 25mins).

CHICHESTER – LYME REGIS

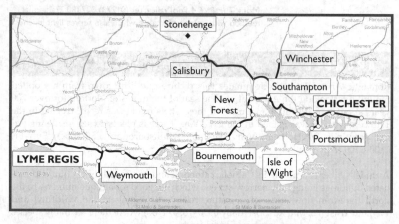

CHICHESTER–LYME REGIS

TRANSPORT	FREQUENCY	JOURNEY TIME
Train and Bus	9–10 daily (4 on Sun)	4hrs 28mins

CHICHESTER–PORTSMOUTH
ETT TABLE 110

TRANSPORT	FREQUENCY	JOURNEY TIME
Train	38–51 daily (35 on Sun)	28mins

PORTSMOUTH–SOUTHAMPTON
ETT TABLE 137

TRANSPORT	FREQUENCY	JOURNEY TIME
Train	18–35 daily (17 on Sun)	48mins

SOUTHAMPTON CENTRAL–BOURNEMOUTH
ETT TABLES 108/127

TRANSPORT	FREQUENCY	JOURNEY TIME
Train	49–63 daily (39 on Sun)	37mins

BOURNEMOUTH–WEYMOUTH
ETT TABLE 108

TRANSPORT	FREQUENCY	JOURNEY TIME
Train	16–19 daily (13 on Sun)	56mins

WEYMOUTH–LYME REGIS

TRANSPORT	FREQUENCY	JOURNEY TIME
Bus	16 daily (7 on Sun)	1hr 36mins

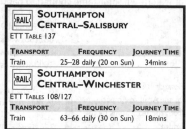

SOUTHAMPTON CENTRAL–SALISBURY
ETT TABLE 137

TRANSPORT	FREQUENCY	JOURNEY TIME
Train	25–28 daily (20 on Sun)	34mins

SOUTHAMPTON CENTRAL–WINCHESTER
ETT TABLES 108/127

TRANSPORT	FREQUENCY	JOURNEY TIME
Train	63–66 daily (30 on Sun)	18mins

Notes

There are no trains to Lyme Regis. Buses from Weymouth to Lyme Regis are First Southern National services 31/X31/X53.

An alternative is to take a train to Dorchester and travel by bus from Dorchester to Lyme Regis, First Southern National services 31/X31.

This largely coastal route from Chichester takes in the great maritime centres of Portsmouth and Southampton and the popular seaside resorts of Bournemouth and Weymouth with their miles of sandy beaches. On the way there plenty of opportunities for interesting side trips, mostly accessible by train. Inland, the cathedral cities of Winchester and Salisbury have an extraordinarily rich heritage of historic buildings, while Salisbury Plain is littered with many reminders of a much earlier civilisation, notably Stonehenge.

The Isle of Wight, with its attractive beaches and varied scenery, is only a short ferry hop from Portsmouth and merits at least a day's exploration. Beyond Southampton the route passes through the tranquil ancient woodland of the New Forest. Good rail links make train travel here feasible, although a car is needed to explore off the beaten track, and is the best way to discover the Dorset coast beyond Weymouth to Lyme Regis.

CHICHESTER

Chichester's Roman origins are evident in the city wall encircling the town, partly rebuilt in medieval times, and the **Wall Walk** is a good way to orient yourself. The four main streets – North, South, East and West – dividing the city centre into quadrants, are also Roman, and meet at the 16th-century **Market Cross**. **Chichester Cathedral**, smaller than most, is largely Norman and Early English, and has a graceful nave, some outstanding Romanesque sculpture, stained glass by Chagall and an unusual detached belfry. Donation requested, West St; open daily 0730–1900 (1700 in winter).

Much of the town's architecture is Georgian, and both within the tranquil cathedral precinct and elsewhere there are some fine 18th-century houses, especially around beautiful **Pallant House** (££, 9 North Pallant; open Tues–Sat 1000–1700), which has a good modern art collection. **Chichester Festival Theatre** is one of the most renowned outside London and has a festival season in July; tel: (01243) 780192 for details.

> **CANALSIDE WALK**
> The 4-mile (6.5-km) walk alongside the canal to **Chichester Harbour** is rich in wildlife and makes an excellent stroll.

i **Tourist Information Centre** 29A South St; tel: (01243) 775888; website: www.chichester.gov.uk; e-mail: chitic@chichester.gov.uk. Open Mon–Sat 0930–1700 all year; Sun 1000–1600 (Apr–Sept).

The station is at Southgate, a 10-min walk from the Market Cross. There are frequent trains from Brighton (45 mins) and Portsmouth (30 mins).

FISHBOURNE ROMAN PALACE

The largest Roman residence ever found in Britain, Fishbourne has some remarkable mosaic floors and a reconstructed dining room and garden. ££, open daily 1000–1600/1800. The palace and museum are a 10-min walk from Fishbourne station, 3 mins out of Chichester.

There is a good choice of B&Bs, but pre-book in July.
Friary Close ££ Friary Lane; tel: (01243) 527294; e-mail: friaryclose@argonet.co.uk. Convenient B&B in Georgian house.
Encore ££ 11 Clydesdale Ave; tel: (01243) 528271. B&B in central yet quiet townhouse.

Chichester has a very good choice of restaurants and cafés, including:
The Crypt ££ 12a South St. Imaginative brasserie in historic surroundings.
Café Coco £ 13 South St. French café selling filling snacks, baguettes, etc.
Chichester Delicatessen £ Sadler's Walk, East St. The best place for sandwiches.

PORTSMOUTH

Once the maritime capital of England, Portsmouth – otherwise a rather unappealing port – has put its heritage to good use and the **Historic Dockyard** complex merits a full day. It has three star attractions, each a draw in itself: Nelson's flagship **HMS Victory**, veteran of the Battle of Trafalgar; Henry VIII's warship *Mary Rose*, which sunk in 1545 and was raised to the surface in 1982; and the revolutionary iron warship of 1860, **HMS *Warrior***. The **Royal Naval Museum**, also in the dockyard, charts the history of British seaborne defence over 800 years. The entrance is beside the tourist office in The Hard. Free entry to dockyard, ££ per ship or £££ for all three plus museum. Open daily 1000–1730 (Apr–Oct); 1000–1700 (Nov–Mar). Visits to HMS *Victory* by guided tour.

You can gain a sense of what the 18th-century town was like from the cobbled streets and Tudor and Georgian houses of **Old Portsmouth**, a short walk south of Portsmouth Harbour station at the end of the High St.

Further south-east along the waterfront is **Southsea**, Portsmouth's seaside resort with a shingle beach. The **D-Day Museum** on Clarence Esplanade contains the magnificent Overlord Embroidery, a depiction of the D-Day story inspired by the Bayeux Tapestry. ££, open daily 1000–1730 (Apr–Sept); 1000–1700 (Oct–Mar). Adjacent **Southsea Castle**, built by Henry VIII to protect the harbour, may have been Henry's vantage point as he watched the *Mary Rose* go down; £, open daily 1000–1730 (Apr–Oct).

Guided walks – most lasting 1½ hours – are very good value, and can be booked at The Hard Tourist Information Centre.

i **Tourist Information Centre** The Hard. Also at Clarence Esplanade, Southsea. For both: tel: (023) 9282 6722; website:

www.portsmouthharbour.co.uk; e-mail: tic@portsmouth.gov.uk.
Open daily 0930–1745 (1715 in winter).

🚆 **Portsmouth Harbour** station, The Hard, is convenient
for the dockyard and about 20 mins walk from the centre of
town. **Portsmouth Southsea**, on Commercial Rd, is in the
town centre.

🛏 There is plenty of B&B accommodation, mostly in Southsea.
Budget options include:
Portsmouth and Southsea Backpackers Lodge
£ 4 Florence Rd, Southsea; tel: (02392) 832495; website:
www.portsmouthbackpackers.co.uk. Near the seafront.
Portsmouth Youth Hostel £ is some way out at Old
Wymering Lane, Cosham (0.5 mile/1 km from Cosham
station), tel: 0870 7706002 (e-mail: portsmouth@yha.org.uk).
Greenacres Guest House ££ 12 Marion Rd; tel: (02392)
353137. Large guesthouse close to the seafront.

🍴 Osborne Rd in Southsea has many cafés and restaurants,
including **Barnaby's Bistro** ££ at no. 56.
Country Kitchen £ 59a Marmion Rd, Southsea. Wholefood
restaurant.
Spice Island Inn £ Bath Sq., Old Portsmouth. Historic inn
with a good range of food, and seating outside from which to
watch comings and goings on the Solent.

ISLE OF WIGHT

A popular holiday destination, the **Isle of Wight** is a diamond-shaped island (21
miles by 13/34 km by 21) an easy 20-min ferry trip from Portsmouth. It is a good
place to relax for a day or two. There are plenty of safe, sandy beaches and many
marked footpaths across the chalk downlands. The island also boasts excellent bus
services if you prefer to get around without hiring a car. The best beaches are on the
east coast, with **Shanklin Cline** a popular walking spot, while to the west the
Freshwater Peninsula tapers to the dramatic chalk pinnacles of the **Needles**.

The island was made fashionable by Queen Victoria who built Italianate **Osborne
House** as her seaside retreat overlooking the Solent. Today this is one of the island's
main attractions, giving a remarkable insight into the family life of Victoria, Albert
and their many children. £££, open daily 1000–1800 (Apr–Sept); 1000–1700 (Oct). At
the heart of the island is impressive **Carisbrooke Castle**, scene of Charles I's imprisonment before his execution; ££, open daily 1000–1800 (Apr–Sept); 1000–1700 (Oct);
1000–1600 (Nov–Mar).

Ryde, where the Portsmouth ferry docks, itself has many typical seaside town attractions and makes a convenient base. An alternative is **Yarmouth**, an attractive sailing port with a Tudor castle guarding the harbour. There is a ferry service from here to Lymington.

i **Tourist Information Centre** 81–83 Union St, Ryde; tel: (01983) 813818; website: www.islandbreaks.co.uk; e-mail: info@islandbreaks.co.uk. Open Mon–Sat 0900–1730, Sun 0900–1700 (summer); daily 1000–1600 (winter). Bus timetables available here.

RAIL The passenger ferry to Ryde departs from the jetty at Portsmouth Harbour station; Ryde Pier Head station is about 1 mile (1.6 km) north of town. A train service runs down the east coast between Ryde and Shanklin. Cars can be rented from **Esplanade Garage**; tel: (01983) 562322.

Accommodation is mainly in B&Bs and guesthouses. There are two HI hostels, one on each side of the island: Fitzroy St, Sandown; tel: 0870 7706020 (e-mail: sandown@yha.org.uk); and Hurst Hill, Totland Bay; tel: 0870 7706070 (e-mail: totland@yha.org.uk).

WINCHESTER

Capital of England in pre-Norman times, **Winchester** remained an important religious centre throughout the Middle Ages. Now a peaceful town, its attractions remain relatively uncommercialised and the medieval centre is very well preserved. Only 15 miles inland from Southampton, it's well worth a day trip and possible overnight stop.

All the key sites are within easy walking distance of the centre. **Winchester Cathedral** is one of the finest in England: the present structure, begun in 1079, contains many precious treasures and is thought to be the second longest medieval building in the world. Look out for the cheeky carvings on the 15th-century choir stalls. ££ (donation requested); open daily 0730–1830; tours available. Down College St at no. 8 is the house where Jane Austen died in 1817; she is buried in the north aisle of the cathedral. Further east along the street is **Winchester College**, one of England's oldest public schools, founded in 1382; £, chapel and cloisters open daily 1000–1300, 1400–1700 (except Sun mornings). Beyond the present Bishop's Palace are the ruins of **Wolvesey Castle**, headquarters of the powerful medieval bishops of Winchester and now a pleasant spot for a picnic; £, open daily 1000–1800 (Apr–Sept); 1000–1700 (Oct). A beautiful 1-mile (1.6-km) wander through the river Itchen's watermeadows south of here leads to the **Hospital of St Cross**, a 15th-century almshouse; £, St Cross Rd; open Mon–Sat 0930–1700 (Apr–Oct); 1030–1530 (Nov–Mar).

The **Great Hall** is all that survives of Winchester's Norman castle, which contains a 13th-century Round Table, allegedly King Arthur's (Castle St, free, open daily 1000–1700 (Apr–Oct); Sat–Sun 1000–1700 (Nov–Mar).

[i] **Tourist Information Centre** Guildhall, The Broadway; tel: (01962) 840500 or (01962) 848277 (24 hrs); website: www.visitwinchester.com; e-mail: tourism@winchester.gov.uk. Open Mon–Sat 1000–1800, Sun 1100–1400 (summer); Mon–Sat 1000–1700, closed Sun (winter).

[RAIL] The station is on Station Rd, 10 mins walk west of the centre. Trains run about every ¼ hour from Southampton and take about 20 mins.

[🛏] **Wykeham Arms** £££ 75 Kingsgate St; tel: (01962) 853834. Characterful coaching inn serving good food, near the college. **Winchester Youth Hostel** £ City Mill, 1 Water Lane (just across the Itchen); tel: 0870 7706092. Popular hostel, close to the Tourist Information Centre, in a restored water mill.

[🍴] **Cathedral Refectory** £ Visitors Centre, Inner Close, Winchester Cathedral. Good home cooking in an informal atmosphere.
Harvey's ££ 31B The Square. Restaurant and wine bar serving both full meals and snacks.

SALISBURY

Salisbury's lovely **cathedral** is the purest example of Early English style, built entirely between 1220 and 1258, apart from the leaning spire, added 1334–80, which is the tallest in the country. Donation requested; open Mon–Sat 0700–2015, Sun 0700–1815 (Jun–Aug); daily 0700–1815 (Sept–May).

The intrepid can climb 360 steps up the tower to the spire's base. From here, look north towards the massive ramparts of **Old Sarum**, where the city was originally founded before wind and lack of water forced the city fathers to remove in the early 13th century to New Sarum, modern Salisbury. Back to earth, take time to explore the cloisters, the octagonal chapter house and the peaceful, walled **Cathedral Close**, the largest and most harmonious in England with its happy mix of 13th–18th-century houses. These include the Queen Anne **Mompesson House**, ££, open Mon–Wed 1200–1730 (Apr–Oct) with its fine furnishings.

Don't miss the **Salisbury and South Wiltshire Museum**, housed in the 13th-century King's House, £, open Mon–Sat 1000–1700 all year; Sun 1400–1700 (July–Aug), which contains many archaeological treasures from Stonehenge and Old Sarum. North of the cathedral towards **Market Square** is a network of medieval streets and alleys, with many overhanging half-timbered houses. Walk south-west across the meadows for the painter John Constable's famous view across the river Avon.

> 𝑖 **Tourist Information Centre** Fish Row; tel: (01722) 334956; website: www.visitsalisbury.com; e-mail: visitorinfo@salisbury.gov.uk. Open Mon–Sat 0930–1700 (1800 June–Sept); Sun 1030–1630 (May–Sept). **Tourist Information Centre** Railway Station. Open Mon–Sat 0930–1630 (Easter–mid-Sept).

> [RAIL] The station is ¼ mile (0.4 km) west of the centre on South Western Rd.

> 🛏 There are many B&Bs on Castle Rd, heading north out of town.
> **Clovelly Hotel** ££ 17–19 Mill Rd; tel: (01722) 322055; e-mail: clovelly.hotel@virgin.net. Convenient hotel near the station.
> **Old Bakery** ££ 35 Bedwin St; tel: (01722) 320100. Central B&B in 15th-century cottage.
> **Salisbury Youth Hostel** £ Milford Hill, tel: 0870 7706018 (e-mail: salisbury@yha.org.uk) is centrally placed.

> [TO] There are many restaurants in the Market Sq. area, such as **The Loft** £ for snacks and **Harper's** ££–£££ Ox Row, with a good choice of set-price menus.

THE NEW FOREST

English monarchs from William the Conqueror onward have protected and enlarged the New Forest which covers about 145 sq miles (373 sq km) and is in fact a mix of woodland, heath, free grazing and marsh. It is well known for its scenery, coastal views, friendly ponies, deer and other wildlife.

Lyndhurst is effectively the capital of the forest and at the centre of one of the main areas of woodland. However, **Brockenhurst**, 4 miles (6.5 km) away, has a railway station and makes a better base if you are using public transport. Brockenhurst station in its centre has frequent trains from Southampton (15 mins away) and is well

EXPLORING EAST DORSET

Arriving on this route at Bournemouth you enter the county of Dorset, which has some of England's finest coastal scenery (all of it followed by the South West Coast Path), and is the heart of the countryside of Thomas Hardy's novels. **Bournemouth** itself is far from typical, being a large seaside resort of no great interest (although it does have excellent sandy beaches and the delightfully quirky Russell-Cotes Art Gallery and Museum). Things get more interesting beyond Wareham (rail station), where you can take the hourly bus to **Corfe Castle**. This beautiful stone-built village, squeezed in a notch in the long ridge of the Purbeck Hills, takes its name from the castle that is now a spectacularly jagged medieval ruin that can be seen from far around (££, open daily). There are several B&Bs in the village, and a couple of good pubs serving food.

There's much more in the way of accommodation at the nearby seaside resort of **Swanage** (hourly buses from Wareham, Corfe Castle or Bournemouth; steam train on the Swanage Railway from Corfe Castle – tel: (01929) 425800 for times and prices). The town makes a great base for walking. To the west it gets very rugged and remote around the dizzying cliffs of St Aldhelm's Head (best reached from Worth Matravers). The coast path north leads up Ballard Down, past the chalk pinnacles of Old Harry Rocks and on to the village of Studland, flanked by the largest of Dorset's heathlands. Swanage's **youth hostel** is at Cluny Crescent; tel: 0870 7706058 (e-mail: swanage@yha.org.uk), on the south side of town, 10 mins from the station.

Reached by bus 29 or 30 from Wool rail station (10 buses daily, 3 on Sun) is **Lulworth Cove**, a huge scoop in the coastline; a short walk west leads to the natural sandstone arch of Durdle Door, while to the east the wild coast is often closed for army training but is open most weekends and daily in July and Aug and at Easter. Just inland, Lulworth's **youth hostel** is in School Lane, West Lulworth; tel: 0870 7705940.

Dorchester, Dorset's county town and a railway junction, was the Casterbridge of Thomas Hardy's novels; you can visit **Hardy's Birthplace** (£, closed Nov–Mar and Fri and Sat; frequent buses pass within ¹/₂ mile/1 km), a lone thatched cottage in the forest at Higher Bockhampton, and **Max Gate** (£, 1 Apr–30 Sept, Mon, Wed, Sun, 1400–1700; frequent buses), the house he designed for himself just east of the town. At nearby **Stinsford** his heart is buried in the churchyard. In town his study has been reconstructed in the **Dorset County Museum** (££, High West St, closed Sun Nov–Apr). Just south of town **Maiden Castle** (free, always open) is Europe's largest Iron Age hillfort, encircled by vast ramparts.

served by buses. There is a train service to Lymington Pier for the Isle of Wight ferry link with Yarmouth. The **Rufus Stone**, 3 miles (5 km) north-west of Lyndhurst, reputedly but implausibly marks the spot where the unpopular king William Rufus was killed while hunting in 1100.

Some of the most popular spots in the New Forest lie towards its south-east corner. The **Beaulieu** estate (pronounced 'Bewley') includes the remains of a Cistercian abbey and the Palace House. But it is the **National Motor Museum** which is the biggest attraction here, with 250 vehicles including the record-smashing *Bluebird*. £££, open daily 1000–1800 (May–Sept); 1000–1700 (Oct–Apr); website: www.beaulieu.co.uk. Brockenhurst station is about 5 miles (8 km) away; for a taxi, tel: (01590) 623122, or there are buses from Lyndhurst.

Further down the Beaulieu river is the picturesque hamlet of **Buckler's Hard**, where from Elizabethan times huge men of war were built from New Forest oaks – several of Nelson's fleet were launched here. A **Maritime Museum** (included in the ££ admission price to the village) relates the story. Open daily 1000–1730 (May–Sept); 1000–1630 (Oct–Apr).

ON TWO WHEELS

An ideal way of exploring the New Forest is by bicycle – there are over 100 miles of traffic-free cycle routes. Bikes can be hired from **AA Bike Hire**, Gosport Lane, Lyndhurst; tel: (02380) 283349, or from **New Forest Cycle Experience**, 2–4 Brookley Rd, Brockenhurst, tel: (01590) 624204; website: www.cyclex.co.uk.

ℹ️ **New Forest Museum and Visitor Centre** Main Car Park, Lyndhurst, tel: (023) 8028 2269; website: www.thenewforest.co.uk; e-mail: information@nfdc.gov.uk. Open daily 1000–1800 (Apr–Oct); 1000–1700 (Nov–Mar).

🛏️ Both Brockenhurst and Lyndhurst have plenty of accommodation, including:
Cater's Cottage ££ Latchmoor, Brockenhurst; tel: (01590) 623225. B&B on the south side of town in secluded setting.
Penny Farthing Hotel £££ Romsey Rd, Lyndhurst; tel: (02380) 284422; e-mail: stay@pennyfarthinghotel.co.uk. Large B&B in the centre of town.

WEYMOUTH

Like many other seaside resorts Weymouth has a 19th-century feel, having been favoured by George III, whose striking statue stands on the Esplanade. Though smaller than Bournemouth, its beautiful bay and clean sand make it a good family resort. Many of the attractions here are geared towards the young, including **Brewers Quay** and **Timewalk Journey** ££, Hope Sq.; open daily 1000–1730 (2130 in high season), and a **Sea Life Park**, £££, east of the Esplanade, open Mon–Fri 1100–1600, Sat–Sun 1000–1700 (summer only).

Just south of Weymouth lies the **Isle of Portland**, a limestone peninsula 4 miles (6 km) long and under 2 miles (3 km) wide. **Portland Bill** at its tip, with its famous **Lighthouse**, makes a rewarding destination. Beyond the peninsula lies **Chesil Beach**, an extraordinary natural phenomenon – the 18-mile (29-km) bank of shingle, 40-ft (12-m) high in places, is unique in Europe. **Abbotsbury**, near its western end, has a fascinating **Swannery**. ££, open daily 1000–1800 (mid-Mar–Oct). The walk up the hill to St Catherine's Chapel is rewarded by good views over Chesil Beach. Beyond Bridport, the cliffs, frequently subject to landslips, become ever more dramatic; at the very edge of Dorset lies Lyme Regis.

[i] **Tourist Information Centre**, The King's Statue, The Esplanade; tel: (01305) 785747; website: www.weymouth.gov.uk; e-mail: tourism@weymouth.gov.uk. Open daily 0930–1700 (Apr–Sept); 1000–1600 (Oct–Mar).

[RAIL] The station is very central, on King St, with hourly services from Bournemouth (50 mins) and Southampton (90 mins).

LYME REGIS

Built into a hillside and wedged between famously fossil-filled cliffs, Lyme Regis is a seaside resort unlike any other. A fashionable 18th- and 19th-century resort, it retains a Regency feel with its steep narrow streets and pretty seafront cottages. Literature has ensured that **The Cobb**, Lyme's curving breakwater, is known far and wide: here Jane Austen (in *Persuasion*) allowed Louisa Musgrove to have a nasty fall, with far-reaching consequences, while more recently Meryl Streep brooded soulfully in the film adaptation of John Fowles' *The French Lieutenant's Woman*.

The **Philpot Museum** provides some background on all those fossils. £, Bridge St; open daily 1000–1700 (Easter–Oct); closed Sun 1200–1430. **Dinosaurland** (££, Coombe St; open daily 1000–1700) also offers fossil-hunting walks.

[i] **Tourist Information Centre** Guildhall Cottage, Church St; tel: (01297) 442138; website: www.lymeregis.com; e-mail: e-mail@lymeregistourism.co.uk. Open Mon–Sat 1000–1700, Sun 1000–1600 (summer); Mon–Sat 1000–1600, closed Sun (winter).

[≜] There are plenty of places to stay, including:
Old Lyme Guest House ££ 29 Coombe St; tel: (01297) 442929; e-mail: oldlyme.guesthouse@virgin.net. Comfortable rooms in a 17th-century building at the heart of the old town.

[IO] Fish and chips are available everywhere. The **Pilot Boat** pub serves excellent meals, including vegetarian (££ Bridge St), while **The Beach House Café** offers all-day snacks and meals (£ 24 Marine Pde).

WHERE NEXT?

You could continue east to the university town of Exeter (see p. 129), either by car or by National Express bus, and join the route to Plymouth, from where the Pilgrim Fathers set sail (see p. 135). Alternatively, head north to beautiful Bath (see p. 126).

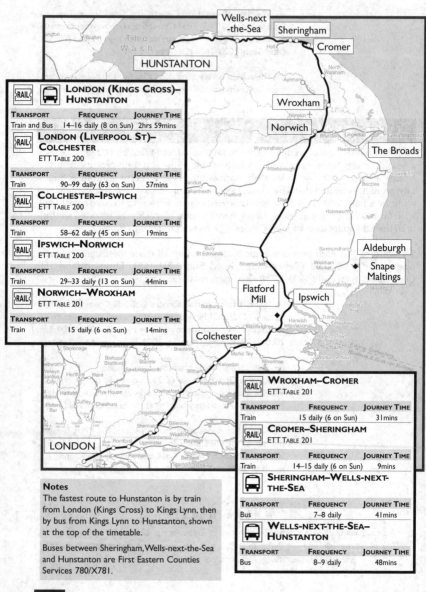

RAIL 🚌	**LONDON (KINGS CROSS)– HUNSTANTON**		
TRANSPORT	**FREQUENCY**	**JOURNEY TIME**	
Train and Bus	14–16 daily (8 on Sun)	2hrs 59mins	

RAIL	**LONDON (LIVERPOOL ST)– COLCHESTER** ETT TABLE 200		
TRANSPORT	**FREQUENCY**	**JOURNEY TIME**	
Train	90–99 daily (63 on Sun)	57mins	

RAIL	**COLCHESTER–IPSWICH** ETT TABLE 200		
TRANSPORT	**FREQUENCY**	**JOURNEY TIME**	
Train	58–62 daily (45 on Sun)	19mins	

RAIL	**IPSWICH–NORWICH** ETT TABLE 200		
TRANSPORT	**FREQUENCY**	**JOURNEY TIME**	
Train	29–33 daily (13 on Sun)	44mins	

RAIL	**NORWICH–WROXHAM** ETT TABLE 201		
TRANSPORT	**FREQUENCY**	**JOURNEY TIME**	
Train	15 daily (6 on Sun)	14mins	

RAIL	**WROXHAM–CROMER** ETT TABLE 201		
TRANSPORT	**FREQUENCY**	**JOURNEY TIME**	
Train	15 daily (6 on Sun)	31mins	

RAIL	**CROMER–SHERINGHAM** ETT TABLE 201		
TRANSPORT	**FREQUENCY**	**JOURNEY TIME**	
Train	14–15 daily (6 on Sun)	9mins	

🚌	**SHERINGHAM–WELLS-NEXT-THE-SEA**		
TRANSPORT	**FREQUENCY**	**JOURNEY TIME**	
Bus	7–8 daily	41mins	

🚌	**WELLS-NEXT-THE-SEA–HUNSTANTON**		
TRANSPORT	**FREQUENCY**	**JOURNEY TIME**	
Bus	8–9 daily	48mins	

Notes

The fastest route to Hunstanton is by train from London (Kings Cross) to Kings Lynn, then by bus from Kings Lynn to Hunstanton, shown at the top of the timetable.

Buses between Sheringham, Wells-next-the-Sea and Hunstanton are First Eastern Counties Services 780/X781.

Three of England's oldest and most historic towns, together with superb coastal areas along the North Sea, are the highlights of this route. There are also classic and unique landscapes, traditional family seaside resorts, quaint villages and picture postcard harbours.

Colchester, Britain's oldest recorded town, was the scene of Queen Boudicca's terrible revenge on the Romans. Ipswich has a number of ancient buildings, as well as a lively waterfront and a nightlife area. Norwich, a superbly preserved city, with medieval streets and a magnificent cathedral, also has wonderful shopping and a vibrant social scene.

Between these major centres are fascinating rural and coastal regions – places like the Stour Valley and the Broads National Park, both an inspiration to major British painters, the Suffolk Coast around Aldeburgh, and North Norfolk, an area of stunning seascapes and picturesque villages west of Cromer. Most of the route can be covered by train, but the last stretch – 34 miles (55 km) between Sheringham and Hunstanton – has no rail services. Instead there is a regular bus service.

LONDON

See p. 40.

COLCHESTER

Britain's first recorded town, Colchester was a substantial settlement even before the Romans arrived; in AD 49 they made it the capital of Britannia. Since then Saxons, Normans, 16th-century Dutch weavers, Royalists and Parliamentarians have all left traces visible to this day. Modern Colchester is a lively shopping centre with excellent facilities – all surrounded by the remains of a Roman defensive wall, which is the oldest in the country. A walk around the town will take about 90 mins and cover most of its architectural, archaeological and historic sights.

The town's history is imaginatively interpreted using hands-on displays, at **Castle Museum**, housed in Europe's largest Norman keep, ££, Castle Park, High St. Open Mon–Sat 1000–1700 (all year), Sun 1100–1700 (Mar–Nov). After a £500,000 refurbishment **Hollytrees Museum**, re-opened to feature life in Colchester over the last three centuries. Youngsters can dress up in period costumes. Free, High St, open Mon–Sat 1000–1700, Sun 1100–1700.

Colchester-made clocks of the 18th and 19th centuries within a restored 15th-century timber-framed house are on display at **Tymperleys Clock Museum**. Free, Trinity St, open Mon–Sat 1000–1700, Sun 1100–1700. Hands-on techniques help visitors to learn more about the local flora and fauna and to follow the development of the local environment in the **Natural History Museum**. Free, High St. Open Mon–Sat 1000–1700, Sun 1100–1700.

Also worth a look are the ruins of the medieval **St Botolph's Priory**, St Botolph's St, the first Augustinian house in England. The award-winning **Colchester Zoo**, set in 60 acres, is home to 200 species of animals from around the world. £££, Maldon Rd, open daily 0930–1730 (closes one hour before dusk Oct–Apr).

A WOMAN SCORNED

The Iceni, a native tribe living in Norfolk, were at first friendly with the Romans, but the colonialists turned against them, giving their queen, Boudicca (Boadicea), a public flogging and raping her two daughters. In AD 60 Boudicca led a major rebellion against the Romans, attacking Colchester and slaughtering the population. She went on to destroy London and St Albans.

i **Visitor Information Centre** 1 Queen St; tel: (01206) 282920; fax: (01206) 282924; website: www.colchester.gov.uk; e-mail: vic@colchester.gov.uk. Open Mon–Tues, Thur–Sat 0930–1800, Wed 1000–1800, Sun 1000–1700 (Easter–early Nov); Mon–Sat 1000–1700 (early Nov–Easter).

There are over a dozen hotels and masses of B&Bs, but pre-booking is necessary during university graduation (July) and Cricket Week (Aug). You can get a copy of the comprehensive *Places to Stay* guide from the Visitor Information Centre.

Globe Hotel ££–£££ 71 North Station Rd; tel: (01206) 502502; fax: (01206)506506. Town centre hotel with 12 *en suite* rooms. Restaurant caters for vegetarians.

Peveril Hotel ££–£££ 51 North Hill; tel/fax: (01206) 574001. This family-run hotel, in the town centre, has 17 rooms and a restaurant with a vegetarian menu.

The closest **campsite** is **Colchester Camping and Caravan Park** Cymbeline Way, Lexden; tel: (01206) 545551.

Colchester has a very wide variety of restaurants, cafes, pubs, clubs and bars. A list of restaurants and advice on eating and drinking is available from the Visitor Information Centre.

SIDE TRIP FROM COLCHESTER On the borders of Essex and Suffolk just 8 miles (13 km) or so from Colchester (easily reached by train from Colchester to Manningtree, Dedham or East Bergholt) lies the **Stour Valley**. Now better known as Constable Country, it is the area immortalised in the paintings of John Constable, who was born at East Bergholt in 1776. His parents are buried in the Church of St Mary the Virgin, East Bergholt.

Nearby is **Flatford Mill**, scene of *The Hay Wain*, Constable's best-known work. The mill is a National Trust property but is leased to the Field Studies Council and not open to the public. However, it can be viewed from the outside and there is a National Trust tea shop. Rowing boats on the River Stour can be hired at Flatford and Dedham and there are several local walks to view the valley.

IPSWICH

One of England's oldest towns, Ipswich has been continuously settled since Saxon times and is now a busy port. The Victorian Wet Dock area, which combines a commercial port and a marina, is a pleasant place for a stroll, with a good selection of restaurants and bars.

Much of Ipswich was built or rebuilt in the 19th century, but 12 medieval churches survive, as well as some fine timber-framed buildings. The **Unitarian Chapel** dates from 1699. Occasional art exhibitions are staged in the elaborately plastered **Ancient House** (1670), Buttermarket. Another interesting old building (1548), the **Christchurch Mansion,** Christchurch Park, houses the **Wolsey Art Gallery**. Originally an Augustinian priory and confiscated for private use in the 16th century, it has period rooms and a fine selection of British art of all kinds, notably the Suffolk painters – with important collections of Constable and Gainsborough. Free, open Tues–Sat.

Ipswich Museum (free, High St, open Tues–Sat 1000–1700) houses many excellent displays, including *Anglo-Saxons come to Ipswich* and *Romans in Suffolk*. Other exhibits range from a woolly mammoth to a fork used by cannibals.

If you enjoy real ale, don't miss a guided tour (with tastings) of the **Tolly Cobbold Brewery**, ££, Cliff Rd; tel: (01473) 231723; website: www.tollycobbold.co.uk. It is one of the finest Victorian breweries in Britain. Tour details from the tourist information centre. **Ipswich Transport Museum**, £, Cobham Rd, open Sun and Bank Holidays 1100–1700 (Apr–Nov), Mon–Fri 1300–1600 (school holidays). The museum is housed in the old trolleybus depot and all the vehicles, from old fire engines to forklift trucks, were made locally.

A BRIGHT SPARK

The word 'electric' was coined by William Gilberd, who was born in Colchester in 1544 and subsequently became Chief Physician to Queen Elizabeth I. Gilberd conducted some of the earliest experiments in electromagnetism. Tymperleys, now the town's clock museum, was one of his properties.

[i] **Tourist Information Centre** St Stephen's Church, St Stephen's Lane; tel: (01473) 258070; website: www.ipswich.gov.uk; e-mail: tourist@ipswich.gov.uk. Open Mon–Sat 0900–1700. The centre has leaflets on themed trails around Ipswich and can provide details of open top bus tours and cruises on the rivers Deben, Orwell and Stour.

Ipswich has a reasonable selection of hotels and a good range of guest houses and B&Bs.
Lattice Lodge ££ 499 Woodbridge Rd; tel: (01473) 712474; fax: (01473) 272239; e-mail: lattice.lodge@btinternet.com. Nine rooms in an elegant Edwardian house, a 15-min walk from the town centre.
Redholme Guest House ££ 52 Ivry St; tel: (01473) 250018; fax: (01473) 233174. Non-smoking Victorian house with four en suite rooms.

TO The town has an abundance of eating places to suit all pockets. The trendiest area for bars, bistros and restaurants is **St Nicholas St**. A list of eating places is available from the tourist information centre.

Brewery Tap ££ Cliff Rd. This traditional pub, adjoining the Tolly Cobbold Brewery, serves bar snacks and prepared meals as well as a full range of the brewery's beers.

SIDE TRIPS FROM IPSWICH **Suffolk's coastal region** is a 40-mile (64-km) strip of out-standing natural beauty punctuated by the estuaries of five rivers – the Blyth, Deben, Alde, Ore and Orwell – and dotted with small market towns, quaint villages and coastal resorts. It's a perfect area for those keen on sailing and birdwatching. **Sutton Hoo**, near Woodbridge, is the site of an important Anglo-Saxon ship burial with an exhibition hall and guided tours of the burial mounds. The East Suffolk Railway runs a service between Ipswich and Felixstowe and local bus services connect Ipswich and coastal communities.

Felixstowe has managed to retain much of its Edwardian charm, with more than 4 miles of seafront, beautifully tended public gardens, a pier and a safe beach of sand and shingle. Trains run hourly from Ipswich and take 25 mins. **Orford**, on the River Alde, is a lovely village dominated by a magnificent keep built by Henry II – a climb up 200 stone steps affords wonderful views. **Orford Ness**, the largest vege-tated shingle spit in Europe, is home to a number of rare plants and a haven for breeding and migratory birds.

The quiet but ever windy coastal resort of **Aldeburgh** is famous for its annual music festival in June, founded by the composer Benjamin Britten, who settled in the town and who is buried in the churchyard. The festival's larger concerts and recitals are staged at **Snape Maltings**, 6 miles (10 km) inland. A pleasant walk from Aldeburgh along the shingle beach leads to the strange village of **Thorpeness**, built in the early 20th century as an upmarket seaside resort, its cottages all in the Tudor rustic style of olde England. Near its lake stands the astonishingly tall seven-storey House in the Clouds, a water tower adapted as a house; water was pumped to it for Thorpeness by means of the adjacent windmill. You can return to Aldeburgh by strolling along a former railway track.

Southwold is a captivating coastal resort and though many may feel it is the epito-me of the English seaside, there is nowhere quite like it anywhere else. It is ranged around a series of greens and dominated by the Victorian brewery of Adnams and the little white lighthouse nearby; the town seems stuck in a 19th-century time warp, with its characterful old pubs, Sailors' Reading Room of 1864 (full of ship models and old photos) and multi-coloured beach huts. The rebuilt pier is fun and offers classic views of Southwold. From late May to September a boatman rows people across the river Blyth to Walberswick, giving scope for walks through the sandy heaths and reedy marshes that dominate the landscape hereabouts.

i **Tourist Information Centre** 69 High Street; tel: (01502) 724729; website: www.waveney.gov.uk; e-mail: southwoldtic@ waveney.gov.uk.

NORWICH

Norwich was already an important town at the time of the Norman conquest, and during most of the Middle Ages rivalled London and York in size and wealth. This has left a heritage of medieval buildings, including the cathedral, the castle and over 30 fine churches, which is unsurpassed by any British city. It also has lots of arty shops and cafés and is a delight to explore.

The splendidly-named **Cathedral Church of the Most Holy and Undivided Trinity** towers over Norwich. Its foundations were laid in 1096 and the 15th-century spire, rising 315 ft (96 m), is the second highest in England. The cloisters, built in the 14th and 15th centuries, are England's largest. The cathedral's interior is an architectural treasure house with a magnificent stone-vaulted roof and 1200 carved stone bosses illustrating the Bible story. The cathedral has a shop and restaurant and guided tours are available. Free, open daily 0730–1800 (mid-Sept–mid-May); daily 0730–1900 (mid-May–mid-Sept).

The **Riverside Walk** is a waymarked route which runs for about a mile and a half from St George's St along the River Wensum to Carrow Bridge. It passes **Cow Tower**, formerly a river toll-house and prison, **Pull's Ferry**, the 15th-century water-gate to the Cathedral Close and the medieval **Bishop Bridge**.

Elm Hill is a winding cobbled street with antique and craft shops, leading to historic **Tombland**, a street whose name has nothing to do with graves, but comes from an old word for market. **Norwich Castle**, Castle Meadow, dating from 1120, now houses a superb museum and art gallery. The museum is home to the world's largest collection of British ceramic teapots. The art gallery has a wonderful collection of works by the famed early 19th-century Norwich School of landscape painters. ££, open Mon–Sat 1030–1700, Sun 1400–1700.

The church of **St Peter Mancroft**, near the market place, was founded in 1430 and is an exceptionally beautiful and imposing example of the Perpendicular Gothic style. Facing the church, and in complete contrast to it, is **The Forum**, the city's 21st-century showpiece, all metal and glass. It houses the Tourist Information Centre, the library and **Origins**, an interactive local history exhibition (££, tel: (01603) 727923, www. originsnorwich.com). Nearby is the 15th-century **Guildhall**, which was the seat of the city's council until **City Hall**, now dominating the market place, was built in 1938.

After 500 years of obscurity, it is now possible to enter **Dragon Hall** and admire such things as the magnificent medieval timber-framed Great Hall and intricate carvings.

£, 115–123 King St, open Mon–Sat 1000–1600 (Apr–Oct), Mon–Fri 1000–1600 (Nov–Mar). Local trades and industries over the past 200 years – including food production, iron foundries, shoe-making and textiles – are featured in the **Bridewell Museum**, which contains reconstructions of a pharmacy of the 1920s and a 1930s pawn shop. £, Bridewell Alley, open Tues–Sat 1000–1700 (closed Oct–Mar).

The story of one of Norfolk's best-known products is told in **Colman's Mustard Shop**, where an integrated museum tells how the company's founder started his mustard production in the early 19th century and improved social conditions for his workers. There is mustard memorabilia and a gift shop. Free, 15 Royal Arcade, open Mon–Sat 0930–1700 (closed public holidays).

TRANSPORT

Most of the city's attractions are within walking distance of each other in the centre. Bus services are mainly operated by Eastern Counties from the central bus station, Surrey St; tel: (01603) 622800.

The Sainsbury Centre for Visual Arts is a superb building that has won awards for its designer, Sir Norman Foster. The remarkable Sainsbury Collection comprises over 1000 paintings, sculptures and ceramics. £, University of East Anglia, Watton Rd, open Tues–Sun 1100–1700 (closed throughout the university's Christmas break). The Sainsbury Centre is 3 miles (5 km) west of the city centre, on several main bus routes.

i **Tourist Information Centre** The Forum, Millennium Plain; tel: (01603) 727927; website: www.norwich.gov.uk; e-mail: tourism.norwich@gtnet.gov.uk. Open Mon–Sat 1000–1800 (1730 in winter), 1030–1630 Sun.

NORMAN MARKET

Norwich market – the largest in the country – has been trading six days a week since it was founded by the Normans nearly a thousand years ago. The city's focal point, it is a maze of narrow alleyways with brightly striped awnings, where colourful stalls offer almost anything you would care to buy.

Norwich has several budget hotels in the city centre and a wide choice of B&Bs, most of which are on the outskirts.
Alpha Hotel ££ 82 Unthank Rd; tel/fax: (01603) 621105; website: www.norfolksbroads.com/alphhotel; e-mail: alphahotel_norwich@hotmail.com. A former Victorian rectory with 19 rooms a 10-min walk from city centre.
Wedgewood House ££ 42 St Stephen's Rd; tel: (01603) 625730; fax: (01603) 615035. Family-run hotel with 13 rooms, a 3-min walk to city centre.
Norwich Youth Hostel £ 112 Turner Rd, tel: 0870 7705976 (e-mail: norwich@yha.org.uk) is in the western suburbs.

TO Norwich has an enormous range of eating places and cuisines and once had, the locals claim, a pub for every day of the year. **Tombland**, the area around the cathedral, has the greatest concentration of restaurants and is the place for nightlife, though it can get very lively after midnight. Pick up a *Where to Eat* guide at the tourist information centre or log on to www.norwich2nite.com for pub details.

SIDE TRIP FROM NORWICH To the north-east and south-east, between Norwich and the coast, lies the **Broads National Park**, a complex of slow-moving rivers and some 40 shallow lakes providing more than 130 miles (209 km) of navigable waterways. An important wetlands area, the Broads look totally natural but in fact are man-made – the result of peat digging in the Middle Ages.

Today, the Broads are the centre of a range of waterborne and outdoor leisure pursuits – sailing, boating, hiking, birdwatching, etc. – with lots of pretty little towns and villages, and waterside pubs to enjoy.

The focal point of activity in the Broads is the small but always busy town of **Wroxham**, 8 miles (13 km) north-east of Norwich, which can be reached by train on what is known as the Bittern Line to Cromer and Sheringham. From Wroxham you can also travel on the narrow gauge **Bure Valley Railway** to the market town of Aylsham, an engaging 10-mile (16-km) journey through some of Norfolk's loveliest scenery.

Cromer lifeboat station stands at the end of the pier and visitors can examine the lifeboat from a viewing gallery in the boathouse. On the cliff path there's a bust of Henry Blogg, legendary coxswain of the lifeboat from 1909 until his death in 1954. Tough, fearless and totally dedicated to saving lives at sea, Henry became Britain's most decorated lifeboatman. He was awarded the George Cross, the nation's highest bravery award for civilians, and the British Empire Medal. Three times the Royal National Lifeboat Institution awarded him the Gold Medal, its highest award. Donations, open daily 1000–1600 (Easter–Oct; also 1800–2000 Aug).

CROMER

Cromer is both a popular sea and sand holiday resort and a workaday community of fisherfolk whose livelihood depends chiefly on the famous Cromer crab. Traditional seaside entertainment, spiced up with performances of pop, rock and jazz, flourishes at the **Pavilion Theatre** on the pier.

A row of fishermen's cottages next to the parish church houses **Cromer Museum** which tells the town's story from prehistoric times, including the history of fishing and tourism. There is a reconstruction of a Victorian fisherman's gas-lit cottage. £, Tucker St, open Mon–Sat 1000–1700, Sun 1400–1700.

i **Tourist Information Centre** Bus Station, Prince of Wales Rd; tel: (01263) 512497; website: www.north-norfolk.gov.uk; e-mail: jn@north-norfolk.gov.uk. Open Mon–Sat 0930–1730, Sun 0930–1700 (mid-July–Aug); Mon–Sat 1000–1700, Sun 1000–1600 (mid-Mar–mid-July) and Sept–late Oct); daily 1000–1300 and 1400–1600 (late Oct–mid-Mar).

There is no shortage of reasonably priced accommodation in Cromer and the surrounding area. The Tourist Information Centre will supply a list.
Cambridge House Hotel ££–£££ Sea Front, East Cliff; tel: (01263) 512085; website: www.broadland.com.cambridgehouse.

An attractive non-smoking Victorian house overlooking the pier. Evening meal available.

Crowmere House ££ 4 Vicarage Rd; tel: (01263) 513056. This friendly B&B is a five min walk from the beach.

Wellington Hotel ££ Garden St; tel: (01263) 511075; fax: (01263) 513750. A traditional Victorian pub with a loyal and friendly band of local 'regulars'.

🍴 **Cromer crabs** are famous far beyond Norfolk, but here you will be eating them fresh from the North Sea. The crabs are not particularly big in diameter, but the deep shell holds a generous portion of delicious white meat. The season runs from spring to mid-winter, when you will have no difficulty finding crab served in a variety of styles in restaurants in the town and all along the North Norfolk Coast.

Rumbletums ££ 7 Hamilton Rd. Fresh Cromer crabs in season as well as snacks, steaks, roasts and vegetarian fare year round. Breakfast served all day. Fully licensed. Closes 1800 in winter.

Le Moon ££–£££ 5A Prince of Wales Rd. As a change from crab, you might like to try the licensed restaurant's Cantonese and Peking cuisine; take-away available.

SHERINGHAM

The railway ends at this quiet little town on the north Norfolk coast. There's a working fishing harbour with a compact old centre. Though there's not a huge amount to detain you here, Sheringham stands on the threshold of a wonderful stretch of coast, made up of salt marshes, tidal flats and vast sandy beaches, running westwards to Hunstanton. It is one of Europe's most important bird habitats, both for permanent and visiting species, and a string of bird reserves is dotted along the way.

Steam trains or vintage diesels of the **North Norfolk Railway** regularly run the 5 miles (8 km) between the relaxing resort of Sheringham and the elegant Georgian market town of Holt, with daily services June–Aug and a varied timetable operating during other months. Dubbed the Poppy Line because of the great swathes of scarlet blooms in summer, the track passes through pine forest and heathland with sea views. There are stops at the villages of Weybourne and Kelling Heath and a Rover ticket, £7.50, provides unlimited all-day travel. Sheringham station has a museum of railway memorabilia. From Holt station you can take a horse-drawn bus into the town centre. North Norfolk Railway, tel: (01263) 820800; timetable, tel: (01263) 820808; website: www.nnr.co.uk.

i **Tourist Information Centre** Station Approach; tel: (01263) 824329; website: www.north-norfolk.gov.uk; e-mail:

jn@north-norfolk.gov.uk. Open (summer only) Mon–Sat 1000–1700, Sun 1000–1600.

🏠 **Sheringham Youth Hostel** £ 1 Cremer's Drift, tel: 0870 7706024 (e-mail: sheringham@yha.org.uk), is 5 mins from the rail and bus stations.

VISITING THE NORTH NORFOLK COAST There are no rail services between Sheringham and King's Lynn, but buses run regularly along the coast road; contact **Norfolk Bus Information Centre**, tel: 0500 626116. Alternatively it's a great area for exploring under your own steam: the **North Norfolk Coast Path** takes in the best of it, while for cyclists there are some quiet back roads – some followed from Norwich to King's Lynn by part of the signposted National Cycle Network route 1 (website: www.sustrans.org.uk).

Cley-next-the-Sea is a pleasant village with a windmill overlooking the marshes, and well placed for breezy walks along to the spit of Blakeney Point. **Wells-next-the-Sea** is larger but just as pretty, with an old grain tower by the harbour and some quiet little streets leading inland. The steam-hauled narrow-gauge **Wells & Walsingham Light Railway** snakes south to the old pilgrimage town of Little Walsingham.

Between Wells and **Burnham Overy Staithe** is one of the loveliest stretches of coast, where low tides leave a desert of sand; there is handy access to the coast at Holkham Gap, near the stately Palladian mansion of **Holkham Hall** (££, Sun–Thur afternoons, plus Sun and Mon at Easter), home in the 18th century of the great agricultural 'improver' Thomas Coke (there's a museum to him); the large, impressive if rather gloomy park is open free daily.

HUNSTANTON

Hunstanton is set on low, crumbly cliffs, and is the only town on Britain's east coast to face west. It is a sedate if not over-exciting place.

🏠 **Hunstanton Youth Hostel** £ 15 Avenue Rd; tel: 0870 7705872, is centrally placed.

WHERE NEXT?

*Continuing south from Hunstanton, you reach King's Lynn (see pp. 94–95) after 16 miles (26 km). About halfway is **Sandringham House**, ££, Sandringham; tel: (01553) 772675, country retreat of the royal family. The house is open to the public mid-Apr–mid-Oct but only between royal visits. From King's Lynn you can carry on south by road or rail to Cambridge (see pp. 90–94).*

CAMBRIDGE AND THE FENS

The architectural heritage of Cambridge, both scholastic and ecclesiastical, is a magnet for the city's visitors. Most colleges are open to the public even in term time, except when examinations are in progress. Like all major long-established university centres, Cambridge gets packed with visitors. Thankfully, most traffic is kept out of the city from 1000–1600, and a park and ride scheme operates from four bases. Apart from academic sights there is good shopping, with a predictably wide selection of bookshops.

Peace, if not solitude, is found at The Backs behind a grouping of ancient colleges, where the River Cam, shaded by willows, flows gently by the lawns and water meadows. Punts, rowing boats and canoes can be hired here.

Tranquility of a different sort is offered by the Fens; a unique farmland area in the region of the Wash, mainly in Cambridgeshire and Lincolnshire and part of west Norfolk. This low-lying land, which has been tamed by artificial drainage since the 17th century, can be eerily atmospheric.

GETTING THERE AND GETTING AROUND

Cambridge railway station – served by direct trains to London (Kings Cross and Liverpool Street), Peterborough, Ipswich, Norwich, Leicester and Birmingham – is about a mile (1.6 km) from the city centre. However, there is a very frequent bus service (*Citi* services 1 and 3; 12 journeys an hour Mon–Sat, 3 an hour on Sun) linking the station to bus stops in the centre.

The **bus and coach station** is more centrally situated, at Drummer St.

Most of the city is pedestrianised Mon–Sat 1000–1600, and some streets are permanently closed to traffic. City centre car parks offer limited short-stay parking. Motorists are encouraged to use the park and ride system on the city's outskirts at Cowley Rd (A1309) in the north, Newmarket Rd (A1303) in the east, Babraham Rd (A1307) to the south and Maddingley Rd (A1303) to the west. All these free car parks are well signposted. Buses leave every 10 or 15 mins daily 0700–2000. Information: Stagecoach Cambus, tel: (01223) 423554; website: www.stagecoach-cambus.co.uk.

Cycling is the traditional way of getting around the city. There are several bike hire outlets; try Geoff's Bike Hire, 65 Devonshire Rd, near the railway station, tel: (01223) 365629, or get a list from the tourist information centre.

INFORMATION

CITY MAP
– inside back cover

Tourist Information Centre The Old Library, Wheeler St; tel: (01223) 322640; website: www.cambridge.gov.uk/leisure/tourism; e-mail: tourism@cambridge.gov.uk.

SAFETY While you should take the personal security precautions you would at home, Cambridge is generally pretty safe. Watch out for cyclists when you cross the road.

ACCOMMODATION

It is advisable to make a reservation – Cambridge is always busy. The tourist information centre runs a **hotline booking service**; tel: (01233) 457581 Mon–Fri 0900–1600. £3 booking fee and a 10% non-refundable deposit. Book at least five days before your visit. The central hotels tend to be pricey, but there are a couple of small good-value budget properties, both with en suite facilities. One is the **Hamilton Hotel** ££ 156 Chesterton Rd; tel: (01233) 365664; website: www.hamiltonhotelcambridge.co.uk; e-mail: enquiries:hamiltonhotel.co.uk. The other, a converted granary, is **Sleeperz Hotel** ££ Station Rd; tel: (01233) 304050; website: www.sleeperz.com; e-mail: info@sleeperz.com. Non-smoking. **Cambridge Youth Hostel** £ 97 Tenison Rd, tel: 0870 7705742 (e-mail: cambridge@yha.org.uk) is near the rail station. The *Cambridge and Beyond* guide, available from the TIC, lists about 70 city guest houses and B&Bs, mostly ££.

FOOD AND DRINK

Special occasion fine dining on a grand scale is available as well as restaurants specialising in the cuisines of various countries and fast food chains. Most of the pubs serve bar snacks and more substantial fare – get in early to avoid a long wait. Claiming to offer the best breakfasts and fry-ups in town, **Café Eleven** ££ 11 Burley St, by the Grafton Centre, can be relied for a cheap and cheerful meal. **Charlie Chan Chinese Restaurant** ££–££ 14 Regent St, has seafood dinners on its menu and offers an economic express lunch menu.

HIGHLIGHTS

For an informative overview of the city, take a guided walking tour (££–£££) or join a Guide Friday bus (££) for a circular tour with commentary, hopping on or off to see whatever interests you. The tourist information centre has details on walking tours, including evening drama tours (Tues evenings in July and Aug). Costumed characters animate Cambridge's history, so participants may encounter anyone from Henry VIII or Sir Isaac Newton to William the Conqueror or Samuel Pepys.

FOR FREE

Other Cambridge museums (all free) are:

Museum of Geology
School Lane, open Mon–Fri 1415–1645.

Sedgwick Museum
Downing St, open Mon–Fri 0900–1300 and 1400–1700; Sat 1000–1300. A large collection of fossils and some mounted dinosaur skeletons.

University Museum of Archaeology and Anthropology, Downing St, open Mon–Fri 1400–1600; Sat 1000–1230.

Anyone wanting more than a cursory look at the major colleges and other architectural highlights will need to devote several days to Cambridge. As well as the colleges and some specialist museums and galleries, the city has the **Round Church** dating from 1130, one of only four circular churches surviving in England. The church has a brass rubbing centre. **St Benet's Church** Tower St has one of the country's few remaining Saxon towers, believed to date from King Canute's reign.

MUSEUMS Works by Rembrandt, Canaletto and other world-renowned artists, as well as an important Egyptian section and collections of medieval illuminated manuscripts are displayed in the **Fitzwilliam Museum**. Free, Trumpington St, open Tues–Sat 1000–1700. The museum has a shop and café.

Cambridge and County Folk Museum presents a wide range of artefacts in a former 16th-century farmhouse. £, 2–3 Castle St, open year round, hours vary. Some important 20th-century paintings and sculptures and changing exhibitions of contemporary art are to be seen in the gallery **Kettles Yard** (£, Castle St, open Tues–Sat 1330–1630, Sun 1400–1630 Apr–Aug; shorter hours rest of year, closed Easter and Christmas). Sculpture, paintings, textiles, furniture and crafts by recognised artists may be viewed at **Cambridge Contemporary Art**, £, 6 Trinity St, open all year Mon–Sat 0900–1730.

Of interest both to the specialist and to the public is the collection of scientific instruments and related items at the **Whipple Museum of the History of Science**. Free, School Lane, open Mon–Fri 1330–1630. Times may vary during university vacations (closed public holidays). **Cambridge Museum of Technology**, £, The Old Pumping Station, Cheddars Lane, is a Victorian pumping house with Hawthorn Davey steam pumping engines, a working letterpress print shop and electrical equipment. Open Sun 1400–1700 (mid-Apr–late Oct).

YOUNG STUDENTS

In former times students were admitted to Cambridge's colleges from their early teens. The poet John Milton was at Christ's College from 1625 (when he was 13) until 1632. It is said that he wrote *Lycidas* while seated beneath a mulberry bush in the college grounds.

THE COLLEGES For a general view of some of the loveliest colleges, stroll along The Backs between Queen's Rd and the west bank of the River Cam. Most people make a beeline for **King's College Chapel**. The real glories of this beautiful chapel, founded by King Henry VI in 1441, are its wonderfully delicate fan-vaulted ceiling, stained glass windows and the *Adoration of the Magi* by Rubens which hangs behind the altar. ££, King's Parade. Open normally Mon–Fri 0930–1530, Sat 0915–1415, Sun 1315–1415 (term time); Mon–Sat 0930–1630, Sun 1000–1700 (vacations). Because the chapel is sometimes closed for choir recordings and broadcasts, you may wish to check times on the number above.

Magdalene (pronounced 'Mawdlen') **College**, Magdalene St, has two courts which are pleasant to wander in. Charles Kingsley, the novelist, was a student at Magdalene, but the main reason for a visit here is its Pepysian Library. It has more than 3000 books collected by Samuel Pepys and left to the college on his death in 1702. Among them was his famous diary, written in code, which was eventually deciphered and published in 1825.

Sir Christopher Wren designed the chapels at **Pembroke College**, Trumpington St, and **Emmanuel College**, St Andrew's St. **Jesus College**, founded in 1497 by a Bishop of Ely, has an attractive courtyard which is open on one side. Thomas Cranmer, Archbishop of Canterbury under Henry VIII, and the poet Coleridge are associated with Jesus College.

The earliest college, **Peterhouse**, Trumpington St, received its charter in 1284 and still has a Tudor fireplace. Most of the original buildings were lost during 19th-century restoration work. The Great Court at **Trinity College**, Trinity St, is the largest court in either Oxford or Cambridge. The college, founded by Henry VIII, has a string of prime ministers and poets among its former students. Byron is said to have been sent down for cavorting naked in the fountain.

SHOPPING Stalls in the busy Market Square offer fruit, vegetables, fish, flowers, clothing, books and other goods Mon–Sat. On Sun crowds are attracted by crafts, antiques and bric à brac sold alongside a farmers' market. Another regular Sat craft market is held at All Saints Gardens and on extra days in summer and at Christmas. Many of the individual gift shops and major stores are in the pedestrianised streets. The Grafton Centre is an indoor shopping mall.

ENTERTAINMENT AND EVENTS Theatre, cinema, classical concerts and clubs provide entertainment in the city. The Corn Exchange, Wheeler St, is a combined concert hall, pop venue, theatre and cinema. Live music takes place in several of the pubs. Special events include Rag Week in February, a beer festival in May, Pop in the Park and the Cambridge Folk Festival, both in July, and the world-famous Festival of Nine Lessons and Carols at King's College Chapel at Christmas.

SIDE TRIPS FROM CAMBRIDGE

DAY TRIPS The National Horseracing Museum, ££, at Newmarket offers tours of the National Stud led by experts. The Imperial War Museum at Duxford, £££, a former Battle of Britain fighter station, has 180 aircraft on show and you can ride in a simulator. It encompasses the American Air Museum and the Land Warfare Hall. Children and parking are free and there's a free bus service from Cambridge railway station. Of special interest to US visitors is the American Cemetery at Madingley, which commemorates American servicemen and women who died in World War II.

Greene-King's brewery, based in Bury for 200 years, offers brewery tours. One of the brewery's pubs, The Nutshell, in the town centre, is named in the *Guinness Book of Records* as the smallest pub in Britain.

BURY ST EDMUNDS Named after a 9th-century Saxon king, **Bury St Edmunds** has the graceful ruins of a 12th-century Benedictine abbey. The Abbey Gardens, with their award-winning floral displays are open free all year. Close by is St **Edmundsbury Cathedral** (guided tours). Among the town's historic buildings is the **Athenaeum**, opened in 1741, where Charles Dickens gave readings from his books. Cultural life flourishes, with a number of galleries and museums. The popular Theatre Royal is one of the country's smallest working theatres. There are 11 trains daily from Cambridge (6–8 Sat and Sun), taking 40 mins.

ELY Fifteen miles (24 km) from Cambridge, and easily reached by a 15-min train journey, **Ely**, England's smallest city, is crammed full of medieval buildings in daily use. Dominating them, and visible from miles of surrounding countryside, is the magnificent **cathedral**, dating from the late 11th century. Within are the Stained Glass Museum and a brass rubbing centre. Ely's modern face includes an attractive River Great Ouse water-side. Other amenities are a sports centre, fitness club, swimming pool, a general market and craft market and good shopping with family-run specialist shops. All parking in the city is free.

A 25% saving is made by buying a joint ticket to the cathedral, Stained Glass Museum, Ely Museum and Oliver Cromwell's House (children under 12 free).

KING'S LYNN King's Lynn, on the wide estuary of the River Great Ouse, has 900 years of maritime history and is still a thriving port. Trains run hourly from Cambridge taking 45 mins. A Millennium Commission scheme has provided the waterfront area near the Custom House at Purfleet Quay with a boardwalk and The

Green Quay, a discovery centre depicting local wildlife and creatures of the Wash.

The 17th-century **Custom House** houses the tourist information centre and a Maritime Museum. True's Yard is a museum of fisherfolk traditions, with restored cottages. Local history can also be traced at Lynn Life and, more gruesomely, at The Old Gaol House. King's Lynn has good shopping, mainly pedestrianised. People from miles around throng to the busy stalls at the Tuesday Market Place and Saturday Market Place.

King's Lynn Youth Hostel £ College Lane, tel: 0870 7705902, is a 500-year-old building by the quay.

THE FENS

In Roman and Anglo-Saxon times people lived on the isolated islands of the region. Still sparsely populated, and criss-crossed by dykes, the Fens has pockets of civilisation in small towns and villages of some character. Agriculture and horticulture thrive in its rich dark earth, which has some of the most fertile land in England. Root crops, cereals, fruit, bulbs and flowers are grown in huge quantities. The area around Spalding (see p. 107), formerly known for its bulbs, is called South Holland.

It was the advent of steam power in the 1820s that enabled the Fen dwellers to keep the water at bay with some success. Today, electric pumps capable of quickly moving thousand of gallons of water are used, but restored land drainage stations of the early 19th century can be seen at Pinchbeck, Stretham and Prickwillow.

To get an idea of how the Fens looked before they were drained, visit **Wicken Fen**, the country's oldest nature reserve and owned by the National Trust (££, daily, dawn–dusk). For centuries villages cut the reeds for use in thatching, and the reserve is carefully managed today in the interests of nature conservation. A great range of birds, mammals and plants can be seen in this watery wilderness, and there are bird hides as well as a boardwalk trail. There's no bus here, but you can hire a bike in Cambridge, ride the train to Ely and cycle the flat 9 miles (14.5 km) from there.

GETTING AROUND

TRAIN Central Trains, tel: 08700 006060 (tickets); 08457 484950 (timetables and fare enquiries), run regular services to Spalding, Peterborough, Whittlesey, March and Ely. Most services to destinations in the Fens are connections from mainline services at Peterborough or Cambridge. WAGN services from Cambridge go to Ely, Littleport, Downham Market and King's Lynn.

Bus Local tourist information centres have information on bus services, or contact the national bus enquiry service; tel: 08706 082608. National Express Coaches, tel: 0990 808080, go from Peterborough to Spalding, Boston, Wisbech and King's Lynn. Coach services operated in the Fens by Stagecoach include Peterborough–March via Whittlesey; Wisbech–Cambridge via March, Chatteris and Ely; and King's Lynn–Cambridge via Downham Market, Littleport and Ely. For information tel: 08706 082608.

[i] **Spalding Tourist Information Centre** (see p. 107) provides pamphlets on a selection of the special interests catered for in the Fens, including cycling, angling, wildfowl and wildlife, flora and gardens, boating and towers. These towers range from ecclesiastical to working windpumps once used for drainage, and industrial and clock towers. Panoramic views can be observed from some of them.

[🛏] Good value accommodation in the little market town of Soham, between Ely and Newmarket, is provided at **The Fountain** ££ 1 Churchgate St, Soham; tel: (01353) 720374. Bar snacks and evening meals are served in the lounge.

[🍴] People flock by river and road to the **Jenyns Arms** £–££ Sluice Bank, Denver Sluice, Downham Market, historically popular with pilots who guided craft along the tidal river. There's plenty of choice at – take a breath – the **Five Miles from Anywhere No Hurry Inn** £–£££ Upware, Wicken, Cambs, midway between Stretham and Soham; tel: (01353) 721654; website: www.fivemiles.co.uk.

Wisbech, dubbing itself 'the capital of the Fens', has the Fenland Museum with displays of local history, geology and archaeology. **March** has a double hammer-beam roof and 120 carved angels in its 15th-century St Wendreda Church. Throughout the Fens are historic churches, many of which hold splendid flower festivals. **Downham Market**, at the centre of the Norfolk Fens, is near Denver Sluice, which clears floodwater from 800,000 acres (324,000 ha) of fenland. People enjoy a variety of watersports at Denver and guided tours take you right to the top of the newly-restored Denver Windmill. It's 30 mins from Cambridge; trains run hourly.

WHERE NEXT?

From Cambridge you can travel via Ely to Peterborough, at the start and finish of the East Midlands Roundabout route which explores the English Shires (see p. 97).

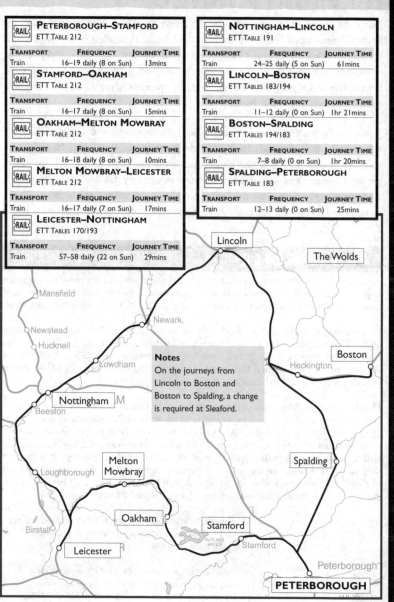

RAIL	**PETERBOROUGH–STAMFORD** ETT TABLE 212		
TRANSPORT	**FREQUENCY**	**JOURNEY TIME**	
Train	16–19 daily (8 on Sun)	13mins	

RAIL	**STAMFORD–OAKHAM** ETT TABLE 212		
TRANSPORT	**FREQUENCY**	**JOURNEY TIME**	
Train	16–17 daily (8 on Sun)	15mins	

RAIL	**OAKHAM–MELTON MOWBRAY** ETT TABLE 212		
TRANSPORT	**FREQUENCY**	**JOURNEY TIME**	
Train	16–18 daily (8 on Sun)	10mins	

RAIL	**MELTON MOWBRAY–LEICESTER** ETT TABLE 212		
TRANSPORT	**FREQUENCY**	**JOURNEY TIME**	
Train	16–17 daily (7 on Sun)	17mins	

RAIL	**LEICESTER–NOTTINGHAM** ETT TABLES 170/193		
TRANSPORT	**FREQUENCY**	**JOURNEY TIME**	
Train	57–58 daily (22 on Sun)	29mins	

RAIL	**NOTTINGHAM–LINCOLN** ETT TABLE 191		
TRANSPORT	**FREQUENCY**	**JOURNEY TIME**	
Train	24–25 daily (5 on Sun)	61mins	

RAIL	**LINCOLN–BOSTON** ETT TABLES 183/194		
TRANSPORT	**FREQUENCY**	**JOURNEY TIME**	
Train	11–12 daily (0 on Sun)	1hr 21mins	

RAIL	**BOSTON–SPALDING** ETT TABLES 194/183		
TRANSPORT	**FREQUENCY**	**JOURNEY TIME**	
Train	7–8 daily (0 on Sun)	1hr 20mins	

RAIL	**SPALDING–PETERBOROUGH** ETT TABLE 183		
TRANSPORT	**FREQUENCY**	**JOURNEY TIME**	
Train	12–13 daily (0 on Sun)	25mins	

Notes
On the journeys from Lincoln to Boston and Boston to Spalding, a change is required at Sleaford.

Contrasts in size and tempo could be the theme for this circular route through the English Shires. At one extreme there is Rutland, England's smallest county, with a rural landscape of sleepy villages and its county town of Oakham – and the country's largest man-made lake. At the other, there are the vast rolling acreages of Leicestershire, Lincolnshire and Nottinghamshire, the sweeping openness of the Wolds and a fragment of Robin Hood's Sherwood Forest.

There are lively cities, as well as atmospheric market towns whose quaintness is the genuine echo of an eventful past. Much of the route covers parts of the Midlands, with roots firmly embedded in English history. But on the east coast at Boston, Lincolnshire, are the foundations of America's pre-Revolutionary history in a small port that gave its name to a great transatlantic city. Trains can take you round the entire course – with some back-tracking – but you could do the bit between Lincoln and Boston by bus or car.

PETERBOROUGH

Although Peterborough, a largely modern and greatly expanded town on the main London–Edinburgh line, is unlikely to entice people to make a prolonged stopover, it does have a briefly interesting historic core dominated by the 12th-century cathedral.

Peterborough Cathedral (donation requested, Minster Precincts, open daily 0830–1715) is a fine example of Norman ecclesiastical architecture, famous for its unique 13th-century triple-arched west front. It contains the tomb of Katherine of Aragon, first wife of Henry VIII, and was the original burial place of Mary, Queen of Scots. A permanent exhibition tells the cathedral's story.

Flag Fen, 3 miles (5 km) east of the city centre (signposted), is a 3000-year-old Bronze Age site with archaeological excavations in progress and a recreated farmstead of 1000 BC, ££, open daily 1000–1700. The finds here have been very enigmatic indeed – the remains of a long wooden causeway across what was a shallow lake, beside which hundreds of superbly crafted metal objects have been unearthed. It is thought that the act of deliberately casting these precious items into the water was some kind of ritual. The best specimens are on display in the site museum. Flag Fen is also the current resting place of the wooden Sea Henge rescued from the North Sea.

[i] **Tourist Information Centre** 3–5 Minster Precincts; tel: (01733) 452336; website: www.peterborough.gov.uk; e-mail: tic@peterborough.gov.uk.

[✉] Peterborough Association of Small Hotels and Guest Houses has an accommodation list on its website: www. peterboroughaccommodation.co.uk; tel: (01733) 703703.

PETERBOROUGH BEER FESTIVAL

The Peterborough Beer Festival takes place during the last full week of August each year, Tues–Sun, by the river Nene, a few minutes' walk from the city centre. Some 300 draught real ales from independent breweries all round the country, ciders, fruit wines and European bottled beers are on sale. Entry is free at lunchtimes, £–££ evenings. Tel: (01733) 564296; www.beer-fest.org.uk.

Anchor Lodge ££ 28 Percival St; tel: (01733) 312724. Family-run guest house, 10-min walk from city centre. Rooms have colour TV and tea and coffee-making facilities.

Brandon Hotel ££ 161 Lincoln Rd; tel/fax: (01733) 568631. Handy for the city centre and bus and rail stations. Eight en suite rooms; full English breakfast; evening meal by arrangement.

There are lots of pubs, modern café bars, family restaurants, plush brasseries and even floating eateries on the River Nene. A good food source for picnickers is the **City Market**, Northminster. Open Tues–Sat 0830–1600.

Ask ££ 30 Priestgate. Popular Italian chain restaurant, generous and tasty.

The Brewery Tap ££–£££ 80 Westgate. Said to be Europe's largest brew pub, the Brewery Tap specialises in genuine Thai food for lunch and evening meals.

Saffron ££–£££ 12–14 Broadway. Flavourful, not too hot Tandoori/Nepalese dishes in relaxed modern space.

STAMFORD

Ancient Stamford has always enjoyed a good write-up. Sir Walter Scott described it as 'the finest scene between London and Edinburgh'. For the poet Sir John Betjeman it was 'England's most attractive town', and when it was declared a conservation area in 1967 it was officially proclaimed 'the finest stone town in England'.

Flanking the tranquil river Welland are streets lined with mellow stone buildings, mainly from medieval and Georgian times. The church spires and towers punctuating the skyline indicate Stamford's importance as a religious centre in the past.

LEGENDS

With more than 600 listed buildings, Stamford has the lofty air of an ancient seat of learning, and legend has it that a university thrived here from around 800 BC until 1335 when it was suppressed to favour the upstart universities of Oxford and Cambridge. Another legend claims that a network of ancient tunnels beneath the town links the medieval monasteries and convents.

Browne's Hospital contains ancient almshouses founded by a local wool merchant in 1483 and still in use. Its **museum** illustrates almshouse life. £, Broad St, open Mon–Fri 1000–1700, Sat–Sun 1100–1600 (May–Sept). The town's history is told in **Stamford Museum**. A special section features life-size effigies of the diminutive 'General' Tom Thumb and Daniel Lambert, once the largest man in England, weighing in at 53 stone (337 kg). Free, Broad St, open Mon–Sat 1000–1700, Sun 1400–1700. Closed Sun (Oct–Mar).

Burghley House, a mile south of the town centre, is one of England's grandest stately homes. A renowned collection of paintings, porcelain and tapestries is on view in 18 rooms. The Elizabethan building stands in a beautiful deer park landscaped by Capability Brown. Open daily 1100–1630 (Apr–Oct) £££. There is no charge for walking around the extensive grounds and sculpture garden.

BURGHLEY HORSE TRIALS

The three-day international event (dressage, cross-country and show jumping) is held in the grounds of Burghley House at the end of August/early September each year. The top names come here to compete, and the cross-country on Saturday draws big crowds who follow the course for close-up views of the competitors (with a bit of posh shopping in between...). For details of this year's event, tel: (01780) 752131 or visit www.burghley-horse.co.uk.

i **Tourist Information Centre** Stamford Arts Centre, 27 St Mary's St; tel/fax (01780) 755611; website: www.southwest-lincs.com; e-mail: stamfordtic@skdc.com. Open Mon–Fri 0930–1700, Sat 0930–1600, Sun 1100–1600. Closed Sun in winter.

🛏 The town has half a dozen small hotels and a range of reasonably priced B&Bs.
Cringleford £ 7 Exeter Gardens; tel: (01780) 762136. B&B in a detached house on the outskirts. No en suite facilities.
Dolphin Guest House ££ 12 East St; tel: (01780) 481567; e-mail: mikdolphin@mikdolphin.demon.co.uk. Eight en suite rooms; continental or full English breakfast.

🍽 Reasonably-priced meals are available in pubs, cafés and restaurants dotted around the town centre and picnic material from shops offering local produce, pies and cheeses. Market days: Fri, Sat. Early closing: Thur.
Dolphin Inn ££ 60 East St. Family-run grill house.
Frangipani's £ 3 Red Lion Sq. Light lunches, tea and cakes.

OAKHAM

The county town of Rutland, England's smallest county, Oakham is mentioned in the Domesday Book and is a classic market town. **Oakham Castle** was completed in 1190 and houses a collection of horseshoes given to the Lord of the Manor by peers of the realm and royalty passing through Oakham, a custom that continues today. Free admission, off Market Pl., open Mon–Sat 1000–1300 and 1330–1700, Sun 1300–1700 (late Mar–late Oct; closes 1600 rest of year). **Rutland County Museum** is set in the former indoor riding school of the Rutland Fencibles, a volunteer cavalry regiment raised in 1794, and features the county's agriculture and rural life. Free, Catmose St, open Mon–Sat 1000–1700, Sun 1400–1700 (to 1600 late Oct–late Mar).

i **Tourist Information Centre** Flore's House, 34 High St; tel/fax: (01572) 724329; website: www.rutnet.co.uk; e-mail: info@rutnet.co.uk. Open Mon–Sat 0930–1700, Sun 1000–1500 (Apr–Sept); Mon, Wed, Fri, Sat 1000–1600, Tues and Thur 1000–1300 (Oct–Mar). The centre is based in Oakham's oldest house, built in the mid-13th century.

EAST MIDLANDS ROUNDABOUT

🛏 Oakham has only a handful of hotels, but is better off for B&Bs and guest houses. There is a wider choice in neighbouring villages, especially near Rutland Water.

Milburn Motel ££ South St, Oakham; tel: (01572) 723330; website: www.rutnet.co.uk/milburnmotel. Modern establishment with ten *en suite* rooms and one with private bath.

Osbaston ££ 3 Peterborough Ave; tel: (01572) 755371. Large non-smoking B&B near town centre. Guest lounge has tea and coffee-making facilities.

🍽 The town's pubs are the best bet for reasonably priced meals. The **Colonel's Café** £ in Rutland County Museum (see p. 100) serves light refreshments and lunches.

SIDE TRIP FROM OAKHAM Oakham's major attraction is nearby **Rutland Water**, a vast man-made lake where visitors can enjoy a wide range of outdoor activities year round, including boating, fishing, bird-watching (ospreys at Egleton spring to late summer; always lots to see), cycling and rock climbing. Information Centre: Sykes Rd, Empingham (5 miles/8 km east); tel: (01572) 653026. Open daily Easter–end Sept (variable opening in winter).

MELTON MOWBRAY

Melton Mowbray is famed for hand-raised pork pies and Stilton cheeses, so it's no surprise to learn that its major attractions are food shops, closely followed by the town's twice-weekly street market. **Ye Olde Pork Pie Shoppe** has become a shrine to the pork pie. Visitors can watch demonstrations of hand-raising pork pies and even have a go themselves. Free, 10 Nottingham St, open Mon–Sat 0800–1700.

PORKIES – THE TRUTH

Melton Mowbray owes its status as the true home of the pork pie to the much older craft of Stilton cheese production. Cheese making produces whey, which local pig farmers fed to their animals, resulting in top quality pork. Edward Adcock began baking pork pies in the town in 1831 and the first factory opened in 1860. Melton Mowbray pork pies became popular with local hunts and their fame spread to such an extent that in 1893 Queen Victoria ordered some for Christmas.

St Mary's Church, the largest and most stately parish church in Leicestershire, is noted for its fine collection of stained glass and for the organ recitals held year round on the first and fourth Tuesday of each month. The world-renowned conductor Sir Malcolm Sargent was organist and choirmaster here 1914–24. Burton St, open Mon–Sat 1000–1200 and 1400–1600 and for Sun services. Free, including recitals (donations appreciated).

i **Tourist Information Centre** Windsor House, Windsor St; tel/fax: (01664) 480992; website: www.melton.gov.uk; e-mail: mmtic@btinternet.com. Open Mon–Fri 1000–1700, Sat 1000–1600, Sun closed.

TO You can buy pork pies and Stilton cheeses in Melton Mowbray's **street market**. Open Tues and Sat 0830–1530. Traditional Blue Stilton, hand-made speciality cheeses from the Vale of Belvoir and delicatessen items can be bought at the **Clawson Cheese Shop**, Windsor St.

LEICESTER

Leicester has been a major commercial and cultural centre since Roman times. Its past is reflected in Danish street names, medieval turrets, Georgian terraces and ornate Victorian buildings. Leicester's 'old town' is **Castle Park**, a historic area of gardens, churches, riverside walks, ancient walls and cultural centres. Leicester Cathedral and the medieval Guildhall can be found here.

The city's social history is featured at **Newark Houses Museum**. Displays include a re-created Victorian street and a 1940s grocery. Free, open Mon–Fri 1200–1700, Sat 1030–1700, Sun 1300–1700 (closes 1600 Oct–Mar). **New Walk Museum and Art Gallery** houses dinosaur skeletons, Egyptian mummies and a fine collection of German Expressionist paintings. Free, New Walk area, open Mon–Sat 1030–1700, Sun 1300–1700 (closes 1600 Oct–Mar).

LEICESTER'S LEAR

King Lear is said to have come from Leicester, where he ruled the land, once known as Leirchestre, in 800 BC, spelling his name 'Leir'. Legend claims that daughter Cordelia buried his body in a vault under the River Soar. Leicester folk say William Shakespeare was inspired to write the great tragedy after hearing the tale when acting at the city's Guildhall.

Leicester's newest attraction is almost certain to become the city's biggest draw for tourists. The **National Space Science Centre** opened at Exploration Drive in 2001. Built at a cost of £52 million, it is the first centre in Britain totally dedicated to space. £££, open Tues–Sun 0930–1600 (last entry).

i **Tourist Information Centre** 7–9 Every St, Town Hall Sq.; tel: (0116) 299 8888; website: www.discoverleicester.com; e-mail: info@discoverleicester.com. Open Mon–Fri 0900–1730, Sat 0900–1700, Sun closed.

🛏 The tourist information centre can provide a list of accommodation. There is a good range of budget places to stay. **Beaumaris Guest House** ££ 18 Westcotes Drive; tel: (0116) 254 0261; e-mail: beaumarisgh@onmail.co.uk. Family-run guest house near city centre, with six rooms (one en suite). **The Gables Hotel** £££ 368 London Rd; tel: (0116) 270 6969;

fax: (0116) 270 3988; e-mail: gableshtl@aol.com. Handy for the city centre, the hotel has 36 en suite rooms (some non-smoking), a restaurant and bar.

> 🔳 The range of cuisines available reflects Leicester's multi-cultural character. Chinese, Creole, Greek, Italian, Mexican, Spanish – even traditional English – it's all there in the city centre. For an authentic taste of India visit Belgrave Rd, more colourfully known as the **Golden Mile**.

NOTTINGHAM

Renowned as the home of the legendary rebel Robin Hood and later as the centre of a thriving lace industry, Nottingham today sees itself as a Renaissance city – a place of culture and technology. The warehouses of the historic Lace Market now house scores of creative companies, and Castle Wharf, the old canal basin, has been transformed into an attractive waterfront centre where business meets pleasure.

Nottingham Castle Museum and Art Gallery is high above the city, in the castle where Charles I raised his standard at the start of the Civil War. The museum tells the town's story and permanent and temporary exhibitions are staged in the art gallery. Free weekdays; £ weekends, off Friar Lane, open daily 1000–1700 (closed Fri Nov–Feb). At the foot of the sandstone rock upon which the castle stands is one of the most plausible contenders for the title of oldest pub in England, **Ye Olde Trip to Jerusalem,** which was used by the Crusaders (1189).

The **Museum of Nottingham Lace** has working machinery and audio-visual demonstrations. £, High Pavement, open daily 1000–1700. The **Costume and Textiles Museum** displays costumes from the 1730s to the 1960s in period rooms. Free, 51 Castle Gate, open Wed–Sun and bank holidays 1000–1600.

To experience what it was like to be on the receiving end of 19th-century justice – from sentence to meeting the hangman – visit the award-winning **Galleries of Justice**. ££, Shire Hall, High Pavement, open Tues–Sun and bank holidays 1000–1700.

The Tales of Robin Hood is a themed museum where visitors are taken in adventure cars on a search for the legendary hero (allow at least 90 mins). You can try your hand at archery and brass rubbing. ££, 30–38 Maid Marian Way, open daily 1000–1800.

If you're interested in seeing a working windmill, visit **Green's Mill and Science Centre**, Windmill Lane, Sneinton, off the A612, a couple of miles east from the city centre. The 19th-century mill, once owned by George Green, mathematician and miller, houses interactive science displays. Free, open Wed–Sun and Bank Holidays 1000–1600.

A unique set of man-made caves, used for different purposes over 750 years, can be explored: with hard hat and audio tape. **The Caves of Nottingham** are beneath the Broadmarsh Shopping Centre. ££, open Mon–Sat 1000–1615 (last admission), Sun 1100–1600.

The **D H Lawrence Heritage Centre** features the terraced cottage where the author was born, gives an insight into Victorian school life and portrays the realities of a coal miner's working day. £, open daily 1000–1700 (1600 in winter).

i **City Information Centre** 1–4 Smithy Row; tel: (0115) 915 5330; website: www.visitnottingham.com; e-mail: tourist.information@nottinghamcity.gov.uk. Open Mon–Fri 0900–1730, Sat 0900–1700 (year round), Sun 1000–1500 (Apr–Sept).

Most of the cheaper accommodation located in West Bridgford (1 mile south) and Beeston (4 miles west). Budget accommodation in the city centre includes:
YMCA £ 4 Shakespeare St; tel: (0115) 956 7600; website: www.ymca.org.uk/gallery/nottingham; e-mail: admin@nottingham.ymca.org.uk.
Igloo Backpackers Hostel £ 110 Mansfield Rd; tel: (0115) 947 5250; website: www.igloohostel.co.uk; e-mail: reception@igloohostel.co.uk.

More than 200 restaurants offer menus to suit every taste and pocket. The range of eating and drinking establishments is so great that the tourist information centre provides a 64-page booklet, *Hair of the Dog – Nottingham's guide to having a good time*. The best areas for pubs and eateries are **Canal Wharf**, the **Lace Market** and **South Side**.

SIDE TRIP FROM NOTTINGHAM Robin Hood's hide-out has become **Sherwood Forest Country Park**, 20 miles (32 km) north, and a fun place for a family day out. There's a visitor centre with exhibitions, shops and a restaurant, and waymarked forest trails. Most visitors make their way to the Major Oak, a massive tree said to be more than 800 years old. The country park is off the B6034 at Edwinstowe, near Mansfield; tel: (01623) 8244 4490; website: www.sherwood-forest.org.uk. To get there by bus, contact the Buses Hotline; tel: (0115) 924 0000.

LINCOLN

Famous for its medieval cathedral, which is recognised as among Europe's finest, Lincoln also has a well-preserved castle built by William the Conqueror. Its beautiful

EVENTS

historic centre has cobbled streets, a wealth of speciality shops, modern shopping centres and plenty for the visitor to see and do.

A half-hour boat trip with commentary aboard *The Belle*, built in 1922, provides a good introduction to the city. It takes you along the River Witham into the expanse of Brayford Pool, which in Roman times was an inland port. If you then take a Guide Friday tour bus ride, getting on and off to see the sights of your choice, or go on a guided walk, you will have absorbed a good working knowledge of Lincoln's present and past.

The city is on two levels. At the top are the cathedral, Bishop's Palace, the castle and most of the antique shops and boutiques and galleries. The direct route is up Steep Hill (well-named as your calf muscles will testify) which links historic 'uphill' with commercial 'downhill'.

CITY HAUNTS

The haunting charms of Lincoln are shared with visitors who can join a guided ghost walk, take a ghost cruise on the river on summer Thur evenings, and drink at the 14th-century Green Dragon riverside pub, which claims a resident ghost.

At the **Cathedral** allow at least an hour to take in the carved angels on the west front, the Chapter House, St Hugh's Choir, the Bishop's Eye window, and the Angel Choir, where the notorious Lincoln Imp is carved among the heavenly throng. Free Sun and for services, open daily 0715–2000 (summer), 0715–1800 (winter).

One of the four surviving copies of Magna Carta, signed by King John in 1215, can be seen at **Lincoln Castle**, Castle Hill. The Norman keep has many interesting features. £, open Mon–Sat 0930–1730, Sun 1100–1730 (closes 1600 winter).

i **Tourist Information Centre** 21 Cornhill; tel: (01522) 873256; website: www.lincoln-info.org.uk; e-mail: recreation@lincoln.gov.uk. Open Mon-Thur 0930–1730, Fri 0930–1700, Sat 1000–1700. **Tourist Information Centre** 9 Castle; tel: (01522) 873213. Open daily all year, hours as at Cornhill tourist information centre plus Sun 1000–1700.

ABC Charisma Guest House ££ 126 Yarborough Rd; tel/fax: (01522) 543560; e-mail: abcguesthouse@ukonline. No-smoking house, a 10-min walk from historic area.
The Reindeer Hotel ££–£££ 8 High St; tel: (01522) 546945. Rooms in a pub one mile from the cathedral.
YHA £ 77 South Park; tel: 0870 7705918;

e-mail: lincoln@yha.org.uk. Youth hostel with a total of 46 beds, some in family rooms.

🔟 **PJ's Fish and Chip Restaurant** £–££ 259 High St. Open Mon–Thur 1130–1630 (Sat to 1700), also Fri and Sat 2300–0300. Eat in or take away.

Green Dragon £–£££ Waterside North. Riverside pub serving wholesome food all day and up to 0130 Fri and Sat. Entertainment most nights.

The **Women's Institute market** is held every Fri at Bailgate Methodist Church 0830–1200. Get there early for a choice of the wonderful range of produce and home-cooked foods.

SIDE TRIP FROM LINCOLN Between the county town and the coast, and up to the river Humber, are the **Wolds**, where you can find out how flat Lincolnshire isn't. This chalky region, which includes the Battle of Britain Memorial Flight visitor centre at RAF Coningsby, Market Rasen Racecourse, Tattershall Castle and Woodhall Spa, rises to more than 550 ft (180 m) above sea level.

BOSTON

Boston, Massachusetts, owes its name to this ancient port, now some 5 miles (8 km) inland from the Wash. In 1607 the Pilgrim Fathers were arrested and imprisoned in the town's 15th-century Guildhall. Then, in 1630 about 10% of the town's population emigrated to New England where they named their new settlement after their home town.

The story of the Pilgrim Fathers and Boston's American connections is told in the **Guildhall Museum**, South St (temporarily closed for conservation and development work, scheduled to reopen 2004/5). Boston's best-known building is the impressive 14th-century St Botolph's Church with its 272-ft (83-m) tower, known as the **Boston Stump** and a landmark for miles around. For a fee (££) visitors may climb the tower's 365 steps for a magnificent view of the Wash and on a good day Lincoln Cathedral, 32 miles (51 km) away. Open Mon–Sat 0830–1630. The Market Place, next to the church, has a colourful market on Wed and Sat, and medieval lanes radiate from the square.

England's tallest working mill, the **Maud Foster Windmill**, dates from 1819 and was restored in 1988. Unusually, it has five sails. You can climb to the top and see the machinery and millstones working. £, Willoughby Rd, open Wed 1000–1700, Sat 1100–1700, Sun 1300–1700 (year round); Thur and Fri 1100–1700 (July–Aug); bank holiday Mon 1000–1700.

ℹ️ **Tourist Information Centre** Market Place; tel/fax:
(01205) 356656; website: www.boston.gov.uk;
e-mail: tourism@bostongb.freeserve.co.uk. Open Mon–Sat
0900–1700, Sun closed.

🏠 Boston has a small range of hotels, inns, B&Bs and guest
houses, so it's wise to book ahead if you plan to stay. The TIC
has a list. The nearest campsite is **Pilgrim's Way Camping
and Caravan Site** Fishtoft, 2 miles (3 km) north; tel: (01205)
366646. **Orchard Park Caravan Park** is at Hubberts Bridge,
3 miles (5 km) west; tel: (01205) 290328; fax: (01205) 290247.

SPALDING

Formerly the centre of Britain's bulb and flower industry, Spalding draws thousands
of visitors in early May when the town stages its annual **flower parade** (although
nowadays all the flowers are shipped in from the Netherlands for the purpose).
Colourful, flower-bedecked floats, marching bands and dancers follow a 4½-mile
(7 km) circular route through the town. Spalding is a peaceful market town on the
banks of the River Welland with a pleasing mix of historic and modern buildings
and an attractive riverside walk.

Ayscoughfee Hall Museum and Gardens, Churchgate, is a late-medieval wool merchant's house set in 5 acres (2 ha) of walled gardens dating from the 1420s, when the
hall was built. The museum has displays featuring local agriculture and horticulture,
history and people. Free, open Mon–Fri 0900–1700, Sat 1000–1700 (closed winter weekends). The beam engine at **Pinchbeck Engine and Land Drainage Museum**, West
Marsh Rd, Pinchbeck, 2 miles (3 km) north, is a unique survival of the steam-powered
pumping stations which once drained the Fens. Built in 1833, it was in use until 1952
and has now been restored to working order. Free, open daily 1000–1600 (Apr–Oct).

ℹ️ **Tourist Information Centre** Ayscoughfee Hall,
Churchgate; tel: (01775) 725468; website: www.sholland.gov.uk;
e-mail: info@sholland.gov.uk. Open Mon–Fri 0900–1700 all
year plus Sat 1000–1700 and Sun 1100–1600 in summer.

WHERE NEXT?

Peterborough, a major rail centre, offers a choice of additional routes. You can travel west via
Leicester to Birmingham (see pp. 158–162), east across the Fens and South Norfolk to
Norwich (see pp. 85–87), or you can go north, joining the East Coast Route between London
and Aberdeen (see pp. 108–109).

LONDON – ABERDEEN: THE EAST COAST ROUTE

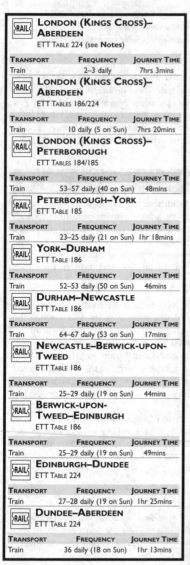

RAIL LONDON (KINGS CROSS)– ABERDEEN		
ETT TABLE 224 (see **Notes**)		
TRANSPORT	FREQUENCY	JOURNEY TIME
Train	2–3 daily	7hrs 3mins

RAIL LONDON (KINGS CROSS)– ABERDEEN		
ETT TABLES 186/224		
TRANSPORT	FREQUENCY	JOURNEY TIME
Train	10 daily (5 on Sun)	7hrs 20mins

RAIL LONDON (KINGS CROSS)– PETERBOROUGH		
ETT TABLES 184/185		
TRANSPORT	FREQUENCY	JOURNEY TIME
Train	53–57 daily (40 on Sun)	48mins

RAIL PETERBOROUGH–YORK		
ETT TABLE 185		
TRANSPORT	FREQUENCY	JOURNEY TIME
Train	23–25 daily (21 on Sun)	1hr 18mins

RAIL YORK–DURHAM		
ETT TABLE 186		
TRANSPORT	FREQUENCY	JOURNEY TIME
Train	52–53 daily (50 on Sun)	46mins

RAIL DURHAM–NEWCASTLE		
ETT TABLE 186		
TRANSPORT	FREQUENCY	JOURNEY TIME
Train	64–67 daily (53 on Sun)	17mins

RAIL NEWCASTLE–BERWICK-UPON- TWEED		
ETT TABLE 186		
TRANSPORT	FREQUENCY	JOURNEY TIME
Train	25–29 daily (19 on Sun)	44mins

RAIL BERWICK-UPON- TWEED–EDINBURGH		
ETT TABLE 186		
TRANSPORT	FREQUENCY	JOURNEY TIME
Train	25–29 daily (19 on Sun)	49mins

RAIL EDINBURGH–DUNDEE		
ETT TABLE 224		
TRANSPORT	FREQUENCY	JOURNEY TIME
Train	27–28 daily (19 on Sun)	1hr 25mins

RAIL DUNDEE–ABERDEEN		
ETT TABLE 224		
TRANSPORT	FREQUENCY	JOURNEY TIME
Train	36 daily (18 on Sun)	1hr 13mins

Notes

There are 2–3 through trains from London to Aberdeen Mon–Sat; the others involve a change at Edinburgh and/or York.

LONDON – ABERDEEN: THE EAST COAST ROUTE

The journey from London to Aberdeen can easily be made in one day. If you drive, it will take you something over 10 hrs, while the train will whisk you from the frenetic heart of the capital to the chilly charms of the 'granite city' in about 7 hrs. The temptation for many visitors who are anxious to see the Highlands will be to make the journey as fast as possible. However, to do so would be to miss out on the extraordinary variety that Britain has to offer, as you pass through so many historic towns and cities, and so many different landscapes en route.

The impression you may get from the first hours is that Britain is entirely flat. From the northern suburbs of London until way beyond York there is barely more than a mild undulation. Yet it is not devoid of interest, with the great cathedrals of **Peterborough** (see pp. 98–99), **York** (see pp. 249–254) and **Durham** (see p. 263) in view from the train.

Beyond Durham the scenery improves as the train passes over the Tyne into central **Newcastle** (see pp. 258–262) and hugs the Northumberland coast to cross the Scottish border just beyond **Berwick-upon-Tweed** (see pp. 270–271), once the scene of fierce fighting between the English and the Scots.

Then you're over the border and into Scotland, still following the coast for long stretches before coming into the Scottish capital, **Edinburgh** (see pp. 272–280), dominated by its sturdy castle and with enough attractions to keep you occupied for several days. About 15 mins after leaving Edinburgh, the train crosses the Forth Bridge – a masterpiece of Victorian engineering – and enters Fife, where the main attraction is **St Andrews** (see pp. 284–285), the home of golf and Scotland's oldest university. Leaving Fife, you cross the Tay to Dundee then travel around the coast to **Aberdeen** (see pp. 287–288), gateway to the splendour of the Grampian Mountains and the fairytale castles of Royal Deeside.

There's no shortage of alternatives to the straight run up the east coast line. You could start by travelling from London to the historic university city of **Cambridge** (see pp. 90–94), then from Cambridge via **Ely** to **Peterborough**, near which you can detour into the delightful old town of **Stamford** (see pp. 99–100). Other options are to leave the main line at Newark for the short trip to the cathedral city of **Lincoln** (see pp. 104–106), or to explore the coast of the **North York Moors National Park** (see pp. 254–257) from Scarborough (from where there are good bus services northwards up the coast to Whitby), itself at the end of a branch off the main line at **York**.

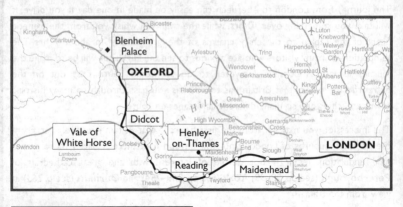

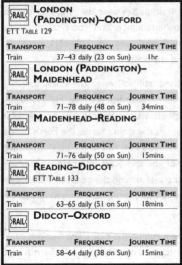

RAIL	LONDON (PADDINGTON)–OXFORD		
ETT TABLE 129			

TRANSPORT	FREQUENCY	JOURNEY TIME
Train	37–43 daily (23 on Sun)	1hr

RAIL	LONDON (PADDINGTON)– MAIDENHEAD		

TRANSPORT	FREQUENCY	JOURNEY TIME
Train	71–78 daily (48 on Sun)	34mins

RAIL	MAIDENHEAD–READING		

TRANSPORT	FREQUENCY	JOURNEY TIME
Train	71–76 daily (50 on Sun)	15mins

RAIL	READING–DIDCOT		
ETT TABLE 133			

TRANSPORT	FREQUENCY	JOURNEY TIME
Train	63–65 daily (51 on Sun)	18mins

RAIL	DIDCOT–OXFORD		

TRANSPORT	FREQUENCY	JOURNEY TIME
Train	58–64 daily (38 on Sun)	15mins

A trip to Oxford is usually high on the list of any first-time visitor to Britain, and deservedly so. Scenically, however, this part of south central England is sometimes overlooked; it is worth spending some time en route, or adding a day or so to your stay in Oxford.

You could pause at Maidenhead or Henley to take in some of the loveliest reaches of the River Thames, while the chalk uplands of the Chiltern Hills to the north offer superb walking country and some tiny, picturesque villages. South-west of Oxford, the Vale of White Horse, rich in prehistoric remains, is worth another detour. And of all the stately homes in the region, Blenheim Palace, just north of Oxford, is both the grandest and the most accessible.

LONDON

See p. 40.

MAIDENHEAD

It is worth taking one of the slower trains on the Oxford route that stop off at Maidenhead, where the main attraction is the **river Thames**. Trains run every 10–20 mins from London, taking about ½ hour. The graceful villas with their gardens backing onto the water are redolent of a less frenetic age. The town boasts two fine bridges – an 18th-century stone road bridge and Brunel's red-brick railway bridge. A pleasant 1½-mile (2.4-km) stroll along the towpath leads to **Boulter's Lock**, a well-known beauty spot and popular rendezvous for pleasure boats.

A VILLAGE IN ART

Nearby Cookham is where the artist Stanley Spencer (1891–1959) lived and worked. He immortalised the village as the setting for biblical scenes in his visionary paintings. The **Stanley Spencer Gallery** has a number of his works. £, High St; open daily 1030–1730 (Easter–Oct); weekends only 1100–1700 (Nov–Easter).

i **Tourist Information Centre** Central Library, St Ives Rd; tel: (01628) 796502; website: www.maidenhead.gov.uk; e-mail: maidenheadtic@rbwm.gov.uk. Open Mon–Fri 0930–1700, Sat 0930–1600 (summer); Mon–Sat 0930–1600 (winter). Sun closed (all year).

Shoppenhangers Rd, south of town centre.

Clifton Guest House £££ 21 Craufurd Rise, Maidenhead; tel/fax: (01628) 623572; e-mail: clifton@aroram.freeserve.co.uk. Friendly, family-run guest house.

Wylie Cottage ££ School Lane, Cookham; tel: (016280) 520106. Small B&B with garden.

HENLEY-ON-THAMES

This most picturesque of Thames-side towns is a good alternative base from which to explore the Chilterns (see p. 118). It is best known for the world-famous **Henley Regatta**, held in June–July, where the rich, famous and aspiring like to be seen. Hourly or half-hourly services run the 5 miles (8 km) from Twyford on the London–Reading line, taking just over 10 mins.

The obsession with rowing is apparent everywhere, and well-documented at the **River and Rowing Museum**, ££, Mill Meadows; open daily 1000–1730 (May–Aug); 1000–1700 (Sept–Apr). Boat trips can be arranged with Hobbs & Sons, Station Rd, tel: (01491) 572035.

Henley's streets with their 18th- and 19th-century brick and timbered architecture – New St and Hart St in particular – make for pleasant strolling. St Mary's Church and the five-arched Georgian bridge are especially fine.

i **Tourist Information Centre** King's Arms Barn, Kings Rd; tel: (01491) 578034; website: www.henley-on-thames.org.uk; e-mail: henleytic@hotmail.com. Open Mon–Sat 0930–1800, Sun 1000–1800 (summer); Mon–Sat 0930–1700, Sun 1100–1600 (winter).

The station is on Station Rd, 5 mins south of Hart St in the centre of town.

Alftrudis £££ 8 Norman Ave; tel: (01491) 573099; e-mail: bandb@alftrudis.fsnet.co.uk. Quiet and central B&B. **Lenwade** ££ 3 Western Rd; tel: (01491) 573468; e-mail: lenwadeuk@compuserve.com. Comfortable B&B in Victorian town house.

The pubs on Hart St are the best bet for food.

READING

Reading – famous in its Victorian industrial heyday for three 'b's: biscuits, beer and bricks – is today a railway hub and has one of the largest shopping centres in southern England. The one sight worth stopping for is the free museum; recently refurbished and including remarkable finds from the nearby Roman town of Silchester.

On display is the only full-size replica in the world of the famous **Bayeux Tapestry** depicting the events of the Battle of Hastings (see pp. 62–63). Made by the ladies of the Leek Embroidery Society in 1885, it is a close copy of the original – apart from the little naked figures of the wounded and the dead in the borders, which the squeamish Victorian ladies felt obliged to clothe in decent woollen shorts.Town Hall, Blagrave St; open Tues–Sat 1000–1600 (Thur until 1900); Sun 1100–1600. Reading is host to two major music festivals – WOMAD (World Music and Dance) in July, founded by Peter Gabriel, and the Reading Festival later in the summer.

> ℹ️ **Tourist Information Centre** Town Hall, Blagrave St; tel: (0118) 956 6226; website: www.readingtourism.org.uk; e-mail: touristinfo@reading.gov.uk. Open Mon–Fri 1000–1700, Sat 1000–1600, closed Sun.

> 🚆 The station is close to the town centre, with frequent trains to London.

> 🍴 There are many cafés, bars and restaurants, with the main concentration around Town Hall Square and St Mary's Butts. King's Walk has several quality restaurants.

DIDCOT

An unremarkable town which owes its 19th-century development solely to the arrival of the Great Western Railway, Didcot is nevertheless well worth a stop if you are a railway buff. You can relive the age of steam at the famous **Railway Centre**, which has a large collection of Great Western steam and diesel engines and carriages. ££ (£££ on steam days), Station Yard; open daily 1000–1700 (Easter–Oct); Sat–Sun 1000–1600 Nov–Easter.

> ℹ️ **Tourist Information Centre** Car Park, Station Rd, Didcot; tel/fax: (01235) 813243. Open daily 1000–1600; closed Sun (Oct–Mar).

> 🚆 Didcot station is on Station Rd, ¼ mile (400 m) north of the town centre.

OXFORD

CITY MAP
– inside back cover

The world-famous city of Oxford offers plenty for the visitor to do, from punting on the River Cherwell to exploring some of England's greatest architecture in the university buildings and colleges. Oxford's venerable university claims origins some 50 years before those of Cambridge, when in 1167 a number of English scholars expelled from the Paris Sorbonne settled here. Today there are 39 colleges, with romantic buildings and mysterious ancient academic traditions.

Oxford offers riverside walks and some fine museums. Yet it is also an industrial city – the nearby Cowley plant produced Britain's first popular car in the 1920s. Today, driving anywhere in Oxford is a lost cause – Oxford's traffic problems are acute and exacerbated by too many buses clogging up the High St. So stay on foot, watching out for bicycles; if you are driving, use the Park and Ride schemes. You could easily pass several days here, and then hire a car to explore the Chilterns (see p. 118); the Berkshire Downs, or the Cotswolds (see pp. 154–155).

i **Tourist Information Centre** 15–16 Broad St; tel: (01865) 726871; website: www.oxford.gov.uk; e-mail: tic@oxford.gov.uk. Open Mon–Sat 0930–1700 all year; sun and public holidays 1000–1600 (summer).

OXFORD V. CAMBRIDGE
The traditional rivalry between the two ancient and most prestigious universities in England is still maintained in several sporting traditions. Most famous is the Boat Race, rowed in March on the Thames in London, with Cambridge currently having a clear lead in the tally of victories. Running it close is the Varsity rugby match played at Twickenham in the autumn, when the two teams battle it out in the mud.

RAIL Oxford station, Park End St, about ¼ mile (400 m) west of the city centre. (A shuttle bus service runs to the centre.) Fast trains from London (1 hr) run every 30 mins – hourly.

This tends to be more expensive towards the centre of town. There are plenty of B&Bs in the Iffley Rd area – contact the tourist information centre for a full list.
Newton House £££ 82–84 Abingdon Rd; tel: (01865) 240561; e-mail: newton.house@btinternet.com. Victorian house convenient for Christ Church.
Isis Guest House ££ 45–53 Iffley Rd; tel: (01865) 248894; e-mail: isis@herald.ox.ac.uk. Good value accommodation just across Magdalen Bridge.
Oxford Backpackers ££ 9a Hythe Bridge St; tel: (01865) 721761; e-mail: oxford@hostels.demon.co.uk. More central than the youth hostel.
Oxford Youth Hostel £ 2a Botley Rd, tel: 0870 7705970 (e-mail: oxford@yha.org.uk) is virtually next to the rail station (turn right out of the station approach, along the main road and under the rail bridge, and it is immediately on the right).

TO The number of students here ensures a bewildering choice, and plenty of reasonably priced places to eat. There is a good range of sandwich bars in the Covered Market.
Brown's ££ 5–11 Woodstock Rd; tel: (01865) 511995 (no advance booking). Ever-popular informal restaurant serving tempting meals and snacks amidst jungly greenery. An Oxford institution.

BUS TOURS

City Sightseeing Oxford run open-topped bus tours every 15 to 20 minutes. There are 20 stops and a day ticket allows you to hop on and hop off at will. You can join it at the rail station. Cost £9 (16–21 yrs/students £7). Bear in mind though that the city centre really is compact enough to walk around, so you might prefer to use your feet instead.

Café Coco ££ 23 Cowley Rd. Mediterranean food, lively atmosphere.

Café MOMA £ Museum of Modern Art, 30 Pembroke St. Stylish, light café with good cakes and vegetarian options.

The Nosebag £ 6 St Michael's St. Long-established café serving wholesome food with good vegetarian options.

Le Petit Blanc £££ 71–72 Walton St; tel: (01865) 510999. Raymond Blanc's stylish brasserie serves breakfasts and teas as well as imaginative set-price meals.

The Perch ££ Binsey Lane. It's worth the walk across Port Meadow (north-west) to this bustling canalside thatched inn serving good food.

Pizza Express ££ Golden Cross, Cornmarket. The usual high standard at this consistently good chain.

THE COLLEGES Visitors usually head first for the **university colleges** in the heart of Oxford, city of 'dreaming spires'. Most are within an easy walk of the centre and open in the afternoons and during vacations (though closures are liable at short notice). You should respect the fact that these are places of study, and heed privacy notices. A few colleges charge for admission. Daily Blue Badge guide walking tours departing from the Tourist Information Centre are a good way to see the colleges; they leave every 15 mins in summer, 30 mins in winter.

Most of the historic colleges lie east of the north–south axis of St Giles, Cornmarket and St Aldates. The most famous, starting from the south, is **Christ Church** (or 'The House'), founded in 1525 by Cardinal Wolsey. It has the largest quadrangle in Oxford, known as Tom Quad after the bell, great Tom, in Christopher Wren's Tom Tower. Great Tom still rings 101 times at 2100 each night, marking a long-defunct undergraduate curfew. The college chapel doubles as **Christ Church Cathedral**, the smallest cathedral in England, which predates the college. Mainly Norman, it has a magnificent Early English chapter house and the first spire in England. £, St Aldates; college and cathedral open all year Mon–Sat 0900–1730; Sun 1300–1730 (cathedral closes 1630). **Christ Church Picture Gallery** includes Italian, Flemish and

MESSING ABOUT ON THE RIVER

Visiting Oxford without taking a trip in a punt on the Cherwell (narrower and less daunting than the Thames) would be unthinkable. Punts are flat-bottomed boats for about six people, propelled and steered from the back with a large pole, easily ceded to the muddy river bottom. You can have a go yourself, if prepared to risk public embarrassment. Punts can be hired (£££ per boat) from Magdalen Bridge, or for shorter queues from Cherwell Boathouse to the north, off Banbury Rd (by Wolfson College); tel: (01865) 515978. Arrive early to avoid queues in season. Chauffeured punts are also available.

Dutch paintings, with works by Dürer and Michelangelo; £, open Mon–Sat 1030–1300 and 1400–1630 (Oct–Easter); daily, closing 1730 (Easter–Sept). To the south and east of Christ Church spreads the bucolic **Christ Church Meadow**.

East of here along Merton St is 13th-century **Merton College**, one of the oldest in Oxford; its peaceful gardens are partly enclosed by the old city wall. Beside Magdalen Bridge, **Magdalen College** (pronounced 'Mawdlen') is perhaps the most attractive in the city. Its buildings have changed little since the 15th century apart from the addition of the harmonious 'New Buildings' in 1733. At sunrise on May Day the college choir sings from the top of the gargoyled tower. Magdalen has its own **deer park**.

Back along the High St are **Queen's College**, with buildings by Wren and Hawksmoor; **St Edmund Hall**, with a dining hall of 1659; and the university church of **St Mary the Virgin**, whose 13th-century tower offers the best viewpoint in Oxford (£, open daily 0900–1700; until 1900 (July–Aug). Queen's Lane leads to **New College**, famed for its gardens, hall and cloister. The **Bridge of Sighs**, spanning New College Lane and modelled on its Venetian counterpart, forms part of **Hertford College**.

Shopping

Oxford's main shopping area is compact and easy to explore on foot. The main chain stores are centred around **Carfax** – Oxford's central crossroads – along Cornmarket (for the Clarendon Shopping Centre) and west along Queen St to the Westgate Shopping Centre.

Not surprisingly, there is a wonderful selection of **bookshops** here. World famous Blackwells (48–51 Broad St) is one of the largest anywhere; the Oxford University Press bookshop at 116–17 High St sells all the press's titles; and there are many smaller vendors selling either new or secondhand titles.

For foodies the **Covered Market** is paradise – tucked between the Cornmarket and Turl St, it is full of specialist shops selling every delicacy imaginable. There is also an open market every Wed at Gloucester Green.

Westward along Broad St are famous rivals, neo-Gothic **Balliol College** and **Trinity College**. **St John's**, around the corner on St Giles and the wealthiest Oxford college, is renowned for its gardens. Worth a slightly longer walk up Parks Rd is the polychromatic-brick **Keble College**, a contrast to all that sandstone. Once regarded as an eyesore, it is now seen as a Victorian *tour de force*.

The **Bodleian Library**, the oldest in the world, receives a copy of every book published in Britain and currently houses over 5.5 million volumes. Parts of this vast edifice, including the original Duke Humphrey's Library (1480), are open to the public (££ with guided tour; Broad Street; open Mon–Fri 0900–1700; Sat 0900–1230). Nearby are two of central Oxford's most striking architectural landmarks. The great, domed **Radcliffe Camera**, built in 1737, acts as one of the reading rooms and the imposing

Sheldonian Theatre, designed by Sir Christopher Wren in 1664 to resemble a Roman theatre is used for university functions and concerts. £, Broad St; open 1000–1230 and 1400–1630 (1530 Nov–Feb), when not in use for ceremonies.

MUSEUMS Oxford's superb museums are worth some of your time. The biggest and most famous is the **Ashmolean Museum** on Beaumont St (free, open Tues–Sat 1000–1700; Sun 1400–1700). The oldest museum in Britain, first opened in 1683, it houses some priceless treasures from the time of early man to 20th-century paintings. The **Oxford University Museum of Natural History** on Parks Rd is housed in an imposing Victorian Gothic building; free, open daily 1200–1700. Adjoining is the eccentric **Pitt Rivers Museum**, an assembly of ethnographic curios (free; open Mon–Sat 1300–1630; Sun 1400–1630). By total contrast is **Modern Art Oxford** (30 Pembroke St; open Tues–Sat, 1000–1700, Sun 1200–1700), housed in a stylishly converted brewery and with temporary modern art exhibitions, talks and live music; admission is free. The imaginatively presented **Oxford Story** tells the city's story from a moving medieval scholar's desk; £££, 6 Broad St, open daily 0930–1700 (Apr–Oct); 0900–1800 (July–Aug); 1000–1630 (Nov–Mar).

A 17th-century gateway off the High St (near Magdalen Bridge) leads into the **University Botanic Garden**, founded in 1621. Its rockeries, pools and greenhouses full of exotic plants provide a tranquil haven from the bustle outside. Free (£ Apr–Aug); open daily 0900–1700 (Apr–Sept); 0900–1630 (Oct–Mar). To the north, close to the University Museum, are the peaceful **University Parks** where you can picnic on the banks of the Cherwell.

SIDE TRIPS FROM OXFORD

BLENHEIM PALACE Seven miles north of Oxford is the attractive town of **Woodstock**, home of the monumental **Blenheim Palace**. Blenheim was Queen Anne's reward for war hero John Churchill, the first Duke of Marlborough, in gratitude for his defeat of the French at Blenheim in 1704. The work of Baroque architect Sir John Vanbrugh, it is the only English palace not built for royalty and was the birthplace of Sir Winston Churchill in 1874.

There are guided tours of the somewhat lifeless interior, with its fine portraits, lavish furnishings and Churchill memorabilia, and you can wander at will through the formal gardens and vast parkland, landscaped by Capability Brown. The lakeside makes an ideal spot for a picnic. Sir Winston is buried in **Bladon churchyard** nearby.

The palace, £££, is open daily 1030–1730 (mid-Mar–Oct). Park (£ for pedestrians) open daily (0900–1700). Take a bus (every ½-hr) to Woodstock from Gloucester Green.

> *i* **Tourist Information Centre** Oxfordshire Museum,
> Part St, Woodstock; tel: (01993) 813276; website:

www.westoxon.gov.uk; e-mail: tourism@westoxon.gov.uk.
Open Mon–Sat 0930–1730 (summer); 1000–1700 (winter); Sun 1300–1700 (all year).

THE CHILTERNS The Chilterns, a range of chalk uplands, runs about 50 miles south-west from near Luton, north of London, to peter out towards the Thames near Reading. The eastern slopes are more heavily developed with commuter-belt, upmarket suburbs. Beyond the ridge to the west there are pretty villages, pleasant beechwoods and wonderful walking country – the **Ridgeway**, a prehistoric track and now a national trail, runs the length of the Chiltern hills and follows the ridge most of the way.

To the north (from Oxford head via the A40 and A418 to Thame), highlights include **Bledlow Ridge**, east of Chinnor, and **Coombe Hill**, near Wendover, one of the highest points. Nearby Chequers, glimpsed from afar, is the country residence of British prime ministers. From Bledlow Ridge the road continues to the picturesque village of **West Wycombe**, which is now owned by the National Trust. Just north of High Wycombe on the A4128 in beautiful parkland is **Hughenden Manor**, home of Victorian prime minister Benjamin Disraeli. ££, open daily 1200–1700; house from 1300 daily (Apr–Oct); Sat–Sun (Mar); park open all year. South of the M40 (take the B4009 from Chinnor to Watlington, an appealing Georgian village), some of the most attractive scenery can be enjoyed around **Turville** and **Nettlebed**, which also have good pubs.

THE RIDGEWAY

Information on the national trail and its history, as well as facilities and accommodation in the area, is available from the National Trails Office, Holton, Oxford; tel: (01865) 810224; website: www.nationaltrails.gov.uk.

WEST WYCOMBE

West Wycombe Park is an Italianate mansion refashioned by Sir Francis Dashwood MP in the mid-18th century. Sir Francis is better known as founder of the Hell Fire Club, a secret society with himself and fellow rakes as members. Black magic and debauchery were the main features of their meetings, which sometimes took place in West Wycombe Caves or inside the huge ball on top of the church tower.

i **Tourist Information Centre** Market House, North St, Thame; tel/fax: (01844) 212834. Open Mon–Fri 0930–1700, Sat 1000–1600.

THE VALE OF WHITE HORSE The chalk downland on the Oxfordshire–Berkshire borders is rich in archaeological remains. On the popular walking route of the ancient Ridgeway path, which continues from the Chilterns across the Berkshire Downs, **Uffington Castle** is the earthworks of an Iron Age camp, and **Wayland's Smithy** is a Neolithic burial site. In the green hillside above Uffington is carved a stylised **White Horse**, thought to be Britain's oldest chalk carving, and possibly dating to 3000 BC. The top of Uffington Hill is a superb viewpoint. The quiet market town of **Wantage**, supposedly birthplace of King Alfred the Great, has a tourist information centre within the **Vale and Downland Museum** (£, 19 Church St; open same hours as the tourist information centre) which gives a good regional overview.

If driving from Oxford, take the A420 south-west and branch off at the A338 to Wantage. There, turn right on the B4507 along the Vale of White Horse. The White Horse, Uffington Castle and Wayland's Smithy are on the left after 6 miles. Turn right to Uffington village, and return to the A420 via Fernham.

> ### CAR HIRE
>
> To see either the Chilterns or the Vale of White Horse properly you need a car for a day or two. Oxford has the greatest choice of agents: Avis, Hertz, Budget and National (for tel. nos see p. 24) all have offices here. Directions are given here from Oxford, but tourist information centres can help with car hire and routes from Didcot, Maidenhead or Henley.

> *i* **Tourist Information Centre** Vale and Downland Museum, 19 Church St, Wantage; tel/fax: (01235) 760176. Open all year Tues–Sat 1030–1630, Sun 1430–1700.

WHERE NEXT?

You could continue from Oxford north-west to Worcester and the charming Cotswolds (see pp. 154–155). Alternatively, from Reading head to the scenic south coast via Southampton (see p. 70).

Bristol is arguably England's most attractive large city. It has long been prosperous, with its fortunes closely linked to its role as an important port. Not all of its history is glorious, however; in the 18th century, Bristol was heavily involved in importing slaves from Africa. Today, its exciting harbourside area, full of history and atmosphere, has a whole new lease of life with shops, restaurants and visitor attractions, and is constantly evolving.

Bristol is a centre for finance and technology, which continues the city's long tradition of innovation and engineering — Isambard Brunel, architect/designer of the Clifton Suspension Bridge, Temple Meads station and the SS *Great Britain*, lived here. Architecture is another of its strong points; despite heavy bombing during the Blitz, many Georgian buildings remain. The city's two universities result in a young and vibrant population. It has a burgeoning arts culture, a myriad of inexpensive places to eat and no shortage of things to do.

GETTING THERE

Bristol International airport is 9 miles (14 km) from the city centre. There's a regular, direct bus service (daily 0530–2230) from the airport to Bristol Temple Meads railway station and to the bus station, which takes about 20 mins. Taxis can be booked; tel: (01275) 474 888.

'I feel that people here enjoy life. There is not that terrible dreariness which is probably the chief curse of our provincial towns... It is a genuine city, an ancient metropolis... Bristol lives on, selling us Gold Flake [tobacco] and Fry's chocolate... And the smoke from a million Gold Flakes solidifies into a new Gothic Tower for the university; and the chocolate melts away to leave behind it all the fine shops down Park Street and the pleasant villas out at Clifton, and an occasional glass of Harvey's Bristol Milk for everybody.'

J B Priestley, *English Journey* (1933)

The main railway station is Bristol Temple Meads, which has connections to Bath, Gloucester and Cheltenham, the Midlands, the north of England and Scotland, as well as London Paddington, Cardiff, Exeter, Plymouth and Southampton. A 15-min walk or buses 8/508 or 9/509 will take you to the city centre. The Bus and Coach Station is located just north of Broadmead Shopping Centre. Bristol is easy to reach by road, via the M5, junction 18 or the M4, junction 19, following the M32 to the city centre.

GETTING AROUND

Most attractions are within walking distance of the city centre but there's a good bus system. If you're fit (Bristol is quite hilly), hiring a bicycle is a sensible choice. Bristol is home to Sustrans, the HQ of the Britain's cycling network, which makes the city particularly cycle friendly. As with all large towns, locking your bike is a sensible precaution. Ferries also operate daily all year round, a pleasant – and cheap – way to get from A to B. Bus information – city centre and rural areas – tel: 0870 608 2608.

> *i* **Tourist Information Office** The Annexe, Wildscreen Walk, Harbourside; tel: 0906 586 2313 (calls charged at 60p per minute); www.visitbristol.co.uk; e-mail: ticharbourside@ bristol-city.gov.uk. Open daily Mon–Sun 1000–1800 (Mar–Oct), Mon–Sat 1000–1700, Sun 1100–1600 (Nov–Feb).

ACCOMMODATION

Bristol's Tourist Information Office can help with booking a place to stay, whether you want a luxury hotel or basic hostel. There's a good range of low budget accommodation and reasonably priced B&Bs.

From July to mid-Sept, the University of Bristol offers **self-catering flats** (£–££) for rent. The University halls are situated in the elegant Clifton area (Goldney Hall); tel: (0117) 903 4873, about a mile out of the city or Stoke Bishop (University Hall); tel: (0117) 903 3730, 3 miles (5 km) from the city centre. They are particularly good value for groups of five to six people.

> **Avon Gorge Hotel** £££ Sion Hill, Clifton; tel: (0117) 973 8955; e-mail: info@avongorge-hotel-bristol.com. A comfortable hotel with unrivalled views of the Clifton Suspension Bridge and a large sun terrace with a play area for children.
>
> **Bristol Backpackers** £ 17 St Stephens St; tel/fax: (0117) 925 7900; e-mail: info@bristolbackpackers.co.uk; website: www.bristolbackpackers.co.uk. Centrally located 56-bed hostel with 6–12 bed dormitories.

BRISTOL

Bristol International Youth Hostel £ 14 Narrow Quay; tel: (0117) 922 1659; e-mail: bristol@yha.org.uk. Central, well-equipped hostel in a converted warehouse on the waterfront. Private four/five/six bed rooms available. Maximum stay six days. The TIC provides information on **camping and caravan sites**. Baltic Wharf Campsite on Cumberland Rd is close to SS *Great Britain*; tel: (0117) 926 8030, fax: (0117) 921 0457. Open all year round. Two and a half-acre (1-ha) site: advance booking essential.

FOOD AND DRINK

Bristol has a wide range of restaurants and pubs. **Clifton village** has many one-off upmarket restaurants, whilst cheaper eating places cluster around the studenty **Whiteladies Road/Cotham Hill** area, with everything from Mexican to Indian and Pan-Asian. The cobbled **King Street** area has a good selection of long-established restaurants and traditional pubs, whilst the **harbourside** brims with trendy, minimalist bars and restaurants of the converted warehouse and funky art variety.

If you want to pack up a sunny day picnic and head off to the Downs, the food stalls in **St Nicholas Markets** – bread, olives, organic of every variety, pasta, homemade soups – are an unbeatable starting point. Smiles is the locally brewed beer and that Sunday schoolteacher's tipple, Harvey's Bristol Cream, was also born here.

Brazz ££–£££ 85 Park St; tel: (0117) 925 2000; www.brazz.co.uk. Brasserie, bar and café in one, open seven days for coffee and cookies, a quick lunch, 'graze menu' of nibbles and wine, dinner or Sunday brunch. Supremely versatile. Student deals available.

Browns Restaurant £££ 38 Queen's Rd, Clifton; tel: (0117) 930 4000. Large, friendly restaurant in a listed Venetian style building, serving traditional English food with a trendy, often Mediterranean, twist.

Budokan ££–£££ 31 Colston St (city centre) and Whiteladies Rd, by Clifton Down railway station. No booking. Billed as a 'Pan-Asian fuelling station', eating here is quick-service Japanese, Thai and Malaysian.

Deasons ££–£££ 43 Whiteladies Rd, tel: (0117) 973 6230; www.deasons.co.uk. Acclaimed contemporary restaurant with interesting and popular dishes stylishly presented. Open for lunch and dinner six days, also Sunday lunch.

Internet Exchange £ 23–25 Queen's Rd, Clifton. The place to come for a *caffè latte* and a quick on-line chat. Also try **Internet Café** £ 140 Whiteladies Rd and **Next Life** £ 27–29 Baldwin St.

Llandoger Trow £–££ King St. Named after the flat-bottomed sailing barges once used by merchants, this traditional

PLASTICINE HEROES
Bristol is the home of the much-loved plasticine characters *Wallace and Gromit*, who are brought to life by Nick Park and colleagues at the Aardman Animation Studios. It is not possible to visit the production studios, but for news of what's going on and an insight into animation work, check out www.wallaceandgromit.com.

timber building dating from 1664 is an atmospheric place to eat good English pub grub.

Mud Dock Cycleworks and Café ££–£££ 40 The Grove. An unusual, trendy café that combines the owners' two passions: bikes and food. The menu includes everything from smoked salmon breakfast bagels to a selection of tapas.

Rajpoot £££–££££ 52 Upper Belgrave Rd; tel: (0117) 973 3515. Upmarket Indian with out of the ordinary dishes and an extraordinary reputation. A pretty terrace overlooks the Downs for outdoor summer dining.

The Cottage Inn ££ Cumberland Rd. Worth considering if you are visiting SS *Great Britain*. Serves good English food and makes a great starting point for a walk along the waterfront with great views up to the rows of rainbow coloured houses on the other side of the river.

HIGHLIGHTS

Many of Bristol's more interesting tourist attractions (and its tourist office) are down by the newly redeveloped harbourside area, part of a £450 million rejuvenation scheme, which makes it a good starting point for exploring the city. If you're looking for something to keep all the family entertained, it's hard to beat the three-part **At-Bristol** attraction, located on Millennium Square.

Explore is a brilliant, state of the art interactive science centre – the ultimate touch, pull, press, prod paradise for kids with plenty for adults to discover too. Run on an oversized hamster wheel; walk through a tornado and make your own mini TV programme. **Wildwalk** is of particular interest to children aged 7+. It's a hi-tech, atmospheric, interactive journey through the story of evolution, encompassing everything from how spiders webs work to how tadpoles grow legs, illustrated by videos, a tropical garden, live animals and more. There's also an **IMAX** giant screen film theatre. There are family tickets and a ticket covering all three attractions (valid for two consecutive days); ££–£££. Open daily 1000–1800.

Animal lovers are well catered for in Bristol, with over 300 species of wildlife at **Bristol Zoo Gardens**. This delightful zoo, set in landscaped gardens, is big on conservation. Highlights include the Seal and Penguin Coasts, with an underwater viewing area, Zona Brazil, and two Asiatic lions; ££–£££, Clifton Down, open daily 0900–1730 (summer), 0900–1630 (winter). Bus 8(508), 9(509), 586 and 587.

Bristol has long played an important role in merchant shipping and seafaring and it was from here that a Venetian merchant living in Bristol, John Cabot, sailed aboard *The Matthew* to discover Newfoundland in Canada in 1497. A replica of his boat, as well as the original **SS *Great Britain***, designed by Brunel, can be seen at the Great Western Dockyard. The SS *Great Britain* was built in Bristol's dockyards in 1839–43, returning there to rest when it was rescued from the Falklands in 1970. It was the world's first iron-built, screw-propelled luxury transatlantic cruise liner, 100 ft (30.5 m) longer than any other of the era. Today you can climb up on deck, see the tiny cabins and replica ladies boudoir and first class dining saloon, plus the restoration work taking place. ££–£££, Gas Ferry Rd, open daily 1000–1730 (Apr–Oct), 1000–1630 (Nov–Mar). Ticket includes entry to Maritime Heritage Centre and both ships.

A recent important addition to the cultural scene is the **British Empire and Commonwealth Museum**, Clock Tower Yard, Temple Meads. It explores all aspects of the British Empire and Commonwealth in a lively and enjoyable way. There are 16 main sections, so be selective. ££, open 1000–1700 every day except Christmas Day and Boxing Day; tel: (0117) 925 4980; www.empiremuseum.co.uk.

TOURS The Bristol Ferry Boat Co., tel: (0117) 927 3416, runs inexpensive round-trip **tours on the historic harbour**. £, open daily (Apr–Sept and school holidays), weekends only (Oct–Mar). The Bristol Packet, tel: (0117) 926 8157, runs a **city docks boat tour** (£). On selected Saturdays throughout the summer, it also operates a 3-hr Avon Gorge cruise (£££), or a 5-hr (one way) boat trip to Bath (£££). Cruises leave from Wapping Wharf, near SS *Great Britain*. Booking recommended for Avon Gorge and Bath cruise.

Hop-on, hop-off, City Sightseeing **open-top bus tours** depart from the city centre and take in all the main sights from SS *Great Britain* to Bristol Zoo. ££, daily 1000–1700, with small discounts off various attractions. If time is limited, it's a fun and informative way to see all the main sights, including some that are a little far flung, such as Sea Walls.

BRUNEL

Isambard Kingdom Brunel is Bristol's most famous son, designing not only the Clifton Suspension Bridge but also SS *Great Britain* and Temple Meads station. He died in 1859, aged 53, worn out by hard work and 40 cigars a day before the bridge project was finished. Such was his eye for detail, the road level is 1m higher at the Clifton end than the Leigh Woods end of the bridge to give the appearance of being absolutely horizontal.

FOR FREE Six city museums are free: the City Museum and Art Gallery, Bristol Industrial Museum, The Georgian House, The Red Lodge, Blaise Castle House Museum and King's Weston Roman Villa. For more details, tel: (0117) 922 3571; www.bristol-city.gov.uk/museums.

It is fun to explore the older areas of Bristol on foot. Clifton is particularly attractive – look out for the **Royal York Crescent** and **Caledonia Place** with its intricate wrought iron balconies. More grand old houses line the edge of the Downs. Start at the top end of Whiteladies Rd and wander past the zoo and down to the **Clifton Suspension Bridge**. This bridge over the Avon Gorge is a world famous sight, designed by Isambard Kingdom Brunel and built 1831–64. There are viewing points near the bridge, as well as one on the Downs, known as Sea Walls (on Circular Rd), which offers a magnificent panorama.

If you'd like an idea of what the beautiful town houses were like inside, head for **The Georgian House**. Built in the 18th century for a wealthy Bristol sugar merchant and Caribbean plantation owner, it still retains many original features. Free, 7 Great George St, open Sat–Wed 1000–1700 (Apr–Oct).

Back indoors, there's a myriad of free cultural experiences to be enjoyed. **Bristol Cathedral** on College Green (open daily 0800–1800) is worth a look for its Norman Chapterhouse and Early-English Lady Chapel. Founded in 1140 as an Augustinian monastery, it became a cathedral in 1542 and is now a mixture of styles.

For contemporary visual arts, dance and film, head to the **Arnolfini** at Narrow Quay. Housed in a waterfront 1830s tea warehouse, exhibitions change every six weeks or so, followed by a two-week closure period, so ring ahead. Free tours take place at 1400 every Saturday during exhibitions. It also has a wonderful bookshop containing cutting edge books and magazines on design, film, fashion and art. Open Mon–Wed, Fri–Sat 1000–1900, Thurs 1000–2100, Sun 1200–1900; tel: (0117) 929 9191; website: www.arnolfini.demon.co.uk.

Other free galleries include the **City Museum and Art Gallery**, Queen's Rd; tel: (0117) 922 3571, and **Spike Island**, 133 Cumberland Rd; tel: (0117) 929 2266.

And if you want to venture further afield, hop on a bike and head to the Roman city of **Bath** (see pp. 126–127) along the 12½-mile (20-km) traffic-free Bristol and Bath Railway cycleway. It winds through gorgeous countryside, with plenty of watering holes *en route*. It's a really enjoyable way to get a feel for the surrounding landscape – and you can always catch a train back.

SHOPPING

Bristol has two modern shopping centres, **The Mall**, at Cribbs Causeway, Junction 17, just off the M5, and **Broadmead** in the city centre. For a more eclectic shopping experience, head to **St Nicholas markets**, Corn St (open Mon–Sat, 0930–1700), where you can browse for food, secondhand books, stylish homeware and jewellery. Next door, a covered arcade has everything from photoframes to secondhand cycling gloves. There's also a **farmer's market** in Corn St every Wed 0930–1530. **Clifton** is a good place for individual boutiques, antiques and arty shops.

EVENTS AND FESTIVALS

Bristol has many festivals throughout the year. Many major events take place at Ashton Court Estate, Long Ashton, about 2½ miles (4 km) south-west of the city. Buses 350/353/354/36. July sees a large music event, the **Bristol Community Festival**, followed by the magnificent **Bristol Balloon Fiesta** in August when about 150 hot air balloons take to the sky. There's also an **International Kite Festival** in September.

NIGHTLIFE

Pick up a free Bristol Entertainments diary from the tourist information centre, galleries and cafés for the latest events. Bristol's theatre, the **Old Vic**, King St; tel: (0117) 987 7877 has a great reputation; it is the oldest working theatre in the county, and there are backstage tours and talks. The **Hippodrome**, tel: 0870 607 7500, hosts everything from opera to mainstream musicals, and many concerts – classical and pop – also take place at **Colston Hall**, Colston St; tel: (0117) 922 3686. The **Old Duke** pub in King Street offers live jazz and blues five nights a week and Sunday lunchtime.

SIDE TRIPS

BATH Fifteen miles (24 km) away (a 20-min car journey, 17-min train ride, or 1-hr bus ride) lies the delightful Georgian spa town of **Bath**, a World Heritage Site. The Romans were the first to take the waters here, and founded the spa of Aquae Sulis. In the 18th century the health-giving properties of the springs were rediscovered and Bath became the height of fashion, with elegant terraces of golden-stone houses erected – the finest architectural set pieces being **The Circus** and the **Royal Crescent**, where **No 1** is a museum house furnished in period style; ££, open Tues–Sun 1030–1700 (mid-Feb–Oct); Tues–Sun 1030–1600 (early–late Nov).

The original spa is an extraordinary place: beyond the genteel 18th-century **Pump Room**, where you can sip tea or hot spa water to the accompaniment of chamber music, are the **Baths** (£££, open daily 0900–2100 (July and Aug); 0900–1700 (Mar–June and Sept–Oct); 0930–1630 (Nov–Feb) – a mixture of Roman and 18th-/19th-century reconstructions, with a fascinating museum display: this is one of Britain's top Roman sites. And now, thanks to money from the Millennium Commission, it is again possible to bathe in the thermal waters at **Bath Spa**, though it is an expensive experience with prices starting from just below £20 (for details, tel: (01225) 477710). Close by the Pump Room, 15th-century **Bath Abbey** (£) is famed for its fan-vaulting in the Perpendicular style; it is known as the Lantern of the West because of its rich stained glass, including the great east window.

Bath is full of museums. One of the best is the **Museum of Costume and Assembly Rooms** (££, Bennett St, open daily 1000–1700), with a sumptuous display showing the history of costume up to the present day. The **Jane Austen Centre** (££, Gay St, open Mon–Sat 1000–1730, Sun 1030–1730) chronicles the great novelist on whose work Bath and its inhabitants were a profound influence. Just south-east of the city, the **American Museum** (££, closed Mon and in mornings) at Claverton Manor is the only museum in Britain focusing exclusively on the USA, and covers folk art, the Native Americans, the Shakers and American period house interiors.

On the south side of the city **Prior Park Landscape Garden** (££; £1 reduction for bus travellers; closed Tues; Dec, Jan open Fri–Sun only) is an 18th-century garden being restored by the National Trust; unusually they don't allow car parking here, and encourage visitors to take the bus (Bath Bus Co. S1 or First Badgerline 2 or 4). The garden occupies a valley and has superb views over Bath. Another pastoral pleasure is to take a **boat trip** along the Avon from Pulteney Bridge, or to hire a punt or rowing boat.

---

i **Tourist Information Centre** Abbey Chambers, Abbey Church Yard; tel: (01225) 477101 or 0906 711 2000 (50p a minute). Websites: www.visitbath.co.uk or www.bath.info; e-mail: tourism@bathnes.gov.uk. Open Mon–Sat 0930–1700 (1800 May–Sept), Sun 1000–1600.

🏠 **Bath Youth Hostel** £ Bathwick Hill; tel: 0870 7705690; e-mail: bath@yha.org.uk; just east of the centre (bus 18 from the rail station).
St Christopher's Inn £ 9 Green St, tel: (020) 7407 1856; www.st-christophers.co.uk. A hostel with an excellent central location.

CHEDDAR GORGE Venture into the country with a trip to **Cheddar Gorge** (A38 south of Bristol to the A371, a 40-min drive; no direct bus from Bristol, 25-min bus ride from Wells, bus 126). Here you can enjoy a cliff top gorge walk, explore the caves (££, open daily 1000–1700 (May–Sept) 1030–1630 (Apr–Oct), and climb the 274 steps of Jacob's Ladder. The cavernous **Cheddar Showcaves** are also worth a visit.

WELLS Further along the A371 is Britain's smallest city, **Wells** (a 45-min drive from Bristol or bus 376, approx. 1hr), famed for its historic buildings and stunning 12th-century cathedral. Inside the lofty, hushed interior look out for the astronomical clock that lurches into life every quarter of an hour. The limestone caves at **Wookey Hole**, a few miles northeast of Wells, are very popular. But don't go if highly commercial tourist attractions turn you off.

GLASTONBURY The A39 from Wells takes you to **Glastonbury** (a 55-min drive from Bristol or bus 376 (via Wells), approximately 1¼ hrs). This little Somerset town is best known as host to Europe's largest music festival. It has an evocative ruined **abbey**, once the richest in the country (£), and strong connections with King Arthur. **Glastonbury Tor** rears up from the flatness of the Somerset levels. Topped by a ruined 14th-century church tower, it affords astonishingly far-reaching views. There's a prehistoric village below the Tor and finds from this settlement are displayed in **The Tribunal**, a well-preserved 15th-century courthouse.

WHERE NEXT?

Bristol is superbly placed for trips to many interesting towns. Just a short trip away by train is the cathedral city of Gloucester (see pp. 149–150) and the beautifully preserved Georgian town of Cheltenham. Or you can head to south into Devon for an altogether more rural experience, as well as some of Britain's finest coastline (see pp. 128–136).

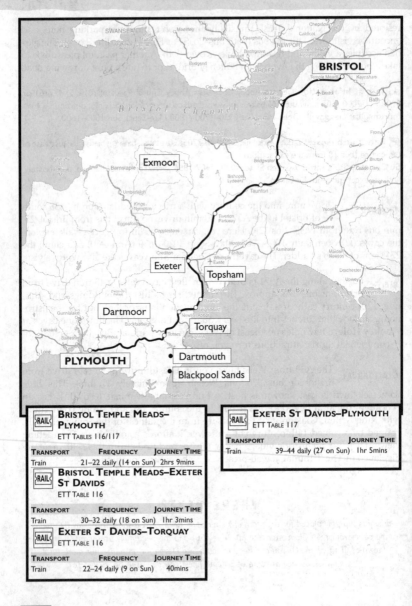

This route covers an immensely varied section of the UK. The Devon coast offers wonderful seascapes, where quaint fishing villages and pretty coves slot in between long stretches of perpendicular cliffs, raucous with the cries of gulls. Dartmoor National Park, a wilderness area covering more than 700 sq miles (1813 sq km), has a sombre, compelling beauty. In the depths of winter the moor can be so empty it's possible to imagine that the rest of the world must be hibernating. The university town of Exeter is packed with history and in Plymouth, visitors can walk down the Mayflower Steps, where the Pilgrim Fathers left all that was familiar behind when they set sail for the New World.

BRISTOL

See p. 120.

EXETER

The compact university town of Exeter isn't as buzzing as you might expect given its large student population. Nevertheless, it's an extremely appealing place. It has been inhabited since Roman times, making it one of the oldest cities in England. Stout walls from Roman times still guard its core, and fine buildings from Tudor, Georgian and Victorian times create immense aesthetic appeal.

Exeter Cathedral's astronomical clock is said to have been the inspiration for the famous nursery rhyme that begins: 'Hickory Dickory Dock, the mouse ran up the clock …'

The 850-year-old **Exeter Cathedral** is a particularly fine specimen. It has the world's longest run of unbroken gothic vaulting and England's tallest Bishop's throne, which is a lofty 59 ft (18 m) high. The **Exeter Domesday Book** is on display in the Cathedral Library. The city has connections with two of Britain's most famous seafarers, Sir Walter Raleigh and Sir Francis Drake – Mol's Coffee House in the attractive **Cathedral Close** and the Ship Inn in St Martin's Lane were favourite haunts of theirs.

INSPIRATIONAL EXETER
Much of Charles Dickens' *Pickwick Papers* was inspired by the characters he met while drinking in the Turks Head pub. Bram Stoker also drew creative inspiration from the city, beginning his story of the fearsome Count Dracula here.

For an unusual element to your visit, there's a guided tour of the fascinating **Underground Passages**, a medieval labyrinth of water conduits believed to date back to the 13th century. Shopping in Exeter is a lot of fun, with its interesting little individual outlets huddled in cobbled back streets. Other points of note include the old

Custom House on the quayside. Built during the reign of Charles II, it is the oldest surviving example in England. The quay was once the hub of the valuable cloth exporting industry. **The Quay House Visitor Centre** delves into the history of the waterfront as well as shedding light on Exeter's history right the way back to Roman times. It's possible to explore the **Exeter Canal** on foot, by bicycle or in a canoe. Paddles and Saddles on King's Wharf can fit you up with the appropriate transport; tel: (01392) 424241.

i **Tourist Information Centre** Civic Centre, Paris St; tel: (01392) 265700; website: www.exeter.gov.uk; e-mail: tic@exeter.gov.uk. Open Mon–Fri 0900–1700, Sat 0900–1700 (closed 1300–1400 in winter); Sun 1000–1600 (summer only).

🛏 For somewhere with a touch of charm and individuality at a very reasonable price, there's **SilverSprings** ££ 12 Richmond Rd; tel: (01392) 494040.
Another central option is the family run **Trees Mini Hotel** £ 2 Queen's Crescent; tel: (01392) 259531. Evening meals.
For a very cheap option check out B&B at the **University of Exeter** £ The Holiday Booking Office, University of Exeter, Hospitality Services, Devonshire House, Stocker Rd; tel: (01392) 211500. It's only a mile (1.6 km) from the centre and it's set in 300 acres (121 ha) of landscaped grounds.
Exeter Youth Hostel £ 47 Countess Wear Rd, tel: 0870 7705826 (e-mail: exeter@yha.org.uk): between Exeter and Topsham; bus 57 or 85 from Exeter Central rail station.
For places slightly further afield there's **B&B in Reka Dom** £–££ 43 The Strand, Topsham; tel: (01392) 873385, a 17th-century merchant's house with views over the estuary and log fires in winter. High teas and dinners for special occasions are laid on. **Drakes Farmhouse** £–££ Ide; tel: (01392) 256814 is a very attractive listed 15th-century building within easy reach of a number of pubs and restaurants.

🍴 For a decent coffee, along with food from breakfast until dinner time try the **Boston Tea Party** £ 84 Queen St. You can drink your coffee in the comfort of the sofa lounge upstairs.
For top-notch cuisine in terribly stylish surroundings make for **The Royal Clarence Hotel** ££–££££ Cathedral Yard; tel: (01392) 310031. There's also a bar and a lunchtime carvery.
Another popular slot for good food, as well as accommodation is **St Olave's Court Hotel** £££ Mary Arches St; tel: (01392) 413054.
The **White Hart Hotel** ££–£££ South St; tel: (01392) 279897 has been around for 400 years. It's located within the old city wall, through which Henry VI entered in 1452. Meals can be

taken in the bars or the restaurant and ale can still be had in half-gallon jugs (about 2 litres).

SIDE TRIPS FROM EXETER Just 3 miles south of Exeter, on the Exe Estuary, you'll find **Topsham**. This charming town has a warren of narrow streets and some very unusual 17th- and 18th-century merchants' houses built in the Dutch style with curved gables. It is also well endowed with pubs, restaurants and tea-shops. **Topsham Museum** has a home in a 17th-century furnished house with a courtyard and gardens overlooking the estuary. It documents the town's maritime history, as well as giving useful information on the wildlife found in and around the Exe Estuary. Topsham is about 15 mins by car and 25 by (regular) bus from Exeter (enquiries for this service, Devon Bus Line; tel: (01392) 382800).

Killerton House in Broadclyst outside Exeter is a must for fans of historic houses and gardens. Killerton is awash with rare trees and shrubs collected by the Veitch family in their horticultural forays around the globe. Riotous planting prevents the garden from being formal and the house with its comfy furnishings is welcoming too. Walks through the parkland give glimpses over the beautiful **Clyst and Culm Valleys**. A path also meanders through a wooded valley to a tiny sea cove. Killerton House (££, open daily 1100–1700 except Tues) is 10–15 mins drive from Exeter and is accessible only by car.

For a highly unusual journey through the Axe Valley why not give the Seaton Tramway a whirl? This unique narrow gauge tramway leaves from Seaton to take visitors on a 3-mile (5-km) journey through the pretty Axe Valley. Tram driving lessons are also available; tel: (01297) 20375.

The East Devon countryside is mellow and rolling, while the coastal region offers some spectacular sea cliffs interspersed by pleasant resort towns like **Seaton**, **Sidmouth**, **Budleigh Salterton** and **Exmouth**. All around a 45 min drive from Exeter, they are not accessible by train but there is a reasonably regular bus service. On the Dawlish road is **Powderham Castle**, an imposing medieval fortress set in a tranquil deer park, with wildly opulent state rooms.

Torquay, on what's known as the English Riviera, is hard to mention without a snigger because the infamous *Fawlty Towers* was located there. Fans of the eternally popular British TV comedy series might go there to pay homage, but sadly they won't find Basil Fawlty goose-stepping or Manuel hyperventilating at yet another dining room calamity. Torquay with its attractive harbour and stately Victorian buildings tends to be popular with families.

DARTMOUTH

An affluent little enclave tucked away on the mouth of the beautiful river Dart, Dartmouth's smart shop and chic eating houses give it a sleek, upmarket feel. The

Magnificent steam trains chug their way through the supremely scenic Dart Valley. It's possible to do a round trip by taking the ferry to Kingswear, Dartmouth's mirror image on the opposing river bank. Here, hop on the train to Paignton (don't be tempted to linger), catch a bus to Totnes and then take a boat trip back to Dartmouth.

medieval town clings to a steep hillside and cradles an exceptionally pretty natural harbour. Its prosperous maritime history began in the 1100s, when it was one of England's principal ports and many of its beautifully preserved buildings were commissioned by wealthy merchants. The tourist board publishes a helpful leaflet with a suggested **'Dartmouth Trail'** which points out interesting spots such as the cobbled **Bayard's Cove**, setting for the sea-faring TV series *The Onedin Line*.

As you walk around Dartmouth, be sure to keep your head raised as the upper sections of the medieval buildings are magnificent. Look out for **The Butterwalk** too. It's difficult to believe now, but in 1635 ships were able to sail right up here. A nifty 5-minute boat trip takes you from the harbour to **Dartmouth Castle,** which looms over the river mouth. Built by Edward IV in the 15th century, it was one of the most sophisticated strongholds of its day. You can also see the remains of the 14th-century **Hawley's Castle**. John Hawley was the model for the infamous merchant in Chaucer's *'A Shipman's Tale'*. His exploits included capturing and sinking foreign ships and the citadel was built to protect his own assets from a similar fate.

Crime writer Agatha Christie is the town's most famous export. Her unlikely sleuths, Hercule Poirot and Miss Marple, have gained recognition throughout the world. The Royal Castle Hotel on the quay in Dartmouth features in *Ordeal by Innocence* and *The Regatta Mystery*.

From the castle you can stroll along the coast to **Sugary Cove** or visit **Gallant's Bower**, a wooded mound that was once a Royalist fortress. **Dartmouth Pottery** above Warfleet Cove is home to the famous Gurgle Jug, so called because of the water-down-the-plughole noise the vessel makes whilst pouring.

i **Tourist Information Centre** The Engine House, Mayor's Ave; tel: (01803) 834224; e-mail: enquiries@dartmouth-tourism.org.uk. Open Mon–Fri 0900–1730, Sat 0900–1800, Sun 1000–1600 (summer); Mon–Sat 0900–1700 (winter).

The Carved Angel ££ 2 South Embankment; tel: (01803) 832465 is an internationally acclaimed restaurant with the added bonus of excellent views over the River Dart. Confusingly, there's also **The Carved Angel Café** £ 7 Foss St; tel: (01803) 834842 serving light lunches and suppers as well as morning coffee and afternoon teas.
Dartmouth's oldest building dates back to 1380 and also happens to be a great pub. **The Cherub** £ Higher St; tel: (01803) 832571 is the perfect place for a glass of ale and a good meal.

For fish, **Hooked** ££ 5 Higher St; tel: (01803) 832022 cannot be faulted. It's located in a beautiful old building and the surroundings are stylish yet friendly.

Cafe Cache £–££ 24 Duke St; tel: (01803) 833804 is another worthwhile place to eat, serving good food at reasonable prices. For a fun atmosphere and a wonderful location on the River Dart, head for **The Gunfield Hotel, Restaurant and Bar** ££ Castle Rd; tel: (01803) 834843. The food is excellent and it isn't prohibitively expensive either.

The Royal Castle ££ The Quay; tel: (01803) 833033 started life as two merchant houses in the 1630s, but the crenellations were added by the Victorians. Previous guests include Donald Sutherland, who stayed here whilst filming the Agatha Christie thriller, *Ordeal by Innocence*.

THE WORM THAT TURNED

An extraordinary event that might be worth looking out for if you happen to be in the area is the International Worm Charming Championships at Blackawton. It usually takes place during the first May Bank Holiday and participants have to goad these creatures to the surface without using digging implements. Permitted techniques include singing, dancing and chanting. Insobriety is no handicap to this kind of activity, so feel free to partake of the locally brewed ale.

SIDE TRIPS FROM DARTMOUTH If you're looking for an idyllic beach, make for the pine-fringed **Blackpool Sands**, which is only 10 mins by car from Dartmouth, or a lovely cliff-top walk taking around an hour. The obelisk on the edge of **Slapton Sands** was presented to the local inhabitants who were evacuated while the area was being used for battle practice prior to the Normandy Landings. The fresh water lagoon at **Slapton Ley** is protected from the sea by a 3-mile (5-km) long sandbar; the reedbeds and lake are now a nature reserve.

Avid horticulturalists should consider early retirement to South Hams, where plants grow with lush abandon. Failing that you can always ogle someone else's plot. **Coleton Fishacre** near Kingswear is a 24-acre (10-ha) portion of pastoral bliss designed by Rupert and Dorothy D'Oyly Carte in the 1920s. Tender and exotic plants are a particular feature and winding paths descend to the sea. Three miles from Kingswear (Dartmouth's opposite number), a car is the only practical option of getting to the gardens. ££, open Wed–Sun 1030–1730 (dusk in winter) end Mar–end Oct.

The eyecatchingly rugged coastline in this region is great for walking and bird watching. Bite sized circular walks, designed for those who are less inclined to route march, are outlined in handy leaflets published by South Hams Tourist Office; tel: (01803) 861234. One such walk kicks off at **Prawle Point** (the most southerly part of Devon) and takes in the enigmatically named Ship's Graveyard and Gammon Head, before veering inland along ancient bridleways.

DARTMOOR

Dartmoor is a place of austere beauty. The wind gallops unchecked over swathes of open moorland and rattles around the awesome granite tors which loom fortress-like on the skyline. But there's a benign side to Dartmoor too. Cosy villages full of thatched cottages and snug pubs with big log fires huddle on its periphery. And this region of peaceful valleys and pretty rivers provides a pleasant antidote to the desolate drama of the heartland. It is best explored by car, which will give you access to the many worthwhile walks.

A bus service does operate to certain villages – running diagonally across the moor from the Plymouth end – Yelverton – to Exeter. However, most services only run at weekends. Further details are available from Princetown tourist information centre, tel: (01822) 890414, and from the public transport info line 0870 6082 608.

Fox Tor Mire, a treacherous section of blanket bog on Dartmoor, was the inspiration for Conan Doyle's Sherlock Holmes escapade *The Hound of the Baskervilles*, and people are said to have disappeared forever in this voracious pea soup.

On a clear day, walk up to **Yes Tor** and **High Willhays** (both over 2000 ft/610 m) for impressive views, but when it's cold and blustery it's better to avoid the high ground and make for somewhere sheltered like the wooded **Bovey Valley**.

Dartmoor is littered with relics of prehistoric times – menhirs, burial chambers, standing stones, hut circles and the rutted remains of ancient field systems. The Bronze Age settlement at **Grimspound** is particularly impressive and gives some sense of how life must have been for the people who eked out a living on this bare hillside. Tread the length of the stone rows at **Merrivale** if you want to steep yourself in the mysteries of the very distant past. The setting is magnificent too, with the jagged outcrop of King's Tor standing sentinel on the skyline. Incidentally, nearby Merrivale Quarry supplied stone for the building of New Scotland Yard.

The infamous Okehampton by-pass lops off a slice of countryside uncomfortably close to the moor, but the ruins of **Okehampton Castle** are still worth a look. In a deliciously sinister legend, Lady Howard makes a nightly journey from the castle in a coach made from the bones of her four dead husbands. Continuing this spectral theme, **Moretonhampstead** is reputed to be the most haunted town on the moor. A headstone in St Andrews Churchyard marks the grave of a French prisoner of war billeted in the town at the time of the Napoleonic Wars. He used to entertain the locals by playing his fiddle under the boughs of the **Dancing Tree**. Sadly, the soldier died the day before his exchange papers arrived and he never saw his homeland again. If you visit the Dancing Tree on a quiet night, you might well catch the wistful strains of the soldier's ghostly fiddle.

[i] **Dartmoor National Park Information Centre**
On the B3112, Postbridge; tel: (01822) 880272; website:
www.dartmoor-npa.gov.uk. Open daily 1000–1700 (Easter–Oct).

[🛏] **The Cherrybrook Hotel £–££** near Two Bridges,
Dartmoor; tel: (01822) 880260 scooped the 1999 award for
the warmest welcome in Dartmoor. The comfy surroundings
and homely cooking make it a pleasure to stop off.
Garden lovers will be delighted with the 14th-century **Tor
Down House £** Belstone, Okehampton; tel: (01837) 840731
with its delightfully unruly array of plants. This is one of only
125 traditional longhouses remaining in Devon.

[🍽] The exquisitely pretty **Castle Inn ££** in Lydford,
Okehampton; tel: (01822) 820242 oozes character with its
low-slung ceilings and flagstone floors. It has a bar (serving
food) a restaurant and rooms, plus an attractive garden.
The Dartmoor Inn £–££ Lydford, Okehampton; tel: (01822)
820221 is a 16th-century coaching inn which has earned a
fearsome reputation for the quality of its food. There's no
accommodation.

PLYMOUTH

The Pilgrim Fathers set sail from Plymouth's Mayflower Steps on their momentous
voyage to the New World. Walter Raleigh, Francis Drake and Charles Darwin also
set off on historic journeys from Plymouth and **Plymouth Sound**, formed from five
separate river mouths, remains one of Europe's finest anchorages. Central Plymouth
is post-war and only the attractive meandering alleys of the waterside region known
as the **Barbican** survived World War II bombing. From the Barbican you can climb
up the steps to the grassy sweep of land known as **The Hoe**, where the **Royal
Citadel** is a superb example of 17th-century military architecture and is still in use
(guided tours on Tues, 1430, late May–Sept). There are great views of the harbour
here, and during Feb–Nov (daily) **boat tours** from Phoenix Wharf take in the harbour and head up river. The **Plymouth Dome** gives a high-tech presentation of the
city's history and admission to **Smeaton's Tower**, the lighthouse, is included. The
National Marine Aquarium (£££, open daily 1000–1800 Apr–Oct; 1000–1700 Nov–
Mar) is Britain's biggest such attraction. Just outside the confines of the city, **Mount
Edgecumbe** is actually over the border in Cornwall and can be reached by catching
the Cremyll ferry from Plymouth Harbour which takes hardly more than 5 minutes.
Although it was rebuilt after bomb damage in World War II and there's not much of
interest inside, the huge landscaped grounds give choice waterside views of
Plymouth and entrance is free. Walks can extend on to **Rame Head** and the quaint
Cornish fishing villages of **Cawsand** and **Kingsand**.

$\boxed{i}$ **Tourist Information Centre** Island House, 9 The
Barbican; tel: (01752) 304849. Open Mon–Sat 0900–1700, Sun
1000–1600 (summer); Mon–Fri 0900–1700, Sat 1000–1600
(winter). Also at Plymouth Discovery Centre, Crabtree; tel:
(01752) 266030; same hours as The Barbican.

🏨 **Berkeley's of St James** ££ 4 St James Place East; tel:
(01752) 221654 offers high quality rooms in a quiet square on
The Hoe.
In the same region is **Citadel House** ££ 55 Citadel Rd, The
Hoe; tel: (01752) 661712, an elegant Victorian property, and
Four Seasons ££ 207 Citadel Road East; tel: (01752) 223591,
a friendly and attractive place to stay.
Athenaeum Lodge ££ 4 Athenaeum St; tel: (01752) 665005
is an attractive Georgian townhouse that once belonged to a
sea captain.
If you want a hotel, there's the **Duke of Cornwall** £££
Millbay Rd; tel: (01752) 275852.

🍴 **Chez Nous** ££–£££ 13 Frankfurt Gate; tel: (01752)
266793 is the only restaurant in the city mentioned in all the
good food guides.
It's worth booking as far ahead as possible if you want a
weekend table at **Tanner's Restaurant** ££, Prysten House,
Finewell St; tel: (01752) 252001. Local produce is a speciality,
with fish bought freshly from the quay daily.
For fish try **Piermaster's** ££ 33 Southside St, Barbican; tel:
(01752) 229345 and for Italian food **Bella Napoli** £–££
41–42 Southside St, Barbican; tel: (01752) 667772.

SIDE TRIPS FROM PLYMOUTH **Buckfast Abbey** is a living Benedictine Monastery in
the Dart Valley. It has a magnificent Abbey Church,
peaceful gardens, a number of interesting shops and a very decent restaurant. Free,
open daily all year; it's around 30 mins drive from Plymouth and you need a car to
get there.

WHERE NEXT?

From Plymouth the logical progression is to cross the Tamar Bridge into Cornwall (see p. 138).
The Cornish coast with its rugged beauty and endearing little fishing ports is well known, but
it can also be very attractive inland, with deep lanes boxed in by high hedges, and smothered in
wild flowers.

EXMOOR NATIONAL PARK

Exmoor, the countryside immortalised by R D Blackmore's novel *Lorna Doone*, straddles the border between Devon and Somerset. Although it does fill up in summer, you get the feeling that it is not nearly as discovered as other parts of the south-west peninsula. It is an enticing mix of cosy-looking cob and thatch villages, rolling green hills, moors and above all a rugged coast with cliffs rising higher than any others on the British mainland and offering excellent scope for walking – particularly along the coast path. Although seaside towns just outside Exmoor, notably Ilfracombe and Minehead, are busy beach resorts, there's nothing brash or commercialised about anywhere in the national park itself.

Lynton, the main coastal town, is pleasantly sleepy. If you are without a car, this is the best base, as there are plenty of B&Bs as well as bus services 309 and 310 from Barnstaple (10 services a day), the nearest rail station. The less frequent bus 300 (daily, 3 a day Jun–Sept; weekends only in other months) continues along the coast road through Porlock and Allerford to Minehead, from where hourly services run to Taunton; there's also the diesel and steam services of the **West Somerset Railway** (rail passes not accepted) which leads from Minehead to Bishop's Lydeard, from where there are buses to join the main rail network at Taunton; through tickets for bus and train from Taunton to Minehead are available. The Devon bus map (free from tourist information centres) covers the Somerset parts of Exmoor too; for more bus information, tel: 0870 608 2608 (website: www.devon.gov.uk/devonbus).

Lynton is connected by cliff railway to its immediate neighbour **Lynmouth**, on the sea some way below (though it hardly takes any longer to walk up). A short walk along the coast west leads into the **Valley of Rocks**, a wonderful coastal moorland punctuated by great crags; you can return over Hollerday Hill for a panorama of the area. To the east, another rewarding path leads along the Lyn River to **Watersmeet**, where two rivers join by a strategically sited café; the most exciting route back is on the path high above the valley to the south.

Inland, **Dunkery Beacon** is one of the great West Country viewpoints, and is an easy stroll up from the road, or a longer walk through woods south from Porlock. Another worthwhile excursion is to **Dunster**, one of Somerset's showpiece towns – a tiny place with a handsome broad main street, and an ancient octagonal yarn market at its centre. Its church has the widest medieval screen in England, and a different carillon for every day of the week. The National Trust owns a working 18th-century watermill here (£, Apr–Oct, closed Fri), as well as Dunster Castle (££, open daily; closed Jan), looming high over the town, which is of various ages, but mostly 17th century and 19th century.

ℹ️ **Tourist Information Centre** Town Hall, Lee Rd, Lynton; tel: (01598) 752225; fax: (01598) 752755. Open daily 0930–1800 (summer); Mon–Sat 1010–1600, closed Sun (winter).

🛏️ **Lynton Youth Hostel** Lynbridge, Lynton, tel: 0870 7705942, fax: 0870 7705943.

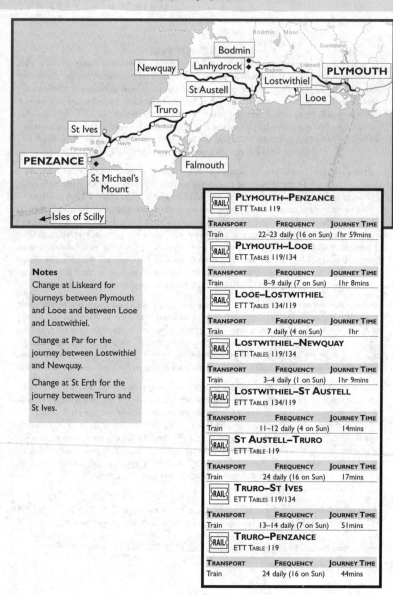

Notes

Change at Liskeard for journeys between Plymouth and Looe and between Looe and Lostwithiel.

Change at Par for the journey between Lostwithiel and Newquay.

Change at St Erth for the journey between Truro and St Ives.

RAIL
PLYMOUTH–PENZANCE
ETT TABLE 119

TRANSPORT	FREQUENCY	JOURNEY TIME
Train	22–23 daily (16 on Sun)	1hr 59mins

RAIL
PLYMOUTH–LOOE
ETT TABLES 119/134

TRANSPORT	FREQUENCY	JOURNEY TIME
Train	8–9 daily (7 on Sun)	1hr 8mins

RAIL
LOOE–LOSTWITHIEL
ETT TABLES 134/119

TRANSPORT	FREQUENCY	JOURNEY TIME
Train	7 daily (4 on Sun)	1hr

RAIL
LOSTWITHIEL–NEWQUAY
ETT TABLES 119/134

TRANSPORT	FREQUENCY	JOURNEY TIME
Train	3–4 daily (1 on Sun)	1hr 9mins

RAIL
LOSTWITHIEL–ST AUSTELL
ETT TABLES 134/119

TRANSPORT	FREQUENCY	JOURNEY TIME
Train	11–12 daily (4 on Sun)	14mins

RAIL
ST AUSTELL–TRURO
ETT TABLE 119

TRANSPORT	FREQUENCY	JOURNEY TIME
Train	24 daily (16 on Sun)	17mins

RAIL
TRURO–ST IVES
ETT TABLES 119/134

TRANSPORT	FREQUENCY	JOURNEY TIME
Train	13–14 daily (7 on Sun)	51mins

RAIL
TRURO–PENZANCE
ETT TABLE 119

TRANSPORT	FREQUENCY	JOURNEY TIME
Train	24 daily (16 on Sun)	44mins

The train leaves Plymouth and Devon to cross the Tamar Bridge, the gateway into Cornwall, at the south-west toe of Britain. While there's plenty of interest on the main line, rather more lies off it, some accessible by rail and much more within reach by local buses. You can detour along branch lines to the seaside resorts of Looe, Falmouth, Newquay and St Ives, while the main line skirts the moonscape china clay workings above St Austell and the former tin-mining towns of Redruth and Camborne.

> 'Cornwall little known, of small significance, remains the tail of England, still aloof and rather splendidly detached from the activity across the Tamar hailed as progress.'
> Daphne du Maurier,
> *Vanishing Cornwall* (1967)

Other parts of north Cornwall have scant bus services, but if you have your own transport you could venture to Launceston, with its commanding hilltop Norman castle, and Tintagel, the spectacularly sited coastal castle ruin linked with King Arthur. The finale is the port of Penzance and the archaeology-strewn moors and dramatic cliffs of Penwith, culminating at Land's End.

PLYMOUTH

See p. 135.

LOOE

In the eastern part of this seaside resort you'll find the characterful old town, with its grid of narrow alleys, fishing harbour and adjacent sandy beach. West Looe is almost entirely modern by contrast. Looe's a nice enough place to hang out for a day or so, but local expeditions are likely to be of more interest. **Boat trips** from the harbour leave for St George's Island and on shark-fishing jaunts.

Westwards along the coast **Polperro** is one of the most appealing of all West Country fishing villages, crammed tightly into a valley, with gulls perching on fishermen's cottages and cats dozing in alleys. To avoid the hordes arriving by car, you might like to follow the coast path from West Looe. It's an easy and delightful walk, taking a couple of hours. To get there or back you can take bus no. 73 to Looe and Liskeard (hourly; three a day on Sun).

> *i* **Tourist Information Centre** The Guildhall, Fore St, East Looe; tel: (01503) 262072. Open daily 1000–1700; closed winter.

Cornwall Tourist Board, Pydar House, Pydar St, Truro, Cornwall; tel: (01872) 274057; website: www.cornwall touristboard.co.uk.

For a free **public transport map** of the whole of Cornwall, showing frequencies of services, contact the Passenger Transport Unit, New County Hall, Truro, Cornwall TR1 3AY; tel: (01872) 322000; enclose £1.50 to cover postage.

🛏 Centrally located B&Bs in the old part of town include:
Sea Breeze Guest House ££ Lower Chapel St; tel: (01503) 26313; e-mail:johnjenkin@sbgh.freeserve.co.uk.
St John's Court ££ East Cliff; tel/fax: (01503) 262301; e-mail: stjohnscourt@looecornwall.freeserve.co.uk.

🍴 Most of the town's restaurants are in the alleys of East Looe, including, as you would expect, some excellent fish eateries. For pub food, the **Olde Salutation** ££ Fore St is good value.

SIDE TRIPS FROM LOOE A preserved standard-gauge steam railway, the **Bodmin and Wenford Railway** (££) runs from Bodmin Parkway along the Fowey valley into Bodmin. There's not a massive amount in Bodmin itself, though the free local museum and its huge parish church with striking Norman font are worth a look. Bus no. 55 (hourly; four a day on Sun) runs from Bodmin Parkway to **Lanhydrock**. This vast 17th-century pile was adapted by the high-living Victorian owners. You get a lot for your money here, with dozens of rooms, and similarly lavish grounds. £££, open Tues–Sun and bank holiday Mon 1100–1730 (end March–early Nov).

LOSTWITHIEL

This amiably dozy place has shrunk in importance from its medieval heyday as a busy port and stannary town (where tin was brought for official stamping). There's a cluster of granite Georgian cottages and a town **museum** £, open Mon–Sat 1030–1230; 1430–1630 (Easter–end Sept) in the former prison in Fore St. Fewer Norman castle ruins look more romantic than **Restormel Castle** £, open daily 1000–1800 (Apr–Sept); 1000–1700 (Oct), a 1¼-mile (2-km) walk along a country lane north of the town. Built to control the crossing of the Fowey River, it became a Parliamentarian stronghold during the Civil War. Miraculously the structure has escaped major stone-robbing and the walls stand to their original height.

ℹ️ **Tourist Information Centre** Community Centre, Liddicoat Rd; tel/fax: (01208) 872207; e-mail: lostwithieltic@ visit.org.uk. Open daily 0930–1700; closed Sun (winter).

PAR

A busy, dusty china clay port, definitely not worth stopping off for. Change here for trains to Newquay.

NEWQUAY

One of Britain's big surfing destinations, Newquay is a lively, big seaside resort which fills to capacity in high summer. Although not charming in the manner of St Ives or Fowey, it is loaded with family-oriented attractions and with excellent sandy beaches in a series of bays beneath the town's neat municipal lawns and flower beds. From the fishing harbour you can walk up past the lifeboat station to Towan Head to look into Fistral Bay and its long beach that is a mecca for surfers.

Newquay Zoo (££, Trenance Park; open daily all year 0930–dusk) is on an ambitious scale, with a big selection of exotic species. You can get joint tickets for the nearby adjacent Waterworld fun pool. The environs of Newquay are a bit disappointing, with postwar sprawl and caravan parks scarring the much of the coast. However, the **beaches** along the stretch to Padstow (an enchanting little fishing town facing the mouth of the Camel estuary) are superb even by Cornish standards.

> *i* **Tourist Information Centre** Municipal Offices, Marcus Hill; tel: (01637) 854020; website: www.newquay.co.uk; e-mail: info@ newquay.co.uk. Open Mon–Sat 0900–1800, Sun 1000–1700 (summer); Mon–Fri 0930–1630, Sat 0930–1200, Sun closed (winter).

> ✈ **Newquay Airport** is served by no-frills airline Ryanair, with departures from London Stansted: out of season you can get amazingly cheap flights. The airport is about 4 miles (6.5 km) north-east of town, served by buses.

> 🛏 No shortage of guesthouses, but book ahead in July and Aug. Cheaper places include:
> **Fistral Surf Lodge** £ Headland Rd; tel: (01637) 879163; website: www.fistralsurflodge.co.uk. Self-catering rooms, lounge, Internet, close to Fistral Beach.
> **St Christopher's Inn** £ 35 Fore St, tel: (020) 7407 1856; www.st-christophers.co.uk. A hostel right in the middle of the action.
> **St Mawes Hotel** ££ 5–7 Springfield Rd; tel: (01637) 872574. Near beach; no single supplement.

> 🍴 **Fort** £ Fore St. Characterful pub (former master mariner's house) overlooking the sea in the town centre with inexpensive snacks and vegetarian food.

ST AUSTELL

Several mega attractions are reached from here, though St Austell itself is a workaday, unenticing town and the headquarters of the Cornish china clay industry.

THE EDEN PROJECT

The Eden Project, near St Austell, is an astonishing recreation of plant habitats housed in three gigantic glasshouses known as 'biomes' intended to stimulate awareness about the relationship between plants, people and resources. There's lots else going on, including workshops, sculpture and live music. £££, open daily 1000–1800 (Mar–Oct); 1000–1630 (Nov–Feb). Bus from St Austell station; tel: (01872) 273 453 for details.

SIDE TRIPS FROM ST AUSTELL

A preserved standard-gauge steam railway, the **Bodmin** South of St Austell and reached by bus no. 24 (half-hourly; hourly on Sun, via Par) is the captivating resort of **Fowey** (pronouced 'Foy'). Its position is everything: stacked up steeply on the hillside at the mouth of the Fowey River, with steep alleys and paths zigzagging down to Fore Street and the water's edge. It's a great place to stay, though it does get very full for the August regatta, and has some superb local walks. Take the ferry to Polruan and walk around the Pont Pill estuary northwards to Bodinnick for the ferry back. Or walk the coast path to Gribbin Head.

Another excursion from St Austell is by bus no. 26/26A (hourly, every day) to **Mevagissey**. It's a likable if self-conscious fishing village full of souvenir shops and postcard racks, but good fun, and with plenty of character around its harbour.

Bus no. 26 (five times a day, not Sun) continues on to Gorran Haven via the **Lost Gardens of Heligan**, ££, open daily 1000–1800; last tickets 1630 (summer); 1000–1700; last tickets 1530 (winter). The gardens were indeed lost from 1914 to 1991, but have been painstakingly restored to their original magnificence in the largest project of its kind in Europe.

i **Tourist Information Centre** Southbourne Rd; tel/fax: (01726) 76333; website: www.cornish-riviera.co.uk; e-mail: tic@cornish-riviera.co.uk. Open daily 0930–1700; closed Sun (winter).

Buckingham House ££ 17 Tregoney Hill, Mevagissey; tel: (01726) 843375; website: www.buckinghamhouse.fsnet.co.uk. Characterful old B&B near the harbour.
For a splurge go to the **Marina Hotel** £££ The Esplanade, Fowey; tel: (01726) 833315; e-mail: marina.hotel@dial.pipex.com. Superb estuary views from the front, and very centrally placed.

Sharksfin Waterside Restaurant ££ The Quay, Mevagissey. Good for locally caught fish, right beside the water's edge.
The Galleon ££ Town Quay, Fowey. Pub serving fresh fish.
Close by is **Food for Thought** ££ The Quay, Fowey, with well-prepared food in pleasant surroundings.

TRURO

Truro is more interesting for its surroundings than the place itself, with good transport links making it a useful base. It doesn't take long to walk around the highlights. The obvious central reference point is the **cathedral**, 30 years in the building until its completion in 1910 – it is a clever use of a cramped site with its three spires soaring elegantly.

Truro's best Georgian street, **Lemon Street**, is an essay in honey coloured Bath stone and a reminder of the heady days of the 18th and 19th centuries when tin and copper mining brought a lot of money into the town. In River St the **Royal Cornwall Museum** reflects on the county's past, with a look at archaeology, smuggling and mining as well as paintings from the Newlyn school. £, open Mon–Sat 1000–1700 (all year).

i **Tourist Information Centre** Municipal Building, Boscawen St; tel: (01872) 274555; fax: (01872) 263031. Open Mon–Fri 0900–1700 (all year); Sat 0930–1300 (summer).

🛏 **Palm Tree House** ££ Parkins Terrace, St Clement Street; tel: (01872) 222733; e-mail: bodybusiness@freeuk.com. A centrally located Victorian house.

🍽 Make for the **Old Ale House** £ Quay St; a pleasantly old-fashioned pub with inexpensive hot food.

FALMOUTH

Cornwall's largest town stands at the mouth of Carrick Roads, a huge estuary filled with small boats. The best views of Falmouth are from the water. You can take the ferry to Truro or St Mawes, or venture on a 2-hour boat trip, ££, tel: (01326) 374241. The major attraction here is **Pendennis Castle**, a spectacular fortification built by Henry VIII to guard against the French and adapted over 400 years. As well as being an outstanding example of military architecture it gives superb views. ££, open daily 1000–1800; 1000–1600/1700 (Oct–Mar).

The **National Maritime Museum Cornwall**, Discovery Quay, provides an interesting picture of Cornwall's maritime heritage, designed to appeal to adults and children alike. ££, open every day 1000–1700; tel: (01326) 313388; www.nmmc.co.uk.

SIDE TRIPS FROM FALMOUTH Reached by ferry, **St Mawes Castle** is the best preserved of all Henry VIII's chain of coastal fortresses. £, open daily 1000–1800 (Apr–Sept); daily 1000–1700 (Oct); Fri–Tues 1000–1300 and 1400–1600 (Nov–Mar).

Bus no. T4/T8 (hourly; four a day on Sun) take you to two dream-like, semi-exotic gardens that adjoin each other just beyond Mawnan Smith. **Glendurgan Garden**, created in the 1820s, slopes towards the Helford River, with banks of rhododendrons, a laurel maze and a lily pond. ££, open Tues–Sat plus bank holiday Mon 1030–1730; last admission 1630 (mid-Feb–early Nov). **Trebah** has towering rhododendrons and palms, with paths zigzagging around Mediterranean blooms and tunnelling through gigantic Brazilian rhubarb. ££, open daily 1030–1700.

Bus no. T4 continues to Helston via Gweek, where the **National Seal Sanctuary**, ££, open daily, cares for orphaned and injured seals before releasing them into the ocean.

> *i* **Tourist Information Centre** 28 Killigrew St; tel: (01326) 312300; e-mail: falmouthtic@yahoo.co.uk. Open Mon–Sat 0900–1730 (summer); Mon–Fri 0900–1730 (winter).

> 🏠 There are plenty of guesthouses, especially in the western part of town around Gyllyngvase Beach, including **Chellowdene** ££ Gyllyngvase Beach; tel: (01326) 314950; May–Oct.

> 🍽 The **Quayside Inn** £ Arwenack is a characterful town-centre pub with a good range of real ales and decent-value bar food.

ST IVES

Oozing with fishing-port charm and endowed with firm, sandy beaches, St Ives is a captivating resort that has attracted many artists for its almost Mediterranean light. Turner, Sickert and Whistler worked here; in the 1930s it drew in such names as Ben Nicholson, Naum Gabo and Barbara Hepworth, and it's still home to many artists' studios today. Though fishing plays second fiddle to tourism, there's an atmospheric web of tiny alleys that makes up the old fishing quarter of Downalong.

Paintings and sculpture from the St Ives school are on display with modern art in the **Tate Gallery St Ives**, Porthmeor Beach, housed in a stunning modern building overlooking the Atlantic. ££, open Tues–Sun plus bank holidays, and Mon (July and Aug). In the Lady Chapel of the parish church is a sculpture by Barbara Hepworth. The **Barbara Hepworth Museum** in the house where she worked, and died in a fire in 1975, is an intensely personal tribute to the great sculptor and her back garden is filled with her art. ££, open same times as Tate Gallery St Ives.

For surfers, Porthmeor Beach is renowned. If you want to sample the **Cornish Coast Path** it gets immediately rewarding as you leave the town on the western side above the cliffs. A great half-day walk is along here to Zennor, from where you can return to St Ives by buses nos 8/8A/15 (6–9 journeys daily; three on Sun). Zennor itself is home to the entertaining **Wayside Folk Museum** with all manner of bygones. £, open daily; closed Nov–Mar and Sat.

i **Tourist Information Centre** The Guildhall, Street-an-Pol; tel: (01736) 796297; website: www.penwith.gov.uk; e-mail: ivtic@penwith.gov.uk. Open Mon–Sat 0900–1800, Sun 1000–1600 (summer); Mon–Fri 0900–1700, Sat 1000–1300 (winter).

🍴 **The Sloop Inn ££** The Wharf is a pleasant, popular pub with local fish and bar food. There are plenty of cafés and inexpensive eateries around Fore St.

🛏 There are plenty of guesthouses in town and in adjoining Carbis Bay. Near the beaches and town centre are:
Chy-Roma ££ 2 Seaview Terrace; tel: (01736) 797539; website: www.connexions.co.uk/chyroma.
The Cobbles ££ 3 Back Rd West; tel: (01736) 798206.

PENZANCE

This busy port and shopping town makes an excellent base for exploring some of the most dramatic coastline in the West Country, plus a range of prehistoric sites and other attractions in the hinterland. There's a reasonable spread of bus services to get you around, notably to Land's End, St Michael's Mount and the Lizard Peninsula, plus ferries to the Isles of Scilly.

Penzance itself has some attractive corners. Particularly notable is Chapel St where there's an absorbing **Maritime Museum** (£, closed Sat), an old town house remodelled into a four-deck 18th-century man-of-war, while nearby is the wildly exuberant Egyptian House of 1835 (not open).

Run by Trinity House, the organisation that maintains Britain's crucial chain of (now fully automated) lighthouses, the **National Lighthouse Centre** paints a full technical and historical picture. £, open Sun–Fri 1030–1630 (Easter–end Oct).

i **Tourist Information Centre** Station Rd; tel: (01736) 362207; website: www.penzance.co.uk. Open Mon–Fri 0900–1700, Sat 0900–1600, Sun 1000–1300 (summer); Mon–Fri 0900–1700, Sat 1000–1300, closed Sun (winter).

🛏 **Penzance Youth Hostel £** Castle Horneck, Alverton; tel: 0870 7705992; e-mail: penzance@yha.org.uk. A Georgian

manor house on edge of town, 1 mile (1.6 km) west of the station. Buses no. 5B, 6B, 6C and 10B from rail station stop within a 10-min walk.
Treventon Guest House ££ Alexandra Place; tel: (01736) 363521 is a Victorian house near the sea.

🍽 Plenty of cafés in the town centre. For local fish, try **Harris's** ££ New St. For pub food, the cosy **Turk's Head** ££ Chapel St is central.

SIDE TRIPS FROM PENZANCE

In Mount's Bay just east of town is **St Michael's Mount**, a castle atop an island, reached by a walk across the causeway at low tide from Marazion (tide times are posted) or by ferry at high tide. Though incredibly crowded in season, it really is worth seeing, from the outside at least. Owned in medieval times by the monks of Mont-St Michel in Normandy, it then had a church on its summit; later replaced with a castle. It was adapted as a residence by the St Aubyn family, the owners since 1659. ££, open Mon–Fri 1030–1730; last admission 1645 (early Apr–early Nov); tel: (01730) 710 265 for tide and ferry info. Bus nos 2/2A running between Penzance and Helston (half-hourly, 1–2 per hour on Sun) make the journey.

> **THE MINACK THEATRE**
> With its backdrop of cliffs and the Atlantic, this open-air theatre at Porthcurno is a stunningly beautiful venue for Shakespeare, modern drama, musicals and opera. The season lasts May–Sept, and if there's no play on you can visit the Exhibition Centre. For tickets, tel: (01736) 810181.

Just west of Penzance, **Newlyn** is Cornwall's main fishing port, not as squalidly picturesque as in the 19th century when artists used to set up their easels here. Take bus no. 5A/5B/6A/6B (every 15 mins; half-hourly on Sun) from Penzance. The **Pilchard Works**, £, open Mon–Fri 1000–1800 (mid-Apr–end Nov), takes looks at Cornwall's fishing heritage and the Newlyn Arts and Crafts movement. Bus nos 6A and 6B (half-hourly; hourly on Sun) carry on to the improbably pretty fishing village of **Mousehole**.

The granite upland of the Land's End peninsula harbours some delectable scenery, though bus services are a bit sporadic. If you have time, spend a couple of days walking the Coast Path from **Penzance** to **St Ives**. Highlights are **Treen** with its huge rocky headland, **Porthcurno** with the cliffside outdoor Minack Theatre and the entire, awe-inspiring stretch from there to **Land's End**, at the end of mainland Britain. Land's End (bus no. 1 from Penzance; hourly, every day) is over-visited and home to theme-park attractions that dilute the atmosphere, but it disappears as you round the corner towards Sennen Cove.

Another superb bit of coast to head for is around St Just (buses no. 10/10A/10B, every 20 mins, hourly on Sun). Here you can stride out to see relics of the old tin mines on the cliffs at **Cape Cornwall** and **Levant Mine** near **Botallack** – where the clifftop engine that pumped water from the mines has been restored to working order by the National Trust.

Inland, Penwith is a primaeval landscape of dry-stone walled fields and rolling moors punctuated by shells of old mine buildings and a remarkable concentration of **prehistoric sites**. Just off the road north-west from Penzance to Morvah are **Lanyon Quoit**, a Neolithic burial chamber, **Chûn Castle**, an impressive Iron Age fort, and **Men-an-Tol**, a mysterious holed stone.

Between Penzance and Zennor, **Chysauster** is the site of a 2000-year-old Iron Age village with the oldest identifiable village street in England. £, open daily 1000–1800 (Apr–Sept); 1000–1700 (Oct). Take bus no. 8A/8B from Penzance and get off at New Mill, from where it is a 1½-mile (2-km) walk (2–5 journeys a day; Mon–Sat only).

The Lizard Peninsula stretches to the Britain's southern extremity, Lizard Point. The peninsula has a rugged western side, with granite cliffs sheltering choice beaches such as **Kynance Cove** and **Mullion Cove**. Beyond the thatched village of Cadgwith, eastern Lizard is by contrast mellow and verdant, with the wooded estuary of the Helford River. Flat inland Lizard is dominated by the futuristic **Goonhilly Earth Station**; the world's largest satellite station. ££, open daily (except Nov–Mar). Buses no. 2 and 2A run frequently from Penzance to Helston, from where frequent daily buses serve the Lizard Peninsula.

THE ISLES OF SCILLY

Lying off Land's End, this archipelago of granite isles makes an idyllic getaway from Penzance if you like gentle walks or cycle rides, bird-watching, wild flowers and pottering around on beaches, though there's little in the way of formal sightseeing. Of the five inhabited islands, **St Mary's** is the largest, and home to an array of prehistoric burial chambers. Its village-sized capital, Hugh Town, is a starting point for cruises to bird and seal colonies.

Car-free **Tresco** is much visited for the subtropical gardens of **Tresco Abbey** (££, open daily 1030–1700, year round) that make the most of the mild Scillies climate. The other islands are **St Martin's**, **St Agnes** and **Bryher**. They are distinctly on the quiet side, although each has its own character.

Ferries serve each island. They take 2 hrs 30 mins from Penzance to St Mary's (end Mar–mid-Nov). Skybus flights depart from Bristol, Exeter, Plymouth, Newquay and Land's End. For information, contact Isles of Scilly Travel, tel: 0845 710 5555; website: www.ios-travel.co.uk.

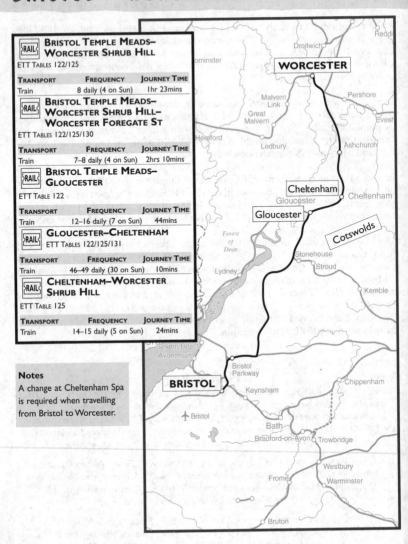

RAIL **BRISTOL TEMPLE MEADS–**
WORCESTER SHRUB HILL

ETT Tables 122/125

Transport	Frequency	Journey Time
Train	8 daily (4 on Sun)	1hr 23mins

RAIL **BRISTOL TEMPLE MEADS–**
WORCESTER SHRUB HILL–
WORCESTER FOREGATE ST

ETT Tables 122/125/130

Transport	Frequency	Journey Time
Train	7–8 daily (4 on Sun)	2hrs 10mins

RAIL **BRISTOL TEMPLE MEADS–**
GLOUCESTER

ETT Table 122

Transport	Frequency	Journey Time
Train	12–16 daily (7 on Sun)	44mins

RAIL **GLOUCESTER–CHELTENHAM**
ETT Tables 122/125/131

Transport	Frequency	Journey Time
Train	46–49 daily (30 on Sun)	10mins

RAIL **CHELTENHAM–WORCESTER**
SHRUB HILL

ETT Table 125

Transport	Frequency	Journey Time
Train	14–15 daily (5 on Sun)	24mins

Notes

A change at Cheltenham Spa
is required when travelling
from Bristol to Worcester.

This route passes through some magnificent English countryside along the Severn Vale, with the Forest of Dean and the Malvern Hills to the west and the Cotswolds rising to the east. It takes in the cathedral city of Gloucester and Worcester, standing on the banks of the River Severn. Cheltenham, the most complete Regency town in Britain, is exceptionally attractive and makes an ideal sightseeing base for this area.

The Cotswolds epitomise the rural English landscape — a picturesque patchwork of farmland divided by dry stone walls and woodland; a mixture of rolling hills and deep wooded valleys. Dotted with villages and market towns built from honey-coloured Cotswold stone, it's a fertile area for tea-shops, country pubs and rose covered cottages. Some of the best walks in Britain pass through this area, including part of the Severn Way — the longest riverside walk in Britain (210 miles/338 km) and the Cotswold Way, a 100-mile (160-km) route from Chipping Campden to Bath.

BRISTOL

See p. 120.

GLOUCESTER

Gloucester was capital of its own shire in the Anglo-Saxon period, flourished as an important religious centre during Norman times and was a thriving commercial hub in the medieval era. The opening of the Gloucester and Sharpness canal in 1827 made it a viable inland port until the late 19th century.

During the war, Gloucester suffered some damage, but escaped fairly lightly considering it was home to the Gloster Aircraft Company, which built Hawker Hurricanes and Typhoons and the first British jets. Today's city is a blend of quaint historical streets and modern roads, some of which owe more to concrete than to creativity. One of the buildings which escaped damage is the 11th-century **cathedral** (free, open Mon–Fri 0730–1800, Sat–Sun 0730–1700). Highlights include the East Window (*c*.1350) with its enormous expanse of medieval glass; the Norman nave and the magnificent 14th-century fan-vaulted cloister. It's also one of the locations for the film *Harry Potter and the Philosopher's Stone*. Guided tours are available.

Nearby is **The House of the Tailor of Gloucester**, £ adults, children free, 9 College Court, open 1000–1700 (Apr–Oct), 1000–1600 (Nov–Mar). It is the very house sketched by Beatrix Potter in 1897 for her story of the helpful mice. The downstairs is a treasure trove of merchandise covered in her trademark mice, hedgehogs and rabbits. Upstairs is a tiny museum.

Five minutes walk south-west of the cathedral, Gloucester's historic docks house several museums in restored Victorian warehouses. Right by the docks is the **National Waterways Museum**, (££, open daily 1000–1700). It contains interesting displays of Britain's canal network and interactive screens for everything from working a lock to decorating your own barge. The museum also runs boat trips through the docks, taking 45 minutes.

You can also join a free guided tour of the ancient **City East Gate** from the City Museum and Art Gallery, on Sat (1015, 1115, 1515, 1615), May–Sept.

From the dockside by the National Waterways Museum, you can take a 45-min **boat trip** (££) down the canal on the *Queen Boadicea*, a Dunkirk 'little ship' built in 1936. Trips depart several times a day at weekends only before Easter, then daily until Oct; tel: (01452) 318 054. Throughout the summer, guided walks of the city run from the tourist information centre in Southgate St.

i **Tourist Information Centre** 28 Southgate St; tel: (01452) 421188/396572; e-mail: tourism@gloscity.gov.uk. Open Mon–Sat 1000–1700.

🛏 There's a wide range of accommodation in Gloucester, which is easily booked on arrival except during festivals (see box) and the Cheltenham Gold Cup in March. Ask the tourist information centre for the *Stay on a Farm* leaflet if you fancy a B&B with countryside views.
Briarfields £ Gloucester Rd; tel: (01242) 235324 (1 mile from junction 11 on M5). Five-acre caravan and camping site, with restaurant, bar and 18-room motel on site. Open all year.
Lulworth Guest House ££ 12 Midland Rd; tel: (01452) 521 881. Comfortable guest house half a mile from the city centre. Family rooms available.
Springfields Farm £–££ Little Witcombe; tel: (01452) 863 532. A pretty farmhouse 5 miles (8 km) east of the city centre with single, double and family rooms.

🍽 Don't leave without trying the local specialities – Gloucester sausage, Double Gloucester cheese and Severn elvers.
Westgate St offers a choice of restaurants, and there are several historic inns serving good pub grub such as the 16th-century **Golden Cross** £ Southgate St.
On Long Smith St, **Bearland Wine Bar** (££–£££) offers a trendy Mediterranean menu of the 'salsa, pan-fried, tartlet' variety. Upstairs is a lovely fern-filled conservatory; downstairs a vaulted, intimate restaurant.

SIDE TRIP FROM GLOUCESTER **Wildfowl and Wetlands Trust**, ££, Slimbridge. Open 0930–1700 (summer) 0930–1600 (winter). There is only a Sunday bus service (no. 91A) from Gloucester; otherwise take a train to Dursley and Cam (3 miles/5 km from Slimbridge) and then a taxi. A peaceful haven by the Severn River, its the largest collection of ducks, geese and swans in the world, including the near-extinct Hawaiian goose.

CHELTENHAM

Although the spa water was discovered as far back as 1716, Cheltenham only became fashionable after King George III visited in 1788. Writers – Jane Austen and Charles Dickens – and aristocrats – the Duke of Wellington and Princess Victoria (before she was queen) – were among the many elite figures to patronise the town. Today, Cheltenham retains a genteel, upper class air; a fitting location for the private girl's school, Cheltenham Ladies' College, established in 1853.

Right from the outskirts of the town, it's evident that this is no ordinary place. Instead of the usual dreary suburbs, the roads into Cheltenham are lined with Regency town houses, with high windows and intricate ironwork balconies. Most of the town centre is a conservation area, with several beautiful parks and an abundance of flowers. As the majority of attractions are within walking distance, the best way to enjoy the town is simply by strolling the streets.

FESTIVE TOWN

A wide range of festivals takes place in Cheltenham throughout the year. There's a folk festival in February, followed by an international jazz festival in May and an international festival of music and fringe in July. In October there's a two-week festival of literature.

In summertime, Cheltenham is a riot of colour, winning many awards in the annual 'Britain in Bloom' competitions. **Pittville Park** is carpeted with crocuses in the spring. Set around a lake, with a children's play area and mini-aviary, it's overlooked by the magnificent **Pump Room**. The building is open to the public (free, open Wed–Mon 1100–1600), but apart from the ornate main hall where you can still taste the spa water, the other rooms are pretty bare. Other parks worth visiting are **Montpellier Gardens**, with its tree-lined broadwalk, and the **Imperial Gardens** with a stunning floral display each year and a lovely beer garden in summer. There's a great play area for children at **Sandford Park**, and a summer open-air lido (open daily May–Oct 1100–1930).

The **Cheltenham Art Gallery and Museum** in Clarence St (free, open Mon–Sat 1000–1720, Sun 1400–1620) contains a good arts and crafts gallery and displays about Cheltenham's history.

For a change of scene, head to the **Cheltenham Racecourse**, ££–£££, at Prestbury Park; tel: (01242) 513 014. The season runs October to April, with 15 days of racing. The most prestigious event is the three-day National Hunt Festival featuring the Cheltenham Gold Cup in March.

> i **Tourist Information Centre** 77 Promenade; tel: (01242) 522878; website: www.cheltenham.gov.uk; e-mail: tic@cheltenham.gov.uk. Open Mon–Sat 0930–1700, Sun 0930–1300 (summer); Mon–Sat 0930–1700, Sun closed (winter).

Contact Cheltenham tourist information centre for details of **scenic coach tours** (June–Sept), to the North Cotswolds, South Cotswolds, Stratford-upon-Avon, Bath, the Forest of Dean and the Wye Valley, Worcester and the Malvern Hills.

🛏 Cheltenham tourist information centre offers a free accommodation booking service; tel: (01242) 517 110.
Cheltenham YMCA £ 6 Vittoria Walk; tel: (01242) 524 024. Near the town centre, this hostel and fitness centre has 56 single rooms.
Freedom Camping and RV Park £ Bamfurlong Lane; tel: (01452) 712 705; e-mail: info@freedom-motorhomes.co.uk; website: www.freedom-motorhomes.co.uk. Two miles (3 km) west of Cheltenham, this modern 3-acre (1.2 ha) site for tents and caravans is open all year.
Hunters Lodge £–££ Cheltenham Racecourse, Prestbury Park; tel: (01242) 513 345. In the grounds of Cheltenham Racecourse, a friendly hotel ideal for families.

🍴 There's an enormous choice of places to eat. Trendy wine bar style eateries abound in the Montpellier area, as well as a range of patisseries (not cafés, darling). The area around Suffolk Rd brims with small individual restaurants and bistros, whilst Bath Rd is home to a myriad of Indian restaurants.
Choirs ££–£££ 5–6 Well Walk; tel: (01242) 235578. Tiny restaurant in a beautiful Georgian building, specialising in fish and seafood. Great value. Booking advisable.
The Daffodil ££–£££ 18-20 Suffolk Parade. Worth a visit as much for the building, a converted art deco cinema, as for the English food with a Mediterranean influence. You can have a drink in the Circle Bar upstairs whilst the chefs work their magic 'on stage'.
Olives ££ 14 Montpellier Arcade. A brilliant starting point for a picnic in the park … as the name suggests, olives with everything – as well as fancy cheeses and speciality bread.
Le Petit Blanc Brasserie £££ The Promenade; tel: (01242) 266 800. Authentic French cuisine. The à la carte menu can be pricey but there is a *Blanc Vite* menu (fresh fast food) and reasonably priced set menus. Very child-friendly.
Storyteller £ 11 North Place. Set in a bright conservatory, the menu is modern Mediterranean-cum-Asian. Mellow music, comfy settees and a warm welcome for kids.

Shopping is an integral part of the Cheltenham experience. The Promenade has swish designer labels, while the Montpellier area offers specialist food outlets, secondhand bookshops and antique shops. Car boot sales and antiques fairs regularly take place at Cheltenham's Racecourse on Sundays.

WORCESTER

Worcester's town centre is modern, interspersed with attractive historical buildings. These include the 18th-century **Guildhall** on the High St (free, open Mon–Sat 0830–1630) and the timber-framed **Greyfriars** built in 1480. £, Friar St, open Wed–Thur and bank holidays 1400–1700 (Apr–Oct).

Most attractions are within walking distance of the town centre and the eye is naturally drawn to the **Cathedral** (open daily 0730–1830) with its 170-ft (52-m) 14th-century tower, standing proudly by the river Severn. Nearby in Severn St are Victorian buildings housing the porcelain industry, founded in the city in 1751. The **Museum of Worcester Porcelain** (£, open Mon–Sat 0900–1700, Sun 1100–1700) traces the history of the china from its beginnings to the present day and you can also watch artists at work in the Manufactory, with the chance to paint your own plate (extra cost). Hour-long guided tours of the working factory (££, Mon–Fri; booking recommended; no children under 11; no tours during factory shutdowns; tel: (01905) 21247).

History and military buffs will enjoy the **Commandery Civil War Centre**, Sidbury, (££, open Mon–Sat 1000–1700, Sun 1330–1700) which tells the story of England's Civil War in the 17th-century. The city's location offers great riverside walks along the banks of the River Severn – the tourist information centre has leaflets and books, and throughout the summer 45-min **boat trips** run from the south quay near the Cathedral (£).

Side Trips From Worcester

Ten miles (16 km) north-west of Worcester on the A443 (take the bus for Tenbury Wells) is **Witley Court**, the spectacular ruin of a vast 19th-century Italianate mansion. The shell has an eerie atmosphere, redolent of high society balls and extravagant living. The grounds offer woodland trails, a delightful sculpture park and stunning fountains. ££, open daily 1000–1800 (Apr–Sept) 1000–1700 (Oct), Wed–Sun 1000–1600 (Nov–Mar).

Three miles (5 km) west along the A44 is the country cottage housing **Elgar's Birthplace Museum**, Crown East Lane, Lower Broadheath, packed with personal possessions and an intriguing insight into the composer's life. £, open daily, 1100–1700, closed four weeks in winter; tel: (01905) 333224.

i **Tourist Information Centre** The Guildhall, High St; tel: (01905) 726311; website: www.cityofworcester.gov.uk; e-mail: mphillips@cityofworcester.gov.uk. Open all year Mon–Sat 0930–1700, closed Sun.

The tourist information centre can help with booking accommodation – there is a good choice of B&Bs and guest houses.

King Charles II Restaurant ££ 29 New St, serves continental food in an atmospheric listed building.
The 15th-century **Cardinal's Hat** £–££ 31 Friar St, is Worcester's oldest pub, serving real ale and good food.

Hostel/Campsites

The nearest youth hostel to Worcester is **Malvern Hills**, 18 Peachfield Rd, Malvern Wells; tel: 0870 770 5948; e-mail: malvern@yha.org.uk.

The closest campsites to Worcester are: **Millhouse** £ Hawford, 3 miles (4.8 km) north; tel: (01905) 451 283, open Apr–Oct. There's a smaller site at **Lenchford Meadow Park** £ Shrawley, 7 miles (11.3 km) north-west; tel: (01905) 620 246, open Mar–Nov.

Browns Restaurant 24 Quay St; tel: (01905) 26263. Popular riverside restaurant. Set menu £38.

Little Venice ££ 1 St Nicholas St offers a wide range of pizza and pasta dishes, with a good value set menu at lunchtime (except Sat).

Ostlers at No. 1 ££–£££ 1 Severn Terr; tel: (01905) 612300. Excellent food in a romantic atmosphere.

SIDE TRIP TO THE COTSWOLDS

The Cotswolds is a geological area defined by a gorgeous honey-coloured limestone that spreads south-west to north-east, covering an area roughly bounded by Bath and Cirencester to the south, Woodstock (and arguably Oxford) to the east, Chipping Campden to the north and Cheltenham and Stroud to the west. The scenery is mild and manicured rather than spectacular, although the steep western escarpment has some moments of drama: for walkers the Cotswold Way (103 miles/166 km), from Chipping Campden to Bath, takes in the best of the local landscapes. But it is the man-made features that are memorable: timeless village greens, manor houses behind high boundary walls, landscaped country estates, cottage gardens, rolling fields enclosed by dry-stone walls, and handsome market towns. The stone-built Cotswold house or cottage is the area's unmistakable hallmark.

The easiest way of exploring is by car (it is also excellent cycling terrain, with plenty of quiet back roads), as public transport is a bit limited. Railways skirt the Cotswolds, but do not penetrate far. Useful **rail stations** are Moreton-in-Marsh (Oxford–Worcester line), Cheltenham Spa (Birmingham–Bristol line) and Kemble (Cheltenham–Swindon line). From these there are some regular **buses** (the Gloucestershire bus map, available free from tourist information centres, shows routes and frequencies for most of the Cotswolds). From Moreton-in-Marsh it's a short ride to Stow-on-the-Wold, Chipping Campden and Bourton-on-the-Water, and you can carry on to Cirencester; from Cheltenham buses go via Cleeve Hill to Winchcombe, east to Bourton-on-the-Water and south to Painswick and Cirencester; Kemble also has buses to Cirencester.

In the north, **Chipping Campden** is one of the showcase small towns, with its wide main street and old market hall, and Perpendicular-style 15th-century church built in the prosperous heyday of the local wool trade. Stow-on-the-Wold has a youth hostel (tel: 0870 7706050; e-mail: stow@yha.org.uk) in the market square of the pleasant old town; close by, **Bourton-on-the-Water** may be too self-conscious and over-run for some tastes, but is undeniably pretty, with its brook running along the central street; there are a host of attractions to visit, including the Cotswold Motor Museum and Toy Collection (£; closed Nov–Apr). A pleasant walk can be had by following paths to the nearby villages of **Upper Slaughter** and **Lower Slaughter**, similarly photogenic as Bourton-on-the-Water but nothing like as touristy.

Cirencester was founded by the Romans as Corinium, and though there's little physical trace of the original town remaining, the Roman presence is admirably documented in the Corinium Museum (£; closed until spring 2004 for refurbishment; tel: (01285) 655611). It's a pleasant town with a very grand church; the adjacent central square hosts a market on Mon and Fri. Beyond Cecily Hill, the town's most beautiful street, you can stroll for free in the vast grounds of Cirencester Park; nearby, in the town, is an open-air swimming pool (£, May–Sept).

Painswick has a surreal churchyard dotted with yew topiary (99 yews in all) and a remarkable array of tombs. The houses have a more silvery look compared with the golden hues further north. Nearby are the restored 18th-century **Painswick Rococo Gardens** (££, daily May–Sept, Wed–Sun rest of year; closed Dec).

North of Cheltenham, **Cleeve Hill** is a hillside hamlet beneath the hill itself – the highest point in the Cotswolds, and a favourite place for horse-riding and kite-flying. It's actually no great height, but does have a colossal view over towards the Welsh border. Further north, **Winchcombe** is another appealing town, and abuts the estate of **Sudeley Castle**, birthplace of Katherine Parr (the sixth wife of Henry VIII, who survived him), The building is a blend of medieval and 19th century, with paintings by Turner and Van Dyck, and there are ten separate gardens in the grounds (£££, Apr–Oct; gardens open Mar).

If you have your own transport, further recommended excursions include **Chedworth Roman Villa**, with its fine mosaics and antiquated Victorian museum (deliberately kept that way by the National Trust; ££, closed Mon and all mid Nov–end Feb); **Bibury** (another perfect stone-built village); and **Snowshill Manor** (a highly eccentric National Trust-owned house crammed full of all sorts of unrelated bits and pieces – including old bicycles, clocks and Samurai armour; ££; garden and restaurant closed Mon and Tues and all Nov–Mar, house closed until 2005 for restoration).

> *i* There is no single tourist office covering the whole of the Cotswolds but the website www.cotswold.gov.uk covers accommodation and sights. For the south Cotswolds: Cirencester, tel: (01285) 654180; for the north: Stow-on-the-Wold, tel: (01451) 831082.

WHERE NEXT?

From Worcester it is a short journey west to Hereford (17–18 trains daily, 9 on Sun; journey time about 45 mins) to join the Bristol–Chester route (see pp. 168–175). On the way the train passes through the Victorian spa and hill resort of Great Malvern and the quaint old market town of Ledbury (see p. 171).

LONDON – GLASGOW: THE WEST COAST ROUTE

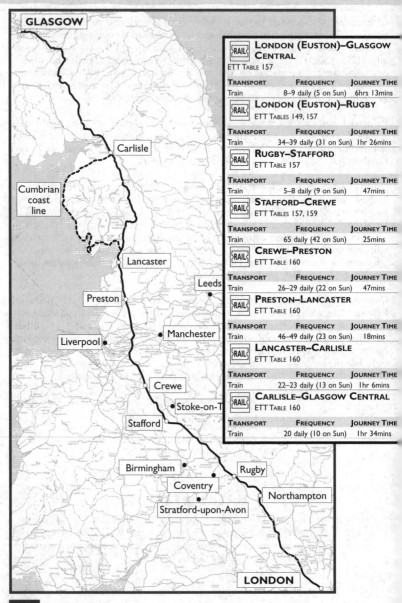

GLASGOW

Carlisle

Cumbrian coast line

Lancaster

Leeds

Preston

Manchester

Liverpool

Crewe

Stoke-on-T

Stafford

Birmingham

Coventry

Rugby

Northampton

Stratford-upon-Avon

LONDON

🚆RAIL	**LONDON (EUSTON)–GLASGOW CENTRAL**		
ETT TABLE 157			
TRANSPORT	**FREQUENCY**		**JOURNEY TIME**
Train	8–9 daily (5 on Sun)		6hrs 13mins

🚆RAIL	**LONDON (EUSTON)–RUGBY**		
ETT TABLES 149, 157			
TRANSPORT	**FREQUENCY**		**JOURNEY TIME**
Train	34–39 daily (31 on Sun)		1hr 26mins

🚆RAIL	**RUGBY–STAFFORD**		
ETT TABLE 157			
TRANSPORT	**FREQUENCY**		**JOURNEY TIME**
Train	5–8 daily (9 on Sun)		47mins

🚆RAIL	**STAFFORD–CREWE**		
ETT TABLES 157, 159			
TRANSPORT	**FREQUENCY**		**JOURNEY TIME**
Train	65 daily (42 on Sun)		25mins

🚆RAIL	**CREWE–PRESTON**		
ETT TABLE 160			
TRANSPORT	**FREQUENCY**		**JOURNEY TIME**
Train	26–29 daily (22 on Sun)		47mins

🚆RAIL	**PRESTON–LANCASTER**		
ETT TABLE 160			
TRANSPORT	**FREQUENCY**		**JOURNEY TIME**
Train	46–49 daily (23 on Sun)		18mins

🚆RAIL	**LANCASTER–CARLISLE**		
ETT TABLE 160			
TRANSPORT	**FREQUENCY**		**JOURNEY TIME**
Train	22–23 daily (13 on Sun)		1hr 6mins

🚆RAIL	**CARLISLE–GLASGOW CENTRAL**		
ETT TABLE 160			
TRANSPORT	**FREQUENCY**		**JOURNEY TIME**
Train	20 daily (10 on Sun)		1hr 34mins

LONDON – GLASGOW: THE WEST COAST ROUTE

Trains on the west coast route from London to Glasgow take around 5½ hours to cover 402 miles (646 km). The route skirts the main places of interest, but you do get to see the transition from the Home Counties (the area around London) to the industrial heartlands of the Midlands (around Birmingham) and north (around Manchester). The scenery improves north of Lancaster, and soon the line runs through the Howgill Fells, a spectacular upland area flanking the east side of the Lake District.

Leave the main route at **Rugby** for a detour into **Birmingham** (see pp. 158–162), England's second city – not exactly a beauty but with some worthwhile sights – as well as visits to war-ravaged Coventry, with its post-war cathedral, and **Stratford-upon-Avon** and **Warwick**. All these places are reachable by train and are described in the Birmingham chapter. Additionally you can leave the main line at **Stafford** for a visit to the potteries town of **Stoke-on-Trent** (see pp. 165–167), where you don't need to be an *aficionado* of ceramics to enjoy a visit to the outstanding Gladstone Pottery Museum.

The main line steers a course through industrial Warrington and Wigan, though if you want to see some of the great northern cities it's worth detouring to **Liverpool** (see pp. 212–219) and **Manchester** (see pp. 206–211). At **Preston** you can divert east (while the main line carries on north) on to trains to **Leeds** (see pp. 240–242) via Bradford. This line gives wonderful views of **Calderdale**, a long, scenic Pennine valley with stone-built mill towns such as Hebden Bridge and Halifax. From Leeds you can rejoin the main London–Glasgow line by taking the famous train journey via **Settle**, over the high, bleak hills of the Pennines and along the Eden valley to Carlisle: this is one of the most scenic rail journeys on the national network.

Another highly recommended diversion is to change at Lancaster onto the Cumbrian Coast line, that crosses over a series of low viaducts around the treacherous quicksands of vast Morecambe Bay to Ulverston: it's an amazing feat of engineering. The stations at Arnside and Grange-over-Sands both lie close to small hills that are easily climbed but give superb panoramas. Beyond Barrow the line heads along the coast and around the west side of the **Lake District**, passing Ravenglass, where you can change onto the narrow-gauge private Ravenglass & Eskdale Railway that will take you into Eskdale, in the Lake District proper. The Cumbrian Coast line meanwhile carries on through Whitehaven (a characterful port developed in the 17th–19th centuries) to rejoin the main line at the cathedral city of **Carlisle** (see pp. 222–223).

From **Glasgow**, one of Britain's liveliest and most fashionable cities (see pp. 311–317), there is scope to explore the scenery of the Highlands by riding the train to Mallaig.

BIRMINGHAM

England's second city sprawls inelegantly across the industrial Midlands. It merges imperceptibly with Wolverhampton in the 'Black Country' to the west, and is flanked by war-blitzed Coventry to the east. For a long time 'Brum', as it's nick-named, was considered unglamorous. The nightmare of roads beneath the M6 – 'Spaghetti Junction' – and brutalist 1960s buildings exemplified the worst of postwar planning. Yet suddenly things have got better: civic pride has returned. The streets are full of modern sculptures and the web of canals has witnessed a renaissance with new walkways, shoppng and public areas, and even tourists.

Birmingham makes an excellent introduction to Britain's rich industrial legacy, with some good museums in the city. Dudley and Stoke are feasible as day trips and Stratford and Warwick are within close range. Canals are prolific – eight of them in the city boundaries – their city centre towpaths provide some of the best walks.

GETTING THERE

More or less hidden inside a large shopping mall in the very centre of the city, Birmingham New Street station (main entrance in Station St) stands at the hub of Britain's cross-country rail network. As well as fast and stopping trains to and from London Euston via Coventry, this very busy station also handles frequent long-distance services to all parts of the country. Also in the city centre, the smaller Snow Hill and Moor Street stations have stopping and semi-fast services to and from London Marylebone via Warwick.

There are express coach services to Birmingham from London, Heathrow and Gatwick airports and many UK cities. The coach station is at Digbeth, close to the city centre.

INFORMATION

Visitor Information Centre 130 Colmore Rd; tel: (0121) 693 6300;
e-mail: piazza@bmp.org.uk. Open daily 0930–1800 (1000–1600 Sun in winter).

Convention & Visitor Bureau 2 City Arcade; tel: (0121) 643 2514; e-mail: ticketshop@ bmp.org.uk. Open Mon–Sat 0930–1730, closed Sun. Website for both: www.birmingham.org.uk.

ACCOMMODATION

The suburbs of Edgbaston and Harborne, south-west of the centre, have numerous B&Bs, including **Cook House** ££ 425 Hagley Rd, Edgbaston; tel: (0121) 429 1916; **Woodville House** ££ 39 Portland Rd, Edgbaston; tel: (0121) 454 0274; and Grasmere ££ 37 Serpentine Rd, Harborne; tel: (0121) 427 4546.

Hostels: Men and women can stay at either **YMCAs** or **YWCAs** £ with single, double and treble rooms.
YMCAs: 300 Reservoir Rd, Erdington; tel: (0121) 373 1937 (ages 18–30; bus 102/104 from Priory Queensway to Six Ways Island). 200 Bunbury Rd; Northfield; tel: (0121) 475 6218 (ages 18 – 30; bus 61/62/63 from Rotunda; get off at Church Rd and take bus no. 18 to Bunbury Rd).
YWCA 27 Norfolk Rd, Edgbaston; tel: (0121) 454 8134 (over 18s only; bus no. 9 from Colmore Row to Norfolk Rd).

FOOD AND DRINK

The Ladypool Rd vicinity features a famous concentration (the country's largest) of some 50 **Kashmiri/Pakistani Balti restaurants** (£–££). You can usually get in without booking, although Friday and Saturday nights tend to be busy.

There's a compact Chinatown near the markets on the south side of the city centre, with numerous **Chinese** eateries £.
Two city centre museums with free admission are particularly good for lunch. The **Ikon Gallery** £ has a very stylish café serving Spanish food, including tapas, while the **City Museum and Art Gallery's tea room** £ is a wonderful high-ceilinged hall with good-value hot food such as carrot and coriander soup, hot pot and fruit crumble.
The **Fiddle and Bone** £–££ 4 Sheepcote St is a large musical instrument theme pub by the canal, handy for Symphony Hall.

HIGHLIGHTS

CITY CENTRE Victoria Square and Centenary Square constitute the obvious central point, with the Italianate, domed, mosaic-embellished Council House and Grecian-style former **Town Hall**, where Mendelssohn's *Elijah* was first

TOURS

Themed **walks** are run year round by the Birmingham Convention and Visitor Bureau, 130 Colmore Row, Victoria Sq.; tel: (0121) 693 6300. Guide Friday operate hop-on hop-off open-top **bus tours**, ££, stopping at many of the city's top attractions, and there are **canal boat tours** from Gas Street Basin.

performed. In Chamberlain Square near the fountain containing a statue of a female (nicknamed 'the floozie in the jacuzzi') you'll find the **Museum and Art Gallery**. Free (admission for Gas Hall exhibitions; variable rates); open Mon–Thurs and Sat 1000–1700, Fri 1030–1700, Sun 1230–1700. This exuberant Victorian building is famed for its stunning collection of some of the world's best-known Pre-Raphaelite paintings (Millais' *The Blind Girl* and Ford Madox Ford's *Last of England* among them), which alone justify a visit to the city. Other collections include glass and ceramics, European old masters, natural history, archaeology and local history. The museum encompasses the Gas Hall, a gallery with changing exhibitions, and the Water Hall modern art gallery.

In a revamped canalside setting, the glass-roofed blue-scaffold of the **International Convention Centre** houses **Symphony Hall**, home of the City of Birmingham Symphony Orchestra. It is usually possible to peep in through the open doors during the day to glimpse one of the most acoustically advanced concert halls in the world. Nearby, the **Ikon Gallery**, free, 1 Oozells Square, Brindleyplace (open Tues–Sun 1100–1800; closed Mondays except bank holidays) is a stylish contemporary art venue, with a changing programme of exhibitions and events.

One earlier legacy is the baroque 18th-century **cathedral** in Colmore Row, endowed with stained glass by the Pre-Raphaelite artist Burne-Jones. North of the centre, and a pleasant canalside walk, the **Jewellery Quarter** is a grid of streets containing hundreds of specialist jewellery workshops. The whole area narrowly escaped complete redevelopment a few decades ago. One of the workshops, **Smith and Pepper**, which made bangles from 1899 to 1981, is now the **Museum of the Jewellery Quarter** (£, 75–79 Vyse St, Hockley; open Mon–Fri 1000–1600; Sat 1100–1700). Skilled jewellers show you round, giving an entertaining spiel of social history, technical know-how and gossip. They explain how the gold dust that settled on the floor was carefully swept up and the resulting 'sweep' was a big perk for the bosses, and how the tea lady brewed up in a room containing a box of cyanide. The miserly owners clearly modernised nothing, hence the survival of this time-warp of a factory.

OUT OF THE CENTRE Reached by bus nos 74/78/79 from the city centre, **Soho House** (£, Soho Ave, Handsworth; open Tues–Sat 1000–1700, Sun 1200–1700; closed Mon except bank holidays) is

the place to learn about Birmingham's industrial beginnings. Within this pleasant Georgian house lived industrial pioneer Matthew Boulton from 1766 to 1809, close to his now vanished 'manufactory' where he developed one of the first successful attempts at mass production. Here he hosted the Lunar Society and met with some of the great important scientists, engineers and thinkers of the day. The house boasted innovations far ahead of its time, including a WC, a steam-heated bath and a central heating system.

Incongruous in the midst of concrete jungle suburbia and within sight of Spaghetti Junction is the former country mansion of **Aston Hall** (free, Trinity Rd, Aston; open daily 1400–1700 end Mar–end Oct; train to Witton). It gives its name to the famous Aston Villa Football Club, based at nearby Villa Park. Erected 1618–35, it is an outstanding and ostentatious example of Jacobean style, with sumptuous plasterwork, a huge Long Gallery, a grand carved oak staircase, and rooms with period furnishings and art.

> **'THE FATHER OF ENGLISH POTTERS'**
>
> The great pottery manufacturer **Josiah Wedgwood** (1730–95) was a philanthropist and a champion of the movement to abolish slavery. He also attended meetings with other men of science at Soho House (see pp. 160–161). There were evidently brains in the family: his grandson was Charles Darwin, who formulated the theory of evolution.

A short train ride to University station in the suburb of Edgbaston takes you to the University of Birmingham, and its outstanding **Barber Institute of Fine Arts** (free, open Mon–Sat 1000–1700, Sun 1400–1700). Established in 1932 by Lady Barber 'for the encouragement of art and music' it's an unrushed, quiet gallery, giving an impressive survey of Western art, including works by Bellini, Martini, Claude, Turner, Monet and Magritte. There's also a programme of concerts, lectures and events.

For a verdant contrast to the largely treeless city centre, **Birmingham Botanical Gardens** is the prime plant collection in the Midlands, with glasshouses full of exotica and themed gardens, plus brass band concerts on Sundays in summer. ££, Westbourne Rd, Edgbaston; open 0900–1900, or dusk; Sun open 1000. Buses 10/10A/20/21/21A/22/23/29/103 from city centre).

Cadbury World (££, Linden Rd; tel: (0121) 451 4159 for opening days, times and admission prices and to reserve admission) is located at Bournville (near Bournville station), where the philanthropic Victorian founder of the celebrated chocolate factory established a cottagey garden village to house his workers. Cadbury World itself is a nicely presented journey into all things chocolate, with chocolate-making demonstrations, a tempting shop and an exhibition on the social history of the Cadbury empire. Be aware that it's massively popular (booking advised) and it's not a factory tour – there's no admittance to the nearby modern Cadbury's factory itself.

Another great place to spend the whole day is the **Black Country Living Museum** (££, Tipton Rd, Dudley; open daily 1000–1700 Mar–Oct; Wed–Sun 1000–1600

BIRMINGHAM

Nov–Feb. Bus no. 126 from Birmingham, or train to Tipton, then bus or walk 1 mile/1.6 km). It brings to life the past lifestyles of the industrial Black Country with real flair. There's masses going on here, including a period canalside village peopled by costumed actors, an old-style fairground, a mine, a Victorian school, tram and charabanc rides and a 1930s fish and chip shop.

NIGHTLIFE AND EVENTS

Major venues include **Ronnie Scott's**, Broad St (mostly jazz), **The Glee Club**, Arcadian Centre, Hurst St (comedy) and the **National Indoor Arena** and **NEC Arena** (major events including rock concerts). Leading theatre venues include the **Birmingham Repertory Theatre**, Broad St. If you're into classical music, try to get tickets for the prestigious City of Birmingham Symphony Orchestra, who play at **Symphony Hall**, a wonderful modern building. The **Hippodrome** is home of the Birmingham Royal Ballet.

There's no shortage of **cinemas** in the city centre. Near the M6, Warner Village Megaplex at StarCity, 100 Watson Rd, Nechells, tel: (0121) 326 0246, rates among the world's largest, with 30 screens, seating more than 6000 people.

The leading **soccer** team is Aston Villa, who play at Villa Park, north of the city centre. Other local teams are Birmingham City, West Bromwich Albion and Walsall; Coventry City, Wolverhampton Wanderers and Kidderminster Harriers are nearby. Warwickshire play **cricket** at the Edgbaston ground, which also stages test (international) matches, for which tickets are expensive and sell out well in advance.

Pick up a free copy of 'What's On' from the tourist office, for all city listings. **Birmingham Ticket Shop and Tourist Information**, 2 City Arcade, tel: (0121) 605 7000 can get you tickets for most theatres and concerts.

SIDE TRIP TO WARWICK

A recommended stopover on the way to Stratford-upon-Avon, Warwick is a worthy destination in its own right. Trains run hourly from Birmingham Snow Hill taking around 60 mins. In 1694 a massive fire destroyed most of the town, but spared a couple of medieval gateways. There is the impressive collegiate **Church of St Mary** with its fan-vaulted chapel and Norman crypt, and the spectacularly leaning half-timbered pile in High St known as **Lord Leycester's Hospital**. The hospital was a hospice founded in 1571 for retired soldiers; it houses a chapel, a galleried courtyard, a pretty garden and a regimental museum (£, open Tues–Sun, bank holiday Mon 1000–1700, 1600 in winter). Most of the town was rebuilt with a pleasing, early 18th-century uniformity and is a delight to wander around. The **Warwickshire County Museum** has a good local collection (free, Market Place, open Mon–Sat 1000–1730; plus Sun May–Sept 1100–1700).

Above all Warwick is famed for **Warwick Castle**, £££, open daily 1000–1800 (Apr–Sept); 1000–1700 (Nov–Mar). Founded in 1068 and much rebuilt, it was then adapted into a stately home in the 19th century. It looks at its most magnificent from the River Avon. You might content yourself with this free waterside view, as inside it can be a bit too crowded and given over to such contrivances as the Tussaud's waxworks of a royal weekend house party and a sounds and smells-style exhibition on a household preparing for battle. The grounds were landscaped by Capability Brown and make for very pleasant strolling.

> *i* **Tourist Information Centre** The Court House, Jury St;
> tel: (01926) 492212; website: www.shakespeare-country.co.uk;
> e-mail: warwicktic@btinternet.com. Open daily 0930–1630.

SIDE TRIP TO STRATFORD-UPON-AVON

As the birthplace of William Shakespeare, Stratford is one of the world's foremost literary sites. It's an attractive town, but it is massively touristy. Hourly trains run from Birmingham, journey time 50 mins; there are 9–10 trains daily from Warwick (three on Sun), taking 25 mins. **Open-topped bus tours** of the sites run 2–4 times an hour, allowing you to get on and off at will – you'll need a long day to fit them all in. Apart from Anne Hathaway's Cottage and Mary Arden's House, the sites are all within walking distance from the station. **Avon Boating** offers 30-min river cruises and rowing boat hire (£) from near the Royal Shakespeare Theatre.

The five houses associated with Shakespeare are open daily 0900/0930–1700 and 1000–1600/1700 Sun except around Christmas (ticket covering all properties £££, valid for 12 months). The half-timbered building known as **Shakespeare's Birthplace**, Henley St, has an array of Shakespeare-related items inside, though obviously the interior has changed since his day. Shakespeare's daughter Susanna and her husband Dr Hall resided at **Hall's Croft** (££), for which the ticket also covers **Nash's House**, Chapel St, a typical Tudor house adjoining a knot garden marking the site of **New Place**, the house where Shakespeare died. He was baptised and buried nearby at **Holy Trinity Church**, where there's a memorial to him, holding a quill pen.

The Royal Shakespeare Company (RSC; website: www.rsc.org.uk) stages works in three theatres by the River Avon. The Royal Shakespeare Theatre, tel: (01789) 205301, is the main theatre; the others are the Swan Theatre and the smaller Other Place. Get a great insight into Stratford's theatrical world by taking the '**Behind the Scenes with the RSC backstage tour**', with displays of costumes and props. ££, daily, usually 1330 and 1730. Sometimes you can join a group visit after a performance; check on tel: (01789) 403405.

Not far from the Royal Shakespeare Theatre, in the Bancroft Gardens, is the 19th-century **Gower Memorial**, a statue of Shakespeare surrounded by four of his

'ALL THE WORLD'S A STAGE'

William Shakespeare (1564–1616) grew up, married and raised a family in Stratford but spent his working life in London. There he thrived as an actor, playwright and leading member of the Lord Chamberlain's Men, later the King's Men, performing at the Globe and Blackfriars theatres. He wrote some 38 plays and numerous sonnets. He retired to Stratford, where he died and was buried in Holy Trinity Church. He is considered England's greatest dramatist and his plays are still widely performed and loved today.

The Shakespeare Birthplace Trust website has more information on the man and the Stratford houses: www.shakespeare.org.uk.

characters: Hamlet, Lady Macbeth, Falstaff and Prince Hal, representing philosophy, tragedy, comedy and history. Colourful canal boats are moored alongside.

Just out of town at Shottery is **Anne Hathaway's Cottage** (££), the home of Shakespeare's wife before her marriage. The quaintness of the famous thatched cottage and its romantic garden pulls in the visitors, and you may have to wait in line to get in. The Bard's mother spent her childhood at Wilmcote in a farmhouse now known as **Mary Arden's House and the Shakespeare Countryside Museum** (££), given over to displays of rural life, with rare farm breeds.

[i] **Tourist Information Centre** Bridgefoot; tel: (01789) 293127; website: www.shakespeare-country.co.uk; e-mail: stratfordtic@shakespeare-country.co.uk. Open Mon–Sat 0900–1800, Sun 1100–1700 (Apr–Oct); Mon–Sat 0900–1700, Sun 1000–1500 (Nov–Mar).

[🏠] **Stratford-upon-Avon Youth Hostel** £, Alveston; tel: 0870 7706052; e-mail: stratford@yha.org.uk, is a fine Georgian mansion 1½ miles (2.5 km) from the town centre.

[🍴] Many restaurants offer good-value pre-theatre dinner menus, from 1730/1800. Try **Russons** ££–£££ 8 Church St, tel: (01789) 268822, for good soups, salads and risottos. Arrive early or book. Closed Sun–Mon.

SIDE TRIP TO IRONBRIDGE

Located 35 miles (56 km) outside Birmingham, Ironbridge has so much to see that it's worth staying a night or two. There's no station here, but there are buses from Telford Central rail station (bus no. 44 runs every 10 mins to the bus station, from where Ironbridge buses leave, taking 20–30 mins). For a slow but fascinating journey, get the train to Kidderminster, change on to the steam-hauled **Severn Valley Railway**, which runs 16 miles (26 km) to Bridgnorth, then take bus no. 9 or 99 to Ironbridge (daily; hourly; last bus 1545).

Widely recognised as the birthplace of the Industrial Revolution, Ironbridge is a town in the scenic Severn gorge, spanned by the world's earliest iron bridge (1779). At neighbouring Coalbrookdale 70 years earlier Abraham Darby first successfully smelted iron ore with coke instead of charcoal, paving the way for mass production in iron. In the 18th and 19th centuries the gorge became an industrial heartland, thick with smoke from the furnaces and ceramics works.

Ironbridge Gorge Museums; tel: (01952) 433522; website: www.ironbridge.org.uk. Most sites open all year 1000–1700; some sites closed Nov–Mar; call before visiting. Passport ticket to all sites, valid indefinitely £££, student/child ££.

The factories have all closed now, but many are re-opened as visitor attractions, including **Jackfield Tile Museum**, the **Coalport China Museum**, the **Broseley Pipeworks** (where clay pipes for smokers were made) and the **Museum of Iron**. The biggest museum site of all is **Blists Hill Victorian Town**, where some relics have survived in situ. Period-dressed guides show you round and answer questions, and you can seek out a steep railway connecting the canal with the the gorge, down which trucks hurtled to be unloaded at the bottom. The passport ticket also covers the **Darby Houses**, former homes of the ironmasters, and the **Tar Tunnel**, where bitumen was extracted. **Enginuity** is a wonderful interactive design and technology centre, with lots of actitivities for children. On bank holiday Suns and Mons, a bus service takes you round all the sites; otherwise you have to walk (the Severn Valley Way, along an old railway track, connects Ironbridge and Coalport) or use public buses.

EN ROUTE

Bridgnorth is a town built on a cliff, with the pleasant old 'high town' reachable by cliff railway. It boasts former cave dwellings inhabited until the 1830s as well as an alarmingly tilting castle ruin blown up in the Civil War.

i **Tourist Information Centre** The Wharfage; tel: (01952) 432166; website: www.ironbridge.org.uk; e-mail: info@ironbridge.org.uk. Open Mon–Fri 0900–1700, Sat–Sun 1000–1700.

🛏 **Ironbridge Gorge Youth Hostel** £ High St, Coalport; tel: 0870 7705882; e-mail: ironbridge@yha.org.uk, is on two sites by Coalport China Museum.

SIDE TRIP TO THE POTTERIES

Another highly worthwhile trip with an industrial flavour is the so-called Potteries – known in entirety as **Stoke-on-Trent**. Immortalised by Arnold Bennett's novels of the 'five towns', the Potteries are now a conurbation of six towns, though it needs local knowledge to pinpoint where one ends and the next begins. They are: **Tunstall** (the main tile-producing area), **Burslem** (specialising in teapot production), **Hanley** (the city centre), **Stoke** (home to Portmeirion and Spode), **Fenton**, and **Longton** (specialising in bone china production).

Up to the 1950s it was the smokiest, grimiest place imaginable, but only 47 of the old bottle kilns that once numbered some 3000 have survived, and the air has cleared. The potteries, however, are still very much in business and you can visit a large number of them. Many have factory shops offering price reductions of anything from 20% to 80%. Twelve potteries offer factory tours, Mon–Fri (not factory holidays), and include three visitor centres (Spode, Wedgwood and Royal Doulton). With the exception of Wedgwood it's advisable to book ahead.

If you're arriving by train, you'll need to rely on buses for **getting around** – it's no fun walking here, though three of the city's best sights are within walking distance of stations: Spode (Stoke station), Etruria Industrial Museum (Etruria station) and the Gladstone Pottery Museum (Longton station). For bus information contact First Bus PMT; tel: (01782) 270999.

The **Gladstone Pottery Museum**, ££, Uttoxeter Rd, Longton, open daily 1000–1700, except Christmas to New Year (short walk from Longton rail station) is the area's only remaining Victorian pottery factory, where you can see inside a bottle kiln and try your hand at throwing a pot or making clay flowers (with plenty of guidance from the experts). There's plenty that evokes the past, including an office of 1910, a restored doctor's surgery, a tile exhibition and probably the world's most eye-catching assembly of household toilets, in a display titled 'Flushed with Pride'. Allow at least half a day.

A short distance east, **Royal Doulton Visitor Centre** makes all those hand-crafted figurines you see in colour supplements (the visitor centre has the world's largest collection), as well as fine bone china. £, Nile St, Burslem, open Mon–Sat 0930–1700, including factory and bank holidays, except Christmas week; Sun 1030–1630. Tours £££ Mon–Thur 1030 and 1400, Fri 1030 and 1330 except factory holidays; prior booking essential; tel: (01782) 292434; no children under 10.

Pride of the **Potteries Museum and Art Gallery** is the ceramics section, with 5000 items on display representing about a fifth of the museum's total stock. There are also reconstructed old shops and a Spitfire plane designed by Reginald Mitchell, the local engineer whose work did much to win the Allies superiority of the skies in World War II. Free, Bethesda St, Hanley; open Mon–Sat 1000–1700, Sun 1400–1700; closes 1600 Nov–Feb; closed Christmas to New Year.

Sandwiched between two canals near Etruria rail station, **Etruria Industrial Museum** is Britain's last surviving steam-powered potter's mill. It is powered by an 1820s beam engine, where flint was crushed for use in the ceramics process. £, Lower Bedford St, Etruria; open Wed–Sun 1000–1600, except Christmas to New Year. The modern mill that succeeds it stands alongside and is still in use.

Spode is located in its original 18th-century factory. It is the only pottery to be on its original site and the only one to use the old method of 'underglaze transfer printing' – all explained on the excellent tour. Within these blackened old brick buildings Spode produces the celebrated bone china. Free, Church St, World of Spode visitor centre, Stoke; open Mon–Sat 0900–1700, Sun 1000–1600. Tours ££ Mon–Thu 1000 and 1330; booking essential; tel: (01782) 744011.

The most famous potter of all was Josiah Wedgwood, who set up a factory in Etruria. Nowadays the famous blue and white **Wedgwood** pottery is made at a modern factory on the edge of the city at Barlaston. Like the other visitor centres you can try your hand at pottery or painting flowers. The display features a magnificent historic collection of Wedgwood. Wedgwood Story £££ (includes self-guided factory tour), open daily 0900–1700; weekends from 1000.

The novels of Arnold Bennett (1867–1931) encapsulate the 'pitheads, chimneys and kilns, tier above tier, dim in their own mists' of the Potteries. His best-known works are *Clayhanger* and *Anna of the Five Towns.*

i **Tourist Information Centre** Quadrant Rd, Hanley, Stoke-on-Trent; tel: (01782) 236000; website: www.stoke.gov.uk; e-mail: stoke.tic@virgin.net. Open Mon–Sat 0930–1700, closed Sun.

Two places within walking distance of Stoke rail station are **Rhodes Hotel** ££ 42 Leek Rd; tel: (01782) 416320 and **L Beez Guest House** ££ 46 Leek Rd; tel: (01782) 846727.

The **Gladstone Pottery Museum** £–££ has a recommendable restaurant, serving some local specialities such as 'lobby' (a meat stew) and savoury oatcakes.

SIDE TRIP TO COVENTRY

Blitzed during World War II, Coventry is a shadow of its former self, but among the drab streetscapes it's worth seeking out the postwar cathedral, the masterpiece of architect Sir Basil Spence. Situated by the bombed ruins of the old cathedral, it is striking for its modern art, notably the stained glass by John Piper and the tapestry by Graham Sutherland. Trains from Birmingham take about 28 mins.

i **Tourist Information Centre** Bayley Lane; tel: (024) 7622 7264; website: www.coventry.org; e-mail: tic@coventry.org. Open Mon–Fri 0930–1700 (1630 in winter), Sat–Sun 1000–1630.

WHERE NEXT?

There are good rail links in all directions. Join the Bristol–Chester route (see pp. 168–175) by travelling west to Shrewsbury or south-west to Hereford. The latter journey takes you via the cathedral city of Worcester, Great Malvern (where there's a superb walk along the ridge of the Malvern Hills) and the attractive town of Ledbury. Alternatively, travel north to Chester (see pp. 174–175), Liverpool (see pp. 212–218) and Manchester (see pp. 206–211). Heading south-east, carry on beyond Warwick to historic Oxford (see pp. 113–117).

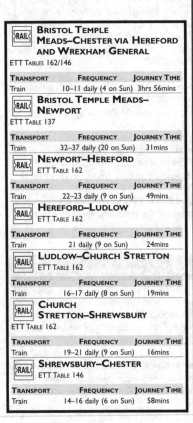

RAIL **BRISTOL TEMPLE MEADS–CHESTER VIA HEREFORD AND WREXHAM GENERAL**

ETT TABLES 162/146

TRANSPORT	FREQUENCY	JOURNEY TIME
Train	10–11 daily (4 on Sun)	3hrs 56mins

RAIL **BRISTOL TEMPLE MEADS–NEWPORT**

ETT TABLE 137

TRANSPORT	FREQUENCY	JOURNEY TIME
Train	32–37 daily (20 on Sun)	31mins

RAIL **NEWPORT–HEREFORD**

ETT TABLE 162

TRANSPORT	FREQUENCY	JOURNEY TIME
Train	22–23 daily (9 on Sun)	49mins

RAIL **HEREFORD–LUDLOW**

ETT TABLE 162

TRANSPORT	FREQUENCY	JOURNEY TIME
Train	21 daily (9 on Sun)	24mins

RAIL **LUDLOW–CHURCH STRETTON**

ETT TABLE 162

TRANSPORT	FREQUENCY	JOURNEY TIME
Train	16–17 daily (8 on Sun)	19mins

RAIL **CHURCH STRETTON–SHREWSBURY**

ETT TABLE 162

TRANSPORT	FREQUENCY	JOURNEY TIME
Train	19–21 daily (9 on Sun)	16mins

RAIL **SHREWSBURY–CHESTER**

ETT TABLE 146

TRANSPORT	FREQUENCY	JOURNEY TIME
Train	14–16 daily (6 on Sun)	58mins

Notes
The through journey from Bristol Temple Meads to Chester involves changing trains at Newport and/or Shrewsbury.

The rural tranquillity of the Welsh Marches belies a much more savage past. The remains of impregnable fortresses, the emblem of Wales and her border country, tell of a fierce fight to subdue this remote, hilly country and her recalcitrant population. Now, of course, the Marcher lords are long since dead and their strongholds reduced to being photogenic relics from a distant age. The modern visitor to this corner of the UK will find a laid-back atmosphere; country pubs stocking distinctive regional ales, remarkably attractive villages crammed with ancient timber-frame cottages and an abundance of opportunities for enjoying the great outdoors.

BRISTOL

See p. 120.

NEWPORT

Newport is not exactly Wales' most prepossessing town, best seen purely as a kicking off point. However, should you have time on your hands a handful of places will liven up your stay. One of the best is the **Transporter Bridge** that straddles the river Usk, carrying vehicles across the water in an ingenious aerial gondola.

> i **Tourist Information Centre** Museum and Art Gallery, John Frost Sq.; tel: (01633) 842962; e-mail: newport-tic@ tsww.com. Open Mon–Sat 0930–1700.

SIDE TRIP FROM NEWPORT **Caerleon**, a stone's throw from Newport, might make a more pleasing place to stay the night. This little town is awash with Roman history. The main site is Caerleon Roman Fortress (£, closed 24–26 Dec, 1 Jan). Although British Roman ruins can't compete with the ancient sites of the Mediterranean, this is one of the better preserved ones, with impressive remains of the amphitheatre and bath-house. Finds are displayed in the town's Legionary Museum. The Priory, ££–£££, High St; tel: (01633) 421241, has rooms as well as a restaurant that cooks your meat and fish to order.

THE LOWER WYE VALLEY At Newport you can change for trains to Chepstow (12 trains daily, 7 on Sun; journey time 20 mins) to explore the lower Wye Valley, where the river Wye snakes through a densely wooded sandstone gorge and for some of the way defines the border between England and Wales. It's deeply romantic and beautiful, and good bus services along the valley link key places such as Chepstow, Tintern and Monmouth.

Chepstow (just inside Wales) is a hilly little border town which has its best moments by the river, with its elegant Regency bridge and above all the massive castle (£, daily except 24–26 Dec), built by the English in Norman times to guard over the Welsh. It perches on a rock with its towers, gatehouses and barbicans (added in later centuries) standing to their original height and the original Norman keep at the core of the site. During the Civil War in the 17th century it was further adapted for cannon and musketry. Further upstream is another notable stone ruin, **Tintern Abbey** (£, daily except 24–26 Dec) is one of the most graceful of Britain's ruined monasteries as well as the most complete abbey in Wales. Its beauty inspired Wordsworth to write one of his best-known poems, *Lines composed a few miles above Tintern Abbey*.

Monmouth is a likeable town on the Welsh side of the Wye where the smaller river Monnow flows into the valley. Spanning the Monnow is a rare fortified 13th-century bridge, which looks like something out of southern France. In Agincourt Square are statues to two local heroes – Henry V and Charles Rolls (holding a model aeroplane) of Rolls-Royce fame, while the Nelson Museum (£, daily but closed Sun mornings, 24–26 Dec, 1 Jan) houses a vast collection of Nelson memorabilia.

> *i* **Tourist Information Centre** Castle Car Park, Bridge St, Chepstow; tel: (01291) 623772; website: www.chepstow.org.uk; e-mail: chepstow-tic@tsww.com. Open daily from 1000 (summer); from 0930 (winter).
> **Tourist Information Centre** Shire Hall, Agincourt Sq., Monmouth; tel: (01600) 713899; website: www.monmouth.org.uk; e-mail: monmouth-tic@tsww.com. Open daily from 1000 (summer); from 0930 (winter).

> 🛏 The most obvious places to stay in the valley are Chepstow and Monmouth, both of which have tourist offices and a good supply of bed and breakfast accommodation. If you are hostelling, do not miss a night at **St Briavels Castle Youth Hostel** (tel: 0870 7706040; e-mail stbriavels@yha.org.uk), in the small village of St Briavels 2 miles (3 km) from the valley and on the English side – one of the most amazing hostel buildings in the country: it's a moated medieval castle once used as a hunting lodge by King John, and full of period details, even dungeons!

HEREFORD

Hereford is a small cathedral city at the centre of Herefordshire, known for cattle and cider. It has some pleasant river scenery and streets of Georgian and other buildings (notably the handsome **Old House**, a Jacobean house in High Town with period furnishings, open free), though the effect is a bit spoiled by the inner ring road. At its heart, the sandstone **cathedral** is famed for its 13th-century map of the world known as the Mappa Mundi – the largest map of its date in the world. It is displayed in a dimmed room, and there is a good interpretative exhibition (££, closed winter Suns). Also look in at the cathedral's chained library (that is, books with chains on them to stop you 'borrowing' them), with 1500 volumes including manuscripts from the Dark Ages.

THE CIDER ROUTE

Herefordshire is one of the UK's most rural counties and is famous for its apple orchards and hop yards. Visitors are invited to take the Cider Route, stopping off at the major producers, and of course, knock back a drop or two. To the denizens of Herefordshire, The Big Apple is a weekend celebration of apple growing and cider production taking place in October. Alternatively (or as well as) you could try the Hop Trail and sample the wares of local brewers who produce ales such as Dorothy Goodbody and Bravo Bitter. Information from Shrewsbury tourist information centre. American readers please note: unlike cider in the US, English cider is alcoholic, and quite a bit stronger than beer!

Since cider is such a theme in Hereford, you might like to look in at **Bulmer's Cider Mill**, a modern plant open for tours and tastings (££, 1030, 1415, 1930; by appointment, tel: (01432) 352000). The ticket covers entry to the **Cider Museum** (Ryelands St; £ for separate entry, open daily except Christmas, and closed Mon in winter), telling the story of cider-making through the centuries.

The **river Wye** patrols the border between England and Wales, making forays into both countries, offering 100 miles (161 km) of navigable waterway. Canadian canoes can be hired on the Wye and there is a way-marked 112-mile (180-km) long-distance **walking route** following its course.

i **Tourist Information Centre** | King St; tel: (01432) 268430; website: www.hereford.gov.uk; e-mail: tic-hereford@ herefordshire.gov.uk. Open Mon–Sat 0900–1700, Sun (summer only) 1000–1600.

There are several B&Bs close to the heart of Hereford. The closest to the centre is **Montgomery House** ££–£££ 12 St Owen St; tel: (01432) 351454. Another convenient B&B is **Charades** ££ 34 Southbank Rd; tel: (01432) 269444, just a 10-min walk from the centre.

For a light bite in Hereford's core there's **Cafe @ All Saints** High St; tel: (01432) 370415. The menu changes daily and it serves wine, good coffee and locally made apple juice. The elegant **Castle Room Restaurant** ££–£££ Castle St, Hereford; tel: (01432) 356321, has won awards for its food.

SIDE TRIPS FROM HEREFORD

The train east from Hereford joins the Bristol–Worcester route (see pp. 148–155) at Worcester (18–19 trains daily, 8 on Sun; journey time 40 mins). On the way, you pass through two minor gems. **Ledbury** is an agreeable place with a fine timber-framed market hall punctuating its main street, and a quaint narrow medieval alley leading from there to the church with its separate tower. There's not a lot in the way of formal sights, but if you want to see an unspoilt English market town it is well worth stopping off for an hour or so. Nearby **Eastnor Castle** is also worth a visit. **Great Malvern** is a

Victorian spa town nestling directly beneath the slopes of the **Malvern Hills**, a stretch of friendly upland with a delectable walk along its spine. The composer Edward Elgar was among the many who have found inspiration by wandering up here. On a clear day you can see well into Wales to the west, and far across the west Midlands to the Cotswolds to your east. There is a rewarding walk from Ledbury to Great Malvern, returning by train.

A reasonable network of **bus services** fans out from Hereford, and is shown on the public transport map for Herefordshire (free from tourist information centres and from the bus station). Southwards, bus 416 (5 daily, not Sun) travels to **Monmouth** (see p. 170) in the scenic lower Wye Valley, from where there are bus connections to Tintern and Chepstow. A great journey westwards is to **Hay-on-Wye** (bus no. 39, 5 daily, 3 on Sun; 55 mins), a tiny border town tucked just inside Wales and famed among bibliophiles as a world centre for second-hand books. Virtually every other shop seems to sell dusty tomes of one type or other; even the castle and former cinema are now given over to the trade, and though it is run by dealers who clearly know their stock, there are plenty of bargains to be had. Hay-on-Wye also hosts a high-profile Literary Festival each May–June (tel: (01497) 821299, www.hayfestival.co.uk). Additionally, the town is a good centre for walking, being on the long-distance Offa's Dyke Path and just inside the north-east corner of the **Brecon Beacons National Park** (see p. 183). It is not an easy area to explore without a car, but bus no. 39 takes you to Brecon at the centre of the national park.

> *i* **Tourist Information Centre** Oxford Rd, Hay-on-Wye; tel: (01497) 820144; website: www.hay-on-wye.co.uk. Open daily 1000–1300, 1400–1700 (Easter–Oct); daily 1100–1300, 1400–1600 (Nov–Easter).

LUDLOW

Often cited as the most perfect English small town, Ludlow occupies a hilltop site, topped by its castle, market place and almost cathedral-like church set in a pretty close behind the butter market. Sloping down is a grid of delightful streets laid out in medieval times. The town harbours a rich legacy of domestic architecture, predominantly from the 17th and 18th centuries, though with some earlier buildings such as the spectacularly ornate half-timbered hotel known as **The Feathers** (in the Bull Ring). **Broad Street** is the most visually satisfying of all the town's streets.

In Castle Square, **Castle Lodge** has a much-panelled interior that gives a good idea of how a 16th-century town house looked (£, daily). **Ludlow Castle** (£, closed 25 Dec and weekdays in Jan), finely set above the river Teme, has retained a large amount of its medieval fabric and hosts outdoor performances of Shakespeare plays during the **Ludlow Festival** in June/July. Close by in Castle St is the free Ludlow Museum, with an entertaining display of local history (closed Nov–Mar, and Sun except Jun–Aug).

STOKESAY CASTLE

The stormy history of the Marches has left a legacy of castles. Shropshire alone has 32. One of the most photogenic is Stokesay Castle, a 14th-century fortified manor (7 miles/11.3 km from Ludlow; open daily 1000–1800 Apr–Oct; 1000–1600 Wed–Sun, Nov–Mar).

i **Tourist Information Centre** Castle St, Ludlow; tel: (01584) 875053; fax: (01584) 877931. Open daily 1000–1700 (summer); Mon–Fri 1000–1700, Sat 1000–1600 (winter).

CHURCH STRETTON

The scenery is the thing here: the Long Mynd is a startlingly sudden upland that rears straight out of the demure little town of Church Stretton. The walks are numerous: the best known is into the Cardingmill Valley, although the equally beautiful and deeply set Ashes Hollow is just as scenic.

i **Tourist Information Centre** Church St, Church Stretton; tel: (01694) 723045. Open summer only.

SHREWSBURY

Shrewsbury has some enigmatically named streets – Fish, Milk, Butcher Row and, best of all, Grope Lane. The place is stuffed with those wonderful tilting black and white houses the Marches are renowned for, so it's spectacularly picturesque. Guided tours around the city depart from the tourist information centre and give broad insights to the town's extensive history. Themed tours are another feature and fans of the Ellis Peters mysteries can follow in the footsteps of the medieval sleuth Brother Cadfael on a special tour. Shrewsbury's other claim to fame is that it is the birthplace of Charles Darwin. Look out for the unusual round Georgian church of St Chad's too.

i **Tourist Information Centre** The Music Hall, The Square; tel: (01743) 281200; website: www.shrewsburytourism.co.uk; e-mail: tic@shrewsburytourism.co.uk. Open Mon–Sat 1000–1800, Sun 1000–16000 (summer); Mon–Sat 1000–1700, Sun closed (winter).

The Lion £££ Wyle Cop; tel: (01743) 353107, has been ushering guests through its doors for 350 years. It serves coffee and afternoon tea, as well as lunch and dinner. All 59 bedrooms are en suite. The 16th-century coaching inn, the **Lion & Pheasant Hotel** ££ 49–50 Lower Wyle Cop; tel: (01743) 236288, is also full of character.
Shrewsbury Youth Hostel £ The Woodlands, Abbey Foregate, tel: 0870 7706030, e-mail: shrewsbury@yha.org.uk, is a former Victorian ironmaster's house in the eastern outskirts, a mile or so from the bus and train stations.

**SHROPSHIRE
SPECIALITIES**

Shropshire is famous for
regional delicacies such as
damson gin, whinberry pie
and Shropshire Blue cheese.
Devotees of regional beers
can partake in a real ale trail
called Looking at Shropshire
Through a Glass; tel:
(01743) 462462, while
Shrewsbury hosts a Real
Ale Festival; tel: (01743)
352842.

🆃🅾 Shrewsbury isn't short of good eating houses. Here's just a
small selection.

The Real Art Gallery & Coffee Shop £ Castle Gates; tel:
(01743) 270123, houses a decent collection of arts and crafts
as well as providing good food and drink.

For Mediterranean-style cuisine, there's **Traitor's Gate
Brasserie** £–££ Castle St, St Mary's Water Lane; tel: (01743)
249152, and for authentic Italian cuisine **La Trattoria** £–££
7 Fish St; tel: (01743) 249490. For a touch of style, try
Chambers Restaurant & Bar £–££ Church St; tel: (01743)
233818. Another star-rated cafe/bar/restaurant is the 15th-
century **Peach Tree** £–££ 21 Abbey Foregate; tel: (01743)
355055. For a wholefood and vegetarian option, try
The Goodlife Wholefood Restaurant £ Barracks Passage;
tel: (01743) 350455.

CHESTER

Established by the 20th Roman Legion as the city of Deva, Chester was a prosperous port in medieval times before the river Dee was silted up. Today it is one of
England's great historic cities and is a delightful place to walk around. Everywhere
you are confronted with layer upon layer of history: fragments of the Roman presence (particularly the street network), medieval remains and Georgian architecture.

Chester is particularly famed for two features. The old city is ringed by one of the
most complete **medieval city walls** in Britain, which you can walk along or beside
for a fascinating tour (parts of the north and east sections date back to Roman times).
Within the walls are **The Rows**, a series of galleried shopping streets running above
the street-level shops; this unique feature of British townscape has medieval origins.

It is an easy place in which to get your bearings. The city centre is effectively a simple staggered criss-cross of streets, with Watergate St leading into Eastgate St and
running west-east and Northgate St running north to south and continuing beyond
the central Cross as Bridge St and Lower Bridge St. Around The Cross is the hub of
activity, and it's from here that **The Rows** radiate; the exuberant Tudor-looking
black and white buildings hereabouts are mostly rather good 19th-century fakes,
though there are some genuine ones in Lower Bridge St and elsewhere.

Heading along Eastgate St you'll see the ornate clock erected over the **Eastgate** itself,
one of the city's original gateways, for Queen Victoria's Diamond Jubilee in 1897.
This is one of several possible starting points for exploring the **city wall**, which
along this stretch is followed by a walkway along the top. If you turn right along it
you'll soon cross Newgate, where it is worth a detour just outside the wall to see the
partly excavated site of the **Roman Amphitheatre** and the nearby **Roman Garden**,

with its resurrected Roman columns. There follows a pretty section along the river Dee, where the graceful **Grosvenor Bridge** was the largest single-span bridge in the world when it opened in 1832. Nuns Rd and City Walls Rd take you along the western side, close to the **Roodee**, the world's oldest race course (with ultra-fashionable races in May). At the north-west corner the **Water Tower** gives views into the Welsh hills; you can then rejoin the walkway along the walls, high above the Shropshire Union Canal. Beyond Northgate, **King Charles' Tower** takes its name from Charles I who one day in 1645 stood there and watched his army being defeated on Rowton Heath. Before returning to Eastgate, you pass the precincts of the sandstone **cathedral**, which has lost much of its medieval character through heavy restoration but retains some wonderful carved 14th-century choir stalls.

For more on Chester's past, visit the excellent **Grosvenor Museum** (free, closed Sun morning) in Grosvenor St; it includes locally crafted furniture, an entire Georgian house and a gallery of Roman tombstones. **Dewa Roman Experience** (££, Pierpoint Lane, daily) re-creates Roman Chester's streets, forts and bath-houses with sights, sounds and smells, and ends with an exhibition of archaeological finds.

🚆 About 15 mins walk from the city centre, via City Rd and Foregate St, or take a bus.

ℹ️ **Chester Visitor Centre** Vicar's Ln.; tel: (01244) 402111; website: www.chestertourism.com; e-mail: tic@chestercc.gov.uk. Open Mon–Sat 0900–1730 (1000–1700 Oct–Mar), Sun and bank holidays 1000–1600. **Tourist Information Centre** Town Hall, Northgate St. Open same times as Chester Visitor Centre except closed Sun (Oct–Mar).

🏨 **Chester Youth Hostel** £ 40 Hough Green; tel: 0870 7705762, fax: 0870 7705763, e-mail: chester@yha.org.uk. A large Victorian house on the south-west side of the city (about 20 mins walk from the centre, or take a bus).
Edwards House ££ 61 Hoole Road; tel: (01244) 318055, fax: (01244) 318055, e-mail: steanerob@supanet.com. Elegant, early Victorian house with well-proportioned rooms, all en suite (close to city centre).
Alton Lodge £££ 78 Hoole Road; tel: (01244) 310213. Family-run hotel with à la carte restaurant (close to city centre).

WHERE NEXT?

From Chester it's just a hop and a skip to Liverpool, a charismatic city with wild night life, magnificent buildings and a population with a gift for humour. And yes, you can take a ferry across the Mersey (see p. 213).

CARDIFF

Europe's youngest capital is possibly one of the most under-rated cities in the UK. The last decade or so has seen the place emerge from the rubble of its industrial past and evolve into a lively city with a 'craic' (pronounced 'crack') like Dublin's and a population whose gift for humour can be compared to that of the Liverpudlians.

The city and its environs were rated fourth in the UK for quality of life by a recent University of Glasgow survey. It can also lay claim to having more parkland per head than any other British city; an unreservedly over-the-top baroque castle; elegant Victorian and Edwardian shopping arcades; the largest collection of Impressionist paintings outside Paris and the biggest free festival in Europe. The latest addition to modern Cardiff is the Millennium Stadium, or Cardiff Arms Park, whose futuristic presence dominates most overviews of the city.

GETTING THERE AND GETTING AROUND

Cardiff International **Airport** is located in Rhoose about a 20-min drive from the city. For further information tel: (01446) 711 111. Cardiff has good connections with other parts of Wales, the Midlands and the West of England, with the M4 as the key to most routes in and out of the city.

City maps can be purchased at Waterstones Bookstore; tel: (029) 2066 5606, on The Hayes. Most of the attractions in town are within walking distance or an easy bus journey from the city centre. The rapidly growing Cardiff Bay development area is about a mile south of the centre.

Most **bus** services operate from the Central Bus Station, Central Square. The main local operator is Cardiff Bus; tel: (029) 20 666 444. Passenger information and time-tables can be obtained by calling Traveline; tel: 0870 608 2608, daily 0700–2100. Services are good in the city centre and to the suburbs, running until 2300 on the most popular routes, with reduced services on Sun. Cardiff Bus issues a City Rider ticket costing £2.95 a day, covering all its services. For **train** services call National Rail Enquiries; tel: 08457 484950; Wales and Border Trains; tel: 0870 9000 773.

Useful **car hire** numbers include Charter Vehicle Hire on (029) 2055 3111. The main **taxi ranks** can be found at Central Station, The Hayes, Park Place and St Mary St. Useful numbers include Capital Cars (029) 2077 7777, Amber (029) 2055 5555 and Black cabs (029) 2034 3343.

INFORMATION
CITY MAP – inside back cover

Cardiff Visitor Centre 16 Wood St (opposite central railway and bus station); tel: (029) 2022 7281; website: www.cardiffmarketing.co.uk; e-mail: enquiries@cardifftic.co.uk. Open Mon–Sat 0900–1700 (1800 in summer), Sun 1000–1600. You can purchase the Cardiff Card here and save pounds by gaining free access to all the top attractions in and around the city along with free public transport. It's valid for 48 hours and is also available from post offices, stations and selected hotels, attractions and shops. **Cardiff Bay Visitor Centre** Harbour Dr., Cardiff Bay; tel: (029) 2046 3833. Open Mon–Fri 0930–1700 (1930 in summer), Sat–Sun and bank holidays 1030–1700 (1930 in summer). For what's going on in Cardiff look up the website: www.virtualcardiff.co.uk, which is updated daily. *The Western Mail* and *South Wales Echo* carry arts pages and listings sections.

ACCOMMODATION

Cardiff is pretty well served on the accommodation front. However, it's worth checking if there's a rugby international on, when beds will be scarce. Sampling the city centre after a match isn't for the faint-hearted either.

The Lincoln House Hotel ££ 118 Cathedral Rd; tel: (029) 2039 5558. On an attractive tree-lined road, a mere 5-min walk from the centre. A comfortable option.

Another mid-range solution is **The Big Sleep** ££ Bute Terrace; tel: (029) 2063 6363. A very decent place, it's part owned by John Malkovich, although the chances he'll be staying there are probably remote!

For budget options there's the **Cardiff International Backpacker** £ 98 Neville St, Riverside; tel: (029) 2034 5577. A gloriously vivid purple exterior and high quality services.

Cardiff Youth Hostel £ 2 Wedal Rd, Roath Park, tel: 0870 7705751 (e-mail: cardiff@yha.org.uk) is in the student area of Cardiff, about 15 mins walk from Heath High Level or Heath Low Level rail stations.

FOOD AND DRINK

Cardiff's new-found affluence is reflected in the rash of restaurants and cafés mushrooming throughout the city. Although many serve truly excellent food, as in any city, choosing a place at random can be something of a lottery. It is worth getting hold of a copy of *Eat Well in Wales: The Red Book*, an independent good food guide that includes a chapter on the best in Cardiff's dining.

Brava £ 71 Pontcanna St. This is a café in true European style where you can linger endlessly over an espresso or a glass of wine at your pavement table. The food is very imaginative too.

Café Jazz £–££ St Mary St; tel: (029) 2038 7026. Listen to live jazz in the city centre (Thur nights tend to be best). Food served until 2200, which is head and shoulders above that served in a number of famous London jazz clubs.

Chapter Arts Centre £ Market St; tel: (029) 2031 1050. Eclectic arts venue with an excellent cinema and buzzy bar. This venue isn't afraid to push the boat out with avant-garde exhibitions and theatre shows – Orlan and Annie Sprinkle are two controversial names to have graced this venue. It's perfectly OK, if not outstanding, for a bite to eat too.

Greenhouse £–££ 38 Woodville Rd, Cathays; tel: (029) 2023 5731. This Lilliputian seafood and vegetarian café is tucked away in the city's student quarter. Although diners sit cheek by jowl, the atmosphere is cosy and the food is encouragingly inventive.

Izakaya Japanese Tavern £–££ Mermaid Quay, Cardiff Bay; tel: (029) 2049 2939. An excellent place to sample a broad range of Japanese cuisine at very reasonable prices. Try eating 'tapas' style by ordering two or three dishes at a time.

Madhav £ Lower Cathedral Rd. This little shop sells freshly cooked hot snacks like spicy potato balls in gram flour batter that are reputed to be the best you'll find outside Bombay. Sit and eat them in Despenser Gardens, within a stone's throw of the Millennium Stadium.

HIGHLIGHTS

Cardiff Castle in the city centre is a wildly flamboyant testimony to the huge wealth gleaned by the Bute family courtesy of the once booming coal industry. The third Marquess of Bute lavished much of his substantial fortune on creating this exuberant folly. Architect William Burges was commissioned to carry out the work and his distinctive stamp can be seen in the castle's garishly opulent appartments. ££, open daily 0930–1800 (fee includes an interesting guided tour).

The National Museum and Gallery of Wales is set within the neoclassical splendour of the civic centre. Apart from housing a fine collection of Impressionist paintings, including works by Monet, Renoir, Cézanne and Van Gogh, the museum is also home to one of Rodin's versions of his famous statue *The Kiss* and a decent collection of contemporary paintings. Around £26 million have been spent on developing the museum, which is reflected in the fascinating 'Evolution of Wales' wing, an excellent Natural History section and an interactive gallery. Free, open Tues–Sun and bank holidays 1000–1700.

Techniquest in Stuart St in Cardiff Bay is a hands-on science discovery centre that really brings science to life. Children are certain to have a great time (and they can't break anything) and it's sufficiently entertaining for adults to enjoy too. (££, open daily Mon–Fri 0930–1630; Sat–Sun; Bank Holidays 1030–1700.)

Llandaff Cathedral is tucked away in a green hollow a little out of the city centre close to the river Taff. Begun in the 12th century by Bishop Urban, the cathedral wasn't completed until the 15th century and you'll find miscellaneous medieval ecclesiastical styles lurking here. Sir Jacob Epstein's statue *Christ in Majesty* dominates the interior. People either love it or hate it.

An extensive oasis of quiet in the heart of the city, **Bute Park Arboretum** encircles the castle and is perfect for a picnic lunch on a sunny day. (Free, open dawn 'til dusk.) If you fancy it, you can stroll along the river Taff to Llandaff Cathedral, 2 miles (3 km) away.

Extraordinary though it may seem, it is possible to go **fly-fishing** within the confines of the city centre and almost imagine yourself in the country. The river Taff rising on a sandstone escarpment in the Brecon Beacons National Park is home to salmon, sea trout, brown trout (both wild and stocked) and grayling. The death throes of the coal industry have spelt good news for this particular river, which now runs clean and pure from the hills. Day tickets are available from Garry Evans Tackle Shop; tel: (029) 2061 9828.

Cardiff Bay is the birthplace of Shirley Bassey, but Tiger Bay, the run-down docks area where she was born, is long since demolished. Now distinctly upmarket with its cafés, bars and restaurants, it is also home to the Welsh Assembly. A barrage scheme ensures permanent high water, much to the chagrin of those who believe that the permutations of the tidal flow are infinitely preferable to stagnant water. Whatever your opinion on the barrage, the Bay area is a fascinating combination of Cardiff's prosperous past (such as the Coal Exchange where the world's first £1 million deal was struck) and its hopes for an equally illustrious future.

Open-top bus tours of the city are operated by Leisurelink, in association with Guide Friday, ££, tel: (029) 2052 2202; Easter–Oct. Tours start at the castle gates.

CARDIFF

Boat trips round the Bristol Channel area are run by Waverley Excursions, ££, tel: (0141) 243 2224. An afternoon's jaunt to Ilfracombe on the historic pleasure steamers *Waverley* and *Balmoral* is only possible during the summer months, usually from mid-May through to late Aug.

SHOPPING

There's no doubt about it, you can shop until you drop in this city, or at least until your credit card reaches its limit. Cardiff's attractive Victorian arcades house scores of unusual shops. One of the most appealing is the balconied **Castle Arcade**, home to street-smart clothing store Gokyo, the condom emporium, Johnnies, Claire Grove Buttons, hair designers Zoo, an organic juice bar and the Celtic Cauldron, a café specialising in Welsh fodder like laverbread with bacon, Penclawdd cockles and Anglesey eggs.

Listen out for the characteristic exploding consonant sounds of the Welsh language being spoken in the streets. Welsh is one of Europe's oldest languages and the Welsh flag, with its scarlet fire-breathing dragon, one of its oldest national flags.

Eccentrix in the **High Street Arcade** is a shoe fetishist's paradise. For anyone wanting kinky boots or any number of high-heeled thrillers, Eccentrix is your kind of place. For designer names like Betty Barclay, Paul Costelloe et al, the department store Howells has the lot under one roof.

Stylish modern shopping malls like the **Capitol Centre** and the **Queen's Arcade** will also supply an adrenalin shot for devotees of retail therapy. **Jacob's Market** on West Canal Wharf has 50 shops selling anything from antiques and bric-à-brac to vintage clothing.

Then, for anyone who's looking for the living, breathing version of the record store in Nick Hornby's *High Fidelity*, there's **Spiller's Records** on The Hayes. It also claims to be the oldest record shop in the world – it was founded in 1894.

NIGHTLIFE

There's no shortage of hedonistic fixes to be had in Cardiff. The likes of super-cool chick Cerys from Catatonia, the Manic Street Preachers and The Stereophonics have helped Wales look hip in the eyes of a broader public for the very first time.

Cardiff's nightlife is diverse enough to satisfy everyone in terms of age and taste. There are venues for the young and happening as well as places for 30 pluses to relax without feeling they've got one or both feet in the grave. The New Theatre provides orthodox theatre and The Sherman and Chapter varying degrees of alternative entertainment. Cardiff is also home to the world-renowned Welsh National Opera. Check the New Theatre for details of their dates.

Toucan Club in Womanby St is a great venue with a truly friendly vibe that's home to Latin and salsa sounds as well as a smattering of jazz and funk. A good atmosphere is guaranteed. In the same street, **Clwb Ifor Bach** is also known as 'The Welsh Club' although naturalisation is not a prerequisite. This is a prime venue for genuine music lovers who don't want to get kitted out to the hilt for a night out.

Club X, Charles St, is the city's best known gay/mixed venue sporting two dance floors, a balcony, a garden and its own café. It's very popular with the dance scene too. There's no attitude and you can be yourself. In the same street, **Minsky's Show Bar** is a cabaret bar with some spectacular drag acts from Thur to Sat.

One of Cardiff's best-kept secrets is **Rajah's**, Riverside. It has excellent live music most nights and only costs a quid to get in. **Bar 38**, Mermaid Quay, is a super-trendy café bar with a balcony overlooking the bay where the hippest people hang out on a warm summer's night. Attached to the rather off-puttingly ostentatious Angel Hotel, **Angel Tavern**, Castle St is one of the few old-style, traditional pubs left and it oozes character.

SIDE TRIPS

Cardiff is a relatively small city (population something over 300,000), so its periphery is easily reached by rail, bus or even cab.

THE COAST   The coast west of Cardiff includes two fine and reasonably accessible stretches that have been designated Heritage Coasts by virtue of their high landscape value.

The **Glamorgan Heritage Coast** stretches from West Aberthaw to Porthcawl and includes some striking candy-striped cliffs full of blow-holes and fissures; low tides leave a strange moonscape of rock, when you can appreciate the cliffs from below. Good places to head for are Nash Point, where you can walk along the coast to St Donat's Castle (now a college), and Ogmore Castle just outside Bridgend.

The **Gower Heritage Coast** includes the peninsula of Gower, just west of Swansea from which it is served by buses (there are frequent trains and buses from Cardiff to Swansea). This is a fascinating area, with superb sandy beaches, castles and some spectacular landforms. A coastal path takes you round the most scenic part (around the southern and western coasts; the north is marshy and low-lying), and there's even a moorland ridge known as Cefn Bryn which is studded with antiquities and has far-ranging views. Threecliff Bay and Mewslade Bay are majestically set with jagged limestone rocks and sublime sands, while on the west side Rhossili Down shelves steeply down to a long beach that attracts surfers. Oxwich is a small resort village offering waterskiing, sailing and other water sports, and has a small 14th-century castle that is open to the public.

MUSEUM OF WELSH LIFE IN ST FAGANS Not to be missed, this museum is an absolute delight. Exhibits have been reconstructed stone by stone and include a 17th-century farmhouse painted a livid pink to ward off evil spirits, a rough-hewn quarryman's cottage from North Wales, a working bakehouse selling fresh bread and a village store stocked with local cheeses and handmade chocolate. Free, open Mon–Sun 1000–1700. A short 15-min drive; it is also possible to go by bus from Cardiff Central Station.

THE RHONDDA HERITAGE PARK This is another must-see. Due for demolition when it closed in 1983, the **Lewis Merthyr Colliery** was reprieved at the eleventh hour by an ambitious proposal to turn it into a living history museum. The story of coal is now graphically told via an underground visit conducted by ex-miners.

No visit to Cardiff is complete without a visit here as the city owes its existence to the wealth generated by the hard graft of generations of miners who worked the seams of Lewis Merthyr and other collieries in the South Wales Valleys. In the hey-day of coal a miner was killed every 6 hrs and a man injured every 2 mins. (££, open daily 1000–1800). It's 20 mins by car or an easy train journey. Catch a Rhondda train from Cardiff Central Station and get off at Trehafod (Valleys Lines; tel: (0292) 044 9944; National Rail Enquiries, tel: 08457 484950).

CASTELL COCH If Cardiff Castle and its overwhelmingly lavish decor appealed to you, then Castell Coch provides another opportunity to witness architect William Burges' flights of fancy, on the north-west edge of Cardiff. Slightly more restrained than the castle – this was only a summer picnic house after all – it nevertheless bears the opulent Burges hallmark. Constructed on the site of a Norman fortress deep in the heart of dense woodland, it looks like it has stepped straight from the pages of *Grimm's Fairytales* with its tall turrets and spires. (£, open daily 0930–1700; tel: (0292) 081 0101).

CAERPHILLY CASTLE This castle is a particularly grand specimen. Built in the late 13th century, it has everything a good castle should from its classic concentric design, to high towers and a broad moat. It even has a tilting tower that leans almost as alarmingly as the one in Pisa. (£, open daily 0930–1700.) The castle is only a 15-min drive from Cardiff, 25 mins or so by bus or train (then a 10-minute walk from the station).

BLAENAVON Well worth the journey from Cardiff (bus or train to Newport, then bus to Blaenavon), this former coal- and iron-producing village has been designated a World Heritage Site by UNESCO. The older of the two sites to visit is the **Blaenavon Ironworks** (£, daily 0930–1630, late Mar–end Oct), established in 1788 and the most complete industrial site of its type and date surviving in Europe. The **Big Pit National Mining Museum** (free; open daily 0930–1700, mid-Feb–end Nov) offers an outstanding visit to a coal mine that closed in 1980. Ex-miners take you down on a cage lift and show you into the depths of the mine, while on the surface are colliery buildings, a smithy and the pithead baths.

BRECON BEACONS NATIONAL PARK Located some 40 miles (65 km) north of Cardiff and the highest land in South Wales, the Brecon Beacons rise to 2907 ft (886 m). There's a wonderful sense of space and remoteness here. Public transport is limited to the services along main roads, with the cheerful small town of **Brecon** as the obvious touring centre; from here buses link Cardiff (via Storey Arms), Abergavenny (via Talybont on Usk and Crickhowell), Llandovery, Hay-on-Wye and Bridgend (via Glyn-neath). The sandstone summits including the highest point, **Pen y Fan** (together known as the Brecon Beacons), make a superb walk from the Storey Arms on the A470. Further west is the bleak moorland of Fforest Fawr and the clifflike ridge of the **Carmarthen Fan**, while eastwards lie the **Black Mountains** – a series of deep, secretive valleys harbouring the ruins of Llanthony Priory (free access). Tucked into the north-east corner of the national park, and almost in England, is the town of **Hay-on-Wye** (buses from Brecon; see p. 172). In the south of the area, the **Brecon Beacons Waterfall Country** is a series of ferociously gushing waterfalls within the deep, wooded gorges of the Hepste, Nedd and Mellte rivers: Pontneddfechan (off the A465 near Glyn-neath) is a useful starting point for walks.

> *i* **Tourist Information Centre** Cattle Market Car Park, Brecon, tel: (01874) 623156; www.breconbeacons.org.

WHERE NEXT?

Leaving Cardiff behind, you can travel by rail to Bristol (see pp. 120–126) and southwest England, or head west along the Welsh coast via Swansea to Carmarthen for the beautiful Pembrokeshire coast (see pp. 185–190). Alternatively, you can travel east to Chepstow (12 trains daily, 6 on Sun; journey time 35 mins) for the Lower Wye Valley (see p. 169).

CARMARTHEN – CARDIGAN

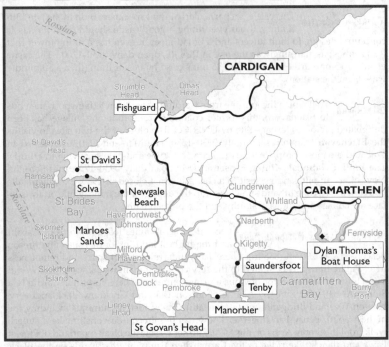

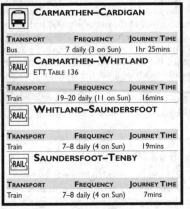

CARMARTHEN–CARDIGAN

TRANSPORT	FREQUENCY	JOURNEY TIME
Bus	7 daily (3 on Sun)	1hr 25mins

CARMARTHEN–WHITLAND
ETT TABLE 136

TRANSPORT	FREQUENCY	JOURNEY TIME
Train	19–20 daily (11 on Sun)	16mins

WHITLAND–SAUNDERSFOOT

TRANSPORT	FREQUENCY	JOURNEY TIME
Train	7–8 daily (4 on Sun)	19mins

SAUNDERSFOOT–TENBY

TRANSPORT	FREQUENCY	JOURNEY TIME
Train	7–8 daily (4 on Sun)	7mins

CARMARTHEN–FISHGUARD

TRANSPORT	FREQUENCY	JOURNEY TIME
Train/Bus	6–7 daily (0 on Sun)	1hr 51mins

FISHGUARD–CARDIGAN

TRANSPORT	FREQUENCY	JOURNEY TIME
Bus	12 daily (1 on Sun)	38mins

Notes

Between Carmarthen and Cardigan, First Cymru/ Richards Brothers run bus services nos 460/461.

Between Carmarthen and Fishguard, travel by train to Haverfordwest, then by bus to Fishguard: Richards Brothers service 412.

Between Fishguard and Cardigan, Richards Brothers service 412.

This route takes in the Pembrokeshire Coast, Britain's only coastal national park and an area of exceptional natural beauty. The Park runs for around 180 miles (290 km) from Amroth close to Tenby in the southerly reaches, to St Dogmael's near Cardigan in the north. The coastal path follows almost its entire length. Off the coast are islands like Skomer, a nature reserve with global clout, is home to the world's largest breeding colony of Manx shearwaters. Inland, Pembrokeshire has wonderful scenery; the lonely beauty of the Preseli Hills and the tranquil Gwaun valley are as diverse as they are compelling. Innumerable places of interest are dotted around the region, including ancient burial sites.

CARMARTHEN

The market town of Carmarthen is a staging post en route to Pembrokeshire National Park. It's a convenient place to stop off for lunch or maybe for the night as you work your way down to the coast. Carmarthen has plenty of vitality and a long history. It was the Romans' most westerly fortress in the UK and the **Roman Amphitheatre** in Priory St is one of only seven in Britain. Nott Square is home to **The Guildhall** with its imposing façade and just off the square are the ruins of the castle.

Seven miles east of Carmarthen is the newly opened **National Botanic Garden of Wales** sited at Middleton Hall near Llanarthney. This is the first modern botanic garden in the UK to be constructed with conservation as its primary aim. It boasts the largest single span glasshouse in the world and a magnificent collection of all the Mediterranean floras of the world. Addictively delicious chocolates are hand-crafted at **Pemberton's Victorian Chocolates** near Llanboidy. Demonstrations are given and, better still, the wares can be sampled.

The rivers Towy (near Carmarthen) and Teifi (near Cardigan) are famous for their coracles – a small one-man boat with a basketwork frame clad in leather that predates the Roman era. Fishermen work in pairs, casting a net across the water from their tiny cockle shell shaped boats, in the hope of capturing sewin or sea trout. An annual Coracle Regatta is held on these rivers in the summer.

i **Tourist Information Centre** 113 Lammas St; tel: (01267) 231557; website: www.carmarthenshire.gov.uk; e-mail: carmarthentic@carmarthenshire.gov.uk. Open daily from 0930 (summer); Mon–Sat 1000–1600 (winter).

For pub accommodation with a bit of character and atmosphere there's **The Drovers Arms** £ Lammas St; tel: (01267) 237646.
A few miles outside Carmarthen guests can take advantage of a lovely old house in the attractive Towy Valley by booking into **Capel Dewi Uchaf Country House** ££ Capel Dewi; tel: (01267) 290799. No nonsense home cooking is served around a large communal table in comfy surroundings.

TO **The Quayside Brasserie** £–££ The Quay; tel: (01267) 223000 has a deck where guests can sit out and watch the river Towy flowing by; the interior is just as pleasing. Look out for the interesting Welsh cheeses.

SIDE TRIP FROM CARMARTHEN Dylan Thomas's poetic play *Under Milk Wood* has charmed audiences the world over. The inspiration for his whimsically eloquent piece of work is **Laugharne** on the Tâf estuary. Thomas's **Boat House**, where he lived with his wife, the fiery, passionate Caitlin, and their children is now a museum (£, tel: (01994) 427420) and incorporates the writing shed next to the Thomas home, where the writer penned some of his most famous works. Laugharne is in a particularly glorious setting and oozes a quirky, off-beat charm.

SAUNDERSFOOT

A commercial resort and popular sailing and watersports centre, Saundersfoot attracts visitors in their droves. Seven trains run daily from Whitland, taking 20 mins. Nearby attractions include **Folly Farm** in Kilgetty, based on a working dairy farm. Children are usually captivated by the fluffy creatures in the animal pens and an indoor play area makes it a good wet weather retreat for families.

TENBY

The delightful little town of Tenby really is an idyllic seaside resort. It's a half-hour walk along the coast from Saundersfoot, or a 25-min train journey from Whitland (7–8 daily, 4 on Sun). Extremely elegant, with brightly painted harbour-front Georgian homes and tiny winding streets, it also has a lively atmosphere, lovely beaches, a medieval castle and town walls and a formidable fort. The **Tudor Merchant's House** is a fascinating three-storey building dating back to the 15th century, and is thought to be Tenby's oldest building. This legacy is testimony to Tenby's prosperous past as an important trading port.

Wales is littered with castles and, arguably, two of the most spectacular are in this region. **Carreg Cennen Castle** in Trapp near Llandeilo is built atop a towering crag with a commanding view. This 13th-century citadel has an unusual feature, a walled passageway in the cliff that leads to a cave beneath the castle. **Kidwelly** is a remarkably well-preserved medieval stronghold. The enormous three-storey gatehouse is awesome and Kidwelly's concentric structure makes it look very much like the perfect castle – a fact that hasn't bypassed film-makers.

Tenby Harbour is a magnet for visitors during the summer (don't even think about taking the car, leave it in the multi-storey facility on the edge of town) and from here you can take a boat trip to nearby **Caldey Island**. The island is home to a thriving Cistercian abbey where the monks busy themselves making perfume and chocolate and taking conducted tours. In sunny weather you could easily spend an entire day pottering around the island.

---

i **Tourist Information Centre** The Croft, Tenby; tel: (01834) 842402; website: www.pembrokeshire.gov.uk; e-mail: tenby.tic@pembrokeshire.gov.uk. Open daily from 1000.

🖳 Accommodation can get quite booked up in Tenby during the main season. If you plan on staying as long as a week it might be worth looking at self-catering accommodation. There are some very attractive properties overlooking the harbour. For fine views, hotels and guesthouses hugging Tenby's clifftops can't be beaten.

The Park Hotel ££ North Cliff; tel: (01834) 842480 overlooks the gleaming expanse of North Beach as does **Castle View Hotel**; tel: (01834) 842666 while the **Belgrave Hotel** ££ The Esplanade; tel: (01834) 842377 looks out over South Beach.

🏧 Tenby has an extraordinary range of good eating houses and fun cafés for such a small place. One of the nicest is **Plantagenet House** £–££ Quay Hill; tel: (01834) 842350, located in one of Tenby's higgeldy-piggeldy back streets. It's open for coffee, lunch and dinner, where local fish is a strong contender. The wine list is extensive and thoughtfully selected. The jolly Mediterranean style **Reef Café** ££ St Julian St serves informal lunches (baguettes and ciabatta, for instance) and more sophisticated selections for dinner. Tapas nights can be enjoyed from time to time as well.

On a warm summer's night **The Mews** £–££ Upper Frog St; tel: (01834) 844068 is great as you can sit outside amongst tubs of colourful flowers beneath the cosy warmth of terrace heaters. Sumo's Seafood Scones and the home made bread are worth travelling for.

MANORBIER AND ST GOVAN'S HEAD

Working your way around the coast, which is ideally explored by car, **Manorbier** boasts a friendly pub (The Castle Inn), a striking castle, a cluster of pretty cottages and a very appealing cove. The coastal walking in this area is stunning. The dramatic headland known as **St Govan's Head** offers heart-stopping views down perpendicular cliffs. Tucked away at the foot of the cliffs is the ancient religious site **St Govan's Chapel**, reached by steep steps. If you suffer from vertigo, don't go!

Nearby is the magnificent sea arch the **Green Bridge of Wales**, which can be observed from the safety of a viewing platform. Also worth a visit is **Bosherston**, famous for its large lily ponds. These lakes are reached via a pleasant walk through woodland and if you'd like to see the lilies in bloom, try timing your visit for June. The path eventually leads down to **Broad Haven** beach, sheltered by the might of St Govan's Head.

BEACHES AND NATURE RESERVES

Marloes Sands has to be one of the most beautiful beaches in Wales. The sweeping arm of sand dotted with odd-shaped columns of rock and presided over by the craggy Gateholm Island (which can be reached at low tide) is especially lovely. The unique nature reserves on **Skomer**, **Skokholm** and **Grassholm** islands are of international importance. Skomer is famous for its immense colonies of puffins and Manx shearwaters, while Grassholm, 10 miles (16 km) offshore, is home to 30,000 pairs of gannets. Trips to these islands leave from Martin's Haven and Dale; tel: (01646) 636754 or (0795) 0025586.

Further up the coast, surfers love the vast open beach at **Newgale** where the waves come pounding in with considerable force. Newgale itself is little more than a shop and a camp-site, however. Anyone looking for an inland sojourn might try **Llysyfran Country Park**, a 20-min drive from Haverfordwest. Set on a reservoir it offers sailing, canoeing, windsurfing and fishing. This expanse of fresh water (187 acres in total) has attracted many different species of bird, so it's worth taking binoculars.

Solva lies deep inside a tidal inlet, perfectly sheltered from the rigours of the weather on the open coast. The harbour, dotted with a multitude of different types of craft, is overlooked by dome-shaped lime kilns, where lime was burnt in the 19th century for agricultural purposes. For a meal out, **The Old Pharmacy Restaurant**, tel: (01437) 720005, is worth digging in your pocket for.

ST DAVID'S

With its dolls' house size cottages and narrow back streets, St David's, Britain's smallest city, certainly doesn't fall short in the charm stakes. A lively surfing community helps funk up the atmosphere and a flourishing artistic community bears comparison to that in Cornwall during the 1930s. **St David's Cathedral**, a fine example of medieval craftsmanship, sits in a grassy hollow that screens it from the main city. This sacred site has been a place of pilgrimage for almost a thousand years.

i **National Park Visitor Centre** The Grove; tel: (01437) 720392; website: www.pembrokeshirecoast.org.uk; e-mail: enquiries@stdavids.pembrokeshirecoast.org.uk. Open daily from 0930 (from 1000 in winter).

🏨 All St David's hotels incorporate a restaurant open to non-residents.

For a B&B in a traditional Georgian town house try the centrally located **Alandale** ££ 43 Nun St, St David's; tel: (01437) 7200404.

Also in Nun St is **The Glenydd** ££; tel: (01437) 720576. This guest house also has its own bistro.

FISHGUARD

Fishguard's most picturesque part is the lower quayside where quaint cottages huddle beneath a steep hillside. It is notorious as being the site of the last invasion of British soil; however, the attempted breach of the defences was so bungled as to be laughable. A formidable local woman called Jemima Nicholas managed to capture 12 of the invading French troops armed only with a pitchfork. Nearby attractions include **Llangloffan Farmhouse Cheese Centre** in Castle Morris where flavoursome Welsh cheese is made from the farm's own herd of cows. There are cheese-making demonstrations every morning. There's also the 18th-century **Tregwynt Woollen Mill** in St Nicholas. Nestling in a lovely setting, this working mill produces traditional Welsh weaves. For a walk on the wild side take a hike to **Strumble Head** a dramatically beautiful promontory capped with a lighthouse that's accessible by a footbridge.

i **Tourist Information Centre** Town Hall, The Square, Fishguard Town; tel: (01348) 873484; website: www.pembroke shire.gov.uk; e-mail: fishguard.tic@pembrokeshire.gov.uk. Open daily (except Sun in winter) from 1000.

🏨 For a B&B high on a hill overlooking the harbour there's **Cri'r Wylan** ££, Penwallis, Fishguard; tel: (01348) 873398. Or, in downtown Fishguard, **Esme** ££ 72 High St; tel: (01348) 872559.

On the edge of Goodwick, joined at the hip to Fishguard, **Glanmoy Country House Hotel** ££–£££ Treswrgi Rd, Goodwick; tel: (01348) 872 844 is in a quiet location with pretty gardens.

🍴 **Three Main Street** £–££ Main St, Fishguard; tel: (01348) 874275. This restaurant with rooms is very elegant yet far from formal, with super food and a hospitable environment. Another option combining delectable food and quality accommodation is the **Manor House** £–££ Main St, Fishguard; tel: (01348) 873260.

CARDIGAN

The market town of Cardigan sits at the mouth of the river Teifi and was once an important port. Its days of sea-faring lustre are long gone, but it still has some points of interest: the delightful sculpture of an **otter** presented to the town by naturalist David Bellamy, for instance, and the former **Guildhall** with its collection of market stalls. **Theatr Mwldan** puts on a lively entertainment schedule. Practically on the doorstep you'll find **Poppit Sands**, a great beach for swimming. **Cilgerran** is within spitting distance of Cardigan too and it has a wonderful castle which crowns a lofty crag overlooking the **Teifi Gorge**. Five miles of trails dissect a variety of habitats at the **Welsh Wildlife Centre** near Cilgerran. There is a large reedbed, a conservation garden and a tree nursery. Wildlife (maybe even otters if you're lucky) can be viewed from hides and an overview of the 270-acre (109-ha) site can be had from a tree-top hide.

i **Tourist Information Centre** Theatr Mwldan, Bath House Rd; tel: (01239) 613230; website: www.ceredigion.gov.uk; e-mail: cardigantic@ceredigion.gov.uk. Open daily from 1000.

An old coaching inn in the heart of Cardigan, **The Black Lion** ££ High St, Cardigan; tel: (01239) 612532, offers rooms, bar food and a pleasant drinking haunt.
Alternatively, there's a handy B&B called **Highbury** ££ Pendre, Carmarthen; tel: (01239) 613403.

Just a mile or so outside the town is the lovely little pub, the **Ferry Inn** £ St Dogmaels; tel: (01239) 615172. It's too small to provide rooms, but great care is taken over its very good freshly cooked food.

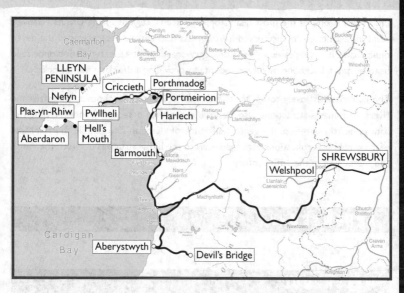

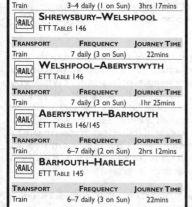

RAIL SHREWSBURY–PWLLHELI
ETT Tables 146/145

TRANSPORT	FREQUENCY	JOURNEY TIME
Train	3–4 daily (1 on Sun)	3hrs 17mins

RAIL SHREWSBURY–WELSHPOOL
ETT Tables 146

TRANSPORT	FREQUENCY	JOURNEY TIME
Train	7 daily (3 on Sun)	22mins

RAIL WELSHPOOL–ABERYSTWYTH
ETT Table 146

TRANSPORT	FREQUENCY	JOURNEY TIME
Train	7 daily (3 on Sun)	1hr 25mins

RAIL ABERYSTWYTH–BARMOUTH
ETT Tables 146/145

TRANSPORT	FREQUENCY	JOURNEY TIME
Train	6–7 daily (2 on Sun)	2hrs 12mins

RAIL BARMOUTH–HARLECH
ETT Table 145

TRANSPORT	FREQUENCY	JOURNEY TIME
Train	6–7 daily (3 on Sun)	22mins

RAIL HARLECH–PORTHMADOG
ETT Table 145

TRANSPORT	FREQUENCY	JOURNEY TIME
Train	6 daily (3 on Sun)	19mins

RAIL PORTHMADOG–CRICCIETH
ETT Table 145

TRANSPORT	FREQUENCY	JOURNEY TIME
Train	6 daily (3 on Sun)	8mins

RAIL CRICCIETH–PWLLHELI
ETT Table 145

TRANSPORT	FREQUENCY	JOURNEY TIME
Train	6 daily (3 on Sun)	13mins

Notes
If travelling through from Shrewsbury or Welshpool to Pwllheli, change at Machynlleth.

For journeys from Aberystwyth to Barmouth, change at Dovey Junction.

SHREWSBURY — LLEYN PENINSULA

Mid Wales is one of the most heartstoppingly scenic regions in the UK. Its relatively scant infrastructure has preserved it from mass tourism and the ravages of the developer's hand. It has miles upon miles of craggy coastline interspersed with blonde sand beaches and a backbone of rugged mountains providing a dramatic framework.

The hinterland is lovely too, with its lush valleys, isolated farmhouses, waterfalls and rivers. Man-made attractions also deserve more than a second glance. A clutch of handsome towns reflect the genteel affluence of Victorian times while the remnants of many robust fortifications bear testimony to the bitter struggles between the Welsh and the English in the 13th century.

SHREWSBURY

See p. 173.

WELSHPOOL

This pleasant market town sits close to the Wales/England border and its architectural styles reflect both influences. Its main thoroughfare has a number of interesting buildings. Look out for the 15th- and 16th-century **Buttery** and **Prentice Traders** with their delicately carved wooden frontages. The hexagonal **cockpit** was used for cock fighting until the sport was banned in 1849. Welshpool's railway station is a flamboyant paean to the glory days of rail travel, while a second station serves the narrow-gauge **Welshpool and Llanfair Light Railway**.

Welshpool stands on the Montgomery Canal and boat trips depart from the town wharf. The former dock warehouse is now home to the **Powysland Museum and Montgomery Canal Centre**, giving interesting snippets of local history. A mile or so south-west of the town is **Powis Castle** and if you take the route through parkland (starting from the High St) it's a pleasant walk. This ostentatious mansion features lofty mock battlements towering over a flight of Italianate terraces cut into the steep slope beneath them. Created between 1688 and 1722, they are the only formal gardens of this date in Britain to survive in their original form.

Six narrow-gauge railways operate in Mid Wales: the **Fairbourne and Barmouth**, the **Welshpool and Llanfair**, the **Talyllyn**, the **Bala Lake**, the **Vale of Rheidol** and the **Teifi Valley**.

[i] **Tourist Information Centre** Vicarage Garden, Church St; tel: (01938) 5520043; website: www.powys.gov.uk; e-mail: weltic@powys.gov.uk. Open daily from 0930 (summer); Mon–Fri 0930–1700, Sat–Sun 1000–1700 (winter).

ABERYSTWYTH

Aberystwyth is frequently dubbed the capital of Mid Wales, a rather more appropriate title than the 'Biarritz of Wales', as it has been known. This seaside town's image is certainly more staid than racy. Its traditional Victorian promenade ends abruptly at **Constitution Hill**. The views from the top are wonderful. If you're feeling energetic you can reach the 430 ft (131 m) summit on foot. Or you can take the dignified Victorian alternative, the **Cliff Railway**, which ascends the hill's 1-in-2 gradient at a very sober 4 mph (6.5 km/h). At the top is another legacy from the ever-enterprising Victorians, the **Camera Obscura**, a device whose mirror and lens system produces moving pictures of the surroundings. This new model casts its eye over immensely beautiful countryside.

Aberystwyth Arts Centre; tel: (01970) 623232, is worth looking up for performances, exhibitions and cinema. Don't forget to take a look at the magnificent new wing, which is particularly stylish. Also worth seeing is Edward I's stronghold, **Aberystwyth Castle**, a fortress built as part of the monarch's campaign to suppress the Welsh. The narrow-gauge **Vale of Rheidol Railway** takes passengers from Aberystwyth to **Devil's Bridge**, the steam engine puffing its way through magnificent scenery that culminates at the Devil's Bridge waterfalls.

Devil's Bridge itself is said to have been built by the devil so that an old woman could cross the gorge and retrieve her cow. Of course the devil's motives were far from altruistic. He stipulated that he would own the first living creature to cross the bridge. The old woman didn't fall for this ruse, outwitting the devil by throwing a crust of bread over the bridge, which her dog chased. The devil got the dog instead of the woman.

> **i** **Tourist Information Centre** Terrace Rd;
> tel: (01970) 612125; website: www.ceredigion.gov.uk;
> e-mail: aberystwythtic@ceredigion.gov.uk. Open daily
> 1000–1800 (summer); Mon–Sat 1000–1700 (winter).

> 🛏 Prime examples of stately Victorian architecture can be
> found on the seafront. One such establishment is the **Belle
> Vue Royal Hotel** ££ Marine Terrace; tel: (01970) 617558. On
> a fine evening the sunsets over Cardigan Bay are magnificent.
> **University** accommodation £ Penglais Campus is available
> during the holidays; tel: (01970) 623111.

> 🍴 **The Treehouse Restaurant** £–££ Baker St serves excel-
> lent organic food; tel: (01970) 615791. Informal and bustling,
> lunchtimes feature predominantly vegetarian food with one
> meat option. Evenings (open only Thur–Sat) are more formal
> and feature a broader range of meat and fish dishes.

For pub style grub there's **Bar Essential** on Portland St and **Scholars** on Queen's Rd.

SIDE TRIPS FROM ABERYSTWYTH As you journey northwards from Aberystwyth it's worth taking a detour to the **National Centre for Alternative Technology**, tel: (01654) 702400, near Machynlleth, one of Wales' most popular tourist attractions. A once derelict slate quarry has become home to an almost entirely self-sufficient community generating 80% of its own power from the wind, sun and water. In addition to day-visitors and an award-winning vegetarian café, the centre offers residential courses.

The charming little seaside town of **Aberdovey** (Aberdyfi) snakes its way along a spit of land backed by steep hills. It was the birthplace of the outward-bound movement in 1941. The sheltered waters of the bay make it a popular spot for sailing and other watersports. Also in the confines of the Dyfi estuary is **Ynyslas** and the dunes of the **Dyfi National Nature Reserve** which stand out like pyramids in this low-lying region of sand and saltmarsh.

BARMOUTH

A little further up the coast is the delightful little town of **Barmouth** standing on the spectacular Mawddach Estuary. It has a picturesque harbour and acres of clean sand, ideal for the bucket-and-spade brigade. The houses are built on a steep hillside so that they seem to be stacked one on top of each other. Across the estuary is **Fairbourne**, home to the **Fairbourne and Barmouth Steam Railway**, which has the narrowest of narrow gauges at only 12¼ in (311 mm). These locomotives stop off en route at the station with the world's longest name, as confirmed by the *Guinness Book of Records*. Here goes: Gorsafawddachaidraigodanheddogleddollonpen-rhynareurdraethceredigion.

🛏 **Ty'r Graig Castle Hotel** ££ Llanaber Rd, Barmouth; tel: (01341) 2800 00470 is perched on a hillside overlooking the sea. The atmosphere is friendly and there is also a restaurant. Surrounded by countryside, yet two minutes from the beach is **Bryn Melyn Hotel** ££ Panorama Rd; tel: (01341) 280556, which also has a restaurant.

🍴 **Llwyndu Farmhouse** ££ Llanaber; tel: (01341) 2800 00144 is a lovely old building located slightly north of Barmouth combining, as many rural establishments do now, accommodation and food. Peter and Paula Thompson make an excellent job of both. Guests can look forward to eating delectable food amid oak panelling, beams and massive fireplaces.

The Indian Clipper Balti House £–££ 2 Church St; tel: (01341) 280252 is a balti house of note that eschews the formulaic offerings that many serve. The naan is made to order and is excellent for mopping up the juices in a *Macchi Sebz* – white fish with crisp aubergine and a fennel and sesame seed sauce.

HARLECH

Harlech's main attraction is its magnificent and highly atmospheric castle. Perched on a tall crag, the views from its ramparts are breathtaking. Built by Edward I in 1283, it now rates as a World Heritage listed site. Golfing fans could give the Royal St David's golf club a try, while Harlech beach affords yawning swathes of yellow sand. Nearby (about 1½ miles/2.4 km south of Harlech) you'll find **Muriau'r Gwyddelod** (Irishmen's Walls), a cluster of prehistoric dwellings that probably won't be easy to locate without an Ordnance Survey map. There's also the **Old Llanfair Slate Caverns**, a relic of North Wales' once mighty slate industry.

> *i* **Tourist Information Centre** Gwyddfor House, High St; tel/fax: (01766) 780658; website: www.gwynedd.gov.uk; e-mail: ticharlech@hotmail.com. Open summer only, daily from 1000.

> 🏠 The diminutive **Castle Cottage Restaurant with Rooms** ££ Pen Lleth, Harlech; tel: (01766) 780479 shelters in the shadow of Edward I's awesome fortress. The food here is sublime and it's worth spending the night to enjoy it.

> 🍽 **Plas Café** £–££ High St, Harlech; tel: (01766) 780204 serves decent, wholesome food from morning to night and there are marvellous views from the tea garden. A small wine list and draught beers are also on offer.

PORTMEIRION

Colour-washed façades, neoclassical colonnades, a Pantheon and cupolas, all flouncing around a Mediterranean piazza. This is Portmeirion, an eccentrically incongruous, but surprisingly pleasing, 20th-century architectural flight of fancy grafted onto the Welsh countryside by Sir Clough Williams-Ellis, whose descendants are responsible for the eponymous pottery.

It's in a wonderful location, but unfortunately during the summer months the rest of the planet thinks so too and the village can clock up as many as 3000 visitors per day. Another surreal aspect to Portmeirion is the fact that the 1960s cult series *The Prisoner* was filmed there and fans of this bizarre TV drama congregate for a weekend every autumn for a convention. A fun way to arrive is by taking the steam-hauled Ffestiniog Railway (Blaenau Ffestiniog–Porthmadog; mainline stations at both ends) to Boston Lodge, from which it is about 10 minutes' walk.

> 🍴 For a bite to eat and a drink there's **Castell Deudraeth** £–££ in the grounds of Portmeirion; tel: (01766) 770000, serving everything from morning coffee to bar meals and suppers. Local seafood is a speciality, no pre-booking is required and children are welcome. Closed during the winter months.

THE LLEYN PENINSULA

PORTHMADOG Porthmadog is an attractive little town with a small harbour. Although there isn't a great deal to see there, it's conveniently placed for exploring the peninsula and Snowdonia National Park. This is the terminus for the **Ffestiniog Railway**, where steam locos take a highly scenic route to the slate-mining village of Blaenau Ffestiniog, from where you can head further by rail to Betws-y-Coed in the heart of Snowdonia.

> ℹ️ **Tourist Information Centre** Y Ganolfan, High St; tel: (01766) 512981; website: www.gwynedd.gov.uk; e-mail: porthmadog.tic@gwynedd.gov.uk. Open daily from 0930 (1000 in summer).

> 🏨 **The Royal Sportsman** ££ 131 High St; tel: (01766) 512015 has newly refurbished non-smoking rooms and an award-winning restaurant along with bar meals cooked to order. **The Owens Hotel** ££ 71 High St, Porthmadog; tel: (01766) 512098 is also located on the town's main thoroughfare.

> 🍴 For an imaginative à la carte menu and generous range of vegetarian options try **The Grapevine** ££ 152 High St, tel: (01766) 5144230.
> There's a boisterous atmosphere and a very decent menu (take a good look at the specials) at **Yr Hen Fecws** £–££ 15/16 Lombard St; tel: (01766) 514625.

CRICCIETH A quiet little town on the Lleyn Peninsula, Criccieth was popular in Victorian times as a seaside resort and this era is reflected in its respectable bay-fronted houses. It caters for those who want a low key break rather than hustle and bustle. The summer music festival has earned a good reputation. The ruined fortifications of Criccieth Castle, a fortress which has served both English and Welsh, sits on the headland separating the town's two beaches, with far-reaching views over Tremadog Bay.

🍴 For those with a penchant for seafood, **Tir-a-Mor** ££ 1–3 Mona Terrace, Criccieth; tel: (01766) 523084 shouldn't be missed, with fresh line-caught sea-bass and fat local scallops.

PWLLHELI Pwllheli is much busier than most other places on the peninsula. A popular sailing centre, it boasts a capacious modern marina and sailing club. Old Pwllheli, with its narrow streets, has retained a more traditional ambience. For those who want laid-on entertainment, nearby **Starcoast World** offers the thrills of the 'Boomerang' roller coaster as well as a wet weather option of a tropical pool complete with rapids and whirlpool.

ℹ️ **Tourist Information Centre** Min y Don, Station Sq.; tel: (01758) 613000; website: www.gwynedd.gov.uk; e-mail: pwllheli.tic@gwynedd.gov.uk. Open daily from 1000 (summer); Mon–Wed, Fri–Sat (winter).

🏠 **Plas Bodegroes** ££ Nefyn Rd, Pwllheli; tel: (01758) 612363 is another place in this little corner of Wales with an excellent reputation for fine food and charming accommodation.

SIDE TRIPS FROM PWLLHELI **Abersoch** is another resort popular with the yachting fraternity, although its sandy beaches and extremely attractive location give it a universal appeal.

🏠 **Porth Tocyn** £££ Abersoch; tel: (01758) 713303 is a treat of a place in a wonderful location overlooking Cardigan Bay and the mountains of Snowdonia. It's also well known for its delicious food and has been featured in a number of good food guides. The dining room is open to non-residents.

A must-see on the south-west of the Lleyn Peninsula is the delightful manor house **Plas-yn-Rhiw**. This compact structure is medieval in origin but most of the existing edifice is 17th-century. It overlooks a wild coastline, yet is surrounded by verdant woodland and intricate ornamental gardens. **Hell's Mouth** or **Porth Neigwl**, to give it its proper moniker, is a magnificent bay where the surf pounds in over the sands. A wild, exposed spot, it's gloriously exhilarating on a windy day.

Porth Oer, a couple of miles north of Aberdaron on the Lleyn Peninsula, is also known as Whistling Sands. The grains of sand on this pretty little beach squeak underfoot. However, it's supposed to work best if you run on damp sand in bare feet!

The whitewashed cottages in **Aberdaron** village gleam appealingly when the sun shines. Although remote and unassuming, this outpost at the very tip of the Lleyn was once a very important stopping place for pilgrims making their way to **Bardsey Island**, 2 miles (3 km) offshore. It was said that three pilgrimages to

Bardsey equalled one to Rome. It might have been safer getting to Rome as many of the devoted drowned while crossing the treacherous Bardsey Sound. Legend has it that Bardsey is the burial place of 20,000 saints, although it doesn't specify how many of these died getting there.

The safe anchorage of **Porthdinllaen** has missed its chance to feature on the map in a big way. A 19th-century plan aimed to turn it into a major sea port sheltering shipping to and from Ireland – but that distinction went to Holyhead. Porthdinllaen's loss is the visitor's gain, because it really is a very attractive spot with its old pub and myriad trails leading over the headland.

Nearby **Nefyn** with its steep streets once made its living from herring, now it's the tourists who provide the income. The village of **Nant Gwrtheyrn** is worth a visit too. Until fairly recently its appeal lay in the fact that it had been abandoned when quarrying ceased to pay. Its sense of isolation was compounded by the fact that it could only be reached via a footpath. Now it has a new purpose in life, as a Welsh language study centre, but its charm is retained by the unspoilt location and the fact that you are still obliged to walk there, only these days not on a rough track.

WHERE NEXT?

Link up with the Colwyn Bay — Snowdonia National Park route in reverse for Wales's highest mountain and dramatic scenery as well as sand beaches (see p. 199). You could then continue to the Isle of Anglesey, with its lush pastureland and spectacular rocky coastline.

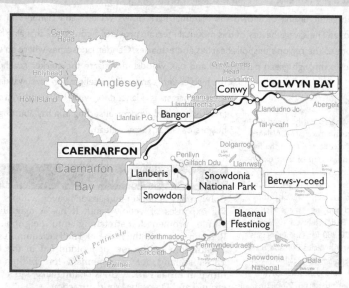

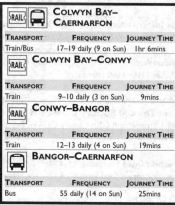

RAIL 🚌 **COLWYN BAY–**		
CAERNARFON		
TRANSPORT	FREQUENCY	JOURNEY TIME
Train/Bus	17–19 daily (9 on Sun)	1hr 6mins

RAIL **COLWYN BAY–CONWY**		
TRANSPORT	FREQUENCY	JOURNEY TIME
Train	9–10 daily (3 on Sun)	9mins

RAIL **CONWY–BANGOR**		
TRANSPORT	FREQUENCY	JOURNEY TIME
Train	12–13 daily (4 on Sun)	19mins

🚌 **BANGOR–CAERNARFON**		
TRANSPORT	FREQUENCY	JOURNEY TIME
Bus	55 daily (14 on Sun)	25mins

Notes

From Colwyn Bay to Caernarfon, travel by train to Bangor, then by bus to Caernarfon: First Cymru services 5/5A/5B/5X. Conwy is a request stop.

Colwyn Bay – Snowdonia National Park

The gaunt drama of Snowdonia National Park draws walkers and climbers in their droves. The savage beauty of this mountain terrain provides a constantly changing backcloth to the region's unspoilt beaches and estuaries. Gentler landscapes where streams trickle through green pastureland and oak woodland mitigate the starker reaches of the high country and offer excellent low level walking. In total contrast is Llandudno, with its grand Victorian architecture and wonderful setting in a bay abutting the heights of Great Ormes Head.

A bus service called Sherpa is a godsend in such a rural area. Walkers are collected from the finishing point of their excursion and taken back to their car or hotel. It's also a useful means of getting to outlying villages such as Beddgelert; tel: (01286) 870 880 for further details. An All Wales Bus and Train Enquiry Line called Travel Line is another useful option; tel: 0870 6082608.

COLWYN BAY

Colwyn Bay is bucket-and-spade heaven with its gaping expanses of yellow sand. It has a magnificent 3-mile promenade, stretching into neighbouring Rhos-on-Sea (also the home of The Harlequin Puppet Theatre, one of the few of its kind left in the UK). Those seeking out entertainment for children will thrive in **Eirias Park** with its boating lake, kid's playground and Dinosaur World attraction.

i **Tourist Information Centre** Imperial Buildings, Station Sq., Prince's Dr; tel: (01492) 530478; website: www.colwyn-bay-tourism.co.uk; e-mail: colwynbay.tic@virgin.net. Open Mon–Sat 0930–1700, Sun Aug only1000–1700 (summer); Mon–Sat 0930–1600, Sun 1100–1600 (summer)

Lovers of American-style harness racing might be surprised to find a track right here in coastal North Wales – the Tir Prince Raceway on the Towyn road. This might be a long way from the USA, but visitors aren't short-changed on showbiz glitz and hype.

For upmarket accommodation, superb views and delicious food, look out **The Old Rectory Country House** £–££ Llanrwst Rd, Llansantffraid Glan Conwy, Colwyn Bay; tel: (01492) 580611.

Café Nicoise £ 124 Abergele Rd; tel: (01492) 53155, with its arty blue exterior, serves food worthy of a decent French bistro.

SIDE TRIP FROM COLWYN BAY **Llandudno** really is a classic British seaside resort. Dignified in the extreme with its rows of elegant Victorian buildings, pier and promenade, it has avoided the crass development of so many maritime locations. It has an old-fashioned, rather staid ambience, and you'll find that it still offers donkey rides on the beach and Punch and Judy shows. It's possible to ride on a tram to The Great Orme, a massive limestone cliff rearing up from the sea. In Norse, the word 'orme' means sea monster. The Great Orme Mines show how copper was retrieved in ancient times.

i **Tourist Information Centre** 1-2 Chapel St, Llandudno; tel: (01492) 876413; website: www.llandudno-tourism.co.uk; e-mail: llandudno.tic@virgin.net. Open daily from 0930 (summer); Mon–Sat from 0900 (winter).

🛏 **Cranberry House** ££ 12 Abbey Rd, Llandudno; tel: (01492) 879760 is a centrally located B&B, as is **Abbey Lodge** ££ 14 Abbey Rd, Llandudno.

🍴 For the bustling informality of a pub, take a look at the **Queen's Head** £ Glanwydden, Llandudno Junction; tel: (01492) 546570. The emphasis is on simple, well executed dishes for hearty appetites.

CONWY

Approaching Conwy from Llandudno, one gets a magnificent view of the medieval castle, the estuary, its wooded banks and the mountains of Snowdonia. **Conwy Castle**, power base of Edward I, is a World Heritage Site. Most of the town is embraced by fearsome town walls, some sections of which can still be walked and offer excellent views. Architecturally speaking, Conwy's 800 years of history has produced some delights. The Smallest House in the UK, set on the quayside, for instance, and the Elizabethan town house, Plas Mawr.

i **Conwy Castle Visitor Centre**, Castle Buildings, Castle St; tel: (01492) 592248; website: www.conway.gov.uk; e-mail: conway.tic@virgin.net. Open daily from 1000 (summer); Mon–Fri 0930–1600, Sat–Sun 1100–1600 (winter).

🛏 **Conwy Youth Hostel** £ Sychnant Pass Rd, tel: 0870 7705774 (e-mail: conwy@yha.org.uk) is up on the west side of town, a short walk from the town centre and station.

🍴 At **Richard's Bistro** £–££ 7 Church Walks; tel: (01492) 875315 there's a choice of an easy-going downstairs area or a slightly smarter alternative upstairs. Either way, the food is worth a visit.

There's a great view over the Conwy estuary from **La Paysanne** ££ 147 Station Rd, Deganwy; tel: (01492) 582079. The menu offers hearty French influenced dishes, plus a well-chosen wine list.

The superb gardens at **Bodnant** shouldn't be missed. There's a wonderful mix of styles, from formal terraces to a wild garden with a stream tumbling through. The outlook over the Conwy Valley and Snowdonia is breathtaking. Another great feature is the Laburnum Arch. In early summer the great golden tails of the laburnum avenue form an impressive canopy. Bodnant is 8 miles (13 km) south of Llandudno (Arriva Cymru Alpine bus 25 via Llandudno Junction station passes by); the nearest station to Bodnant is Tal-y-Cafn (1.5 miles/2.5 km).

BANGOR

The university town of Bangor sits on the narrow strip of water separating Anglesey from the mainland, the Menai Strait. Its Victorian pier has been renovated to a high standard. Bangor itself is pleasant enough but not particularly remarkable, but there are some interesting places around and about. **Penrhyn Castle** is a neo-Norman pile built by the Pennant family after they amassed an indecently large fortune courtesy of the local slate quarries. The interior is incredibly lavish, with its hand-painted Chinese wallpaper and gargantuan Great Hall.

> [i] **Tourist Information Centre** Town Hall, Deiniol Rd; tel: (01248) 352786; website: www.gwynedd.gov.uk; e-mail: bangor.tic@gwynedd.gov.uk. Open daily from 1000 (summer); Fri–Sat only (winter).

> [🏠] **Goetre Isaf Farmhouse** £–££ Caernarfon Rd; tel (01248) 364541. This is a worthy choice for good value, home-made food and pleasant accommodation in an attractive old farmhouse.
> **Bangor Youth Hostel** £ Tan-y-Bryn, tel: 0870 7705686 (e-mail: bangor@yha.org.uk) is on the east side of town, near the Penrhyn Castle estate.

> [🍽] For a coffee or a glass of wine over a newspaper, a breakfast of bagels with smoked salmon and scrambled egg, or a main meal (served until 2100), try **Herbs** £ 162 High St; tel: (01248) 351249.

CAERNARFON

Caernarfon Castle is the mightiest of all Edward I's impressive fortresses, in a superb location with the sea lapping at its feet. It was built in triumph after the defeat of the native Welsh prince Llywelyn the Last. Like Conwy Castle, it is now listed as a World Heritage Site. Secure 13th-century walls encase the town, showing that King Edward really did mean business. Even earlier history can be found at the **Segontium Roman Fort and Museum** (walking distance from Caernarfon centre free, open Mon–Sat 1000–1700 and Sun pm April–Oct), while the **Caernarfon**

Maritime Museum unveils the town's seafaring past. An old dredger moored up at the dock is one of the exhibits (£, open Sun–Fri 1100–1600 in summer).

> **ℹ Tourist Information Centre** Oriel Pendeitsh, Castle St; tel: (01286) 672232; website: www.gwynedd.gov.uk; e-mail: caernarfon.tic@gwynedd.gov.uk. Open daily from 1000 (summer); Thur–Tues from 0900 (winter).

SNOWDONIA NATIONAL PARK

The Snowdonia National Park with its lofty peaks, tumbling rivers, attractive narrow-gauge railways, neat stone cottages and panoramic views to the open sea, is truly magnificent.

LLANBERIS Llanberis is a mecca for climbers and walkers, as reflected by the number of outdoor shops and droves of people clad in goretex and shouldering rucksacks. The Llanberis Pass, snaking its way between towering fortresses of rock, is dramatic by anyone's standards. Set at the foot of **Snowdon**, the highest peak in England and Wales (3560 ft/1085 m), Llanberis hugs the shores of two lakes, Llyn Peris and Llyn Padarn. The latter boasts a narrow-gauge line and an appealing little train that chugs along its scenic shores – the **Llanberis Lake Railway**. The longest, but easiest walking route up Snowdon departs from Llanberis as does the Snowdon Mountain Railway, the cop-out route for those who want to enjoy the spectacular views without straining their cardiovascular systems.

Llyn Idwal, a lake accessible only by a footpath leaving from Ogwen Cottage, can look very sombre on a dark day. It's shadowed by tall mountains and the lumpy outcrop looming above it is known as the Devil's Kitchen. Legend has it that no bird will ever fly over it. A fanciful 18th-century writer even went as far as to suggest that these surroundings were enough to inspire murderous thoughts. Others feel differently; the area around the lake became Wales' first National Nature Reserve.

Overlooking Llyn Peris is the brooding ruin of **Dolbadarn Castle** and, for those who prefer to admire modern technology, there's **Electric Mountain**, a hands-on visitor centre explaining the mysteries of hydroelectric power. The underground tour (£) of the largest pumped-storage power station in Europe is spectacular. In the 19th century, slate quarrying was to North Wales what coal mining was to the south. In its glory days Dinorwig Slate Quarry was one of the largest; with a workforce of more than 3000 men working unfeasibly long hours to supply the world with roofing slate. Now its workshops have been preserved as the **Welsh Slate Museum** (free, open daily open 1000–1700).

> **ℹ Tourist Information Centre** 41b High St, Llanberis; tel: (01286) 870765; website: www.gwynedd.gov.uk; e-mail: llaberis.tic@gwynedd.gov.uk. Open daily from 1000 (summer); Wed–Sun and first Tues every month 1000–1600.

🏨 Popular with outdoor types with a lively atmosphere is **The Heights** ££ 74 High St; tel: (01286) 87179. It has hotel accommodation, a bunkhouse and busy bar.
Bron-y-Graig ££ Capel Coch; tel: (01286) 872 073 provides comfortable B&B facilities in a pleasant setting.
Llanberis Youth Hostel £ Llwyn Celyn, tel: 0870 7705928 (e-mail: llanberis@yha.org.uk) is about 10 mins walk from the centre, via Capel Coch Rd (off High St by Spar shop, then fork left). There are also youth hostels around the coast at Conwy, Rowen and Bangor; and close to the mountains at Capel Curig, Betws-y-Coed, Pen y Pass, Snowdon Ranger, Bryn Gwynant and Idwal Cottage.

EN ROUTE

The mineral-rich waters of **Trefriw** (between Conwy and Betws-y-Coed) were discovered by the Romans. In their eagerness to get their hands on this healing liquid they tunnelled into the mountain to reach the source. The Victorians, equally excited by the medicinal properties of these waters, arrived by the shedload to wallow in them. Modern visitors can tour the original Roman cave and see the rather awesome stone bathhouse with its austere slate bath, reached by a 20-min drive from Conwy.

🍽 **Y Bistro** £–££ 43/45 High St; tel: (012860) 871278 provides a haven for those craving a decent bite. Don't be put off by the rather unprepossessing exterior. The restaurant has three rooms and the owners can also fix up visitors with self-catering accommodation.

BLAENAU FFESTINIOG Once a major industrial centre; remnants of those times can still be seen in the mountains of blue-black slate that dominate the town. The **Ffestiniog Railway** also leaves from here, taking the visitor on an extremely lovely 13-mile (21-km) journey through Snowdonia National Park to Porthmadog on the coast.

BETWS-Y-COED This attractive little town crouches on the floor of a steep, wooded valley. It is a tourist honey-pot as well as being popular with anglers and walkers. There are some excellent walking routes starting right in the town centre. Waymarked trails lead through some exceptionally attractive countryside. Nearby **Swallow Falls** are worth a visit – one daring individual descended this foaming cascade in a canoe.

Then there is Ty Hyll, the **Ugly House**, which is actally very cute, being diminutive and constructed haphazardly in local stone. **Penmachno** is a quarrying village famous for its working woollen mill (open to the public). Just 2 miles (3 km) north-west is the 16th-century National Trust property **Ty Mawr Wybrnant**. This unpretentious stone cottage is birthplace of Bishop William Morgan, who did much to keep his native language alive by translating the Bible into Welsh.

ℹ️ **Tourist Information Centre** Royal Oak Stables; tel: (01690) 710426; website: www.gwynedd.gov.uk; e-mail: betwstic@hotmail.com.

🛏 The former coaching inn, **Ty Gwyn Hotel ££** Betws-y-Coed; tel: (01690) 710383, has the option of a four-poster bed (at a slightly higher price than their average rooms). Well located, **The Royal Oak £–££** Holyhead Rd, Betws-y-Coed; tel: (01690) 710219 has a cocktail bar as well as a more earthy option in its converted stables. Spacious rooms with sofas are little more than the price of an ordinary bedroom.

🍽 For a delightful hotel and brasserie nip up the lovely Conwy Valley to **Prince's Arms Country Hotel ££** Trefriw, nr Betws-y-Coed; tel: (01492) 640592.

BEDDGELERT Pretty **Beddgelert** is a famous tourist magnet associated with a legend of dubious credentials. It goes like this. A nobleman went off hunting leaving his dog to guard his infant son. On returning, he found the dog's jowls dripping with blood. He slew the unfortunate hound instantly, thinking he had eaten the baby, only to discover the child safe and sound under his crib and a dead wolf lying close by. Stricken by remorse, he never smiled again. Cynics say a canny pub owner made up the story to attract visitors. Nevertheless, you can see Gelert's Grave on the riverbank, and if you carry on, the waterside walking is very pleasant.

ℹ **Tourist Information Centre** Canolfan Hebog; tel/fax: (01766) 890615; website: www.gwynedd.gov.uk; e-mail: ticbedgelert@hotmail.com. Open daily from 0930 (1000 in summer).

BALA LAKE Wales' very own version of the Loch Ness Monster allegedly lives in **Llyn Tegid** (Bala Lake). You can circumnavigate this splendid water feature on the narrow-gauge Bala Lake Railway – it's a nice outing, even if you fail to spot the beast. Your best way of getting there is by car, and you can break your journey at several points along the route and go for a swim, have a picnic, take a stroll or try your hand at fishing. Bala village is at the eastern end of the 4-mile (6.4-km) long waterway.

ℹ **Tourist Information Centre** Penllyn, Pensarn Rd, Bala; tel/fax: (01678) 521021; website: www.gwynedd.gov.uk; e-mail: bala.tic@gwynedd.gov.uk. Open daily from 1000 (summer); Fri–Mon from 1000 (winter).

WHERE NEXT?

Most trains passing through Colwyn Bay (18–19 daily, 9 on Sun; journey time 57 mins) and Conwy (request stop; 7–8 trains daily, 1 on Sun; journey time 53 mins) continue to Holyhead, at the far side of the isle of Anglesey, for ferries to Ireland (8 daily to Dublin, 4 daily to Dún Laoghaire).

MANCHESTER

The Lancashire cotton industry transformed Manchester from a small country town into a great industrial city in the 19th century. Decay and insensitive post-war redevelopment have not been kind to its face, but a mega-million-pound project funded by the National Lottery has revitalised the central area known as the Millennium Quarter. Manchester has a China Town and a thriving gay quarter, one of the world's most famous soccer teams and a smattering of good sights – including the Museum of Science and Industry in Castlefield and the amazing modern architecture of the crowd-pulling Lowry Centre in the hitherto depressed district of Salford.

To walk around and drink in the atmosphere, begin in Albert Square and take a peek into the Town Hall, a grandiose statement of Victorian self-confidence and commercial might. Head into St Ann's Square, a legacy of 18th-century Manchester, and seek out the glass and iron Victoriana of Barton Square shopping arcade and the hall of the Royal Exchange, in its day the largest hall for business transactions in the world and now home to the Royal Exchange Theatre. Carry on past the Art Gallery in Princess St and follow the atmospheric Rochdale Canal to the canal basin at Castlegate.

GETTING THERE AND GETTING AROUND

Manchester's award-winning International Airport is 10 miles (16 km) from the city centre and serves around 95 airlines. Take the lift down to the railway station and you'll be able to catch a cheap train ride straight into the heart of the city. Alternatively, though slightly costly, a taxi ride to the city centre should take about 10 mins. Hire cars also operate from the airport.

The main railway station is **Manchester Piccadilly**, just east of the city centre, with direct services to, amongst other places, Liverpool, Preston, Glasgow, Edinburgh, Leeds, York, Sheffield, London, Birmingham, North and South Wales, as well as Manchester Airport. The services to and from Liverpool and Preston also call at Manchester **Oxford Rd**.

North of the city centre, and connected to Piccadilly by frequent trams, is **Victoria**

station which, while mostly serving local destinations, also has alternative services to Liverpool, Leeds and York by different routes.

Manchester's recently rebuilt long-distance coach station is in Chorley St.

INFORMATION

TOURIST OFFICES **Manchester Visitor Information Centre,** Town Hall Extension, Lloyd St; (0161) 234 3157; website: destinationmanchester.com; e-mail: manchester-visitor-centre@notes-manchester.gov.uk.

Manchester Airport Information Centre (Terminal 1); tel: (0161) 436 3344; (Terminal 2) (0161) 489 6412.

SAFETY Although much has been done to improve visitor safety in Manchester, common sense dictates that you should be aware of your surroundings at all times. As a general rule, avoid the Salford and Moss Side areas and be vigilant around the Northern Quarter after midnight. However, in this ever-changing city it pays to get the most up-to-date advice from the front desk of your hotel.

MONEY The main banks in the city centre include Barclays, 51 Mosley St; Lloyds TSB, 53 King St; Midland, 100 King St; National Westminster, 11 Spring Gardens; and Royal Bank of Scotland, 38 Mosley St. Open Mon–Fri 0900–1630; the NatWest is also open on Sat 0930–1330.

Several bureaux de change are located within Thomas Cook branches; there are five in the city centre including Piccadilly and Market St. Tel: (0161) 236 8575 for details.

POST AND PHONES Manchester Post Office, 26 Spring Gdns; tel: (0161) 839 0687 or Brazenose Post Office, 21 Brazenose St; tel: (0161) 832 6753.

ACCOMMODATION

Britannia Hotel ££ 35 Portland St; tel: (0161) 228 2288.

Campanile Hotel & Bistro Restaurant ££ 55 Ordsall Lane, Regent Rd, Salford Quays; tel: (0161) 833 1845; fax: (0161) 833 1847.

Elton Bank Hotel ££ 62 Platt Lane, Rusholme; tel: (0161) 224 6449; fax: (0161) 225 6446.

Ibis Manchester ££ Charles St; tel: (0161) 272 5000; fax: (0161) 272 5010; e-mail: h3143-gm@accor-hotels.com.

Monroe's pub and guest house **££** 38 London Rd; tel: (0161) 236 0564.

Premier Lodge (City Centre) Manchester ££ North Tower, Victoria Bridge St, Salford; tel: 0870 700 1488; fax: 0870 700 1489; e-mail:

tracy.salisbury@junglelink.co.uk.

The Rembrandt £££ 33 Sackville St; tel: (0161) 236 1311.

Travel Inn ££ Garden Court, Outwood Lane; tel: (0161) 498 0333. Fri, Sat and Sun rooms for one night only for up to four people sharing.

Youth Hostel £ Potato Wharf, Liverpool Rd, Castlefield; tel: 0870 7705950; website: www.yha.org.uk; e-mail: manchester@yha.org.uk.

FOOD AND DRINK

Cord £ 8 Dorsey House, Dorsey St, off Tibb St; tel: (0161) 832 9494. A modern twist on the traditional pub, this bar serves a wide range of beers and delicious home-made soups and stews at reasonable prices.

Dimitri's Tapas Bar Taverna £££ Campfield Arcade, Tonman St, Castlefield; tel: (0161) 839 3319. A beautiful Greek restaurant just off Deansgate. The meat and sea platters come well recommended.

Eighth Day Vegetarian Café ££ 107–111 Oxford Rd; tel: (0161) 273 1850. A workers co-op since 1976, this friendly establishment serves excellent cheap food from all over the world.

Manchester Craft and Design Centre ££ 17 Oak St; tel: (0161) 832 4274. The café inside the centre serves excellent fried breakfasts, excellent sandwiches and hot, tasty stews.

The Ox ££, situated behind the Deansgate in Liverpool Rd, serves consistently tasty gourmet pub grub at reasonable prices.

Tampopo Noodle Bar £££ 16 Albert Sq.; tel: (0161) 819 1966. A staple favourite amongst those who regularly eat out in Manchester for the Thai, Japanese and Chinese menu.

HIGHLIGHTS

The **Millennium Quarter** links the small historic core of pre-Industrial Revolution Manchester around the **cathedral** with the 19th-century city centre, with its grand architecture such as the stupendous Town Hall, the iron and glass shopping arcade of Barton Arcade, and the classical Royal Exchange. The centrepiece of the Millennium Quarter is **Urbis** (££, open daily), an impressive glass structure housing displays on life in great cities around the globe.

Canal St, which stretches roughly from the foot of Piccadilly train station to Princess St, is the lively hub of the **Gay Village**. A lot of independent money has been invested, both in building some of Manchester's most beautifully designed bars and restaurants and in ensuring that a real community feel thrives in the area. Nightclubs, gyms, loft apartments, offices, various drop-in centres and societies all operate happily on and around the street.

FOR FREE

The big free attractions that everyone is talking about are the **Lowry** and **Imperial War Museum North**, both in Salford (see p. 210). In Manchester proper, there's a good choice of free visits. **Chetham's Library** (Long Millgate) is a public library founded in 1653 and originally a college for priests. At Platt Hall, Rusholme, the **Gallery of Costume** charts 400 years of fashion, while two good visits for social history are the **Jewish Museum** (Cheetham Hill Rd) and the **People's History Museum** (Bridge St). The **Manchester Art Gallery** (Mosley St) houses a magnificent collection, including Pre-Raphaelite paintings and modern British works. There's more art in the **Whitworth Art Gallery** (Oxford Rd) including British watercolours, textiles and wallpapers. Also in Oxford Rd is the wide-ranging **Manchester Museum**.

This isn't a gay ghetto and people from all over Britain flock to sup beer in what is easily one of the most entertaining parts of Manchester. Wednesday night is drag night and the cabaret show in the famous New Union pub is a highlight. Although always busy, during summertime Canal St really blooms. At night the area teems with revellers by day, with so many al fresco bars, the street is a fantastic place to spend an afternoon watching the world go by. Situated in the bohemian Northern Quarter, **Oldham St** is the focal point for Manchester's young, creative beings. Design studios, 17 record shops, a Buddhist centre and numerous independent clothing outlets all sit on or around the street where you're likely to shop next to international DJs, producers, fashion designers or the next Liam Gallagher. Afflex Palace is a real hotch-potch emporium of second-hand clothing, piercing parlours and skate shops, while Café Pop is a real must with hoards of kitsch paraphernalia from the 1960s onwards hanging from the walls.

A £42-million state-of-the-art building, the **Bridgewater Hall** is home to the famous Halle Orchestra and an impressive 22-tonne organ which can be heard in a suspended 2340-seat auditorium. The sound quality really has to be experienced to be believed and if classical recitals aren't your bag, refer to the programme as full orchestral accompaniment to classic silent movies, jazz, or film music are just three examples of the diversity of this beautiful venue. Lower Mosely St; tel: (0161) 907 9000; website: www.bridgewater-hall.co.uk.

A real urban oasis built around Britain's first man-made canal, **Castlefield** is well worth visiting on a lazy afternoon. Best accessed by the small wooden staircase on Oxford Rd (opposite the Palace Theatre) or the entry behind Quay bar in Deansgate Rd, this quiet canal walk is popular with Mancunians looking for easy respite from the hustle and bustle of the city. The Bridgewater canal basin, a large half-amphitheatre of water, doubles as a live venue lying under the shadow of impressive Victorian railway viaducts. The huge stone steps are a popular gathering point for those wanting to soak up some sun in the summer. Above and behind the steps is a replica of the original Roman fort built hereabouts.

The world-famous **John Rylands Library** opened in 1900, resplendent with intricate modern Gothic architecture. It is home to some of the world's oldest books (including Caxton's edition of Chaucer's *Canterbury Tales* which was one of the earliest books to have been printed in England) and rarest manuscripts. St John's Fragment lies here, the earliest known fragment of the New Testament in any language. General access is tricky, but guided tours (£) take place every Wednesday at noon. No prior booking is required, but spaces are limited so arrive early. 150 Deansgate; tel: (0161) 834 5343; rylibweb@man.ac.uk/spcoll.

Joined on to Manchester, but technically a separate town, **Salford** has some of the most deprived areas of housing in Britain. However, rejuvenation has been spearheaded by the recent opening of two architecturally magnificent attractions on the waterfront, meriting a full day in themselves. **The Lowry**, an arts centre completed in 2000, takes its name from the 20th-century local painter, L S Lowry, whose haunting and immensely popular paintings of working-class life, with matchstick men set against bleak industrial landscapes, are on display in one of the galleries. Linked to the Lowry by a bridge over the Manchester Ship Canal, the **Imperial War Museum North** is an innovative building representing three 'shards' of fractured steel to a globe shattered by conflict on land, sea and air. Displays focus on the impact of war since 1900 – including the role of women in war, and medical advances – making it one of the most thought-provoking museums of its kind.

Many consider a night spent sampling the spicy delights of Rusholme's neon-lit **Curry Mile** an unmissable treat. Competing to become Britain's curry restaurant of the year is a cut-throat affair and large banners are proudly displayed by victorious venues. A predominantly Pakistani community, Wilmslow Rd becomes clogged during Eid, two holy festivals where jubilant Islamic communities celebrate the conclusion of Ramadan, a lunar month of fasting around 27 Dec and the Rites of Hajj around 5 March. The colourful material shops and markets fill up while a funfair is erected on Platt Fields. At night whole families go out to eat while exuberant younger generations drive up and down the strip waving flags and honking their horns.

SHOPPING

Manchester offers everything from designer shops and big name stores to antique emporiums, trend-setting music stores and individual craft shops and markets. For designer clothing try **King St** and **St Ann's Sq.**; for retro vintage clothing try the **Northern Quarter**, where you will find Afflecks Palace and Pop Boutique. Manchester's shopping experience is continuing to expand with the arrival of Selfridges in the city centre; Harvey Nichols is due here in 2003.

NIGHTLIFE

Manchester is famously idiosyncratic and the birthplace of whole culture movements. As a result, the night-clubs can reflect both the best of what's happening in the world whilst also completely disregarding trends elsewhere. In terms of bands or dance music, Manchester has its own superstars of which Mancunians are fiercely proud (including 808 State, DJ Justin Robertson and Badly Drawn Boy) so expect more than big billboard names to be dominating the scene.

Planet K, **The Music Box** and **Sankeys Soap** consistently deliver the latest in dance music, while **The Roadhouse** and **Night & Day Café** are gritty yet essential venues for live music. More upmarket is **Life Café** for live music and **Tiger Tiger** and **Ampersand** night-clubs. The Deansgate area is quite dressy, mainly as the bars along this road are popular with footballers, soap stars and the Cheshire Set, a loose description for the young and rich who travel in from Britain's most affluent county.

SIDE TRIPS

A grand stately home worth making the trip to see is **Lyme Park**, Disley, Stockport; infoline: (01633) 766492; website: www.nationaltrust.org.uk. It was used as Pemberley House in the British film production of Jane Austen's *Pride and Prejudice*.

If hats are your thing, you will love **Hat Works**, Wellington Mill, Wellington Rd South in Stockport; tel: (0161) 355 7770. This imaginative new museum in the town centre has fully restored working machinery, displays of historical and contemporary hats, hat-making demonstrations, textile workshops and a rolling programme of special exhibitions.

If there is alien life in outer space, it will be the Lovell telescope at **Jodrell Bank Science Centre and Arboretum** that breaks the news to the world. The giant dish (250 ft/76 m in diameter) looks silently into space, constantly recording every sound and movement in our galaxy. At the Science Centre 'star cities', the solar system and the Apollo moon missions are explained. In addition visitors can see how the universe was born in 3-D at the second largest planetarium in the country. Macclesfield; tel: (01477) 571695.

The **Peak National Park** (see pp. 236–239) is easily reached by rail, with frequent sevices for Sheffield via New Mills, Esdale and Hope.

LIVERPOOL

Liverpool is a city of contrasts – and not always in the most flattering sense. Yes, it's a place most definitely worth visiting, not only because it spawned the four most famous and influential musicians in the history of the world (The Beatles, of course), but also because it is rich in culture and nightlife. Chosen to be European Capital of Culture in 2008 and home to the second-most museums, theatres and galleries outside London, Liverpool also houses one of Britain's most popular nightclubs, Cream.

But, outside of the centre and the waterfront of the river Mersey, Liverpool is not always the prettiest of cities, for all its pockets of striking architectural brilliance. Fortunately, though, Liverpool is undergoing massive regeneration and there is an air of renewed positivity about the city. The area around the docks on the north side of the Mersey, in particular, has already been transformed into a fashionable hinterland of premium warehouse-style apartments and leisure and entertainment facilities based within the original dockland buildings.

GETTING THERE AND GETTING AROUND

Liverpool John Lennon Airport, tel: (0151) 288 4000, is 8 miles (13 km) south-east of the city centre, with flights to and from several European cities, including Dublin, Geneva and Madrid, and the Isle of Man on the north-west coast. Manchester Airport is an hour away by bus or train and offers more choice in flights and destinations.

The journey into the centre takes 20 mins by taxi, ££–£££. Every 30 mins, the no. 500 coach drives directly to the main coach station in the city centre at Norton St. Otherwise, to reach Lime St from the airport, take Merseytravel bus no. 80A (180 and 80 on Sundays) which goes to Garston Station from where trains depart every 15 mins for Liverpool Central station, next to Lime St.

Lime St **railway** station connects to most main English, Welsh and Scottish destinations. Tel: 08457 484950 or www.thetrainline.co.uk. Within Liverpool, the extensive Merseyrail network runs to local stations across the city and below the river Mersey into the Wirral region. There are regular **coaches** connecting to the rest of mainland UK from Norton St. Contact 0990 808080 or www.nationalexpress.co.uk. Fairly frequent **bus** services serve all areas of Merseyside. You will need the correct change to travel.

There's a commuter **ferry** service across the river Mersey during peak hours (see Highlights). You can also travel as a (foot or car) passenger on one of the many boats to and from Dublin; Merchant Ferries; tel: 0870 600 4321.

Tel: (0151) 236 7676 for bus, train and airport enquiries, open daily 0800–2000. Ask about Saveaways, one–day tickets for use on buses, trains and ferries at off–peak times.

INFORMATION

TOURIST OFFICES **Tourist Information centre,** Queen Square Centre, Queen Square. Open Mon, Wed–Sat 0900–1730, Tues, Sun 1030–1630. Also at Atlantic Pavilion, Albert Dock. Open daily 1000–1730. Both tel. 0906 680 6886 (25p a min); accommodation enquiries tel: 0845 601 1125 (local rate); website: www.visitliverpool.com; e-mail: askme@visitliverpool.com.

SAFETY General Liverpool crime rates have been halved recently and the city centre is probably on a par with other main British cities (car crime is probably the most common problem, so don't leave valuables visible on seats). Outside the centre, there are a few areas, such as Toxteth, where crime is more of a problem and normal precautions should be scaled up.

MONEY **Thomas Cook** shops with money-changing facilities: 75 Church St and 55 Lord St, open Mon–Fri 0900–1750 .

POST/PHONES One of the main post offices is at St John's, Houghton Way, open Mon–Sat 0900–1730. *Poste restante* facilities are available. Liverpool's telephone area code is 0151.

ACCOMMODATION

A 5- or 10-min walk out of the city centre, you'll find plenty of B&Bs on Mount Pleasant, while the road that runs alongside the docks is home to numerous new, no-frills hotels and the YHA hostel. The following prices quoted are for single rooms.

CITY CENTRE **Belvedere Hotel ££** 83 Mount Pleasant; tel: (0151) 709 2356. Family-run guest house, no en suites. Comfortable and central.
Embassie Independent Hostel £ 1 Falkner Sq.; tel: (0151) 707 1089. Dorm sleeping in Georgian terrace. Games room and TV–lounge. Many bars within walking (but not shouting) distance.
Feathers Hotel ££ 119–125 Mount Pleasant; tel: (0151) 709 9655, www.feathers.uk.com. Very reasonably priced and

personable. Not all rooms en suite.

YHA Liverpool (youth hostel) ££ 25 Tabley St, off Wapping; tel: 0870 7705730 (e-mail: liverpool@yha.org.uk). Twenty-five rooms of 4–6 beds, all en suite, modern building, with full meals service and table licence.

OUT OF THE CENTRE There is a ring of reasonably priced, grand old hotels built from merchants' homes around Sefton Park itself (Aigburth Dr.), a couple of miles south of the city centre (and round the corner from the many restaurants and pubs of Lark Lane, see Food and Drink pp. 216–217).

With its old shell – including wood-panelled bar – and modern, nicely decorated rooms, the **Alicia** is recommended. £££ 3 Aigburth Dr, Sefton Pk; tel: (0151) 727 4411.

University of Liverpool ££ Greenbank Hse, Greenbank; tel: (0151) 794 6440. B&B and self catering available April and mid-June–Sept only. Set in private parkland, 3 miles (4.8 km) from city centre.

HIGHLIGHTS

THE DOCKS The docks provide a fine starting point to explore Liverpool's cultural offerings (although everything listed below is within walking distance of the town centre). Take the almost obligatory **ferry across the Mersey** made famous by Gerry and the Pacemakers. £ from Pier Head (behind the famous Liver Building), 1000–1500 daily weekdays, 1000–1800 weekends.

Then head for **Albert Dock**, an imaginatively restored Victorian dock where the former warehouses are now given over to attractions, shops and eateries, and where there are two excellent sights. At the **Merseyside Maritime Museum** Liverpool's crucial role in slavery, immigration and emigration and war is movingly portrayed through the experiences of individuals. The **Tate Gallery Liverpool** is the largest gallery of contemporary art outside London (free; closed Mon). Also in the Albert Dock is **The Beatles Story**, a poignant journey through the band's success. If you're not a fan, the hefty admission price may be too much to learn nothing the world doesn't already know about the band. ££, open 1000–1800 (Apr–Sept), 1000–1700 (Oct–Mar). Tickets are on sale at the Atlantic Pavilion for tours on the **Liverpool Ducks**, cheery yellow amphibious World War II vehicles that take in the city sights before plunging into the Mersey.

CITY CENTRE The civic centre of Liverpool is indeed grand, with a glut of wonderfully designed classical buildings around the main, Liverpool Lime Street train station. In front of the station is **St George's Hall**, tel: (0151) 707 2391, one of the finest neo-classical buildings in the country, with an amazing Minton tiled floor. £, open mid-July–end Aug, Mon–Sat 1030–1630. The nearby **Town Hall**, tel: (0151) 707 2391, features fine staterooms with all the necessary chandeliers and works of art but has extremely limited opening. Admission free.

To the side of St George's, on William Brown St, are the newly refurbished **Liverpool Museum and Walker Art Gallery**. The Museum features exhibits on the natural world and outer space, while the Gallery contains works from Rubens, Rembrandt, Cézanne and Degas, with a great Pre-Raphaelite collection and wonderful furniture and sculptures. Admission to both by NMGM pass, both open Mon–Sat 1000–1700, Sun 1200–1700, closed 23–26 Dec and 1 Jan.

Liverpool is unique in having two 20th-century cathedrals, both only a short walk from the town centre. The **Anglican Liverpool Cathedral** at St James Mount is massive; imposing and Victorian Gothic in style (it took 74 years to build) with a 10,000-pipe organ (it also holds concerts). The **Catholic Metropolitan Cathedral** of Christ the King on Mount Pleasant is desperately modern, the first to be built in a round shape and features a central tower of multi-coloured glass and separate bell tower. Appropriately situated either end of Hope St, both are architecturally impressive for entirely different reasons.

In the shadow of Liverpool Cathedral, you'll find **Chinatown** at Nelson St. Liverpool is

HISTORICAL PARKLAND

Merseyside was at the forefront of the creation of municipal parks; the first in the world was opened in 1847 across the Mersey in Birkenhead. Set in over 125 acres (51 ha), **Birkenhead Park** was the inspiration for New York's Central Park. It features six lodges built in different styles, a lake that twists and curves like a river and an ornate, Swiss-style bridge. Back in Liverpool, **Sefton Park** has just seen the reopening of its Palm House conservatory after a £2.5 million facelift, in which the 3720 panes of glass were replaced. Concerts will be held there.

THE DOCKS

If Liverpool's heart lies in its musical heritage, the region's lifeblood flows through the docks – at least it did until the 1960s, when Southampton took its place as the main port in England for carrying transatlantic passengers. Liverpool began life around its beloved river when King John created a borough from a small fishing village in 1207. The first docks were built in 1705 and grew during the years of the slave trade through the Industrial Revolution when Liverpool became established as a major port and second city of the empire.

Now they are at the centre of its cultural renaissance. **Albert Dock** is the most important as it contains several of the best museums and galleries and the most restaurants and bars. But the neighbouring **Kings Waterfront** is due to undergo massive redevelopment worth £200 million over about five years and looks set to include the new Everton football stadium. Once completed, it will make Liverpool's waterfront one of the most exciting in Europe.

Liverpool

home to the oldest Chinese community in Europe (the first settlers came in the 1860s). This was commemorated by a fabulous millennium arch made by craftsmen from Shanghai – the largest outside China. Garish and ornate, it sits uncomfortably in a desolate environment – once the home of the rope-making industry for the ships.

BEATLES' HOUSES John Lennon's childhood home 'Mendips' opened to the public in 2003, restored by the National Trust. The Trust runs combined tours of the Lennon home and the family home of Paul McCartney, 20 Forthlin Rd, by minibus from Albert Dock and Speke Hall. ££–£££, Wed–Sun, Mar–Oct; tel: (0151) 708 8574 for morning tour, (0151) 427 7231 for afternoon tour.

FOOD AND DRINK

CITY CENTRE

Bechers Brook Restaurant ££££ 29a Hope St. Highly commended in regional awards. Modern food, featuring European and oriental dishes. Intimate atmosphere with antique furniture. Booking recommended; tel: (0151) 707 0005.

Casa Italia ££ 40 Stanley St. Filling Anglicised Italian food in a functional, brightly lit, roomy environment and staff with personality.

Everyman Bistro ££ Hope St. Award-winning, substantial bistro food and extensive vegetarian selection. Famous for its puddings. Laid-back, friendly and lively. Open same hours as bar (see Nightlife p. 217).

Jenny's Seafood Restaurant ££ The Old Ropery, Fenwick St. Well-established and popular with locals. Silver cutlery and linen tablecloths and traditional meals (fresh seafood with freshly made sauces). Open Mon–Fri lunch, Tues–Sat dinner.

Liverpool Cathedral Refectory £ St James Mount (see Highlights). Award-winning, home-cooked food. Great for Sunday lunch. Open 1000–1600, 1200–1700 Sun.

LIVERPOOL'S MOST FAMOUS LANDMARK
The most important landmark in Liverpool is formed by three buildings on the waterfront, nicknamed the Three Graces. The first to be built, in 1908, was the head office of the Port of Liverpool, followed by the head office of Cunard in 1916. But the most famous – and most treasured by Liverpudlians – is the **Liver Building**, built in 1912 for Royal Liver Insurance. It features a clockface bigger than Big Ben's and watchful birds perched on top that are part cormorant – to signify the city's dependence on the sea and part eagle – as a reminder of the charter from King John that first gave the area recognition back in 1207.

Ziba ££–£££ 15 Berry St. Fashionable modern food (British, with a continental twist) and décor (used to be a car showroom). Booking recommended; tel: (0151) 708 8870. Closed Sun.

LARK LANE Three miles (5 km) out of the centre near Sefton Park, this area offers a surprising choice of menus within a few hundred yards of each other. Here you'll find Greek, Indian, Chinese, French and Spanish alongside pub grub, pizzas and takeaways. Some is only passable, but **L'Alouette**, £££, Lark Lane, is sublime with a great wine list and imaginative, thoughtfully prepared food. Also on Lark Lane, **Keith's**, £, is a wine bar/basic restaurant much favoured by the bohemian locals. Lark Lane is also ideal for plain, no-frills pubs.

SHOPPING

The centre is large and filled with the usual chains, occasional designer shops and many shopping centres. The wonderful **Quiggins market** on School Lane is currently an indoor collection of independent units selling retro and unusual clothing, furniture, collectibles and gifts. The **Heritage Market** at Stanley Dock is a ragtag collection of stalls selling cheap, ordinary household goods and clothes in wonderful, delapitated old warehouse buildings. Open Sun only.

NIGHTLIFE

A night on the town is a serious activity for Liverpudlians. It's better to err on the side of smartness, because jeans or trainers are not allowed in some bars. The main areas are around **Hardman St** (very young and brash); **Slater St** (trendy); **Bold St** and **Concert Square** (glamorous); **Hope St** (down-to-earth) and **Albert Dock** (older, slightly more sophisticated).

The Cavern, 8–10 Mathew St, is a must for Beatles fans, although the building that stood atop the original site was demolished after the band split up and this is the 'reproduction'. Live music (not necessarily Beatles tracks) three nights a week. Tel: (0151) 236 9091; www.cavern-liverpool.co.uk.
In terms of nightclubs, **Cream**, is the forerunner. One of the most famous dance clubs in Britain, Cream is legendary for its atmosphere and music. Wolstenhome Sq., off Slater St; tel: (0151) 709 1693, open Sat 2200–0400. Be prepared to queue.
The **Everyman**, Hope St, is more than a bar (it opens past midnight, usually with a DJ, with bistro food available) and can be relied on to provide an affable, comfortable environment.

LIVERPOOL

PAY BEFORE YOU GO
Many petrol stations and some restaurants (particularly those in Chinatown late at night) require patrons to pay before filling up. This is not the norm in most of England. And don't be surprised to walk into a newsagent or off licence to find yourself separated from the goods by a defensive plastic wall that requires the assistant behind it to do your shopping for you in case you forget to pay before leaving.

Life Café Bar, Bold St, attracts a well-dressed crowd drinking cocktails (there's a late-opening bar downstairs with live music) and the casts from locally filmed TV soaps such as *Family Affairs*, *Hollyoaks* and *Brookside*.

Modo, Concert Square, is relaxed but busy, with comfortable armchairs and sofas in modern, fashionable surroundings.

The **Philharmonic Pub**, Hope St, is relaxed and definitely worth a drink just to see its fabulously ornate, original interior (the urinals in the gents' loos are exquisite).

Wonderbar, Slater St, is known for its lively atmosphere and trendy, pre-club crowd. Queues likely.

EVENTS

The **Grand National**, one of the world's greatest horse races, takes place in April, Aintree Racecourse, Ormskirk Rd, Aintree; tel: (0151) 523 2600. The race captivates the entire country and is apparently watched by more people around the world than any other sporting event. Liverpool is fully booked for this weekend.

The **Mersey River Festival** is held in June, at the Albert Dock, and features fireworks, tall ships, street entertainment and air balloons; tel: (0151) 233 6354.

The **Merseyside International Street Festival** happens in August; tel: (0151) 709 3334.

SIDE TRIPS

BLACKPOOL Liverpool is the gateway to many coastal towns, the biggest of which is **Blackpool**, which rakes in a living as Britain's humorous answer to Las Vegas. Blackpool is tacky, fun and a truly British experience. Trains run regularly from Piccadilly station and take about 30 mins.

SOUTHPORT Much nearer than tacky Blackpool is Southport. The **beaches** are plain and sandy – with a massive oil rig bewilderingly positioned on the horizon. There is surprisingly good shopping on Victorian parades (Lord St in particular). There is also an amusement park, **Pleasureland**, that is unsophisticated but offers a charming mix of rickety-feeling old rides from decades back (the park opened in 1913) and super modern – the white-knuckle Traumatizer is the tallest and fastest suspended looping rollercoaster in the country.

i **Tourist Information Centre**; 112 Lord St; tel: (01704) 533333; website: www.visitsouthport.com;

e-mail: southport_tic@btinternet.com. Open all year round
Mon–Fri 0900–1730, Sat 1000–1700, Sun 1200–1600.

PORT SUNLIGHT On the railway line to Chester and on the much built-up Wirral peninsula (get off at Port Sunlight station), Port Sunlight is a fascinating 19th-century factory village (a precursor to the garden city movement) built by Lord Leverhulme, whose Sunlight Soap factory was established here. It was a grand gesture of philanthropy, with the accent on health, clean air, greenery and sanitation – and what is really striking is the amount of green space and parkland in between rows of neat, Tudoresque, Elizabethan and Queen Anne style vernacular cottages. There is a conspicuous lack of pubs or other distractions: instead, the central focus is the Lady Lever Art Gallery (free, closed Sun morning), intended to improve the workers' minds with its works by Turner, the Pre-Raphaelites and others. Today the village is a highly desirable commuter paradise, and every brick is jealously preserved as the whole place is a conservation area.

ISLE OF MAN Between Liverpool and Northern Ireland (reachable by sea or air), this small, self-governing island is 40% uninhabited and great for a quiet break full of castles, countryside, beaches and spectacular views. The capital, **Douglas**, is a grand Victorian resort and harbour, but **Peel**, on the west coast, with its tiny lanes, is considered more characterful. There are picturesque, sandy beaches, particularly at Port Erin in the south, and 17 coastal and mountain glens, including Dhoon Glen with its verdant waterfall in the north-east. Other attractions include quaint trams and steam and electric railways; take the Snaefell Mountain Railway along a gorgeous 5-mile (8km) trek up steep gradients.

> [i] **Tourist Information Centre** Sea Terminal Buildings,
> Douglas; tel: (01624) 686766; website: www.gov.im/tourism;
> e-mail: tourism@gov.im. Open daily (May–Sept); Mon–Fri
> (Oct–Apr).

WHERE NEXT?

From Liverpool there are rail services every 30 mins (journey time 40 mins) to the historic walled city of Chester (see pp. 174–175). The M62 motorway links directly to the main M6 which travels through from the Midlands of England past the border into Scotland. It's only a short train journey to Manchester (see pp. 206–211). Or, for a complete contrast, head for Colwyn Bay and explore the north coast of Wales and Snowdonia National Park (see pp. 203–205).

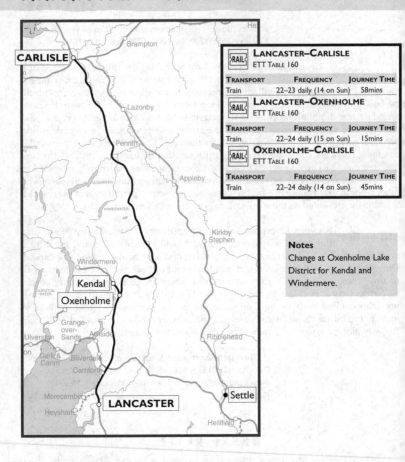

LANCASTER–CARLISLE
RAIL | ETT TABLE 160

TRANSPORT	FREQUENCY	JOURNEY TIME
Train	22–23 daily (14 on Sun)	58mins

LANCASTER–OXENHOLME
RAIL | ETT TABLE 160

TRANSPORT	FREQUENCY	JOURNEY TIME
Train	22–24 daily (15 on Sun)	15mins

OXENHOLME–CARLISLE
RAIL | ETT TABLE 160

TRANSPORT	FREQUENCY	JOURNEY TIME
Train	22–24 daily (14 on Sun)	45mins

Notes

Change at Oxenholme Lake
District for Kendal and
Windermere.

It's only 68 miles (109 km) from the lively university town of Lancaster to Carlisle, the western gateway to Scotland, but this route takes you past some of England's most stunning scenery. To the west lies the jewel in England's crown – the Lake District, with its pretty villages and poetic landscapes. To the east lies the unspoilt Eden Valley and the wilds of the North Pennines. The M6 motorway and the main line railway speed you through here in about an hour, giving you just a taste of the magnificent mountains and lonely fells that characterise this area. Driving along the A6 takes about 1 hr 40 mins, but takes in the attractive market town of Kendal, an eastern gateway to the Lake District.

LANCASTER

Lancashire's county town had its origins as a Roman camp and later became a prosperous port. Today it is a lively university city. In its historic centre stands **Lancaster Castle,** formerly a prison, now used as a crown court and museum. Many prisoners convicted here were transported to Australia. ££ open daily (mid-Mar–mid-Dec). On the waterfront is the **Maritime Museum,** £, open daily 1100–1700 (Apr–end Oct); 1230–1600 (winter).

i **Tourist Information Centre** 29 Castle Hill; tel: (01524) 32878; website: www.lancaster.gov.uk; e-mail: csailsbury@ lancaster.gov.uk. Open Mon–Sat 1000–1700 (summer); 1000–1600 (winter).

The 555 Stagecoach bus service runs from Lancaster to Carlisle via many of the Lake District's most popular sites like Grasmere, Ambleside and Kendal. An Explorer ticket, ££, allows you to break your journey during the day.

There are a few hotels as well as a small range of B&Bs and guesthouses. During the holidays you can also stay at Lancaster University. Accommodation can be booked through the Tourist Information Centre.
Edenbreck House £££ Sunnyside Lane; tel: (01524) 32464.
The Old Rectory ££ Claughton, nr Hornby; tel: (01524) 221150.
The Priory £££ 15 St Mary's Parade, Castlehill; tel: (01524) 845711.

Crow's £ 10a King St. Café/wine bar offering light meals and tapas.
Marcos ££ 27 North Rd. Italian restaurant with a lively atmosphere.

SIDE TRIP FROM LANCASTER **Morecambe Bay** is only a short drive from Lancaster along the A683. A huge area of tidal sand and mudflats, it is one of Britain's most important breeding and feeding grounds for wading birds. The sands have caused many deaths over the years as the tides gallop in and out, and quicksand and sea fogs make crossing the sands extremely hazardous. Today, experienced local guides offer escorted walks over the crossing in summer. Never try this unaccompanied. On the Central Promenade of Morecambe is the **Eric Morecambe** statue, a monument to one of Britain's most popular comedians.

KENDAL

Change at Oxenholme to visit this attractive market town, once home to the great fell walker Alfred Wainwright. At the south end of the main street are **Abbot Hall Art Gallery** (£, open daily 1030–1700 Apr–Oct; 1030–1600 Nov–Mar) and the **Museum of Lakeland Life and Industry** (£, open daily 1030–1700). Further up the main street the **Kendal Museum** provides background on the Lakes (£, open Mon–Sat 1030–1700, closes at 1600 winter).

i **Tourist Information Centre** Town Hall, Highgate; tel: (01539) 725758; e-mail: kendaltic@southlakeland.gov.uk. Open Mon–Sat 0900–1700, Sun 1000–1600.

🛏 There are plenty of hotels, B&Bs and farmhouses in and around Kendal. The tourist information centre can book your accommodation.
Kendal Youth Hostel £ 118 Highgate, tel: 0870 7705892; e-mail: kendal@yha.org.uk, is a Georgian house in the centre of town, close to the Brewery Arts Centre.

🍴 Kendal is well supplied with restaurants, bistros and tea shops.

CARLISLE

Guarding the western end of England's border with Scotland, Carlisle is well worth a day's stopover. There is the historic **Castle** which was once home to Mary, Queen of Scots (£, open daily 0930–1800 Apr–Sept; 1000–1700 Oct; 1000–1600 Nov–Mar) and a magnificent **Cathedral**, which was founded in 1122 (open Mon–Sat 0730–1815, Sun 0730–1700).

i **Carlisle Visitor Centre** Old Town Hall, Green Market;
tel: (01228) 625600; website: www.historic-carlisle.org.uk;
e-mail: tourism@carlise-city.gov.uk. Open Mon–Sat 0930–1700,
Sun 1030–1600 (summer), Mon–Sat 1000–1600, Sun closed
(winter).

🛏 **Carlisle Youth Hostel** £ Old Brewery Residences,
Bridge Lane, Caldewgate, tel: 0870 7705752 (e-mail: carlisle
@yha.org.uk) is a university hall that becomes youth hostel
accommodation during early July–early Sept.

WHERE NEXT?

*From Carlisle you can continue north over the Scottish border to Glasgow (see pp. 311–317).
Alternatively head down the Cumbria coast line via the Georgian port of Whitehaven and
the coastal village of Ravenglass (on the west side of the Lake District) to Barrow, and
then rejoin the main line at Carnforth: this is a scenic route, with some fine coastal views once
you are past Whitehaven, and after Ulverston you cross over Morecambe Bay's quicksands via
a series of low viaducts. Another beautiful route is from Carlisle to Settle, and then on to
Leeds: this famous railway line leads along the Eden Valley and through the wilds of the
Pennines and Yorkshire Dales National Park, and owes its survival to a spirited campaign by a
band of enthusiasts. Rail passes are accepted for all these routes, which form part of the
national rail network.*

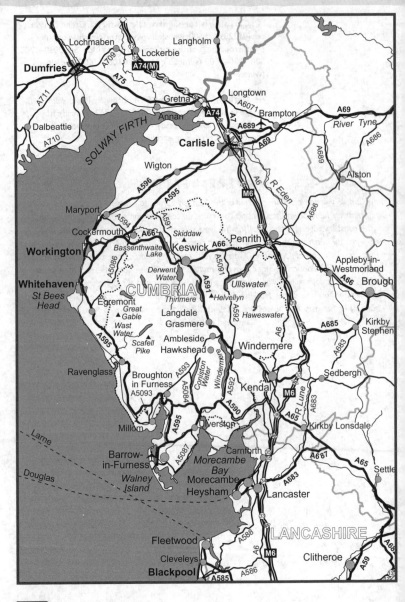

This spectacular area of glaciated lakes and brooding mountains is squeezed into a surprisingly small corner of north-west England. Just 40 miles (64 km) across, the Lake District contains an extraordinary variety of landscapes and is a highly desirable holiday spot. Walking, climbing and sailing are popular activities, as are less vigorous pursuits such as lake cruises and visiting museums and gardens. If the weather is bad, there are plenty of undercover attractions for the whole family, plus interesting shops, pubs, cafés and restaurants. The beauty of the area has inspired writers and poets for hundreds of years and literary associations can be found everywhere. William Wordsworth, Beatrix Potter, Samuel Taylor Coleridge, Robert Southey were all here.

Easily accessed from both the M6 motorway and the west coast main line railway, the eastern sector of the Lake District National Park is much visited and Kendal, Ullswater and Windermere can get very crowded. However, it is always possible to find the kind of solitude Wordsworth wrote about in his poem *Daffodils*: 'I wandered lonely as a cloud ...'. This is particularly true if you head for the wilder, western parts of the area such as Buttermere, Crummock Water and Eskdale. The best way to escape the crowds in any part of the Lake District is to get out of the car and walk or cycle.

GETTING THERE

Virgin trains run regular services from London, Glasgow and Carlisle to the Lake District. Oxenholme is the main station, from which First North Western run connecting trains to Kendal and Windermere. A number of these trains are through services from Manchester.

By car from London take the M1 motorway, then join the M6 which runs very close to the eastern sector of the Lake District. Smaller roads then lead into the heart of the Lakes.

If you are travelling by coach, National Express Rapide services run from London Victoria to Kendal. National Express Enquiries, tel: 08705 808080.

GETTING AROUND

There is no doubt that a **car** is the most convenient way to explore the more remote areas of the Lake District. However the roads can get extremely congested at peak periods. Generally, the further west you go the less crowded the roads.

There are plenty of ways of covering the Lakes by public transport, though, with Windermere the most useful rail station. From there, frequent buses connect the

THE LAKE DISTRICT

main points in the area, including Ambleside, Grasmere, Coniston and Keswick, and elsewhere there are useful bus services to Langdale and Buttermere. Ambleside and Keswick are good bases for bus travellers. The Cumbrian Coast rail line (Lancaster to Carlisle via Barrow) skirts the west side of the area with fine views for much of the way, with Ravenglass an interchange for narrow-gauge trains into Eskdale (see p. 228).

A range of Explorer tickets are available on **Stagecoach Cumberland Buses**. Tickets are available from most tourist information centres. For all public transport enquiries in the Lake District contact Traveline; tel: 0870 608 2608.

INFORMATION

For general information on the Lake District contact the **Cumbria Tourist Board**, Ashleigh, Holly Rd, Windermere, Cumbria LA23 2AQ; tel: (015394) 40414; fax: (015394) 44041; website: www.gocumbria.co.uk; e-mail: info@golakes.co.uk.

Main tourist information centres:
Ambleside: Central Buildings, Market Cross; tel: (015394) 32582; e-mail: ambleside-tic@southlakeland.gov.uk. Open daily 0900–1730 (summer); 0930–1700 (winter).
Kendal: Town Hall, Highgate; tel: (01539) 725758; e-mail: kendaltic@southlakeland.gov.uk. Open Mon–Sat 0900–1700, Sun 1000–1600.
Keswick: Moot Hall, Market Square; tel: (017687) 72645; website: www.keswick.org; e-mail: keswicktic@lake-district.gov.uk. Open daily 0930–1730 (1630 winter).
Windermere: Victoria St; tel: (015394) 46499; website: www.windermere.co.uk; e-mail: windermeretic@telinco.co.uk. Open daily 0900–1800 (Apr–Oct); 0900–1700 (Nov–Mar).

SAFETY Before setting off for a walk in the Lake District mountains make sure that you are suitably equipped with good walking boots, waterproof clothing, a map, compass and a whistle for attracting attention if you get into difficulties. Let people know where you intend to go. The weather can change quickly on the hills so it is worth checking the **Lake District Weather Service**; tel: (01768) 775757.

ACCOMMODATION

The Lake District is so popular that accommodation can be scarce at peak times, so it is worth booking in advance. The Cumbria Tourist Board has a **booking hotline**; tel: 0808 100 8848, alternatively local TICs can source accommodation for you. The area has a good choice of accommodation ranging from country house hotels to bed and breakfasts, farmhouses and inns. There are also camp sites and self catering cottages.

CENTRAL AND SOUTHERN LAKES

Borwick Lodge ££ Outgate, Hawkshead, Ambleside; tel: (01539) 436332; website: www.smoothound.co.uk/hotels/borwick.html; e-mail: borwicklodge@talk21.com. Award winning country house with great views of the lakes and mountains.

Haisthorpe House ££ Holly Rd, Windermere; tel: (01539) 443445; e-mail: haisthorpe@clara.net. Good value B&B in popular location.

Garnett House Farm ££ Burneside, Kendal; tel: (01539) 724542. A 15th-century farmhouse on a working sheep and dairy farm.

Rowanfield Country House £££ Kirkstone Rd, Ambleside; tel: (01539) 433686; website: www.rowanfield.com; e-mail: e-mail@rowanfield.com. Immaculately kept farmhouse in beautiful location, serving excellent food.

NORTHERN AND WESTERN LAKES

The Old Vicarage ££ Church Lane, Lorton; tel: (01900) 85656; website: www.oldvicarage.co.uk; e-mail: enquiries@oldvicarage.co.uk. Friendly and helpful B&B in one of the most tranquil parts of the Lake District.

Swinside Lodge £££ Newlands, Keswick; tel: (01768) 772948; website: www.swinsidelodge-hotel.co.uk; e-mail: info@swinsidelodge-hotel.co.uk. Ultra-smart guesthouse with top-notch cooking in secluded and glorious scenery.

Wasdale Head Inn £££ Wasdale, Near Gosforth; tel: (01946) 726229; website: www.wasdale.com; e-mail: wasdaleheadinn@msn.com. Rugged walkers' pub in remote but stunning location. Lots of character and climbing history.

YOUTH HOSTELS

There are over 20 hostels in the Lake District, many in superb country locations; for details see www.yha.org. Those in main tourist centres include **Ambleside**, tel: 0870 7705672 (e-mail: ambleside@yha.org.uk), **Buttermere**, tel: 0870 7705736 (e-mail: buttermere@yha.org.uk), **Grasmere**, tel: 0870 7705837 (e-mail: grasmere@yha.org.uk), **Keswick**, tel: 0870 7705895 (e-mail: keswick@yha.org.uk) and **Windermere**, tel: 0870 7706094 (e-mail: windermere@yha.org.uk).

FOOD AND DRINK

The Lake District offers everything from fine food in country house hotels to simple but substantial pub meals. The more touristy areas are packed with tea shops as well. Sunday lunch is very popular in many pubs and it is worth booking in advance.

The Lake District is noted for regional specialites such as air-cured ham, Cumberland sausage and Herdwick lamb. However, its most famous food product must be Kendal Mint Cake, a sticky, sugary confection used by generations of walkers to give them instant energy out on the fells.

CENTRAL AND SOUTHERN LAKES

Kirkstile Inn ££ Loweswater, Cockermouth; tel: (01900) 85219. Old fashioned inn with a log fire and simple but tasty bar meals and snacks.

Mason's Arms ££ Strawberry Bank, Cartmel Fell, nr Windermere; tel: (01539) 568486. Popular pub renowned for extensive selection of beers and adventurous food, including vegetarian specialities.

Punch Bowl £££ Underbarrow, Kendal; tel: (01539) 568237. A 16th-century inn serving imaginative food.

Queen's Head £££ Troutbeck, nr Windemere; tel: (01539) 432174. Traditional British dishes in Tudor country inn.

NORTHERN AND WESTERN LAKES

Dog and Gun ££ Lake Rd, Keswick; tel: (01768) 773463. Characterful pub with log fires serving good bar meals.

Quince & Medlar £££ 13 Castlegate, Cockermouth; tel: (01900) 823579. Accomplished vegetarian restaurant with friendly, relaxing service. Open evenings only Tues–Sun.

Yew Tree Restaurant £££ Seatoller, Borrowdale, nr Keswick; tel: (01768) 777634. Quality local dishes served in a couple of old miners' cottages. Vegetarian dishes and afternoon teas.

CENTRAL AND SOUTHERN LAKES

WINDERMERE Windermere is the largest lake in England and a giant holiday playground all summer. Bowness, the Victorian resort on the lake's eastern shoreline, is home to the **Windermere Steamboat Museum** combines displays of historic steam and sail boats. ££, Rayrigg Rd, Bowness, tel: (01539) 445565; open daily 1000–1700 (mid-March–late Oct). From early April to October you can take a trip on the **Lakeside and Haverthwaite steam railway**, tel: (01539) 531594, starting at Lakeside, and then link with a cruise around Windermere with **Windermere Lake Cruises**, tel: (01539) 531188, which runs all year round and starts from several points on the lake, including Ambleside. A relaxing way of enjoying the lakeland scenery. ££ (train); £££ (train and boat). Family tickets available.

The miniature **Ravenglass and Eskdale Railway** uses steam engines to carry visitors from the coast to the foot of the Lake District's highest mountains. You can use it to access many walks in Eskdale. £££ daily Mar–Oct from Ravenglass and Dalegarth stations. Tel: (01229) 717171, website: www.ravenglass-railway.co.uk.

Just outside the nearby town of Ambleside, **Townend** (£, 1300–1700, closed Sat, Mon and all Nov–Mar) is an evocative Cumbrian farmhouse owned by one family for 300 years up to 1943 and where remarkably little has changed over the years.

GRASMERE About 20 mins from Windermere by car (or bus no. 555 from Lancaster, Kendal, Ambleside and Windermere) is postcard-pretty Grasmere, a village synonymous with William Wordsworth, the most celebrated of all the Lake poets. He lived with his sister Dorothy at **Dove Cottage,** ££, Grasmere, where he wrote much of his best known poetry. The beautifully preserved cottage is adjacent to an award-winning **Wordsworth Museum**, £, which displays manuscripts, portraits and memorabilia. Dove Cottage is just off the A591, just south of Grasmere Village. Visitors are offered guided tours of the cottage. Open daily 0930–1730 (last tour 1700). The evidence of poverty in Dove Cottage (including walls papered with newspapers of the day) contrasts with the grander **Rydal Mount** where he spent his last years. The house is still owned by one of his descendants and there are extensive gardens landscaped by the poet. Off A591 1 mile (1.6 km) from Ambleside. ££, open daily 0930–1700 (Mar–Oct), 1000–1600 (Nov–Feb); closed Tues in winter. Joint tickets with Dove Cottage are available.

HAWKSHEAD Hawkshead is a showcase village where Wordsworth went to school and its cobbled streets and squares are lined with restored Tudor buildings. Today the village is devoted to the memory of **Beatrix Potter** who lived in the neighbouring village of Near Sawrey, 2 miles (3 km) south of Hawkshead. Her 17th-century farmhouse **Hill Top**, where she wrote many of her children's stories, has been kept exactly as she left it. ££, open daily 1100–1630, except Thur and Fri (31 Mar–31 Oct); 1030–1700 (Mar–May and June–Aug); 1100–1630 (Sept–Oct). Family tickets available.

LANGDALE In a gorgeous double valley, Langdale is ringed by spectacular mountains with names like Crinkle Crags and Pike o'Stickle. It attracts serious walkers and climbers. Great Langdale has more striking scenery, but Little Langdale is quieter and has some excellent walks. The hamlet of Elterwater is a pretty spot for a pub lunch or a picnic.

NORTHERN AND WESTERN LAKES

KESWICK On Derwent Water, Keswick is the main centre for the Northern Lakes, ideal for exploring rugged Borrowdale or the smooth slatey fells of Skiddaw. It is an excellent place to look for outdoor gear. A mostly Victorian town of grey slate, it prospered on textiles and leatherworking, then on local graphite deposits. The Derwent pencil factory houses an entertaining Pencil Museum, ££, and the Keswick Museum, £, has a varied collection of Victorian memorabilia.

COCKERMOUTH This lively market town is an excellent base for exploring the quieter north-western parts of the Lake District. Wordworth was born here in 1770 and **Wordsworth House**, a handsome Georgian building on the main street, is open to visitors. ££, open weekdays 1030–1630 (early Apr–early Nov), plus Sat in June, July and Aug. Nearby is **Castlegate House**, an art imaginative gallery and

Fletcher Christian was born at Moorland Close, Eaglesfield near Cockermouth. He achieved lasting fame for his part in the mutiny on the *Bounty*, ending his days on remote Pitcairn Island.

sculpture garden, whose owner has a real eye for good artists. Open daily in summer; website: www.castle-gatehouse.co.uk.

BUTTERMERE A necklace of watery jewels forms one of the Lake District's best-loved scenes between Lorton Vale and the Honister Pass. With a magnificent setting, amid awesome fells, Buttermere is one of the prettiest of all the lakes. Linked with **Crummock Water** and **Loweswater**, the three once formed a single lake. The stone village of Buttermere makes a popular starting point for family walks; easy footpaths fringe the waterline. Scale Force near Crummock Water is the Lake District's highest waterfall, plunging 125 ft (38 m) in a single drop.

Buttermere church contains a window plaque commemorating **Alfred Wainwright** the great fell-walker. The fell called Haystacks is visible through the window on a clear day. This is where his ashes were scattered after his death in 1991, in accordance with his final wishes.

WASDALE Its remote location entails a special effort but Wasdale is well worth it. A dead-end single track road runs along the western shore of England's deepest lake, the mysterious Wast Water. Above the lakehead looms the perfect pyramid of Great Gable and Scafell Pike, England's highest peak.

ULLSWATER Ullswater is often rated the most beautiful of all Cumbria's lakes. Victorian pleasure steamers ply a triangular course around the lake in summer, while countless sailboats, kayaks and wind-surfers battle with the unpredictable wind. Gowbarrow Fell, near Aira Force on the northern shore, is where Wordsworth and his sister first saw those famous daffodils.

A number of companies offer small group guided tours of the Lake District which can be an excellent introduction to the area. A choice of full and half day tours are available. You can book direct or through any TIC. Operators include:

Furness Adventure Tours; tel: (01229) 474547

Lakeland Safari Tours; tel: (01539) 433904

Mountain Goat MiniCoach Tours; tel: (01539) 445161

TOURS The National Trust runs **Landscape Minibus Tours** taking in classic sites and scenic views. These provide a great introduction to the Lake District and are led by informative drivers. Full and half day tours depart from Keswick and Ambleside. To book, tel: (01768) 773780. For out of season enquiries, tel: (01539) 463810, £££, concessions for Trust members.

The National Trust has renovated *Gondola*, a steam yacht first launched in 1859. It is now used to provide **passenger cruises** of Coniston Water. Coniston was the location for Donald Campbell's tragic assault on the

The traditional sport of **Cumbrian wrestling** can be seen in the Lakes during summer, expecially at gatherings like the Grasmere Sports. The opponents try to topple each other over by a skilful application of strength and balance. Another popular pastime is **fell running**, which must count as one of the most masochistic pursuits ever devised.

world water-speed record in 1967. Happier memories are shared by devotees of Arthur Ransome, whose *Swallows and Amazons* stories were set on Coniston and its islands. ££, sailings from Coniston Pier starting at 1100 weekdays, 1200 Sat (end Mar–mid-Dec); tel: (01539) 463856.

Walking really is the best way to enjoy the beauty of the Lake District – and it's free. There are a bewildering array of **walks** to follow and there is something to suit everyone. Helvellyn is the most popular mountain to climb but a head for heights and experience is needed. There are plenty of short, low level walks to choose from and maps and guides are available in bookshops and tourist information centres.

The **Cumbria Cycleway** is a 259-mile (417 km) circular route around Cumbria. It is mainly on minor roads and forms links with railway stations. Other cycleways have opened up throughout the Lake District and are continually being developed. Many companies offer cycles for hire. Further details on cycling in the region can be obtained from tourist information centres and also from: Groundwork West Cumbria, tel: (0194) 6813677; Country Lanes Cycle Centre; tel: (01539) 444544.

THE WORLD'S BIGGEST LIAR

The Lake District is the location for the World's Biggest Liar competition, which is held every November at the Bridge Inn, Santon Bridge. It is held in commemoration of Will Ritson, innkeeper at the Wasdale Head Inn who was famous for his tall tales. Politicians are barred from the amateur event on the grounds that they are professionals.

WHERE NEXT?

The Cumbrian coast does not offer the spectacular scenery of the Lake District but there are still some attractions worth investigating. **Whitehaven** houses The Rum Story, a visitor attraction telling the story of the port's role at the heart of the British rum trade. To the east of the Lake District, on the M6, is **Penrith** a pleasant old centre of warm red sandstone. It is close to the family attraction of Rheged, which takes visitors on a journey back to the days of King Arthur. Alternatively, join up with the short but stunning route from Lancaster to Carlisle (see p. 220).

SHEFFIELD AND THE PEAK DISTRICT

John Ruskin, the famous British author, described Sheffield as 'the dirty picture within a golden frame'; the Peak District a beautiful border to the rather grimy industrial city. But today that picture has been sympathetically restored. Landscaped gardens and civic squares have enhanced its heart. Ugly concrete buildings are making way for galleries and museums in marble and glass, and sports stadia have replaced the giant steel mills with their blazing furnaces and belching chimneys. Even its twin cooling towers now stand in the shadow of a huge shopping mall and are more fondly remembered for their cameo role in the hugely successful 1997 film *The Full Monty* about unemployed steel workers.

Sheffield's reputation as a producer of quality steel and fine cutlery remains. Surprisingly, Sheffield produces more steel than ever, but in a cleaner environment and, sadly, with only a fraction of the workforce. Sheffield is a green city and a high one too (rising to half the height of the UK's tallest mountain). A little like Rome, it is built on seven hills and five valleys. Steep hills and leafy suburbs mark the west of the city and it's easy to feel how closely Sheffield nestles to the moors and peaks of the Peak District National Park.

Two universities and over 60,000 students have helped Sheffield become an upbeat city with a growing cosmopolitan feel and a bright nightlife. Sheffield is the fourth largest city in the country, with a population of 500,000, but its proud traditions and friendly locals mean its reputation as the largest village in England is well deserved.

GETTING THERE AND GETTING AROUND

Sheffield City Airport is 3 miles (5 km) east of the city centre; tel: (0114) 201 1998. There are direct flights from London City Airport, Dublin and Belfast. Buses are infrequent so ordering a taxi is recommended and will cost £8–£10. Transfer time to the centre is 15 mins. Car hire must be arranged in advance; tel: (0114) 276 8888. Flights from **Manchester International Airport**; tel: (0161) 489 3000 arrive from all over the world and transfer time to Sheffield is approximately 90 mins.

Trains run from Manchester Piccadilly and London St. Pancras railway stations direct to Sheffield. For National Rail Enquiries, tel: 0845 7484950. Travelling time from London is approximately 2 hrs 25 mins.

There are **National Express coach services** direct from Manchester and London to the city bus station, known as Sheffield Interchange. Sheffield is served by Stagecoach and First Mainline **buses**; tel: Travelline: (01709) 515151. Sheffield

Supertram connects the railway station and the city centre with major venues including City Hall, the Cathedral, Sheffield Arena, Don Valley Stadium and Meadowhall shopping and entertainment complex. A Day Rider ticket for one day's unlimited travel costs £2. Supertram stops running at 2330.

INFORMATION

Destination Sheffield Visitor Information Centre I Tudor Square; tel: (0114) 221 1900 or (0114) 201 1011; website: www.destinationsheffield.org.uk; e-mail: info@www.destinationsheffield.org.uk. Open Mon–Fri 0930–1700, Sat 0930–1600, closed Sun.

SAFETY Sheffield city centre is pretty safe, even late at night. After dark it's best to avoid areas east of the city. The Wicker and parts of Attercliffe are unsavoury rather than unsafe.

MONEY Thomas Cook branches are at: 37 Fargate, Sheffield; tel: (0114) 260 7700 (open Mon–Sat 0900–1730); 119 Pinstone St, Sheffield; tel: (0114) 260 7600 (open Mon–Sat 0900–1730); Meadowhall, 83 High St, Sheffield; tel: (0114) 260 7000 (open Mon–Fri 1000–2100, Sat 1000–1900, Sun 1100–1700).

POST/PHONES The main Post Office is at GT News, Norfolk Row; tel: (0114) 281 4713. Open Mon–Sat 0830–1730, Wed 0900–1730. (Closed Bank Holidays.)

ACCOMMODATION

The Visitor Information Centre has lists of guesthouses, hotels and self-catering accommodation. They offer a free reservation service; tel: (0114) 201 1011.

Hotel Bristol £££ Blonk St, Sheffield; tel: (0114) 220 4000; website: www.bhg.co.uk; e-mail: sheffield@bhg.co.uk. Economy hotel by Victorian quayside. Weekend breaks available.

Guest Boat Ruby £££ Victoria Quays, Wharf St, Sheffield; tel: (0114) 244 4136; website: www.rubysheffield.com; e-mail: info@rubysheffield.com. Narrowboat accommodation moored on Sheffield's restored canal basin.

University of Sheffield £ 12 Claremont Crescent, Sheffield; tel: (0114) 222 0260; website: www.shef.ac.uk; e-mail: self-catering@sheffield.ac.uk. University self-catering accommodation available Jun–Sept. Minimum stay two nights.

Westbourne House Hotel £££ 25 Westbourne Rd, Sheffield; tel: (0114) 266 0109; website: www.westbourne-househotel.com. AA 5 diamond rating. Serves evening meals.

Woodseats Farm ££ Bradfield, Sheffield; tel: (0114) 285 1429. Moderately priced accommodation on a working farm.

FOOD AND DRINK

The *Sheffield Telegraph*, published every Friday, has a dining out section. It's worth checking out the area west of the city known as the **Devonshire Quarter** (5 mins walk from the centre). Popular with students, it contains many pubs and café-bars.

The Forum ££, Devonshire St, is a café-bar in a converted warehouse containing trendy retail units. A great place for people watching.

The Frog and Parrot £, Division St, is an old fashioned pub. Ask for a glass of 'Roger and Out' ale – so strong they only sell it in third of a pint glasses.

Havana £, Division St, is an Internet café ideal for a lunchtime snack.

The **Mediterranean £££**, Sharrow Vale Rd; tel: (0114) 266 1069. You'll need to book at this seafood and tapas restaurant. The clam chowder comes highly recommended.

The **Olive Garden ££**, Surrey St, is a vegetarian restaurant above a healthfood and herbalists.

HIGHLIGHTS

In the heart of the city, the **Peace Gardens** are the main public square with ornate stone carvings and water features. Opposite is **Tudor Square** – home of the **Crucible Theatre** and the restored Victorian **Lyceum Theatre**. Just 2 mins walk away are the **Millennium Galleries**. This new £15 million cultural attraction exhibiting treasures from the Victoria and Albert Museum in London, features the city metalware gallery and the renowned John Ruskin collection.

Sheffield has more woodland than any other English city and four times as many mature trees as people.

The grandly named **Cultural Industries Quarter** is a revamped area by the railway station where nightclubs and galleries exist alongside design and photography businesses. **The Showroom Cinema** housed in a 1930s art deco building is the largest independent cinema outside the capital (the one in London has just six more seats) and shows arthouse productions and mainstream films. The nearby **Site Gallery** specialises in exhibitions of contemporary art and new media.

In the **Cathedral Quarter**, the Anglican **cathedral** is not the grandest of city cathedrals, though its Tudor memorials and striking stained glass are worth a look. It faces the **Cutlers' Hall**, £, home of the Cutlers' Company's superb collection of silver (open to pre-booked parties only); tel: (0114) 272 8456. Round the corner is **Orchard Square**, a charming, though not exactly unique, shopping courtyard. Children may enjoy watching the Swiss style clock which chimes every quarter of an hour.

Sheffield Ski Village is the largest artificial resort in Europe, with slopes, snow-boarding and toboggan run. Bus nos 77, 80 from Flat St.

A 10-min walk or a 2-min tram ride will take you to **Victoria Quays**. Colourful boats are moored on this restored part of the canal and there are designer shops in the refurbished arches. Three mins back to **Ponds Forge Leisure Centre** and you can board Supertram for the 10-min ride to **Sheffield Arena** – an entertainment venue hosting pop concerts, musical theatre, ice shows, basket-ball and ice-hockey; tel: (0114) 256 5656. Nearby is its even larger neighbour **Don Valley Stadium**, home to major outdoor pop concerts and international athletics; tel: (0114) 256 0607. **Kelham Island** museum celebrates Sheffield's industrial heritage with traditional craftspeople in small workshops on a restored cobbled street. Open Mon–Thur 1000–1600 and Sun 1100–1645; tel: (0114) 272 2106. Bus nos 77, 80 from Flat St.

In Sheffield's **Norfolk Park** you may encounter the **ghost of Spring Heeled Jack** who is said to jump over hedges to surprise courting couples.

TOURS Many of Sheffield's historic buildings and attractions can be explored on foot. There are no daily city tours but if you want to find out more about Sheffield's history and architecture, a Blue Badge Guide is recommended; tel: (0114) 289 0922. The Visitor Information Centre has details of the **Sheffield Round Walk**, a scenic 14-mile (23-km) circular walk linking local parks and woodland. Boats can be hired at Victoria Quays to explore Sheffield's canals.

FOR FREE

The **Graves Art Gallery**, Surrey St, has touring exhibitions and is home to the city's collection of modern art; tel: (0114) 278 2600, open Mon–Sat 1000–1700. The **City Museum** and **Mappin Art Gallery** are an Aladdin's cave of decorative arts, natural and social history collections with renovated galleries containing beautiful Old Masters. Weston Park; tel: (0114) 278 2600, open Tues–Sat 1000–1700, Sun 1100–1700 and Bank Holiday Mon. **Upper Chapel** Norfolk St, open Tues and Sun, is a 300-year-old chapel with stained glass and sanctuary gardens with bronze statues. The **Botanical Gardens** have 5000 species of plants inside Pavilions designed by the architect of London's Crystal Palace. Bus no. 50 from Sheffield Interchange. Clarkehouse Rd; tel: (0114) 267 6496, open daily 0800–dusk.

SHOPPING

City centre shopping is bland and rather unappealing. Instead try the **Devonshire Quarter** (a 5 min walk), a vibrant shopping district with a mix of shops and café-bars oozing with artistic flair and offering designer labels and furnishings. **Abbeydale Road** (15 mins walk from the centre) is well known to bargain hunters for its craft

EVENTS AND FESTIVALS
The *Sheffield Telegraph* has an excellent listings section. The Visitor Information Centre has a what's on freesheet or you can visit www. sheffieldcity.co.uk/ what'son.

and bric-à-brac shops. It is also home to the **city's antiques quarter**. The huge shopping mall **Meadowhall** is great for casual browsers or serious shoppers. Locals sometimes call it 'Meadowhell'. Visit on a busy Saturday, and you'll soon see why. Open Mon–Fri 1000–2100, Sat 0900–1900, Sun 1100–1700.

NIGHTLIFE

Check out the comprehensive club listings in the *Sheffield Telegraph* or log on to www.thesteellounge. co.uk. Most of the action is in the Devonshire and Cultural Industries Quarters. Amongst several late night venues you'll find the Republic, Arundel St, the popular Leadmill, Leadmill Rd. and Bed, London Rd. If you want live music head for The Boardwalk, Snig Hill, The Casbah, Wellington St or the Ju Ju Club, Snig Hill. There's also a Comedy Club at the Lescar Pub, Sharrow Vale Rd.

THE PEAK NATIONAL PARK

Dark moors with blazes of purple heather, towering gritstone cliffs, white limestone walls, sweeping patchwork fields and water worn valleys characterise the Peak District. It was Britain's first **National Park** in 1951 and is extraordinarily beautiful, but don't expect a wilderness experience. This area is a product of intensive human activity over thousands of years. Farming, lead mining, quarrying, reservoirs and textile mills have helped form the landscape you see today. This is reflected in the symbol of the national park – the 'millstone' or grinding wheel.

Geologically, the area is divided into two – the **Dark Peak** in the north and the **White Peak** in the south.

GETTING AROUND **Rail** access is via Grindleford, Hathersage, Hope or Edale stations on the Sheffield to Manchester Line. Travelling time by train to Hathersage from Sheffield is 18 mins. National Rail Enquiries, tel: 0845 7484950.

Travel by **bus** is generally good between villages. For timetable enquiries, tel: 0870 6082608. Bus no. 272 from Sheffield Interchange is direct to Castleton via Hathersage and Bradwell; travelling time is approx 45 mins. Buses for Bakewell (no. 240) leave Sheffield Interchange and take approx 45 mins. Buses for Buxton and Tideswell (no. 65) depart from Sheffield Interchange and take 1 hr.

It may also be worth hiring a **car** to reach places such as Dovedale, the Roaches and Chatsworth.

SHEFFIELD AND THE PEAK DISTRICT

ℹ️ **Peak District National Park Authority,** Aldern House, Baslow Rd, Bakewell, Derbyshire DE45 1AE; tel: (01629) 816200; fax: (01629) 816310. website: www.peakdistrict-npa.org; e-mail: aldern@peakdistrict-npa.gov.uk.

🛏️ Accommodation is plentiful and varied, from campsites and guesthouses to working farms, pubs and hotels. Tourist information centres keep detailed lists. There are youth hostels at Alstonefield, Bakewell, Bretton, Castleton, Edale, Elton, Eyam, Gradbach Mill, Hartington Hall, Hathersage, Ilam Hall, Langsett, Matlock, Ravenstor, Shining Cliff and Youlgreave.

🍴 Most villages have a pub that serves food and there are many cafés, restaurants and shops. Information on places to eat can be found in the free *Peak Advertiser*.

THE DARK PEAK   Named for its peat moors and gritstone edges, the Dark Peak was for a long time out-of-bounds to the workers of Manchester and Sheffield; it was reserved for the rich to raise and shoot grouse and protected by game-keepers. It was here that the idea of 'access' was born, with mass trespass committed at many sites. The most famous of these was at **Kinder Scout**, which is a plateau of moorland edged by the villages of **Hayfield** and **Edale**. The gruelling **Pennine Way** – Britain's first long-distance path – begins at **Edale** (near the railway station) and stretches 250 miles (402 km) across some of the wildest moors and worst bogs in the country. The walk traditionally starts with a pint of ale at **The Nags Head** pub in the village.

The villages of this part of the peak are well represented by **Hathersage** and **Eyam**. **Hathersage**, 11 miles west of Sheffield, has the grave of Robin Hood's confederate **Little John** in its graveyard. Charlotte Brontë used the village as a location for the novel *Jane Eyre*. Hathersage is a good base if you intend to do any climbing.

At **Eyam** (pronounced 'Eem' and known as 'the Plague village') you will find a tragic but inspiring story. In 1665 the 'Black Death' arrived carried in a bolt of cloth from London. Starting in one household it decimated the village, killing half the inhabitants and was prevented from spreading throughout the Peak District by the self-sacrifice of the villagers who put themselves into isolation. You will still see rock-hollows where money to pay for food was left in vinegar to disinfect it, many graves and the **Plague Cottages**. A café and craft shops are in the courtyard of **Eyam Hall**, ££, and the hall is open for tours May–Oct on Tues, Wed, Thur, Sun and Bank Holidays 1100–1600.

THE WHITE PEAK   Dotted with sheep and enclosed by white limestone walls, the White Peak is gentler on the eye than its dark northern cousin. The plateau is high with round green shapes, while the dales cut into the limestone, leaving tall white cliffs, scree slopes covered in grass and rivers which disappear into the porous rock beneath.

One of these rivers emerges in **Castleton** – named after **Peveril Castle** – on the border of the dark and white peak. Castleton is noted for **Blue John** stone mined in two of the four local show caves and the dramatic gorge of **Winnats Pass** and **Mam Tor** – known locally as the shivering mountain due to the vast landslides that make up its southern face. If you only have time for one cavern, try **Speedwell**. An old lead-mine, it is the only one of the caverns visited by boat. You float through half a mile of tunnels (helmets are provided but watch your head) to the Bottomless Pit Cavern, open daily 0930–1730 (Easter–Oct), daily 1000–1700 (Nov–Easter). However, it is also worth taking a look at the huge entrance to **Peak Cavern** (also known more memorably as the Devil's Arse), in a tiny gorge at the edge of Castleton, beneath the ruins of Peveril Castle. Ropemakers used to work in the entrance; the cave itself is by far the largest in the area, but has no limestone concretions (££, closed weekdays Nov–Mar).

From here head south to **Bakewell**, the only market town inside the National Park. You'll find good shopping, cafés, a livestock market and the Bakewell showground, which hosts a large agricultural show every summer. Bakewell is home to the famous pudding. A cook at a local hostelry confused his pastry and pudding mixes, putting them together upside down and so the Bakewell Pudding was born. Incidentally, don't confuse the pudding with the tart, they're very different, as any local pudding shop will be pleased to show you. Just south of Bakewell is **Haddon Hall**, ££, open daily 1030–1700 (April–Sept), a superbly preserved medieval house with a panelled gallery, chapel and walled garden jutting out over the river Wye. If historic houses and gardens are to your taste you'll have to go a long way to better **Chatsworth House**, £££, and grounds. Open daily 1100–1730 (Easter–Oct), 4 miles (6.4 km) east of Bakewell. The home of the Duke and Duchess of Devonshire has gardens designed by Capability Brown and incorporates the pretty estate village of **Edensor**.

From Monyash you could go west to **Longnor** and visit the craft centre in the old market hall with its gallery

From May to September, local towns and villages practice the ancient custom of **Well Dressing.** Believed to be a form of water worship or a fertility ritual, 5-ft (1.5-m) high pictures made of flower petals are pressed into clay and attached to local springs. Among the best are those held at **Tideswell, Tissington** and **Ashford-in-the-Water**. Contact **Bakewell Tourist Information Centre**, Old Market Hall, Bridge St; tel: (01629) 813227. Open daily 0900–1730 (summer); 0930–1700 (winter).

From Bakewell try a trip to The Old Smithy café at Monyash – home of the folk group Smithy's Brew and voted to have the best breakfast in the Peak District. Muddy walking boots and wet dogs are welcome.

If you enjoy walking try the defunct railway line – **The Monsal Trail** – which flirts with Bakewell and runs for 8 miles (13 km) through wooded gorges and limestone valleys and is mostly suitable for pushchairs and wheelchairs.

and fabulous woodwork. Then head for **Hartington**, home of good local cheeses, and at the head of a series of green dales that reach a climax at **Dovedale** with its rock spires and stepping stones. The valley floor provides the best-known walk in the Peak District: at weekends it fills to capacity, especially at the southern end. If you want to avoid the worst of the crowds, a good starting point is Alstonefield, from where a lane leads past the church and drops to Milldale, at the north end of Dovedale itself. Nearby **Wetton** is a perfect example of a Derbyshire farming hamlet with a good pub (The Royal Oak) and nearby **Thors Cave** set dramatically high in a cliff above the Manifold valley. Further west are gritstone outcrops of **The Roaches**, famous for their climbing routes, long views to Tittesworth reservoir.

South of the former spa of **Matlock**, the river Derwent carves a course through a craggy gorge. At **Matlock Bath** a cable car whisks you up to the Heights of Abraham, a country park with views and caves. Just to the south of here, **Cromford** is an early industrial village where in 1771 Richard Arkwright set up the world's first water-powered cotton mill, now a UNESCO World Heritage Site and museum (free; tours available).

Buxton, though technically outside the Peak National Park, makes an excellent base for the area, with good connections by rail and bus, and plenty of accommodation. Buxton today is a gracious spa, predominantly Victorian in character although its most famous range of buildings, The Crescent, dates from the 1780s when the Roman spa site was revived. You can still sample the (extremely pure-tasting) waters for free at St Ann's Well near the former spa building. Pavilion Gardens is full of period charm, with its glass pavilion and backdrops of the mosque-like dome of the former Devonshire Royal Hospital and the huge Palace Hotel. The Buxton Museum and Art Gallery (£, daily except Mon except Bank Holidays) gives an excellent introduction to the Peak District. On the southern edge of town, Poole's Cavern ranks as the best of the Peak District show caves, with some spectacular limestone concretions and the longest horizontal view of any cave in Britain (££, daily; closed Nov–Feb).

WHERE NEXT?

Buxton and other points in the Peak District (including Hathersage, Hope and Edale) have good rail connections to Manchester (see pp. 206–211) via Stockport. Trains go through New Mills, an old mill town dramatically sited over a gorge of the rivers Goyt and Sett – it is well worth stopping off to walk along the trail along the floor of the gorge, past atmospherically decaying old mill buildings. At Stockport you can change onto the main line south (towards London), stopping off at Macclesfield where Paradise Silk Mills and Museum features an astonishing time-warp silk mill (closed Mon except Bank Holidays).

LEEDS AND THE YORKSHIRE DALES

Leeds is the liveliest city in Yorkshire and has a reputation for great shopping. It is not a real tourist draw in itself, but it has good transport links to the beautiful limestone uplands of the Yorkshire Dales which feel surprisingly peaceful, even lonely in places. There are over 20 identifiable 'dales', some familiar and well publicised, others obscure and remote. They consist of placid sheep farming country, interspersed with patches of barren moorland, limestone pavement and brooding hills. Pretty towns and villages nestle in the dales and a maze of soft grey drystone walls spreads across the landscape like a giant fishing net.

Further east you find the civilised spa of Harrogate with its elegant shops, stately architecture and gardens, while historic Ripon and Richmond have castles and cathedrals to explore. There are grand monastic ruins at Bolton, Jervaulx and Fountains. And just west of Leeds is Haworth, famed throughout the world as the home of the Brontë sisters, whose work was inspired by the bleak beauty of the surrounding countryside.

GETTING THERE AND GETTING AROUND

Leeds/Bradford Airport is situated 8 miles (13 km) north west of Leeds and receives scheduled flights from many cities including London, Edinburgh, Glasgow, Amsterdam and Brussels. A regular Airlink coach runs to the city centre.

The **bus and coach** station is situated in New York St in the centre of Leeds. Regular National Express coaches run to destinations throughout Britain, tel: 0990 808080, while First Leeds is the major bus operator buses in the area, tel: (0113) 245 1601. For local bus times call Metroline, tel: (0113) 245 7676; www.wymetro.com.

Leeds has a busy **railway** station with regular services running to all parts of Britain. The journey from London takes around 2 hrs 25 mins. There is an excellent service of local trains ('Metro') connecting the city with the rest of West Yorkshire. For times contact Metroline, tel: (0113) 245 7676; www.wymetro.com.

INFORMATION

Gateway Yorkshire Regional Travel and Tourist information centre, The Arcade, City Station; tel: (0113) 242 5242; website: www.leeds.gov.uk; e-mail: tourinfo@leeds.gov.uk. Open Mon–Sat 0900–1730, Sun 1000–1600.

MONEY Foreign exchange is available in Leeds Post Office in the City Square and also at Thomas Cook branches on Cambridge Rd and James St in Harrogate.

Post Leeds Post Office is in the City Square. There are post offices in Harrogate and the main towns in the Dales.

ACCOMMODATION

Glengarth Hotel £££ 162 Woodsley Rd; tel: (0113) 245 7940. Family-run hotel a short walk from the city centre.

Malmaison ££££ Sovereign Quay; tel: (0113) 398 1001; e-mail: leeds@malmaison.com. Stylish hotel on the waterfront.

FOOD AND DRINK

One of the most famous sights in Leeds is **Headingley Cricket Ground**. The first cricket match was played here in 1890. The ground is the home of the Yorkshire County Cricket Club and Test matches are still played here.

Art's Café £££ 42 Call Lane; tel: (0113) 243 8243. Well-established bistro in trendy part of town.

Brio £££ 40 Great George St; tel: (0113) 246 5225. Modern Italian cuisine in bright, spacious surroundings.

Bryan's Fisheries ££ 9 Westwood Lane. Good old fish, chips and mushy peas.

Fourth Floor Café and Bar ££ 107 Briggate. Fashionable café in the Leeds branch of Harvey Nichols.

Bradford is known as the curry capital of the UK and it is well worth visiting to try some of its excellent ethnic restaurants. Trains run regularly from Leeds and the journey only takes 20 mins. **Mumtaz Paan House Restaurant £££** 390 Great Horton Rd, Bradford. Classic Indian food, no alcohol allowed.

HIGHLIGHTS

Leeds was at the heart of the Industrial Revolution and became the centre of the cloth trade, growing wealthy in the process. Today it is a busy university city and has firmly established itself as the shopping centre of the North.

Royal Armouries Museum, ££, family tickets, Armouries Drive, open daily 1030–1730. This attraction is one for all the family with interactive exhibits, live action events and costumed demonstrations bringing 3000 years of arms and armour to life. Displays include Henry VIII's tournament armour.

The **City Art Gallery** has a collection that includes famous Victorian paintings, French post-Impressionist

TOURS

There are regular themed guided walks of Leeds and its immediate surroundings, led by official guides. Details available from Leeds tourist information centre.

works and contemporary British art. It is linked to the Henry Moore Institute, which is devoted to sculpture of all periods. Free, The Headrow, open Mon–Sat 1000–1700, Wed 1000–2000, Sun 1300–1700. The **Thackray Medical Museum** is a fascinating but gruesome museum depicting, in sometimes graphic detail, how medicine has affected the lives of ordinary people. ££, Beckett St, frequent bus service from city centre, open Tues–Sun 1000–1700.

SHOPPING

Leeds boasts a branch of the exclusive department store Harvey Nichols, situated on Briggate, the city's main shopping street. Other shops along here include designer names like Paul Smith, Dolce and Gabbana and Vivienne Westwood in The Victorian Quarter, and a branch of Fraser's which stocks designer clothes by Paul Costello and Max Mara.

NIGHTLIFE

There are plenty of pubs, bars, cafés and clubs in Leeds – **Exchange Quarter** is the city's trendy meeting place. **City Varieties** in Swan St is one of the last traditional music halls in Britain. Artists who have performed here over the years include Lillie Langtry, Harry Houdini and Charlie Chaplin. There is a music hall season every April and October.

SIDE TRIPS FROM LEEDS

HAREWOOD HOUSE Harewood is the home of the Queen's cousin, the Earl of Harewood, and is one of the most magnificent houses in England. The interior of the house is lavish with Chippendale furniture, fine porcelain and works of art by Turner, Tintoretto and Titian. Then there are the landscaped grounds, designed by Capability Brown in the 18th century, and a Lakeside Bird Garden with over 120 rare and endangered species. £££, open daily 1000–1600; grounds, 1100; house – last admission 1600. Bus no. 36 runs every 20 mins from Leeds and Harrogate during opening hours.

SKIPTON This lively market town, easily reached by Metro train from Leeds, is the gateway to the southern Dales. Its name means 'sheeptown', an allusion to its farming traditions. Set above a dramatic gorge is romantic **Skipton Castle** (££, open daily 1000–1800, Sun 1200–1800, closes 1600 Oct–Feb) with well

Pennine Boat Trips ££; tel: (01756) 790829. From Skipton you can take a cruise along the Leeds and Liverpool Canal, Britain's longest inland waterway. It is a relaxing way of seeing the countryside and you can choose from 2- to 6-hr cruises. Cruises start and finish at the Wharf in Coach St.

preserved medieval, Tudor and Stuart sections. The church of Holy Trinity has a bossed 15th-century roof and a fine rood screen. **The Craven Museum**, Town Hall is a quirky museum with a fascinating assortment of local history. ££, open Wed–Mon 1000–1700, Sun 1400–1700 (Apr–Sept); daily except Tues and Sun 1330–1700, Sat 1000–1600 (winter). Steam trains run from the nearby station of Embsay to **Bolton Abbey** (££, open daily 0730–dusk), where you can explore the medieval ruins or walk along the river Wharfe.

HAWORTH Situated high on the Pennine Moors, the little village of Haworth is famed throughout the world for its connection with the Brontë sisters. It was here that Charlotte wrote *Jane Eyre* and Emily penned the romantic *Wuthering Heights*. The village is dominated by their memory, becoming extremely busy during peak times. Surrounded by bleak moorland, the heart of the village is dominated by **Haworth Church**, where the Brontës' father was parson. The neighbouring house where the family lived, and where the sisters wrote their novels, is now preserved as the **Brontë Parsonage Museum** (££, open daily 1000–1930 Apr–Sept, 1100–1700 Oct–Mar). The museum contains the Brontës' own furniture and the daughters' writing desks.

You can reach Haworth on the historic **Keighley and Worth Valley Railway** (£££, day ticket provides unlimited travel, family tickets available; includes admission to Museum of Rail Travel at Ingrow; tel: (01535) 645214), which connects at Keighley with the Metro train from Leeds. This 5-mile (8-km) branch line has six atmospheric old gas lit stations, and runs lovingly restored steam locomotives which carry both local people and tourists. It terminates at Oxenhope. It is worth getting off at **Oakworth**, the preserved Edwardian station which featured in the classic film *The Railway Children*.

You can stroll round the village, which is packed with tea shops and gift shops and which still contains the chemist's where Branwell Brontë bought his supplies of opium to feed his addiction. There are plenty of **walks** that start here including the 40-mile (64-km) Brontë Way. The most famous part of the walk leads on to the moors and over to Top Withens, a ruin which is said to be the setting for the farm in *Wuthering Heights*.

> *i* **Tourist Information Centre** 2–4 West Lane; tel: (01535) 642329, e-mail: haworth@ytbtic.co.uk. Open daily 0930–1730 (Apr–Oct), closes 1700 (Nov–Mar).

> **Ashmount** ££ Mytholmes Lane, Haworth, Keighley; tel: (01535) 645726; website: www. members.aol.com/ashmount haworth; e-mail: ashmounthaworth@aol.com. Victorian villa, only 5 mins walk from the Brontë village of Haworth.

BRADFORD Bradford is easily reached from Leeds and is the home of the acclaimed **National Museum of Photography, Film and Television** (free, open

Leeds and the Yorkshire Dales

Tues–Sun 1000–1800). It contains interactive exhibits taking you inside the world of the media that dominated the 20th century.

SALTAIRE A planned industrial village (reached by Metro train from Leeds, approximately 15 mins), Saltaire was built in the 19th century by Victorian businessman and philanthropist, Sir Titus Salt. The village was designed to provide clean housing and living conditions for the workers at the neighbouring woollen mill, a Utopian alternative to the slums in neighbouring Bradford and Leeds. Walking around the village gives an insight into the lives of the inhabitants of the village of the time – and you can pick up self guided walking leaflets from Saltaire Tourist Infomation Centre, 2 Victoria Rd, tel: (01274) 774 993, open daily 1030–1730. The village's main attraction is the former mill, **Salts Mill** (free, open daily 1000–1800), which houses the 1853 Gallery devoted to the works of Bradford-born artist David Hockney. The mill also has a diner and some speciality shops.

> The **Leeds–Settle–Carlisle Railway** is one of the most scenic railways in Britain and provides an excellent way of enjoying the Yorkshire Dales. Completed in 1876, the railway line quickly became a favourite with Victorian and Edwardian passengers. The line's most famous landmark is the Ribblehead Viaduct, a picturesque triumph of engineering. The line goes via Keighley, Skipton and Dent and the journey takes under 3 hrs. With a 'Freedom of the Line' ticket (£), valid for 3 days, you can explore the countryside and villages along the route. A network of buses connects stations with villages, with a programme of guided walks from selected stations. Tel: (01729) 825037; website: www.settle-carlisle.co.uk.

Fountains Abbey and Studley Royal Water Gardens

One of England's most romantic ruins, this former Cistercian monastery enjoys a wonderful setting in the wooded valley of the river Skell (off B6265, nr Ripon; about an hour by car from Leeds). Founded in 1133, it grew to be the wealthiest abbey in the country. Surrounding the abbey are the 17th-century Fountains Hall and the intricate 18th-century water gardens of Studley Royal. This combination of Elizabethan mansion and Georgian water garden simply enhances the magic of the abbey, with lakes, temples and cascades drawing the eye. The parkland approach provides a beautiful walk to the abbey. The complex is now a World Heritage Site. ££ (free to National Trust and English Heritage members), open daily 1000–1900 Apr–Sept, 1000–1700 Oct–Mar, closed Fri Nov–Jan.

> Every night at 2100 Ripon's resident red-coated bugler blows a horn in the market square. This custom dates from Saxon times and assures the residents of their safety for the night. Elsewhere in the Dales, in Bainbridge, a similar evening horn was blown to guide travellers through the thick woods in darkness or bad weather.

Fountains Abbey is close to **Ripon**, a market town with a huge cathedral containing fine wood and stone carving as well as a 7th-century crypt.

YORKSHIRE DALES NATIONAL PARK

This ever-popular area of green sheep-grazed turf, dry-stone walls and former lead-mining villages represents a deeply traditional landscape, best enjoyed on foot or by cycle. If you are without a car, there's a reasonable network of buses; Skipton (with mainline rail services) is a useful gateway, with bus services to Malham, Grassington, Settle and elsewhere (for online information visit the website www.lineone.net/~travelinfo/dales).

i **Tourist Information Centre**, Dales Countryside Museum, Station Yard, Hawes; tel: (01969) 667450; e-mail: hawes@ytbtic.co.uk. Open 1000–1700 (summer); 1100–1500 (winter).

🛏 The Yorkshire Dales have many excellent B&Bs, many of them on working farms, as well as self catering accommodation and bunk barns.

There is also a good network of youth hostels (£) in the Yorkshire Dales. In Wensleydale: **Aysgarth Falls** Aysgarth, tel: 0870 7705679 (e-mail: aysgarth@yha.org.uk); **Hawes** Lancaster Terrace, tel: 0870 7705854 (e-mail: hawes@yha.org.uk). In Swaledale: **Grinton Lodge** £ Grinton, tel: 0870 7705844 (e-mail: grinton@yha.org.uk); **Keld**, tel: 0870 7705889. In Wharfedale: **Kettlewell**, tel: 0870 7705897 (e-mail: kettlewell@yha.org.uk); **Linton**, tel: 0870 7705920. Also: **Dentdale**, tel: 0870 7705790(e-mail: dentdale@yha.org.uk); **Ingleton**, Sammy Lane, tel: 0870 7705880 (e-mail: ingleton@yha.org.uk); **Malham**, tel: 0870 7705946 (e-mail: malham@yha.org.uk); **Stainforth**, tel: 0870 7706046 (e-mail: stainforth@yha.org.uk).

Carr End House ££ Countersett, Wensleydale; tel: (01969) 650346. 17th-century house in the heart of the Dales.

Simonstone Hall £££ Simonstone, Hawes; tel: (01969) 667255; website: www.simonstonehall.co.uk; e-mail: e-mail@simonstonehall.demon.co.uk. Lavishly furnished country house with magnificent views.

🍴 Yorkshire is well served with traditional **pubs**, which generally offer good, traditional dishes at low prices. There are also plenty of **tea rooms** serving cakes, scones and light meals.

Wensleydale Heifer ££ West Witton, Wensleydale. Yorkshire pub in the heart of a popular village.

Waterford House £££ Kirkgate, Middleham; tel: (01969) 622090. Restaurant with rooms near village square. Super cooking in unpretentious French style.

WENSLEYDALE Wensleydale is a broad, pastoral valley, with well-wooded slopes and classic Pennine villages. It is one of the richest of the Dales and the most popular with visitors. Several waterfalls punctuate the course of the river Ure, particularly at Aysgarth Falls. The dale is full of variety, with romantic ruins such as the old Cistercian house of **Jervaulx Abbey** (£, open daily) and the splendour of **Middleham Castle** (£, open daily 1000–1800 Apr–Oct), the childhood home of Richard III. Wensleydale sheep, with their long, curly fleeces are an economic mainstay and at Masham, local breweries such as Theakston (££, open daily, ring to confirm tour times; tel: (01765) 689057) and Black Sheep (££, ring to confirm tour times; tel: (01765) 680100) offer tours and tastings.

WENSLEYDALE CHEESE
Wensleydale cheese has been made in the dale ever since the 12th century. The special recipe was brought here by the French Cistercian monks of Jervaulx Abbey. They made the cheese until the dissolution of the monasteries in the 16th century – by which time the art had been passed on to local farmers' wives. The dairy at Hawes – the **Wensleydale Creamery**, Gayle Lane (£, open daily 0900–1730 summer, 0930–1630 winter) – was established in the 19th century and is still producing cheese today. There is a visitor centre where you can watch as the cheese is made and then taste the finished product. In the shop you can buy cheeses to take home.

🖳 **Helm**, £££ Askrigg, Leyburn; tel: (01969) 650443; website: www.helmyorkshire.com; e-mail: holiday@helmyorkshire.com. Quiet stone guesthouse with wonderful views.

The market town of **Hawes** makes an excellent base for touring, with superb drives and walks on its doorstep, including the dramatic Buttertubs Pass to the north and a wild route to Langstrothdale. Hardraw Force just outside the town is England's tallest single-drop waterfall. You can walk right behind the cascade on a rock ledge.

SWALEDALE **Richmond** is one of the most attractive towns in England, with a striking castle perched on a precarious-looking site above the river Swale. It was built soon after the Norman conquest and has been little altered since. The atmospheric Market Square is surrounded with Georgian buildings and little shops, while cobbled streets run down to the river. The Georgian Theatre Royal (£, open Mon–Sat 1030–1430) still has the original proscenium.

Richmond is the gateway to **Swaledale**, a more rugged dale than Wensleydale. It features attractive villages like Reeth, home to the **Swaledale Folk Museum** (£, open daily 1030–1700 Easter–end Oct) and Keld, a typical stone village on the Pennine Way. Traditional stone hay barns are a classic feature of the landscape and there are plenty of traditional craft workshops to visit. Richmond and Swaledale are best reached by car.

WHARFDALE This long natural corridor is lush and wooded at its southern end, around the ruins and active church of Bolton Abbey and Strid Woods but bracingly open further up. Grassington, served by buses from Skipton, is its busy hub, packed full of tourists and walkers in summer and at weekends, and with a reasonable choice of places to stay. There are easy village-to-village walks in the dale, along the river or through pastures; Kettlewell, Buckden and Hubberholme are good places to hike to, each with a good pub.

MALHAMDALE Some of northern England's greatest natural wonders are in the area around the village of Malham. **Malham Cove** is a huge cliff, at the base of which the river Aire re-emerges after running underground: you can trace its course by heading up the Pennine Way, above the Cove where there is an impressive **limestone pavement**. Beyond is the dry valley of **Watlowes** where streams drop into sink holes, and above that is the small lake of Malham Tarn. It is also worth walking east past the tufa-encrusted waterfall of **Janet's Foss** to **Gordale Scar**, where a stream performs a somersault between rocks before dropping into a huge valley.

> **MARKETS**
> Many of the towns in the Dales have excellent traditional markets. They are great places to browse, purchase fresh local produce and meet local people. Ripon, Skipton, Masham, Richmond and Settle are just some of the market towns worth visiting.

THE THREE PEAKS Yorkshire's highest trio of summits – Whernside, Ingleborough and Pen-y-ghent – rise to 2414 ft (736 m) on the western side of the Yorkshire Dales. Pen-y-ghent, arguably most interesting of the three, can be climbed from Horton-in-Ribblesdale rail station (on the famously scenic Settle–Carlisle line): on the way up you encounter entrances to potholes, while the final ascent is exhilaratingly craggy. Ingleborough is also rewarding, and best done by climbing out of Ingleton to the summit, then dropping past the entrance to Gaping Gill, an immense underground chamber, and Ingleborough show caves to end at the attractive village of Clapham, from where buses take you back. Another fascinating walk is into Ingleton Glen (£, daily), with its series of spectacular waterfalls – reached from Ingleton itself.

HARROGATE

Harrogate must be the most elegant town in Yorkshire. It became a spa in the 18th century and by the mid-19th century was attracting 30,000 visitors a year. With its palatial Assembly Rooms, Opera House and grand hotels, the town still has a prosperous air. The **Royal Pump Room Museum** (£, open Mon–Sat 1000–1700 Apr–Oct, Sun 1400–1700, closed Mon in winter) records the history of the spa – and gives you the chance to taste the pungent sulphur waters that were taken as a 'cure'. The town is strong on tearooms and toffee and renowned for its specialist shops and beautiful gardens. **Harlow Carr Botanical Gardens**, Crag Lane (££, open daily 0930–dusk) are the Northern Horticultural Society's superbly planted headquarters with an impressive range of ornamental gardens.

Just 3 miles (4.8 km) east of Harrogate, or about 45 mins by train from Leeds, is **Knaresborough**, a historic town with a dramatic setting over the Nidd gorge; its battered Norman **Castle** (£, open daily 1030–1700 Easter–Sept) poised on the cliff edge.

Harrogate is a good base from which to explore **Nidderdale**, one of the smaller dales and an Area of Outstanding Natural Beauty. It is an excellent place for walking and has a variety of attractions. There is Ripley Castle (££, tel: (01423) 770152 for opening times) situated in the attractive village of Ripley and **The Nidderdale Museum** at Pateley Bridge (£, open daily 1400–1700 Easter–Nov, 1100–1700 Aug). Natural features worth exploring include the dramatically shaped **Brimham Rocks** near Pateley Bridge and **Stump Cross Caverns**, Greenhow (£, open daily 1000–1800 Mar–Oct) a 500,000-year-old cave with a striking collection of stalactites and stalagmites.

Mother Shipton's Cave, the mystical birthplace of a 16th-century prophetess, is a popular and busy tourist attraction (£££, open Easter–Halloween, daily 0930–1745).

| *i* | **Tourist Information Centre** Royal Baths Assembly Rooms, Crescent Rd; tel: (01423) 537300; website: harrogate.gov.uk; e-mail: tic@harrogate.gov.uk. Open Mon–Sat 0900–1800, Sun 1000–1300 (Apr–Sept), Mon–Fri 0900–1700, Sat 0900–1600 (winter).

The Ruskin Hotel £££ 1 Swan Rd, Harrogate; tel: (01423) 502045; e-mail: ruskin.hotel@virgin.net. Small Victorian hotel, well placed for exploring elegant Harrogate.

Bettys £–££ 1 Parliament St, Harrogate; tel: (01423) 502746. Gorgeous cakes and light meals. A Yorkshire institution; be prepared to queue.

Drum and Monkey £££ 5 Montpellier Gardens, Harrogate. Good central restaurant with accomplished seafood cooking.

SHOPPING Harrogate is an elegant centre with many individual shops, including several antique stores, while shops in the towns and villages of the Dales are great places to pick up outdoor gear and local food and drink.

EVENTS The **Nidderdale Festival** takes place in late June or early July and is a celebration of the dale's rich culture. There is music, walks, talks and various outdoor activities. In August **St Wilfrid's Procession** passes through the streets of Ripon, commemorating the safe return of St Wilfrid from exile in 686. September sees the **Harrogate Autumn Flower Show**, an extremely popular event with stunning displays of flowers.

WHERE NEXT?

Eleven miles (18 km) north of Harrogate is the market town of Ripon with its famous cathedral which is well worth a visit. From here you could then explore the North York Moors (see pp. 254–257). Alternatively, travel to the western part of the Yorkshire Dales and then move into Cumbria and the Lake District (see pp. 224–231).

YORK AND THE NORTH YORK MOORS

York's significance far outweighs its status as a county town. Two thousand years of history have turned it into something of an open air museum and its quaint, traffic-free streets, including Saxon Whip-ma-whop-ma-gate, recall the past at every turn. The Romans founded the city in AD 71, naming it *Eboracum* (the Archbishop of York still adds 'Ebor' to his official signature). The Vikings made the thriving inland port the foremost city of the Danelaw. Fortified with walls and castles by the Normans, York continued to prosper in medieval times on the back of its wool trade. Now chocolate and tourism are the town's main concerns.

The surrounding countryside is glorious and scattered with abbeys, castle, stately homes and picturesque stone villages. To the north is the North York Moors National Park, while to the east are long stretches of heritage coastline. Consider tackling the area as two separate trips, one concentrating on the coast and wolds, the other exploring the National Park interior. The best inland scenery is accessible only via a maze of minor roads through sheep-strewn pastureland. Just about any lane reveals an unexpected view: clouds of spring daffodils, an ancient stone cross, or the kilns and trackbeds of Rosedale's old ironstone industry. Some roads are hair-raisingly steep.

GETTING THERE AND GETTING AROUND

Leeds/Bradford Airport is the most convenient airport for York. It receives flights from many cities including London, Edinburgh, Amsterdam and Brussels. A regular airlink coach runs to Leeds city centre from where there are connecting trains to York.

Most **buses** run from York railway station. Regular **National Express** coaches run from destinations throughout Britain, tel: 0990 808080; for local buses, tel: Businfo (01904) 551400. **Yorkshire Coastliner** runs services to Leeds, Scarborough and Whitby, tel: (01653) 692556; **Harrogate and District** operates services to Harrogate and Ripon, tel: (01423) 566061. **East Yorkshire Buses** runs services to Bridlington, tel: (01482) 327142.

York is on the East coast main **railway** line and there are regular services to and from London, Newcastle and Edinburgh. National Rail Enquiries, tel: 08457 484950.

INFORMATION

Yorkshire Tourist Board See p. 409.

York Tourism De Grey Rooms, Exhibition Square; tel: (01904) 621756; website: www.york-tourism.co.uk; e-mail: tic@york-tourism.co.uk. Open daily 0900–1800 (summer); Mon–Sat

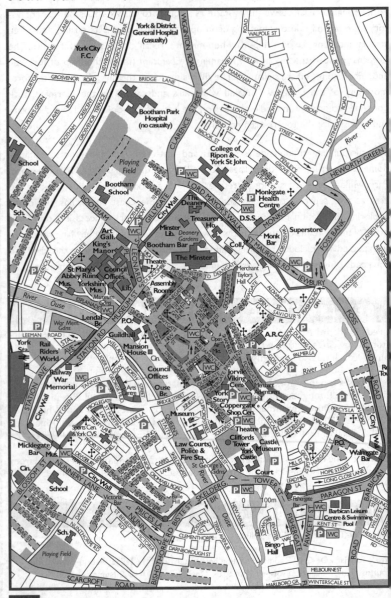

0900–1700, Sun 0930–1600 (winter). There is also a branch at the Railway Station; tel: (01904) 621756. Open daily 0900–1800 (summer); Mon–Sat 0900–1700, Sun 1000–1600 (winter).

Easingwold Tourist Information Centre, Chapel Lane; tel: (01347) 821530; e-mail: easingwold@ytbtic.co.uk. Open Mon–Sat 1000–1600 (summer only).

Malton Tourist Information Centre, 58 Market Place; tel: (01653) 600048; e-mail: malton@ytbtic.co.uk. Open Mon–Sat 0930–1730 (Mar–Oct); Mon–Wed, Fri–Sat 0930–1630 (Nov–Mar).

Money Foreign exchange is available from Thomas Cook in Stonegate. You can also change money at the tourist information centres in Exhibition Square and at the railway station.

Post The main Post Office is in Lendal.

ACCOMMODATION

The Bar Convent ££ 17 Blossom St, York; tel: (01904) 643238; e-mail: info@bar-convent.org.uk. Refurbished Georgian listed convent offers unusual B&B.

Easton's ££ 88–90 Bishopthorpe Rd, York; tel: (01904) 626646; e-mail: eastonsbbyork@aol.com. Centrally located B&B with period furnishings.

Hollies Guest House ££ 141 Fulford Rd, York; tel: (01904) 634279; website: www.hollies-guesthouse.co.uk; e-mail: enquiries@hollies-guesthouse.co.uk. Friendly service in refurbished Edwardian residence.

Romley House ££, 2 Millfield Rd, York; tel: (01904) 652822; website: www.romleyhouse.co.uk; e-mail: info@romleyhouse.co.uk. Comfortable accommodation close to city centre.

The Walmgate Hotel ££ 16 Barbican Rd, York; tel: (01904) 659976; website: www.walmgatehotel.co.uk; e-mail: walmgatehotel@yahoo.com. Reader-recommended address; 11 rooms with TV, continental self-service breakfast; 10–15 mins' walk to city centre.

York Youth Hostel £ Water End, Clifton; tel: 0870 7706102; e-mail: york@yha.org.uk. 20-min walk from rail station; has singles, twins and family rooms plus dorms.

FOOD AND DRINK

Bettys £–££ 6–8 St Helen's Square, York. A branch of Yorkshire's famous café/tea rooms serving cakes and light meals.

Blake Head Bookshop and Vegetarian Café ££ 104 Micklegate, York. Well reviewed vegetarian café serving snacks, salads and substantial meals during the day.

Café Concerto £££ 21 High Petergate, York. Friendly café/bistro where you can relax with a cappucino during the day or eat French style food at night.

El Piano ££ 15–17 Grape Lane, York. Relaxed place serving a mix of Hispanic and vegetarian food. Not licensed.

Meltons Too ££ 25 Walmgate, York. Contemporary café, bar and bistro. Sister to Meltons serving light meals and snacks.

Rish £££ 7 Fossgate, York; tel: (01904) 622688. Restaurant serving modern British food with a Middle Eastern influence.

The Treasurer's House ££ Minster Yard, York. Home baking in atmospheric medieval National Trust property opposite the Minster.

HIGHLIGHTS

York's medieval city walls, built to protect the city, are the best preserved in England and make a popular walking circuit. The 'bars' or gateways are still intact, as are the many towers – including the Red Tower built in the 1490s and once used to make gunpowder. The tourist information centre produces a leaflet on the City Walls Trail, £.

At **York Castle** little survives of the two original fortresses built by the Normans in York except a keep, known as **Clifford's Tower**, £, Tower St (open daily 1000–1800 Apr–Sept; 1000–1700 Oct; 1000–1600 Nov–Mar) from which you get great views over the city. Immediately beside it stands **York Castle Museum** (tel: 0345 660280 for prices; open daily 0930–1700 Apr–Oct; 0930–1630 Nov–Mar), a splendidly eclectic social history museum. There are re-created Victorian and Edwardian streets and exhibits covering everything from ancient armour to the history of chocolate.

You could probably spend a day just exploring **York Minster**, Deangate (free entry to main body of the church, free guided tours; charges requested for museum, treasury, chapterhouse, crypt and tower; open daily 0700–1800). It is the largest medieval cathedral in northern Europe and took two centuries to build. The present structure was begun in 1220 and additions continued until the central tower was completed in 1470. The building has a stupendous array of medieval glass. Climb up the 275 spiral steps to the Central Tower and you will be rewarded with stunning views of York and the surrounding countryside.

One of York's best-loved attractions is **Jorvik, The Viking City**, £££, Coppergate (open daily 0900–1730 Apr–Oct; 1000–1630 Nov–Mar). Recently refurbished at a cost of nearly £ 5 million, this attraction uses 21st-century technology to take you back to the days of 10th-century Viking York. It brings the city to life with real archaeological evidence combined with authentic sights, sounds and smells.

At **Fairfax House**, ££, Castlegate (open Mon–Thur and Sat 1100–1700; Fri by guided tour only 1100–1400; Sun 1330–1730 mid-Feb–early Jan) you can explore a classical 18th-century townhouse. Its collection of furniture and clocks is said to be one of the best private collections in the country.

Art lovers should head for **York City Art Gallery**, £, Exhibition Square (open daily 1000–1700) which has an extensive collection of European paintings including works by Reynolds, Lowry, Nash and Hockney.

Just a 5-min walk from the railway station is the **National Railway Museum** (free, open daily 1000–1800), which brings the history of rail travel to life. There are interactive exhibits, historic carriages and gleaming steam engines. The impressive collection includes a replica of Stephenson's *Rocket*, Queen Victoria's Royal carriage and a Bullet train from Japan. The *Mallard* loco is also based here; it reached 126 mph (203 km/h) in 1938, breaking the world steam locomotion speed record.

Yorkwalk run themed guided walks (££) through the city, which often give you access to areas you would not otherwise see. Tours last from one and a half to two hours and start at the Museum Gardens Gate on Museum Street just north of Lendal Bridge.

Tours Two companies run open top bus tours of the city, and tickets are valid all day so you can get on and off as often as you like.

Discover York by Guide Friday, ££, family tickets. You can purchase tickets from tourist information centres, Thomas Cook Hotel and Reservations (Platform 3 York Station) or on the bus. Complete tour lasts one hour.

York City Sightseeing, ££, family tickets; tel: (01904) 692505. Purchase tickets on the bus. Departures every 15 mins.

You can also take a one hour guided boat trip around the city on the River Ouse with **Yorkboat**, ££; tel: (01904) 628324. Trips sail daily from Feb–Nov and leave from King's Staith Landing and Lendal Bridge Landing. Evening cruises also available.

SHOPPING

York's most famous street is the **Shambles**, a picturesque cobbled street lined with overhanging, half timbered buildings. It has a charming, medieval appearance, yet its origins were brutal. It got its name from the Saxon word *shamel* meaning slaughterhouse and used to be the local butchery. Today it is full of shops selling souvenirs and sweets.

Newgate Market is a daily market in the centre of York near the Shambles. It sells everything from vegetables to bric-à-brac – great for browsing.

York's main shopping streets are **Stonegate**,

Parliament St and Coney St. All general High Street names are here and also in the covered Coppergate Centre. For specialist food and fashion shops try Swinegate. If you're looking for antiques, the Red House Antiques Centre, Duncombe Place, has over 60 antique dealers selling their goods.

NIGHTLIFE

York doesn't have the metropolitan buzz of a big city but there is still plenty to do at night. There are lots of places to drink, ranging from modern chain pubs to chic wine bars and traditional, real ale pubs – which often feature live music. La Plaza at the De Grey Rooms, Exhibition Square, has a wide range of entertainment from tea dances to salsa dancing. Theatre lovers should check out the **Theatre Royal**, St Leonard's Place, where you can see drama, comedy and panto. **The Grand Opera House**, Cumberland St, also puts on a wide range of productions.

SIDE TRIPS FROM YORK

Castle Howard must be one of the grandest houses in Britain. Best known from the British TV serialisation of *Brideshead Revisited*, Castle Howard represents the summit of Sir John Vanbrugh's achievement. His ambitious design of 1699 dominates the formal grounds and ornamental lake. The Great Hall is topped by a gilded dome and the Long Gallery is hung with family portraits. The house is surrounded by 1000 acres of parkland with fountains, woodland gardens and the famous Temple of the Four Winds designed in 1724. £££, 15 miles (24 km) from York off the A64; occasional buses from York, for details, tel: 0870 608 2608. Open daily Mar–Nov; last admission 1630; grounds open most days in winter.

Eden Camp, ££ (off A64 at A169 Pickering/Malton junction; occasional buses from York, for details; tel: 0870 608 2608 open daily 1000–1700). This unusual museum transports you back to wartime Britain, allowing you to experience the sights and smells of the time. The museum stretches over six acres (2.4 ha), and includes exhibits on the blitz and the blackout. Visits generally take around four hours. The nearby market town of **Malton** is also worth a visit, with an excellent **Museum**, £, open 1000–1600 Mon–Sat (Easter–Oct) in the Market Place.

NORTH YORK MOORS

The **North York Moors** is the largest stretch of heather moorland in England. There are several different species of heather, which flower in a glorious expanse of pink and purple between July and September. The moors are sparsely populated but show many signs of earlier occupation: prehistoric burial mounds, Roman roads, old mine-workings and medieval stone crosses.

The most rewarding of the lush dales for motorists are **Rosedale**, **Farndale**, **Ryedale** and **Eskdale** – although they can get very busy at weekends and during holiday times. (Some bus services now run there, especially during the summer, to try and cut down on congestion.) Farndale is famous for its wild daffodils in spring, protected in a 2000-acre (810-ha) nature reserve. Rosedale's scenery is steeper and more austere. The Stape–Goathland road is one of the wildest moorland routes, leading past the Roman earthwork training grounds of the Cawthorn Camps to a clearly preserved mile-long trackway known as Wade's Causeway or the Wheeldale Roman road. To see it you must take to your feet. One of the most popular parts of the area is **Goathland**, made famous as the setting for the popular British TV series *Heartbeat*.

Hutton-le-Hole, with its long, uneven village green grazed by sheep, is one of the most photogenic corners of the area. Its main sight is the **Ryedale Folk Museum** (££, Easter–late Oct), where a number of historic buildings from the area have been brought, reassembled and safeguarded. They include a photographer's studio, a farm worker's cottage, a cobbler's, a tinsmith's and a gypsy caravan. Close by, the church at **Lastingham** has a real surprise – from the present church, steps lead down into an astonishingly unaltered 11th-century crypt.

On Sundays and during summer school holidays, from Easter to September, **Moorsbus** services run between towns, villages and attractions on the North York Moors. Information from Sutton Bank National Park Centre; tel: (01845) 957426. Some Royal Mail **Postbus** services also operate in the area; tel: (01325) 341306.

i **North York Moors National Park Authority** The Old Vicarage, Bondgate, Helmsley, YO62 5BP, tel: (01439) 770657; fax: (01439) 770691; website: www.northyorkmoors-npa.org; e-mail: info@northyorkmoors-npa.gov.uk.

Tourist Information Centre Unit 3, Pavilion House, Valley Bridge Rd, Scarborough; tel: (01723) 373333; website: www. scarborough.gov.uk; e-mail: scarboroughtic@scarborough.gov.uk. Open daily 0930–1800 (May–Sept); 1000–1630 (Oct–Apr).

Tourist Information Centre Langborne Rd, Whitby; tel: (01947) 602674; www.scarborough.gov.uk; e-mail: whitbytic@scarborough.gov.uk. Open daily 0930–1800 (summer); 1000–1630 (winter).

Laskill Farm Country House £££ Laskill Farm, Hawnby, tel: (01439) 798268; e-mail: suesmith@laskillfarm.fsnet.co.uk. Country house set in an acre of garden with ducks, swans and peacocks.

Moorlands House £££ Hutton-Le-Hole, YO62 6UA; tel: (01751) 417548; website: www.moorlandshouse.com; e-mail: welcome@moorlandshouse.com. Welcoming Georgian guesthouse with streamside garden, log fires, homemade cake…

Oldstead Grange £££ Oldstead, Coxwold; tel: (01347) 868634; website: www.yorkshireuk.com; e-mail: anne@yorkshireuk.com. Spacious accommodation in a 17th-century farmhouse.

White Horse Farm £££ Rosedale Abbey, nr Pickering; tel: (01751) 417239; website: www.whitehorsefarmhotel; e-mail:

One of the most enjoyable ways of seeing the countryside is on the **North Yorkshire Moors Railway**, the most popular heritage railway in Britain. The line runs for 18 miles (29km) from the market town of **Pickering** to the village of **Grosmont** (buses run from York to Pickering) with restored steam trains stopping at various stations including Levisham and Goathland. The best way to enjoy the trip is to buy an all-day rover ticket which allows you to get on and off the train at will. £££, family tickets available (daily Mar–Nov; tel: (01751) 472508; website: www.northyorkmoorsrail way.com.

sales@whitehorsefarmhotel.co.uk. Traditional inn overlooking some of the best scenery in the North York Moors.

Youth hostels: Boggle Hole Youth Hostel £, tel: 0870 7705705 (e-mail: bogglehole@yha.org.uk). Idyllically sited near the beach close to Robin Hood's Bay. **Helmsley Youth Hostel** £, tel: 0870 7705860 (e-mail: helmsley@yha.org.uk). In the centre of a characterful market town. **Lockton Youth Hostel** £, tel/fax: 0870 7705939. Primitive and rural, former village school. **Osmotherley Youth Hostel** £, tel: 0870 7705983 (e-mail: osmotherley@yha.org.uk). In a village near Osmotherley station. **Scarborough Youth Hostel** £ Burniston Rd, tel: 0870 7706022 (e-mail: scarborough@yha.org.uk). **Whitby Youth Hostel** £ East Cliff, tel: 0870 7706088 (e-mail: whitby@ yha.org.uk). Near the abbey ruins and coast path.

HELMSLEY Helmsley is a pretty market town right on the edge of the North York Moors National Park. Close to the market square are the ruins of a 12th-century **Castle** which is most famous for its huge earthworks. £, open daily 1000–1800 (Apr–Sept); 1000–1700 (Oct); Wed–Sun 1000–1600 (Nov–Mar). About half a mile away is the neo-classical splendour of **Duncombe Park**, ££, (open Sun–Thur 1030–1800 Apr–Oct), which has a unique 18th-century landscaped garden and offers great views of the surrounding countryside.

West of Helmsley is **Rievaulx Abbey**, an evocative monastic ruin standing serenely in the wooded valley of the river Rye; ££, open Apr–Sept, daily 1000–1800, Aug 0930–1900, Oct 1000–1700, Nov–Apr 1000–1600. Founded in 1131, Rievaulx was one of the earliest and grandest Cistercian foundations in England and soon became one of the wealthiest, by exploiting local ironstone deposits and farming sheep. The abbey's prime splendour is the choir, dating from about 1225. Rievaulx Terrace, to the east, gives an excellent overview from a long lawn graced at either end by 18th-century 'temples', one erected as a banqueting house. The Terrace is owned by the National Trust (££, daily 1030–1800 late Mar–Sept; 1030–1700 Oct).

Colour Section

(i) Punch and Judy show on the beach, Blackpool (p. 218)

(ii) Tarn Howes, Lake District (pp. 224–231); Hartington village in the Peak District (p. 239)

(iii) Hadrian's Wall, Northumberland (pp. 264–265); Edinburgh Castle, Scotland, with pipers (pp. 272–280)

(iv) Entrance to the Glasgow School of Art, designed by Charles Rennie Mackintosh (pp. 311–317)

SCARBOROUGH This civilised seaside town with a Georgian conservation area and elegant Regency terraces lies around two fine sandy bays on either side of a castle-crowned headland. The town pioneered sea bathing as early as 1660 and is still a popular resort, catering for all ages and interests. As well as the obvious attractions of the beach, there is

The Cleveland Way
(website:
www.countrygoer. org/
nymoors/cwayymap is a
waymarked walking trail
that runs from Helmsley,
across the North York
Moors and on through
Scarborough to Filey. The
full route is 110 miles
(177 km) long. A guide to
the route is available from
tourist infomation centres.

12th-century **Scarborough Castle**, £, Castle Rd (open daily 1000–1800 (Apr–Oct); Wed–Sun 1000–1600 (Nov–Mar). **Scarborough Museums and Gallery** (£, c/o Londesborough Lodge, the Crescent, open Easter–Oct Tues–Sun 1000–1700, reduced opening in winter) is three museums in one covering everything from local history to art.

WHITBY **Whitby**, is the gem of Yorkshire's coast. Still a busy fishing port, it is dominated by **Whitby Abbey** (£, open daily 1000–1800 Apr–Sept; 1000–1700 Oct; 1000–1600 Nov–Mar) and **St Mary's Church**. They sit high on the East Cliff guarding an attractive huddle of pastel washed houses and tiny streets around the mouth of the river Esk. Whitby has strong associations with Captain James Cook and the house where he lodged as an apprentice is now the **Captain Cook Memorial Museum**. £, Grape Lane, open daily 0945–1700 (Apr–Oct).

Other places of interest include the **Whitby Museum** which has fascinating collections including the famous Whitby jet, a black semi-precious stone popularly used in Victorian jewellery. £, Pannett Park, open Tues 1000–1300, Wed–Sat 1000–1600, Sun 1400–1600 (Oct–Apr); Mon–Sat 0930–1730, Sun 1400–1700 (May–Sept). There is also an old **Victorian Jet Works** (open daily 1030–1700) on Church St.

ALONG THE COAST Apart from the resorts of Whitby and Scarborough, virtually the entire stretch of coast in the national park is bounded by formidable cliffs. The Cleveland Way steers a course along the top. The frequent bus service connecting points along the coast makes it easy to explore on foot and return to the starting point. **Robin Hood's Bay** is a wonderfully evocative fishing and former smuggling village, with a huddle of red roofs and tiny alleys. Low tide reveals a fascinating beach for browsing in rock pools and fossil hunting. North of Whitby, **Runswick Bay** is another fishing village clinging to an improbable looking slope, and it is only an hour's walk north along the coast path from there to **Staithes**, squeezed into a long valley leading to the sea, where small fishing craft known as cobles are moored near the bright-red sandstone cliffs.

WHERE NEXT?

From Whitby, trains run across the North York Moors to Middlesbrough, from where you can continue to Darlington, on the main east coast line from London to Edinburgh. Scarborough has regular services to York; you can take the less direct route through Beverley – a gem of a town and not that well known, with two superb medieval churches (including Beverley Minster); the route continues through Hull and Selby to York.

NEWCASTLE

A busy commercial city, Newcastle lies at the heart of a sprawling conurbation along the river Tyne. The city grew famous as a coal exporting port – hence the saying 'coals to Newcastle' – and was once an important centre for heavy industry, although these sadly went into sharp decline after World War II. However, the city has plenty more to offer than appears at first, including well preserved Georgian terraces, a Norman castle, some excellent museums and great shopping. It also has a reputation as one of the best party cities in the world.

Newcastle is a good base from which to explore the invigorating border country with its wild scenery and grim history. You can visit Hadrian's Wall, the northernmost frontier of the Roman Empire and the most important Roman monument in Britain. It stretches from Newcastle in the east, to Carlisle and the Solway Firth in the west. Surrounded by bleak but magnificent moorland, it ranks alongside the Taj Mahal and other treasures as a World Heritage Site. South of Newcastle is the ancient city of Durham, home of one of England's oldest universities. With its magnificent cathedral, imposing castle and historic centre it is a real 'must' on any itinerary.

GETTING THERE AND GETTING AROUND

Newcastle **Airport** is just a 15-min drive from the city centre and handles flights from UK and European airports. There are frequent buses to the city as well as an excellent Metro link.

National Express, tel: 0990 808080, run regular **coach** services to cities throughout the UK. There are also plenty of **buses** within the city centre and services to other parts of Northumbria. For information call Northumberland County Council Public Transport Enquiries, tel: (01670) 533128.

Newcastle is on the main London–Edinburgh **railway** line and there are frequent services to the city. The journey from London takes around 3 hrs. There is an excellent Metro service in the city. For details contact the Passenger Transport Travel-line, tel: (0191) 232 5325.

FERRY Newcastle is linked by **ferry** to Holland, Scandinavia and Germany. For sailings contact:

DFDS Seaways, tel: 08705 333000, or Fjordline, tel: (0191) 2961313.

INFORMATION

Northumbria Information Hotline; tel: 0906 683 3000 Mon–Fri 0900–1700 (calls charged at 25p per min); website: www.visitnorthumbria.com.

Newcastle Information Centre Central Exchange Building 5, 132 Grainger St; tel: (0191) 277 8000; website: www.newcastle.gov.uk; e-mail: tourist.info@newcastle. gov.uk. Open Mon–Wed, Fri 0930–1730, Thur 0930–1930, Sat 0900–1730, and June–Oct Sun 1000–1600. Also at, Central Station; tel: (0191) 277 8000. Open Mon–Fri 0930–1700, Sat 0900–1700.

Gateshead Tourist Information Centre Central Library, Prince Consort Rd; tel: (0191) 477 3478; webstie: www.gateshead.gov.uk; e-mail: enquiries@libarts. gatesheadmbc.gov.uk. Open Mon, Tues and Thur, Fri 0900–1900, Wed 0900–1700, Sat 0900–1300, closed Sun. Also at **Portcullis**, 7 The Arcade, MetroCentre, tel: (0191) 460 6345; e-mail: portcullis@gateshead. gov.uk. Open Mon–Wed, Fri 1000–2000, Thurs 1000–2100, Sat 0900–1900, Sun 1100–1700.

South Shields Tourist Information Centre (for Jarrow), Museum & Gallery, Ocean Rd; tel: (0191) 454 6612; e-mail: museum.tic@s-tyneside-mcb.gov.uk. Open all year 1000–1700, Sun 1300–1700 (summer).

MONEY Foreign exchange is available in Newcastle Post Office in Eldon Square, Percy St and also at Thomas Cook in Northumberland St.

POST The main Post Office is in Eldon Square, Percy St.

ACCOMMODATION

The Esplanade Hotel £££ Whitley Bay; tel: (0191) 252 1111; website: www.esplanade-hotel-freeserve.co.uk; e-mail: Esplanade. Hotel@btinternet.com. Refurbished hotel on the sea front.

Newcastle Youth Hostel £ 107 Jesmond Rd, tel: 0870 7705972 (e-mail: newcastle@yha.org.uk) is a short walk from Jesmond Tyne & Wear metro station; dorms plus five twins.

The Plough Inn £££ Stamfordham Rd, Eachwick, Ponteland; tel: (01661) 853555; website: www.the-plough-ponteland.co.uk; e-mail: stay@the-plough-ponteland.co.uk. Family run 17th-century coaching inn on the outskirts of Newcastle.

Royal Station Hotel £££ Neville St; tel: (0191) 232 0781; website: www.royalstationhotel.com; e-mail: info@royalstation hotel.com. Comfortable Victorian hotel in the city centre.

FOOD AND DRINK

Blakes Coffee House £ 53 Grey St. A New York deli-style café where you can relax over coffee and sandwiches with the papers.

Dragon House £££ 30-32 Stowell St. Very popular Cantonese restaurant in the heart of the city's Chinatown.

The Metropolitan ££££ 35 Grey St. This contemporary restaurant serves traditional English dishes with a modern twist.

Parisa ££££ Quayside. Relaxed café/bistro serving French style dishes.

HIGHLIGHTS

Hancock Museum, Barras Bridge, ££, open Mon–Sat 1000–1700, Sun 1400–1700. This natural history museum has an enormous collection of mammals, fossils and insects, as well as special exhibitions such as Land of the Pharaohs and Living Planet. The **Museum of Antiquities** at Newcastle University might sound a bit worthy but is one of the best places to see artefacts from Hadrian's Wall. There are models of the wall and a reconstruction of a Roman temple. Free, open Mon–Sat 1000–1700. **St Nicholas Cathedral** in St Nicholas St dates from the 14th and 15th centuries and is famous for its lantern tower.

For fine views over the Tyne make for **Castle Keep**, St Nicholas St, Castle Garth. This fine example of a Norman keep was built by Henry II in the 12th century on the site of the New Castle which gave the city its name. £, open Tues–Sun 0930–1730 (Apr–Sept), Tues–Sun 0930–1630 (Oct–Mar). From here you get superb views of the six famous bridges across the Tyne. The best known are Robert Stephenson's double-decker **High Level Bridge** (1849), for both rail and road, and the 1920s single-span **Tyne Bridge**.

The premiere art collection in the North-East is at **Laing Art Gallery**, which includes amazing works by local visionary artist John Martin, interactive displays and a children's gallery. Free, New Bridge St, open Mon–Fri 1000–1700, Sun 1400–1700. **Trinity Maritime Centre** is the place to learn about the ancient maritime heritage of Newcastle and the River Tyne. 29 Broad Chare, Quayside, free, open Mon–Fri 1100–1600 (Apr–Oct). For more general history about Newcastle, including displays on science, ships, pioneers, fashion and more, **Newcastle Discovery** is the place. This is like visiting several museums in one and is a favourite with families. Blandford House, Blandford Square, free, open Mon–Sat 1000–1700, Sun 1400–1700.

South of the Tyne lies **Gateshead**, where you will find the striking sculpture the **Angel of the North**, adopted as the symbol of the North-East. Designed by Antony Gormley, it is 66ft (20m) high and has a 177ft (54m) wing span. Gateshead suffered from neglect for many years but is now being regenerated. In 2002 the **Baltic Centre for Contemporary Art**, Quayside, opened in a converted grain warehouse to display the largest collection of international contemporary art outside London. There is also the **Shipley Art Gallery**, Prince Consort Rd, Gateshead, free, open Mon–Sat 1000–1700, Sun 1400–1700. As well as paintings, and an exhibition on the history of Gateshead, it has a large collection of contemporary craft, including ceramics, jewellery and furniture. The **Millennium Bridge** is a sleek, coat-hanger shaped pedestrian bridge linking Newcastle and Gateshead.

South-east of the Tyne, about 30 mins by metro, is **Jarrow**, the starting point for the famous Jarrow March of the 1930s when men walked to London to protest about the deprivation caused by high unemployment. It was once the home of the famous monk known as the Venerable Bede, an 8th-century historian. The visitor attraction **Bede's World** brings alive the Northumberland of his time. ££ family ticket, Church Bank, open Mon–Sat 1000–1730, Sun 1200–1730 (Apr–Oct), Mon–Sat 1000–1630, Sun 1200–1630 (Nov–Mar) You can visit the ruins of Bede's home, **St Paul's Monastery**, founded in 682, and **St Paul's Church**, an Anglo Saxon church which has been in continuous use for 1300 years.

Another family attraction is **Life Interactive World**. It has lots of interactive exhibits, 3D, and a sound and light show. £££, Times Square, Scotswood Rd, open daily 1000–1800. **Bessie Surtees House** provides a good example of domestic Jacobean architecture. It once belonged to a wealthy local merchant whose daughter, the eponymous Bessie, defied her family and eloped to Scotland with the impoverished son of a coal merchant. 41–44 Sandhill, free, open Mon–Fri 1000–1600.

TOURS **North of England Tours**, 4 Eskdale Place, Newton Aycliffe; tel: (01325) 308094.

You can take a trip on the river Tyne on the **Shields Ferry**, which runs from North and South Shields on summer afternoons, tel: (0191) 203 3315.

The **Tanfield Railway**, ££, Old Marley Hill, Sunniside, Gateshead, tel: (0191) 388 7545, opened in 1725 and is the oldest existing railway in the world. It was built to take coal to the river Tyne. Originally horses used to pull wagons along wooden tracks, they were replaced by locomotives and metal rails in the 19th century. There are historic steam trains and carriages; trains run on Sun, Bank Holidays and Wed and Thur during school summer holidays. Bus from Eldon Sq. station, Newcastle, takes about 45 mins.

SHOPPING

The main shopping area in Newcastle City Centre is the **Eldon Square** Shopping Centre, which has all the usual High Street chains, plus some more exclusive stores in Eldon Garden. Northumberland St, Grey St and Grainger St are also worth exploring. The city has several interesting **markets** including Grainger Market, which has the last Marks and Spencer Penny Bazaar. Then there is the **Metro Centre** in Gateshead, one of the largest shopping centres in Europe. There are frequent buses and trains from Newcastle.

NIGHTLIFE

Newcastle is noted for its nightlife – it was voted eighth best party city in the world. It is full of bars and pubs and gets extremely lively, even rowdy, at night, especially around Bigg Market – the drinking heartland of the city. There are also plenty of clubs to visit such as Baja Beach Club, Quayside and Foundation, Melbourne St. A variety of theatrical productions take place at the Theatre Royal, Grey St, and also at Live Theatre, Broad Chare, Quayside. The Hyena Café, Leazes Lane, is a popular comedy café, often featuring top acts from the stand-up circuit.

SIDE TRIPS

BELSAY HALL, CASTLE AND GARDENS The Belsay estate is off the main tourist track but is well worth a visit, particularly for its extensive 19th-century gardens which include a famous Quarry Garden. You can also visit the 14th-century castle and the neo-classical Belsay Hall. The Hall is unfurnished but frequently hosts exhibitions. There is a tea room in the old kitchen. ££, Belsay (west of Newcastle on the A696; Arriva bus 508 runs on Sun only in summer from Newcastle) open daily 1000–1800 (Apr–Sept); 1000–1700 (Oct); 1000–1600 (Nov–Mar).

SOUTH SHIELDS The area around South Shields is often known as Catherine Cookson country as this is the area where the famous novelist lived and worked. The **South Shields Museum and Art Gallery** has a reconstruction of the street where she grew up as well as exhibitions on the natural and industrial history of the area. Free, open Mon–Sat 1000–1700 (Nov–Mar), Mon–Sat 1000–1730, Sun 1300–1700 (Apr–Oct). You can also visit **Arbeia Roman Fort and Museum** (free) an original Roman fort plus an archaeology centre. Take the metro from Newcastle to South Shields, then it's about a 10-min walk, or catch a bus. Along the coast is **Souter Point Lighthouse** (£, open daily except Fri 1100–1700 Apr–Oct), a lighthouse built in 1871. You can go inside and see the engine room and light tower.

DURHAM Durham is a delightful city in which to wander – large enough to provide plenty of interest and small enough to be easily accessible (48 trains from Newcastle daily, 34 on Sun; journey time is around 15 mins). Its crowning glory is its Norman **Cathedral** (free, donation requested, open Mon–Sat 0930–1815, Sun 1230–1700 – later in summer; tours available). It is the greatest piece of Norman church architecture in Britain and possibly in the world. No other church has preserved so much period character and the rich ornamentation on the pillars and arcades is unforgettable. It houses the **Treasures of St Cuthbert** (£), an exhibition of manuscripts, altar plate and other objects associated with 900 years of cathedral history, as well as the relics of St Cuthbert, the most revered of northern saints.

The city's other major attraction is **Durham Castle** (£, guided tours Mon–Sat 1000–1230 and 1400–1600, Sun 1000–1200 and 1400–1600 Mar–Oct). Dating from 1072, it guards the approach to the historic city and was once the seat of the powerful Prince Bishops who ruled this area. Now it is part of Durham University. The 15th-century kitchen is still in use and you can see the imposing Great Hall and 'Black Staircase' which is made entirely from oak.

Durham University dominates the city and it has two museums that you can visit. The most unusual is the **Oriental Museum** (£, open Mon–Fri 1000–1700, weekends 1200–1700). Devoted entirely to Oriental art and antiquities, it includes a 'Marvels of China' gallery and displays on the art of Japan, Tibet and the Islamic world. There is also a **Museum of Archaeology** (£, tel: (0191) 374 3623 for opening hours) which illustrates the history of the city through artefacts discovered through excavations.

A wander along the **river Wear**, which makes a great loop around the old town, is highly recommended for the tremendous views up to the cathedral which looms high above from a clifftop setting. On the west side of town, South Street gets some of the best photo opportunities of all across to the cathedral and castle.

> *i* **Tourist Information Centre** Market Place; tel: (0191) 384 3720; website: www.durhamcity.gov.uk; e-mail: touristinfo@durhamcity.gov.uk. Open Mon–Sat 1000–1730, Sun 1100–1600.

> 🛏 The **University of Durham** also offers accommodation during the summer; tel: (0191) 374 7360; website: www.dur.ac.uk/conference_tourism; e-mail: conference.tourism@durham.ac.uk.

> 🍴 **The Almshouses** £ Palace Green. Excellent value at this café/restaurant beside the Cathedral, which is very popular with staff and students of the university.

BEAMISH The award-winning **Beamish Open Air Museum** is one of the main attractions in County Durham and you can easily spend a day here.

It recreates life in the North of England during the early 1800s and 1900s. There is a working pub, sweetshop and bank, a railway station and a chapel. You can take a tour of a real 'drift' mine in the Colliery Village and peep into the rooms of traditional pit cottages. £££, open daily 1000–1600 (Apr–Oct), closed Mon and Fri (Oct–Mar) – reduced admission in winter; tel: (01207) 231811.

BARNARD CASTLE This appealing little Pennine town takes its name from the imposing medieval castle (£, open daily) sited above the sylvan river Tees. The town is full of characterful corners, including old textile mills and 17th- and 18th-century town houses. **The Bowes Museum** (££, open daily 1100–1700) is a magnificent French-style chateau built by a relative of the late Queen Mother. Its superb collection of paintings, furniture and ceramics is of national importance.

HADRIAN'S WALL The most important monument built by the Romans in Britain, Hadrian's Wall, is 73 miles (117 km) long, nearly 2000 years old and a magnificent sight, although only parts of the wall have survived. Along its route, from Wallsend in the east to Bowness in the west, are many features of interest – milecastles, forts, bathhouses and even Roman flushing latrines.

It is believed that the Emperor Hadrian ordered the building of the wall after he visited Britain in AD 122. A Roman biographer of Hadrian suggested it was 'to separate the Romans from the Barbarians', but the most generally agreed theory is that Hadrian wanted to mark the northern boundary of his great empire. The wall took six years to build. Sentries and guards kept watch from the milecastles and turrets, keeping a check on who and what was crossing the frontier. Forts built along the wall strengthened control and served as crossing points and civilian settlements grew up around them. Hadrian's Wall was abandoned towards the end of the 4th century.

One of the most attractive towns to visit is **Corbridge**, just off the main line of the wall. Once a Roman garrison town, it has some lovely stone buildings and individual shops in which to browse. **St Andrews Church,** Market Place, dates back to the 7th cen-

> ## ROMAN SITES YOU CAN VISIT
> **Housesteads Roman Fort**, Haydon Bridge, which has the only example of a Roman hospital as well as some well preserved communal latrines, £, open daily 1000–1800 (Apr–Sept); 1000–1700 (Oct); 1000–1600 (Nov–Mar).
>
> **Vindolanda**, Bardon Mill, ££, open daily 1000–1700 (Feb–Nov), with the remains of several forts and civilian settlements, plus a museum packed with rare Roman writing tablets and textiles.
>
> **Chesters Roman Fort**, Chollerford £, open daily 0930–1800 (Apr–Sept); 1000–1700 (Oct); Wed–Sun 1000–1300 and 1400–1600 (Nov–Mar).
>
> There is a special **Hadrian's Wall Bus** that runs from Newcastle to many of the main sites along the wall. Tel: (01434) 322002, website: www.hadrians-wall.org.

It is possible to walk the waymarked **Hadrian's Wall Path National Trail**, staying at B&Bs along the way; six days are recommended for the 84-mile (135-km) route from Segedunum Roman Fort near Newcastle to Bowness-on-Solway, Cumbria. The most spectacular section of the Wall is the 12-mile (19-km) stretch between Sewingshields and Greenhead; tel: (0191) 261 1585. For more information tel: (01434) 322002, www.hadrians-wall.org. You can also pick up leaflets from tourist information centres that explain station-to-station walks along the wall.

tury and has many Saxon features. You can also visit **Corstopitum**, an extensive Roman site less than half hour an hour's walk from the town (£, open daily 1000–1800; 1000–1700 Oct; Wed–Sun 1000–1600 Nov–Mar). **Hexham** is a busier town, also off the main line of the wall itself, but well worth a visit if only to see **Hexham Abbey**, open daily 0900–1900 (May–Sept); 0900–1700 (Oct–Apr). It has a Saxon crypt and contains inscribed stones from Corstopitum. Trains from Newcastle run to Corbridge and Hexham.

i **Corbridge Tourist Information Centre** Hill St; tel: (01434) 632815. Open summer only Mon–Sat 1000–1800, Sun 1300–1700.

Hexham Tourist Information Centre Wentworth Car Park; tel: (01434) 652220; www.tynedale.gov.uk; e-mail: hexham.tic@ tynedale.gov.uk. Open Mon–Sat 0900–1800, Sun 1000–1700 (summer). Mon–Sat 0900–1700, closed Sun (winter).

Haltwhistle Tourist Information Centre Railway Station, Station Rd, tel: (01434) 322002. Open Mon–Sat 1000–1800, Sun 1300–1700 (summer), Mon, Tues, Thur–Sat 1000–1530, closed Sun (winter).

Laburnum House ££ 23 Leazes Crescent, Hexham; tel: (01434) 601828; e-mail: laburnum.house@virginnet.co.uk. Spotless, comfortable, friendly B&B in Hexham. Excellent value. **Once Brewed Youth Hostel** £, tel: 0870 7705981 (e-mail: oncebrewed@yha.org.uk). By the B6318 at the turn for Vindolanda, and well placed for exploring Hadrian's Wall.

WHERE NEXT?

Hadrian's Wall is crammed with places of interest such as Segedunum, the recreated Roman baths, at Wallsend, Birdoswald Roman Fort and Hexham Herbs at Chollerford. There are also plenty of industrial heritage sites near Durham and Newcastle. On the coast is the traditional resort of Whitley Bay. From Newcastle you can head north to the Northumberland National Park (see pp. 267–268) and Edinburgh (see pp. 272–280).

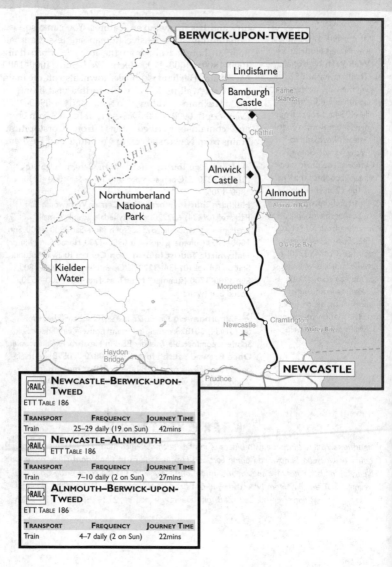

BERWICK-UPON-TWEED

Lindisfarne

Bamburgh
Castle ◆

Farne
Islands

Chathill

The Cheviot Hills

Alnwick
Castle ◆

Alnmouth

Alnmouth Bay

Northumberland
National
Park

Druridge Bay

borders

Kielder
Water

Morpeth

Cramlington

Newcastle

Whitley Bay

Haydon
Bridge

Prudhoe

NEWCASTLE

RAIL	**NEWCASTLE–BERWICK-UPON-TWEED**
ETT TABLE 186	

TRANSPORT	FREQUENCY	JOURNEY TIME
Train	25–29 daily (19 on Sun)	42mins

RAIL	**NEWCASTLE–ALNMOUTH**
ETT TABLE 186	

TRANSPORT	FREQUENCY	JOURNEY TIME
Train	7–10 daily (2 on Sun)	27mins

RAIL	**ALNMOUTH–BERWICK-UPON-TWEED**
ETT TABLE 186	

TRANSPORT	FREQUENCY	JOURNEY TIME
Train	4–7 daily (2 on Sun)	22mins

Too many people race through Northumberland in their hurry to reach Scotland – which is a pity as this is one of the most unspoilt parts of England. It's 67 miles (108 km) from Newcastle to Berwick-upon-Tweed and the journey takes only 45 mins by direct train, however it is well worth breaking your journey to explore the surrounding countryside. To the west is the wild sweep of the Northumberland National Park, where majestic moody moorland combines with dense conifer forests. To the east is the glorious coastline, dotted with romantic castles, magical islands and gloriously unspoilt beaches that are a treat for walkers and naturalists. You will need a car if you want to explore the National Park – this is one place where the phrase 'getting away from it all' means just what it says.

NEWCASTLE

See p. 258.

NORTHUMBERLAND NATIONAL PARK

Remote, empty moorland or bilberry and bracken rise in glacier-rasped contours to the Cheviot watershed – the National Park and adjoining Border Forest Park covering over 400 sq miles (1036 sq km). There are no major towns or villages and visitor facilities are sparse, but it is this wild beauty that makes this area so appealing. Deep in the forest, **Kielder Water**, (website: www.kielder.org) Europe's largest man-made lake at over 9 miles (14km) long, offers relaxing watersports and the surrounding forest has over 400 miles (644km) of walking and cycling routes. The long-distance walking trail the **Pennine Way** crosses the more scenic areas of the park before tracking a rugged stretch of the border through the grassy Cheviot Hills to its Scottish terminus near Kirk Yetholm.

Northumberland National Park is very remote and there are very limited bus services to the area, so a car is essential. Kielder Water itself can only be reached via minor roads, and the journey takes about 1hr 15mins from Newcastle. The A68 passes through the heart of the National Park. You can join it near Corbridge at Hadrian's Wall, or via the A696 out of Newcastle. The A68 is not the most direct route to Berwick-upon-Tweed but does take you over the Carter Bar – the border with Scotland – and goes on to the Scottish border town of Jedburgh.

At **Kielder Bikes Cycle Centre**, Castle Hill, Kielder Water, tel: (01434) 250392, open daily, you can hire bikes to explore the extensive tracts of forest paths, while **Hawkhirst Adventure Camp**, Kielder Water, tel: (01434) 250217, hires equipment for boating, sailing and kayaking on the lake. **Kielder Castle**, Kielder, tel: (01434)

250209, open daily 1000–1700 (Mar–Oct), Sat and Sun 1100–1600 (Nov–Dec), is an 18th-century castle with exhibitions on wildlife and conservation of Kielder, a tearoom and access to walking trails. **Kielder Water Cruises**, Kielder (tel: (01434) 250312, open daily Apr–Oct), run cruises on the lake.

i **Northumberland National Park Centre** Once Brewed, Military Rd, Bardon Mill; tel: (01434) 344396, website: www.nnpa.org.uk; e-mail: tic.oncebrewed@nnpa.org.uk. Open daily 0930–1700 (mid-Mar–early Nov); Sat–Sun 1000–1500 (early Nov–mid-Mar).

Northumberland National Park Centre, Church House, Church St, Rothbury; tel: (01669) 620887; e-mail: tic.rothbury@ nnpa.org.uk. Open daily 1000–1700 (mid-Mar–early Nov); Sat–Sun 1000–1500 (early Nov–mid-Mar).

🛏 **The Pheasant Inn** ££££ Stannersburn, Kielder Water; tel: (01434) 240382; e-mail: thepheasant@ kielderwater.demon.co.uk. Traditional family-run inn in the National Park.

Farm Cottage, ££ Thropton, Rothbury; tel: (01669) 620831; website: www.farmcottage.ntb.org.uk; e-mail: joan@farmcottage44.fsnet.co.uk. Award-winning B&B in country cottage. Home cooking and evening meals.

Lee Farm ££ Nr Rothbury, Longframlington; tel: 01665 570257; website: www.leefarm.co.uk; e-mail: enqs@leefarm.co.uk. Comfortable, award-winning farmhouse B&B on the edge of the National Park.

Tosson Tower Farm ££ Great Tosson, Rothbury; tel: (01669) 620228; website: www.tossontowerfarm.com; e-mail: ann@ tossontowerfarm.com. Great views from this farmhouse B&B which was once a drovers' inn. Self-catering cottages available.

ALNWICK

Change at Alnmouth, a quiet coastal resort, to reach nearby **Alnwick** (pronounced 'Annick'), an unspoilt market town with a medieval feel. Its main attraction is the majestic **Alnwick Castle** (£££, open daily 1100–1700 Apr–Oct) set on the river Aln, which has been the home of the Percy family – the Dukes of Northumberland – since 1309. It was described by the Victorians as the 'Windsor of the North' and is the largest inhabited castle in England after Windsor. It has a valuable art collection with works by Titian, Canaletto and Van Dyke, and there are extensive grounds designed by Capability Brown, plus an exciting new 21st-century garden in the making (www.alnwickgarden.com).

[i] **Tourist Information Centre** 2 The Shambles; tel: (01665) 510665; website: www.alnwick@gov.uk; e-mail: alnwicktic@gov.uk. Open daily 0900–1700 (Apr–Oct); Mon–Sat 0930–1630 (Nov–Mar).

🏨 **High Buston Hall** £££ Alnmouth; tel: (01665) 830606; website: www.members.aol.com/highbuston; e-mail: highbuston@aol.com. Award-winning B&B in Georgian house.
The Grange at Alnmouth ££ Northumberland St, Alnmouth; tel: (01665) 830401; e-mail: thegrange.alnmouth@virgin.net. This 18th-century house is close to the river and has its own walled grounds.
Ash Tree House ££ The Terrace, Eglingham, Alnwick; tel: (01665) 578533; website: www.ashtreehouse.ntb.org.uk. This peaceful B&B is a convenient base from which to explore both the coastline and the National Park.

🍴 **The Saddle Hotel** £££ 24/25 Northumberland St, Alnmouth. Popular eating place offering bar meals and restaurant food. Accommodation also available.

BAMBURGH

From Alnwick it is worth travelling further up Northumbria's unspoilt coast to the little village of Bamburgh. This is dominated by the impressive and picturesque fortress of **Bamburgh Castle** (££, open daily 1100–1700 Apr–Oct) which sits right on the coast. There has been a settlement here since pre-Roman times, but the present castle was built in the 13th century. It suffered much damage in wars between the English and the Scots and fell into disrepair but was heavily renovated in the 19th century. It has a collection of china, furniture, paintings and armour. In the village is the **Grace Darling Museum**, free, Radcliffe Rd (open Mon–Sat 1000–1700, Sun 1200–1700 Apr–Oct). This commemorates Grace Darling, the lighthouse keeper's daughter who, with her father, made a dramatic rescue of nine survivors from a shipwreck in 1838.

🏨 **Burton Hall** ££ Bamburgh; tel: (01668) 214213.
Farmhouse B&B in peaceful surroundings with great views of Bamburgh Castle.
Waren House Hotel ££££ Waren Mill, Belford; tel: (01668) 214581; website: www.arenhousehotel.co.uk; e-mail: enqiiries@warenhousehotel.co.uk. Elegant country house hotel set in its own grounds.
Olde Ship Hotel ££ 9 Main St, Seahouses; tel: (01665) 720200. Fine old pub in salty setting overlooking bustling fishing harbour. You can stay here or just drop in for a meal.

SIDE TRIP FROM BAMBURGH Just a few miles off the Northumberland coast lie the 28 **Farne Islands**, a precious bird reserve providing a home to around 70,000 pairs of breeding birds. There are terns, cormorants, several types of gull and a large colony of puffins. The islands also have a large colony of grey seals. From Apr–Sept you can take boat trips to the islands and land on some of them, although access is restricted during the breeding season, May–July. Trips run from the little fishing village of **Seahouses** which is close to Bamburgh. Choose calm weather as the seas around the islands are notoriously rough.

LINDISFARNE (HOLY ISLAND)

Twice a day, the sea retreats sufficiently to allow access to this windswept, low-lying stretch of dunes, beaches and quiet grazing land known as Lindisfarne. **Holy Island**, as it is often called, was one of Europe's primary centres of Christianity in Celtic times and is still a place of pilgrimage. The richly illuminated Lindisfarne Gospels created in about AD 700 were carried away for safe keeping in AD 875. The island's 11th-century **Priory** (££, open daily 1000–1800 Apr–Sept; 1000–1700 Oct; 1000–1600 Nov–Mar) was built on the site of the Celtic monastery founded in AD 635 by St Aidan. This is considered to be the birthplace of Christianity in Britain. The other main site is **Lindisfarne Castle** (££, open daily except Fri 1200–1500 Apr–Oct) built in the 16th century. In 1902 it was imaginatively converted into a home by the architect Edwin Lutyens.

An infrequent bus service runs from Berwick to Lindisfarne (operating Wed and Sat – more often during the summer – times are dependent upon the tide); ask at the Berwick tourist information centre (see p. 271). You might find it more convenient to take a taxi. If you are driving yourself be sure that you check tide times before setting off. Every year cars are swept away because drivers think they can beat the tide.

> 🛏 **The Bungalow** £££ Lindisfarne; tel: (01289) 389308; e-mail: bungalow@celtic121.demon.co.uk. B&B close to the centre of the village and the island's main attraction, the Priory.

> 🍽 **The Crown and Anchor** £££ Market Place, Lindisfarne. This island pub offers a reasonable selection of bar meals.

BERWICK-UPON-TWEED

Now England's most northerly town, Berwick changed hands between the English and the Scots over a dozen times in medieval times. It finally became a permanent part of England in 1482. Its sturdy **Ramparts** constructed in the 16th century to replace medieval defences still surround the town. They make a popular walk for visitors, providing great views of the town's bridges (notably the **Royal Border Bridge** built by Robert Stephenson) and also of Berwick's famous colony of swans.

Berwick Barracks were the first purpose-built infantry barracks in Britain, designed by Nicholas Hawksmoor. Today they house several museums and exhibitions including the town's **Museum and Art Gallery**, which includes part of the stunning Burrell Collection donated by Sir William Burrell. It includes paintings by Degas, Venetian glassware and Japanese pottery. £, The Parade, open daily 1000–1800 (Apr–Sept); 1000–1700 (Oct); Wed–Sun 1000–1600 (Nov–Mar).

The Battle of Flodden Field, 1513, was the last pitched battle between England and Scotland and was fought in Northumbria, a short drive from Berwick-upon-Tweed. There are many memories of this battle at the villages of Ford and Etal. Etal Castle (open daily 1000–1800 Apr–Sept; 1000–1700 Oct) has an exhibition on the battle. West of Ford is a monument near Branxton, which commemorates 'the brave of both nations'.

i **Tourist Information Centre** 106 Marygate; tel: (01289) 330733; website: www.berwick-upon-tweed.gov.uk; e-mail: tourism@berwick-upon-tweed.gov.uk. Open Mon–Sat 1000–1800, Sun 1100–1600 (summer); Mon–Sat 1000–1600 (winter).

Clovelly House ££ 58 West St Berwick-upon-Tweed; tel: (01289) 302337; website: www.clovelly53.freeserve.co.uk; e-mail: vivroc@clovelly53.freeserve.co.uk. Comfortable B&B in the centre of the town.

No.1 Sallyport ££ 1 Sallyport, off Bridge St, Berwick-upon-Tweed; tel: (01289) 308827. Award winning B&B in attractive 17th-century townhouse.

The Estate House ££ Ford, Berwick-upon-Tweed; tel: (01890) 820668; e-mail: theeastatehouse@supanet.com. Edwardian house in the village of Ford, close to the Cheviot Hills.

The Old Manse ££ New Rd, Chatton, Nr Wooler; tel: (01668) 215343; website: www.oldmansechatton.ntb.org.uk; e-mail: chattonbb@aol.com. Award-winning B&B in large Victorian house deep in the Northumbrian countryside.

The Tankerville Arms Hotel £££, 22 Cottage Rd, Wooler; tel: (01668) 281581; website: www.tankervillehotel.co.uk; e-mail: enquiries@tankervillehotel.co.uk. Traditional coaching inn offering good bar meals, in the market town of Wooler. Accommodation also available.

Foxtons ££ Hyde Hill, Berwick-upon-Tweed; tel: (01289) 303939. Popular wine bar and bistro, serving light meals at lunchtime and more substantial fare in the evenings.

Popinjays £ Hyde Hill, Berwick-upon-Tweed. Traditional tea shop with a good selection of cakes and buns.

WHERE NEXT?

From Berwick-upon-Tweed you can explore the Scottish Border towns of Jedburgh, Kelso, Melrose and Selkirk. Alternatively you can head further north along the coast to Edinburgh (see pp. 272–280).

EDINBURGH

No tour of Scotland is complete without a visit to Edinburgh, and for many visitors this showcase city is the gateway to the rest of the country. It is one of the most appealing cities in Europe, with a stunning location and a rich history. Offering a feast of things to see and do, Edinburgh is so compact that all its contrasting sights can easily be explored on foot. From the medieval wynds and cobbles of the Old Town to the leafy avenues and Georgian elegance of the New Town, it is always fascinating; no wonder it is often known as 'The Athens of the North'.

The city has been the capital of Scotland for hundreds of years and is now home to the new Scottish Parliament. All the traditional images of Scotland can be found here: tartan, bagpipes, fine malt whisky and dramatic scenery, mingling with contemporary buildings, designer stores and sleek, modern restaurants. This is a thriving, prosperous city with a lively arts scene – most notably celebrated every summer in the Edinburgh International Festival which, together with its irreverent Fringe, is one of the greatest arts festivals in the world. The fire in the old town in December 2002 may have devastated a number of buildings in the Cowgate area, but the city still boasts one of the most perfectly preserved historic cores in Europe, and wandering the old cobbled streets of Edinburgh is a great pleasure.

GETTING THERE AND GETTING AROUND

Edinburgh International **Airport** is only 8 miles (13 km) west of the city centre. It has regular services from airports throughout the UK and some airports in Europe. There are frequent airport buses to the city centre – the journey takes about 20 mins.

There are regular **coach services** from London and other UK cities. Coaches leave from St Andrew Square in the city centre. For information contact Scottish Citylink, tel: 08705 505050, and National Express, tel: 08705 808080.

There are frequent **buses** throughout the city centre and to some outlying areas. Information from Lothian Buses, tel: (0131) 555 6363, and First Edinburgh, tel: 08708 727271.

Edinburgh Waverley is the main **railway** station in the city and has a regular service to London – the journey taking about 4 hrs 30 mins with GNER, tel: 08457 225225. There are good connections to other main cities on the east coast (such as York), and fewer services to west coast destinations. Trains also run to major Scottish cities and to outlying areas such as the seaside resort of North Berwick. Scotrail, tel: 08457 484 950, also run overnight rail sleeper services between Edinburgh and London.

INFORMATION
CITY MAP
– inside back cover

Edinburgh and Scotland Information Centre 3 Princes St, Edinburgh; tel: 0845 22 55 121, fax: (01506) 832 222; website: www.edinburgh.org; e-mail: info@visitscotland.com. Open Mon–Sat 0900–1800, Sun 1000–1800 (Apr & Oct); Mon–Sat 0900–1900, Sun 1000–1900 (May, June & Sept); Mon–Sat 0900–2000, Sun 1000–2000 (July & Aug); Mon–Wed 0900–1700, Thurs–Sat 0900–1800, Sun 1000–1700 (Nov–Mar). *The List* is the local weekly entertainment and events guide, available from most newsagents. The publishers also produce an annual eating and drinking guide.

Tourist Information Desk Edinburgh International Airport; tel: (0131) 344 3213; fax: (0131) 344 3466. Open daily 0630–2230 (Apr–Oct); 0730–1930 (Nov–Mar).

MONEY Foreign exchange is available in the St James Centre and Frederick St branches of the Post Office, and also at Thomas Cook branches on Hanover St and Frederick St.

POST The main Post Offices in Edinburgh are in the St James Centre, in Hope St and on Frederick St.

ACCOMMODATION

Apex International Hotel ££££ 31–35 Grassmarket, Edinburgh; tel: (0131) 300 3456; fax: (0131) 220 5345; website: www.apexhotels.co.uk; e-mail: international@apexhotels.co.uk. Popular contemporary hotel in the heart of the Old Town.

Ard-na-Said £££ 5 Priestfield Rd, Edinburgh; tel: (0131) 667 8754; fax: (0131) 667 7815; e-mail: jimandolive@ardnasaid. freeserve.co.uk. B&B in quiet residential area a short distance from the city centre.

Balmoral Guest House ££ 32 Pilrig St, Edinburgh; tel: (0131) 554 1857; fax: (0131) 553 5712; website: www.balmoralguest house.co.uk; e-mail: bookings@balmoralguesthouse.co.uk. Recently restored friendly B&B close to the city centre and a short bus ride from trendy Leith.

Brodies Hostel £ 12 High St, Edinburgh; tel: (0131) 556 6770; website: www.brodieshostels.co.uk. Right on the Royal Mile in a very central location. Booking ahead essential.

Buchan Guest House £££ 3 Coates Gardens, Edinburgh; tel: (0131) 337 1045/1775; fax: (0131) 313 0330; e-mail: michael@ haymarket-hotel.co.uk. Family run B&B close to Haymarket and the west end of Edinburgh.

Caledonian Hostel £ 3 Queensferry St, Edinburgh; tel: (0131) 441 6628; website: www.edinburghhostels.com. Just behind Princes St and handy for the main shopping district, as well as the railway and bus stations.

Castle Rock Hostel £ 15 Johnstone Terr., Edinburgh; tel: (0131) 225 9666; e-mail: castle-rock@scotlands-top-hostels.com. Excellent location in the shadow of the castle, amid the city's lively nightlife.

Channings ££££ 12–16 South Learmonth Gardens, Edinburgh; tel: (0131) 315 2226; website: www.channings.co.uk; e-mail: reserve@channings.co.uk. Stylish and comfortable Edwardian town house close to the city centre.

Cockle Mill ££ 10 School Brae, Cramond, Edinburgh; tel: (0131) 312 7657; fax: (0131) 336 1488; e-mail: bnbmill98@aol.com. Converted mill on the riverside in Cramond, a residential district about 4 miles (6.5 km) out of the city centre.

Davenport House £££ 58 Great King St, Edinburgh; tel: (0131) 558 8495; fax: (0131) 558 8496; website: www.davenport-house. com; e-mail: davenporthouse@btinternet.com. Elegant town-house in the heart of the Georgian New Town.

Edinburgh Residence ££££ 7 Rothesay Terr., Edinburgh; tel: (0131) 226 3380; fax: (0131) 226 3381; website: www.townhouse company.co.uk. Luxurious and spacious apartment suites with internet special rates. Good value for the quality.

Kingsburgh House £££ 2 Corstorphine Rd, Murrayfield, Edinburgh; tel: (0131) 313 1679; fax: (0131) 346 0554; website: www.thekingsburgh.com; e-mail: bookings@kingsburgh.com. Plush B&B in restored Victorian house a short bus ride from the city centre.

St Christopher's Inn £ 9–13 Market St; tel: (020) 7407 1856; website: www.st-christophers.co.uk. Cheap and fantastically central – a few paces away from the main rail station.

Stuart House £££ 12 East Claremont St, Edinburgh; tel: (0131) 557 9030; fax: (0131) 557 0563; website: www.stuartguesthouse. co.uk; e-mail: june@stuartguesthouse.co.uk. Traditional comfort-able guest house a short walk from the city centre.

No.38 £££ 38 Dublin St, Edinburgh; tel: (0131) 557 1789; fax: (0131) 557 6307. B&B in Georgian house in Edinburgh's New Town. Four star B&B.

FOOD AND DRINK

Eating out is becoming increasingly popular in Edinburgh and booking is always advised at weekends and during the Festival.

The Apartment ££££ 7–13 Barclay Place; tel: (0131) 228 6456. One of the hottest restaurants in the city, serving Mediterranean style food. Very busy even during the week.

Bann UK ££ 5 Hunter Sq., popular café and restaurant offering modern vegetarian cooking.

Black Bo's £££ 57–61 Blackfriars St; tel: (0131) 557 6136. Innovative vegetarian food in the heart of the Old Town. Excellent vegetarian Haggis.

Café Hub, ££ Castehill, Royal Mile. The official centre for the Edinburgh Festival, The Hub also has a popular café/bistro where you can get light meals as well as more substantial fare.

Clarinda's £ 69 Canongate. A traditional tearoom, serving good home baked cakes and scones.

Elephant House £ 21 George IV Bridge. Relaxed, studenty café serving coffees and light meals. Good views from window tables.

Howies £££ 208 Bruntsfield Pl.; tel: (0131) 221 1777. Part of a popular, good value Edinburgh chain offering modern Scottish food in a bistro atmosphere. Other branches in Waterloo Pl., Glanville Pl. and Victoria St.

Kalpna £££ 2–3 St Patrick's Sq., tel: (0131) 667 9890. Acclaimed Indian vegetarian restaurant. Going for over 20 years.

Lost Sock Diner ££–£££ 11 East London St, tel: (0131) 557 6097. A bizarre place to eat, inside a launderette, but the food is good value and filling and you can do your washing while you wait ...

Oloruso £££–££££ 33 Castle St; tel: (0131) 226 7614. Stunning views of the castle and city rooftops from the outdoor terrace on a sunny day. Buzzing atmosphere and a new favourite of the local smart set, ideal for a blowout.

Patisserie Florentin £ 8 St Giles St. Laid back café serving good croissants and pastries.

Rick's ££££ 55A Frederick St; tel: (0131) 622 7800. Very trendy bar/restaurant serving modern-global food. Come for cocktails if you don't want to eat.

The Waterfront £££–££££ 1c Dock Place, Leith; tel: (0131) 554 7427. Long established bar and restaurant in trendy Leith.

Witchery £££–££££ Castlehill; tel: (0131) 225 5613. One of the best modern Scottish restaurants in the country, with the intimate Secret Garden a candlelit highlight.

Princes Street is Edinburgh's main thoroughfare. Although it is no longer the smartest shopping street in the city, it is home to **Jenners**, the long-established department store that is Scotland's answer to Harrods. Opposite Jenners is the **Scott Monument**, the striking Gothic monument to Sir Walter Scott. One side of Princes St is given over to Princes St Gardens, which nestle beneath the Castle and provide a convenient place for picnics on warm days.

HIGHLIGHTS

Perched high on Castle Rock, **Edinburgh Castle** is probably Scotland's most famous sight. It has been home to royalty since the 11th century, although few of the original structures remain. Tiny St Margaret's Chapel (12th century) is dedicated to Malcolm III's queen and is thought to be the oldest building in the city. In the Palace Block is the chamber where Mary, Queen of Scots gave birth to James VI of Scotland (later James I of England). The Castle contains the Scottish Crown Jewels and the Stone of Destiny. In the sinister Vaults, formerly used as a prison, is the great 15th-century cannon, Mons Meg. £££, Castle Hill, open daily 0930–1800 (Apr–Sept), 0930–1700 (Oct–Mar).

For centuries **St Giles Cathedral** was the only church in the Old Town. It was here that the reformer John Knox served as minister and from here that he launched the Reformation in Scotland. Royal Mile, free, open Mon–Fri 0900–1900, Sat 0900–1700, Sun 1300–1700 (Easter–Sept), Mon–Sat, 0900–1700, Sun 1300–1700 (Oct–Easter).

The **Palace of Holyroodhouse**, the Queen's official residence in Scotland, lies at the end of the Royal Mile and as it is still a working palace, is closed if she is in residence. Surprisingly understated inside, the most interesting rooms are those used by Mary, Queen of Scots – particularly the room adjoining her bedchamber where her secretary David Rizzio was murdered. Canongate, Royal Mile, ££, family tickets available, open daily 0930–1630 (Nov–Mar); 0930–1800 (Apr–Oct).

THE SCOTTISH PARLIAMENT

The debacle over the construction of the Scottish Parliament at Holyrood, at the bottom of the Royal Mile, has been a major embarrassment for the fledgling devolved government. Originally the plan was to give the city an affordable and world-class building that it could be proud of, but the project has been beset with difficulties. The cost has spiralled as the ambitions of the construction have receded, with the date for its completion being constantly pushed further and further back.

Among the fascinating exhibits at the **Museum of Scotland** are some of the Lewis chess pieces, carved in the 12th century, and many items associated with the Jacobite rebellion. This is a spacious modern museum telling the history of Scotland from prehistoric times to the present day. Allow plenty of time for a visit here. Chambers St, £, open Mon–Sat 1000–1700, Sun 1200–1700, late opening Tues until 2000. Admission price includes the Royal Museum.

Adjacent to the Museum of Scotland is the **Royal Museum of Scotland**. This grand Victorian building houses a rich international collection. Exhibits include natural history, archaeology, costume and decorative art. £, opening times as the Museum of Scotland, to which admission price allows access.

Edinburgh's **New Town** is no modern housing estate but an elegant Georgian residential area. It was designed by architect James Craig in the 18th century as a means of relieving the squalor and overcrowding of the medieval Old Town. Its wide streets and spacious Georgian houses soon became the most fashionable place to live in the city: Sir Walter Scott and Robert Louis Stevenson were among its residents. One of the most delightful squares is **Charlotte Square** which was designed by Robert Adam.

National Gallery of Scotland, The Mound, free, open Mon–Sat 1000–1700, Sun 1200–1700. There is an extensive collection here, featuring works from the Renaissance to Post Impressionism and including paintings by Rembrandt, Turner and Van Gogh as well as many Scottish artists. Pride of place goes to Canova's *The Three Graces* and Botticelli's *The Virgin Adoring the Sleeping Christ Child*.

The Georgian House, 7 Charlotte Square, ££, open Mon–Sat 1000–1700, Sun 1400–1700. This typical New Town residence has been restored to its late-18th-century splendour by the National Trust for Scotland. Among the rooms you can see is an airy drawing room, a dining room laid for dinner and a large kitchen, equipped with curious gadgets of the time.

Dean Gallery, Belford Rd, free, open Mon–Sat 1000–1700, Sun 1200–1700. A gallery of modern art housed in a palatial 19th-century building that was once an orphanage. There is a collection of Dada and Surrealist works, as well as many sculptures by Edinburgh artist Eduardo Paolozzi.

Opposite the Dean Gallery is a neo-classical building containing an extensive collection of modern art. The **Scottish National Gallery of Modern Art** is particularly noted for its works by Scottish artists such as Fergusson, Peploe, Hunter and Cadell – the Scottish Colourists. Belford Rd, free, open Mon–Sat 1000–1700, Sun 1200–1700.

Put faces to the names of Scotland's kings, queens, heroes and literary giants at the **Scottish National Portrait Gallery**.This celebration of Scottishness is housed in a Victorian Gothic Revival building and includes many fine portraits of famous people right up to the present day. 1 Queen St, free, open Mon–Sat 1000–1700, Sun 1200–1700. A celebration of Scotland's literary heritage, with collections on Robert Burns, Sir Walter Scott and Robert Louis Stevenson is found at the **Writers' Museum**, Lady Stair's Close, Lawnmarket, Royal Mile, free, open Mon–Sat 1000–1700. During the Festival also open on Sun 1400–1700.

Our Dynamic Earth, Holyrood Rd, £££, open daily 1000–1800 (Apr–Oct); Wed–Sun 1000–1700 (Nov–Mar). This hi-tech visitor attraction brings to life the history of the planet from the very beginning of time. Interactive exhibits are a favourite of children. **Shaping a Nation,** Fountainpark, Dundee St (££, open Mon–Sat 1000–1700, Sun 1100–1700), is a new attraction looking at innovation and creativity in Scotland using hi-tech interactive technology.

> One of the best views in Edinburgh is from **Calton Hill** at the east end of Princes St. This is a volcanic outcrop on which are dotted neo-classical monuments such as the National Monument, modelled on the Parthenon, and the Dugald Stewart memorial which resembles a circular Greek temple. From here you can see right over the city and also get a great view of **Arthur's Seat**, a magnificent volcanic outcrop that looms over the city.

The former royal yacht at **The Royal Yacht** *Britannia*, Ocean Terminal, Leith, gives a fascinating insight into the life of the royal family, showing their private rooms as well as the public areas used for entertaining visiting dignitaries. Pre-booking is advised, tel: (0131) 555 5566, and buses run direct from Princes St. £££, open Mon–Fri 1030–1630, Sat, Sun 0930–1630 (Mar–July and Sept, Oct); until 1930 on Fri, Sat, Sun (Aug); Mon–Fri 1030–1530, Sat, Sun 1030–1630 (Nov–Feb). The Ocean Terminal complex has a range of shops, cafés and the Terence Conran-run Zinc Bar & Grill, as well as facilities for modern cruise shipping.

Royal Botanic Garden, 20A Inverleith Row, free, open daily from 0930, closes at 1600 (Nov–Jan), 1700 (Feb), 1800 (Mar and Sept), 1900 (Apr–Aug). This is Scotland's most important botanic garden. There are extensive grounds as well as 11 glasshouses, in which grow exotic plants from all over the world. The café is very popular with residents for lunch or tea.

TOURS There are plenty of tours of Edinburgh to choose from, ranging from classic open-topped bus tours to specialist walking tours of the city. Bus tours are operated by **Lothian Buses**, tel: (0131) 553 6363, and **Edinburgh Bus Tours**, tel: (0131) 556 2244, and details are available from the tourist information centre.

Walking tours include the **Edinburgh Literary Pub Tour**, £££; tel: (0131) 226 6665. This has professional actors who bring Edinburgh's literary heritage to life while stopping at selected pubs along the way. The same company also offers **Inspector Rebus Tours**, based on the fictional

> ## ON FOOT
> Edinburgh is a great city in which to walk. **Holyrood Park** next to Holyrood Palace is popular with visitors and locals alike and is crowned by **Arthur's Seat**, which is a steep climb but gives you great views over the city. The **Water of Leith**; tel: (0131) 455 7367, is a river which runs through the city and into the surrounding countryside. It is possible to walk most of its length and is great escape from the bustle of the centre. Then there are the **Pentland Hills** which can be seen from the city and can easily be reached by bus. There are plenty of walks to follow here – just look for guides in the tourist information centre and in local bookshops.

detective who stars in Ian Rankin's novels. The tours take in some of the more inter-esting of the unconventional detective's haunts, including his favourite pub. Ghost tours of the city are also popular and are run by **Robin's Ghost and History Tours**, tel: (0131) 557 9933; **The Cadies-Witchery Tours**, ££, tel: (0131) 555 2500; and **Auld Reekie Tours**, tel: (0131) 557 4700. Further details available from the tourist infor-mation centre.

Mary King's Close is one of the city's most unusual sights. It is part of an under-ground city that grew up due to overcrowding in the Old Town. Architects who had already built upwards created dwellings beneath the Royal Mile. The inhabitants here were generally the poorest in the city. A myth grew up that Mary King's Close was sealed up (with its residents) during an outbreak of the plague – in fact it was inhabited until the 19th century. The Close is said to be haunted and there are creepy tours organised by **Mercat Walking Tours**; tel: (0131) 557 6464.

SHOPPING

Whisky lovers will be spoilt for choice in Edinburgh. Royal Mile Whiskies on the Royal Mile stocks hundreds of different types of whisky, while the **Scotch Whisky Heritage Centre**, Castehill (££, open daily 1000–1700) gives you the chance to taste various types of whisky as well as to learn all about how it is produced.

Edinburgh is a great shopping city as it is compact enough to shop on foot yet large enough to support a wide range of shops. If you are looking for souvenirs the best place is the **Royal Mile**, which is lined with shops selling tartan, shortbread and whisky. Then there are quirky specialist shops along **Victoria Street** and the **Grassmarket** in the Old Town, where you can browse for hours looking at secondhand books, antiques, clothes and food. **Princes Street** is full of standard high street chain stores. It has a large branch of the book chain Waterstones and **Jenners**, the city's oldest department store, which has a great food hall. **George Street** is the most fashionable shopping street and is the place to come to splash out on designer clothing. A branch of **Harvey Nichols** opened at the east end of George Street in St Andrews Square in 2002. The rooftop restaurant and brasserie at Harvey Nichols so far seems to be more successful than the actual store, with London prices putting off many of the local cognoscenti. On the western fringes of the city is the **Gyle Centre**, a large mall complex where many locals come to do their weekly shopping. Also home to a variety of clothing stores.

EVENTS AND FESTIVALS

In August, Edinburgh becomes the Festival City and pulsates non-stop with both official and impromptu performances and events. The **Edinburgh International**

EDINBURGH

Festival, tel: (0131) 473 2000, website: www.eif.co.uk, offers music, theatre and dance from top performers around the world. Close on its heels is the **Festival Fringe**, tel: (0131) 226 5257, website: www.edfringe.com, an avant-garde gathering of artists, musicians, actors and comedians. At the same time the **Edinburgh Military Tattoo** takes place on the Castle Esplanade and the Film, Book and Jazz festivals are held in venues throughout the city. Other festivals include the **International Science Festival** (tel: (0131) 530 2001, website: www.edinburgh-festivals.com) which is held every April, and the **Hogmanay** celebrations which run from the end of December until the beginning of January. Note that the main Hogmanay street party on 31 December is a strictly ticket-only affair (tickets available in advance from www.edinburghshogmanay.com).

NIGHTLIFE

There is more than enough to keep you occupied in Edinburgh at night. As well as restaurants, bars and pubs, there are plenty of cinemas and some excellent theatres. These include **The Festival Theatre**, Nicolson St, which stages major opera, ballet and dramatic performances, and the **Playhouse**, Greenside Place, which generally shows large-scale productions such as musicals. The **Traverse Theatre**, Cambridge St, is Scotland's leading new writing theatre and presents innovative productions. The city's main concert hall is the **Usher Hall** on Lothian Rd. Clubs include Po Na Na on Frederick St, The Vaults on Niddrie St and The Venue on Calton Rd.

SIDE TRIPS

NORTH BERWICK This pleasant seaside town is just a 35-min train ride from Edinburgh. It is the place to come for old-fashioned pleasures such as eating ice cream cornets, fish and chips and sticky pink rock and making sand-castles. The beaches are spotless and the town has several restaurants and cafés in which to eat. It is home to the **Scottish Seabird Centre**, The Harbour (££, family tickets available, open daily 1000–1600 winter, 1000–1800 summer). This is a hi-tech birdwatching centre, which has interactive cameras trained on islands in the Firth of Forth. These allow you to observe the resident puffin and gannet colonies – moving the camera yourself to get the best view.

SOUTH QUEENSFERRY This town on the Firth of Forth, is a 15-min train journey from central Edinburgh (take the train to Dalmeny). It is dominated by the mighty **Forth Bridges** – the 1888–92 railway bridge (one of the masterpieces of 19th-century engineering) and the 1964 suspension bridge that replaced a 900-year-old ferry service across the Forth. Just beneath the rail bridge is the recently renovated Hawes Inn where Robert Louis Stevenson wrote his famous adventure story *Kidnapped*. From the pier you can take a boat trip on the *Maid of the Forth* (££, Apr–Oct) to **Incholm Island** which has a colony of grey seals and a ruined abbey.

On the edge of the town is **Hopetoun House** (££), the ancestral home of the Earls of Linlithgow, and one of the finest stately homes in Scotland. As well as visiting the house you can stroll in the extensive grounds.

TRAQUAIR HOUSE Traquair is one of the most interesting houses in Scotland. Once home to the Scottish kings, the present owners are the Maxwell-Stuarts who have lived here since the 15th century. The house contains fascinating Jacobite memorabilia, as the family's Catholic principles led them to play a significant part in the Jacobite movement. The house also has its own brewery from which it produces Traquair Ale. ££, Innerleith, nr Peebles, open daily 1230–1730 (Apr, May, Sept, Oct); 1030–1730 (June–Aug); website: www.traquair.co.uk.

There are plenty of firms that offer tours from Edinburgh to other areas of Scotland such as the Highlands.

The Authentic Sir Walter Scott Tour, tel: (0131) 468 8505, offers full and half day tours of Sir Walter Scott's Border country.

Ossian Archaeology Tours, tel: (0131) 553 7574, take you out to explore historic monuments in the Lothians.

Dunedin Guided Tours, tel: (0131) 662 9497, run tours to the Borders and the Highlands.

Rabbie's Trail Burners, tel: (0131) 226 3133, offer minicoach tours to the Highlands and Islands.

Scotline Tours, tel: (0131) 557 0162, run tours to Loch Lomond, Loch Ness and St Andrews.

Heart of Scotland Tours, tel: (0131) 558 8855, run one- and two-day minibus tours from Edinburgh into the Highlands.

WHERE NEXT?

Interesting attractions close to Edinburgh include Linlithgow Palace, the birthplace of Mary, Queen of Scots; Lennoxlove House near Haddington, the seat of the Duke of Hamilton, and Rosslyn Chapel, Roslin, a tiny gem of a church which has strong links to the Knights Templar, a warrior order of priests. Further afield you can visit the vibrant city of Glasgow (see pp. 311–317), travel north to Aberdeen (see pp. 287–288) or go south to explore the lush green countryside of the Scottish Borders. Here you can visit ancient abbeys such as those in Jedburgh and Kelso, go to Abbotsford House near Melrose which was once the home of Sir Walter Scott, or simply go walking.

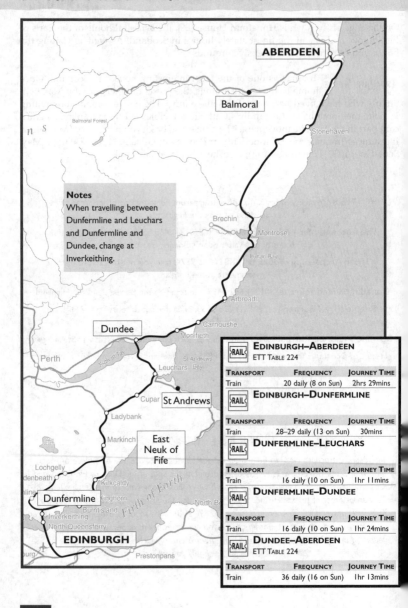

ABERDEEN

Balmoral

Stonehaven

Notes
When travelling between
Dunfermline and Leuchars
and Dunfermline and
Dundee, change at
Inverkeithing.

Brechin

Montrose

Arbroath

Carnoustie

Dundee

Monifieth

Perth

Tay

St Andrews Bay

Leuchars

Cupar

St Andrews

Ladybank

Markinch

East
Neuk of
Fife

Lochgelly

denbeath

Kirkcaldy

Dunfermline

Kinghorn

North B

Burntisland

Firth of Forth

Inverkeithing

North Queensferry

EDINBURGH

burgh

Prestonpans

RAIL	**EDINBURGH–ABERDEEN** ETT TABLE 224	
TRANSPORT	**FREQUENCY**	**JOURNEY TIME**
Train	20 daily (8 on Sun)	2hrs 29mins

RAIL	**EDINBURGH–DUNFERMLINE**	
TRANSPORT	**FREQUENCY**	**JOURNEY TIME**
Train	28–29 daily (13 on Sun)	30mins

RAIL	**DUNFERMLINE–LEUCHARS**	
TRANSPORT	**FREQUENCY**	**JOURNEY TIME**
Train	16 daily (10 on Sun)	1hr 11mins

RAIL	**DUNFERMLINE–DUNDEE**	
TRANSPORT	**FREQUENCY**	**JOURNEY TIME**
Train	16 daily (10 on Sun)	1hr 24mins

RAIL	**DUNDEE–ABERDEEN** ETT TABLE 224	
TRANSPORT	**FREQUENCY**	**JOURNEY TIME**
Train	36 daily (16 on Sun)	1hr 13mins

Soon after you leave Edinburgh the train crosses the famous Forth Railway Bridge and you clatter high over the Firth of Forth into the ancient Kingdom of Fife. Some trains stop at Inverkeithing, where you can change to visit Dunfermline, the ancient capital of Scotland and the birthplace of Charles I. The route then takes you through the centre of Fife and on to Leuchars, a jumping off point for the venerable seaside town of St Andrews, famous as the home of golf and of Scotland's oldest university.

Close to St Andrews is the picturesque East Neuk of Fife, a corner of the coast dotted with traditional fishing villages. From Leuchars the train crosses the Tay Bridge and enters Dundee, a convenient centre for breaking your journey and picking up a car to explore the fertile farmlands of Angus that lie to the north-west. The train then rumbles right along the east coast to the granite city of Aberdeen, gateway to the dramatic hills and castles of Royal Deeside. The 130 miles (210 km) between Edinburgh and Aberdeen can generally be covered in about 2½ hours.

Further west of Inverkeithing, along the coast, is the fascinating settlement of **Culross**, (pronounced Coo-ross). This old royal burgh has been restored by the National Trust for Scotland to its 16th- and 17th-century splendour, when it was a prosperous trading centre, dealing in coal and salt. Much of its trade was with the Netherlands and Dutch influence can be seen in the architecture. You can easily spend a couple of hours exploring the narrow cobbled streets lined with whitewashed house with pantile roofs. The Palace is full of atmosphere and has a fine period garden.

EDINBURGH

See p. 272.

DUNFERMLINE

From Edinburgh you can get a train to Dunfermline, the capital of Scotland during the reign of Malcolm Canmore in the 11th century. **Dunfermline Abbey** was built by David I in the 12th century and although much altered over the years, it contains some of the finest Norman architecture in Scotland. £, open daily 0930–1800 (Apr–Sept), Mon–Wed and Sat 0930–1600, Sun 1330–1600 (Oct–Mar). The abbey church preceded the island of Iona as the burial place of Scottish kings and queens, including Robert the Bruce whose tomb is marked with a brass memorial. The nearby striking pink façade of **Abbot House** (£, open 1000–1700 daily) houses a heritage centre with displays on the town's history. You can also see the remains of the royal palace where Charles I was born.

i **Tourist Information Centre** 13–15 Maygate; tel: (01383) 720999; fax: (01383) 730187. Open Mon–Sat 0900–1800, Sun 1130–1530 (July–Sept); Mon–Fri 1000–1700, Sat 1000–1600 (Oct & Apr–June).

ST ANDREWS AND THE EAST NEUK OF FIFE

If you want to explore St Andrews, get off the train at **Leuchars**, from where you can get a bus or a taxi to this historic city. The centre of the city still follows its medieval layout and is full of atmosphere, with cobbled streets, narrow alleyways and ancient buildings.

HISTORY OF GOLF

The game of golf developed in Scotland as early as the 15th century – in fact James II tried to ban the game because it was preventing people from practising the useful military skill of archery. The land around St Andrews with its grass covered dunes, known as links, provided natural fairways and bunkers. Mary, Queen of Scots occasionally played and her son James VI was a keen player.

St Andrews University is the oldest in Scotland, founded in 1410, and student life dominates the city. Students can still be spotted wearing their traditional red gowns; those who wear their gown off both shoulders – practically trailing it behind them – are final year students. University buildings are dotted around the city. The most attractive parts are St Mary's College and St Salvator's College, both of which have lovely old quads.

St Andrews was founded as a religious settlement by Celtic monks and the ruins of their first church, **St Mary on the Rock**, stand near the harbour. Pilgrims flocked to a shrine holding the relics of St Andrew, who became the country's patron saint. The town was a great ecclesiastical centre in the Middle Ages. The **Cathedral** (grounds open all year), founded in 1160, was the largest religious edifice ever built in Scotland. It was ravaged by the Reformers in the 16th century and only the towering ruins and museum attest to its former splendour. Next to the Cathedral is **St Rule's Tower** (£, open daily 0930–1830 Apr–Sept) from which you can get a great view of the town.

The **Castle** (£, open daily 0930–1800 Apr–Sept) was an infamous place of imprisonment and execution. Joint tickets are available for both the castle and cathedral. St Andrews is also famous for being the home of golf; the game has been played here since the 15th century. The **Royal and Ancient Golf Club** here is the governing body for the games worldwide. Golf lovers might want to visit the British Golf Museum (££, open daily 0930-1800 (Easter–Oct) not far from the clubhouse.

i **Kingdom of Fife Tourist Board** 70 Market St, St Andrews; tel: (01334) 472021; fax: (01334) 478422; website: www.standrews.com; e-mail: fife.tourism@kftb.ossian.net. Open Mon–Sat 0930–1700 (Oct–Mar); Mon–Sat 0930–1700, Sun 1100–1600 (Apr); Mon–Sat 0930–1730, Sun 1100–1600 (May–June); Mon–Sat 0930–1900, Sun 1000–1700 (July–Aug); Mon–Sat 0930–1800, Sun 1100–1600 (Sept).

🛏 There is plenty of accommodation in St Andrews, ranging from swish hotels to self catering cottages. It can get booked up quickly, particularly if the Open Golf is on, so do book in advance if you can.

Cambo Estate £££ Cambo House, Kingsbarns, St Andrews; tel: (01333) 450313; fax: (01333) 450987; website: www.camboestate.com; e-mail: cambohouse@compuserve.com. Both B&B and self-catering accommodation available in large wooded coastal estate.

Castlemount ££–£££ 2 The Scores, St Andrews; tel: (01334) 475579; fax: (01334) 478089; e-mail: castlemount@onetel.net.uk. This Edwardian house is opposite St. Andrews Castle and is convenient for all the attractions in the town centre.

Cleveden House ££ 3 Murray Place, St Andrews; tel: (01334) 474212; website: www.clevedenhouse.co.uk; e-mail: clevedenhouse@aol.com.

Doune House ££ 5 Murray Place, St Andrews; tel: (01334) 475195, e-mail: dounehouse@aol.com.

Fossil House ££ 12–14 Main St, Strathkinness; tel: (01334) 850639; website: www.fossil-guest-house.co.uk; e-mail: the.fossil@virgin.net. Tasteful cottage conversion in little village just outside St Andrews.

Newton of Nydie Farm Bed and Breakfast ££ The High Rd, Strathkiness; tel: (01334) 850204; e-mail: nydiefarmhouse@ talk21.com. Comfortable accommodation in working farmhouse with large garden just 3 miles (4.8 km) outside St Andrews.

Old Manor Country House Hotel £££–££££ Leven Rd, Lundin Links, Fife; tel: (01333) 320368; fax: (01333) 320911; e-mail: enquiries@oldmanor-hotel.co.uk. There are great views over Largo Bay from this comfortable hotel in the seaside village of Lundin Links on the Fife coast.

Todhall House ££–£££ Dairsie, nr Cupar; tel: (01334) 656344; website: www.scotland2000.com/todhall; e-mail: todhallhouse@ukgateway.net. This elegant Georgian house is in a rural location a few miles from St Andrews.

The University offers accommodation throughout the city from June to September. **St Andrews University Holidays ££** 79 North St, St Andrews; tel: (01334) 462000; fax: (01334) 462500; website: www.st-andrews.ac.uk, e-mail: holidays@ st-andrews.ac.uk

🍴 **The Doll's House ££** Church Square, St Andrews. Busy, lively bistro serving good fresh food.

Victoria Café £–££ Market St, St Andrews. Popular student bar/café serving light meals.

From St Andrews you can get some buses (although it is much more convenient to drive) down the coast to the **East Neuk of Fife**, an area of little fishing villages, each with its own distinctive character. **Crail** has a picturesque harbour and is popular with artists and tourists. **Anstruther** is larger and livelier and is home to the Scottish Fisheries Museum, ££, family tickets available (open Mon–Sat 1000–1730, Sun 1100–1700 (Apr–Sept), which portrays the life of the local fisher folk. You can take boat trips from 'Anster', as it is known, to the **Isle of May**, a nature reserve for seals and seabirds. Then there is pretty **Pittenweem** which is still a working fishing port, and further down the coast **St Monans, Elie** and **Lower Largo** (the home of Alexander Selkirk, the inspiration for Robinson Crusoe).

> Between St Andrews and Anstruther is **Scotland's Secret Bunker**, £££, family tickets available, open daily 1000–1700 (Apr–Oct). This was a secret military bunker that would have become Scotland's administrative centre in case of nuclear war. Entrance is through a farmhouse.

🛏 **The Grange** ££ 45 Pittenweem Rd, Anstruther; tel: (01333) 310842; website: www.thegrangeanstruther.fsnet.co.uk; e-mail: pamela@thegrangeanstruther.fsnet.co.uk. Friendly and comfortable B&B in spacious Edwardian villa, situated in the picturesque fishing village of Anstruther.
Beaumont Lodge Guest House ££ Pittenweem Rd, Anstruther; tel: (01333) 310315; website: www.smothhound.co.uk/hotels/beaumnt2.html; e-mail: reservations@beau-lodge.demon.co.uk. This family run B&B offers a high standard of accommodation and good cooking.

🍴 **Anstruther Fish Bar and Restaurant** £ Shore St, Anstruther. Famous and very popular fish and chip shop.
The Cellar ££££ Anstruther; tel: (01333) 310378. High quality seafood in one of Anstruther's oldest buildings.

DUNDEE

There is not a lot to detain you in Dundee itself, but it does have attractions of interest. Most notable is **Discovery Point and RRS Discovery**, ££, family tickets available (open Mon–Sat 1000–1700, Sun 1100–1700 (Apr–Oct); Mon–Sat 1000–1600, Sun 1100–1600 (Nov–Mar). Here you can see Captain Scott's famous polar research ship *Discovery*. It is fascinating to see how Captain Scott and his crew lived and worked for two years, and you can also learn about Antarctica today. Not far from here is **Verdant Works** (££, open Mon–Sat 1000–1700, Sun 1100–1700 (Apr–Oct); Mon–Sat 1000–1600, Sun 1100–1600 (Nov–Mar). This attraction tells the story of Dundee's famous jute industry and shows how the people of Dundee lived over 100 years ago.

Dundee is a good jumping off point for exploring Angus, an attractive rural area with fertile agricultural lands and some beautiful, unspoilt glens such as Glen Clova. The little town of **Kirriemuir** is notable as the birthplace of J M Barrie, the creator of Peter Pan. His childhood home, **Barrie's Birthplace** (£, open Mon–Sat 1100–1730, Sun 1330–1730) is open to the public. North of Kirriemuir is **Glamis Castle** – a tour of the castle lasts about an hour (£££, open daily 1030–1730 Apr–Nov). It has a fairy tale façade and is renowned as the childhood home of the late Queen Mother; there is an exhibition about her life. Glamis has been the seat of the Earls of Strathmore since 1372.

i **Angus & City of Dundee Tourist Board** 21 Castle St, Dundee; tel: (01382) 527527; fax: (01382) 527551; website: www.angusanddundee.co.uk; e-mail: enquiries@ angusanddundee.co.uk. Open Mon–Sat 0900–1700 (Jan–Apr); Mon–Sat 0900–1800, Sun noon–1600 (May–Sept); Mon–Sat, 0900–1700 (Oct–Dec).
Tourist Information Centre 1 Cumberland Close, Kirriemuir; tel: (01575) 574097. Open Mon–Sat, 1000–1700 (Apr–June), Mon–Sat 0930–1730 (July, Aug), Mon–Sat 1000–1700 (Sept).

ABERDEEN

Aberdeen is Scotland's third largest city and the largest coastal holiday resort in Scotland. The village-like 12th-century burgh of Old Aberdeen is centred around its **Cathedral** and university, while the grey stone buildings of the main part of the city earn it the sobriquet 'the Granite City'. The harbour has always been vital to Aberdeen's prosperity, from its days as a medieval trading port to its role today as the offshore oil capital of Europe.

In the **Art Gallery**, Schoolhill (free, open Mon–Sat 1000–1700, Sun 1400–1700), there is a good collection of 20th-century British art, while earlier works featured include paintings by William McTaggart. **Provost Skene's House**, Guestrow (free, open Mon–Sat 1000–1700, Sun 1300–1600), is one of the few surviving examples of Aberdeen's early architecture. A 16th-century house, it has been restored to re-create the style of the house and furnishings of the time. The **Gordon Highlanders' Museum** (£, Viewfield Rd, open Tues–Sat 1030–1630, Sun 1330–1630 Apr–Oct) has exhibits on the famous Scottish regiment, while the city's maritime past is recalled in the award-winning **Maritime Museum** (free, Shiprow, open Mon–Sat 1000–1700, Sun noon–1500). There is an exhibition on the history and lifestyle of the North Sea oil industry, as well as displays on lighthouses, fishing and shipbuilding.

i **Tourist Information Centre** 23 Union St, Shiprow; tel: (01224) 288828; fax: (01224) 586861; website: www.castlesandwhisky.com;

e-mail: info@agtb.org. Open Mon–Sat 0930–1700 throughouth the year; until 1900 and Sun 1000–1600 (July and Aug).
Tourist Information Centre, Old Royal Station, Ballater; tel: (013397) 55306, open Mon–Sat 1000–1700 (later and Sun opening in summer; times vary).

🏨 **Ewood House** £££ 12 Kings Gate, Aberdeen; tel; (01224) 648408; e-mail: ewood@ifb.co.uk. Four star B&B near the west end of the city.
Merkland Guest House ££ 12 Merkland Road East, Aberdeen; tel: (01224) 634451; website: www.smoothhound.co.uk. Friendly guest house 10-min walk from Old Aberdeen.
Struan Hall ££–£££ Ballater Rd, Aboyne; tel: (013398) 87241; e-mail: struanhall@zetnet.co.uk. Spacious house ideally situated for touring Deeside.
Migvie House ££ By Logie Coldstone, Aboyne; tel: (013398) 81313; fax: (013398) 81635, website: www.b-and-b-scotland.co.uk/migvie. Restored farmhouse set on small highland estate.

SIDE TRIP FROM ABERDEEN   West of Aberdeen is **Royal Deeside** where the **Castle Trail** snakes through an area of mountains and forests, studded with historic castles. This area was much loved by Queen Victoria, who spent a lot of her time here. **Balmoral Castle** (££, open daily 1000–1700 Apr–end July) is the summer home of the royal family; you can visit the grounds and see the ballroom here. Not far from Balmoral is **Crathie Kirk**, where the royal family worship when in residence. Other places worth visiting are **Braemar**, a popular resort with plenty of nearby walking trails, best known for the Braemar Gathering – the royal highland games – and **Ballater**, a popular Victorian health spa.

WHERE NEXT?

From Aberdeen you can head north-west to Speyside (see p. 296) and its famous whisky distilleries or go further west to the coastal towns of the Moray Firth and on to Inverness (see pp. 294–295).

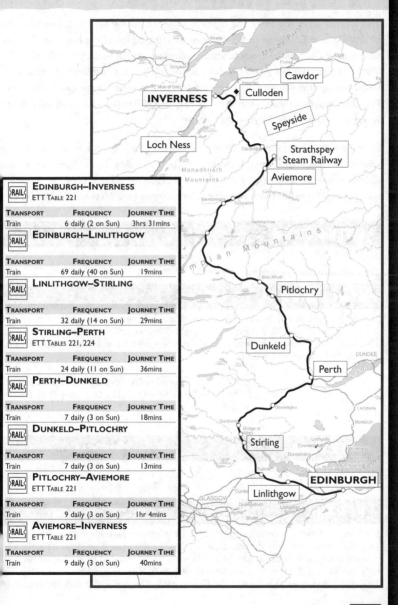

TRANSPORT	FREQUENCY	JOURNEY TIME
Train	6 daily (2 on Sun)	3hrs 31mins

RAIL EDINBURGH–LINLITHGOW

TRANSPORT	FREQUENCY	JOURNEY TIME
Train	69 daily (40 on Sun)	19mins

RAIL LINLITHGOW–STIRLING

TRANSPORT	FREQUENCY	JOURNEY TIME
Train	32 daily (14 on Sun)	29mins

RAIL STIRLING–PERTH
ETT TABLES 221, 224

TRANSPORT	FREQUENCY	JOURNEY TIME
Train	24 daily (11 on Sun)	36mins

RAIL PERTH–DUNKELD

TRANSPORT	FREQUENCY	JOURNEY TIME
Train	7 daily (3 on Sun)	18mins

RAIL DUNKELD–PITLOCHRY

TRANSPORT	FREQUENCY	JOURNEY TIME
Train	7 daily (3 on Sun)	13mins

RAIL PITLOCHRY–AVIEMORE
ETT TABLE 221

TRANSPORT	FREQUENCY	JOURNEY TIME
Train	9 daily (3 on Sun)	1hr 4mins

RAIL AVIEMORE–INVERNESS
ETT TABLE 221

TRANSPORT	FREQUENCY	JOURNEY TIME
Train	9 daily (3 on Sun)	40mins

EDINBURGH – INVERNESS

This journey takes you along one of the most scenic railway lines in Britain, from the beautiful city of Edinburgh to bustling Inverness, the capital of the Highlands. The flat farmlands of Fife soon give way to green rolling hills around Perth (the 'fair city' of Sir Walter Scott's tale) and you know that you are nearly in the Highlands. The train then winds through the heart of the Highlands, stopping at pretty towns like Dunkeld and Pitlochry; it passes through the stunning Pass of Killiecrankie and on to Blair Atholl where you can visit the fairytale Blair Castle.

From here the countryside gets wilder and more dramatic and the train stops at little villages like Dalwhinnie and Newtonmore, before pulling in to Aviemore in the Cairngorms – the jumping off point for one of Scotland's skiing areas. After about 3½ hours you pull in to Inverness, a good base for exploring Loch Ness and the Moray Firth.

EDINBURGH

See p. 272.

LINLITHGOW

The main sight in this small historic town is **Linlithgow Palace** (£, daily except Christmas and New Year Bank Holidays), birthplace of Mary, Queen of Scots in 1542. A fire in 1786 left the building as a roofless ruin, magnificently broody in its site beside Linlithgow Loch.

> *i* **Tourist Information Centre** Burgh Halls, The Close; tel:
> (01506) 844600; fax (01506) 671373. Open daily 1000–1700
> (Apr–Sept).

STIRLING

See p. 318.

PERTH

Perth is an attractive, prosperous city and a convenient base for walking in the surrounding hills. To explore the area easily it is best to hire a car. It was once a great ecclesiastical centre with four monasteries until they were destroyed by rioting mobs, fired by John Knox's Reformation sermons in **St John's Kirk** (open May–Sept, Mon–Sat 1000–1600, Jun–Sept also Sun 1200–1400) in 1559. The River Tay was the source of

Perth's prosperity, with dyeing and bleaching of cloth once a major industry.

The city's **Museum and Art Gallery** (free, open Mon–Sat 1000–1700) is one of the oldest museums in Britain and it is well worth a visit to its decorative arts and natural history displays. There is more art at the **Fergusson Gallery** (free, open Mon–Sat 1000–1700) which is devoted to the works of the Scottish colourist J D Fergusson. **Bell's Cherrybank Gardens** (Cherrybank, £, open Easter–Oct, Mon–Sat 0900–1700, Sun 1200–1600, Oct–Easter, Mon–Fri 1000–1600) has the National Heather Collection. **The Black Watch Museum**, Balhousie Castle, Hay St (free, open Mon–Sat, 1000–1630, May–Sept, Mon–Fri, 1000–1530 Oct–Apr) tells the history of the famous regiment. The **Caithness Glass Factory**, Inveralmond Industrial Estate (free, open Mon–Sat, 0900–1700, Sun, Mar–Nov;1000–1700, 1200–1700, Dec–Feb), is another attraction worth a look.

Perth's main attraction is **Scone Palace** (££, open daily 0930–1715 Apr–Oct) just outside the town. It was here that Kenneth MacAlpin brought the Stone of Destiny in the 9th century when he made Scone the centre of his kingdom. Moot Hill, in the palace grounds, became the crowing place of Scottish kings until 1651, when Charles II was crowned. The palace is the home of the Earls of Mansfield and contains unique collections of *objets d'art*, porcelain and furniture.

A few miles north east of Perth is the little town of **Meigle** which has an outstanding **Museum** (£, open daily 0930–1830 Apr–Sept), containing 25 sculptured monuments of the Celtic Christian period. Also worth a visit is **Huntingtower Castle**, Huntingtower (£, open daily 0930–1830 Apr–Sept; closes 1630, Sun am, Thur pm and Fri Oct–Mar). Its towers date back to the 15th and 16th centuries, and there are fine painted walls and ceilings.

i **Perthshire Tourist Board**, Lower City Mills, West Mill St, Perth: tel: (01738) 450600; fax: (01738) 630416; website: www.perthshire.co.uk; e-mail: perthtic@perthshire.co.uk. Open Mon–Sat 0930–1730, Sun 1100–1600 (Apr–mid-July, Sept and Oct); Mon–Sat 1000–1600 (Oct–Mar).

Almond Villa Guest House ££ 51 Dunkeld Rd, Perth; tel: (01738) 629356; fax: (01738) 446606; e-mail: almondvilla@compuserve.com. Victorian villa close to the town centre.

Park Lane Guest House ££ 17 Marshall Place, Perth; tel: (01738) 637218; fax: (01738) 643519; website: www.parklane-uk.com; e-mail: stay@parklane-uk.com. Georgian townhouse conveniently placed for city centre attractions.

DUNKELD

Dunkeld was proclaimed Scotland's ecclesiastical capital by Kenneth MacAlpin in the 9th century. The majestic, partly ruined **Cathedral** dates back to the 12th century and is the town's main attraction. It contains the tomb of the 'Wolf of Badenoch' Robert II's son who achieved notoriety by leaving his wife, for which he was excommunicated. In revenge he sacked Elgin cathedral.

On the opposite bank of the River Tay is the village of **Birnam**. The young Beatrix Potter spent holidays here and drew inspiration for her ever-popular children's books, including *The Tale of Peter Rabbit*. There is a **Beatrix Potter Exhibition** (£, open daily 1000–1700).

[i] **Tourist Information Centre** The Cross; tel/fax: (01350) 727688. e-mail: dunkeldtic@perthshire.co.uk. Open Mon–Sat 0930–1730, Sun 1100–1600 (Apr–July and Sept, Oct), reduced hours in winter.

PITLOCHRY

South west of Pitlochry is the tiny village of **Fortingall**. In the church-yard is an extraordinary yew tree, which is said to be possibly 5000 years old – one of the oldest living things in the world. Some believe that earthworks on the edge of the village are the remains of a Roman outpost and legend has it that Pontius Pilate was born here when his father, a Roman General, was stationed here.

Pitlochry is a very popular tourist centre that shot to fame in Victorian times. Its most unusual attraction is the **Fish Ladder**, a ladder of 31 stepped pools created when a hydro-electric project threatened to cut off the route that salmon followed to their spawning grounds. To the west of town is the **Dunfallandy Stone**, an 8th-century carved Pictish stone. There are also two distilleries you can visit. **Bell's Blair Atholl Distillery** (£, open Mon–Sat 0900–1700 Easter–Sept and Oct; Sun 1200–1700 from June; Mon–Fri 1000–1600 Nov–Easter) has a visitor centre where you can learn how whisky is made and taste the finished product. **Edradour Distillery** is the smallest distillery in Scotland and offers guided tours and tastings (free, open Mon–Sat 0930–1700, Sun 1200–1700 Mar–Oct; Mon–Sat, 1000–1530 Nov–mid-Dec).

Just north of Pitlochry is the beautiful **Pass of Killiecrankie**, the scene of a fearsome battle in the first

Jacobite uprising of 1689. The Highlanders won the day but their leader, John Graham of Claverhouse, or 'Bonnie Dundee', was killed by a stray bullet and the rebellion floundered. There is a National Trust for Scotland **Visitor Centre** (open daily 1000–1730 Apr–Oct) which has displays telling the story of the battle and the gorge. Among the woodland walks you can do is one to Soldier's Leap, where a government soldier is said to have jumped an extraordinary distance across a gorge to escape the pursuing Highlanders.

> [i] **Tourist Information Centre** 22 Atholl Rd; tel: (01796) 472215; fax: (01796) 474046; website: www.perthshire.co.uk; e-mail: pitlochrytic@perthshire.co.uk. Open Mon–Sat 0900–1800, Sun 1100–1700 (Apr–May, Sept and Oct); closes an hour later May–Sept and an hour earlier/1400 on Sun (Oct–Mar).

> 🛏 **Birchwood Hotel £££** 2 East Moulin Rd; Pitlochry; tel: (01796) 472477; fax: (01796) 473951; website: www.birchwoodhotel.co.uk; e-mail: viv@birchwoodhotel.co.uk. This hotel is set in its own grounds but is only a few minutes walk from the centre of town.

SIDE TRIP TO BLAIR CASTLE You can get off the train at the little village of Blair Atholl to visit **Blair Castle** (£££, open daily 1000–1800 Apr–Oct; from 0930 Jul and Aug). This whitewashed, turreted castle is the home of the dukes of Atholl and makes a striking sight against the green backdrop of the Perthshire hills. It dates from 1269 and has 32 exquisitely furnished rooms filled with collections and memorabilia – with a particularly emphasis on the clan's role in the Jacobite rebellion. The Duke of Atholl is the only person in Britain allowed to have his own private army – the Atholl Highlanders; a privilege granted him by Queen Victoria. A few miles north of the castle are the **Falls of Bruar**, an impressive beauty spot.

EN ROUTE
KINGUSSIE

Kingussie has lots of hotels, restaurants and craft shops and makes a more atmospheric base for exploring the area than Aviemore. The **Highland Folk Museum** (£, open Mon–Sat 0930–1730 Apr–Oct) is a social history museum that depicts the life of the Highlander over the past 400 years.

AVIEMORE

Aviemore is a purpose-built 1960s ski resort (not thick with charm) with mountain sports shops, supermarkets, large hotels and apartments. It is the southern terminus for the **Strathspey Steam Railway** (£££, open Mar–Oct) which runs daily trains from Aviemore to Boat of Garten. At Loch Garten, Boat of Garten, you can visit the **Osprey Centre** (£, open daily 1000–1800 Apr–Aug) where in season you can watch nesting ospreys on a CCTV link.

From Aviemore you can visit the **Cairngorms**, a dramatic granite range of mountains stretching from the

Spey Valley to Braemar. Remote, windswept and wild, the Cairngorms are a formidable challenge to experienced mountaineers and hillwalkers. In winter skiers flock to the **Cairngorm Ski Centre**, just a few miles from Aviemore itself. A funicular railway will take you to the top of the mountains. In summer activities focus on walking, watersports, horse riding, mountain biking and fishing and there are plenty of companies offering equipment hire. One company is **Loch Morlich Watersports**, Glenmore Forest Park, tel: (01479) 861221, which rents watersports equipment and offers tuition.

Behind the village of Aviemore is the **Craigellachie Nature Reserve**, a haven for wildlife with plenty of footpaths to follow. Not far from Aviemore is the **Rothiemurchus Estate**, Inverdruie (open daily; tel: (01479) 810858), where you can enjoy a whole range of outdoor activities from Land Rover safari tours to clay pigeon shooting.

i **Tourist Information Centre** Grampian Rd, Aviemore; tel: (01479) 810363: fax: (01479) 811063; e-mail: aviemore @host.co.uk.
Tourist Information Centre 54 High St, Grantown-on-Spey; tel/fax: (01479) 872773; e-mail: grantown@host.co.uk. Open Mon, Wed, Fri 1000–1600 (Oct–Mar); daily 0900–1700 (Easter–Oct).

As well as hotels and B&Bs, the area around Aviemore has plenty of self catering accommodation in chalets, lodges, caravans and bungalows. The tourist information centre will have details.
Corrour House Hotel £££ Inverdruie, Aviemore; tel: (01479) 810220; fax: (01479) 811500; website: www.corrourhouse.co.uk. Comfortable small hotel serving good food.
Culdearn House Hotel ££££ Woodlands Terrace, Grantown-on-Spey; tel: (01479) 872106; fax: (01479) 873641; website: www.culdean.com; e-mail: culdearn@globalnet.co.uk. This small country house offers good fresh food and very comfortable accommodation.
Glenavon House £££ Kinchurdy Rd, Boat of Garten; tel: (01479) 831213; website: www.host.co.uk; e-mail: glenavonhouse @aol.com. Five-star guest house open from Apr–Oct.

There are plenty of places to eat in and around Aviemore.

INVERNESS

A strategic Highland crossroads, Inverness has been settled since ancient times and is known as the capital of the Highlands. The city centre along the banks of the river

Ness has an attractive charm, although this has been spoiled by unsympathetic 20th-century developments. **St Andrew's Cathedral**, built in the 19th century in neo-Gothic style, has beautiful stained glass over the entrance. **Inverness Castle**, also built in the 19th century, overlooks the river and houses law courts and offices.

Below the castle is the **Inverness Museum and Art Gallery** (free, open Mon–Sat 0900–1700) which has exhibits about the history of the Great Glen and Highland life. Lovers of contemporary art should head for **art.tm** (free, open Tues–Sat 0900–1700), an award-winning gallery with crafts, prints, paintings and ceramics. The **Scottish Kiltmaker Visitor Centre** (£, open Mon–Sat 0900–1700, later in summer) gives an insight into the history, culture and tradition of the kilt. There are workshop presentations on kiltmaking.

> [i] **Tourist Information Centre** Castle Wynd, Inverness;
> tel: (01463) 234353; fax: (01463) 710609; e-mail: inverness@
> host.co.uk. Open Mon–Fri 0900–1700, Sat 1000–1600; open
> later June–Aug, phone to confirm.

> 🛏 **Melness Guest House** ££ 8 Old Edinburgh Rd,
> Inverness; tel: (01463) 220963. Comfortable and homely B&B.
> **Trafford Bank** £££ 96 Fairfield Rd, Inverness; tel: (01463)
> 241414; website: www.ibmpcug.co.uk-cs/guest/trafford/trafford;
> e-mail: traff@pop.cali.co.uk. Award winning B&B in large
> comfortable home.

SIDE TRIPS FROM INVERNESS

LOCH NESS The deep waters of Loch Ness are, of course, famous for sheltering that mythical beast the **Loch Ness Monster**. Tales of 'Nessie', rumoured to be a prehistoric creature with a humped back and snake-like neck, have circulated since the 8th century. Countless expeditions to discover the truth have been made by everyone from amateur obsessives to serious scientists.

You can drive to Drumnadrochit, where there are two visitor attractions devoted to the myth. The **Official Loch Ness Exhibition Centre** (££, open daily 1000–1600, longer hours in summer) uses the latest technology to explore the story of the loch and its monster. The **Original Loch Ness Visitor Centre** (££, open daily 1000–1600, longer hours in summer) has film on the history of the area. You can also book cruises of the loch from here with **Loch Ness Cruises**.

CULLODEN AND THE MORAY FIRTH To the east of Inverness is the tranquil coastal area of the Moray Firth, dotted with attractive little towns and imposing castles. Many of its attractions can easily be visited on a day trip from Inverness. Undoubtedly the most important site is **Culloden Moor** where, in 1746, the Jacobite dream was crushed forever. This was the last major battle fought on mainland Britain. It was not, as many believe, a battle between the Scots and the English, but one between the Highland forces of Bonnie Prince Charlie and the government forces of the Duke of Cumberland (which contained many lowland Scots). Cumberland became known as 'Butcher Cumberland' for his brutal slaughter of innocent bystanders and wounded soldiers in the aftermath of the battle. You can see the battlefield as well as see exhibitions on the Jacobites at the **Visitor Centre** (££, open daily 1000–1600 Oct–Mar; 0900–1800 Apr–Oct).

CAWDOR CASTLE Further along the coast you come to Cawdor Castle (££, open daily 1000–1730 May–Oct) near the pretty town of **Nairn**. This romantic 600-year-old castle was built for the Thane of Cawdor and is still a family home today. The castle was reputedly the place of Duncan's murder in Shakespeare's *Macbeth*.

SPEYSIDE The fertile fields of Speyside (the agricultural area surrounding the river Spey) produce the barley and grain that is needed to make malt whisky, and there are so many distilleries in Speyside that it has earned the name Malt Whisky Country. As well as distilleries there are castles, cathedrals and museums to visit. You can reach the Speyside towns of Forres and Elgin by train from Aberdeen, but to explore the heart of Speyside you need a car.

Forres is the home of the **Dallas Dhu Historic Distillery** (£, open daily 0930–1830 Apr–Sept; reduced hours Oct–Mar). **Elgin** has a picturesque ruined 13th-century **Cathedral**. Other attractions include the **Glenfiddich Distillery**, Dufftown (free, open Mon–Fri 0930–1630 plus Sat 0930–1630 and Sun 1200–1630 from Easter–Oct); the **Speyside Cooperage**, Craigellachie (£, open Mon–Fri 0930–1630); and the **Glen Grant Distillery**, Rothes (£, open Mon–Sat 1000–1600, Sun 1230–1600, Apr–Oct), which is surrounded by a beautiful Victorian garden.

> *i* **Tourist Information Centre** 17 High St, Elgin; tel: (01343) 542666 or 543388; e-mail: elgin@agtb.ossian.net. Open daily 0900–1800 (Apr–Oct); Mon–Sat 1000–1600 (Nov–Mar).

> 🏠 **Sherston House** £££ Hillhead, Forres; tel: (01309) 671087; fax: (01343) 850535. Delightful countryside B&B with large, comfortable rooms.

WHERE NEXT?

From Inverness you can travel west to the Beauly Firth or follow the coastline eastwards and down to Aberdeen (see p. 287). Alternatively, you can continue travelling north to the wilder reaches of the Highlands (see p. 297).

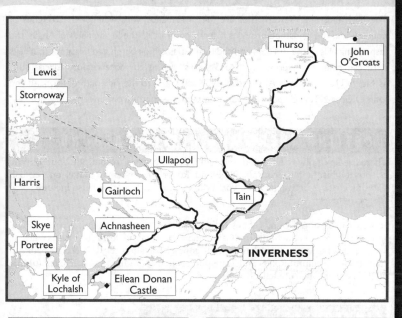

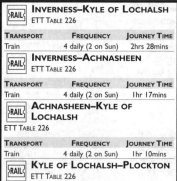

RAIL	**INVERNESS–KYLE OF LOCHALSH**	
	ETT TABLE 226	

TRANSPORT	FREQUENCY	JOURNEY TIME
Train	4 daily (2 on Sun)	2hrs 28mins

RAIL	**INVERNESS–ACHNASHEEN**	
	ETT TABLE 226	

TRANSPORT	FREQUENCY	JOURNEY TIME
Train	4 daily (2 on Sun)	1hr 17mins

RAIL	**ACHNASHEEN–KYLE OF LOCHALSH**	
	ETT TABLE 226	

TRANSPORT	FREQUENCY	JOURNEY TIME
Train	4 daily (2 on Sun)	1hr 10mins

RAIL	**KYLE OF LOCHALSH–PLOCKTON**	
	ETT TABLE 226	

TRANSPORT	FREQUENCY	JOURNEY TIME
Train	4 daily (2 on Sun)	13mins

	INVERNESS–ULLAPOOL	
	ETT TABLE 227	

TRANSPORT	FREQUENCY	JOURNEY TIME
Bus	2–3 daily (0 on Sun)	1hr 20mins

	ULLAPOOL–STORNOWAY	

TRANSPORT	FREQUENCY	JOURNEY TIME
Ship	2–3 daily (0 on Sun)	2hrs 40mins

RAIL	**INVERNESS–TAIN**	
	ETT TABLE 226	

TRANSPORT	FREQUENCY	JOURNEY TIME
Train	3–4 daily (2 on Sun)	1hr

RAIL	**TAIN–THURSO**	
	ETT TABLE 226	

TRANSPORT	FREQUENCY	JOURNEY TIME
Train	3 daily (2 on Sun)	2hrs 25mins

Notes

Frequencies shown are for summer; winter services are less frequent. The bus between Inverness and Ullapool is Scottish Citylink service 961.

Highlands and Western Isles

The Highlands and Western Isles are full of romance, with wild, lonely stretches of countryside. The landscape provides a sharp contrast to the fertile fields of Angus, the lush rolling hills of the Borders and the busy cities of Edinburgh and Glasgow. Journeys here can take you over the sea to Skye, as well as to more remote islands such as North Uist and Lewis. Alternatively you can travel to the far north of Scotland and John O'Groats. This chapter covers three separate routes from Inverness.

GETTING THERE AND GETTING AROUND

There are few railway lines and you will frequently need to continue your journey by bus or hire a car. ScotRail 'Highland Rover' tickets cover travel on Scottish Citylink coaches between Oban, Fort William and Inverness and also include some ferry crossings.

It is easier to travel around by bus than by train. A Scottish Citylink 'Explorer Pass' also offers 50% reductions on Caledonian MacBrayne ferry services; website: www.calmac.co.uk. To plan your journey contact Traveline, tel: 0870 608 2608, or call the extremely helpful Roads and Transport section at Highland Council; tel: (01463) 702695; e-mail: sheila.fletcher@highland.gov.uk.

INVERNESS – SKYE

The journey from Inverness to Skye takes in some stunning scenery. The train journey takes under 2 hours and stops at stations with intriguing names like Garve, Achnashellach and Duirinish. Trains terminate at Kyle of Lochalsh, but coaches from Inverness continue over the Skye Bridge to Plockton, on Skye.

INVERNESS See p. 294.

ACHNASHEEN Achnasheen is the nearest station to the **Beinn Eighe National Nature Reserve** which can only be reached by car (from Achnasheen along the A832 to Kinlochewe, west of which is the Reserve). It was the first National Nature Reserve in Britain and is home to red deer, roe deer, pine marten and wildcat. Birds of prey such as buzzard and golden eagle can also sometimes be seen and there are mountain and woodland trails.

LOCH MAREE

Between Kinlochewe and Gairloch, north of the A832, is **Loch Maree**. Set between the backdrop of the peaks of Beinn Eighe and Ben Slioch, and studded with pine covered islands, it is one of the most beautiful lochs in Scotland. One of the islands on the loch is also the legendary burial place of a Viking Romeo and Juliet who died tragically in the 9th century. Queen Victoria made a famous visit here in 1877.

SIDE TRIP FROM ACHNASHEEN If you continue past Loch Maree on the A832 from Achnasheen, the road brings you to **Gairloch**, a popular tourist centre with some of best beaches in western Scotland. The history of the local crofting community is well told at the **Gairloch Heritage Museum** (£, open Mon–Sat 1000–1700 Apr–Sept; Mon–Fri 1000–1300 Oct). The reconstructed crofthouse is cleverly done and worth a visit.

EN ROUTE
PLOCKTON

Plockton is a picture postcard village popular with tourists and artists. Famous as the setting for the BBC *Hamish Macbeth* series, it is a lovely place to relax. You can take boat trips from here to watch seals with Leisure Marine (££, Harbour St, Apr–Oct).

[i] **Tourist Information Centre** Achtercairn, Gairloch; tel: (01445) 712130; fax: ; (01445) 712071; e-mail: gairloch@ host.co.uk. Open Mon–Sat 1000–1700, Sun 1200–1600 (Apr–June, Oct); daily 1000–1700/1800 (Jun–Sept).

Not far from Gairloch is **Poolewe**, a pretty, laid-back village set on the banks of the River Ewe. It is home to the outstanding **Inverewe Gardens** (open ££, daily 0930–2100 Mar–Oct; 0930–1700 Nov–Mar), among the finest in Europe. The gardens were planted by Osgood Mackenzie on barren ground in 1862 and have grown to encompass 60 acres (24 ha) of woodland and flowering plants that cover the peninsula. Although on the same latitude as Siberia, the warm currents of the North Atlantic Drift have created an oasis for exotic, tropical species. The views over the loch from among the pines are fabulous.

[🏨] **The Plockton Hotel** ££–£££ Harbour St, Plockton; tel: (01599) 544274; fax: (01599) 544475; website: www.host.co.uk.

KYLE OF LOCHALSH This mainland town is the gateway to Skye and the terminus for the railway line from Inverness. Kyle is connected to Skye by the new Skye Bridge.

[i] **Tourist Information Centre** Car Park, Kyle of Lochalsh; tel: (01599) 534276; fax: (01599) 534808; e-mail: kyle@ host.co.uk. Open Mon–Sat 0900–1700 Easter–Oct; daily 0900–1800 mid-July–mid-Aug.

[🏨] **The Old Schoolhouse** £££ Tigh Fasgaidgh, Erbusaig, Kyle; tel: (01599) 534639; website: www.host.co.uk; e-mail: cuminecandj @lineone.net. Restaurant with rooms open Apr–Oct.

SIDE TRIP FROM KYLE OF LOCHALSH If you drive south of Kyle along the A87, you come to **Eilean Donan Castle** (££, open daily 1000–1600 Mar and Nov; 1000–1730 Apr–Oct). One of Scotland's most stunning castles, it is set on an island at the meeting point of Lochs Duich, Alsh and Long. The castle is the ancestral seat of the MacKenzies of Kintail and dates back to the 13th century.

🚌 From Kyle of Lochalsh there are regular shuttle buses over the Skye Bridge to Kyleakin on Skye. You can then change to reach Portree.

🚆 Trains terminate at Kyle of Lochalsh, but coaches from Inverness continue over the Skye Bridge to Plockton, on Skye.

SKYE Skye is the largest of the Inner Hebridean islands and apart from the towns and main attractions is little touched by tourism, remaining the domain of serious climbers and walkers. The central part is dominated by the dramatic, bare peaks of the Cuillin Hills, beyond which is the capital Portree. Skye is one of the most romantic destinations in Scotland, largely due to its association with Bonnie Prince Charlie. Following the massacre of the Jacobites as Culloden in 1746, the 'Young Pretender' fled to the Western Isles. Flora MacDonald then took him from Uist to Skye disguised as her maid.

Exploring Skye is easiest by car. However, there are about four buses each day running between Portree, Broadford and Kyleakin. Near Kyleakin is the **Brightwater Visitor Centre** (free, open Mon–Sat 0900–1800 Apr–Oct) which focuses on the history and wildlife of the conservation island of Eilean Ban and its associations with Gavin Maxwell, author of *Ring of Bright Water*. There are also boat trips to Eilean Ban with the possibility of spotting otters.

PORTREE Portree is the capital of Skye, a pretty little town which manages to accommodate all the tourists who make it their touring base. It is at its most beautiful around the harbour, either in the soft morning light or during one of Skye's tremendous sunsets.

To the south of the town is the **Aros Experience** (£, Viewfield Rd, open daily 0900–1800), Skye's heritage centre which has an exhibition tracing the history of the people of the island.

North-west of Portree is **Dunvegan Castle** (££, open daily 1000–1730 Mar–Oct; 1100–1600 Nov–Mar), the ancestral seat of the MacLeods. It has been occupied for more than 700 years. Among Dunvegan's treasure are the Fairy Flag, said to have been given to the fourth clan chief by his fairy wife. The ancient scrap of silk reputedly holds the power to save the clan from destruction three times – and has been used twice. Another attraction is the **Talisker Distillery**, Carbost (££, open Mon–Fri 1400–1630 Nov–Mar; Mon–Fri 0900–1630 Apr–Jun and Oct; Mon–Sat 0900–1630 Jul–Sept) which is the only distillery on Skye.

ℹ️ **Tourist Information Centre** Bayfield House, Bayfield Rd, Portree; tel: (01478) 612137; fax: (01478) 612141; e-mail: portree@host.co.uk. Open Mon–Sat 0900–1700, Sat

WHERE NEXT?

From Skye you can take a ferry to the islands of Harris and North Uist, or return to the mainland via Mallaig and travel south to Fort William (see pp. 325–236), or along the coast to join ferry services to the island of Mull.

1000–1600 (Nov–Mar); Mon–Sat 0900–1700 (Mar–Easter); Mon–Sat 0900–1730/1800/2000, Sun 1000–1600 (Easter–Oct).

🚇 **Lime Stone Cottage** ££ 4 Lime Park, Broadford, Skye; tel: (01471) 822142; website: www.host.co.uk; e-mail: kathielimepark@btinternet.com.

The Three Chimneys Restaurant and The House Over-By ££££ Colbost, Dunvegan, Skye; tel: (01470) 511258; fax: (01470) 511358; website: www.threechimneys.co.uk; e-mail: eatandstay@threechimneys.co.uk. Luxury restaurant with rooms.

Viewfield House Hotel £££ Viewfield House, Portree, Skye; tel: (01478) 612217; fax: (01478) 613517; website: www.skye.co.uk/viewfield.

Flodigarry Country House Hotel ££££ Staffin, Skye; tel: (01470) 552203; fax: (01470) 552301; website: www.flodigarry. co.uk. Award-winning hotel in secluded grounds.

INVERNESS – ULLAPOOL – LEWIS

There are no trains from Inverness to Ullapool so you have to drive or take a bus. Ullapool, in Ross and Cromarty, is a fishing port that is a convenient gateway for exploring the remote, majestic landscapes of Sutherland to the north. Ferries from Ullapool take you to the island of Lewis, one of Scotland's Western Isles, where Gaelic is still spoken and where strict religious beliefs mean that shops, attractions, bars, restaurants are closed on Sundays.

ULLAPOOL   A delightful seaport on the shores of Loch Broom, Ullapool is the gateway to the Western Isles. It has a lovely waterfront and several pleasant pubs and restaurants. The **Ullapool Museum** (£, open Mon–Sat 0930–1730) has a good audio-visual presentation telling the story of 'Loch Broom – The People of the Loch'. Not far from the town are **Leckmelm Gardens** (open daily 1000–1800 Apr–Sept) where you will find many rare trees and a good display of rhododendrons and azaleas.

ROUTE DETAIL

From Inverness it takes around 1 hr 20 mins to drive to Ullapool. Take the A9 to Tore, then go west along the A835 through Garve. Continue following the A835 into Ullapool, 57 miles (95 km).

ℹ️ **Tourist Information Centre** Argyle St, Ullapool; tel: (01854) 612135; fax. (01854) 613031; e-mail: ullapool@host.co.uk. Open Mon–Fri 1330–1700 (Oct–Mar); Mon–Sat 0900–1700, Sun 1200–1600 (Apr, May); Mon–Sat 0900–1730/1800, Sun 1000–1600/1700 (Jun–Oct).

HIGHLANDS AND WESTERN ISLES

⊟ **Ardvreck Guest House** ££ North Rd, Morefield, Ullapool;
tel: (01854) 612028; fax: (01854) 613000; website: www.host.co.uk.
Bright attractive guest house surrounded by crofting land.
Eilean Donan Guest House ££ 14 Market St, Ullapool; tel:
(01854) 612524; website: www.host.co.uk.

LEWIS Ferries to Lewis from Ullapool arrive at flat, bleak Stornoway with its clear, white sandy beaches and many freshwater lochs. Stornoway has a good museum, **Museum nan Eilean** (free, open Mon–Sat, 1000–1730 Apr–Sept; Tues–Fri 1000–1700, Sat 1000–1300 Oct–Apr), which has exhibits on the life of the island. The main attraction on the island are the **Callanish Stones**, circles of prehistoric standing stones that are considered nearly as important as Stonehenge. A **Visitor Centre** (£, open Mon–Sat 1000–1800 Apr–Sept; Wed–Sat 1000–1600 Oct–Apr) has an audio visual presentation on the stones, as well as a shop and a café.

HARRIS Lewis is connected to the island of Harris by a narrow strip of land. Famous for Harris tweed, this mountainous island offers some challenging walks and climbs. It also has some spectacular beaches.

i **Western Isles Tourist Board** 26 Cromwell Street,
Stornoway, Lewis; tel: (01851) 703088; fax: (01851) 705244;
website: www.witb.co.uk; e-mail: stornowaytic@witb.ossian.net.
Open Mon–Fri 0900–1700 Oct–Mar; Mon–Sat, 0900–1800 &
2000–2100 Apr–Oct.

⊟ **Galson Farm Guest House** £££ South Galson, Lewis;
tel: (01851) 850492; website: www.galsonfarm.freeserve.co.uk;
e-mail: galsonfarm@yahoo.com.
Park Guest House and Garden Rooms ££ 30 James St,
Stornoway, Lewis; tel: (01851) 702485; website: www.witb.co.uk/
links/parkguesthouse. Welcoming guest house with restaurant.
Seaside Villa ££ Back, Lewis; tel: (01851) 820208. Four-star
B&B with great views.
Allan Cottage Guest House £££ Tarbert, Harris; tel: (01859)
502146; website: www.witb.co.uk/links/allancottage.htm.
Dunard £££ Tarbert, Harris; tel: (01859) 502340. Renovated
19th-century villa close to ferry terminal.

WHERE NEXT?

*From Harris you can take
a ferry to the island of
North Uist and then travel
on to Benbecula and
South Uist.*

INVERNESS – THURSO – JOHN O'GROATS

From Inverness it is 143 miles (230 km) to John O'Groats. The train first takes you past the fertile lands of the Black Isle and into Easter Ross, which has picturesque fishing villages dotted along its varied coastline. Soon you reach Sutherland, a land scarred by the memory of the brutal Highland Clearances, and then enter the windswept reaches of Caithness. To the west you can see from the train the empty Flow Country, where vast empty peat bogs form a unique refuge for many birds and plants. After about 3 hrs 25 mins, you arrive at Thurso, from where you can get a bus to John O'Groats, Britain's most northerly village.

TAIN Tain is one of the oldest towns in the Highlands and dates back to at least the 11th century. A medieval pilgrimage centre, it is a good base for exploring the coastline of the Dornoch Firth. Its main attraction is **Tain Through Time** (££, open daily 1000–1800 Mar–Oct; Sat noon–1600 Nov–Mar). This includes a Pilgrimage centre devoted to James IV's many pilgrimages, entry to the Clan Ross Centre and a tour of the Collegiate Church, one of the best preserved medieval churches in the north.

🖳 **Golf View House** ££ 13 Knockbreck Rd, Tain; tel: (01862) 892856; website: www.golf-view.co.uk.

West of Ardgay station is **Croick Church** which has moving messages scratched on a window. They were carved by the residents of Glen Calvie just before they were evicted by the Highland Clearances.

THURSO Thurso was founded by the Vikings and was an important trading centre. During the 19th century it became a major centre for the export of Caithness flagstone, then in the 20th century it had an influx of scientists and engineers with the building of Dounreay nuclear reactor nearby. The coastline here is said to offer some of the best surfing in Europe. You can visit 12th-century **St Peter's Church** and **Thurso Folk Museum** (£, open Mon–Sat 1000–1300 & 1400–1600 June–Sept) which contains a Pictish stone. Ferries leave Scrabster, near Thurso, for the Orkneys.

ℹ️ **Tourist Information Centre** Riverside, Thurso; tel: (01847) 892371; fax: (01847) 893155; e-mail: thurso@ host.co.uk. Open Mon–Sat, 1000–1700 (Apr–May); daily, 1000–1700/1800 (May–July); Mon–Sat 1000–1700, Sun 1100–1600 (Aug–Oct).

🖳 **The Sheiling Guest House**, ££ Melvich; tel: (01641) 531256; website: www.b-and-b-scotland.co.uk/sheiling; e-mail: thesheiling@btinternet.com.

Forss Country House Hotel £££ by Thurso; tel; (01847) 861201; website: www.forsscountryhouse.co.uk; e-mail: jamie@forsshouse.freeserve.co.uk.

CASTLE OF MEY Former summer home of the late Queen Elizabeth, the Queen Mother, this turreted Z-shaped castle stands beside the sea just north of the A836 between John O'Groats and Thurso (Rapson's bus no. 80 calls at Mey Post Office, about ⅝ mile (1 km) from the castle). Since her death in 2002 at the age of 101, the castle has opened its doors to the public in accordance with her wishes. It has a walled garden and fine coastal views. Open late May–early Oct (but closed two weeks in early Aug) Tues–Sat 1100–1700, Sun 1400–1700; tel: (01847) 851227.

JOHN O'GROATS John O'Groats is Britain's most northerly village – its most northerly point is Dunnet Head a few miles away. The town (an hour's bus ride from Thurso station) was named after Jan de Groot, a Dutchman who was granted a charter to run a ferry to the Orkneys in the 15th century. Ferries still run from here (and from nearby Gills) to the Orkneys. You can visit the **Last House in Scotland** (free, open daily, 1000–1630 Mar–Oct; open later in high season), which has a little museum. East of the town is **Duncansby Head**, with high cliffs and a lighthouse. A path leads to the striking sandstone pinnacles of **Duncansby Stacks**.

EN ROUTE

At **Forsinard** there is a huge **RSPB Reserve** in the Flow Country. From the Visitor Centre (open daily 0900–1800 Apr–Sept) you can go on guided walks, learn about the peatlands and the plants and animals of the area.

[i] **Tourist Information Centre** Country Rd, Caithness, John O'Groats; tel: (01955) 611373; fax; (01955) 611448; e-mail: johnogroats@host.co.uk. Open Mon–Sat 1000–1700 Easter–Oct.

▤ **The Bungalow** ££ Bannochmore Farm, Harpsdale, Halkirk; tel: (01847) 841216; website: www.host.co.uk
The Clachan ££ South Rd, Wick; website: www.theclachan.co.uk; e-mail: enquiry@theclachan.co.uk.

WHERE NEXT?

From Scrabster, west of John O'Groats you can catch a ferry to the Orkney Islands
(see pp. 305–308) *and then travel on to the Shetland Islands.*

Although both the Orkney and Shetland Islands are part of Britain, they feel very different – even to Scotland. Both groups of islands have been inhabited for thousands of years and there are many fascinating prehistoric sites to visit. They have a strong Scandinavian influence and many Old Norse words are still used. They are, however, very different in character. Green and fertile Orkney is good farming country, while rugged, barren Shetland has traditionally been peopled by fishermen.

FERRY OPERATORS

P&O Scottish Ferries;
tel: (01856) 850655.
Orkney Ferries;
tel: (01856) 872044.
John O'Groats Ferries;
tel: (01955) 611353.

Both archipelagos can be reached by air from Aberdeen. There are also ferry services from Thurso and John O'Groats to Orkney, and between both Aberdeen and Orkney to Shetland.

ORKNEY ISLANDS

Mysterious and alluring, the Orkneys are an archipelago of 70 islands, 13 of which are inhabited. They have the greatest concentration of prehistoric sites in Western Europe. On the largest island, known to Orcadians as Mainland, is the capital, **Kirkwall**. It is dominated by the splendid **St Magnus Cathedral** (open Mon–Sat, services Sun), the most northerly cathedral in Britain. Built of red sandstone it was founded in 1137 by Earl Rognvald Kolson, the Norse ruler of Orkney.

The **Bishop's Palace** (£, open daily 0930–1830 Apr–Sept) dates back to the 12th century and the **Earl's Palace** (joint entry with Bishop's Palace), which was built by a Scottish Earl in 1600, is a good example of French Renaissance architecture. There are also some interesting museums to visit in the town. The **Orkney Museum**, Tankerness House (free, open Mon–Sat 1030–1230, 1330–1700 Oct–Mar; 1030–1700 Apr–Sept; 1400–1700 May–Sept), is set in the town house of an Orkney laird and tells the story of island life. Close to the harbour is the **Wireless Museum** (free, open Mon–Sat 1000–1630, Sun 1400–1630 Apr–Sept), which has exhibits on wartime communication and a large collection of radios.

Travel east of Kirkwall to the part of the island known as East Mainland, and you come to two reminders of the islands' strategic importance during World War II. Not far from the village of St Mary's, joining Mainland to the islands of Burray and South Ronaldsay, are the **Churchill Barriers**. Built on Winston Churchill's orders by Italian prisoners of war, the immense barriers were erected after a German submarine managed to pass through this channel into Scapa Flow, where it torpedoed and sank HMS *Royal Oak*. On the tiny island of Lamb Holm is the remarkable **Italian Chapel**, built in Nissen huts by Italian prisoners of war.

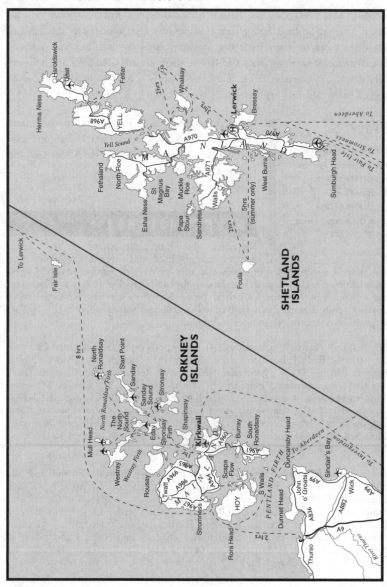

In West Mainland, west of Kirkwall is **Stromness**, Orkney's second largest town. This was a staging post for the Hudson's Bay Company in the 18th century and many Orcadians left from here to work in Canada. Attractions here include the **Stromness Museum** (free, open Mon–Sat 1030–1700, closed 1230–1330 Oct–Apr; daily 1000–1700 May–Sept). Its displays and artefacts on the island's maritime history include the German fleet in Scapa Flow and the Hudson's Bay Company. The **Pier Arts Centre** (free, open daily 1000–1700, closed 1230–1330) is a modern art gallery which often has exhibitions by local artists.

At Sandwick north of Stromness is **Skara Brae** (££, open daily 0930–1830 Apr–Sept; Mon–Sat, 0930–1630, Sun 1400–1630 Oct–Mar), Orkney's most famous attraction. This 5,000-year-old Neolithic village lay buried under the sand dunes at Skaille Bay and was only discovered 100 years ago. The dwellings are perfectly preserved with stone beds, dressers and wall cupboards. A **Skara Brae Visitor Centre** (opening times as Skara Brae) looks at the history of the village and has a replica of one of the houses. Ticket to Skara Brae also includes entry to the 17th-century **Skaill House** (open daily 0930–1830 Apr–Sept). Other ancient sites on Mainland are the **Ring of Brodgar**, a stone circle and **Maeshowe**, Stenness (£, open daily 0930–1830 Apr–Sept; Mon–Sat 0930–1630, Sun 1400–1630 Oct–Mar), a fine chambered tomb built before 2700 BC. It has the largest collection of runic inscriptions in the world.

To the south of Mainland is the island of **Hoy**, famous for its dramatic 450-ft (137-m) sandstone rock stack, the **Old Man of Hoy**. To the north are little islands like Rousay, Eynhallow, Wyre, Westray and Shapinsay. Ferries for many of these Outer Islands leave from Kirkwall. There are also some inter island flights – including the world's shortest scheduled flight between Westray and Papa Westray which has been completed in under a minute.

Buses are there to meet the ferries that arrive at Stromness and Burwick. There are plenty of taxis and car hire firms on Mainland, and many companies also offer bus and boat tours of the islands.

i **Orkney Tourist Board** 6 Broad St, Kirkwall; tel: (01856) 872856; fax: (01856) 875056; website: www.visitorkney.com; e-mail: info@otb.ossian.net. Open Mon–Fri 0830–2000 (May–Sept); Mon–Fri 0930–1700 (Oct–Apr).
Tourist Information Centre Ferry Terminal Building, The Pier Head, Stromness; tel: (01856) 850716; fax: (01856) 850777. Open daily 0900–1600, 2000–2100 (May–Sept); opens to meet ferries 2000–2100 (Oct–Apr).

🏨 **Albert Hotel** ££ Mounthoolie Lane, Kirkwall (Mainland); tel: (01856) 876000; fax: (01856) 875397; e-mail: enquiries@alberthotel.co.uk.
Mill of Eyrland ££ Stenness (Mainland); tel: (01856) 850136; fax: (01856) 851633; website: www.orknet.co.uk/mill; e-mail: kenandmorag@millofeyrland.demon.co.uk. B&B in converted mill.
Girnigoe ££ Shapinsay; tel: (01856) 711256;

e-mail: jean@girnigoe.P9.co.uk. Farmhouse B&B on one of
Orkney's outer islands.
Bellevue Guest House ££ St Margaret's Hope, South
Ronaldsay; tel: (01856) 831294.
Rickla, ££ Harray; tel: (01856) 761575; fax: (01856) 761880;
website: www.rickla.com; e-mail: jacky@rickla.com. Five-star
B&B.
Midhouse ££ Tenston, Sandwick; tel: (01856) 841695; website:
www.midhouseorkney.co.uk; e-mail: midhouse@talk21.com.
B&B in traditional Orkney farmhouse.

SHETLAND ISLANDS

The Shetland Islands are as close to Norway as they are to Scotland and have a distinctly 'foreign' feeling. Shetland was part of the Norse empire for hundreds of years and only became part of Scotland in 1469, when King Christian of Denmark pledged the islands as a dowry for his daughter Margaret, who married James III of Scotland. There are about 100 hundred islands in the archipelago, but only 15 are inhabited.

Shetland's most important attraction is the prehistoric site of **Jarlshof** (open all year) near Sumburgh Head, which was discovered in 1905 when a storm partially uncovered its remains. The site spans 3000 years of settlement: a Bronze Age village, an Iron Age broch and a Viking settlement. The **Jarlshof Visitor Centre** (£, open daily 0930–1830 Apr–Sept) brings the site to life and displays its fascinating history.

The Shetlands are heaven for nature lovers and many seabirds, mammals and wildflowers can be spotted. The sheer cliffs provide homes for species such as puffins, fulmars, storm petrels, kittiwakes and arctic terns while rare birds such as the red-necked phalarope can also be seen. Shetland is also famous for its miniature ponies, and seals, otters, porpoises and dolphins all live in and around the islands.

At **Sumburgh Head Lighthouse** there is an **RSPB Office** (free, open all year), where you have a good chance of spotting puffins and other seabirds between April and mid-August. You can also visit the **Old Scatness Broch Excavations**, Virkie (£, open Sat–Thur

UP HELLY AA

The islands' rich Viking heritage is recalled in the Up Helly Aa festival every January, when islanders celebrate the old new year (before the calendar was changed) with a torch-light procession through the streets. This culminates in the burning of a full size replica of a Viking longship and a lengthy and enthusiastic drinking session. For an introduction to Shetland's Viking festival, visit the **Up Helly Aa Exhibiton** (£, open Tues and Sat, 1400–1600, Tues and Fri 1900–2100 mid-May–mid-Sept) which has a replica galley, costumes and video of the festival.

1000–1700 July–Aug), an on-going archaeological dig where you can get guided tours of an Iron Age village.

Lerwick (the name is Norse for muddy bay) is the capital of Shetland and a busy fishing port. Places of interest include **Fort Charlotte** (free, open daily 0900–2030) which was built to protect the islands from the Dutch, and **Shetland Museum** (free, open Mon, Wed, Fri 1000–1900, Tues, Thur, Sat 1000–1700) which has displays on all aspects of island life, including Pictish and Viking sites, fishing, crofting and knitting. Opposite the museum is the **Town Hall** (free, open variable hours), with beautiful stained glass windows depicting episodes from Shetland's history.

Not far from Lerwick is the **Bod of Gremista** (£, open Wed–Sun, 1000–1300, 1400–1700 June–Sept). This 18th-century fishing booth has been restored as the workplace and residence of the 18th-century factor who was in charge of fish-curing. It was the birthplace of Arthur Anderson, a Shetlander who co-founded P&O Ferries. Also just out of town is the **Clickimin Broch** (free, open 0900–2030 in summer), a defensive fort occupied from 700 BC to around the 6th century. The Bronze Age farmstead was followed by an Iron Age fort. Shetland can be reached by air from Aberdeen and Kirkwall, and also by ferry from Aberdeen and from Stromness. There are plenty of boat trips allowing you to visit the outer islands and you can easily hire a car to get around.

Travel south of Lerwick to Leebitten and you can get a boat to the little island of Mousa (Apr–Sept, arrange with Tom Jamieson, tel: (01595) 431367). This is famous for **Mousa Broch** (free), one of Britain's finest prehistoric relics. It was built in the Iron Age and has chambers, galleries and a staircase. Further south still and you come to the **Croft House Museum**, South Voe, Dunrossness (£, open Mon–Sun 1000–1300, 1400–1700 May–Sept). This restored thatched crofthouse dating from around 1870 is furnished with 19th-century furniture and utensils.

Shetland's other main town is **Scalloway**, the ancient capital, which is dominated by the ruins of **Scalloway Castle**. Other visitor attractions on Shetland include **Tangwick Haa Museum**, Eshaness (free, open Mon–Fri 1300–1700, Sat, Sun 1100–1900 May–Sept), which was once a Laird's house, and the **Bonhoga Gallery**, Weisdale Mill (free, open Tues–Sat, 1030–1630, Sun noon–1630), a former grain mill housing a gallery of arts and crafts.

Orkneys and Shetlands

Alderlodge Guest House ££ 6 Clairmont Place,
Lerwick; tel: (01595) 695705.
Buness Country House £££ Baltasound, Unst; tel: (01957)
711315; fax: (01957) 711815; website: www.users.zetnet.co.uk/
buness-house.
Westayre ££ Muckle Roe, Brae, North Mainland; tel: (01806)
522368.
Whinrig ££ 12 Burgh Rd, Lerwick; tel: (01595) 693554;
e-mail: c.gifford@btinternet.com.

Glasgow is a city that is no longer willing to play second fiddle to Edinburgh. This western metropolis may not be the capital, but is the biggest city in the country and competes with Edinburgh for all major projects, such as new art galleries and infrastructure improvements. It is a gutsy, lively city with plenty of cultural attractions and glorious Victorian architecture. Its Gaelic name, Glas-ghu, means 'dear green place' and it boasts more than 70 parks and gardens. The city is also a good base from which to explore Loch Lomond, the west of Scotland and the Ayrshire coast. Its architectural riches were generated in part by the 18th-century 'tobacco lords', whose wealth from trade funded the city's move into manufacturing and heavy industry in the 19th century. Its industrial heritage gave the city a hard, grimy image for many years.

But during the 1980s it cleaned itself up and reinvented itself, with cool bars, restaurants and shops opening in former warehouses. This renaissance was capped with the designation 'Glasgow European City of Culture' in 1990 and 'UK City of Architecture and Design' in 1999. Today the city is one of Europe's most vibrant cities and is renowned for the range and quality of its fine art galleries and museums. Its fashion-conscious population also ensures that it is an excellent shopping centre, with plenty of designer stores as well as major high street chains. Glasgow's appeal is probably best summed up by the commentator who described the city as 'Manhattan with a Scottish accent'.

GETTING THERE AND GETTING AROUND

Glasgow International **Airport** is just 8 miles (13 km) from the city centre. It receives both scheduled and charter flights from all over the UK, Europe and North America. There are regular shuttle buses to the city centre, and a coach service connects the airport to the national rail network. Prestwick Airport is about 30 miles (48 km) from the city centre and receives flights from London Stansted, Dublin, Paris Beauvais, Frankfurt Hahn and Amsterdam.

GLASGOW

Buchanan Bus Station, Killermont St, is the city's main bus station. Scottish Citylink operate services throughout Scotland, there are also coach services to other parts of the UK. There are also good bus services within the city centre.

There are two main **railway** stations in Glasgow, Central Station and Queen Street, and there are regular services to all parts of Great Britain, as well as to outlying areas of Glasgow. There is a small but efficient underground system – known locally as the clockwork orange – that helps you to get around the city quickly and all-day tickets are available. Scotrail, tel: 08457 484 950, also run daily rail sleeper services between Glasgow and London.

INFORMATION

Glasgow and Clyde Valley Tourist Board 11 George Square, Glasgow; tel: (0141) 204 4400; fax: (0141) 221 3524; website: www.seeglasgow.com; e-mail: enquiries@seeglasgow.com. Open Mon–Sat 0900–1800, Sun 1000–1800 (Easter–May); Mon–Sat 0900–1900, Sun 1000–1800 (June, Sept); Mon–Sat 0900–2000, Sun 1000–1800 (July–Aug); Mon–Sat 0900–1800, closed Sun (Oct–Easter). *The List* is the local weekly entertainment and events guide, available from most newsagents. The publishers also produce an annual eating and drinking guide.

Tourist Information Desk Glasgow Airport; tel: (0141) 848 4440; fax: (0141) 849 1444; e-mail: airport@seeglasgow.com. Open daily 0730–1700.

Argyll, The Isles, Loch Lomond, Stirling & Trossachs Tourist Board Dept SOS, 7 Alexandra Parade, Dunnoon; tel: (01369) 703785; fax: (01369) 706085; website: www.scottish.heartlands.org; e-mail: info@scottish.heartlands.org.

Ayrshire & Arran Tourist Board Customer Information Centre, 15 Skye Rd, Prestwick; tel: (01292) 678100; fax: (01292) 471832; website: www.ayrshire-arran.com; e-mail: info@ayrshire-arran.com.

Dumfries & Galloway Tourist Board 64 Whitesands, Dumfries; tel: (01387) 253862; fax: (01387) 245555; website: www.dumfries-and-galloway.co.uk; e-mail: info@dgtb.ossian.net.

MONEY Foreign exchange is available in the main Post Office on St Vincent St, in the tourist information centre on George Square and at a branch of Thomas Cook on Gordon St.

POST The main Post Office is close to the tourist information centre on St Vincent St.

ACCOMMODATION

The Belgrave Guest House ££ 2 Belgrave Terrace, Hillhead, Glasgow; tel: (0141) 337 1850; fax: (0141) 337 1741; website:

The universities of both Glasgow and Strathclyde offer B&B accommodation in campus residences during university vacations.

University of Glasgow
££, various locations; tel: Freephone 0800 027 2030; (0141) 330 5385; fax: (0141) 334 5465; website: www.gla.ac.uk/ vacationaccommodation; e-mail: vacation@gla.ac.uk.

University of Strathclyde ££, various locations; tel: (0141) 553 4148; fax: (0141) 553 4149; website: www.strath.ac.uk/ departments/rescat/ sales/index.

www.belgraveguesthouse.co.uk; e-mail: belgraveguesthse@ hotmail.com. Small guest house in the trendy area of Hillhead, close to the university.

The Flower House £££ 33 St Vincent Crescent, Glasgow; tel: (0141) 204 2846; fax: (0141) 226 5130, website: www. scotland2000.com/flowerhouse, e-mail: docherty33@ lineone.net. Small three-star B&B in the West End of the city.

Glasgow Youth Hostel £ 7/8 Park Terrace; tel: (0141) 332 3004. Excellent position in a fine West End terrace.

Kirklee Hotel £££ 11 Kensington Gate, Glasgow; tel: (0141) 334 5555; fax: (0141) 339 3828; website: www.scotland2000.com/ kirklee; e-mail: kirklee@clara.net. This Edwardian townhouse full of character is set in the West End's conservation area.

Manor Park Hotel £££ 28 Balshagray Drive, Glasgow; tel: (0141) 339 2143; fax: (0141) 339 5842; e-mail: manorparkhotel@ aol.com. The speaking of Gaelic is promoted in this hotel in the fashionable West End of Glasgow.

The Merchant Lodge £££ 52 Virginia St, Glasgow; tel: (0141) 552 2424; fax: (0141) 552 4747; website: www.hotelsglasgow. com; e-mail: kdmcmillan@msn.com. Former home of one of Glasgow's tobacco lords, now restored and converted into a comfortable hotel.

New Lanark Mill Hotel £££ Mill One, New Lanark, Lanark; tel: (01555) 667200; fax: (01555) 667222; website: www. newlanark.org; e-mail: hotel@newlanark.org. New Lanark is a World Heritage site, a former industrial planned village. The hotel is in a converted 18th-century mill, overlooking the river Clyde. It is about an hour's drive from Glasgow.

The Old School House ££ Gartocharn, by Loch Lomond; tel: (01389) 830373. Comfortable B&B in a rural setting near the village of Gartocharn and a short distance from Loch Lomond.

The Old School House ££–£££ 194 Renfrew St, Glasgow; tel: (0141) 332 7600; fax: (0141) 332 8684. Small hotel situated in a conservation area a short walk from the city centre.

Park House ££ 13 Victoria Park Gdns South, Broomhill, Glasgow; tel: (0141) 339 1559; fax: (0141) 576 0915; website: www.xwf54.dial.pipex.com; e-mail: richardanddi.parkhouse. glasgow@dial.pipex.com. Comfortable B&B in large Victorian house a short distance from the centre of the city.

Radisson £££–££££ 301 Argyle St, Glasgow; tel: (0141) 204 3333, website: www.radisson.com. Opened in 2002, this 4-star hotel boasts Scandinavian chic and a health spa. Internet special rates are good value, especially at weekends.

FOOD AND DRINK

Air Organic ££–£££ 36 Kelvingrove St. Trendy restaurant serving light, Asian inspired meals and using mostly organic produce.

The Ashoka ££–£££ 108 Elderslie St. Family-run Indian that has been going strong for 20 years.

Babbity Bowster £–££ 16–18 Blackfriars St. Long established city bar that also serves substantial meals and sandwiches.

Brel Bar ££ 39–43 Ashton Lane. Brel is a trendy bar serving Belgian beers and Belgian food. There is a food 'happy hour' from 1700–1900 every day.

Café Gandolfi £–££ 64 Albion St. This café/restaurant is a Glasgow institution. It serves mainly Scottish food.

Fratelli Sarti £££–££££ 42 Renfield St. Very popular and atmospheric Italian restaurant.

Grassroots Café £££ 97 St Georges Rd. Imaginative and upmarket vegetarian food.

Killermont Polo Club ££–£££ 20–22 Maryhill Rd. Unusual and delicious Indian cuisine served in stylish surroundings.

Nice 'n' Sleazy ££–£££ 421 Sauchiehall St. Not as nefarious as the name suggests, but good pub food with veggie haggis and huge Scottish breakfasts.

Shish Mahal £££ 60–68 Park Rd. Great Indian food in one of Glasgow's most popular restaurants.

Toast £ 86 Albion St. Contemporary café serving tasty and imaginative snacks on toast.

Ubiquitous Chip ££–££££ 12 Ashton Lane. One of Scotland's most famous restaurants for three decades, serving top-notch modern Scottish in the main restaurant and more informal cuisine in the bar area.

Uisge Beatha £–££ 232–246 Woodlands Rd. The 'Water of Life' has over 120 single malt whiskies, but also good bar food and truly unique Scottish theme décor.

The Willow Tea Room £–££ 217 Sauchiehall St. This traditional tea room is famous for its original Charles Rennie Mackintosh interior. Touristy but worth a visit.

HIGHLIGHTS

Art Gallery and Museum Kelvingrove, free, open Mon–Sat 1000–1700, Sun 1100–1700. This imposing red sandstone building filled with treasures has relics of Scotland's history and prehistory, silver, ceramics, furniture, arms and armour and natural history. There is also an extensive collection of paintings from Britain and Europe. Scottish artists are well represented as are the Impressionists.

CHARLES RENNIE MACKINTOSH

One of Glasgow's most influential figures was **Charles Rennie Mackintosh** (1868–1928), the architect and designer, who helped to shape European Art Nouveau. He was a strong influence on the development of the 'Glasgow style' and enjoyed much critical acclaim. His work can be seen throughout Glasgow in public buildings, houses and tea rooms – and he also created distinctive furniture designs, easily recognisable for their crisp, clean lines.

His masterpiece is the **Glasgow School of Art**, 167 Renfrew St (££, guided tours Sept–Jun, Mon–Fri 1100 & 1400, Sat 1030, 1130; Jul–Aug, Mon–Fri 1100 & 1400, Sat, 1030, 1130 & 1300) – the library is particularly famous. It is also worth taking a trip to **House for an Art Lover,** Bellahouston Park (££, open Apr–Oct, Sun–Thur 1000–1600, Sat 1000–1500), a house built following original designs by Mackintosh. **Scotland Street School Museum**, Scotland St (free, open Mon–Thur & Sat 1000–1700, Fri & Sat 1100–1700), is a former school designed by Mackintosh. It now looks at the history of education and has several recreated classrooms from the Victorian era to the 1960s. **The Lighthouse**, 11 Mitchell Lane (£, open Mon, Wed, Fri & Sat 1030–1730, Tues 1100–1730, Thur 1000–1900, Sun noon–1700): housed in a Mackintosh designed building, this is Scotland's centre for Architecture, Design and the City and has a changing programme of exhibitions and also includes the Mackintosh Interpretation Centre, devoted to the work of the designer. The **Hunterian Art Gallery**, University of Glasgow, 82 Hillhead St, free open Mon–Sat 0930–1700 (Mackintosh House closed daily 1230–1330) contains parts of Mackintosh's former home, together with the original furniture that he designed. The gallery is also worth a visit for its important collection of works by Whistler, as well as paintings by the Scottish landscape painter William McTaggart, the Glasgow Boys and the Scottish Colourists.

The Burrell Collection, Pollok Country Park, 2060 Pollokshaws Rd, free, open Mon–Sat 1000–1700, Sun 1100–1700. This is undoubtedly one of the finest art collections in Britain, if not Europe. It was acquired by one man, Sir William Burrell, a prosperous Glaswegian shipowner, and reflects his personal taste, foresight and achievement. Among the highlights are artefacts from ancient Egypt and Greece, Oriental art, exquisite medieval tapestries, stained glass, paintings and sculpture (including Rodin's famous *Thinker*). The collection is housed in a splendid woodland setting and some artefacts, such as ancient arches, are set into the fabric of the building.

A visit to this elegant Georgian country house can be conveniently combined with a trip to the Burrell Collection. **Pollok House**, Pollok Country Park, 2060 Pollokshaws Rd, Apr–Oct, ££, Nov–Mar free; open daily 1000–1700 (Apr–Oct); 1100–1600 (Nov–Mar). Situated in an extensive country park, its treasures include a fine collection of Spanish painting.

Housed in the Royal Exchange building, the **Gallery of Modern Art** is a collection of contemporary art featuring the works of artists from 1950 to the present day. There are four floors to explore and works by artists such as Beryl Cook and Peter Howson are represented. Queen St, free, open Mon–Thur and Sat 1000–1700, Fri and Sun 1100–1700.

Glasgow

Dating back to the 12th century, **Glasgow Cathedral** is a stunning Gothic gem of Scottish medieval architecture. It is the only medieval Scottish church on the mainland to have survived the Reformation complete. It is associated with St Mungo, Glasgow's patron saint, who founded a church here in the 7th century. Cathedral Square, free, open Mon–Sat 0930–1800, Sun 1400–1700 (Apr–Sept); Mon–Sat 0930–1600, Sun 1400–1600 (Oct–Mar).

St Mungo Museum of Religious Life and Art, 2 Castle St, free, open Mon–Thur and Sat 1000–1700, Fri and Sun 1100–1700. This fascinating small museum provoked controversy when it first opened, for its portrayal of religious and spiritual beliefs and symbols around the world. Exhibits include Salavador Dalí's painting *Christ of St John of the Cross*, Aboriginal paintings and an Islamic prayer rug. Outside is Britain's only authentic Japenese Zen garden.

People's Palace, Glasgow Green, free, Mon–Thur and Sat 1000–1700, Fri and Sun 1100–1700. This entertaining and enlightening museum tells the story of the people of Glasgow and looks at popular culture and working class life. Refurbished galleries contain evocative objects, photographs and film sequences that really bring the city's past to life.

Museum of Transport, 1 Burnhouse Rd, Kelvinhall, free, open Mon–Thur and Sat 1000–1700, Fri and Sun 1100–1700. This popular museum has a delightful array of trains, trams, buses, cars and bicycles. The Clyde room contains models of ships built in Scotland's shipyards and there is also a construction of an imaginary Glasgow street of 1938.

The **Waverley** is the world's last sea-going paddle steamer and was launched in 1947. She was one of a number of Clyde pleasure boats that used to take holiday makers to resorts along the coast and has recently been refitted to her original 1940s splendour. Waverley Excursions Ltd, tel: (0141) 243 2224, are running trips along the Firth of Clyde from June–Aug. Trips last from 1½ hrs to all day and cover the main lochs and islands of the Clyde.

Provand's Lordship, 3 Castle St, free, open Mon–Thur and Sat 1000–1700, Fri and Sun 1100–1700. This is the oldest house in Glasgow, dating back to 1471. It was built as a clergyman's house and has period displays of furniture and a medieval style garden. **The Tenement House**, 145 Buccleuch St, Garnethill, ££, open Mar–Oct, daily 1400–1700. This house is in practically the same condition as it was when its owner Miss Agnes Toward moved in with her mother in 1911 and is a fascinating slice of social history.

Tours You can take classic city bus tours of Glasgow with **Scotguide Tourist Services**, tel: (0141) 204 0444, and **Guide Friday**, tel: (0141) 248 7644. Both companies allow you to hop on and off the bus as often as you want. You can also take an amphibious tour with **glasgowDucks** (£££) tel: (0141) 572 8381 who provide a 90-min road and river tour of the city.

You can also take **walking tours** of the city with Mercat Tours, tel: (0141) 772 0022, who have daily tours on specialised themes such as Historic Glasgow.

SHOPPING

Glasgow is one of the best shopping cities in Britain – particularly for designer clothing. One of the newest shopping centres is **Buchanan Galleries**, Buchanan St, which has a large branch of John Lewis as well as many high street chains such as H&M and Mango.

The **Italian Centre** in the old Merchant City is one of the coolest places to shop, boasting the UK's first Versace store, plus Armani and other designer shops. **Princes Square**, Buchanan St, is an extremely stylish centre set in a renovated 19th-century square. It has a Rennie Mackintosh theme and contains designer stores, classy crafts and cafés. Sauchiehall St and Buchanan St are both bustling with shoppers, while at **Victorian Village**, 93 West Regent St, you can browse for antiques, retro clothing and jewellery.

NIGHTLIFE

There is plenty to do in the city at night, with lots of restaurants as well as cool, trendy bars such as Bar 91, Café Clear, Oko and Strata. Clubs worth checking out include the Arches, Midland St, the gay club Polo Lounge, Wilson St and the unpretentious Fury Murry's on Maxwell St.

Glasgow's Science Centre, 50 Pacific Quay, has Scotland's first IMAX cinema, while the Theatre Royal, Hope St, stages performances by Scottish Ballet and Scottish Opera, as well as drama productions. The King's Theatre, Bath St, presents musicals and pantomimes and the Royal Concert Hall, 2 Sauchiehall St, attracts world famous artistes.

SIDE TRIPS

New Lanark World Heritage Village New Lanark Mills, Lanark (££, open Mon–Sun 1100–1700). New Lanark was built in the 18th century as a planned industrial settlement, using the nearby Falls of Clyde to power lucrative cotton mills. Housing was

It is easy to take a day trip from Glasgow to **Loch Lomond**, Scotland's first national park, although you are best to hire a car as public transport is not very frequent. Heading out from Glasgow, stop at the pretty village of Drymen, where you can have lunch, then drive to Balmaha, a little settlement right on the water's edge. Alternatively, drive along the western bank of the loch to the resorts of Balloch and Luss, where you can take boat trips on the loch. Ben Lomond at the top of the loch is one of the most popular climbs in Scotland.

i **Balloch TIC** Balloch Rd, Balloch; tel: (01389) 753533. Open daily Apr and Sept–Oct 1000–1700, May and June 0930–1800, July 0930–1830, Aug 0930–1800.

Drymen TIC Drymen Library, The Square, Drymen; tel: (01360) 660068. Open daily, May–mid-July and Sept 1000–1700, Jul, Aug 1000–1800.

The train journey from **Glasgow to Fort William** (see pp. 325–326) is very scenic and a great way of exploring the Western Highlands. The train stops at stations such as Ardlui, Crianlarich, Tyndrum, Bridge of Orchy, and Rannoch and essentially follows the same route as the West Highland Way. Places such as Bridge of Orchy are delightful and extremely peaceful, while Rannoch is the stop for the windy, moody expanse of Rannoch Moor. At **Crianlarich** you can get a train to Oban, while trains leave Fort William for Mallaig, one of the most scenic stretches of railway in the world. Highland Rover tickets give you the freedom of the line for four days (to be used within a period of eight days) so that you can get off and explore an area in detail. In the summer 'The Jacobite' steam train runs from Fort William to Mallaig.

i **Tyndrum TIC** Main St, Tyndrum; tel: (01838) 400246. Open daily 1000–1700 Apr; 1000–1800 June; 0930–1800 July–Aug; 1000–1700 Sept–Oct.

🛏 **Bridge of Orchy Hotel** ££–£££, Bridge of Orchy, Argyll; tel: (01838) 400208; fax: (01838) 400313; e-mail: bridgeoforchy@onyxnet.co.uk. This hotel is situated by the Orchy River and has refurbished rooms as well as modern bunkhouse accommodation.

provided for the mill workers. In the early 19th century the new manager Robert Owen turned the village into a Utopian ideal, introducing education for the workers' small children, free medical care and banishing child labour. The village has been carefully conserved and gives a fascinating insight into the past.

You can also walk from the village to the Falls of Clyde, a stunning waterfall situated in a nature reserve. New Lanark can be reached by car, or by train from Glasgow to Lanark and then a bus.

STIRLING

Stirling is one of Scotland's most historic cities and is popularly known as the gateway to the highlands. It can be reached by train from Glasgow but a car will give far more flexibility to allow you to explore the surrounding area.

The great battles of the Wars of Independence – Bannockburn and Stirling Bridge – were fought here, and **Stirling Castle** (££, open Apr–Sept, daily 0930–1830,

Oct–Mar, daily, 0930–1700), favoured residence of the Stuart monarchs, remains the centrepiece of the old town. It dominates the surrounding countryside from a dramatic rocky outcrop.

The other major attraction is the striking **National Wallace Monument** £, open Jan–Feb 1000–1600, Mar–May & Oct 1000–1700, Jun–Sept 1000–1800, July and Aug 1000–1830. This commemorates William Wallace, Scotland's national hero, who defeated the English army at the Battle of Stirling Bridge in 1297. It is a steep climb to reach the tower and you have to climb almost 250 steps if you want to get to the top of the monument itself, but it does provide one of the best viewpoints of the surrounding country. A short drive from Stirling is Bannockburn, the site of Robert the Bruce's victory over the English army in 1314. You can visit the **Bannockburn Heritage Centre**, £, open Mar and Nov–Dec, daily 1100–1500, Apr–Oct, daily 1000–1730, and also see the famous battlesite.

The Trossachs, a national park since 2002, are often described as the Highlands in miniature and the term is used to describe the area roughly from the east of Loch Lomond to the attractive town of Callander. This is Rob Roy country, the area once frequented by the famous Scottish outlaw and cattle rustler. **Callander** and **Aberfoyle** both make good centres from which to explore the Trossachs, particularly if you want to do some of the area's many excellent country walks. Other attractive towns a short drive from Stirling are Dunblane, Doune and Crieff.

i **Royal Burgh of Stirling Visitor Centre** Castle Esplanade, Stirling; tel: (01786) 479901; fax: (01786) 451881; e-mail: info@rbsvc.visitscotland.com. Open daily 0900–1700 (Oct–Mar), 0930–1800 (Apr–mid-Jun), 0900–1830 (Jun–mid-Aug), 0930–1800 (Aug–Oct). There is also a **tourist information centre** at 41 Dumbarton Road; tel: (01786) 475019, ring to check opening times.

Rob Roy & Trossachs Visitor Centre Ancaster Square, Callander; tel: (01877) 330342; fax: (01877) 330784; e-mail: info@callander.visitscotland.com. Tourist information plus exhibition on Rob Roy MacGregor £. Open daily 1000–1700 (Mar–May & Oct–Dec), 0930–1800 (Jun), 0900–2200 (Jul–Aug), 1000–1800 (Sept), Sat & Sun 1100–1630 (Jan–Feb).

Trossachs Discovery Centre Main St, Aberfoyle; tel: (01877) 382352. fax: (01877) 382153; e-mail: info@aberfoyle. visitscotland.com. Tourist information centre and visitor centre open daily 1000–1700 (Apr–Jun & Sept–Oct), 0930–1800 (Jul, Aug), Sat & Sun 1000–1600 (Nov–Mar).

🏠 **Leny House** ££££ Callander, Perthshire; tel: (01877) 331078; fax: (01877) 331335; website: www.lenyestate.com; e-mail: res@lenyestate.com. This historic house is set in its

own grounds and offers luxurious B&B accommodation.
Culcreuch Castle and Country Park £££–££££ Culcreuch
Castle, Fintry, Stirlingshire; tel: (01360) 860555; fax: (01360)
860556; website: www.culcreuch.com. This 700-year-old castle
is set in a huge parkland estate.
Kippenross £££ Dunblane, Perthshire; tel; (01786) 824048;
fax: (01786) 823124. Just a short drive from Stirling, this
Georgian country house offers high quality B&B. It is situated
in secluded parkland.

WHERE NEXT?

*From Glasgow you can head south down the Ayrshire coast to popular holiday resorts such as
Largs, Irvine and Troon, as well as the magnificent stately home Culzean Castle. From
Ardrossan, south of Largs, you can take a ferry to **Arran**, an accessible and popular island
which offers some excellent walking. Further south you come to **Dumfries and Galloway**,
with its strong associations with Robert Burns. Alternatively, you can head east to historic and
lively Edinburgh (see pp. 272–280) or travel north to the beautiful Highlands and Western
Isles (see pp. 297–304).*

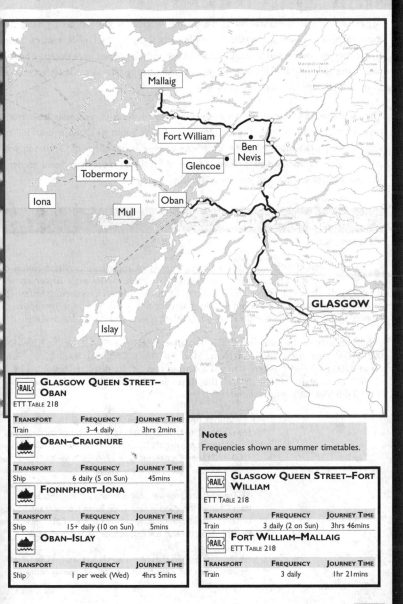

ETT TABLE 218

TRANSPORT	FREQUENCY	JOURNEY TIME
Train	3–4 daily	3hrs 2mins

OBAN–CRAIGNURE

TRANSPORT	FREQUENCY	JOURNEY TIME
Ship	6 daily (5 on Sun)	45mins

FIONNPHORT–IONA

TRANSPORT	FREQUENCY	JOURNEY TIME
Ship	15+ daily (10 on Sun)	5mins

OBAN–ISLAY

TRANSPORT	FREQUENCY	JOURNEY TIME
Ship	1 per week (Wed)	4hrs 5mins

Notes

Frequencies shown are summer timetables.

RAIL **GLASGOW QUEEN STREET–FORT WILLIAM**

ETT TABLE 218

TRANSPORT	FREQUENCY	JOURNEY TIME
Train	3 daily (2 on Sun)	3hrs 46mins

RAIL **FORT WILLIAM–MALLAIG**

ETT TABLE 218

TRANSPORT	FREQUENCY	JOURNEY TIME
Ship	3 daily	1hr 21mins

ARGYLL AND THE INNER HEBRIDES

Argyll's scenery is quintessential Scotland, with wooded slopes bordering delightful lochs and glens. Thanks to the mild climate brought about by the Gulf Stream, rare and exotic species flourish and beautiful gardens have been developed here since the beginning of the 18th century. This area is a very popular touring spot as it is easily accessible from Glasgow and offers plenty of variety.

The busy town of Oban is known as the Gateway to the Isles, as ferries leave from here to the islands of Mull, Tiree, Colonsay and Islay. South of Oban is the Mull of Kintyre, which has more frequent ferry links to Islay. Travel north of Oban and you come to Fort William, which is close to some of Scotland's most magnificent scenery and the start of a scenic rail journey to Mallaig.

GLASGOW – IONA

GLASGOW See p. 311.

OBAN Set around its picturesque harbour, Oban is an important ferry terminal and a popular tourist centre. Its unmissable landmark is **McCaig's Tower**, sometimes called McCaig's Folly, which is a replica of the Roman Colosseum. Intended as a family memorial, it was built by a local banker to provide work for unemployed stonemasons. When the banker died, so did the project, and it remains unfinished.

Other attractions include the **Oban Distillery**, Stafford St (££, open Mon–Sat 0930–1700 Apr–June and Oct–Nov; Mon–Fri 0930–2030, Sat 0930–1700, Sun, noon–1700 July–Sept), where you get a 40-min tour of the distillery followed by a chance to taste the product, and the **Rare Breeds Farm Park** (££, open daily 1000–1730 Mar–Oct, later in summer).

i **Tourist Information Centre** Argyll Square; tel: (01631) 563122; fax: (01631) 564273; website: www.scottishheartlands.org; e-mail: info@oban.org.uk. Open Mon–Fri 0900–1700, Sat–Sun 1000–1700 (Apr–Oct; closes later Jul–Aug); Mon–Sat 0930–1700, Sat 1200–1600 (Nov–Mar).

Ferries leave Oban for Craignure on Mull. You can also sail from Oban to the island of Coll, Tiree, Barra, Colonsay and South Uist. For information on ferry services contact Caledonian MacBrayne; tel: (01475) 650100, website: www.calmac.co.uk.

There is plenty of accommodation in and around Oban, ranging from hotels and B&Bs to hostels and self catering cottages.

Foxholes Country Hotel £££ Cologin, Lerags, by Oban; tel: (01631) 564982; fax: (01631) 570890. Peaceful B&B in secluded glen outside Oban.

Dungallan House Hotel £££ Gallanach Rd, Oban; tel: (01631) 563799; fax: (01631) 566711; website: www.dungallanhotel-oban. co.uk; e-mail: welcome@dungallanhotel-oban.co.uk. Victorian villa with good views over Oban and out to the islands.

Barriemore Hotel ££ Corran Esplanade; Oban, tel: (01631) 566356. Once home of the McCaig family, this restored Victorian house has beautifully appointed rooms.

Lerags House, ££ Lerags, By Oban; tel: (01631) 563381; e-mail: leragshouse@supanet.com. Georgian country house on the shores of Loch Feochan.

🆃🅾 **The Waterfront Restaurant £££–££££,** 1 The Waterfront, The Pier, Oban. Fresh fish and seafood are the specialities at this harbourside restaurant, which also serves light meals and coffees in the morning.

MULL Mull is the second largest island of the Inner Hebrides. Its 300 miles (483 km) of coastline are rocky, jagged and cut by deep sea lochs. The island has some beautiful stretches of coastline, but much of the interior is moorland. **Craignure**, the main ferry terminal, is close to two of the island's main sights.

Torosay Castle (££, open daily, 1030–1730 Apr–mid-Oct), built in 1856, is actually a Victorian mansion. Its highlight is the Italian terraced garden, graced with statues. You can reach the castle from Craignure on the island's **miniature railway** (£, daily 1100–1700 Easter–mid-Oct). Further down the road is **Duart Castle,** Craignure (££, open daily 1030–1800 May–Oct), built in the 13th century and home of the Maclean clan chiefs. In the north of the island at Dervaig, the **Old Byre Heritage Centre** (open daily 1030–1830, Easter–Oct) has tableaux depicting island life through the ages.

The main town on the island, **Tobermory** has a lovely sheltered harbour lined with tall, brightly painted houses. The harbour is a popular yachting centre, as well as a fishing, diving and cruising port. It also contains a lost treasure. In 1588 a Spanish galleon was blown up in the harbour along with its hoard of gold, most of which has never been found. Whisky lovers can take a tour of the island's only distillery, **Tobermory Distillers** (£, open Mon–Fri 1000–1700, Easter–Oct).

ℹ️ **Tourist Information Centre** Main St, The Pier, Tobermory; tel: (01688) 302182; fax: (01688) 302145. Open Mon–Fri 1000–1700, Sat, Sun 1200–1700 (Apr); Mon–Sat 1000–1700, Sun 1100–1700 (May–July); Mon–Sat 0930–1800, Sun 1000–1700 (July–Sept); Mon–Sat 1000–1700, Sun 1200–1700 (Sept–Oct).

🏨 **Highland Cottage** ££££ Breadalbane St, Tobermory; tel: (01688) 302030; fax: (01688) 302727; website: www.highland cottage.co.uk; e-mail: davidandjo@highlandcottage.co.uk. Quality hotel built in the conservation area of Tobermory.
Druimnacroish Hotel £££ Dervaig; tel: (01688) 400274; website: www.druimnacroish.co.uk; e-mail: info-tb@ druimnacroish.co.uk. Country house in a peaceful setting.
Gruline Home Farm ££ Gruline; tel: (01680) 300581; fax: (01680) 300573; website: www.gruline.com; e-mail: stb@ gruline.com. Five-star B&B in former Victorian farmhouse.

IONA

Iona is a tiny island known as the cradle of Scottish Christianity. St Columba landed here from Ireland in 563 and set up a monastery whose influence spread throughout the land. Archaeological evidence suggests that the island had long been a pagan centre of worship as well as becoming the burial place of Scottish kings. The island was viciously sacked by Viking raiders in the 8th century and Columba's original wooden monastery was destroyed. Later the Benedictines established an abbey here in 1203 which fell into disrepair after the Reformation. To reach Iona you need to travel across Mull from Craignure on the A849 to Fionnphort. From here you take the ferry for a 5-min crossing to the island.

ST COLUMBA

St Columba was born in Donegal, Ireland, in AD 521. In 561 he was exiled from Ireland for his part in a family conflict and sailed to Iona with his followers to pursue a monastic life. He is said to have written over 300 books as well as calculating solar and lunar cycles to determine the date of Easter and other Christian holy days. He died on Iona at the age of 75.

The little island contains the ruins of a 13th-century Augustinian **nunnery**, while the restored **Abbey Church** (£, shop open daily 0930–1830, Apr–Sept; 0930–1630, Oct–Mar) is about a 10-min walk away. The tiny **St Columba's Shrine** is said to be the saint's original burial place. Iona's oldest building is **St Oran's Chapel**, set in the early Christian graveyard where kings from Kenneth MacAlpin to Malcolm III are reputedly buried. The **Iona Heritage Centre** (£, open Mon–Sat 1030–1630 Easter–Oct) has displays on crofting, fishing and island life.

🏨 Accommodation is limited on tiny Iona so you are advised to book beforehand.
Argyll Hotel, Iona; tel: (01681) 700334; fax: (01681) 700510; website: www.argyllhoteliona.co.uk, e-mail: reception@argyllhoteliona.co.uk.
St Columba Hotel, Iona; tel: (01681) 700304; fax: (01681) 700688, e-mail: columba@btinternet.com.

ISLAY

Islay is famous for its peaty-tasting whiskies like Laphroaig, Ardbeg and Bowmore. It is also home to large flocks of barnacle and white-fronted geese, as well as red deer, wild goats and otters. At the **Museum of Islay Life,** Port Charlotte (£, open Mon–Sat 1000–1700, Sun 1400–1700 Apr–Oct), you can see fascinating artefacts found on the island dating back to Mesolithic times – 8000 BC. At the **RSPB Loch Gruinart Nature Reserve** Bridgend (free, open daily 1000–1700), you can watch the island's incredible variety of bird life.

⚓ There is only one sailing a week from Oban to Islay. The journey takes about 2 hrs 15 mins and you travel via the small island of Colonsay. Alternatively there are daily sailings from Kennacraig on the Mull of Kintyre.

i **Tourist Information Centre** The Square, Bowmore; tel: (01496) 810254; fax: (01496) 810363; e-mail: info@islay. visitscotland.com. Open Mon–Sat 1000–1700 (Apr); Mon–Sat 0930–1700/1730, Sun 1400–1700 (May–Sept); Mon–Sat 1000–1700 (Sept–Oct); Mon–Fri, noon–1600 (Oct–Mar).

🏠 **Kilmeny Country Guest House** £££ Ballygrant; tel: (01496) 840668; website: www.kilmeny.co.uk **Glenmachrie Farmhouse** £££ Port Ellen; tel. (01496) 302560; website: www.isle-of-islay.com/group/guest/ glenmachrie; e-mail: glenmachrie@isle-of-islay.com.

GLASGOW – MALLAIG

GLASGOW See p. 311.

FORT WILLIAM   Fort William stretches along the shores of Loch Linnhe. Lying at the foot of Britain's highest mountain, Ben Nevis, it is a popular base for climbers and walkers. The fort for which the town was named is long gone, replaced by the train station and the Victorian town that grew up around it. The **West Highland Museum** (£, open Mon–Sat 1000–1600, July and Aug, also Sun 1400–1700) is well laid out and has good Jacobite collections.

i **Tourist Information Centre** Cameron Centre, Cameron Sq; tel: (01397) 703781; fax: (01397) 705184; e-mail: fortwilliam@ host.co.uk. Open Mon–Sat 0900–1900/2030, Sun 1000–1800 (June–Aug); Mon–Sat, 0900–1900, Sun 1000–1800 (Aug–Sept); Mon–Sat 0900–1700/1730, Sun 1000–1600; (Sept–June).

🏠 **Distillery Guest House** ££–£££ Nevis Bridge, Fort William; tel: (01397) 700103; website: www.fort-william.net/ distillery-house; e-mail: disthouse@aol.com.

Guisachan House ££ Alma Rd, Fort William; tel: (01397) 703797; website: www.fort-william.net/guisachanhouse; e-mail: info@stablesrooms.fsnet.co.uk

From Fort William it is only a few miles to the beautiful valley of **Glen Nevis**, which nestles beneath the slopes of **Ben Nevis** – a challenging climb not to be taken by the inexperienced or ill prepared. There is a **Visitor Centre** (open Apr–Oct) at the foot of the road which has an exhibition on the area's natural history and information on walks in the area.

Drive or take a bus south along the A82 and you can also visit **Glencoe**, scene of the infamous massacre of 1692 when William of Orange's soldiers – members of the Campbell clan – took the lives of their hosts, the MacDonalds. It is a haunting and brooding place with a melancholy atmosphere. There is a **Glencoe Visitor Centre** (£, open daily 1000–1700 Mar–Apr and Sept–Oct; daily 0930–1730 May–Aug) which has a film about the massacre.

EN ROUTE

The **Glenfinnan Monument** (£) is a memorial to the sacrifice of the Highlanders in the Jacobite cause. The **Visitor Centre** (open daily 1000–1700 Apr–mid-May and Sept–Oct; daily 0930–1800 mid-May–Aug) tells the story of the Jacobite campaign. **Glenfinnan Station Museum** (£, open daily June–Sept) has exhibitions on the West Highland Railway.

MALLAIG The rail journey from Fort William to Mallaig is one of the most scenic in Britain; taking about 1 hr and 20 mins. Steam trains run along the line June–Sept; to book, tel: Jacobite Steam Train (01463) 239026. The **Mallaig Heritage Centre** (£, open Mon–Sat, 1100–1600 Apr–Oct) has exhibits on fishing and the Knoydart Clearances.

ⓘ **Tourist Information Centre** Mallaig; tel: (01687) 462170; fax: (01687) 462064. Open Mon–Sat 0900–1830, Sun 1000–1700 (May, June); Mon–Sat 0900–2000, Sun 1000–1700 (July–Aug); Mon–Fri 1000–1800 (Sept–Oct); call to check other hours.

🏨 **West Highland Hotel** £££, Mallaig; tel: (01687) 462210; fax: (01687) 462130; website: www.westhighlandhotel.co.uk; e-mail: westhighland.hotel@virgin.net.

WHERE NEXT?

From Fort William you can travel further north to Inverness (see pp. 294–295), or south to the city of Glasgow (see pp. 311–317). From Oban you can visit some of Scotland's other islands such as Coll and Tiree.

Belfast received its borough status in 1613, but its real growth and prosperity took place in the 19th and early 20th centuries. It had the world's greatest shipyard (Harland and Wolff – still a major employer), the most extensive ropeworks ever built and the world's largest weaving and tobacco factories. Linen is still a favourite memento for visitors to take home.

Small and compact, Belfast has blossomed anew since the signing of the Good Friday agreement into a vital, buzzing city. It combines fine Victorian architecture and an absorbing history with quality developments, great entertainment and a not-to-be-missed eating and drinking scene. It is no wonder that Belfast has emerged as a big name in city tourism. You won't meet more hospitable people anywhere.

GETTING AROUND

Belfast Central Railway Station; tel: (028) 9089 9411. Passengers can use their rail tickets for a free bus ride calling at the Europa Bus Centre, Glengall St, and Laganside Bus Centre, near the Albert Clock. It also drops off passengers at Belfast International Hostel, Donegall Rd.

CityBus services, tel: (028) 9024 6485, begin and end around City Hall. A single journey costs under £1. Multi-journey tickets and travel cards are sold at the CityBus kiosk, Donegall Sq., and shops showing the CityBus sticker.

The green **Centralink 100** 'circle line' bus is a boon for visitors. It goes to all the attractions in the main downtown area and the service runs every 12 mins.

INFORMATION

Belfast Welcome Centre, 35 Donegall Pl., Belfast BT1 5AD; tel: (028) 9024 6609; fax: (028) 9031 2424; website: www.gotobelfast.com; e-mail: belfastwelcomecentre@nitic.net. Open Mon–Sat 0900–1900, Sun 1200–1700 (June–Sept); Mon–Sat 0900–1730 (Oct–May).

BELFAST

MONEY Foreign currency can be exchanged at the Thomas Cook bureaux de change at 11 Donegall Pl. and 22–24 Lombard St. Northern Ireland's currency is the pound sterling (as in the rest of the UK). The province has two different designs for its pound coins; one depicting flax and the other showing the gold collar – a famous archaeological find – superimposed on a Celtic cross. Major banks and some tourist information centres also change currency.

POST AND PHONES The main post offices in Belfast, all with *poste restante* facilities, are at Donegall Sq., Castle Pl., and Shaftesbury Sq. There are public payphone kiosks throughout the city and province.

ACCOMMODATION

Accommodation throughout the province and the republic can be booked on freephone, tel: 00080 6686 6866 or 0800 783 5740. Accommodation in Northern Ireland can be booked online; website: www.discovernorthernireland.com.

As well as the usual range of B&Bs and guest houses of a good standard – mostly ££ – budget accommodation can be found at three hostels and two campuses during university vacations. Contact **Belfast Visitor and Convention Bureau** for a booklet listing the city's variety of accommodation.

FOOD AND DRINK

Belfast has more than 450 eating places. Those on a budget can get an all-day breakfast – the famous and fortifying Ulster Fry – from between £2 and £4. You may come across excellent Irish stew in a pub for under a fiver. Vegetarian, French, Chinese, Italian, Mexican, Thai, Indian or Mongolian and traditional Irish – the choice is yours.

HIGHLIGHTS

The big newcomer is **Odyssey**, 2 Queen's Quay, Belfast, a Landmark Millennium Project providing the biggest entertainment and leisure attraction in Ireland. The waterfront development has an indoor arena seating 10,000 for concerts and boxing matches. The arena also stages gymnastics, basketball, soccer, ice hockey, tennis and athletics. Odyssey has an IMAX theatre and the **Pavilion**, a courtyard-style building with transparent roof. It has a 12-screen multiplex cinema, a variety of shops, restaurants, bistros and bars.

People of all ages find themselves on an upward learning curve at the **whowhatwherewhenwhy** experience, mercifully abbreviated to **W5** (££, open Mon–Fri 1000–1800, Sat–Sun 1200–1800, last admission 1700). This is Odyssey's inspirational discovery centre, with interactive involvement related to science, technology and engineering. You build bridges and robots, play the laser harp, create animations and do a host of other interesting things. W5 is run by Museums and Galleries of Northern Ireland.

Belfast City Hall, built of Portland stone, sits like a vast wedding cake in Donegall Sq. On fine summer days local office workers have their picnic lunches on the lawn. In the grounds are a number of statues and a memorial to the victims of the sinking of the glamourous ocean liner *Titanic*, which was built in Belfast. Free public tours of this proud building, which was completed in 1906, are held Mon–Fri 1030, 1130 and 1430, Sat 1430 (June–Sept); Mon–Sat 1430 (Oct–May).

More than 160 rare or endangered species are in enclosures that resemble their natural habitats at **Belfast Zoo**. ££, Antrim Rd, 4 miles (6.4 km) north of the city, on Cave Hill. Open daily 1000–1700 (Apr–Sept); daily 1000–1430 (Oct–Mar).

Ulster Weavers, £, 44 Montgomery Rd, Belfast. This linen factory has an inspection area and a display of linen. Tours are by arrangement and are not suitable for children under 12. A cup of tea or coffee is included in the price. **The People's Museum**, £, Fernhill House, Glencavin Rd, Belfast (2 miles/3 km west), reveals the history of the Shankhill District, covering the Home Rule crisis and the two world wars.

Children will be happily entertained at **Dreamland**, ££, Glenmuchan Pl., Boucher Rd, Belfast. Its attractions include a mini train ride, balloon ride, pirate ship and adventure play area. Open Mon–Fri 1000–2000.

Ulster Folk and Transport Museum, ££ (disabled visitors free). On the A2 at Cultra, 7 miles (11 km) east, this indoor and outdoor museum is a must-see. The Belfast City Hopper Tour bus (see Tours) calls there. Allow a good two or three hours, or more, to see steam locomotives, early bicycles, buses, boats, horse-drawn wagons and other modes of travel. Evocative tableaux trace the way of life of people in past ages, going about their domestic and farm work. Visitors can experience a typical Ulster town of the early 20th century and stroll through the countryside of yesteryear, with authentic farms, cottages, crops and livestock.

WRITING ON THE WALLS
Understand more about all those places you've heard of in the news about The Troubles over the years by seeing Belfast's alternative sights – the political murals in the Protestant Shankhill Rd and the Catholic Falls Rd.

Outside, you can watch great horses pulling the plough, thatchers at work, a forge, bare rural schoolrooms and little churches with boxed pews. Cottages from the 1800s have been rescued from demolition and re-built on the museum site for visitors to tour. Exhibits on the *Titanic*, built in Belfast, and 'Flight Experience' are staged. The museum has a tea room and gift shop. Open Mon–Sat 1030–1800, Sun 1200–1800 (July–Aug); Mon–Fri 0930–1700, Sat

ON RECORD

The Public Record Office of Northern Ireland, tel: (028) 9025 1318, has 30 miles (48 km) of shelves holding documents galore. People from many parts of the world consult files in the search room in the quest to discover their family history.

1030–1800, Sun 1200–1800 (Apr–June and Sept); Mon–Fri 0930–1600, Sat–Sun 1230–1630 (Oct–Mar).

Botanic Gardens, £, Stranmillis Rd, Belfast. Near Queen's University, the extensive gardens are noted for the Palm House, dating from 1839, and the Tropical Ravine, or Fernery (1889). The gardens are accessible daily, dawn to dusk. Palm House and Fernery are open Mon–Fri 1000–1700. Sat–Sun and public holidays 1400–1600 (Apr–Sept). Closed lunchtime.

There's a pets' corner, milking parlour, rides, nature trail, viewing gallery, shop and tea room at the **Streamvale Open Dairy Farm**, ££, 38 Ballyhandwood Rd, Belfast; tel: (028) 9048 3244. The attraction presents a microcosm of an Ulster dairy farm. For animal feeding times, of special appeal to children, phone before you visit. Open Wed, Sat–Sun 1400–1800 (Feb–May and Sept–Oct), daily 1200–1800 (June), daily 1030–1800 (July–Aug).

Lagan Lookout Centre, £, Donegall Quay, Belfast. Hear about the industrial and folk history of the city, the River Lagan and its weir, and find out from computers and videos how the Laganside area has been regenerated. View river activities from a public platform. Open Mon–Fri 1100–1700, Sat 1200–1700, Sun 1400–1700 (Apr–Sept); Tues–Fri 1100–1530, Sat 1300–1430, Sun 1400–1630 (Oct–Mar).

TOURS A number of **bus tours** are operated by Belfast CityBus in summer. For a free colour booklet about all the company's tours, tel: (028) 9045 8484. Belfast City Tour includes City Hall, the shipyard, Queen's University, the new Odyssey Arena and the zoo. There's a Belfast Living History Tour visiting historic places and the city murals. The City Hopper Bus provides you with an opportunity to hop on and off at the City Hall, Belfast Castle, Ulster Folk and Transport Museum and other sites. Half-hourly departures are from Castle Pl.

LATE BUS

On Fri and Sat nights the Late Night bus service operates from Donegall Sq. West until 0230. For information call at the CityBus kiosk in Donegall Sq. or tel: (028) 9024 6485.

Thirty-min **boat tours** around Bangor Bay and Belfast sea lough east of the city, are run by Bangor Harbour Boats (£) 24 Stanley Rd, Bangor; tel: (028) 9145 5321. They sail from Pickie Family Fun Park on Bangor seafront from 1400 Sat and Sun (May, June, Sept and Oct), daily (June and Aug).

Lagan Boat Company, 48 St John's Close, 2 Laganbank Rd, Belfast; tel: (028) 9033 0844, offers a cruise (£) between the Lagan Lookout Centre and Donegall Quay to Stranmillis, aboard a 40-seater boat, *The Joyce*.

The Lagan Experience Tour (££), tel: (028) 9045 8484, provides a close-up look at recent developments, including the Waterfront Hall and the Lagan Weir and Lookout Centre. Fully guided.

Bailey's Belfast Historical Pub Walk; tel/fax: (028) 9268 3665 is a 2-hour tour calling at six pubs of character and interest. ££ (refreshments not included); Thur 1900, Sat 1600 (May–Sept). Details of **walking tours** with Blue Badge guides and other walking, bus or taxi tours are available from Belfast Visitor and Convention Bureau and the tourist information centre.

FOR FREE It's worth climbing to the top of Cave Hill, Antrim Rd, past Neolithic caves, to the ancient earthworks at McArt's Fort for panoramic views from **Cave Hill Country Park**. It was at McArt's Fort in 1795 that Wolfe Tone and United Irishmen swore rebellion, planning independence from England. There are pleasant walks and an adventure playground in the country park. Call in at the Heritage Centre in Belfast Castle, open daily 0900–1800, with its six-storey tower, for information on the park.

> ### IRISH LINEN
> With the arrival of Huguenot weavers at the end of the 17th century, Ulster became a major linen producer, particularly in the 'linen triangle' that stretched from Belfast southwest to Armagh and Dungannon. The industry flourished for over 200 years, but the costly production process eventually led to a decline in demand. Today, only small quantities are produced for the luxury goods market. Dozens of abandoned mills – often called 'beetling mills', after the final stage of the process in which the cloth was hammered to create a sheen – are dotted around the area.

The highly renowned gardens of **Dixon Park** (Upper Malane Rd, South Belfast, freely accessible all year) are a joy to behold when many thousands of roses are in full bloom in summer. **Queen's University Visitors' Centre**, University Rd, stages exhibitions. This grand mid-19th-century building, with its tower entrance and paved cloisters, was designed by Sir Charles Langan, who was responsible for much of Belfast's architecture. Open Mon–Fri 1000-1600, also Sat 1000–1600 (May–Sept only). Tours available by prior arrangement.

Royal Ulster Rifles Museum, 5 Waring St, Belfast; tel: (028) 9023 2086 (appointment advisable). Relics of the regiment and the foot regiments which preceded it are displayed. In the same building is the World War II Museum. Open Mon–Fri 0900–1700. **RUC Museum**, 65 Knock Rd, 3 miles (4.8 km) east of the city; tel: (028) 9065 0222, ext. 22499. Uniforms and equipment of the Royal Irish Constabulary from its founding in 1822 are exhibited. The work of the Royal Ulster Constabulary since its creation in 1922 is depicted.

Hours of interesting browsing are offered at the **Ulster Museum**, Botanic Gardens, Stranmillis Rd, Belfast. It has collections of Irish art, history, natural sciences and archaeology. Exhibits include treasure from a Spanish Armada ship which was wrecked off the Giant's Causeway in 1588. The Early Ireland gallery takes you from 10,000 BC to 1500 BC. Open Mon–Fri 1000–1700, Sat 1300–1700.

Described as 'Hiberno-Romanesque', **St Anne's Cathedral** in Donegall St was partly completed and opened in the 1890s, but not totally completed until a century later. The Gertrude Stein mosaics, the font's angel heads by Rosamund Praeger and the baptistry are among the highlights. Open daily.

A **World War II Exhibition** in the War Memorial Building, 9–13 Waring St, commemorates the province's crucial role through photographs and exhibits. The Belfast blitz and the experiences of a Belfast anti-aircraft battery in Burma are recorded. Open Mon–Fri.

SHOPPING

The **May St variety market**, St George's, is a draw on Fri mornings. In a revitalised part of Belfast, the covered market offers local fresh produce and fish, second-hand videos and discounted clothing among its many wares. For department store browsing and window shopping, go to Donegall Pl. and Royal Ave, the modern mall at **Castle Court**. There are fashion shops in the Golden Mile, around Bedford St, Dublin Rd and up to Lisburn Rd. Linen, Tyrone crystal and hand-knitted goods are among the prestigious local products available.

EVENTS

Belfast Giants have matches in the Ice Hockey League in Jan and Feb at the Odyssey Arena. For details, tel: (028) 9059 1111. 17 March sees the St Patrick's Day parade. The Belfast Marathon is held in early May. The anniversary of the 1690 Battle of the Boyne is celebrated with Orange Day parades (mid-July). The City of Belfast International Rose Trials are held at Dixon Gardens in July. In the autumn the Belfast Festival is Ulster's premier arts event.

NIGHTLIFE

The pubs are alive with the sound of music, especially at weekends, and some every night. The **Rotterdam Bar** in the Docklands attracts all age groups with traditional Irish music sessions. **Madison's**, in Botanic Ave, offers live entertainment Thur–Sun, and there's a basement nightclub for dancing. The **Fly Bar** in Lower Crescent, famous for its cocktails, has resident DJs playing hits. **Bob's**, in the Lisburn Rd, incorporates the Storm nightclub.

TRULY GRAND

The Grand Opera House, Great Victoria St, Belfast, tel: (028) 9024 9129 (programme information), (028) 9024 1919 (tickets), is the lavishly ornate, late Victorian venue for world-class theatre, musicals, ballet, opera, concerts and comedy.

Rock Rhythm and Blues, Country and Western, jazz, Irish and folk – all kinds of musical tastes are catered for in Belfast, and the new **Odyssey** development is adding to the options. Several nightclubs are in the Botanic Ave and Bradbury Pl. vicinity, near Queen's University. Popular venues for gays are Kremlin, The Parliament and the Crow's Nest.

The **comedy** scene flourishes, with stand-up comics delivering their wry Irish humour. Take it in at The Empire, an entertainment pub in Botanic Ave. Variety, drama, concerts, story-telling are all represented at such places as the Grand Opera House, the Lyric Theatre, the Waterfront Hall, Odyssey

WEBSITE BY GASLIGHT

Northern Ireland's best-known pub, the **Crown Liquor Saloon** in Great Victoria St, is an amazingly well-preserved Victorian property, with all the genuine woodwork, glass and tiles. It is owned by the National Trust. And to prove that you're not totally submerged in the 19th century, you can sit in a snug and raise your glass to the multitudes worldwide visiting the Crown's website: www.belfasttelegraph.co.uk/crown. The pub claims to have the only webcam on the Internet operating in a gas-lit bar.

and the Crescent Arts Theatre. Pick up a free 'what's on' guide like *The Big List*, or spend 50p on *Northern Entertainment*.

SIDE TRIPS

Ten miles (16 km) south of Belfast is the pretty little town of **Hillsborough**, where the castle is the official residence of the Secretary of State for Northern Ireland. The castle and gardens are open Apr–Sept (££). North of Belfast is **Carrickfergus**, with its massive 12th-century castle (£). Open all year. A trip through Carrickfergus history by monorail is another option.

Belfast

East of Belfast, the journey along the **Ards Peninsula** goes by Strangford Lough and along the Co. Down coastline to Portaferry. Inland is Downpatrick, where the new St Patrick Centre (££) displays the life of the saint in a state-of-the-art exhibition. From Belfast Laganside Bus Centre services 9 and 10 leave regularly for Portaferry.

On the northern shore of Strangford Lough is **Mount Stewart House and Gardens** (££), childhood home of Lord Castlereagh. Run by the National Trust, the house has interesting features and the gardens are among the finest in Europe.

WHERE NEXT?

By car (or bus) you can travel west along the M1 and then south on the A29 to historic and beautiful Armagh. From here, continue west to Enniskillen, an attractive Georgian town on an island, and pass through dramatic countryside to reach Sligo (see pp. 363–364). Alternatively, embark on the route to Londonderry (see pp. 339–340) or Dublin (see pp. 347–357).

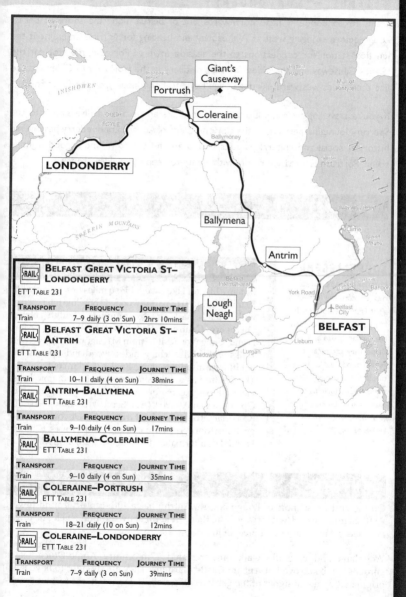

Giant's
Causeway

Portrush

Coleraine

Ballymoney

LONDONDERRY

Ballymena

Antrim

Lough
Neagh

York Road

BELFAST

RAIL BELFAST GREAT VICTORIA ST– LONDONDERRY
ETT TABLE 231

TRANSPORT	FREQUENCY	JOURNEY TIME
Train	7–9 daily (3 on Sun)	2hrs 10mins

RAIL BELFAST GREAT VICTORIA ST– ANTRIM
ETT TABLE 231

TRANSPORT	FREQUENCY	JOURNEY TIME
Train	10–11 daily (4 on Sun)	38mins

RAIL ANTRIM–BALLYMENA
ETT TABLE 231

TRANSPORT	FREQUENCY	JOURNEY TIME
Train	9–10 daily (4 on Sun)	17mins

RAIL BALLYMENA–COLERAINE
ETT TABLE 231

TRANSPORT	FREQUENCY	JOURNEY TIME
Train	9–10 daily (4 on Sun)	35mins

RAIL COLERAINE–PORTRUSH
ETT TABLE 231

TRANSPORT	FREQUENCY	JOURNEY TIME
Train	18–21 daily (10 on Sun)	12mins

RAIL COLERAINE–LONDONDERRY
ETT TABLE 231

TRANSPORT	FREQUENCY	JOURNEY TIME
Train	7–9 daily (3 on Sun)	39mins

BELFAST – LONDONDERRY

Trains to Londonderry head northwards out of Belfast along the shore of Belfast Lough before swinging west at Whiteabbey and heading for Antrim. Coleraine is the junction station for connections to the seaside town of Portrush, the stop for the Giant's Causeway and the oldest whiskey distillery in the world. From Coleraine, the line then heads westward, skirting Lough Foyle to Londonderry, on the River Foyle.

If you're travelling by car, you may wish to make an occasional diversion, into the Sperrin Mountains, perhaps, or the glorious Glens of Antrim. Londonderry has diverse historical, social and cultural pursuits in and around the town and a good nightlife scene. Portrush is a seaside resort with plenty to keep the children happy.

BELFAST

See p. 327.

LOUGH LEGEND

Many of Ireland's 'tall stories' concern the legendary giant Finn McCool. Lough Neagh and the Isle of Man are similar in size and shape, they say, because Finn scooped out a chunk of earth and tossed it into the Irish Sea, forming the island, while the hole filled with water and formed Lough Neagh.

LOUGH NEAGH

Britain's biggest lake covers 153 sq miles (396 sq km), with 75 miles (121 km) of partly-wooded shoreline interspersed with small harbour communities. **Lough Neagh Discovery Centre National Nature Reserve**, Oxford Island, Craigavon (exit 10 from M1, signposted). There are walks with birdwatching hides, woodlands, ponds and wildflower meadows along 4 miles (6.5 km) of footpaths. The Centre has a craft shop, café and panoramic lough views. Free, except for award-winning exhibition (£). Open daily 1000–1900 (Apr–Sept); Wed–Sun 1000–1700 (Oct–Mar). Thirty-min **boat trips** to the Discovery Centre go from Kinnego Marina, also 2-hour cruises to Carey Island. For information for both, tel: (028) 3832 7573.

ANTRIM

On the north-east shore of Lough Neagh, Antrim has a 10th-century **round tower**, 93 ft (28 m) high with a doorway more than 7 ft (2 m) above ground level. The tower is accessible at all times, off Steeple Rd.

Woodland and riverside walks and restored 17th-century Anglo-Dutch water gardens can be enjoyed at **Antrim Castle Gardens**. They are thought to have been originated by the designer of the gardens at Versailles, France. In the former coach-house is the Clotworthy Arts Centre, Randalstown Rd, Antrim. Open Mon–Fri 0930–2130, Sat 1000–1700, Sun 1400–1700 (July–Aug).

> i **Tourist Information Centre** 16 High St, Antrim; tel: (028) 9442 8331; website: www.antrim.gov.uk; e-mail: abs@antrim.gov.uk. Open all year.

BALLYMENA

Morrow's Shop Museum presents displays on the borough's history. It is housed in a former draper's shop with original fittings at 13 Bridge St. Free, open Mon–Fri 1000–1300 and 1400–1700, Sat 1000–1300.

Outside the town, on the A43 Ballymena-Waterfoot road, is the **Glenariff Forest Park**, with beautifully scenic glen walks. Amenities include a visitor centre, shop and restaurant. The park (£) is open daily from 1000 (see notice board for closing times).

The 150-acre (61 ha) **ECOS Environment Centre**, Kernohans Lane, Broughshane Rd, a mile from Ballymena town centre, highlights environmental issues through interactive exhibits, demonstrating alternative energy production from sustainable sources. There are galleries with displays and opportunities for walking, cycling and fishing in the grounds. Wheelchairs are supplied for those with mobility problems. The centre has a restaurant. Open Mon–Sat 0930–1700, Sun 1200–1700 (Easter–Sept); closes 1600 rest of year.

> i **Tourist Information Centre** 76 Church St, Ballymena; tel: (028) 2563 8494; website: www.discovernorthernireland. com; e-mail: ballymenatic@hotmail.com. Open all year.

COLERAINE

Coleraine is a university town on the River Bann, near the coastal villages of Castlerock and Portstewart, where the river flows into the Atlantic Ocean.

The annual **North West 200**, hailed as the world's fastest motorcycle race on public roads, takes place in May. It attracts around 100,000 people. The course is between Portstewart, Coleraine and Portrush. If you wish to attend it – or avoid it – find out the current year's date from the tourist infomation centre.

A bus service from Coleraine goes through Downhill, near Castlerock, where a classical domed building on a clifftop is the library of an 18th-century Bishop of Derry. This is the **Mussenden Temple**, which has survived ocean storms, while the palace which Bishop Frederick Hervey also built on the site has long been in ruins. Free, open Sat, Sun 1200–1800 (Apr–June and Sept), daily (July–Aug); gardens open dawn–dusk.

i **Tourist Information Centre** Railway Rd, Coleraine; tel: (028) 7034 4723; website: www.discovernorthernireland.com; e-mail: coleraine@nitic.net. Open all year.

🏠 **Brown's Country House** ££ 174 Ballybogey Rd, Coleraine, Co. Londonderry; tel: (028) 2073 2777; fax: (028) 2073 1627; e-mail: brownscountryhouse@hotmail.com. En suite rooms in a family-run house handy for the Giant's Causeway and Bushmills

🍽 A good choice of budget eateries to suit the student population and others.

PORTRUSH

Great stretches of clean sandy beaches, with the chance of a donkey ride, keep young children amused at Portrush. There's also **Waterworld** (££) an indoor complex with giant water flumes, whirlpools, water cannon and a pirate ship.

The **Dunluce Family Entertainment Centre** (££) Sandhill Drive, Portrush, is a children's theme park presenting Earthquest and Myths and Legends theatres, simulated thrill rides, an adventure play area and sights and sounds of local wildlife.

Three miles east of Portrush, on the A2, stand the ruins of **Dunluce Castle** (£) dating mainly from the 16th and 17th centuries. A visitors' centre and shop are on site and guided tours are available. Open all year, hours variable; tel: (028) 2073 1938.

i **Tourist Information Centre** Dunluce Centre, Sandhill Dr., Portrush; tel: (028) 7082 3333; website: www.discovernorthern ireland.com; e-mail: portrush@nitic.net. Seasonal opening.

🏠 **Alexandra Guest House** ££ 11 Lansdown Cr, Portrush, Co. Antrim; tel/fax: (028) 7082 2284; e-mail: mcalistermary @hotmail.com. In a quiet crescent with uninterrupted sea views. **Causeway Hotel** £££ 40 Causeway Rd, Bushmills, Co. Antrim; tel: (028) 2073 1226; fax: (028) 2073 2552; website: www.giants-causeway-hotel.com. Modern comforts in an 1839 family hotel with 30 en suite rooms.

🍽 **Cafes**, bars and restaurants along the seafront and in town offer a range of catering.

SIDE TRIPS FROM PORTRUSH The **Giant's Causeway World Heritage Site** is every bit as spectacular as you imagine. Buses take you the short distance from the interesting visitor centre. A daily minibus service operates for wheelchair visitors. Guided walks (£) should be pre-booked, tel: (028) 2073 1159; www.nationaltrust.org.uk. Coastal paths and walks among the 40,000 stones, mostly hexagonal, are accessible all year, free.

The **Giant's Causeway Centre** has an accommodation booking service, tourist information, bureau de change, craft and souvenir shop and audio-visual presentations in five European languages. Open daily 1000–1900 year-round (July–Aug; earlier closing rest of year). Causeway Head on the B146; tel: (028) 2073 1855; e-mail: causeway@nitic.net.

The world's oldest licensed whiskey distillery, **Old Bushmills Distillery**, beside the River Bush, was established in 1608. One-hour guided tours (££) show how the famous whiskey is produced (it's a different method from Scotch whisky) and end with a tot. Distillery Rd, Bushmills, Co. Antrim; tel: (028) 2073 1521; website: www.irish-whiskey-trail.com.

LONDONDERRY

Visible history, ancient and modern, exercises the mind as you walk the mile-long circuit of the walls of Londonderry and speculate on the violence that has erupted here spasmodically. Retaining its 17th-century layout, and four original gates, the city sits on a hill surrounded by its ancient walls. These are 18-ft thick and have withstood successive sieges, one of which lasted for 105 days in 1688.

From the walls you can see the Apprentice Boys' base from which the Orangemen march, and the political murals on the sides of houses painted in the latter years of The Troubles. Explanatory panels are set into the walls. Free access to the walls; guided tours (££) leave from the tourist information centre at 1115 and 1515 (June–Sept) and 1430 (Oct–May).

THE NAME GAME
In the early days of Christianity in Ireland, St Columb arrived from Donegal to found a monastery in Doire (the Gaelic name for an oak grove). At the time of the plantation of Ulster, the City of London sent men and money to re-build the ruined medieval town – and in 1613 it became Londonderry. That is what Unionists still call it. Nationalists opt for Derry.

St Columb's Cathedral, Bishop St Within, dates from 1633. Its wealth of stained glass relates the history of the long siege of 1688–89, and more is learned through audio-visuals. £, open Mon–Sat 0900–1700 (Apr–Sept), Mon–Sat 0900–1300 and 1400–1600 (Oct–Mar).

Tower Museum, Union Hall Place, is a not-to-be-missed experience. Exhibits tracing the area's past include a pre-historic dug-out canoe. Newsreels and other film on the violence perpetrated by both sides in The Troubles in the recent past give an unprejudiced view of the situation. ££, open Tues–Sat and public holidays 1000–1700; Sun 1400–1700, Mon 1000–1700 (July–Aug).

The city's maritime history, including the port's role in World War II, is illustrated with exhibits and audio-visuals at the **Harbour Museum**, Harbour Sq. Free, open Mon–Fri 1000–1300 and 1400–1700.

The Fifth Province, £, Calgach Centre, Butchers St, tells the history of the Celts, the city and the impact of emigrants on the USA. Another aspect of local life is seen at the Workhouse Museum, 23 Glendermott Rd, Waterside. Open Mon–Thur and Sat 1000–1630 (Mon–Sat July–Aug).

Earhart Centre and Wildlife Sanctuary. The field where Amelia Earhart landed as the first woman to fly the Atlantic solo in 1932 is 1½ miles (2.4 km) beyond Foyle Bridge, off the B194. A cottage exhibition is open Mon–Thur 0900–1600, Fri 0900–1300. The sanctuary opens Mon–Fri 0900–dusk, Sat–Sun 1000–dusk.

GETTING AROUND A comprehensive bus service covers the city. At the centre is The Diamond, with a war memorial. The main thoroughfare is Shipquay St, which is very steep.

i **Tourist Information Centre** 44 Foyle St; tel: (028) 7162 7284; website: www.derryvisitor.com; e-mail: info@derryvisitor. com. Open Mon–Fri 0900–1700, Sat 1000–1700 (mid-Mar–June and Oct); Mon–Fri 0900–1900, Sat 1000–1800, Sun 1000–1700 (July–Sept); Mon–Fri 0900–1700 (Nov–mid-Mar).

🛏 The widest choice of modestly-priced guest houses and B&Bs is on the city outskirts and beyond.
White Horse Hotel ££–£££, 68 Clooney Rd, Campsie, Londonderry; tel: (028) 7186 0606; fax: (028) 7186 0371; e-mail: info@white-horse.demon.co.uk. Five miles east (8 km), the hotel has 43 well-equipped en suite rooms.
Edgewater Hotel £££ 88 Strand Rd, Portstewart, Co. Londonderry; tel: (028) 7083 3314; fax: (028) 7083 2224; e-mail: edgewater.hotel@virgin.net. Good beach and ocean views.

🍴 Shipquay St, William St and The Strand have a mix of cafés and restaurants, and many of Londonderry's bars serve food.

WHERE NEXT?

Ballycastle, on Antrim's north coast, is a pleasant harbour town with a ferry service to Rathlin Island and its bird sanctuary. Five miles (8 km) west of Ballycastle, those with a good head for heights can walk across a swinging rope bridge, the Carrick-a-Rede bridge, over a 60-ft (18-m) chasm to a salmon fishery. You could then head south to Dublin (pp. 347–357), one of Europe's liveliest and most friendly cities.

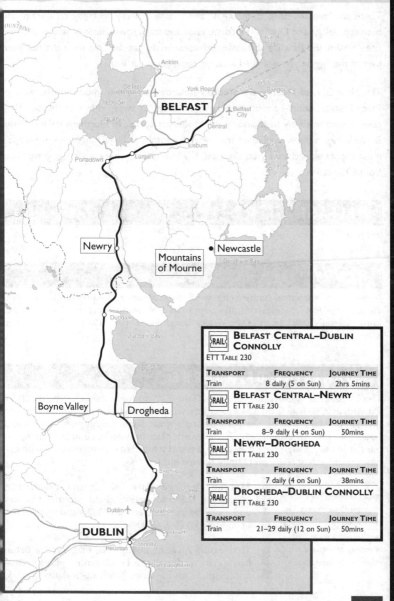

RAIL	**BELFAST CENTRAL–DUBLIN CONNOLLY**	
ETT Table 230		

TRANSPORT	FREQUENCY	JOURNEY TIME
Train	8 daily (5 on Sun)	2hrs 5mins

RAIL	**BELFAST CENTRAL–NEWRY**	
ETT Table 230		

TRANSPORT	FREQUENCY	JOURNEY TIME
Train	8–9 daily (4 on Sun)	50mins

RAIL	**NEWRY–DROGHEDA**	
ETT Table 230		

TRANSPORT	FREQUENCY	JOURNEY TIME
Train	7 daily (4 on Sun)	38mins

RAIL	**DROGHEDA–DUBLIN CONNOLLY**	
ETT Table 230		

TRANSPORT	FREQUENCY	JOURNEY TIME
Train	21–29 daily (12 on Sun)	50mins

BELFAST – DUBLIN

There are long stretches of mountain and coastal scenery to enjoy on a train ride between Belfast and Dublin. The countryside and small towns, historic and prehistoric sites, castles and beaches all demand exploration. To get the best from the northern part of the region you will need a car or some generous lifts.

The Mountains of Mourne are probably Ireland's best-known mountains because of Percy French's song – and they certainly do seem to sweep down to the sea. They cover a comparatively small area in the south-east corner of Northern Ireland. In the Boyne Valley, in the Republic, are the megalithic tombs of Newgrange, one of Europe's most important archaeological sites, and the Hill of Tara, where a passage grave dates from 2000 BC.

BELFAST

See p. 327.

NEWRY

Newry is a commercial centre to the west of the Mourne Mountains. The A25 provides access to them. Newry's arts centre has a **museum** (free) in which Admiral Lord Nelson's table from HMS *Victory* is exhibited. Back Parade, Newry, open Mon–Fri 1030–1630.

MOUNTAINS OF MOURNE

The 12 peaks of Mourne are all over 2000ft (610 m) high, the tallest being Slieve Donard, at 2796 ft (852 m). On a clear day you can gaze from the summit across to the Isle of Man. Two of Northern Ireland's great lakes – Strangford Lough and Lough Neagh – are also in sight. A convenient place to start the climb is from the car park at Bloody Bridge, near Newcastle, a resort which is a convenient base with a 5-mile (8-km) sandy beach and family seaside attractions.

Newcastle, a Victorian resort between the Mourne Mountains and the sea – it has 5 miles (8 km) of sandy beach – has a water park, adventure playground and other family attractions.

Mourne Heritage Trust, 87 Central Promenade, Newcastle, has information about Mourne Country and a year-round programme of talks and walks. Free, open Mon–Fri 0900–1700.

The Seaside Award-winning Blue Flag **Tyrella Beach** has waymarked walks, a beach centre with information displays and a shop. Beach open daily to dusk, centre open (weather permitting) Sat, Sun 0900–dusk (Easter–June), daily (June–Sept). Free. Car park €.

Tollymore Forest Park, Bryansford Rd, Newcastle, provides pleasant walking in the Mournes, with its arboretum, stone follies, bridges and fishing. A barn has wildlife and forestry exhibits, and there's a tea house. Open daily 1000–dusk. € (pedestrian), €€ car park.

The **Silent Valley** and **Ben Crom** reservoirs supply water to Belfast and Co. Down. Private traffic is banned, but people can walk to the top of Ben Crom or, in summer, take a bus daily 1100–1800 (July–Aug), shorter hours and weekends only (Easter–May and Sept–Oct). €, area open daily 1000–1830 (Easter–Sept), 1000–1600 (Oct–Easter).

Ireland is dotted with prehistoric monuments and one of the most dramatic is the **Legananny Dolmen**, a huge slab of stone mounted on a tripod of tall legs in the Mourne Mountains 22 miles (35 km) north of Newcastle and 7 (11 km) miles south of Dromara.

In the south-west corner of the mountain range is the pretty Victorian resort of Rostrevor, in the shadow of Slieve Martin, on the shore of Carlingford Lough. A 2-mile (3-km) forest drive in **Kilbroney Park**, Rostrevor, provides views over the lough. Free, open daily dawn–dusk. The park has a café.

In medieval times **Greencastle**, 4 miles (6 km) south-west of Killeel, was an imposing royal edifice guarding the entrance to Carlingford Lough. It was besieged and plundered in the 14th century and later kept as a garrison for Elizabeth I. €, open Tues–Sat 1000–1800, Sun 1400–1800 (July–Aug).

One of the finest Norman castles in Northern Ireland, **Dundrum Castle**, with views to the sea and the Mourne Mountains, was built by John de Courcey in the 12th century. €, open Tues–Sat 1000–1800, Sun 1400–1800 (Apr–Sept), Sat 1000–1600, Sun 1400–1600 (Oct–Mar).

> *i* **Tourist Information Centre** Newcastle Centre, 10–14
> Central Promenade, Newcastle; tel: (028) 4372 2222; website:
> www.newcastletic.org; e-mail: newcastle@ntic.net.

DROGHEDA

Set on the banks of the River Boyne, its skyline punctuated by the spires of three cathedrals, Drogheda is one of the most attractive medieval towns in the Midlands. It was founded by the Vikings and captured by the Norman Hugh de Lacy, Lord of Trim. By the early 15th century the walled and fortified town was the largest English town in the country. Cromwell launched a savage attack on Drogheda in 1649, and **St Lawrence Gate** is the only sizeable remnant – and a handsome one – of the medieval defences.

On West St, the Gothic Catholic **Church of St Peter's** houses a sad and rather grue-some relic: the head of the martyred saint Oliver Plunkett. Born of a prominent Meath family, he became the Archbishop of Armagh, but was falsely convicted of instigating a 'Popish Plot' and was hung, drawn and quartered in 1681. The mum-mified head is visibly displayed in a side chapel.

The **Millmount Museum** on the outskirts of town has a wonderful collection of guild parade banners, richly coloured and embroidered with slogans and insignia. Craft workshops occupy the buildings around the square. €€, open Mon–Sat 1000–1700, Sun 1430–1700.

> *i* **Drogheda Tourist Information Office** Bus Éireann station, Donore Rd; tel: (041) 983 7070; fax: (041) 984 5340. Open Mon–Fri 0900–1730, Sat 0900–1300.

THE BOYNE VALLEY

The wide, slow-moving river Boyne weaves a twisting path through the counties north of Dublin, and among these green and scenic rolling hills lie some of Ireland's greatest historical sites. This land is the very cradle of Irish civilisation, where Neolithic farmers with a mysterious but sophisticated culture built enormous passage tombs. The prehistoric remains at Brú na Bóinne (Newgrange) are some of the world's most important archaeological remains. The Celts considered the Boyne a sacred river, and for centuries crowned their high kings on the Hill of Tara. Military campaigns were waged here, too: Cromwell's vicious slaughter in the medieval town of Drogheda, and the great turning point in Irish history, the Battle of the Boyne, 1690, when the Protestant army of William III of England defeated the Catholics under the former King James II.

Brú na Bóinne, the 'dwelling place of the Boyne', lies between Drogheda and Slane, surrounded on three sides by a winding stretch of the river. The series of remarkable passage tombs here, built by Neolithic farmers more than 5000 years ago, is one of the world's most important archaeological sites. It is often known by the name of the most famous tomb, Newgrange, but in fact there are some 50 monuments within the area, all on private land.

The enormous passage tomb at Newgrange, built from over 200,000 tons of earth and stone, covers more than an acre and stands 36 ft (11 m) high, and is the only tomb that can be entered. The white quartz that covers the front comes from County Wicklow, 44 miles (71 km) south, and is believed to have been hauled here by coracle along the coast and river. The greatest wonder of Newgrange's construction is the 'roof box': at dawn on the day of the winter solstice, a shaft of sunlight beams through this small opening above the door and penetrates the passage to the very back of the chamber. This undoubtedly had great ritual significance to the Neolithic farmers. €€–€€€, open daily year-round: 0930–1700 (Mar–Apr and Oct); 0900–1830 (May and mid-Sept–end Sept); 0900–1900 (June–mid-Sept); 0930–1700 (Nov–Feb).

Rising more than 300 ft (91 m), the **Hill of Tara** is the legendary seat of the High Kings of Ireland. All that remains is a series of earthworks dating from the Iron Age, so the glory of Tara is left largely to the imagination. Given that the bells of Christianity were Tara's death knell, the statue of St Patrick that stands here today alongside a pillar thought to be the coronation stone of the kings seems somewhat disrespectful of its ancient history. The views from Tara are stupendous, and on a clear day you can see across the central plain to the mountains of Galway. **Hill of Tara Interpretative Centre**, €€, open daily 1000–1700 (May–mid-June and mid-Sept–Oct); 0930–1830 (mid-June–mid-Sept).

Kells, or Ceanannus Mór, is famed for the monastery founded by St Colmcille in the 6th century. Monks from the island of Iona fled here in the 9th century, and it is thought that they were the creators of the Book of Kells, which can be seen at Trinity College in Dublin (see page 353). The remains of the monastery lie west of town.

Founded by St Malachy in 1142, **Mellifont Abbey** was the first Cistercian monastery in Ireland. After the dissolution of the monasteries the abbey was converted into a fortified house, and during the Battle of the Boyne William of Orange made his headquarters here. €€, open daily 1000–1700 (May–mid-June and mid-Sept–Oct); 0930–1830 (mid-June–mid-Sept).

The busy town of **Navan** is at the confluence of the Boyne and Blackwater rivers and was fortified by Hugh de Lacy in the 12th century. A Friday market is held on the green beside the church. There are stocks outside the town hall. **Oldbridge** is the place on the River Boyne where the deposed Catholic monarch of England, James II, challenged the new king, William of Orange, in an attempt to regain his crown. The Battle of the Boyne, which took place on 1 July 1690, was a turning point in Irish history. The Catholic force of Irish and French soldiers, poorly trained and greatly outnumbered, were soundly defeated by the English allies. In the aftermath, Catholic lands were confiscated and discriminatory laws were passed, setting the division of Ireland in motion. A signposted route takes you past significant sites of the battle on a pretty riverside drive.

The Hill of Slane (signposted off the N2) is where St Patrick allegedly lit the paschal fire in 433 to celebrate the arrival of Christianity in Ireland. In doing so he unknowingly disobeyed King Laoghaire at nearby Tara, for this was a night when, according to the Druidic religion, no fires could be lit. When Patrick's fire was seen, one of the Druid leaders prophesied that if the flames were not quenched now they would burn forever and consume Tara – which, figuratively, they did. The Easter fire is still lit here each year. The remains of Slane Abbey stand on the site of a 5th-century monastery, a short walk across the field from the statue of St Patrick. There are panoramic views across the Boyne Valley.

The formidable turreted keep, towers, long curtain wall and drawbridge of Trim Castle made an impressive setting in the Mel Gibson film *Braveheart*.

Situated on the River Boyne, **Trim** is an attractive town with some of the best medieval ruins in Ireland. **King John's Castle**, built by the Norman knight Hugh de Lacy in 1173, is the largest of its era in the country, covering two acres (0.8 ha). On the outskirts of town are the magnificent **Butterstream Gardens**, inspired by those at Sissinghurst in Kent. The visitor centre has an exhibition on medieval Trim. Open Apr–Sept.

i **Trim Tourist Information Office** Mill Street; tel: (046) 37111. Seasonal opening.

⌂ **Birchard B&B** €€, Balrath, Kells, Co. Meath; tel/fax: (046) 40688; e-mail: clarket@iol.ie. Modern farmhouse with en suite rooms; panoramic views, handy for Newgrange and local restaurants.

Drive through Dublin and you might be anywhere in the world, with its stop-and-start traffic flow and cars evidently running on a mixture of adrenaline and testosterone. No wonder people from other parts of Ireland dismiss the place as just another European city. Well, Dublin *is* European. It has O'Connell St, as grand a boulevard as you'll find anywhere on the continent, and wider than all the rest. It has elegant squares, haughty Georgian buildings and a river flanked by picturesque waterfronts and crossed by graceful bridges. It has a castle, three cathedrals and superb museums and art galleries.

Then there's the Irish side: a baffling maze of side streets buzzing with life; street markets crackling with the Dubliners' laconic wit; buskers so talented they should be known worldwide – and next year probably will be. There are streets where genteel people sip tea among potted palms in sedate cafés – and streets where horses run free. And there are pubs – pubs galore! – where you can step aside from life's hurly-burly to enjoy a pint of 'the black stuff' and eavesdrop on conversations bizarre, entertaining *and meant to be overheard.*

GETTING THERE

AIR   **Dublin Airport**, tel: (01) 844 4900, is 7 miles (11 km) north of the city. An inexpensive **Airlink** express bus service runs every 20 mins between the airport and the city's bus and rail stations. The journey takes about 30 mins.

RAIL/BUS   **Connolly Station**, Amiens St, is a 15-min walk from O'Connell St, but well served by a number of bus routes and DART trains (see p. 348). It serves Wexford, Sligo and the North, including Belfast.

Heuston Station, Stevens Lane, is at the end of Victoria Quay on the south side of the River Liffey, a long way from the city centre. It is served by several bus routes, including no. 90, a shuttle service between Connolly and Heuston stations which runs every 10 mins and takes about 15 mins. Heuston Station is the starting point for trains to the West, South and South West. For information on rail services, tel: (01) 836 6222.

Busaras, tel: (01) 836 6111, Store St, near Connolly Station; is the city's central bus station and the hub for Bus Éireann's comprehensive network of services throughout the country.

GETTING AROUND

Many of Dublin's major sights and attractions are within walking distance of **O'Connell Bridge**, more or less in the centre of the city. An excellent large-scale map, with details of places of interest, cinemas and theatres, shopping centres and bus routes, is available from the offices of Dublin Tourism. Suburban bus and rail services are good.

DART – the Dublin Area Rapid Transit system – is an electrical rail service covering 30 stations. It extends from Malahide and Howth in the north to Greystones in the south and connects with outlying suburban rail services. Trains are fast, clean and comfortable. The service runs Mon–Sat 0550–2359 and Sun 0845-2330; tel: (01) 836 6222. A variety of multi-trip ticket options is available. Special-offer tickets can be bought at all DART and suburban rail stations and from the Rail Travel Centre, 35 Lower Abbey St.

Dublin Bus serves the city with about 100 routes. On weekdays services start around 0630 and the last buses leave the city centre at about 2330. Timetables and maps are available from Dublin Bus, 59 Upper O'Connell St, tel: (01) 873 4222, and from newsagents. If you are staying in the city for some time buy a Dublin Rambler card. It provides three days of unlimited travel on all Dublin Bus services, including the Airlink service between the city centre and Dublin International airport. It can be bought at the Dublin Tourism Centre, Suffolk St, and from nearly 250 newsagents. Other pre-paid tickets and passes are available, some allowing unlimited travel on DART and the suburban rail systems.

INFORMATION

CITY MAP
– inside back cover

Dublin Tourism Centre, Suffolk St, Dublin 2; tel: (01) 605 7799; fax: (01) 605 7725; website: www.visitdublin.com; e-mail: information@dublintourism.ie. Open Mon–Sat 0900–1730 (Sept–June); Mon–Sat 0830–1830, Sun and bank holidays 1030–1500 (July–Aug).

The centre has a wide range of leaflets, brochures and maps – many of them free – covering other parts of Ireland, as well as Dublin. Other tourist offices are in the arrivals hall at **Dublin Airport**; open daily 0800–2200 (2230 July–Aug), **Dún Laoghaire Ferry Terminal**; open

Mon–Sat 1000–1800, **The Square Shopping Centre,** Tallaght; open Mon–Sat 0930–1200, 1230–1700 and **Baggot Street Bridge**; open Mon–Fri 0930–1230, 1300–1700.

SAFETY   Violent crime is rare in Dublin, but it's best to take sensible precautions and stay out of its less savoury areas and darker side streets. Ungentrified parts of The Liberties may be hazardous and fashionable Temple Bar can be rowdy after dark, especially on Sat. Tourist office staff will gladly tell you which parts to avoid. As in other cities, pickpockets may be active in busy streets, markets and crowded shopping malls.

MONEY   Banks open Mon–Fri 1000–1600 (1700 Thur). Automatic Teller Machines accepting 'Plus' and 'Cirrus' symbols can be found throughout the city. There are **Thomas Cook bureaux de change** at 51 Grafton St and 118 Grafton St. There are also exchange facilities at Dublin Airport.

POST AND PHONES   Dublin's imposing and historic **Post Office** – it was shelled during the Easter Rising of 1916 – is on O'Connell St. *Poste restante* facilities are available. Open Mon–Sat 0800–2000, Sun 1000–1830. Other post offices open Mon-Fri 0900–1730, Sat 0900–1300 and 1415–1700. Throughout the Republic card phones are cheaper than coin-operated phones and are widely available.

ACCOMMODATION

The city and surrounding area have so much accommodation of all kinds that Dublin Tourism publishes *Where to stay in Dublin,* a 78-page guide. Information is also available on www.visitdublin.com and credit card reservations can be made by e-mail: reservations@dublintourism.ie.

HISTORIC HOTEL

Dublin's most famous hotel – an institution in its own right – is The Shelbourne, on St Stephen's Green. Opened in 1824, the hotel is still accepted as the most distinguished address in Ireland. It has hosted many celebrities and played an important role in Ireland's history. Bullets hummed around it in the Easter Rising of 1916 and in 1922 the Constitution of the Irish Free State was drafted in the hotel.

Brewery Hostel € 22-23 Thomas St, Dublin 8; tel: (01) 453 8600; fax: (01) 453 8616; e-mail: breweryh@indigo.ie. Located beside the Guinness Brewery, a 10-min walk from city centre. Five en suite bedrooms, seven dormitories.

Celtic Lodge Guest House €€–€€€ 81–82 Talbot St, Dublin 1; tel: (01) 677 9955; fax: (01) 878 8698; e-mail: celticguesthouse@tinet.ie. A gracious Victorian residence with 29 en suite rooms. A downstairs bar has traditional music. Temple Bar and city centre attractions nearby.

Charles Stewart Hostel €€ 5-6 Parnell Sq., Dublin 1; tel: (01) 878 0350; fax: (01) 878 1387; e-mail: c.stuart@iol.ie. City centre location with 63 bedroom and two dormitories. Full Irish breakfast.

Kelly's Hotel €€–€€€ 36 South Great Georges St, Dublin 2; tel: (01) 677 9277; fax: (01) 671 3216; e-mail: kellyhtl@iol.ie. Close to fashionable Grafton St and a short walk to Trinity College and Temple Bar; 24 rooms, most of them en suite.

Marian Guest House €€ 21 Upper Gardiner St, Dublin 1; tel: (01) 874 4129. Small, family-run guest house with six centrally-heated bedrooms.

O'Neill's Victorian Pub and Townhouse €€–€€€ 36–37 Pearse St, Dublin 2; tel: (01) 671 4074; fax: (01) 832 5218; e-mail: oneilpub@iol.ie. One of Dublin's oldest family-run pubs, located opposite Trinity College, has eight tastefully furnished en suite rooms. Continental breakfast.

DUBLIN DISHES

Traditional Dublin dishes are Irish stew, bacon and cabbage, soda bread and potato cakes. Champ is chopped scallions (spring onions) stirred into creamy mashed potatoes. Dublin Bay prawns and oysters served with Guinness are renowned delicacies.

FOOD AND DRINK

Unless you are going very upmarket for dinner, you would be advised to eat early in Dublin. By 1800 most middle range restaurants in the city centre are full and by 2000 are lowering the shutters. Nevertheless, there is a wide range of restaurants with modestly-priced menus. Pubs are a good choice for soup and sandwiches at lunchtime.

Temple Bar is the place for lively bistro-type establishments. The **Grafton St** area offers a wide choice of menus and prices. Two Dublin establishments have achieved institutional status: **Beshoff**, renowned for fish and chips, has restaurants at 7 Upper O'Connell St, and 14 Westmoreland St. **Bewley's** on Grafton St, South Great George St and Westmoreland St, is the place for noisy get-togethers over coffee, cream cakes and sticky buns.

Burdock's € 2 Werburgh St. The city's oldest fish and chip shop. Strictly take-away fresh fish with chips made from Irish potatoes. But this is no place for vegetarians – the exquisite chips are fried in beef dripping. Mon–Fri 1230–midnight, Sat 1400–2300, Sun 1600–midnight.

Davy Byrne's €€ 21 Duke St. The pub immortalised in James Joyce's *Ulysses* is also a restaurant renowned for its seafood and traditional Irish dishes.

Juice €€ South Great George Street, serves good vegetarian meals at very affordable prices. Open daily 0900–2300 or later.

Kilkenny Kitchen € 6 Nassau St. You'll find this restaurant in the Kilkenny Shop, serving Irish stew, casseroles, salads and an excellent house quiche. Open 0900–1730.

O'Neill's € 2 Suffolk St, is full of atmosphere and one of Dublin's best-known pubs. Close to the Dublin Tourism Centre, it's full of nooks and crannies and has the best pub carvery in the city. Lunch is served 1200–1430, but get there early to find a seat – the place is a favourite with city workers.

Periwinkle Seafood Bar €€ Powerscourt Townhouse
Centre. Quality seafood in an establishment which has won an
Irish Tourist Board award.

The Runner Bean € Nassau St. Located above a green-
grocery of the same name, this is the place for imaginative
vegetarian dishes.

Jones's Delicatessen, 137 Baggot St Lower. Sells all the
makings for a picnic in any of the area's parks or on the towpath of the Grand Canal.

HIGHLIGHTS

You can gain a good introduction to the city by joining the **Hop on-Hop off tour** run
by Dublin Bus. The complete tour lasts about 75 mins, but you can take all day over it
if you wish, hopping on and off at any of 12 stops, each conveniently near one of the
city's most popular attrac-
tions. The open-top buses
depart hourly from out-
side 59 O'Connell St, and
your ticket (€€) entitles
you to a discount at some
of the attractions en route.

PEDESTRIANS ONLY

While it could hardly be called tranquil, Henry St, off
O'Connell St, is traffic-free, which makes shopping quicker
and more pleasurable. It's a great place for fashion, jewellery,
quality gifts and souvenirs. All you need is money. The lilting
Irish music of buskers should put a spring in your step.

For a guided cycling tour
contact **Dublin Bike
Tours**; tel: (01) 679 0899. A genial insight into Dublin's literature, history and architecture is provided on the **Jameson Dublin Literary Pub Crawl** (€€€). These take
place year round and are led by actors who play some of the city's most colourful
characters as groups progress from pub to pub, starting at The Duke on Duke St.

The **O'Connell Bridge** over the River Liffey forms a dividing line between the north
and the south of Dublin. **O'Connell St**, on the north side, dates from the 1700s and at
150 ft is the widest in Europe. Its two lanes are separated by a pedestrian island which
has several statues and memorials. The **Anna Livia Millennium Fountain**, unveiled
in 1988 to mark Dublin's millennium, has been dubbed 'the Floozie in the Jacuzzi'.
Nearby, at North Earl St, is Marjorie Fitzgibbon's statue of Anna's creator, James Joyce.

Modern Irish history is firmly stamped on O'Connell St. You cannot go into the
General Post Office, buy stamps for your postcards or make a phone call from the
generous row of coin and card phones, without noticing the bullet holes in the portico columns. The GPO was significantly involved in the Easter Rising of 1916.

Dating from the 1750s and originally named Rutland Square, **Parnell Square** provided a prestigious address for aristocrats, MPs, men of the ecclesiastical hierarchy and other notables. In a city of fine Georgian architecture, the Square stands out as a peaceful area of gracious buildings. It provides a contrast with the commercial activities and jostling crowds of O'Connell St, just round the corner.

At the **Dublin Writers Museum**, 18 Parnell Sq., you can study original letters, profiles, portraits, memorabilia and photographs of three centuries of the major figures on the city's literary stage. Open Mon–Sat 1000–1700, Sun 1100–1700 (to 1800 June–Aug).

The **Hugh Lane Municipal Gallery of Modern Art**, Charlemont House, Parnell Sq., is named after a benefactor who, in 1905, decided to donate his collection of Impressionist works to Dublin Corporation, with the proviso that they should be exhibited in a suitable building. The Corporation dragged its heels in finding an appropriate place, so Sir Hugh, losing patience, thought that he would let London have the gift instead. Later he had second thoughts and reverted to the original plan. He added a codicil to his will to this effect, but before it was witnessed, he died as a passenger on the *Lusitania* when it was torpedoed in World War I. It took lawyers half a century to sort it out. Dublin and London now take turns to show the collection. Free, open Tues–Fri 0930–1800, Sat 0930–1700, Sun 1100–1700.

> ### O'CONNELL BRIDGE
> Named the Carlisle Bridge when it was built in the 1790s, the O'Connell Bridge was re-named in 1882 after Daniel O'Connell, anti-Union politician and lawyer who helped bring about Catholic emancipation. A statue, a memorial to O'Connell, was erected near the bridge, more than 30 years after his death.

James Joyce Cultural Centre, 35 North Great George St, is one of several carefully restored Georgian houses in the street. In the reference library and exhibition rooms you can get to know much about Joyce and his work. €, open Mon–Sat, 0930–1700, Sun 1230–1700.

Linking Batchelors Row to Wellington Quay, **Ha'penny Bridge** is officially called the Wellington Bridge after the Duke of Wellington, who died in 1852, but everybody knows it as the Ha'penny Bridge, so called because in days gone by that was the toll charged for crossing it.

Dublin's finest Georgian public building is the **Custom House**, Custom House Quay. It was designed by master architect James Gandon and completed in 1791. Its gleaming façade of Portland stone stretches 374ft (114 m) from end to end. A copper dome rises behind the

central portico, crowned by a statue of Commerce. The interior was badly damaged when Republicans set fire to the building in 1921. Now restored, it is used for government offices, but there is a visitor centre. €, open Mon-Fri 1000–1700, Sat–Sun 1400–1700 (mid-Mar–Nov); Wed–Fri 1000–1700, Sun 1400–1700.

RITA'S CAMPUS

If parts of the Trinity College campus seem familiar, it's probably because this was where much of the 1983 film *Educating Rita* was shot.

South of O'Connell Bridge, Westmoreland St leads into College Green, where you'll find the imposing entrance to **Trinity College**, flanked by statues of Edmund Burke (1729–97), the political writer who became a British Member of Parliament, and Oliver Goldsmith (1728–74), poet and playwright. Both men studied at Trinity, which was founded by Queen Elizabeth I in 1592. The campus covers 42 acres (17 ha) of cobbled squares, gardens and sports grounds. None of the original Elizabethan buildings has survived, but their loss has been amply compensated by magnificent Palladian structures.

The Old Library, built in 1732, contains the Long Room, the largest single chamber library in Europe, measuring 213ft by 42ft (65 m by 13 m). **The Colonnades** exhibition gallery displays the world-famous *Book of Kells*, the 9th-century illuminated manuscript of the Four Gospels. €€, open Mon–Sat 0930–1700, Sun 1200–1630. Among Trinity's newer buildings, the Thomas Davis Theatre houses the **Dublin Experience**, an entertaining outline of the city's history. €€, open daily 1000–1700 (mid-May–Sept).

Opposite Trinity's entrance is the **Bank of Ireland**, said to be one of Europe's greatest public buildings. Purpose-built to house the Irish Parliament, it was Dublin's first Palladian-style building. It was sold to the Bank of Ireland after the Irish Parliament was dissolved in 1800. Free guided tours Mon–Wed and Fri 1000–1600.

A striking statue of Molly Malone wheeling her wheelbarrow marks the start of pedestrianised **Grafton St**, Dublin's most popular thoroughfare. Lined with shops large and small, pubs, flower stalls and buskers, it leads to St Stephen's Green. Two of the city's most famous pubs are in Duke St, just off Grafton St. **The Bailey** was frequented by James Joyce before he left Ireland in 1912. Other famous customers were Brendan Behan, Oliver St John Gogarty and Patrick Kavanagh. Across the street, Davy Byrne's owes some of its fame to the fact that Leopold Bloom, of *Ulysses*, stopped off for a snack on 16 June 1904, now celebrated annually as Bloomsday. The area to the west, between William St South and Grafton St is a cornucopia of shops and eating places.

The **Powerscourt Townhouse Centre**, best entered through the splendid façade of the mansion that once stood here on William St South, is Dublin's most upmarket shopping mall. Nearby George's Arcade, a covered market reaching across to South Great George's St, presents everything from fruit and vegetables to second-hand clothing and books, collectibles and antiques.

DUBLIN

To the east are Dawson and Kildare Streets. Dawson St, the more workaday of the two, is where you will find the official residence of the Lord Mayor of Dublin and elegant St. Anne's Church. Kildare St has Leinster House, home of the Dáil, the Irish Parliament, as well as the National Museum, the National Library, and at no. 30, the one-time home of Bram Stoker, creator of Count Dracula.

St Anne's Church dates from 1720, but its present façade was erected in 1868. In 1723 Lord Newtown left a bequest to the church to buy bread for the poor. The tradition continues today and the bread is distributed from a special shelf erected beside the altar. Members of the public are admitted to **Leinster House** in Kildare St but only through an introduction by a member of the Dáil, or when Parliament is not sitting, but the building can be viewed from the outside from the ornate main gates and from the rotundas on either side.

The **National Museum**, on the south side of Leinster House, houses Celtic antiquities and artefacts from the Iron and Bronze Ages and a wide range of Viking items excavated from sites in Dublin. The Road to Independence is a section of the museum devoted to Ireland's tumultuous political history during the first quarter of the 20th century. Free, open Tues–Sat 1000–1700, Sun 1400–1700.

Exhibitions drawn from its massive collection of books, magazines, newspapers, maps, photographs and manuscripts are mounted in the entrance hall of the **National Library**, which occupies the rotunda on the north side of Leinster House. Free, open Mon 1000–2100, Tues–Fri 1000–1700, Sat 1000–1300.

Dublin's heyday in architecture and town planning was in the 18th and 19th centuries and the city is bejewelled with fine Georgian buildings. The pinnacle of residential development was achieved south of the River Liffey, around Merrion Sq and St Stephen's Green, two spacious areas of public parkland still surrounded by splendid buildings.

The **Natural History Museum**, Merrion St, is one of those superbly old-fashioned museums with a creepy, slightly gothic ambience. Dubliners call it 'the dead zoo'. But it's informative and fun for all that. Here you'll find the skeletons of Irish elk, and those of whales stranded on Irish beaches. There are exhibits of Irish wildlife, and jars filled with things that once wriggled, slithered or squirmed. Free, open Tues–Sat 1000–1700, Sun 1400–1700.

The **National Gallery of Ireland**, Merrion Sq. West, houses collections embracing the 14th to the 20th centuries, including works by Degas, El Greco, Goya, Monet and Picasso. One room is devoted to works by Jack B Yeats, the poet's brother. Many, however, consider the *pièce de résistance* to be Caravaggio's *The Taking of Christ*, discovered in 1992 in the Dublin Jesuit House of Study. Free, open Mon–Wed and Fri–Sat 1000–1715, Thur 1000–2030, Sun 1400–1700.

Dublin's largest square – a quarter of a mile (400 m) in each direction and covering 22 acres (9 ha) – **St Stephen's Green** was a tract of rough common ground until 1664 when the city corporation set it aside as an open space for the use of citizens. The trouble was no one could get there. Access was along a rough lane 'so foule and out of repaire that persons cannot passe'. In 1671 the corporation put the lane in order, and pedestrians have been using Grafton St as the main route to St Stephen's Green ever since.

The oldest part of Dublin, on the south side of the River Liffey, embraces the city's two Protestant cathedrals, Dublin Castle and Temple Bar, once a maze of sweat shops and warehouses but now an area of trendy boutiques, bistros, pubs and art galleries.

The best approach to Temple Bar is to cross Ha'penny Bridge from the opposite side of the Liffey and enter the district through Merchants' Arch. This gives the keenest experience of its medieval bazaar ambience. Temple Bar is home to a number of cultural centres, and there is always something going on – jazz and rock festivals, art exhibitions or open-air theatre. To find out what's happening contact the **Temple Bar Information Centre**, 18 Eustace St; tel: (01) 671 5717.

Dublin's Viking Adventure, Essex St West, presents a fanciful trip through time, re-creating the sights, sounds and even smells of old 'Dyflin', as the Vikings knew it. One section features an important collection of artefacts excavated at nearby Wood Quay and other parts of Viking Dublin. €€, open Tues–Sat 1000–1630.

Christ Church Cathedral, Christ Church Pl., originated as a simple wooden church, built in 1038 by Sitric Silkenbeard, king of the Dublin Norsemen. It was rebuilt in stone in 1169 by the Earl of Pembroke, also known as Strongbow. Donation, open daily 1000-1700.

St Patrick's Cathedral, Patrick's Close, dates from 1191, but a church has stood on the site since 450. The saint himself is said to have baptised converts in a nearby well. Jonathan Swift, author of *Gulliver's Travels*, served as Dean of St Patrick's for more than 30 years and is buried in the nave.

Standing on the site of a Viking fortress, **Dublin Castle**, Dame St, dates from the 13th century. Its State Apartments are used for presidential inaugurations and state functions. €€, open Mon–Fri 1000-1700, Sun 1400–1700. **Chester Beatty Library and Gallery of Oriental Art**, Bermingham Tower, Dublin Castle. Sir Alfred Chester Beatty died in 1968, bequeathing his priceless collection of oriental furniture, decorated manuscripts, paintings and ceramics to the Irish nation. The collection is so large that curators estimate it will take 55 years to display everything in a rotating exhibition.

SHOPPING

Quality is the hallmark of Ireland's irresistible products – crystal, textiles, fine china, knitwear, whiskey, liqueurs, farmhouse cheeses, smoked salmon. Quality is enduring and it doesn't come cheap, so if you're looking for something really special, prepare to dig deep.

Spend time in **Clery's** in O'Connell St and **Arnott's** in Henry St. Both have dedicated Irish shops within the store. Wander around **Brown Thomas** in Grafton St, where everything from a velvet scarf to a cocktail shaker has a classy look. Beautiful Irish crafts, including Waterford crystal, bone china, jewellery and textiles attract visitors to the **House of Ireland** in Nassau St, near Trinity College.

For high fashion, **Grafton St** and its environs certainly won't let you down. Even in the dead of winter the flower stalls are piled high with glorious blooms, and there's nearly always a busker somewhere, playing the fiddle expertly or singing his heart out. It's a place with a joyous atmosphere, and whatever intentions you start out with you'll find yourself in a what-the-hell spending mood.

At the southern end of Grafton St, the **St Stephen's Green Shopping Centre** has three floors of specialist shops and places to eat. On the ground floor is an enormous Dunne's, a good value store with 100 branches throughout the country which the Irish love and trust. Clothes for the whole family, food, booze and what-have-you, can be bought here. Take a look at The Donegal Shop on the top floor. Hand-woven tweed jackets for men and women, homespun tweed caps and hats, traditional hand-knitted polo sweaters, hand-loomed Aran cardigans and sweaters in 100 per cent wool …

People with an eye for the unusual and those who are natural born collectors should make a weekend bee-line for the indoor **Mother Redcap's Market**. All sorts of bric-à-brac, antiques and collectibles and general flea market discoveries are on sale. There are old photographs, good knitwear, furniture, mats, nails and screws, electrical items, paintings, gadgets and heaven knows what. The market is in Back Lane, off Cornmarket. Open Fri–Sun 1000–1730.

NIGHTLIFE

Most of Dublin's nightclubs are in **Leeson St**, off St Stephen's Green. The Burlington Hotel, in Upper Leeson St, features a classy Irish cabaret. The snappy dressers among the young set dance the night away at The **PoD** in Harcourt St. The abbreviation means 'Place of Dance'.

For dancing to music from the 1960s, '70s and '80s, try the **Leftbank Bar** in Anglesea St, Temple Bar. **La Med**, in Essex St, Temple Bar, has a jazz bar. Irish music sessions and dancing nights are held at **Lanigan's Pub** at the Clifton Court Hotel, O'Connell's Bridge. Turf fires and candlelight set the mood.

The **Abbey Theatre**, incorporating the smaller Peacock Theatre, in Lower Abbey St, is noted for its Irish classics and (in the Peacock) the work of new writers. Contemporary works are staged at the **Gate Theatre**, Parnell Sq. Performances of general and family appeal are presented at the **Gaiety Theatre**, South King St, where dance, drama, opera and musicals take place. The **Olympia Theatre**, Dame St, stages music events and family entertainment. Classical music is performed at the **National Concert Hall**, and the occasional gig is held there.

Keep an eye on the major daily newspapers for details of what's on. The fortnightly *Hot Press* gives the low-down on the music scene. Tickets and information on most events, theatres, shows and tours are available from the Ticket Desk, Dublin Tourism Centre. For ticket reservations by credit card, tel: (01) 605 7777.

SIDE TRIPS

Beaches, fishing villages, country towns, castles, monastic remains, bird sanctuaries, boat trips, stately homes and gardens – all these are ideally located for a day out from Dublin. Better still, many of them are accessible by DART (Dublin Area Rapid Transport) which has more than two dozen stations along Dublin Bay.

Almost at the southern limit of DART, 14 miles (23 km) from Dublin, **Bray** has more than a mile of sand and shingle beach. On warm summer days crowds flock along the esplanade and into the amusement arcades. The **National Aquarium** presents a fascinating array of marine life. Thousands of fish and other creatures are exhibited. About 2 miles (3 km) south-west, at Enniskerry, is **Powerscourt House and Gardens** estate. The Palladian-style house, built in the 1730s, was severely damaged by fire in 1974 but there has been some restoration. A garden centre, terrace café, children's playground, picnic area, and 45 acres (18 ha) of formal and walled gardens provide a good day out.

The DART station at **Killiney** is right on the pebbly beach, which stretches for 2 miles (3 km). People come from miles around to swim here. It's worth panting up the hill in Killiney Park for the view of the bay.

Howth is an attractive village at the northern end of the DART line, and is the northernmost point of Dublin Bay. It offers a range of watersports and has a marina for pleasure craft. It is a busy commercial fishing port and is a good strolling area for visitors. The grounds of **Howth Castle**, behind the Deer Park Hotel, are worth seeing, particularly in late spring when countless varieties of rhododendron are in bloom. Here you will find the **National Transport Museum**, exhibiting early horse-drawn commercial vehicles, carriages, fire-fighting appliances, early motor vehicles and the open-top Hill of Howth tram which served the village up to half a century ago.

You can take a feeder bus from Howth DART station to **Malahide**, where the enormous structure of **Malahide Castle** is the big attraction. Its 250-acre (101-ha) grounds include the Talbot Botanic Gardens and the Fry Model Railway Museum, a favourite with children. The castle has stood for more than eight centuries.

WHERE NEXT?

From Dublin's Connolly Station you can travel south, following the Irish Sea coast for much of the route to Waterford (see pp. 388–389). Stops along the way include Wicklow and Wexford, with the neighbouring ferry port of Rosslare. An alternative route to Waterford is from Heuston Station via Kildare (see pp. 379–380), the market town of Carlow, on the River Barrow, and Kilkenny, noted for its medieval castle, cathedral and 6th-century round tower.

1892 Thomas Cook brochure cover

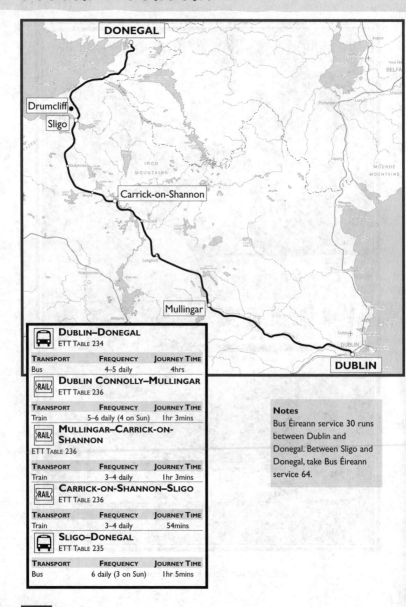

DONEGAL

Drumcliff

Sligo

Carrick-on-Shannon

Mullingar

DUBLIN

🚌 DUBLIN–DONEGAL
ETT TABLE 234

TRANSPORT	FREQUENCY	JOURNEY TIME
Bus	4–5 daily	4hrs

🚆RAIL🚆 DUBLIN CONNOLLY–MULLINGAR
ETT TABLE 236

TRANSPORT	FREQUENCY	JOURNEY TIME
Train	5–6 daily (4 on Sun)	1hr 3mins

🚆RAIL🚆 MULLINGAR–CARRICK-ON-SHANNON
ETT TABLE 236

TRANSPORT	FREQUENCY	JOURNEY TIME
Train	3–4 daily	1hr 3mins

🚆RAIL🚆 CARRICK-ON-SHANNON–SLIGO
ETT TABLE 236

TRANSPORT	FREQUENCY	JOURNEY TIME
Train	3–4 daily	54mins

🚌 SLIGO–DONEGAL
ETT TABLE 235

TRANSPORT	FREQUENCY	JOURNEY TIME
Bus	6 daily (3 on Sun)	1hr 5mins

Notes
Bus Éireann service 30 runs between Dublin and Donegal. Between Sligo and Donegal, take Bus Éireann service 64.

This cross-country route takes you across the capital's fertile hinterland, following the old Royal Canal, now undergoing restoration, to the lively market town of Mullingar, at the centre of Ireland's cattle-raising lands. Continuing north-west through Co. Longford, you enter the region of the majestic River Shannon, flowing from lough to lough on its south-westerly course to the Atlantic Ocean. Carrick-on-Shannon, on the river's upper reaches, is a boating holiday centre but is worth a stopover for landlubbers.

From here, the route threads its way between loughs and mountain ranges to reach Sligo Town on the Atlantic coast. This is the end of the line, as far as rail travel is concerned. Continuing north on the N15 along these rugged but beautiful western shorelines, you cross into Co. Donegal, just before the resort town of Ballyshannon, at the mouth of the north-flowing River Erne, and reach Donegal Town 41 miles (66 km) from Sligo Town.

DUBLIN

See p. 347.

MULLINGAR

There is an energetic, friendly feel to Mullingar, which has become a popular touring base for the Midlands region. The market town's skyline is dominated by the twin spires of the Renaissance-style **Cathedral of Christ the King**, which was completed in 1939. Inside are superb mosaics of St Patrick and St Anne by the Russian artist Boris Anrep, and an ecclesiastical museum. The cathedral opens daily 0900–1730; ecclesiastical museum opens Thur, Sat and Sun 1600–1700, or contact the sacristan; tel: (044) 48402.

Mullingar is a former garrison town, and artefacts from the various conflicts in Irish history, including uniforms and weapons of local units of the old IRA, are displayed in the **Military Museum** (€) in Columb Barracks; tel: (044) 48391. Open by appointment only. Mullingar is at the heart of Ireland's cattle-raising lands, and farmers across the country judge a good cow as 'beef to the heels, like a Mullingar heifer'.

> *i* **Tourist Information Office** Market House, Mullingar;
> tel: (044) 48650; website: www.midlandseastireland.travel.ie;
> e-mail: midlandseastireland@eirecom.net. Open Mon–Fri
> 0900–1800, Sat 0900–1300.

> 🛏 **Greville Arms Hotel** €€€ Mullingar, Co. Westmeath;
> tel: (044) 48563; fax: (044) 48052. Each of the 39 bedrooms in
> this centrally-located hotel is en suite, with colour TV and

direct dial telephone. Most rooms look out on to the garden.
There is a restaurant.

Marlinstown Court €€ Dublin Rd Mullingar, Co.
Westmeath; tel: (044) 40053. In a beautiful setting in its own
grounds, a mile from the town centre, the B&B has five en
suite rooms. Non-smoking rooms available.

Petieswood House €€ Dublin Rd, Mullingar, Co. Westmeath;
tel: (044) 48397. Large attractive house in a tree-lined avenue,
1 mile from the town centre. Three en suite rooms; non-
smoking available.

Woodside €€ Dublin Rd, Mullingar, Co. Westmeath; tel: (044)
41636. A 10-min walk from the town centre, this attractive
family home has four en suite guest rooms and caters for non-
smokers.

CARRICK-ON-SHANNON

The county town of Leitrim, Carrick is a small (population 2000) but attractive town
on the River Shannon, bordering Co. Roscommon. It has some fine Georgian buildings and as Ireland's main centre for river boating holidays is well geared to
tourism. It's also a good centre for walking, cycling, angling and birdwatching.
Apart from boating, the town's major claim to fame is that it has the world's second
smallest chapel. The **Costello Chapel**, Main St, was built in 1877 by Edward
Costello, a local tycoon, as a memorial to his young wife. The couple are interred in
lead coffins, side by side, sunk in the floor and covered by glass.

i **Tourism Information Point** The Quay, Carrick-on-
Shannon; tel: (077) 20170. Seasonal opening.

🛏 **Aisleigh Guest House** €€ Dublin Rd, Carrick-on-Shannon,
Co. Leitrim; tel/fax: (078)20313; www.homepage.eircom.net/
~aisleigh; e-mail: aisleigh@eircom.net. Family-run, the guest
house is a mile from the town centre and has ten en suite
guest rooms. Facilities include a games room and sauna.

Attyrory Lodge €€ Dublin Rd, Carrick-on-Shannon, Co.
Leitrim; tel/fax: (078) 20955; e-mail: attyrorylodge@eircom.net.
Five en suite rooms — some for non-smokers — in a modern
chalet-style B&B. Dinner available.

Bush Hotel €€€ Carrick-on-Shannon, Co. Leitrim; tel: (078)
20014; fax: (078) 21180; www.bushhotel.com; e-mail:
bushhotel:eircom.net. One of Ireland's oldest hotels, located in
the town centre, the Bush has recently undergone a major
refurbishment. It has 28 en suite rooms, bars, coffee shop and a
restaurant.

Corbally Lodge €€ Dublin Rd, Carrick-on-Shannon, Co. Leitrim; tel/fax: (078) 20228; e-mail: valerierowley@ hotmail.com. Four guest rooms – three of them en suite – in a peaceful B&B with antique furnishings on the outskirts of town. If you're trying to trace ancestors, the owner may be able to help.

Moyrane House €€ Dublin Rd, Carrick-on-Shannon, Co. Leitrim; tel: (078) 20325; www.homepage.eircom.net/~ eleanorshortt. Less than half a mile from town, this modern B&B has three en suite rooms and one standard room. Non-smokers accommodated.

TO Catering mainly for boating holidaymakers, Carrick has plenty of eating places, especially pubs, and good provision stores and delicatessens. If you are shopping to feed yourself, Clancy's Supermarket, on the Roscommon side of the bridge, can meet most demands.

SLIGO

The Northwest's largest town spans the River Garavogue and covers the neck of land between Lough Gill and Sligo Bay. It's a lively place, with a booming economy, a college and a compact town centre of traditional façades. The town is also known as a centre for the arts and Irish music. Its greatest appeal for many visitors is its associations with the poet W B Yeats.

At Hyde Bridge, a striking bronze statue of the man by Rohan Gillespie stands across from the Yeats Memorial Building, where the Yeats Summer School of poetry readings, lectures and other events is held in Aug. The **Sligo Art Gallery**, Yeats Memorial Building, Hyde Bridge, holds contemporary art exhibitions. €, open Mon–Sat 1000–1700.

The **Yeats Gallery Library Building**, Stephen St, is home to a large collection of paintings by Jack B Yeats, the poet's brother, and their father John B Yeats. Personal memorabilia is displayed in the museum. €, open Tues–Fri 1000–1700, Sat 1000–1300, 1400–1700.

Founded in 1253, **Sligo Abbey**, is the only medieval building remaining in the town, and most of the ruins date from the 15th century. The cloisters and altar have beautifully carved stonework. Other notable buildings include the court-house, Dominican friary and several churches. €€, open daily 0930–1830 (June–Sept).

i **Tourist Information Office** Aras Reddan, Temple St, Silgo; tel: (071) 61201; fax: (071) 60360. Open Mon–Fri 0900–1300, 14001700. Sat 0900–1300.

THE BROTHERS YEATS

The poet William Butler Yeats (1865–1939) and his artist brother Jack (1871–1957) were members of a prominent Sligo family. Although they spent their childhood in London, where their father John struggled to earn a living as a portrait painter, during summer holidays they visited their maternal grandparents, the Pollexfens, who were merchant shippers in Sligo. This idyllic landscape inspired them throughout their lives.

🛏 Sligo has a breadth of B&B choices, with many handily located near the railway station in the centre of town. Hotels range from one to three stars.

Alverno B&B €€ Cairns Hill Rd, Sligo Town, Co. Sligo; tel: (071) 63893. Three guest rooms (two en suite) in a two-storey Georgian house.

Innisfree Hotel €€€ High St, Sligo Town, Co. Sligo; tel: (071) 4201; fax: (071) 45745. Family-run hotel, in town centre, with 19 en suite rooms. Food available all day.

Lisadorn Guest House €€ Donegal Rd, Sligo Town, Co. Sligo; tel: (071) 43417; fax: (071) 46418; e-mail: cjo'connor@eircom.net. Sligo's first three-star guest house, located within five mins of the town centre. Seven en suite rooms.

Rosscahill B&B €€ 19 Marymount, Pearse Rd, Sligo Town; Co. Sligo; tel: (071) 61744. Located in a quiet cul-de-sac, the house has three en suite guest rooms.

Stradbrook €€ Cornageeha, Pearse Rd, Sligo Town; Co. Sligo; tel: (071) 69674; fax: (071) 69933; www.stradbrook.com; e-mail: stradbrook@futurenet.ie. Four en suite rooms in this family-run B&B.

Treetops €€ Cleveragh Rd, Sligo Town, Co. Sligo; tel: (071) 60160; fax: (071) 62301; www.sligobandb.com; e-mail: treetops@iol.ie. This non-smoking B&B, a 5-min walk from the town centre, has five en suite guest rooms.

🍴 Sligo is well off for reasonably-priced eating places. Most pubs – and the town is famous for them – serve bar lunches. For a real treat – garlic mushrooms, say, or smoked chicken and all sorts of filled baguettes – try the **Yeats River Café** € The Mall (closed Sun).

The **Garavogue** €€ Stephen St, serves pasta, pizzas and a range of modern Mediterranean dishes.

If you are self-catering, there are lots of good food shops, a Friday market and **Cosgrove's** 32 Market Sq., an old-fashioned delicatessen.

Yeats Tavern Restaurant € on the N15 at Drumcliff (see p. 365) is a cheery family-run establishment, with a large pub and adjoining restaurant. Great burgers, salads and a range of meals that are a cut above the usual pub fare. Open daily 1230–2200.

SIDE TRIP FROM SLIGO It's worth taking a trip to Drumcliff, 5 miles (8 km) north of Sligo, where W B Yeats is buried, as he wished, in the Protestant churchyard at the foot of Benbulben mountain. His grave lies just to the left of the entrance to the little church where his grandfather was rector. The tombstone is inscribed with his own epitaph: 'Cast a cold eye/On life, on death,/Horseman, pass by!' St Colmcille founded a monastery here in the 6th century, and a fine carved high cross from this earlier church still stands. Another remnant is the well-preserved round tower, built between 900 and 1200, across the road. **Strandhill**, 5 miles (8 km) west, is a relaxing seaside resort overlooking Sligo Bay. Both places can be reached by bus from Sligo Town.

> **WHERE NEXT FROM SLIGO?**
>
> *You can head by bus to Ballina (see p. 371), which takes 1 hr 30 mins; Mon–Sat.*

DONEGAL TOWN

Donegal Town is a gateway into the wilder parts of the northwest. Its Irish name, Dún na nGall, means 'fort of the foreigners'. Originally, this referred to the Vikings who set up a base here in the 9th century, but seems equally fitting today, considering the number of visitors to this small town. It is set on a crossroads where the River Eske flows into Donegal Bay, and built around the attractive 17th-century market square, known as the Diamond. The 20-ft (6-m) obelisk here commemorates the Four Masters – four Franciscan friars who set out between 1632 and 1636 to preserve as much of Celtic culture as possible and compiled one of the earliest historic texts, the *Annals of the Four Masters*, now in the National Library. The ruins of **Donegal Abbey**, where they laboured, lie a few minutes' walk south of town. Beside the Diamond, **Donegal Castle**, €€, built by an O'Donnell chieftain in the 15th century, has been restored and can be visited. Open daily 0930–1745 (Easter–Oct). The town is also a centre for the tweed industry.

> *i* **Tourist Information Office** Key St, Donegal; tel: (073) 21148; fax: (073) 22762. Open Mon–Fri 0900–1800; Sat 0900–1300 (Easter–Sept).

> 🛏 Donegal has half a dozen medium-sized hotels and about 20 reasonably-priced quality B&Bs.
>
> **Bay-View** €€ Golf Course Rd, Donegal Town, Co. Donegal; tel: (073) 23018. Four en suite rooms in a quiet B&B overlooking Donegal Bay. Golf, fishing, sand beaches and walking trails nearby; 10-min walk to town.
> **Cranaford** €€ Ardeskin, Donegal Town, Co. Donegal; tel: (073) 21455; e-mail: cranaford@ireland.com. This modern family bungalow, in a peaceful residential area, has two en suite rooms and one standard room and is within walking distance of town.

The Harp of Erne **Water Bus** Tour takes you on a scenic 90-minute cruise of Donegal Bay and its islands. Tickets from the booking office at Donegal Pier; tel: (073) 23666.

ALL TWEEDY

Magee of Donegal, established in 1866, is famous for its hand-woven tweed jackets, which are reasonably priced at its shop on the Diamond. Outside town on the Ballyshannon Rd, Donegal Craft Village is a group of workshops making batik, pottery, jewellery and uilleann pipes among other goods.

Island View House €€ Tullaghcullion, Donegal Town, Co. Donegal; tel: (073) 22411; www.eirbyte.com/islandview; e-mail: islandview@eirbyte.com. Overlooking Donegal Bay, a 10-min walk from town, this new two-storey Georgian-style house has four en suite rooms.

Rosearl €€ The Glebe, Donegal Town, Co. Donegal; tel: (073) 21462; e-mail: rosearl@indigo.ie. Four en suite rooms in a modern, spacious home in a quiet residential area, 5 mins walk from the town centre.

McGroarty's Bar €. This traditional bar, housed in a stone building on the Diamond, caters for vegetarians, a rarity in Ireland. Along with smoked salmon and a variety of sandwiches and casseroles, there is a long list of creative vegetarian dishes to choose from, all fresh and prepared to order, including salads, quiches, stir-fry, pitta bread wraps and soups. Lunch is 1200–1700 (May–Sept), 1200–1500 (Oct–Apr); snacks served all day.

WHERE NEXT?

There are no rail services in the north-west of Ireland, but you can travel by road from Donegal Town to Londonderry (there are 3–4 buses run by Bus Éireann, service 64, daily; journey time 1 hr 25 mins). The N15 passes the southern end of Lough Eske and skirts the Blue Stack Mountains, reaching Ballybofey after 17 miles (27 km), then continuing for another 14 miles (23 km) to Strabane, just across the border. From here the A5 follows the line of the Foyle river for 15 miles (24 km) to Londonderry, where it meets the rail link with Belfast (see pp. 327–333).

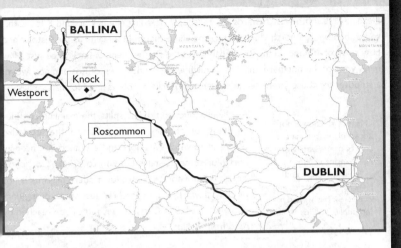

BALLINA

Knock

Westport

Roscommon

DUBLIN

RAIL	**DUBLIN HEUSTON–BALLINA** ETT TABLE 240	
TRANSPORT	**FREQUENCY**	**JOURNEY TIME**
Train	3–4 daily	3hrs 42mins

RAIL	**DUBLIN HEUSTON–ROSCOMMON** ETT TABLE 240	
TRANSPORT	**FREQUENCY**	**JOURNEY TIME**
Train	4–5 daily	1hr 53mins

RAIL	**ROSCOMMON–WESTPORT** ETT TABLE 240	
TRANSPORT	**FREQUENCY**	**JOURNEY TIME**
Train	3 daily	1hr 36mins

RAIL	**ROSCOMMON–BALLINA** ETT TABLE 240	
TRANSPORT	**FREQUENCY**	**JOURNEY TIME**
Train	3–4 daily	1hr 38mins

	WESTPORT–BALLINA	
TRANSPORT	**FREQUENCY**	**JOURNEY TIME**
Bus	2–3 daily	1hr 10mins

Notes

Change at Manulla Junction on the journey between Dublin and Ballina.

Bus Éireann services 51/66/456 between Westport and Ballina.

ROUTE 367

DUBLIN — BALLINA

Heading first south-west towards the racehorse-breeding country around Kildare, this route then sweeps north-west, skirting the Slieve Bloom Mountains to the historic and busy town of Athlone on the River Shannon at the southern end of Lough Ree. Just a few miles west of the northern end of the lough is the county town of Roscommon, worth a stopover for those interested in the ruins of medieval abbeys and Norman castles.

Manulla Junction is not accessible by road and is only of use to passengers changing between Dublin–Manulla and Manulla–Ballina trains and vice versa. The station has no public facilities at all.

At Manulla Junction the line splits, the mainline continuing west for about a dozen miles to the attractive Georgian town of Westport and a branch line heading north for some 25 miles (40 km) to Ballina, Co. Mayo's largest town. Knock, a centre for modern pilgrims, is not on the railway. It lies on the N17, just south of its junction with the N5 at Charlestown and can be reached by road from Ballina.

DUBLIN

See p. 347.

ROSCOMMON

This stone-built market town lies at the heart of an agricultural district. The old **county gaol** in the town centre commemorates the hangwoman 'Lady Betty'. Sentenced to death for the murder of her son in 1780, she escaped her fate by agreeing to take on the unwanted job of executioner, which she fulfilled for 30 years.

Opposite the gaol is the lovely Georgian courthouse, now the Bank of Ireland. South of the centre in Abbey St are the ruins of **Roscommon Abbey**, a Dominican friary built in 1253 by Felim O'Connor, king of Connacht. His tomb in the church is supported by eight sculpted gallowglasses – Scottish medieval warriors hired to repel the Anglo-Norman invaders. To the north of town are the formidable ruins of **Roscommon Castle**, a Norman stronghold.

i **Tourist Information Office** Harrison Hall, Market Sq, Roscommon; tel: (0903) 26342. Open Mon–Sat 1000–1730 (mid-May–mid-Sept).

Regan's Guest House €€ Market Sq, Roscommon Town, Co. Roscommon; tel: (0903) 25339; fax: (0903) 27833. Licensed guesthouse in the town centre with 14 en suite

rooms and two-bedroom self-catering apartments.
Hillcrest House €€ Racecourse Rd, Roscommon, Co.
Roscommon; tel: (0903) 25201. Four en suite rooms in a
modern country house, less than a mile out of town. Non-
smokers accommodated.
Riverside House €€ Riverside Ave, Circular Rd, Roscommon
Town, Co. Roscommon; tel: (0903) 26897. Two en suite rooms in
a modern bungalow within walking distance of the town centre.

KNOCK

In 1879, 15 people witnessed an apparition of the Blessed Virgin in this small impoverished town. It has since become an international Marian Shrine, visited by 1½ million pilgrims seeking cures or forgiveness every year. The basilica built to
accommodate them has 32 pillars, one donated from each of the counties in Ireland;
the four medieval windows represent the four provinces. Pope John Paul II commemorated the centenary of the apparition during a visit here in 1979.

Knock Shrine (€), a programme of ceremonies and devotions takes place late
Apr–mid-Oct; call for information; tel: (094) 88100; www.knock-shrine.ie; e-mail:
info@knock-shrine.ie. To the south of the church, the **Knock Folk Museum** (€€) portrays life in rural Ireland in the 19th century, and documents the story of the apparition. Open daily 1000–1800 (May–June, Sept–Oct); daily 1000–1900 (July–Aug).

> *i* **Tourist Information Office**, Knock; tel: (094) 88193.
> Open daily 1000–1800 (May–Sept).

> 🛏 **Knock International Hotel** €€ Main St, Knock, Co.
> Mayo; tel: (094) 88428. A favourite with pilgrims since 1986, the
> family-run hotel is handy for the Shrine and Knock Airport. Ten
> en suite rooms.
> **Carramore House** €€ Airport Rd, Knock, Co. Mayo; tel;
> (094) 88149; fax: (094) 88154. Family home about a third of a
> mile (500 m) from the Shrine. Six en suite rooms, some non-
> smoking. Light meals.
> **Eskerville** €€ Claremorris Rd, Knock, Co. Mayo; tel: (094)
> 88413. Dormer bungalow with four en suite rooms and one
> standard room. Dinner and partial board available.

WESTPORT

Westport, one of the few planned towns in the Republic, with an octagon, rather
than a square or diamond at its centre, was designed by James Wyatt in the 18th

century. The graceful tree-lined Mall which straddles the Carrowbeg River, the lovely Georgian houses and the bright shop fronts on Bridge St make this heritage town a popular base for visitors.

Westport House and Country Estate, tel: (098) 25430, near the quay, is the home of Lord Sligo, a descendant of the pirate queen Grace O'Malley. The house was built in 1730 and has many outstanding features, including ceilings by Richard Castle, a dining room by James Wyatt and exquisite period furnishings. In the grounds are a children's zoo, a miniature railway and various family attractions. €€€, open Mon–Sat 1400–1700 or 1800 (Easter–late June and late Aug–Sept); Mon–Sat 1130–1800, Sun 1400–1800 (late June–late Aug); call to confirm opening days.

i **Tourist Information Centre** James St, Westport; tel: (098) 25711; fax: (098) 26709. Open Mon–Sat 0900–1800 (June and Sept); Mon–Sat 0900–1700 and Sun 1000–1800 (July-Aug); Mon–Fri 0900–1715 (Oct–May).

🛏 There's no shortage of accommodation in Westport, but it's worth remembering that the town does get busy in summer, so it's a good idea to make reservations.
Augusta Lodge €€ Golf Links Rd, Westport, Co. Mayo; tel: (098) 28900; fax: (098) 28995; www.augustalodge.ie; e-mail: info@augustalodge.ie. A purpose-built, three-star guest house just a five-min walk from the town centre. Ten en suite rooms.
Central Hotel €€€ The Octagon, Westport, Co. Mayo; tel: (098) 25027; fax: (098) 26316; www.thecentralhotel.com; e-mail: centralhotel@anu.ie. Recently renovated, the town centre hotel has 35 en suite rooms and a restaurant. Bar food served all day.
Broadlands €€ Quay Rd, Westport, Co. Mayo; tel: (098) 27377. Close to the town centre and Westport Quay, this large bungalow B&B has five en suite rooms and accommodates non-smokers.
St Anthony's €€ Distillery Rd, Westport, Co. Mayo; tel: (098) 25406; e-mail: edkelly@eircom.net. B&B in an 1820 house standing in an acre of riverside grounds. Five en suite rooms, two with Jacuzzis. Non-smokers accommodated.

🍴 Westport is well geared up to feed its visitors. For self-caterers, a farmers' market is held on Thur mornings at The Octagon, in the town centre.
Kirwan's on the Mall €€ The Mall; tel: (098) 29077, serves adventurous, modern Irish cooking in a converted Methodist church. Closed Sun.
Torrinos €–€€ 10 Market Lane, Middle Bridge St; tel: (098) 28338. You'd be wise to book a table in high season in this

justifiably popular Italian restaurant. There's a wide choice of meat, poultry, pasta and gourmet pizzas and a good wine list.

ENTERTAINMENT The town has a lively entertainment scene, especially from mid-July, which sees the start of the **Westport Street Festival** and end-Sept when the end of summer is marked by the town's **arts festival**. The **Wyatt Theatre**, in the Town Hall, features Irish drama. The best pubs and restaurants are to be found around The Quay and along Bridge St, where **Matt Molloy's**, owned by a member of The Chieftains folk group, is one of the most popular venues for traditional music in Westport.

BALLINA

Standing on the River Moy, and the largest town in Co. Mayo, Ballina is a noted centre for salmon and trout fishing. Largely modern, it still shows some of the planned elegance from its founding by Lord Tyrawley in 1730. There is a pleasant walk beside the river in which salmon trawling takes place.

Near the railway station, a quarter of a mile out of town (400 m), is the **Dolmen of the Four Maols**, said to mark the grave of four foster-brothers who murdered a bishop in the 6th century and were themselves killed by his brother. Ballina marks the start of the **North Mayo Sculpture Trail**, where works by leading sculptors from eight countries and three continents are located in wild and beautiful countryside. The town is a good centre for antiques and shoppers will also find knitwear, tweeds and other craft goods.

WHERE NEXT?

From Ballina you can travel by road north-west on the N59 for 32 miles (51 km) to Sligo (see pp. 363–364) and on by way of the N15 to Donegal (see pp. 365–366). There are direct buses to Sligo (Mon–Sat), taking 1 hr 30 mins.

i **Tourist Information Office** Cathedral Rd, Ballina; tel: (096) 70848. Open Mon–Sat 1000–1800 (Apr–Sept).

🏨 **Downhill Inn** €€€ Sligo Rd, Ballina, Co. Mayo; tel: (096) 73444; fax: (096) 73411; www.downhillinn.com; e-mail: thedownhillinn@eircom.net. Far from going downhill, this family-run 3-star hotel, a mile out of town, is contemporary in design and has 45 en suite rooms, a bar and restaurant.
Rock Guest House €€ Foxford Rd, Ballina, Co. Mayo; tel: (096) 22140; e-mail: therocks@eircom.net. Six en suite rooms in an attractive residence standing in large landscaped gardens with a children's play area and barbecue. The owners can arrange river and sea fishing trips.
Belvedere House €€ Foxford Rd, Ballina, Co. Mayo; tel: (096) 22004. Modern Georgian-style home within walking distance of town, offering B&B in four en suite rooms.

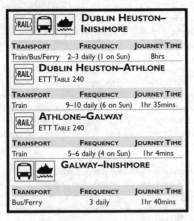

RAIL 🚌 ⛴	**DUBLIN HEUSTON–INISHMORE**	
TRANSPORT	**FREQUENCY**	**JOURNEY TIME**
Train/Bus/Ferry	2–3 daily (1 on Sun)	8hrs

RAIL	**DUBLIN HEUSTON–ATHLONE** ETT TABLE 240	
TRANSPORT	**FREQUENCY**	**JOURNEY TIME**
Train	9–10 daily (6 on Sun)	1hr 35mins

RAIL	**ATHLONE–GALWAY** ETT TABLE 240	
TRANSPORT	**FREQUENCY**	**JOURNEY TIME**
Train	5–6 daily (4 on Sun)	1hr 4mins

🚌 ⛴	**GALWAY–INISHMORE**	
TRANSPORT	**FREQUENCY**	**JOURNEY TIME**
Bus/Ferry	3 daily	1hr 40mins

Notes

Travel by train Dublin Heuston–Galway, by bus Galway–Rossaveal, and by ferry Rossaveal–Inishmore (bus and ferry operated by Island Ferries).

Here's a trip that takes you right across the centre of Ireland – from the far east to the vibrant western city of Galway, then on across romantic Galway Bay to the tranquil and traditional Aran Isles. From Dublin, the train heads south-west through Kildare (see pp. 379–380), then curves northwards to the busy and historic town of Athlone, straddling the River Shannon. On next through cattle-and horse-rearing country to Galway City. From here, you will need to cross the water by air or ferryboat to reach the islands.

To do the trip by road from Dublin, take the N4 for 39 miles (63 km) from Dublin to Kinnegad, then follow the N6 for 39 miles (63 km) to Athlone and continue on this road for a further 57 miles (92 km) to Galway City. Total distance: 135 miles (218 km) (about 3 hrs 15 mins). Remember, vehicles are not permitted to cross to the islands.

DUBLIN

See p. 347.

ATHLONE

Set along the River Shannon at the base of Lough Ree, Athlone is a busy market town and road junction. Its main attraction is the 12th-century **Athlone Castle**, €€, open daily 1000–1700 (May–Sept). The Irish retreated here in 1691 after their defeat at the Battle of the Boyne (see p. 344), and the castle suffered in the subsequent bombardment, but has now been restored. Its museum contains exhibits on the siege, the history of the town and the life of the great tenor, John McCormack (1884–1945), a native of Athlone. Behind the castle, the buildings of the 'Left Bank' date back more than 200 years. The MV *Ross* takes passengers on a 90-min cruise on the River Shannon from Jolly Mariner Marina. Cruises daily (Apr–Sept) €€€.

> *i* **Tourist Information Office** Athlone Castle and Visitor Centre, St Peters Sq, Atholne; tel: (0902) 94630. Open Mon–Fri 0900–1800, Sat 0900–1300 (Apr–Oct).

> 🛏 The town and surrounding area has about half a dozen reasonably priced hotels and plenty of B&Bs.
> **Shamrock Lodge Hotel** €€€ Clonown Rd, Athlone, Co. Westmeath; tel: (0902) 92601; fax: (0902 92737. Manor-style hotel in landscaped gardens a 5-min walk from the town centre; 27 en suite rooms.
> **De Vere House** €€ Retreat Rd, Athlone, Co. Westmeath; tel: (0902) 75376. Three en suite rooms and one standard room in

a modern residence in its own grounds, close to town centre.
Dun Mhuire House €€ Bonavalley, Dublin Rd, Athlone, Co.
Westmeath. An attractive house on the outskirts with two en
suite and two standard rooms.
Heather View €€ Auburn, Dublin Rd, Athlone, Co.
Westmeath. This large bungalow on an acre of ground in a
quiet cul de sac has four en suite rooms.

SIDE TRIP FROM ATHLONE You can take a trip with Rosanna Cruises from Athlone,
tel: (0902) 73383, south along the River Shannon to
Clonmacnoise, the stunning early Christian monastic site, founded by St Ciarán in
548. It has two round towers, several churches and hundreds of early grave slabs.

GALWAY CITY

Galway City, on Galway Bay at the mouth of the River Corrib, is capital of the West
and one of the fastest growing cities in the country. It's a pleasant place, with a compact and colourful centre that still bears traces of its medieval past. Founded in the
13th century, the city became an Anglo-Norman bastion amid the fiercely Irish lands
of Connacht. Today, it's the Irish traditions that hold sway, from the hand-painted
wooden shop signs along its cobbled streets to the traditional music and Irish-
language theatre. The resort of Salthill, with beaches and a splendid promenade, lies
just beyond the city centre.

With its grassy lawns and monuments, **Eyre Square** is a gathering point for
Galwegians. The park is known as John F Kennedy Memorial Park, in honour of the
US president who visited here in 1963. A bronze plaque with his likeness is near the
statue of Pádraic O'Conaire (1882–1928), one of Ireland's most important literary figures. The focal point of the square is the fountain with a striking sculpture representing the rust-coloured sails of a Galway 'hooker', the region's traditional sailing boat.

Galway Cathedral commands the skyline from Nun's Island, formed by channels of
the River Corrib. It was one of the last cruciform churches to be built in Ireland, and
was dedicated in 1965 by Boston's Cardinal Cushing. The **Collegiate Church of St
Nicholas**, Lombard St, was built by the Normans in 1320 on the site of an older chapel.
Tradition claims that Christopher Columbus prayed here before his voyage to the
New World. One of Galway's most famous landmarks, the **Spanish Arch** was built in
the 16th century to protect the quays where Spanish ships unloaded their cargoes.

Salthill is Galway City's seaside resort, 2 miles (3 km) west of the town centre, and
a holiday destination in its own right. Many of the city's large hotels are located
here. It has good beaches, nightlife and family attractions.

> *i* **Tourist Information Office** Forster St, Galway; tel: (091)
> 537700; fax: (091) 537733. Open daily 0830–1745 (May, June,

Sept); daily 0830–1945 (July–Aug); Mon–Fri 0900–1745, Sat 0900–1245. (Oct–Apr).

🛏 Lots of accommodation to suit all pockets can be found in Galway City and Salthill.

A Star of the Sea €€–€€€ 125 Upper Salthill, Salthill, Co. Galway; tel: (091) 525900; fax: (091) 589563; www.astarofthe sea.com; e-mail: astarsea@iol.ie. This family-managed guest house overlooking Galway Bay and within walking distance of the city centre offers a high standard of accommodation in eight en suite rooms, some with superb sea views.

Inishmore Guest House €€–€€€ 109 Fr Griffin Rd, Lower Salthill, Co. Galway; tel: (091) 582639; fax: (091) 589311; www.galway@pop.galway.net; e-mail: inishmorehouse@eircom.net. Six en suite rooms and one standard in a charming family residence a five-min walk from beach and city.

Aras Mhuire €€ 28 Mansells Rd, Taylor's Hill, Galway, Co. Galway; tel/fax: (091) 526210; e-mail: mmtobin@eircom.net. B&B in a peaceful setting overlooking Galway Cathedral; walking distance of town. Two en suite rooms and one standard.

Dunkellin House €€ 9 Grattan Park, Coast Road, Galway, Co. Galway; tel: (091) 589037. Panoramic views of Galway Bay are a feature of this B&B within walking distance of the city centre. Three en suite rooms and one standard room. Non-smokers accommodated.

🍽 Seafood lovers will be in their element in Galway, but there are plenty of places offering fare for all tastes. The pubs are a good bet for lunch.

McDonagh's Seafood Bar €€–€€€ 22 Quay St; tel: (091) 565001. This Galway landmark caters for all budgets and appetites. You can relax over a restaurant meal of fresh mussels, Galway oysters or the catch of the day, or have a cheap and cheerful – but equally delicious – snack from the fish and chips bar.

Tigh Neachtain €€–€€€ 17 Cross St; tel: (091) 568820. This popular bar and bistro is housed in a historic pub in Galway's medieval quarter. The downstairs pub is famous for traditional music and the bistro upstairs serves delicious seafood and steaks.

SHOPPING On Saturday mornings there's a lively market in the pedestrian street beside St Nicholas Church (0800–dusk). Claddagh Jewellers is one of

THE CLADDAGH RING

The Claddagh ring – two hands holding a heart with a crown on top – represents love, loyalty and friendship. The tradition originated in the fishing village of Claddagh, on the west bank of the river. If the ring is worn with the heart pointing inwards, it signifies the wearer's heart is taken. If the heart points outwards, the wearer's heart is open.

many merchants in the area selling the traditional Claddagh rings. The Cornstore in Middle St is a complex of stylish shops; Mulligan, in the same street, has a good selection of traditional music.

ENTERTAINMENT Galway is a city of the arts, with several theatre and dance groups, a film industry and numerous arts events The city also has a vibrant music scene, where you can hear traditional Irish music or check out some excellent night-clubs with a variety of dance music.

ARAN ISLANDS

The three Aran Islands, formed of a limestone base, lie off the south coast of Connemara in Galway Bay. Many age-old Irish traditions are still part of everyday life here, from language and dress to methods of fishing and farming. Aran knitwear, with its distinctive motifs, is highly prized throughout Ireland.

At 8 miles (5 km) long and 2 miles (3 km) wide, **Inishmore** (Inis Mór) is the largest of the three islands. Ferries arrive at Kilronan (Cill Rónáin), its main village, where passengers are met by minibuses and jaunting carts. The **Aran Heritage Centre** (Ionad Árann) is a good place to learn about the history and culture of the islanders. €€, open daily 1100–1700 (Apr–May, Sept–Oct), daily 1000–1900 (June–Aug).

The island's main sight is **Dun Aengus** (Dún Aonghasa), a stone fort dating from the Iron or Bronze Age and one of Europe's most important prehistoric sites. The views from the inner rampart are spectacular. The island is also known for its early Christian ruins. St Enda established a monastery here in the 5th century and for centuries it was the island of saints and hermits. Enda's church and those of St Ciarán and others can be seen. Many sights are near Kilmurvey (Cill Mhuirbhigh), which also has a good beach.

Inishmaan (Inis Meáin), the middle island, with a population of around 300, also has an abundance of ancient monuments, including the fort of **Dun Conor** (Dún Chonchúir). The smallest island, **Inishere** (Inis Oírr), has the ruined church of St Gobnait, the only woman allowed among the early Christian brethren, and the 15th-century **O'Brien's Castle**.

GETTING THERE AND GETTING AROUND Cars cannot be taken to the Aran Islands. Passenger ferries leave daily from Rossaveal for Inishmore, with extra sailings in summer; for Inishmaan and Inishere, daily May–Sept, call for winter and inter-island schedule. Island Ferries; tel: (091) 568903 or 561767. Aer Árann operates daily flights to the Aran Islands year round from Connemara Regional Airport at Inverin, near Spiddal; tel: (091) 593034. One of the best ways to get around the islands is by bicycle. Bicycle hire is available at the quay in Kilronan.

> **_i_ Tourist Information Office** Cill Ronain, Inis Mor, Aran Islands; tel: (099) 61263; fax; (099) 61420. Open Tues–Sun 1000–1800 (mid-Mar–early Oct); daily 1000–1900 (July–Aug).

> **Ard Einne Guest House** €€ Inishmore, Aran Islands, Co. Galway; tel: (099) 61126; fax: (099) 61388; www.dragnet-systems.ie/dira/ardeinne; e-mail: ardeinne@eircom.net. Sweeping views of the mainland coast and mountains from this attractive guest house with 15 rooms (12 en suite).
> **Ard Mhuiris** €€ Kilronan, Inishmore, Aran Islands, Co. Galway; tel: (099) 61208; fax: (099) 61333; e-mail: ardmhuiris@eircom.net. Five mins from the ferry terminal, with restaurants, pubs and beaches nearby, this B&B has six en suite rooms and enjoys a view of Galway Bay. Non-smokers accommodated.
> **Cregmont House** €€ Creig-an-Cheirin, Kilronan, Inishmore, Aran Islands, Co. Galway; tel: (099) 61139. Set in an unspoilt location with a spectacular sea panorama, the B&B has three en suite rooms and one standard room. Dinner available. Non-smokers accommodated.

WHERE NEXT?

Returning to Galway, you could make your way up to Ballina to join the Dublin–Ballina route in reverse. Visit medieval castles and travel through cattle-breeding country before reaching the lively city of Dublin (see pp. 347–357).

Galway is reasonably well provided with buses to other points in western Ireland. There are daily services to Ballina (2 hrs 10 mins; 6 daily) and Limerick (2 hrs 5 mins, hourly), and there are limited services Mon–Sat to Westport (2 hrs).

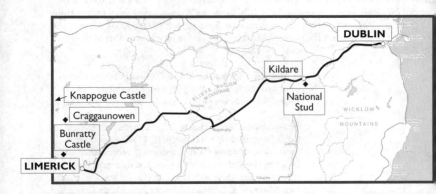

The route begins at Dublin and heads first across rural countryside, which soon becomes the open plain on which the Curragh, Ireland's famous racecourse stands. Kildare is the centre for Ireland's racehorse breeding and training activities, and you can spend an interesting time at the National Stud and the Irish Horse Museum. At Ballybrophy, east of Kildare, some trains travel to Limerick via Roscrea and Nenagh while others continue to Limerick Junction, just north of Tipperary, where passengers change to continue their journey to Limerick. If you are travelling by road, the N7 will take you all the way from Dublin to Limerick by way of Kildare, Port Laoise, Roscrea and Nenagh. Distance: 121 miles (195 km).

DUBLIN

See p. 347.

KILDARE

Kildare on the edge of the broad green pastures of the Curragh, is a pleasant, prosperous town with a population of around 4500. St Brigid, one of Ireland's patron saints, established a religious community here in 490. The 13th-century cathedral named in her honour stands on the site. It has some noteworthy monuments and a stained-glass window depicting Brigid with saints Patrick and Colmcille. You can climb the round tower, at 108 ft (33 m) the second highest in the country, for panoramic views. **Kildare Cathedral** (€) and **Round Tower** (€€) The Square. Open Mon–Sat 1000–1300, 1400–1700, Sun 1400–1700.

The **National Stud**, at Tully, a mile south, covers 958 acres (388 ha). Colonel William Hall-Walker, a Scotsman, began breeding thoroughbred horses here in 1900. He believed that the fate of every creature was dictated by the stars, and so built skylights into the stables so that the heavens could exert maximum influence. However eccentric his ideas seemed to the outside world, they bore fruit with a string of winners. In 1943 he presented the grounds and horses to the state.

Along with a tour of the paddocks and stables, you can visit the **Irish Horse Museum**, in which the skeleton of Arkle, the famous racehorse of the 1960s, is displayed. Adjacent to the National Stud are the superb **Japanese Gardens**, also established by Colonel Hall-Walker and designed by Tassa Eida and his son Minoru. They symbolise stages in the life of man, from birth through death. The National Stud and Japanese Gardens (€€€) are open daily 0930–1800 (mid-Feb–mid-Nov).

> *i* **Tourist Information Office** Market Sq. Kildare; tel: (045) 521240. Open Mon–Fri 0900–1800, Sat 0900–1300 (June–mid-Sept).

⌂ There's little in the way of hotels and guest houses in the area for budget travellers. The following B&Bs are handy for The Curragh, National Stud and Japanese Gardens.

Mount Ruadhan €€ Old Rd, Southgreen, Kildare, Co. Kildare; tel/fax: (045) 521637. Two en suite rooms and one standard room in a bungalow, a mile (1.6 km) out of town. Non-smokers accommodated.

Bella Vista €€ 105 Moorefield Park, Newbridge, Co. Kildare; tel: (045) 431047; fax: (045) 438259; e-mail: belavista@eircom.net. Long-established B&B in a quiet residential area, 5 miles (8 km) east of Kildare. Four en suite rooms; light meals and dinner available.

Seven Springs €€ Hawkfield, Newbridge; Co. Kildare; tel: (045) 431677. Three standard rooms in a bungalow B&B; light meals and dinner available.

Kerryhill €€ Morristown Biller, Newbridge, Co. Kildare; tel: (045) 432433. Two en suite rooms and one standard room in a spacious bungalow. Non-smokers accommodated.

LIMERICK

The Republic's fourth-largest city shot to fame in 1996 as the setting for Frank McCourt's novel *Angela's Ashes*. While some natives take issue with his portrayal of their city, it has none the less sparked visitor interest. The slums of McCourt's childhood have long gone, and Limerick's beautifully renovated Georgian buildings – best seen along the Crescent and O'Connell St – and its prosperous city centre create a fine impression of the city today.

The Great Limerick Tour (€€€) of the city sights by open-top bus runs twice daily at 1100 and 1430 from mid-June through Aug. Contact Bus Éireann; tel: (061) 313333. They also run the *Angela's Ashes* tour.

With its strategic location on the Shannon, Limerick dates back to Celtic times. In its long and often turbulent history it has been settled by the Vikings, walled and segregated by the English, and defended by Irish patriots against Cromwell and during the Jacobite wars. The tourist office has devised two walking tours: 'Limerick – the Past Revisited', which highlights the many places of interest; or you can see the sights on two open-top bus tours, one covering medieval and Georgian Limerick, the other visiting the settings in McCourt's novel.

The **Hunt Museum**, Custom House, Rutland St, has a superb collection of Celtic and medieval treasures as well as Irish and European paintings. €€, open Tues–Sun 0930–1700. **Limerick Museum** also has a fine collection of artefacts, including a brass-topped stone pillar known as 'the Nail', which once stood in the Exchange (now gone), where business transactions were finalised with cash 'on the Nail'. The museum is housed in two of the attractive Georgian buildings at St John's Sq. €, open Tues–Sat.

In the old medieval city, **St Mary's Cathedral**, Bridge St, dates from the 12th century and has interesting tombs. €, open daily in summer 0900–1300, 1400–1700. **King John's Castle**, a Norman fortress, houses good historical exhibitions. €€, open daily 0930–1730; last admission 1630 (Apr–Oct; weekends only Nov–Mar). Alongside the castle is **Castle Lane**, an authentic 18th to 19th-century streetscape. Across Thomond Bridge is the **Treaty Stone**, where the treaty that ended the siege of the Williamites was signed.

Limerick has many beautiful churches. Whether or not you're a McCourt fan, pay a visit to **Mungret Abbey**, where Angela's ashes were finally scattered in the churchyard. These atmospheric ruins lie on the southwest outskirts of town and date from the 6th century.

[i] **Tourist Information Office** Arthur's Quay, Limerick; tel: (061) 317522; fax: (061) 317939. Open Mon–Fri 0930–1300, 1400–1730, Sat 0930–1300 (Sept–May); Mon–Fri 0930–1900, Sat 0930–1300 (June); Mon–Fri 0930–1900, Sat–Sun 0900–1800 (Jul–Aug). Limerick – The Past Revisited (€€) has walking trails through English Town and New Town and is available from the tourist office or the Limerick Civic Trust opposite King John's Castle.

There is an abundance of accommodation to suit all pockets in and around the city.
Cruises House €€ Denmark St, Limerick; tel: (061) 315320; fax: (061) 316995; e-mail: cruiseshouse@eircom.net. Located in the heart of the city, Limerick's largest guest house has 29 rooms (27 en suite). Handy for restaurants, pubs and shops.
Hanratty's Hotel €€– €€€ 5 Glentworth St, Limerick; tel: (061) 410999; fax: (061) 311077. The city's oldest hotel, Hanratty's has retained its Georgian character while meeting modern comfort requirements. It has 22 en suite rooms and a traditional bar with music most nights.
Railway Hotel €€ Parnell St, Limerick; tel: (061) 413653; fax: (061) 419762; www.railwayhotel.ie; e-mail: sales@railway

hotel.ie. Family run, the hotel is located opposite the rail and bus stations. There are 22 en suite rooms, an attractive lounge/bar and a restaurant serving good, home-cooked food.

Glen Eagles €€ 12 Vereker Gdns, Ennis Rd, Limerick; tel/fax: (061) 455521. Four en suite rooms in a spacious B&B close to the city centre.

Santa Cruz €€ 10 Coolraine Terrace, Ennis Rd, Limerick; tel: (061) 454500. A 5-min bus ride from the town centre, this spacious town house has two en suite and three standard rooms. Dinner available. Non-smokers accommodated.

Trebor €€ Ennis Rd, Limerick; tel/fax: (061) 454632; e-mail: treborhouse@eircom.net. A short walk from the city centre, this older style town house has five en suite rooms. Non-smokers welcomed.

LIVE LIKE A LORD
If quaffing mead and feasting on roast beast in a real medieval dining hall strikes your fancy, you've come to the right region.

Bunratty Castle and Knappogue Castle hold medieval banquets twice nightly in season (year-round at Bunratty). These royal repasts are accompanied by music, entertainment and merry-making. Bunratty also holds Traditional Irish Nights in the Great Barn. Contact Shannon Castle Banquets: tel: (061) 360788.

🅣🅞 The Celtic tiger has torn Limerick's eating and nightlife habits to shreds. Not so long ago everyone was tucking in by 1800, the restaurant shutters closed an hour later and the lights went out soon after that. The best places for good, reasonably priced food and a lively night out are the pubs. Here's a sample.

The Brazen Head Sports Bar €€– €€€ 102 O' Connell St, claims to have been an attraction for the city's socialites since 1794. It has two bars, two restaurants and a nightclub. The sports bar-restaurant boasts 30 screens featuring live digital sports coverage. Bar food is served daily 1200–2200. A lunch menu is available until 1500, followed by an à la carte menu.

Dolan's €€–€€€ Dock Rd. A haven of traditional Irish music, played nightly, Dolan's offers good value for breakfast, lunch and dinner, with continuous service from 0800–2100. Its fully licensed restaurant, specialising in Irish fare and seafood, is open nightly and for Sun lunch. Vegetarian dishes available.

SIDE TRIPS FROM LIMERICK

One of Ireland's most popular castles, **Bunratty Castle**, 6 miles (10 km) north-west, on the N18, was built in 1425, though its origins date back to Viking times. It has been restored to its medieval glory and filled with a superb collection of medieval furniture. Highlights include the great hall with its timbered roof and tapestries, the 'murder holes' through which enemies were drenched in boiling oil, and the banqueting hall, where the popular medieval banquets take place. Surrounding the castle is the delightful **folk park**, with re-creations of a village street, fisherman's cottage, farmhouses, a forge and other period buildings illustrating walks of life in the past. €€€, open daily 0930–1900 (June–Aug), 0930–1730 (Sept–May); last admission to castle 1600.

Craggaunowen, about 12 miles (19 km) north-west on the R462, features a reconstructed *crannóg*, a Bronze Age lake dwelling that portrays the lifestyle of the ancient Celts. The project was the brainchild of the late John Hunt, known in his day as one of the best medievalists in Europe. A fascinating piece of recent history is *The Brendan*, the leather-hulled boat in which Tim Severin crossed the Atlantic in 1976 in an effort to authenticate the voyage of St Brendan the Navigator. €€€, open daily 1000–1800 (mid-Mar–Oct; last admission 1700).

Knappogue Castle, 17 miles (27 km) north-west on the N18, was built in 1467 and is a typical example of the fortified tower house favoured by the Irish and Anglo-Irish ruling class. Today its four-storey tower houses the banquet hall, where Knappogue's medieval banquets take place, and the reconstructed rooms of a 19th-century extension. €€€, open daily 0930–1700; last admission 1630 (Apr–Sept).

WHERE NEXT?

From Limerick you could take the N18 for 23 miles (37 km) to Ennis, then follow the N85 for a further 16 miles (26 km) to Ennistimon. From there the N67 passes through the spa town of Lisdoonvarna, also famous for its annual match-making festival, and on across The Burren, an area rocky, wild and beautiful, to Ballyvaghan on the southern shore of Galway Bay. From Kilcolgan you can travel to lively Galway City (see pp. 374–376) and on to the atmospheric Aran Islands (see p. 376).

Limerick Bus Station is a useful departure point, with services to Killarney (2 hrs; 9 direct services; reduced service on Sun), Galway (2 hrs 5 mins; hourly, every day), Dingle (4 hrs to 4 hrs 50 mins, change at Tralee; about four services a day except on Sun) and Cork (1 hr 50 mins (hourly, every day).

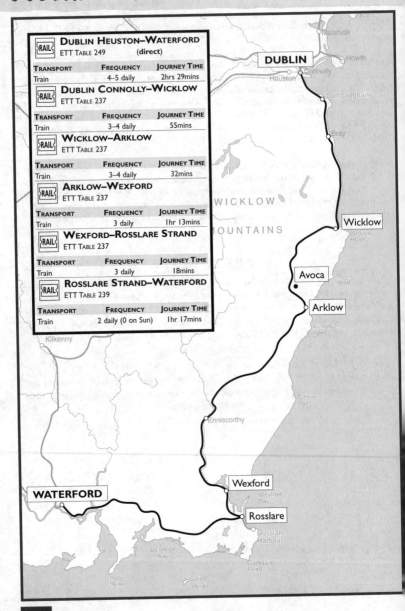

RAIL	DUBLIN HEUSTON–WATERFORD	
	ETT TABLE 249	(direct)

TRANSPORT	FREQUENCY	JOURNEY TIME
Train	4–5 daily	2hrs 29mins

RAIL	DUBLIN CONNOLLY–WICKLOW	
	ETT TABLE 237	

TRANSPORT	FREQUENCY	JOURNEY TIME
Train	3–4 daily	55mins

RAIL	WICKLOW–ARKLOW	
	ETT TABLE 237	

TRANSPORT	FREQUENCY	JOURNEY TIME
Train	3–4 daily	32mins

RAIL	ARKLOW–WEXFORD	
	ETT TABLE 237	

TRANSPORT	FREQUENCY	JOURNEY TIME
Train	3 daily	1hr 13mins

RAIL	WEXFORD–ROSSLARE STRAND	
	ETT TABLE 237	

TRANSPORT	FREQUENCY	JOURNEY TIME
Train	3 daily	18mins

RAIL	ROSSLARE STRAND–WATERFORD	
	ETT TABLE 239	

TRANSPORT	FREQUENCY	JOURNEY TIME
Train	2 daily (0 on Sun)	1hr 17mins

This route first follows the very scenic coastline, with the Irish Sea on one side and the Wicklow Mountains on the other, as far as Wicklow, a quiet historic town overlooking a sweeping bay. From here the line loops inland to meet the coast again at Arklow, where it cuts inland again to lively Wexford, laid out on a Viking street plan. Skirting Wexford Bay, the line heads west for the final leg of its journey to Waterford, on the estuary of the River Suir.

DUBLIN

See p. 347.

WICKLOW TOWN

Wicklow's county town looks out over a wide crescent bay. Founded by the Vikings, its name in Danish, Wykingalo, meant 'Viking meadow'. The town's later history can be traced at **Wicklow's Historic Gaol**, which also houses the Co. Wicklow Heritage and Genealogical Research Centre. €, open daily 1000–1800 (Mar–Oct).

The **harbour** is the town's most interesting area, home to a sailing and yacht club, while the long pebble beach, backed by **Broad Lough**, a wildfowl lagoon, is popular with beachcombers and fishermen. The sprawling ruins of **Black Castle**, built by the Anglo-Norman lord Maurice Fitzgerald in the 12th century, stand on a promontory to the south of the harbour.

i **Tourist Information Office** Rialto House, Fitzwilliam Sq, Wicklow; tel: (0404) 69117; fax: (0404) 69118. Open Mon–Fri 0900–1800, Sat 0930–1300, 1400–1730.

🏨 **Grand Hotel** €€€ Wicklow, Co. Wicklow; tel: (0404) 67337; fax: (0404) 69607; www.grandhotel.ie; e-mail: grandhotel@eircom.net. This town centre hotel has 33 en suite rooms. Food served all day in restaurant and grill room.
Glen Na Smole €€ Ashtown Lane, Marlton Rd, Wicklow, Co. Wicklow; tel: (0404) 67945; fax: (0404) 68155; www.homepage.eircom.net/~byrneglen; e-mail: byrneglen@eircom.net. Dinner and light meals are available in this comfortable family home with four en suite rooms, a mile (1.6 km) out of town. Non-smokers accommodated.
Olanda €€ Dunbur Park, Wicklow, Co. Wicklow; tel: (0404) 67579. Comfortable, non-smoking B&B 5 mins walk from town centre. Two en suite and two standard rooms.

ARKLOW

The Vikings founded a settlement here at the mouth of the River Avoca in the 9th century, and today Arklow is a popular resort with beaches, boating and a golf course. The 1798 Memorial honours the memory of Father Michael Murphy, who died here leading the county's United Irishmen in battle against the English. Arklow's seafaring history is recalled in the **Maritime Museum**, €€, St Mary's Rd. Open Mon–Sat 1000–1300, 1400–1700 (May–Sept); Mon–Fri only (Oct–Apr). Down by the harbour, the **Arklow Pottery Factory**, Ireland's largest, gives guided tours. Open weekdays 0900–1700, weekends 1000–1700.

> *i* **Tourist Information Office** Main St, Arklow; tel: (0402) 32484; fax: (0402) 39773. Open Mon–Fri 1100–1300, 1400–1600.
>
> **Arkglen** €€ Vale Rd, Arklow, Co. Wicklow; tel/fax: (0402) 32454. This luxury bungalow in attractive grounds is a 5-min walk from the town centre and has three en suite rooms and one standard room. Non-smokers accommodated.
> **Vale View** €€ Coolgreaney Rd, Arklow, Co. Wicklow; tel/fax: (0402) 32622; e-mail: pat.crotty@ifi.ie. Four en suite rooms in an Edwardian house with period furnishing, in landscaped gardens. Panoramic views and a rooftop sun lounge. Non-smokers accommodated.

SIDE TRIP FROM ARKLOW The delightful **Vale of Avoca**, where the rivers Avonmore and Avonbeg meet, inspired the poet Thomas Moore (1779–1852) to pen *The Meeting of the Waters* in 1807. At the foot of the vale, Avoca village, 7 miles (11 km) north of Arklow, is the setting for the BBC television series *Ballykissangel*. Avoca Handweavers, which now has shops around the country, and in the United States, occupies the oldest working mill in Ireland, dating from 1723. You can take a guided tour and watch the weavers creating beautiful tweeds. Shop open daily 0930–1730; mill open weekdays 0800–1630.

WEXFORD TOWN

Founded by the Vikings, Wexford flourished as a major port until the harbour silted up in the 19th century. Today, it's is one of the more atmospheric of Ireland's larger heritage towns, with its Viking street plan, and medieval alleys. The **Westgate Heritage Centre** (€€), housed in the only surviving gateway of the old Norman town walls, traces the town's history. Nearby are the ruins of **Selskar Abbey**, a 12th-century Augustinian priory where Henry II is said to have done penance for the murder of Thomas à Becket.

Other sights of interest include the **Franciscan Friary** and the Pugin-designed **St Peter's College Chapel**. Wexford has a lively nightlife. The **Wexford Opera Festival**, held annually in late Oct/early Nov, attracts international artists and opera buffs. This prestigious event is staged over 18 days at the Theatre Royal. Tel: (053) 22144 (booking office) or (053) 22400 (administration).

The mudflats to the east of town contain the 250-acre (100-hectare) **Wexford Wildfowl Reserve**, wintering ground for thousands of geese and other species of birds. €, open daily 0900–1800 (mid-Apr–Sept); 1000–1700. (Oct–mid-Apr).

FEET FIRST

Walking tours of Wexford Town take place in July and Aug Mon–Sat 1100 and 1430; tel: (053) 46506. There are also *ad hoc* tours leaving each evening from the Talbot Hotel; tel: (053) 41081.

i **Tourist Information Office** Crescent Quay, Wexford; tel: (053) 23111; fax: (053) 41743. Open year-round Mon–Fri 0900–1800, Sat 0900–1300.

🛏 There's plenty of accommodation – hotels, guest houses and B&Bs – in and around Wexford.

Faythe Guest House €€ The Faythe, Swan View, Wexford Town; tel: (053) 22249; fax: (053) 21680; www.faytheguesthouse.com; e-mail: faythhse@iol.ie. This 3-star family-run guest house has ten recently refurbished en suite rooms, some with views of Wexford Harbour.

Westgate House €€ Westgate, Wexford Town; tel/fax: (053) 22167; www.wexford-online.com/westgate; e-mail: westgate@wexmail.com. Built as the Westgate Hotel in 1812, the 2-star guesthouse has been refurbished in period style and has ten en suite rooms in a central location.

The Blue Door B&B €€ 18 Lower George St, Wexford Town; tel: (053) 21407; e-mail: bluedoor@indigo.ie. Luxury non-smoking accommodation in a Georgian townhouse handy for restaurants, shops and traditional music pubs. Four en suite rooms.

ROSSLARE

George Bernard Shaw was 'lost in dreams' in this picturesque village, which lies 5 miles (8 km) north of its more famous harbour, and about the same distance from Wexford Town. Its beautiful beach, Rosslare Strand – 6 miles (10 km) long and golden, with an EU Blue Flag – and the fact that it's one of the sunniest places in the country, makes it a popular resort. It also has a championship golf course. Rosslare Harbour became the area's principal port when Wexford's harbour silted up and could no longer handle the big ships. Today it is a busy terminal, serving car and passenger ferries.

i **Tourist Information Office** Rosslare Ferry Terminal, Kilrane; tel: (053) 33232 or 33622; fax: (053) 33421. The office is open year-round to service all sailings.

WATERFORD

Set alongside the river Suir (pronounced 'Shure'), Waterford is a busy, vibrant city with traces of its great heritage woven around its waterfront and modern central shopping district. The attractive quays with their central Victorian clock tower run for nearly a mile along the river. Artefacts from the city's Viking origins and medieval times are displayed at the **Heritage Centre**, Greyfriar's St. €€, open daily 1000–1700 (Apr–Oct, weekdays only Nov–Mar).

At the eastern end of the quays the bulky **Reginald's Tower**, with walls 10 ft (3 m) thick, was a residence for Anglo-Norman kings. Their leader Strongbow captured the city in 1170, married the daughter of the Leinster king, and succeeded to the throne. €€, open daily 1000–2000 (June–Aug); weekdays 1000–1700, weekends 1400–1700 (May and Sept). Some of Waterford's finest Georgian architecture can be seen along The Mall, including town houses, the **City Hall** and the adjacent **Bishop's Palace**.

The neo-classical **Christ Church Cathedral**, with its Corinthian colonnade, was built in the 1770s by the local architect John Roberts. Inside, a gruesome effigy of a rotting corpse marks the tomb of James Rice. Roberts also designed **Holy Trinity**, the city's Catholic cathedral, with a more subdued façade but highly ornate interior.

The first Waterford glasshouse began producing its exquisite patterned glassware in 1783.

On the outskirts of town, the **Waterford Crystal** factory, now the largest of its kind in the world, is a popular attraction. Guided tours daily 0830–1600 (Apr–Oct); weekdays 0900–1515 (Nov–Mar); showrooms open weekdays 0900–1700 (Jan–Feb); daily 0830–1800 (Mar–Oct); daily 0900–1700 (Nov–Mar).

Entertaining **walking tours** (€€) leave from the Granville Hotel, daily at 1200 and 1400 (Mar–Oct); tel: (051) 873711, (fax): 051 850645. On a fine day, a **cruise** along the River Suir is a good way to enjoy Waterford's skyline. Galley Cruises (€€€) tel: (051) 421723, has daily departures from the quay at 1500 (June–Aug), weather permitting.

[i] **Tourist Information Office** 41 The Quay, Waterford; tel: (051) 875823, fax: (051) 877388. Open Mon–Sat 0900–1700, also Sun 0900–1700 (July–Aug).

Waterford has a good range of accommodation, though the choice of budget hotels and guest houses is limited.
Diamond Hill Country House €€ Slieverue, Waterford, Co. Waterford; tel: (051) 832855; fax: (051) 832254. Less than a mile from the city, off the Rosslare road, the refurbished three-star guesthouse, set in its own gardens, has 17 en suite rooms.
Rice Guest House €€–€€€ 35 Barrack St, Waterford City; tel: (051) 371606; fax: (051) 357013; e-mail ricegh@eircom.net. Handy for shops, Waterford Crystal and the train and bus station, the guest house has 21 en suite rooms and offers live entertainment in the lounge most nights.

BY HOOK OR BY CROOKE

As the Anglo-Normans battled for a foothold in the south-east of Ireland, legend has it that in 1170 their leader, Strongbow, vowed he would take Waterford 'by Hook or by Crooke'. He was referring to two buildings on hills near Waterford Harbour: the Tower of Hook on the Co. Wexford side and Crooke Church, across the water near Passage East. He succeeded, and unlike the ruins, his words are still in use today.

Blenheim House €€ Blenheim Heights, Waterford, Co. Waterford; tel: (051) 874115; www.homepage.eircom.net/~blenheim; e-mail: blenheim@eircom.net. Six en suite B&B rooms in a Georgian residence surrounded by lawns and a deer park and furnished throughout with antiques and objets d'art. Two miles from city centre.

Sion Hill House €€–€€€ Ferrybank, Waterford City, Co. Waterford; tel: (051)851558; fax: (051) 851678; e-mail: sionhill@eircom.net. Close to the city centre, this spacious Georgian manor in a 5-acre (2 ha) garden is a non-smoking B&B with four en suite rooms.

City Arms Restaurant and Bar €€–€€€ Arundel Sq. Victorian pub with a fully licensed restaurant with menus to suit all budgets. Food available every day, with lunch specials served 1200–1500 and a full à la carte bar menu 1500–2000.

The Kazbar €€–€€€ John St. Food – snacks and main meals – served in this three-storey themed bar from 1200–1900. Rock music.

The Old Stand €€–€€€ 45 Michael St. Fresh seafood and steaks are the specialities in the Old Stand, which has two atmospheric ground floor bars and an upstairs bar-restaurant. Bar menu available everyday.

WHERE NEXT?

You can travel to Cork (see pp. 390–394) by rail. From Waterford catch the train that runs through Clonmel and Tipperary and change at Limerick Junction. By road, the N25 will take you through the charming old town of Youghal (pronounced 'yawl'), where Sir Walter Raleigh is said to have planted Ireland's first potato, to reach Cork in 108 miles (174 km).

CORK CITY

Cork is the Republic of Ireland's second largest city. Its Irish name, Corcaigh, means 'marshy place', a reference to the estuary of the River Lee, where it grew up on islands in the 6th century. Its heart still lies on an island – known locally as 'the flat' – formed by two channels of the river, and the many bridges give it a continental character. The city prospered from the butter trade in the 17th and 18th centuries, when many of the attractive Georgian buildings with their bow-front windows were built. Until around 1800, when the river was dammed, Patrick St, the Grand Parade and other main streets were still under water.

Cork's independent-minded citizenry gave only nominal obedience to the English crown. A hotbed of the nationalist Fenian movement, 'Rebel Cork' was burned in the War of Independence, 1919–21, but restoration in recent years has created a bright and attractive city with a lively nightlife and an acclaimed arts scene.

GETTING THERE AND GETTING AROUND

Cork airport, tel: (021) 313131, is 4 miles (6 km) south of the city.

Kent Rail Station, tel: (021) 506766, is on the north side of the river, opposite the Custom House.

Cork's one-way traffic system crosses and re-crosses the river and quays, and can be confusing when you drive here for the first time, so arm yourself with a good map before you arrive. Try to avoid rush hours, when you're likely to experience traffic jams. There are several **car-parks** in the city centre, including those at the Grand Parade, South Mall, Lavitt's Quay near the Opera House, Merchant's Quay and across the river at St Patrick's Quay.

Cork's major attractions are either on or close to 'the flat', so **walking** is the best way to get around. In any event, it's an interesting muddle of a place and pedestrians have the edge on vehicular traffic, which is frequently brought to a halt in the narrow, twisting streets.

Local **bus** services operate from the bus station in Parnell Pl, tel: (021) 508188. A standard fare operates within the city area. There are taxi stands near the rail and bus stations and major hotels and opposite the Savoy Centre, Patrick St.

INFORMATION

Cork City Tourist Information Office Grand Parade; tel: (021) 425 5100; fax: (021) 425 5199. Open Mon–Fri 0900–1800, Sat 0900–1300.

POST OFFICE The main Post Office is in Oliver Plunket St; it has bureau de change and *poste restante* facilities. Open Mon–Sat 0900–1730.

ACCOMMODATION

Acorn House €€ 14 St Patrick's Hill, Cork; tel/fax: (021) 450 2474; www.acornhouse-cork.com; e-mail: info@acornhouse-cork.com. Listed Georgian house with nine en suite rooms. The guest house is centrally situated, 3-min walk from theatres and restaurants.

Allcorns Country Home €€ Shoumagh Rd, Blarney, Co. Cork; tel: (021) 438 5577; fax: (021) 438 2828; e-mail: allcorns_blarney@hotmail.com. In a beautiful setting with the Shoumagh River running by, the spacious B&B has three en suite guest rooms. A non-smoking house, it is open Apr–Oct.

Ashley Hotel €€€ Coburg St, Cork; tel: (021) 450 1518; fax: (021) 450 1178; www.ashleyhotelcom; e-mail: ashleyhotel@eircom.net. Family-owned, the 27-room hotel has its own secure car park, restaurant and lively bar.

Killarney Guest House €€ Western Rd, Cork; tel: (021) 427 0290; fax: (021) 427 1010; www.killarneyhouse.com; e-mail: killarneyhouse@iol.ie. Opposite University College, Cork, and a short drive from the airport and ferry, the stylish guest house is also within walking distance of the city centre.

Lough Mahon House €€–€€€ Tivoli, Cork; tel: (021) 450 2142; fax: (021) 450 1804; www.loughmahon.com; e-mail: info@loughmahon.com. The guest house has six well-equipped rooms and is well placed for trips to Fota Wildlife Park, Cobh Heritage Centre, Blarney Castle, Kinsale and Killarney.

Rock Island B&B €€ Kiln Rd, Killeens, Blarney, Co. Cork; tel: (021) 439 9761. A quiet, modern home with private car park 2.5 miles (4 km) from Cork and the same distance from Blarney.

FOOD AND DRINK

Corkonians love eating out and the city has lots of options. One of the best-value places to eat is the café at the **Triskel Arts Centre**, Tobin St, off South Main St, which serves home-made bread, soups and hot dishes for vegetarians and meat-eaters. **The Gingerbread House**, Paul St, is a great stop for coffee or lunch. It serves excellent sandwiches, baguettes and home-made cakes, desserts and ice cream. Needless to say, there's no shortage of pubs in the city – and the 'Black Stuff' here is the locally-brewed Murphy's, rather than Guinness.

HIGHLIGHTS

Crawford Municipal Art Gallery, Emmet Pl., is housed in one of Cork's finest buildings. Its handsome façade of red brick dressed with limestone was built in 1724, and it served as the Custom House until 1832, when Emmet Pl. was still the King's Dock. The building then became a drawing academy and was converted into a gallery for Ireland's finest public art collection outside Dublin. Jack B Yeats, James Barry and Nathaniel Grogan are among the important Irish painters represented. There is also a room dedicated to contemporary Irish artists. The stained-glass rooms on the second floor contain pieces by Harry Clarke, regarded as the country's finest stained-glass craftsman of the time. Special exhibitions are also held here. The gallery café, run by the acclaimed Ballymaloe cookery school, is superb. €, open Mon–Sat 1000–1700.

TOURS

Cork has a sign-posted walking trail, which visitors can follow with the aid of a booklet from the tourist office. Afternoon and evening cruises around Cork Harbour and trips to Fota Islands Wildlife Park take place July–Sept. Details from the tourist office.

Fitzgerald Park is bordered to the north by the River Lee and to the south by the Mardyke, a riverside walk. Housed in a Georgian mansion in the centre of the park is the **Cork Public Museum**, which traces the social and political history of the town, including the conflicts of the 20th century. There are some good archaeological exhibits dating back to 3000 BC, and an important collection of 18th-century silver. €, open weekdays 1100–1300, 1415–1700, Sun 1500–1700.

Visitors climb up the steep north bank to **St Anne's Church** (1722) in Church St, Shandon, to see the Bells of Shandon, made famous in a popular 19th-century tune. The eight bells were cast in Gloucester in 1750. You can climb the 120-ft (36.5-m) tower and ring them, playing a tune with the help of 'music' cards. The weather vane on top of the steeple is shaped like a salmon, the Celtic symbol of knowledge. The clock face is known to locals as 'the four-faced liar' because each face showed slightly different times until it was repaired in 1986. €€, open Mon–Sat 0930–1700 (May–Oct); 1000–1530 (Nov–Apr).

The triple-spired French Gothic **St Finbarre's Cathedral**, Bishop St, is rich in sculptural decoration. It was designed by William Burges and completed in 1878. It was built on the site where St Finbarre, Cork's founder and patron saint, established a monastery in the 7th century. Among its highlights are the west front, mosaic pavements, Bishop's Throne and the beautiful rose window. There is also a 3000-pipe organ. €, open daily 0900–1800.

Founded in 1845 as Queen's College, **University College Cork**, Western Rd, was designed by Sir Thomas Deane in the style of a typical Oxford college and has an attractive riverside quadrangle. The Honan Chapel, built in 1915, was modelled on Cormac's Chapel at the Rock of Cashel. It contains some exquisite stained-glass windows, many by Harry Clarke, as well as fine mosaic, enamel work and other elaborate decoration. The college also has a significant collection of ogham stones on display. €, open weekdays 0900–1700. The chapel may be closed during college holidays; check with the tourist office.

You can experience the sights, sounds and smells of life on the wrong side of the law during the 19th century in **Cork City Gaol**, Sunday Well. €, open daily 0930–1800 (May–Sept). Mon tours at 1030 and 1430, Sat–Sun 1000–1600 (Oct–Apr).

SHOPPING

The major high street chains can be found along **Patrick St**. Roches is the largest department store in town, while Cash's, next door, carries more upmarket fashions. At the top of the street, near the bridge, is a huge shopping complex at **Merchants' Quay**. The **English Market,** off Princes St and the Grand Parade, sells a wonderful variety of foodstuffs, from Irish farm cheeses, smoked salmon, fruit and vegetables to more acquired specialities such as tripe and black pudding. The shops in the old **French Quarter** around Paul St are noted for modern Irish crafts and design, and you will also find a string of antique shops in Paul's Lane. Bargain hunters will be drawn to the open-air flea market on **Coal Quay**.

EVENTS AND FESTIVALS

Despite its no-nonsense, workaday appearance, Cork offers a wide range of cultural experiences. At one end of the scale, there's Gaelic football and hurling in **Páirc Ui Chaomh Stadium**; at the other lunchtime and evening concerts of classical music

Cork City

– details from the tourist office, or check listings in the daily *Cork Examiner* or *Evening Echo*. Drama, musical comedy, ballet and opera are staged at the **Cork Opera House**, Emmet Pl; tel: (021) 272022. The Everyman Palace (tel: 021 501673) with its Victorian interior, the Firkin Crane Centre and the Cork Arts Theatre are smaller venues with a range of productions. The city has an abundance of musical pubs and discos.

Cork keeps the cultural pressure up with a number of world-class festivals. The **Cork International Choral and Folk Dance Festival**, held in City Hall in Apr/May, welcomes choirs and dance teams from around the world. The **Cork Folk Festival and Music** Fair take place in June. The **Cork Film Festival**, Ireland's oldest cinematic event, is held in Sept/Oct. Also in Oct, the great faces of jazz appear at the **Cork Jazz Festival**, a top-rated international gathering.

SIDE TRIPS

CÓBH Cork's neighbour, Cóbh (pronounced 'cove') is less than half an hour from Cork by train (16 trains daily and 7 on Sun). Situated on an island in Cork Harbour and connected to the mainland by a causeway, Cóbh has always had close maritime connections. The Royal Cork Yacht Club, said to be the oldest in the world, was founded here in 1720. From 1750 the town was the embarkation point for thousands of emigrants seeking a new life in Australia, New Zealand, Canada and the United States. In 1912 the *Titanic* made her last stop here on her fateful maiden voyage. Today, it is an important port of call for cruise liners.

The history of the town – and its temporary name change – is told in **The Queenstown Story**, a multimedia exhibition in Cóbh Heritage Centre at the restored Victorian railway station in Westbourne Pl. €€, open daily 1000–1800 (last admission 1700). **St Coleman's Cathedral**, a Gothic Revival edifice designed by Pugin in 1868, soars above the Victorian terraces lining the waterfront. Its carillon of 47 bells is the largest in Ireland. One-hour cruises around Cork Harbour are operated by Marine Transport from Kennedy Pier; tel: (021) 811485. €€€, daily (May–Sept).

> *i* **Cóbh Heritage Centre** Westbourne Pl; tel: (021) 481 3591; fax: (021) 481 3595. Open daily 1000–1800 (Mar–Oct), 1000–1700 (Nov–Feb).

BLARNEY **Blarney Castle** rises up amid the glorious setting of wooded parkland. Built by Cormac MacCarthy in the 15th century, the fortress is a well-preserved ruin. You can let your imagination loose as you climb the spiral stone stairs through the rooms, picturing for yourself what the Young Ladies' Bedroom and the Great Hall must have looked like in their time.

At the top, there are wonderful panoramic views from the ramparts as you approach the famous **Blarney Stone**. Here you must lie on your back and lean your head backwards into a crevasse to kiss the stone, helped by a guard and watched by the castle photographer who will capture this graceless moment for posterity. Take care when descending from the top of the castle, as the winding steps are very narrow and slippery. €€, open Mon–Sat 0900–1830 (May and Sept); 0900–1900 (June–Aug); 0900–dusk (Oct–Apr); Sun 0900–1730 (year round).

KINSALE Kinsale, one of Ireland's most picturesque coastal towns, is set around a large harbour filled with yachts and fishing boats on the estuary of the River Bandon. Narrow streets lined with colourful, up-market shops, restaurants and pubs run back from the waterfront and up into the hills. Kinsale has become known as Ireland's gourmet capital, due to the quality of both the local seafood and the international chefs the town attracts.

A turning point in Irish history occurred at the Battle of Kinsale in 1601, when English forces defeated the rebels and their Spanish allies. The subsequent 'Flight of the Earls', in which the Irish royalty abandoned their lands and left for the Continent, opened the way for English 'plantation'. As you wander through the town, look out for the **Old Courthouse**, now a regional museum; **St Multose Church**, dating from Norman times; and the ruins of **Desmond Castle**. Nearby at Summer Cove is **Charles Fort**, a star-shaped bastion built around 1677 and in use until 1922. It has splendid views of Kinsale harbour. €€, open daily (Apr–Oct).

The **Spaniard Inn**, a long yellow building perched on a hillside opposite the town centre, is an atmospheric pub with log walls, low ceilings, an

GOURMET CAPITAL
Kinsale is the haunt of epicures from around the world early in Oct when this fishing port holds an international four-day Gourmet Festival. Throughout the year the ancient town attracts discerning diners, having firmly established itself as Ireland's Gourmet Capital. It all began in 1975 when 12 restaurants got together to form the **Kinsale Good Food Circle**.

Excellent seafood is served at all of them, but vegetarians can always find something tasty and unusual, like the nettle soup and courgette and herb bake at the **Cottage Loft**, Main St. Locally picked wild spinach and locally farmed mussels are featured on the menu at the **Blue Haven**, on the site of the old fishmarket. Walnut soup is an interesting starter at **The Captain's Table** in Acton's Hotel, and a memorable monkfish in tarragon sauce and white wine is served at **Max's Wine Bar** in Main St.

open fire and sawdust-covered floors. A favourite haunt of local fishermen, it often has traditional music. There is also a restaurant.

> *i* **Tourist Information Office** Pier Rd, Kinsale; tel: (021) 477 2234, fax: (021) 477 4438. Open daily Mon–Fri 0900–1800, Sat 0900–1300 (Mar–Nov).

WHERE NEXT?

As an alternative to the Cork–Dingle Bay rail route (see p. 397), you can follow a fascinating course around the south-western corner of Co. Cork on the N71 road to Killarney, in Co. Kerry. About 30 miles (38 km) from Cork, just east of the pretty village of Rosscarbery you will find the Drombeg Stone Circle, dating from the 2nd century BC. Ten miles (16 km) west is the lively market town of Skibbereen and 13 miles (21 km) beyond there is the pleasant town of Bantry, with the exquisite 18th-century Bantry House overlooking the bay. From here the road traverses mountainous country to Kenmare, where it joins the south-eastern part of the Ring of Kerry to reach Killarney after a total distance of 94 miles (151 km).

Useful bus services from Cork include routes to Waterford (2 hrs 15 mins; hourly, every day), Limerick (1 hr 50 mins; hourly, every day) and Killarney (1 hr 40 mins; hourly, every day).

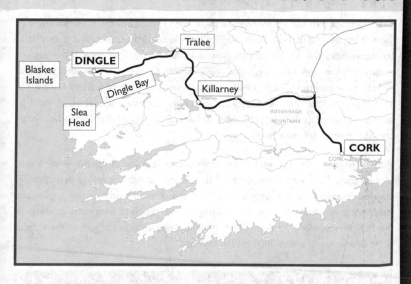

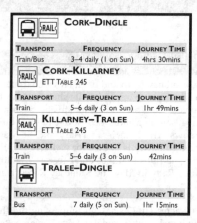

TRANSPORT	FREQUENCY	JOURNEY TIME
CORK–DINGLE		
Train/Bus	3–4 daily (1 on Sun)	4hrs 30mins
CORK–KILLARNEY ETT TABLE 245		
Train	5–6 daily (3 on Sun)	1hr 49mins
KILLARNEY–TRALEE ETT TABLE 245		
Train	5–6 daily (3 on Sun)	42mins
TRALEE–DINGLE		
Bus	7 daily (5 on Sun)	1hr 15mins

Notes

Travel by train from Cork to Tralee, then by bus to Dingle, Bus Éireann service 275.

A change at Mallow is required on some journeys between Cork and Killarney.

CORK – DINGLE BAY

Five fingers jut into the sea in Ireland's south-west corner, and the most northerly of these is the beautiful Dingle Peninsula. The most westerly part of Ireland is also here, and apart from the Blasket Islands, now uninhabited, the next stop is the eastern seaboard of the USA. Killarney, Tralee and Dingle, in Co. Kerry, are all good bases for exploring the peninsula. The region is rich in mountain and coastal scenery and curious little stone 'beehive' huts, or clochans, from early Christian times, possibly built as shelters for pilgrims. It is popular with walkers. Even touring the perimeter by car affords a memorable feast for the eyes.

Modern pilgrims have followed in the footsteps of St Brendan the Navigator, a 6th-century monk born near Tralee, who led an adventurous Atlantic voyage in small, hide-covered 'curraghs'. Some people interpret the accounts of amazing sights and experiences to mean that the Irish may have been the first Europeans to discover North America before the Vikings or Columbus. The pilgrims path goes to the summit of Mt Brendan, more than 3000 ft (914 m) high.

CORK CITY

See p. 390.

KILLARNEY

Killarney, 55 miles (89 km) from Cork, is a busy town and often crowded, but once you're out of the car and on foot you can begin to appreciate its charms. A host of colourful little lanes, some still cobbled, run off the main streets. **St Mary's Cathedral**, designed by Pugin in the 1840s, is a splendid neo-Gothic Revival building with beautiful stained-glass windows. The **Franciscan Friary** and **St Mary's Church of Ireland** are also worth a visit. Killarney is known for its lively nightlife, ranging from traditional music and singing pubs to discos and cabarets. The town is particularly busy during the Killarney Rally in May, the Killarney Races in July and during the Easter folk festival.

Killarney National Park covers 25,000 acres (10,125 ha), encompassing the three lakes of Killarney and the surrounding mountains. It contains Ireland's largest area of natural oak woodlands, and the only remaining herd of native red deer. Among the many places of interest are **Ross Castle** on the shores of Lough Leane, **Innisfallen Island** with its ruined abbey, **Torc Waterfall**, and **Ladies' View**, with its superb vistas over the valley. A spectacular view of the lakes of Killarney can be had from **Aghadoe Hill**, north of the park on the Killarney–Tralee road. There are ruins of a round tower, castle and church.

To the west of the park are the impressive peaks of **Macgillycuddy's Reeks**, which contain Ireland's highest mountain, Carrantouhill, rising 3406 ft (1038 m). The **Gap of Dunloe**, a glacier-carved pass, is a popular walking and horse-riding route, with dramatic views of deep gorges and lakes. It runs from Kate Kearney's Cottage, where 19th-century travellers stopped off for poteen (illegal liquor), to **Moll's Gap**.

Muckross House (€€) near Killarney, is an elegant 19th-century mansion with views to Muckross Lake. In the grounds are Muckross Traditional Farms (€€) demonstrating early 20th-century farming methods. House open daily 0900–1900 (July–Aug), daily 0900–1730 (Sept–June). Farms open weekends 1400–1800 (mid-Mar–Apr), daily 1300–1800 (May), 1000–1900 (June–Sept, 1400–1800 (Oct).

i **Tourist Information Office** Beech Rd, Killarney; tel: (064) 31633; fax: (064) 34506. Open Mon–Sat 0915–1300, 1400–1730 (Sept–May); Mon–Sat 0900–1800 (June); Mon–Sat 0900–2000 (July–Aug).

🛏 **Applecroft House** €€ Woodlawn Rd, Killarney, Co. Kerry; tel: (064) 32782; www.homepage.eircom.net-applecroft; e-mail: applecroft@eircom.net. Award-winning luxury home in a country setting a 15-min walk to town.

🍽 Let Edward Eviston himself tell you about his traditional pub, the **Danny Mann** €€ at 97 New St, Killarney: 'Fabled food, magical portions served in enchanting surroundings, accompanied by musical incantations and singing sorcery …'

🚌 Buses from Killarney include services to Limerick (2 hrs; roughly 9 direct buses a day, with reduced service on Sun) and Cork (1 hr 40 mins; hourly, every day).

TRALEE

The capital of Co. Kerry was made famous years ago by the old Irish ballad, *The Rose of Tralee*. Each Aug the town holds a festival of the same name, in which women from Irish communities around the world compete for the title. Music, dancing, parades and a horse race also mark the event. The National Folk Theatre of Ireland, Siamsa Tíre, is based here and there are performances of traditional music and dance throughout the summer.

Ten miles (16 km) from Tralee, on an inlet of Dingle Bay is **Castlemaine**. For a wonderful view of the town and its harbour go up into the hills from Tralee, skirting the Slieve Mish Mountains. If there is no mist or rain you will be able to see southwards across to the mountains around Killarney.

Kerry the Kingdom tells the county's history from prehistoric times in three combined attractions. The audio-visual show gives an overview of Kerry's sights and scenery. The Kerry County Museum uses modern interpretative media alongside the artefacts and displays. Geraldine Tralee is a time-travel ride through the sights, sounds and smells of medieval Tralee. Ashe Memorial Hall, Denny St. Open daily 1000–1800 (mid-Mar–Dec); to 1900 in Aug.

The **Tralee and Dingle Steam Railway**, €€, is a popular excursion. The train runs for 3 miles (4.8 km) to **Blennerville Windmill**, from Bellyard Station, Tralee; tel: (066) 21064. Departures hourly 1100–1730 (May–Sept and holiday periods). The windmill (€€) has been turned into a visitor centre with interesting activities and exhibits. Open daily (Apr–Oct). The *Jeannie Johnson* was a remarkable 19th-century vessel that transported thousands of emigrants to North America and never lost a single passenger to accident or disease. A full-size replica is now being built at Blennerville which will retrace the Atlantic voyage; the shipyard visitor centre has displays on the ship and emigration. Tel: (066) 27777 for opening times.

i **Tourist Information Office** Ashe Hall, Denny St, Tralee; tel: (066) 712 1288 or 712 1707; fax: (066) 712 1700. Open Mon–Fri 0900–1730 (Sept–June); Mon–Sat 0900–1900, Sun 0900–1800 (July–Aug).

🛏 Beach, bars and restaurants are within walking distance of **Ardkeel House** €€ Ardfert, near Tralee, Co. Kerry; tel/fax: (066) 713 4288; e-mail: ardkeelhouse@oceanfree.net. En suite rooms, dinner by arrangement.

🍽 **The Old Oak** €€–€€€ 13 Rock St, Tralee, serves bar food daily 1100–2100, with Irish and international entertainment on Wed and Sun evenings.

🚌 Buses to Limerick take 2 hrs 5 mins (daily services, about every 2 hrs).

DINGLE BAY

Only 35 miles (56 km), as the crow flies, separate Tralee, county town of Kerry, and Slea Head, at the western point of the Dingle Peninsula. But the spectacular mountain and sea views, the ancient sites, villages with pottery workshops, seafood restaurants and lively pubs – often with impromptu music sessions – make this one of Ireland's premier holiday regions.

In a town known for its traditional music, one name that always pops up is O'Flaherty's (Ua Flaithbheartaigh), on Bridge St, near the town entrance. Its simple, rustic interior is the scene of impromptu *seisiúns* (music sessions) on most summer nights.

This is a Gaeltacht, an area where Irish is the first language. More than 30 years ago, David Lean's hugely successful film *Ryan's Daughter* was shot in the Dingle Peninsula, and from Mar to Oct bus tours still go to the various locations in the movie. In 1992 the Hollywood bandwagon turned up again to film *Far and Away*, starring Tom Cruise and Nicole Kidman, at Dunquin and Clogher Head.

The small streets of **Dingle**, the peninsula's main town, wind up from the fishing harbour and are lined with bright shops, good seafood restaurants and pubs renowned for their traditional music. The Old Presbytery contains historical photos and memorabilia. On the west edge of town, a selection of local crafts are sold at the Ceardlann Craft Village, including leather and handwoven goods and uilleann pipes.

For a worthwhile insight into the history of the Dingle Peninsula, go to the popular holiday village of Ballyferriter, north of Dunquin, where the old school house is a heritage centre with artefacts and old photographs on display.

Dingle is a lively centre with a wide choice of high quality B&B and guest house accommodation at moderate charges.

The most westerly point on the Irish mainland is **Dunmore Head**. From here you can get a great view of the **Blasket Islands**, whose dwindling population of fisherfolk departed for the mainland in 1953. **The Blasket Centre** (€€) at Dunquin recounts the culture, language and traditions of the islanders. Open daily 1000–1800 (Apr–June, Sept–Oct) 1000–1900 (July–Aug). You can ask here about the possibility of being ferried to the islands.

THE LAST PUB
Dunquin boasts the most westerly pub in Europe. **Kruger's**, which offers sessions and set dancing, is named for the late, local hero Kruger Kavanagh, soldier, impresario, storyteller, political activist and bodyguard to Éamonn de Valera.

To the south-east of Dunmore Head is Slea Head, where a dramatic sculpture of the Crucifixion confronts passers-by. Nearby are the mysterious Fahan beehive huts, or clochans, from the early Christian era. More than 400 have been counted in the peninsula. Some are on private land and a small fee may be imposed to see them. The **Gallarus Oratory**, an intriguing dry stone building in the shape of an upturned boat, is near Kilmalked. It is believed to have been built somewhere between 800 and 1200.

CORK – DINGLE BAY

The Dingle Peninsula is rich in ancient monuments whose origin and age are a matter of conjecture. These include the numerous **ogham stones**, inscribed in a cipher consisting of notches, thought to commemorate individuals in early Christian times. At **Riase** are several high crosses and an inscribed pillar stone in what remains of a 7th-century monastic settlement.

WATER SPORTS
Surfing, windsurfing and sub-aqua diving are enjoyed around the Dingle Peninsula, and **The Aquadrome** ££ Dingle Rd, is open daily 1000–2200 (mid-May–early Sept), weekdays 1000–2200, weekends 1100–2000 (rest of year).

i **Tourist Infomation Office** The Pier, Dingle; tel: (066) 915 1188. Seasonal opening.

🛏 **Cois Corraigh** €€ Emila, Ballyferriter, Dingle Peninsula, Co. Kerry; tel: (066) 915 6282; fax: (066) 915 6005; e-mail: coiscorraigh@hotmail.com. Five en suite rooms in a family home handy for restaurants, beaches and archaeological sites.
Dingle Heights €€ Ballinbula, High Rd, Dingle, Co. Kerry; tel: (066) 915 1543; fax: (066) 915 2445; e-mail: dingleheights@hotmail.com. En suite rooms in a home in quiet location overlooking Dingle Bay and harbour. Walking distance of town and amenities.

🍴 Local produce, including fish fresh off the boats, is the pride of **Murphy's** €€, opposite the pier at Strand St, Dingle. A choice of vegetarian food is available.

WHERE NEXT?

Jutting into the Atlantic, south of Dingle, is the Iveragh Peninsula, where the magnificent beauty of the Ring of Kerry draws many thousands of visitors. Try to pick a fine day for a drive along roads winding among green-clad mountains, rock-strewn verges and sudden sea views. Or, you could travel to Limerick and follow the route to Dublin, in reverse (see pp. 378–383).

CONSULAR SERVICES AND EMBASSIES

In Britain, most embassies and consulates are based in London. They can lend a hand in an emergency; if you get arrested or lose your passport, for example.

American Embassy, 24 Grosvenor Square, London W1A 1AE; tel: (020) 7499 9000; e-mail: weblond@pd.state.gov.uk

There are also American consulates in Belfast; tel: (028) 9032 8239; Edinburgh; tel: (0131) 556 8315 and Cardiff; tel: (029) 2078 6633; website: www.usembassy.org.uk

Australian High Commission, Strand, London WC2B 4LA; tel: 0207 379 4334; website: www.australia.org.uk

Canadian High Commission, Canadian House, Trafalgar Square, London SW1Y 5BJ (consular assistance only); tel: (020) 7258 6600; website: www.canada.org.uk

New Zealand High Commission, New Zealand House, Haymarket, London SW1Y 4TQ; tel: (020) 7930 8422; fax: (020) 7839 4580; website: www.newzealandhc.org.uk

South African High Commission, South Africa House, Trafalgar Square, London WC2N 5DP; tel: (020) 7451 7299; fax: (020) 7451 7284; e-mail: general@southafricahouse.com; website: www.southafricahouse.com

Consular section (passports, visas and immigration) is at 15 Whitehall, London, SW1A 2DD, but the postal address is at the commission. Consular enquiries cannot be dealt with via e-mail, only in person or by post; tel: (020) 7925 8900; fax: (020) 7930 1510.

CUSTOMS

GOODS BOUGHT WITHIN THE EU Duty-free allowances on goods bought within the EU have been abolished, so in theory you can bring in as much tobacco or alcohol as you want provided it is for personal use. If you go above the guidance limits – 800 cigarettes, 10 litres of spirits or more than 90 litres of wine – you'll have to prove that it's for your own use.

GOODS BOUGHT FROM OUTSIDE THE EU If you're travelling in from outside the EU, over 17s have duty-free allowances of 200 cigarettes or 100 cigarillos or 250 grams of tobacco. For alcoholic drinks, it's 2 litres of still table wine plus 1 litre of spirits, or 2 litres of fortified or sparkling wine. Perfume, 60ml (2fl.oz), toilet water, 250ml (9fl.oz) and £145 worth of other goods. Personal imports of meat, milk and their products from non-EU countries were banned in 2003; see www.defra.gov.uk/animalh/illegali/allow/allowances.htm.

ALLOWANCES WHEN RETURNING HOME Australia: goods to the value of A$400 (half for those under 18) plus 250 cigarettes or 250g tobacco and 1 litre of alcohol.

Canada: goods to the value of C$300 provided you have been away for over a week and have not already used up part of your allowance that year, plus 50 cigars, plus 200 cigarettes and 1kg of tobacco (if over 16) and 1.14 litres/40oz of alcohol.

New Zealand: goods to the value of NZ$700. Over 17s may also take 200 cigarettes or 250g of tobacco or 50 cigars or a combination of tobacco products not exceeding 250g in all, plus 4.5 litres of beer or wine and 1.125 litres of spirits.

South Africa: goods to the value of R500. Over 18s may take in 400 cigarettes, 50 cigars and 250g tobacco, plus 2 litres wine and 1 litre spirits, plus 50ml perfume and 250ml toilet water.

USA: Goods to the value of US$400 as long as you have been out of the country for at least 48 hours and only use your allowance once every 30 days. Over 21s are also allowed 1 litre of alcohol, plus 100 (non-Cuban) cigars and 200 cigarettes.

VAT Value Added Tax (VAT) is automatically added to many goods and services in the UK at 17.5%. Most prices in shops will already include this. Visitors leaving Britain for a final destination outside the EU can reclaim a VAT refund on large purchases from shops, which operate a Retail Export Scheme (often called Tax-free shopping). Ask the shop to fill in a tax refund form, which you present to customs when you leave (within three months of purchase). Refunds are available at booths in several airports or you can post the form back to the shop for a refund.

ELECTRICITY

Britain and Ireland use the standard European voltage, 230V. Electrical equipment rated at 240V will also work in the UK. Equipment rated at 220V may work, but you should check with the manufacturer first. British plugs are mainly three pin, except for shaving points which are two-pin.

E-MAIL AND INTERNET ACCESS

Many public libraries have computer terminals with Internet access which you can use for a small fee. Otherwise, to log on, look out for cybernet cafés and state-of-the-art photo booths which take passport pictures and also offer e-mail facilities.

EMERGENCIES

For immediate assistance in an emergency – police, ambulance, fire or coastguard – call 999 (or 112, the standard number in the European Union).

ENTRY FORMALITIES

All visitors to the UK must carry a valid passport, except nationals of other EU countries and Austria, Liechtenstein, Monaco and Switzerland, for whom a national identity card suffices. Citizens of the EU and most other Western countries, including Australia, Canada, Japan, New Zealand, South Africa and the US do not need visas. Almost everyone else does. Check your visa requirements at website: www.fco.gov.uk which will tell you instantly whether you need one or not. Alternatively, tel: (020) 7238 3838.

All visitors to the Republic of Ireland must carry a valid passport, except people born in the UK who are travelling direct from there and holders of EU national identity cards. Citizens of Australia, Canada, New Zealand, South Africa and the US need a passport but can stay for up to three months without a visa.

HOTEL CHAINS

There are several good value hotel chains throughout Britain and Ireland. These include:
Heritage Hotels, which are generally more upmarket and individual (tel: 0800 404040; www.heritage-hotels.com).
Holiday Inn – the Express version of the main chain is more basic but good value (tel: 0800 897 121; 1800 553155 in Ireland; www.holiday-inn.com).
Marriott Hotels (tel: 0800 221222; www.marriotthotels.com).
Menzies Hotels (tel: 0870 600 3013; www.menzies-hotels.co.uk).
Swallow Hotels (tel: 0845 600 4666; www.swallowhotels.co.uk).
Travelodge (tel: 08700 850950; www.travelodge.co.uk) which has many family rooms at its 200 hotels throughout the UK.

OPENING TIMES

Shops are generally open Mon–Sat 0900–1730, although in large towns and cities many shops also open for shorter hours on Sunday, typically 1000–1600. Many supermarkets are open 0800–2000 or later in larger towns and cities. Off licences – shops selling wine and spirits – usually stay open until 2230. In villages and small towns, shops often close one midweek afternoon.

Banks are open Mon–Fri 0900–1630/1700, and many larger branches open on Saturday mornings. Many tourist attractions open seven days a week in the summer. Some (including many big theme parks) close completely in the winter or just open at weekends. Museums are generally open Mon–Sat 0900/1000 – 1730/1800 and Sunday mornings. Stately homes and National Trust properties often have different opening times for the gardens and the main house.

PETROL

Most modern cars in Britain run on unleaded petrol, available just about everywhere (look for the green hose) or diesel (black hose). Urban petrol stations are open early till late (0700–2200) including Sundays, with shorter hours in rural areas. Some are 24-hour, especially on motorways, although prices tend to be higher here. Bear in mind that fuel costs in Britain are among the highest in the world.

POSTAL SERVICES

There is an excellent network of post offices and sub post offices (often located in local newsagents). Opening hours are usually Mon–Fri 0900–1730, Sat 0900–1230, with main post offices in towns and cities open longer hours. Many supermarkets, newsagents and hotels sell stamps and large post offices often have stamp machines outside. If you want to receive mail, ask people writing to you to mark their letters *poste restante*, c/o the town's main post office. Letters are usually kept for a month and you will need some form of official identification to claim it (e.g. a passport).

PUBLIC HOLIDAYS

Public holidays are known as 'Bank Holidays' in British English.

England, Wales and Scotland
1 January, Good Friday, Easter Monday, first Monday in May, last Monday in May, last Monday in August, 25 December, 26 December.

Northern Ireland
As England, Wales and Scotland, plus 17 March (St Patrick's Day) and 12 July.

Ireland
1 January, 17 March – St Patrick's Day, Easter Monday, first Monday in May, first Monday in June, first Monday in August, last Monday in October, 25 December, 26 December. Good Friday is not officially a public holiday but often observed as such in many parts of Ireland.

SHOPPING

Very few towns are so remote in Britain that they don't have a supermarket – Tesco, Sainsburys, Safeway and Asda are found all over Britain; Waitrose is the most upmarket. Department stores include Debenhams and John Lewis, with upmarket Selfridges in London and Manchester. Marks & Spencer (M&S) is a good all round store for quality clothing at high street prices.

Farmers' markets, where farmers sell their fresh produce direct to the public, are becoming increasingly popular. Members of the National Association of Farmers' Markets, tel: (01225) 787 914, sell their wares up and down the country – visit www.farmersmarkets.net for details of ones in the areas you're visiting.

And if you like rifling through other people's junk, no Sunday morning (and sometimes Saturday) would be complete without a car boot sale. They're advertised in the local press and are basically junk stalls, with items ranging from good quality secondhand toys and kitchen accessories to rusty tools and chipped crockery!

TELEPHONES

Phone number prefixes

077/078/079 – mobile phones

0800 – freephone

0845 – charged at the rate of a local call

0870 – charged at national call rate

090 – premium rate services (0900 and 0901 are often used for information lines and are charged at up to 60p a minute)

Bright red phone boxes were once as synonymous with Britain as Buckingham Palace, but they are rapidly becoming collector's items. Today's phone boxes are usually grey or black and most take a mixture of coins – minimum 20p – and phone cards (available from newsagents). Many, particularly in high use areas such as railway stations, also take credit cards. Payment must be inserted before you dial – wholly unused coins are returned when you hang up. There are three time bands. Daytime (Mon–Fri 0800–1800) calls are the most expensive and weekend calls (Fri–Sun midnight to midnight) the cheapest. Hotels charge a hefty premium for direct dial facilities from your room.

In the Republic of Ireland, public phones are widespread. Most are card-operated – cards can be bought in denominations of 10, 20 and 50 units from post offices and most newsagents. Coin phones are rarer, but are still found in city centres.

INTERNATIONAL CALLS To make an international call from the UK and the Irish Republic, dial 00 followed by the country code: 62 for Australia, 61 for Canada, 64 for New Zealand, 27 for South Africa and 1 for the USA.

TIME

The following times are based on standard time GMT. Central Europe is one hour ahead of GMT. Visit website: www.greenwichmeantime.com for time differences worldwide.

Australia: New South Wales, Victoria and Queensland GMT +10, Western Australia GMT +8

Canada: British Columbia GMT –8, East Ontario GMT –5, Quebec GMT –5

New Zealand: GMT +12

South Africa: GMT +2

USA: California GMT –8, Texas GMT –6, New York GMT –5, Massachussetts GMT –5

TIPPING

In restaurants check to see if service is included; if it isn't add a 10% tip (unless the service has been appalling) and if paying by credit card be sure to fill in the total box at the bottom. In Ireland tip around 12–15%. Some restaurants charge for service but still leave this box empty in the hope you won't notice and increase the amount by way of a tip. For taxis that you hail in the street, tip the driver 10%, but you don't need to tip drivers of minicabs that you order by phone. Tipping hairdressers 10% or so is entirely optional. Bar staff don't expect tips.

TOILETS

There are public toilets throughout Britain of varying standards. In stations, there will often be a 20p charge. Department stores, garages and large supermarkets usually have toilets, as do large town centre car parks. If you ask nicely, most café and pub owners won't mind you using theirs.

TOURIST INFORMATION

Britain and Ireland have an extremely comprehensive network of tourist offices. Offices (referred to as TICs – tourist information centres) are generally marked with the 'i' symbol. Some are seasonal, open only from Easter to October, or have restricted opening hours in the winter. They can book accommodation, organise tickets for local events, arrange tours, guided walks and sporting activities, often for a small charge.

Listed below are important or regional tourist boards to contact for general information on the area **before** travelling. Some of them are head offices with no facility for personal callers, but they will be able to provide details of local tourist offices in the area you are visiting and many will be able to send out brochures. Local tourist offices are listed in the relevant chapters in the book.

ENGLAND

Cumbria Tourist Board Ashleigh, Holly Rd, Windermere, Cumbria LA23 2AQ; tel: (015394) 40414; fax: (015394) 44041; website: www.gocumbria.co.uk; e-mail: info@golakes.co.uk

East of England Tourist Board Toppesfield Hall, Hadleigh, Suffolk IP7 5DN; tel: (01473) 822922; fax: (01473) 823063; website: www.eastofenglandtouristboard.com; e-mail: eastofenglandtouristboard@compuserve.com

Heart of England Tourist Board Woodside, Larkhill Rd, Worcester WR5 2EZ; tel: (01905) 761100; fax: (01905) 763450; website: www.visitheartofengland.com; e-mail: hetbinfo@bta.org.uk

London Tourist Board, write for a free information pack stating any particular areas of interest (such as shopping, facilities for the disabled or theatre) to London Tourist Board, Glen House, Stag Place, London SW1E 5LT, or fax: (020) 7932 0222, website: www.visitlondon.com

Northumbria Tourist Board Aykley Heads, Durham DH1 5UX; tel: 0906 683 3000, Mon–Fri, 0900–1700, calls cost 25p a min; fax number: (0191) 386 0899; website: www.visitnorthumbria.com; e-mail: enquiries@ntb.org.uk

North West Tourist Board Swan House, Swan Meadow Rd, Wigan Pier, Wigan WN3 5BB; tel: (01942) 321222; fax: (01942) 820002; website: www.visitnorthwest.com; e-mail: info@nwtb.org.uk

South East England Tourist Board The Old Brew House, Warwick Park, Tunbridge Wells, Kent TN2 5TU; tel: (01892) 540766; fax: (01892) 511008; website: www.southeastengland.uk.com; e-mail: enquiries@seetb.org.uk

Southern Tourist Board 40 Chamberlayne Rd, Eastleigh, Hampshire SO50 5JH; tel: (023) 8062 5400; fax: (023) 8062 0010; website: www.visitsouthernengland.com; e-mail: info@southerntb.co.uk

South West Tourism Admail 3186, Exeter, Devon EX2 7WH; tel: 0870 4420880; fax: 0870 4420881; website: www.westcountrynow.com; e-mail: info@westcountryholidays.com

Yorkshire Tourist Board 312 Tadcaster Rd, York YO24 1GS; tel: (01904) 707070 24-hr brochure/enquiry line; manned 0900–1700; fax: (01904) 701414; website: www.yorkshirevisitor.com; e-mail: info@ytb.org.uk

Useful website:

www.visitbritain.com has detailed information on all kinds of information useful for planning a visit, including attractions and tourist information centres (with opening times).

WALES

Wales Tourist Board Visit Wales Centre, Dept VE3, PO Box 113, Bangor LL54 4WW; tel: 08701 211251; website: www.visitwales.com; e-mail: info@visitwales.com

The Isle of Anglesey Tourism Unit Economic Development, Isle of Anglesey County Council, Llangefni LL77 7XA; tel: (01248) 752434; fax: (01248) 752192; website: www.anglesey.gov.uk; e-mail: tourism@anglesey.gov.uk

Cardiff Visitor Centre 16 Wood St, Cardiff CF10 1ES; tel: (029) 2022 7281; fax: (029) 2023 9162; website: www.cardiffmarketing.co.uk; e-mail: enquiries@cardifftic.co.uk

Carmarthenshire Tourism Unit Parc Amanwy, New Rd, Ammanford SA18 3EP; tel/fax: (01558) 824226; website: www.carmarthenshire.gov.uk; e-mail: tourism@carmarthenshire.gov.uk

Ceredigion – Cardigan Bay Ceredigion Tourism and Economic Development Unit, Lisburne House, Terrace Rd, Aberystwyth SY23 2AG; tel: (01970) 612125; fax: (01970) 626566; website: www.ceredigion.gov.uk; e-mail: wtb2002@ceredigion.gov.uk

The Glamorgan Heritage Coast and Countryside Tourism Unit, The Vale of Glamorgan Council, Dock Office, Barry CF63 4RT; tel: (01446) 709328; fax: (01446) 704612; website: www.valeofglamorgan.gov.uk; e-mail: tourism@valeofglamorgan.gov.uk

Llandudno, Colwyn Bay, Rhyl and Prestatyn (for Llandudno/Colwyn Bay) Tourism and Leisure Dept, Conwy County Borough Council Civic Offices, Colwyn Bay LL29 8AR; tel: (01492) 575361/575387; fax: (01492) 513664; websites: www.llandudno-tourism.co.uk, www.colwyn-bay-tourism.co.uk; e-mail: tourism@conwy.gov.uk (for Rhyl/Prestatyn): Marketing and Tourism Unit, West Parade, Rhyl LL18 1HZ; tel: (01745) 344515; fax: (01745) 342255; e-mail: rhyl.tic@denbighshire.gov.uk

Mid Wales and the Brecon Beacons Powys Tourism, Neuadd Maldwyn, Severn Rd, Welshpool SY21 7AS; tel: (01938) 551255; websites: www.tourism.powys.gov.uk, www.brecon-beacons.net; e-mail: tourism@powys.gov.uk

The North Wales Borderlands Mold Tourist Information Centre, Mold Library, Earl Rd, Mold CH7 1AP; tel/fax: (01352) 759331; website: www.borderlands.co.uk; e-mail: mold.tic@virgin.net

Pembrokeshire Holidays PO Box 103, Pembroke Dock SA72 6TQ; tel: (01646) 682278; fax: (01646) 682281; website: www.visitpembrokeshire.com; e-mail: tourism@pembrokeshire.gov.uk

Snowdonia Mountains and Coast Business and Marketing Section (Ref VOW02), Gwynedd Council, Cae Penarlag, Dolgellau LL40 2YB; tel: (01341) 423558; fax: (01341) 424440; website: www.gwynedd.gov.uk; e-mail: tourism@gwynedd.gov.uk

Swansea Tourist Information Centre Plymouth St, Swansea SA1 3QG; tel: (01792) 468321; fax: (01792) 464602; website: www.want2getaway.net; e-mail: tourism@swansea.gov.uk

Travel Directory

The Valleys of South Wales Tourism South and West Wales, Chestnut House, Tawe Business Village, Enterprise Park, Swansea SA7 9LA; tel: (01792) 781212; fax: (01792) 781300; website: www.valley-breaks.co.uk; e-mail: valleys@tsww.com

Wye Valley and Vale of Usk Tourism Section, Environment Dept, Monmouthshire County Council, County Hall, Cwmbran NP44 2XH; tel: (01633) 644842; fax: (01633) 644800; website: www.visitwyevalley.com; e-mail: tourism@monmouthshire.gov.uk

Useful websites:

www.croeso.com has useful descriptions of towns, including information on where to stay, pubs, restaurants, taxis and tourist offices. **www.visitwales.co.uk** is the official Wales Tourist Board site with information or everything from shopping and beaches to crafts.

Scotland

Aberdeen & Grampian Tourist Board 27 Albyn Place, Aberdeen AB10 1YL; tel: (01224) 288828; fax: (01224) 581367; website: www.castlesandwisky.com; e-mail: info@agtb.org

Angus & City of Dundee Tourist Board 21 Castle St, Dundee DD1 3AA; tel: (01382) 527527; fax: (01382) 527551; website: www.angusanddundee..co.uk; e-mail: enquiries@angusanddundee.co.uk

Argyll, The Isles, Loch Lomond, Stirling & Trossachs Tourist Board Dept SOS, 7 Alexandra Parade, Dunoon PA23 8AB; tel: (01369) 703785; fax: (01369) 706085; website: www.scottishheartlands.org; e-mail: info@scottishheartlands.org

Ayrshire & Arran Tourist Board Customer Information Centre, 15 Skye Rd, Prestwick KA9 2TA; tel: (01292) 678 100; fax: (01292) 471832; website: www.ayrshire-arran.com; e-mail: info@ayrshire-arran.com

Dumfries & Galloway Tourist Board 64 Whitesands, Dumfries DG1 2RS; tel: (01387) 253862; fax: (01387) 245555; website: www.dumfriesandgalloway.co.uk; e-mail: info@dgtb.ossian.net

Edinburgh & Scotland Information Centre 3 Princes St, Edinburgh EH2 2QP; tel: 0845 22 55 121; fax: (01506) 832222; websites: www.edinburgh.org and www.visitscotland.com; e-mail: info@visitscotland.com

Glasgow and Clyde Valley Tourist Board 11 George Square, Glasgow G2 1DY; tel: (0141) 204 4400; fax: (0141) 221 3524; website: www.seeglasgow.com; e-mail: enquiries@seeglasgow.com

Highlands of Scotland Tourist Board Peffery House, Strathpeffer IV14 9HA; tel: (01997) 421160; fax: (01997) 421168; website: www.highlandfreedom.com; e-mail: info@host.co.uk

Kingdom of Fife Tourist Board 70 Market St, St Andrews KY16 9NU; tel: (01334) 472021; fax: (01334) 478422; website: www.standrews.com; e-mail: fifetourism@kftb.ossian.net

Orkney Tourist Board 6 Broad St, Kirkwall KW15 1NX; tel: (01856) 872856; fax: (01856) 875056; website: www.visitorkney.com; e-mail: info@otb.ossian.net

Perthshire Tourist Board Lower City Mills, West Mill St, Perth PH1 5QP; tel: (01738) 627958; fax: (01738) 630416; website: www.perthshire.co.uk; e-mail: info@ptb.ossian.net

Scottish Borders Tourist Board Shepherd's Mill, Whinfield Rd, Selkirk TD7 5DT; tel: 0870 6080404; fax: (01750) 21886; website: www.scot-borders.co.uk; e-mail: info@scot-borders.co.uk

Shetland Islands Tourism Market Cross, Lerwick, Shetland ZE1 0LU; tel: (01595) 693434; fax: (01595) 695807; website: www.visitshetland.com; e-mail: shetland.tourism@zetnet.co.uk

Western Isles Tourist Board 26 Cromwell St, Stornoway, Isle of Lewis HS1 2DD; tel: (01851) 703088; fax: (01851) 705244; website: www.witb.co.uk; e-mail: stornowaytic@witb.ossian.net

Ireland

Dublin Tourism Centre Suffolk St, Dublin 2; tel: (01) 605 7799; tel: 1800 668 668 66 (within Ireland); tel: 00800 668 668 66 (from the UK and Northern Ireland); fax: (01) 605 7725; website: www.visitdublin.com;

e-mail: information@dublintourism.ie

East Coast & Midlands Tourism (for Kildare, Laois, Longford, Louth, Meath, North Offaly, Westmeath and Wicklow): Market House, Mullingar, Co. Westmeath; tel: (044) 48650; fax: (044) 40413; website: www.ecoast-midlands.travel.ie; e-mail: info@ecoast-midlandstourism.ie

Ireland West Tourism (for Galway, Mayo and Roscommon): Áras Fáilte, Forster St, Galway; tel: (091) 537700; fax: (091) 537733; website: www.irelandwest.travel.ie; e-mail: info@irelandwest.ie

Irish Tourist Board (Bord Fáilte): Baggot St Bridge, Baggot St, Dublin 2; tel: (01) 602 4000 or 1850 23 03 30; fax: (01) 602 4100; website: www.ireland.travel.ie; e-mail: user@irishtouristboard.ie

Northern Ireland Tourist Board 59 North St, Belfast BT1 1NB; tel: (028) 9023 1221; fax: (028) 9024 0960; website: www.discovernorthernireland.com; e-mail: visitorservices@nitb.com

North West Tourism (for counties Cavan, Donegal, Leitrim, Monaghan and Sligo): Áras Redden, Temple St, Sligo; tel: (071) 61201; fax: (071) 60360; website: www.ireland-northwest.travel.ie; e-mail: irelandnorthwest@eircom.net

Shannon Development (for counties Clare, Limerick, North Kerry, North Tipperary and South Offaly): Shannon Airport Tourist Office, Shannon Airport, Shannon, Co. Clare; tel: (061) 471664; fax: (061) 471661

South East Tourism (for Carlow, Kilkenny, South Tipperary, Waterford and Wexford): 41 The Quay, Waterford; tel: (051) 87582; fax: (051) 877388; website: www.southeastireland.com; e-mail: info@southeastireland.com

South West Tourism (for Cork and South Kerry): Áras Fáilte, Grand Parade, Cork; tel: (021) 425 5100; fax: (021) 425 5199; website: www.corkkerry.ie; e-mail: info@corkkerrytourism.ie

Useful websites:

www.ireland.com, the website of the *Irish Times*; **www.wannabeinireland.com** has the largest choice of accommodation and travel to Ireland

HERITAGE ORGANISATIONS

For details of how to find and gain access to hundreds of historic properties, as well as events and activities happening there, visit the following organisations's websites.

> **The National Trust** (Britain and Ireland) www.nationaltrust.org.uk
> **English Heritage** www.english-heritage.org.uk
> **Historic Scotland** www.historic-scotland.gov.uk
> **Cadw** (Wales) www.cadw.org.uk
> **The Great British Heritage Pass** (only available to non-UK visitors) www.visitbritain.com

WEIGHTS AND MEASURES

Although Britain and Ireland are officially metric countries, most people over 30 still relate more readily to feet and inches and pounds and ounces. Shops are obliged by law to use metric measurements, but many display both. See the conversion tables on p. 412.

CONVERSION TABLES

DISTANCES (approx. conversions)
1 kilometre (km) = 1000 metres (m) 1 metre = 100 centimetres (cm)

Metric	Imperial/US	Metric	Imperial/US	Metric	Imperial/US
1 cm	3/8 in.	10 m	33 ft (11 yd)	3 km	2 miles
50 cm	20 in.	20 m	66 ft (22 yd)	4 km	2½ miles
1 m	3 ft 3 in.	50 m	164 ft (54 yd)	5 km	3 miles
2 m	6 ft 6 in.	100 m	330 ft (110 yd)	10 km	6 miles
3 m	10 ft	200 m	660 ft (220 yd)	20 km	12½ miles
4 m	13 ft	250 m	820 ft (275 yd)	25 km	15½ miles
5 m	16 ft 6 in.	300 m	984 ft (330 yd)	30 km	18½ miles
6 m	19 ft 6 in.	500 m	1640 ft (550 yd)	40 km	25 miles
7 m	23 ft	750 m	½ mile	50 km	31 miles
8 m	26 ft	1 km	⅝ mile	75 km	46 miles
9 m	29 ft (10 yd)	2 km	1½ miles	100 km	62 miles

24-HOUR CLOCK
(examples)

0000 = Midnight	1200 = Noon	1800 = 6 pm
0600 = 6 am	1300 = 1 pm	2000 = 8 pm
0715 = 7.15 am	1415 = 2.15 pm	2110 = 9.10 pm
0930 = 9.30 am	1645 = 4.45 pm	2345 = 11.45 pm

TEMPERATURE
Conversion Formula: (°C x 9 ÷ 5) + 32 = °F

°C	°F	°C	°F	°C	°F	°C	°F
-20	-4	-5	23	10	50	25	77
-15	5	0	32	15	59	30	86
-10	14	5	41	20	68	35	95

WEIGHT
1 kg = 1000 g 100 g = 3½ oz

Kg	Lbs	Kg	Lbs	Kg	Lbs
1	2¼	5	11	25	55
2	4½	10	22	50	110
3	6½	15	33	75	165
4	9	20	45	100	220

FLUID MEASURES
1 ltr.(l) = 0.88 Imp. quarts = 1.06 US quarts

Ltrs.	Imp. gal.	US gal.	Ltrs.	Imp. gal.	US gal.
5	1.1	1.3	30	6.6	7.8
10	2.2	2.6	35	7.7	9.1
15	3.3	3.9	40	8.8	10.4
20	4.4	5.2	45	9.9	11.7
25	5.5	6.5	50	11.0	13.0

MEN'S SHIRTS

UK	Europe	US
14	36	14
15	38	15
15½	39	15½
16	41	16
16½	42	16½
17	43	17

MEN'S SHOES

UK	Europe	US
6	40	7
7	41	8
8	42	9
9	43	10
10	44	11
11	45	12

LADIES' CLOTHES

UK	France	Italy	Rest of Europe	US
10	36	38	34	8
12	38	40	36	10
14	40	42	38	12
16	42	44	40	14
18	44	46	42	16
20	46	48	44	18

MEN'S CLOTHES

UK	Europe	US
36	46	36
38	48	38
40	50	40
42	52	42
44	54	44
46	56	46

LADIES' SHOES

UK	Europe	US
3	36	4½
4	37	5½
5	38	6½
6	39	7½
7	40	8½
8	41	9½

AREAS

1 hectare = 2.471 acres

1 hectare = 10,000 sq metres

1 acre = 0.4 hectares

INDEX

INDEX

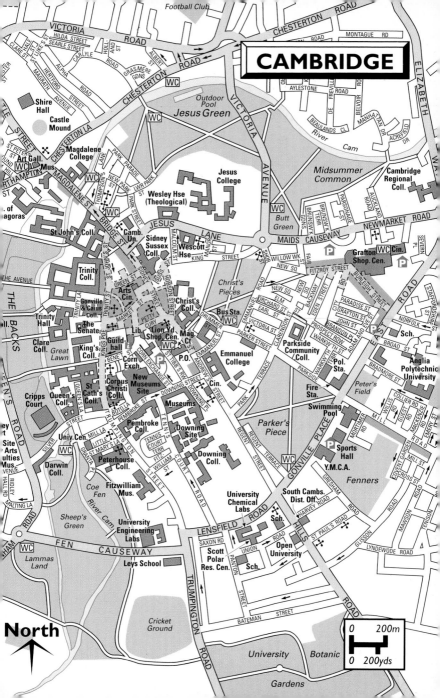

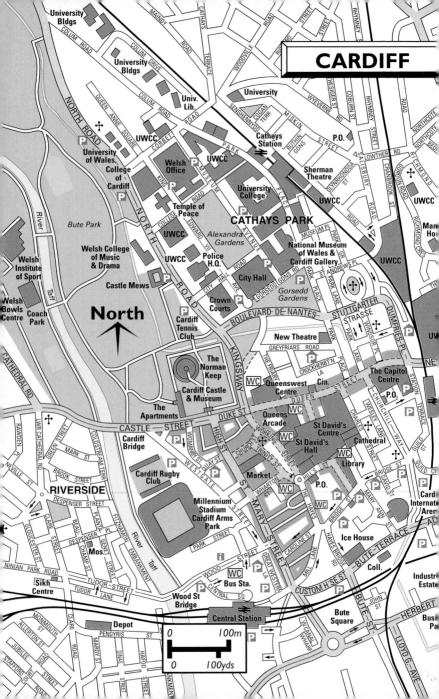

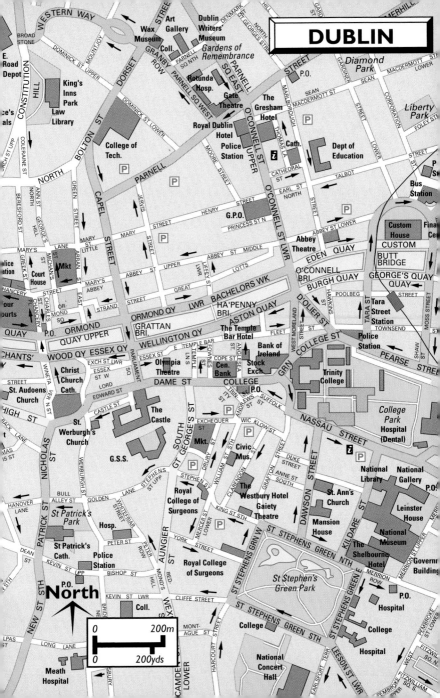

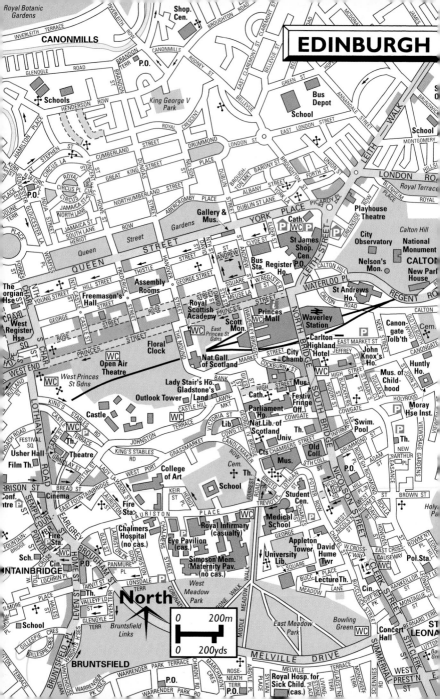

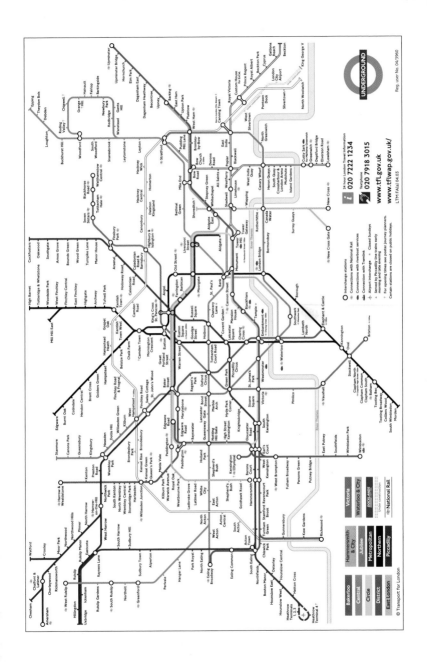

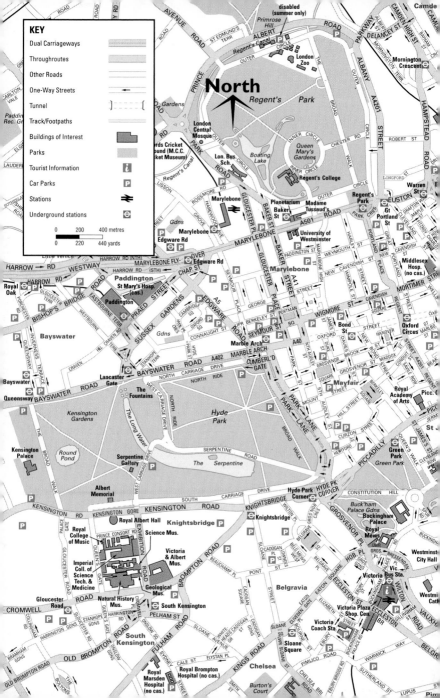

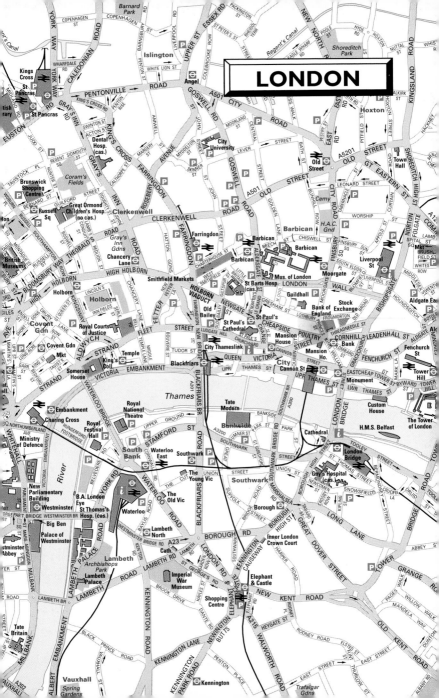

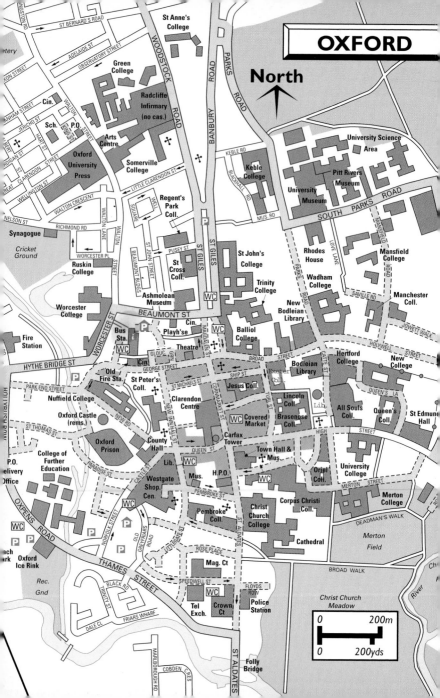